GUIDE TO ARCHITECTURE SCHOOLS IN NORTH AMERICA
Members and Affiliates of the ACSA

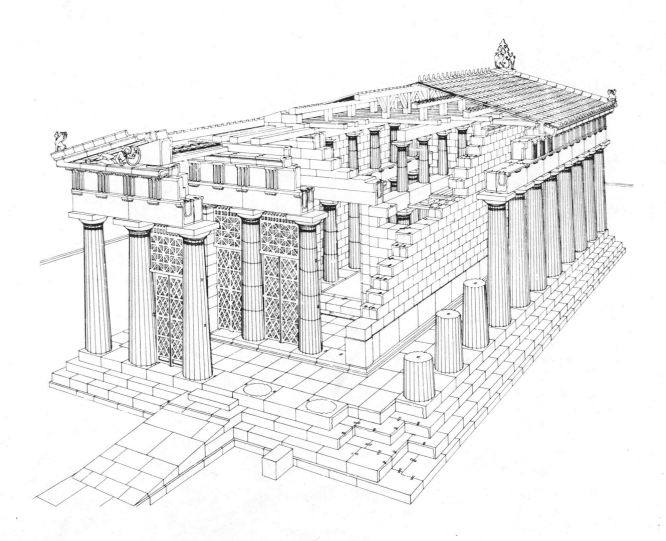

GUIDE TO ARCHITECTURE SCHOOLS IN NORTH AMERICA
Members and Affiliates of the ACSA

EDITOR

Richard E McCommons, AIA

EDITORIAL STAFF

Gerard Martin Moeller, Jr.
Karen L Eldridge
Association of Collegiate Schools of Architecture

Betty J Fishman
Information Dynamics, Inc.

A publication of the
Association of Collegiate Schools of Architecture Press
Washington, DC

Printed in the United States of America.
Published by the Association of Collegiate Schools of Architecture Press.
Distributed by the Association of Collegiate Schools of Architecture,
1735 New York Avenue NW, Washington, DC 20006.

LIBRARY OF CONGRESS
Library of Congress Cataloging-in-Publication Data

Guide to Architecture Schools in North America / editor, Richard E.
  McCommons.
    p. cm.
    Rev. ed. of: Architecture Schools in North America. 3rd ed. c1982.
    Includes index.
    ISBN 0-935437-31-2 : $14.95
         1. Schools of architecture--United States--Directories
    2. Schools of architecture--Canada--Directories.   I. McCommons.
    Richard E., 1941-   . II. Architecture Schools in North America.
    NA2105.G85 1989
    720'.7'1173--dc19   89-12765
                                                         CIP

Illustrations reprinted, with permission, from the following sources:

Cover (except for right center and lower right),
title page, x, xii, xiii, xvii, xviii, and xxii
Sir Banister Fletcher, *A History of Architecture*, 18th ed.
New York: Charles Scribner's Sons, 1975.

Cover (right center and lower right), vii, xi, xiv, xv, xvi, xix, xx,
xxi, and xxiii
Kevin Utsey, ed. *Analysis of Precedent*, vol. 28, 1979, The Student
Publication of the School of Design, North Carolina State University at Raleigh.

viii, ix, and 1
ACSA archives

Contents

Foreword

This book is published for the many people who are interested in pursuing an architecture education and need both career information and academic program descriptions, as well as for those who need a ready reference for the various degrees, faculty statistics, and special programs.

We believe that the many options in both academic programs and careers in architecture have been concisely delineated in this guide, so that the reader can understand the various opportunities and realize the potential of each one relative to his or her own interests and capabilities. As the only publication that brings together statistics on academic programs, career opportunities, and the profession itself, this book should be useful for both prospective architects and professionals in the field.

The material in the 1988 edition of the *Guide to Architecture Schools in North America* covers the full range of programs, schools, degrees, and paths to follow in architecture and its many related fields. The data base is for 1987–88.

All facts, figures, and descriptive materials about the programs in this book were supplied by the schools listed. This book is a publication of the Association of Collegiate Schools of Architecture, which represents all of the 114 professional degree schools of architecture in the United States and Canada, as well as many affiliate member schools.

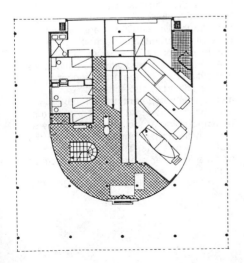
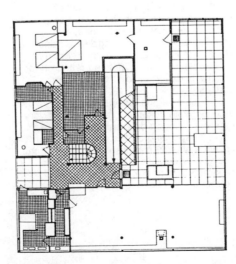
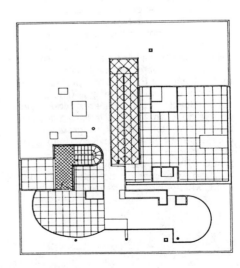

Section I
Architecture Education in North America— A Brief History

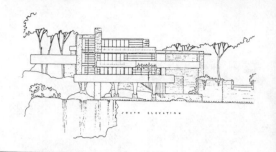

It was 1814 when Thomas Jefferson (the USA's only architect-president) proposed that a professional curriculum in architecture be established in the School of Mathematics of the University of Virginia. Unfortunately, the search for an appropriate architect/mathematician was fruitless and the University of Virginia delayed its entrance into the architectural field for many years. Instead, formal architecture education in the United States began in 1865 at the Massachusetts Institute of Technology, five years after that institution's founding. MIT's action was followed in 1867 by the University of Illinois at Urbana and in 1871 by Cornell University. The Universities of Toronto and Montreal started the first schools of architecture in Canada in 1876.

The Morrill Act, passed by Congress in 1862, was to have great and lasting repercussions for higher education, including architecture. In exchange for land granted by Congress, colleges were expected to provide "practical" education for America's youth. This contrasted strongly with European traditions which more clearly separated education and training: At the university you were "educated" and, once in the office, you were "trained." Of course, not all institutions of higher education founded since then have been "land-grant" colleges, but the tradition the system developed was a pervasive one, particularly in the South, Midwest, and West.

The European tradition, however, is a second important historical thread in American architecture education. The system described above was considered by many to be uncouth. Looking to Europe for a standard, as we often did in the nineteenth century, eyes settled on the prestigious Ecole des Beaux Arts in Paris as the ultimate in architectural training. The Ecole's "true" philosophy was imported to the United States in the form of Beaux Arts professors, and most architecture schools in the early part of this century had at least one Paris-trained professor. If you were the "unfortunate" graduate of a school devoid of such influence, you could always go to an academy in New York and learn the mysteries through a graduate course taught by an exclusively Beaux Arts staff. Or you could go to the Ecole des Beaux Arts for a year, as over five hundred Americans did between 1850 and 1968, when it closed. The grand prize of almost all superior fellowships and competitions of the time was specifically for travel to Europe to study examples of these "masters" and their successors.

Canada was also importing a number of Beaux-Arts-trained teachers at this time, especially in the French-speaking provinces. However, as Canada had stronger ties with England and Scotland than did the United States (not having warred with England), many of the first professors came directly from the British Isles.

The cornerstone of the Beaux Arts system was the "design problem" assigned to the student early in the term and carefully developed with the help of close tutelage. It began as an *esquisse* or sketch problem and ended *en charrette. Charrette,* French for "cart," refers to the carts in which the finished drawings were placed at the deadline hour for transport to the "master" for critique. The Beaux Arts teaching systems relied totally on brilliant teachers and learning-by-doing. Competition was intense and the end results were beautifully drawn projects in traditional styles which were often defensible only on grounds of "good taste" and intuition. The style was mostly neoclassical and the favorite building type was the monument. Projects were judged by a jury of professors and guest architects, usually without the students present. The jurors used the same criterion that the students designed by—"good taste." (Most schools still use some type of "jury" or review system today.)

In the early part of this century, both the US and Canada were developing personalities of their own and outgrowing their European dependence. This powerful notion of individualism affected architecture no less than it did all other aspects of American culture. With the advent of "modern" architecture in Europe, the growing fame of the Chicago skyscraper idiom, and Frank Lloyd Wright's "Prairie School" architecture, intense pressures for change began to build in architecture education.

Like all emerging disciplines, architectural education grew up under very different roofs on different campuses, usually depending on the nature of other colleges already established at the time the decision was made to offer architecture programs. There are separate and autonomous schools or colleges of architecture, departments and programs within graduate schools, schools of art or design, schools oriented toward engineering, technology, or sociology, and, more recently, schools of urban planning and design.

The University of Oregon architecture school, founded in 1914, was the first school in the United States to adopt completely two basic elements of the "modern" movement in architecture education. These are affiliation with all the allied arts (painting, crafts, sculpture, etc.) rather than with engineering, and a noncompetitive, individual approach to learning.

Columbia University made a dramatic shift in 1934 away from the French methods toward those of the modern German movement exemplified by the Bauhaus school. The Bauhaus, formed in 1919, moved to its famous Dessau, Germany, location in 1925, but was closed down by the Nazis in 1933. The effects of that school were felt throughout the world. Its director, Walter Gropius, said that design was neither an intellectual nor a material affair but simply an integral part of the stuff of life. The school embraced modern concepts of mass production and modern technology, which the Beaux Arts had refused to accept. Instruction at the Bauhaus was of a practical nature, providing actual work with materials in the shops and on buildings under construction.

In 1936, Walter Gropius came to the United States and from 1938 to 1952 was head of the architecture department at Harvard University. Also in 1936, Harvard integrated into a single school architecture, landscape architecture, and urban planning—the triangular model of many schools of environmental design today. Gropius' distinguished colleague from the Bauhaus, Ludwig Mies van der Rohe, also came to the United States and became the head of the architecture school of the Illinois Institute of Technology in 1938.

As architecture education expanded the curriculum beyond the art of rendering to include utilitarian subjects such as mechanical equipment and structural analysis, the standard four-year program began to bulge at the seams. Also, there was a growing tendency to include work in crafts and fine arts. The first school to adopt a five-year professional program of study in architecture was Cornell University, which did so in 1922. By 1940

almost all architecture schools had a standard course of five years leading to a Bachelor of Architecture degree.

The last thirty years have taught us that there is a great deal more to the disciplines of building than ever realized in the previous 2,000 years. In the forties, Harvard's Joseph Hudnut made a list of all the subjects that he deemed essential for a sound and complete architecture education. When the list was complete he figured out the length of time it would take to learn everything on it. It came to twenty-two years. While this is ridiculously long, the pressures for the modern architect to know more and be responsible for more have had their effect—even when tempered with the realization that it need not all be learned in school.

The "four-plus-two" program became a model for expanding the professional curriculum in the sixties. This program usually takes the form of a four-year course of study in environmental design followed by two years with a strong concentration in architecture. A report by the AIA's Special Committee on Education published in 1962 has been generally recognized as the impetus behind this development. The first such programs in the United States were developed at the University of California, Berkeley, and Washington University in St. Louis. However, many schools have stayed with the five-year Bachelor of Architecture program, confident that within its time constraints they can provide a liberal and professional education.

Another pattern that emerged in the 1960's recognized the possibilities of studying architecture solely at the graduate level. Many schools offer graduate professional education for students whose undergraduate degrees are in fields as diverse as philosophy, languages, and physics. The idea of professional programs offered exclusively at the graduate level recognizes the option of having a solid university education before embarking on a professional education.

Another interesting trend that emerged in the sixties was the notion of the free clinic for urban problems and architectural design. The movement really began with something called "CDCs" or community design centers. As architecture, along with other professions, woke up to social responsibilities, the non-profit CDCs began to provide architectural and planning

services for the disadvantaged, usually in urban areas. Some CDCs were born of negative responses—for example, to stop a thoughtlessly planned freeway—while others were born with positive motives such as creating playgrounds or low-cost housing. At any rate, by the late sixties it became clear that the market for non-profit design services was larger than originally thought and extended beyond minorities to many segments of society. This gave rise to the "clinic" notion, a logical extension of the original CDC. The clinic may be in the school of architecture or exist as a separate but related institution. Normally it is staffed by members of a school's faculty and provides students an opportunity to work on "real" projects with "real" clients, often with local architects. Successful CDCs are now operating at several schools. Although many are located in large urban areas, rural problems deserve equal attention, and the challenge has been taken up wherever resources permit.

Architecture in our century continues to increase in complexity. Projects in general are larger, often involving greater areas of land. The nature of the client is also changing. In the old days even very large projects were identified with single clients—individuals whose intentions and needs could easily be made clear. Today's client is more likely to be a board of directors or trustees, a special committee, or representatives of a government

agency. There are also many new technological developments, such as automatic control systems for air conditioning, complicated structural systems for long spans, and elaborate factory prefabrication. The concern for efficient use of energy has also become a permanent consideration.

Perhaps the most complex issues in architecture of recent times are not new at all but rather matters that were obvious to any sharp observer all along. These are the impacts of social, psychological, political and economic issues on the man-made environment. It is obvious that architecture and planning broadcast messages, often loudly and clearly. Architecture, like anything else man-made, embodies values and cultural priorities. Archaeologists have for years been trying to reconstruct the values of ancient cultures from their artifacts. Only recently have we begun to examine this process in the present, before it becomes ancient history. Today, 114 schools in the United States and Canada offer professional degrees in architecture, and probably over a hundred offer nonprofessional one- or two-year programs in architectural studies or technology. The vast demands of the profession and the corresponding range of programs provide the entering student with an excellent opportunity for finding the program best suited to his/her talents and interests.

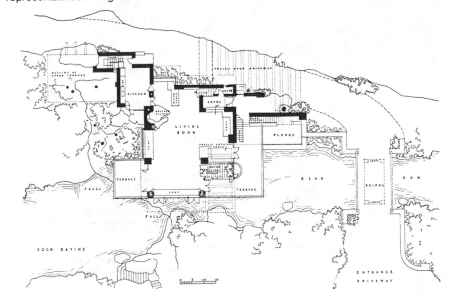

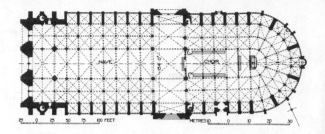

Ideally, the beginning architecture student will have a solid background in the physical sciences, including mathematics; be able to "conceptualize" at an above-average level; have a strong proficiency in oral and written communication; demonstrate a breadth of interest in the humanities; and be able to draw and sketch with ease. It is doubtful that such a student exists—but even three out of five isn't bad.

Drawing is probably the most easily acquired skill of the above, and math probably takes the highest toll of beginning students. Most architecture programs assume the entering student has had at least trigonometry and one course of physics in high school. The majority of architects, perhaps surprisingly, are not highly proficient in mathematical skills, and those whose forte is math (and hence structural design) often possess lower than average ability in drawing or design skills. Architecture is a highly diversified, multi-faceted profession, and the opportunities for specialization are many. So even if you do not excel in mathematics (or drawing, or writing), you may still become an outstanding architect. The time necessary to maintain a high proficiency in more than one or two specific areas of professional practice is generally prohibitive. If you spot a weakness in your preparation, do not despair—but do not assume it is unimportant, either.

The admissions adviser is probably more interested in a student's previous class rank and aptitude scores than specific courses or skills. A big plus for the prospective student is achievement beyond regular requirements that might demonstrate a high level of organizational ability, creativity, or other unique capability.

The potential student should have an ample background in English and other humanities. A good course in freehand drawing will ultimately prove more valuable than drafting; one semester of drafting is probably more than adequate. Botany is highly recommended for those interested in landscape architecture. Courses in geography, history, philosophy, and government are useful to everyone. Foreign languages are seldom required in architecture programs, but most accept a language as an elective. Because many schools have opportunities for study abroad, the appropriate language can have considerable practical use even before

graduation. A course in industrial arts can be helpful, but is not essential. Speech or debate classes are very useful, as architects must often express or explain complex ideas verbally, sometimes in trying circumstances.

A summer job in building construction is a very useful experience to the architectural student, and is usually easier to find than a job in a professional office. If this or other opportunities in related building trades are not available, highly motivated individuals should avail themselves of books and magazines on architecture from a public or university library. A common deficiency of many "average" architecture students is their lack of interest in reading—a habit probably started long before high school.

Ideally, the student enters the field of architecture because it is something he or she wants to study or do, not because someone else, particularly a parent, thinks it is a good idea. Most entering students have a considerable number of misconceptions regarding both the study and practice of architecture. For some, the truth is disappointing, for others exciting. Whatever architecture is, and there are many descriptions, it is not drafting. If you are not interested in academic subjects, the study of architecture (which draws heavily on many academic areas) will probably be of little interest to you.

Because you have "designed" a plan for your parents' home or for a high school class requirement that has received considerable praise, do not be deluded into thinking you necessarily have a natural gift. Such beginning capabilities are not unique and are easily acquired. While "design" is the primary emphasis of study in most programs, the faculty does not expect you to be a good designer when you enter—only when you leave. They do expect you to be above average in intelligence, desirous of knowledge, interested in learning, self-motivated, possessing broad interests, and capable of imposing strong self-discipline.

Architecture students have historically worked many evening and late-night hours in the studio on architectural projects. Design and drawing are time-consuming processes, so that there is often little time for extracurricular activities and/or part-time employment. Although long in hours, the work is enjoyable, and those with discipline find little difficulty in their

new regimen. For students who do poorly in architecture the unwillingness to spend sufficient time is often more critical than actual ability. The advantages of studying architecture are many, not the least of which is developing close relationships with other students and some of the faculty members. The satisfaction that comes from creating a tangible product is a major benefit of architecture studies, and of the profession as well.

Probably because of the widespread interest in environmental issues and the built environment, the number of applicants for admission to most architecture programs has increased significantly in recent years. Consequently, admission to architecture programs is highly competitive and only the best qualified applicants are assured of acceptance.

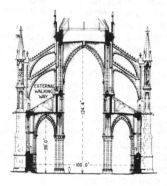

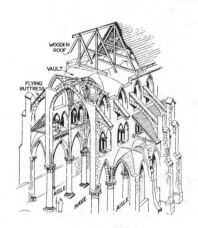

Section III
Selecting A
School

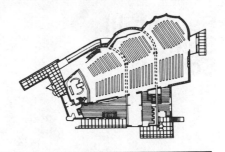

BASIC FACTS

There are one hundred fourteen schools offering professional architecture degree programs. Out of necessity you will need to limit carefully the number of choices you wish to investigate. In selecting a school there are several facts concerning architectural registration and many educational variables to consider. Some of these issues are personal and others pertain to the schools you are considering. We will begin here with the basic facts about licensure.

• *Routes to licensure*

To begin with, you should know some of the facts dealing with the overall route to becoming a registered architect. The entire process requires approximately eight to nine years; five to six years in school and three years as an intern. After you meet the internship requirements you will be required to pass a comprehensive four-day examination. The internship years are spent as a salaried employee in an architectural or related practice setting working under the supervision of registered professionals. Individuals who acquire degrees in other disciplines may enroll in a graduate professional architectural degree program of three-to-four years in duration. Subsequent to these degrees, a three-year internship is generally required. Detailed descriptions of each of these paths will be presented later. Once you fulfill the education, internship and examination requirements of a jurisdiction, you can become a "licensed" or "registered" architect.

You should be aware that each state or jurisdiction registers architects by its own set of requirements. In general, the requirements are the same for most states, but there are variations. These variations should not be an influence in your selection of any architectural program. All jurisdictions have an education requirement which may be satisfied by earning a professional degree in architecture accredited by the National Architectural Accrediting Board (NAAB). The National Council of Architectural Registration Boards (NCARB) has established standards and criteria which licensing boards have adopted as their standard for admission to licensing examinations. These criteria meet the most restrictive requirements of any board and, therefore, facilitate initial and subsequent reciprocal licensure.

• *NAAB-accredited professional degree*

The final issue to understand before you begin your selection process concerns the notion of "accredited professional degree program." Schools or departments of architecture may offer several different degree programs. Not all degree programs within a school or department may be accredited by NAAB. For example, a school of architecture may offer a program in historic preservation or architectural engineering as well as the accredited professional architecture degree program. Much of the course work may be the same but unless the program in which you are enrolled is "the NAAB-accredited professional degree program" you may encounter registration difficulties later in your career. It is not as complicated as it might sound at first. A few simple questions put to the schools you are considering will give you a very clear picture of their NAAB accreditation status. Suggested questions are listed at the end of this section.

Those are the basic facts that apply to everyone pursuing a career as a registered architect. Now it becomes a little more difficult because you must also deal with the variables. For example, not all students studying architecture will become registered architects. Some may decide during their studies that they would rather be landscape architects or perhaps they would rather manage architectural offices than practice architecture in the traditional sense. The good part of having to consider these and other variables is that choosing a career in architecture is not just choosing a single track; many career options are available because schools of architecture celebrate and encourage diversity in their programs.

THE ARCHITECTURE DEGREES

• All degrees outside of the field of architecture are referred to as *non-architecture degrees.* This title generally describes degrees in fields such as philosophy, biology, engineering and also undesignated Bachelor of Arts and Bachelor of Science degrees. These undesignated BA or BS degrees often provide opportunities for a major or minor

in architectural studies or environmental design offered through a liberal studies program. The proportion of architectural studies in the BA or BS major usually does not exceed 50% of the four-year program and may or may not provide for advanced standing in a professional architecture degree program.

• Architecture degrees are referred to as one of four types:

1) **Pre-professional architecture degrees** - The term refers to architecturally-focused four-year degrees that *are not* the professional degrees. These degrees have such titles as BS in Architecture, BS in Architectural Studies, BA in Architecture, Bachelor of Environmental Design, Bachelor of Architectural Studies, etc.; the amount of work in architecture in the program may vary from institution to institution and will determine the length of time required to complete the professional program.

2) **Professional architecture degrees** - These are the degrees that may be received after successfully completing an architecture program accredited by the NAAB. These accredited degrees are those which many states require for licensure as an architect. These degrees are either the NAAB-accredited undergraduate Bachelor of Architecture degree or the NAAB-accredited graduate Master of Architecture degree. The Bachelor of Architecture normally requires five years to complete and is sometimes referred to as the "five-year professional degree." The Master of Architecture requires from two to four years to complete depending on the type of undergraduate degree and the extent of professional content that precedes the Master's degree. When the Master's degree follows a four-year pre-professional architecture degree, it represents the "two" in the term "four + two" program, and is the final portion of the professional phase of the study program.

3) **Post-professional architecture degrees** - These are graduate degrees offered to students who already have a professional degree in architecture. These degree programs *are not* accredited by NAAB. The degrees may be in highly specialized areas of study such as design theory, health care facilities, preservation, interior design, solar design, etc. This type of degree can be either a Master's degree or, in a few cases, a PhD or Doctorate; and

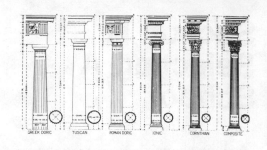

4) **Non-professional graduate architecture degrees** - This title refers to graduate degrees in architecture offered to students who do not have a professional degree and wish to pursue non-professional graduate work in architecture. These programs vary widely in duration and degree title.

There are three paths to obtaining a **professional** degree.

1) Obtaining the five-year professional degree.

2) Obtaining a four-year pre-professional degree + a two-year professional degree; this program is commonly referred to as the four + two route.

3) Obtaining the four-year non-professional degree + a three-to-four-year professional Master of Architecture degree.

The majority of students enter architecture through the first two routes; however, a detailed explanation is merited for all three options.

• **The Professional Bachelor of Architecture Degree** is often the most expeditious means of obtaining the professional degree required for licensure. On the other hand, speed is not necessarily synonymous with what may be best for every individual. Many five-year programs begin with a concentration of architecture courses in a fairly prescribed manner, although some schools begin with a general course of instruction. Electives tend to be few and exposure to other fields limited. As a result, the approximately 50 percent of entering students who do not complete the program may have difficulty moving into another area without considerable loss of credit.

Many five-year programs, however, have devised curriculum structures which allow for quite a bit of flexibility. These programs are broken into yearly components of 2+3, 1+4, 3+2, 4+1, etc. These breaks indicate logical entry and exit points from the various phases of the full five-year program. In most schools the student's work is carefully reviewed before advancement to the next phase. Such points provide a relatively easy means of transfer into an architecture program; transfer to another institution, particularly between degrees; or transfer to another academic discipline. The logical break points may also be used by the faculty to terminate students who have demonstrated little progress. The early segments of the

curriculum mix "pre-professional" design courses with liberal arts and often serve as a common base for several different environmental design disciplines such as architecture, landscape architecture, industrial design, graphics design, etc. Most professional degree programs also accept transfer students at the designated break points but transfer credit is usually evaluated on an individual course-by-course and case-by-case basis.

While the structure of some programs makes it relatively easy for a professional school to accept transfer students from both junior colleges and other colleges, it is recommended in most instances that a student considering an architecture degree start directly at the professional school. Most "feeder" programs cannot match the academic depth, library and faculty resources, and extracurricular activities of the professional schools. Cost should not be an automatic deterrent, because most schools are able to offer financial aid, although some students may find it financially necessary to begin their college education at a community or junior college. For students who are sure that architecture is to be their chosen career field, the five-year professional degree programs offer excellent opportunities. Students seeking slightly more flexibility should also examine five-year programs offering logical curriculum decision points.

• **The pre-professional plus professional Master's degree** is the other predominant route to obtaining a professional architecture degree. This route normally requires six years to complete, followed by a three-year internship. The flexibility in the program is readily apparent. At the end of four years the student has a college degree. He may decide to continue in architecture and get the professional Master's degree, spend a year or two working for an architect, or change disciplines and go into another Master's program to study other design-related fields. He may also decide at this point to shift careers completely and seek an advanced degree outside the design field.

Pre-professional programs are not professionally accredited and vary widely with respect to title, emphasis, electives, requirements and specific architecture offerings. They are, however, preparatory for advanced architectural or other environmental design fields. The four-year pre-professional program may be

subdivided into two phases, usually of two years each. The pre-architecture program may have only basic introductory courses in architecture with the majority of the course work focusing on the arts, humanities and sciences. The typical program, as well as the subdivided five-year professional programs, offers a highly flexible program that matches individual levels of achievement by providing a general education in the early years. While this may frustrate many who want to immerse themselves quickly in architecture, it does provide time for viewing a wider range of subject materials, allowing the maturing student a better opportunity to make career choices. Ideally, the extra courses in the humanities and social sciences will give students a broader background from which to start their professional education.

For those who ultimately receive advanced degrees in design areas other than architecture—or in non-architecture subjects altogether (such as business or structural engineering)—the four-year degree may be preferable to the five-year professional program in minimizing course work and time. One other advantage of a 4 + 2 program is the potential for earning the professional degree at an institution other than where the undergraduate work was completed.

The graduate degree component of the four-plus-two path is the professional NAAB-accredited degree. This degree is most appropriate for students who have a four-year pre-professional undergraduate degree in architecture. The course of study generally takes two years; however, at some schools, up to three years is required. These programs are designed to provide the professional education of the student as well as provide an opportunity for independent and creative exploration. It is imperative that the Master's degree be the professional NAAB-accredited Master's degree if the student wishes to obtain the professional degree through the four-plus-two path.

• **The non-professional degree plus professional Master's degree** path is the third route available but is the least travelled option. This route is usually taken by those who have embarked on a career other than architecture and later decide to study architecture. Many people enter the profession this way; their average age is in the late twenties and their undergraduate

backgrounds range across every imaginable discipline. Students entering the profession this way are usually quite mature and very serious about their studies. This course of study usually requires three to four years beyond the undergraduate degree. The immersion into architecture is quick and very intense. Some schools provide all of the education at the graduate level, while others will admit degree holders into their two-year professional Master's program with deficiencies. This means that preparatory undergraduate course work must first be successfully completed.

PROGRAMS OF STUDY

Now that the degrees have been described, the next step is to understand what courses you will be taking. There exist as many curricula as there are programs in architecture, and in many schools there are a number of options that lead to the completion of the degree requirements. The following illustrations are not selected from actual schools and are not intended as ideals. They simply describe the more common components of the study of architecture at most schools.
• In a five-year Bachelor of Architecture program, and to a lesser extent in the four-year nonprofessional degrees, the primary concentration is design, in both credit hours and time. In some schools "design" may be a required course every semester. It is almost always a studio course, and certain aspects of an actual or hypothetical architectural problem are emphasized. The student, either individually or as a member of a team, finishes a project with a preliminary design solution for the problem, which is graphically presented. For centuries "juries" of faculty and professionals have been used to discuss and evaluate the student solutions—undoubtedly the best-remembered experiences of nearly all students. Ideally, knowledge from other courses is applied in the design studio.

Typically several non-architectural disciplines play key roles in determining architectural solutions—the behavioral sciences, engineering (structural and mechanical), and economics, to name a few of the more obvious. While some schools have made concerted efforts to teach these and other disciplines in an integrated studio situation, in most

programs the actual instruction is provided in separate, discrete courses—sometimes in the architecture department, sometimes in other colleges.

Most architecture graduates do not become principal designers in architectural offices, and there is some criticism that too much emphasis is placed on the design studio without enough attention given to technical instruction. Others fervently argue that the role of the architecture school is not to develop technical skills; rather, it is to provide a broad framework of knowledge and a basic understanding of the desired objectives—realizing that five or six years of formal education cannot possibly provide all the necessary training an architect will ultimately need. But nearly everyone working on an architectural project will at some point be required to make a decision about what materials should be used or how they will be applied. Literally thousands of details must be resolved before the building is completed. To this extent everyone is a "designer," and this in part explains the emphasis on design in architecture schools.

A typical architecture program will recognize the importance of graphic skills, and early instruction will be given in freehand drawing and graphic delineation. Various media will be explored, including pencil, ink, color and often computer graphics. Many programs will require at least one course in basic design or composition preparatory to architectural design, sometimes offered by the art department, to develop a fundamental understanding of both two- and three-dimensional forms. This course or courses may conclude with direct applications to a specific architectural problem, beginning the transition to more complex design problems. Common to many schools is an introductory course in architecture, which may range from a sampling of various aspects of the profession to an overview of the historical development of man's building activities. In a sense it is a preview of future courses.

The problem of designing a structure to withstand the forces of gravity, wind, and earthquakes is usually addressed through another series of courses. Beginning with algebra, trigonometry and physics, most schools require at least one course in calculus and descriptive geometry before the introduction of engineering statics (a

development of the study of vector forces, from elementary physics). There may be an additional course on structural materials, particularly in engineering-oriented programs. The actual structures courses may be taken in various sequences by reference to the type of structural element (beam, column, etc.) or the structural material itself (timber, steel, reinforced concrete). Each material has different characteristics and requires separate considerations, but the ultimate objective in the engineering sense is to determine the most efficient and economical system that can be coordinated with the design solution. Obviously, the design affects the structural system and vice versa. Today, most final structural calculations are done by engineering specialists. A mastery of structures is not essential for the architect, but an understanding is. Again, the emphasis in this area will vary widely from program to program.

Specialists exist for nearly every aspect of professional practice: programming, specifications, contracts, cost estimating, construction supervision, site planning, interiors, acoustics, lighting, heating and air conditioning, and electrical and structural design. And if you look through the offerings in the catalogs of several programs you will probably find courses covering each of these and other subjects. They may be either required or optional, or may be integrated into a broader course such as "architectural technology," "professional practice," "contract documents," or "building systems."

Fundamental to most programs is a sequence of courses in architectural history, sometimes including "theory." In a few instances these courses are taught in art departments, but nearly always include discussion of not only what mankind has constructed since the pyramids but how and why. A thorough understanding of the differences in style and technology of our predecessors provides the foundation for understanding our present culture relative to its building needs.

Communication is essential to human endeavor. Some schools may require or suggest a speech or writing course in addition to English requirements; a good command of English is indispensable. Most architects spend a great deal of time communicating their ideas in both writing and speech. You might be surprised, in fact, that it is not uncommon for several of

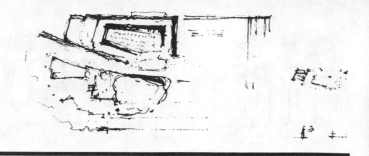

the senior architects in a large firm to have offices without drawing boards!

Interspersed with architectural or technical support courses are the electives. Most programs offer a solid rationale for a strong education in the humanities and social sciences to parallel the professional offerings. While the demand for skills often tends to crowd out the so-called liberal arts offerings, most educators and professionals realize that architecture should not and cannot be practiced independently of the rest of our culture. A school may require the student to select a "directed" sequence of perhaps three courses in one field as well as attempt to provide a diverse exposure to some of the many studies important to architecture—such as psychology, philosophy, history, geography, economics, literature, sociology, and political science. The first two years in undergraduate architecture programs typically have a greater emphasis in the elective areas to establish a student's academic breadth. It is not uncommon to find programs that have few, if any, architecture courses in the first two years, particularly in the schools whose first degree in architecture is pre-professional.

The actual number and designation of courses, their prerequisites, and sequences are the subject of many hours of discussion by virtually every faculty. Some schools will have far greater concentrations in some areas and offer little, if anything, in other areas.

The general study described above, however, is basically descriptive of most programs whether they are 5-year B Arch or 4 + 2 BA or BS in Architecture or Environmental Studies followed by an M Arch. Despite the major differences and minor nuances in the programs of the professional schools in the US and Canada, their graduates collectively have fundamentally similar attributes with, of course, a wide variance in achievement across the range of graduates.

• Several private institutions are not directly affiliated with a university but have architecture programs that are accredited by NAAB, demonstrating the quality and breadth of their offerings. The Boston Architectural Center is an example of such an institution. The BAC, along with Drexel University, offers its course work almost entirely in the evenings, allowing students to work nearly full-time while completing their academic requirements.

• There are probably over one hundred programs in the United States alone that offer programs in architecture study of two years' or less duration; most of these, but not all, are in junior and community colleges. These programs are extremely diverse in both quality and direction. Some are closely linked with professional schools, in Florida and California, for example, and may serve as the first year or two of study for a later degree. Others are specifically established to train architectural technicians or draftsmen, rather than to educate people who wish to become professional architects. As these latter programs are terminal rather than preparatory, transfer to professional schools with credit may be very difficult.

Unfortunately, there is no national body that accredits or approves these one- to two-year programs relative to their architectural training, although the institution itself may be accredited. Since it is the prerogative of the professional school to accept or reject transfer credits, the prospective student should check this possibility very carefully before enrolling in any program at a non-accredited or a nonprofessional school.

NARROWING THE CHOICES

Now to making the selection! This book provides an outline of each school's program, explaining the basic administrative structure, costs, and enrollment requirements. The inclusions for ACSA member schools describe opportunities and resources available to students, special activities, financial aid, educational philosophy, programs of study, and faculty. Each of the schools supplied the information presented.

After carefully reviewing this material, select a half dozen or so likely possibilities and write for the college catalogs and other information for more scrutiny. When writing for the college catalogs also ask if there are special brochures prepared by the department or school of architecture. These are usually carefully prepared and should be read thoroughly before visiting a school.

In addition to your readings, practicing architects are another excellent source of information. Visit several local offices. You will find architects are busy but eager to help students. You will get opinions about what's right, what's wrong, which schools to pick, and "if I had it to do over again"

musing. All of these comments may be right for the person making them but not always right for you. Temper their remarks with your own expectations and situation. Also, if possible, talk to some intern architects and very young practitioners; they are much closer to the school situation you will be entering than the seasoned professional who may have graduated twenty or thirty years ago. Each of these people will have valuable and perhaps different insights on selecting a school and career in architecture.

If at all possible, visit the schools which interest you. Walk around the campus and the school of architecture. Ask yourself if this environment is the kind of place you are willing to spend five or six years of your life. After all, you will "live" here for quite a few years. Talk to students in the program. Sometimes it's difficult to start, but just explain that you are considering coming there and simply ask them what it's like. Listen carefully for their enthusiasm about architecture and their particular programs. Plan, if possible, to visit the school when classes are in session and talk to a variety of students at different levels of study. Spend some time on campus; informal discussions in the lounge, library, or in the studios in the evenings can provide considerable insight into the life of the architecture student and the school.

Having talked with everyone possible, there are other steps you can take which will give you additional insight. Many institutions have summer programs for high school students interested in architecture studies. These programs, lasting for several weeks, are designed to be microcosms of the way you will study architecture. Going through one of the programs helps dispel a lot of misconceptions about what architects do and how they learn to do it. A list of summer programs is available by writing to the Association of Collegiate Schools of Architecture.

Finally, just a few words about your personal situation. There are basic things to consider such as your family's income. Most universities offer financial aid but if money is a very serious consideration remember that it costs a lot of money to come home for holidays and summer vacations. Such things as how far from home you want to be versus how much your family can afford to spend on travel

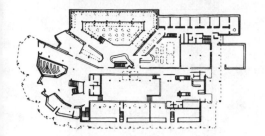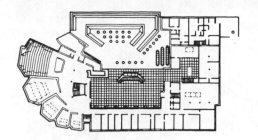

could affect your day-to-day outlook while at school.

Schools of architecture are located within a larger university context. Many of your general courses will be taken across the campus. Will you be more comfortable in a large or small university setting? The same question can be asked of the architecture department. Also, schools are located in a variety of local environments from small towns to big cities. Which of these environments will offer you the most opportunity to grow as a person and also allow you to get the most out of your university education?

The following is a bit of general advice and a synopsis of questions and answers that may help you select the school that best fits your needs.

• *The Advice:*

1. If you have doubts about which field of study you wish to pursue but are currently leaning toward architecture, a 4 + 2 program might be preferable to a five-year professional program. With it you will be freer to sample other subject areas and, should you change majors, it will be easier to transfer (particularly to other design professions) during or after your first four years. Another alternative for maximum flexibility is to first obtain a non-architecture four-year degree (in history, philosophy, geography, etc.) and then pursue a three-and-a-half-year professional graduate degree in architecture.

2. If you are coming directly from high school and are absolutely certain that a primary concern is to become licensed in minimum time, a five-year Bachelor of Architecture degree program will be shorter by one year in many cases.

3. A school with a professionally accredited degree program is generally preferable to a school without one. However, a new, unaccredited program should not be eliminated from your consideration if it can demonstrate quality or certain advantages for you. Since a program cannot be accredited until it has offered instruction for several years, a new program may become accredited by the time you receive your degree.

4. Tuition, fees, and living costs can understandably be a major determinant in

school selection. Most schools can provide some students partial financial assistance, in either scholarships or loans. Graduate students also may receive teaching or research assistantships. You can determine the basic institutional costs from this book, but you should ask a school directly about its potential for providing assistance. The American Institute of Architects has scholarship programs applicable to all schools in the United States; one program is specifically aimed at minorities. The only other source of information for architecture scholarships or assistance is the individual school or university. A list of the AIA's scholarship opportunities is provided later in this book.

5. You should note that there may be great schools of architecture in universities you consider average. Conversely, the notoriety of a given university does not necessarily extend to every department.

• *Questions to ask - Answers you need:*

I. What are the educational degree options and the minimum number of years required to obtain each degree?

There are basically three routes to obtaining a professional architecture degree that will give you the educational requirements to become eligible to take the registration exam. They are:

1. Bachelor of Architecture professional degree: This path requires 5 years in an NAAB-accredited architecture program.

2. Pre-professional degree (e.g. Bachelor of Environmental Design, Bachelor of Science in Architecture, etc.) + Master of Architecture professional degree: This path requires a 4-year undergraduate degree in "Pre-Architecture" plus 2 years for the Master of Architecture professional degree in an NAAB-accredited program.

3. Any Non-Architecture Undergraduate degree + Master of Architecture professional degree: This path requires 4 years for an undergraduate degree in a non-related field, plus 3-4 years in an NAAB-accredited Master of

Architecture professional program. This option requires a total of 7-8 years of education.

II. What are the steps in becoming a licensed/registered architect?

Step 1. Obtain a professional NAAB-accredited architecture degree. Five or six years are usually required.

Step 2. Serve an internship in an architect's office. Usually 3 years are required, but in some cases advanced study or alternative professional or teaching experience can be applied to the internship requirements. Many states require graduates to fulfill the specific criteria established by the Intern-Architect Development Program.

Step 3. Pass the registration exam. In general, you are eligible to take the exam if you have a *professional NAAB-accredited degree* and have met the internship requirements.

III. The following are questions you should ask of schools to which you are interested in applying. **Note:** These are only basic technical questions and do not fully address the quality of the education offered at any institution. Please read all the available material, visit the school, if possible, and formulate your own questions based on your personal aspirations and requirements. All of the information you obtain will help you know if a particular school is right for you.

Accreditation:
1. Is the program accredited by the National Architectural Accrediting Board (NAAB)?

2. If not, what is the school's current status with the National Architectural Accrediting Board (NAAB)?

3. If the school is now accredited by NAAB, what is the term of accreditation given on the last visit? How many years is the term?

4. Can I be reasonably assured that the school will be NAAB-accredited during the time I am in school?

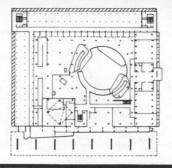 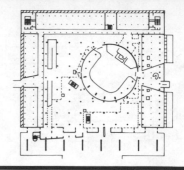

Degree Options:

5. Is the first degree that I receive an NAAB-accredited professional degree which will fulfill the educational requirement to be eligible for registration?

6. If the first degree is not a professional degree, what is the title of the pre-professional degree offered?

7. Is the pre-professional degree one that will allow me to apply for the professional architectural degree at this school or other schools?

8. Is the pre-professional degree one that will allow me to proceed naturally to professional or graduate design programs in other disciplines such as Landscape Architecture, Urban Design, Historic Preservation, etc.?

9. How many years will this pre-professional degree normally require?

10. If I decide not to go on with the professional program or the graduate professional degree program, or if I am not allowed to continue because of not meeting academic criteria, what are my career alternatives with the four-year pre-professional Bachelor's degree?

Curriculum Options:

11. Are there special offerings at this school that allow me to focus on a particular interest such as design, computers, energy, preservation, etc.?

12. Are there special offerings at this school that allow me to take advantage of its geographic location?

13. Are there special enrichment programs such as foreign or off-campus study opportunities?

14. Are there special lab facilities or an outstanding library that would help with my special interests?

15. What are the notable accomplishments of the faculty?

16. What are the average numbers of students in the design studios and the lecture classes?

17. Who will teach my classes? Full-time faculty? Part-time? Graduate students?

18. What are the advantages of this school's teaching system?

IV. There are many other questions you should ask of yourself and others that will help you determine your compatibility at a particular university and school of architecture.

1. How far away from home do I want to be?

2. What is the cost of education?

3. Are scholarships available - academic or need-based?

4. Do I thrive best in a small school environment or large? Rural or urban?

5. Am I certain that I want to be an architect or would I like a program that is broad-based in the first two years to allow for testing various educational options?

6. Am I more liberal arts or technically oriented? This also is a good question to ask of the school and university about its direction.

Nearly every school has at least one designated administrator or faculty member who is assigned specifically to visit with potential applicants. They can answer your questions and tell you a great deal about that school and usually several others, the directions its graduates are pursuing, and what is expected of successful applicants.

After all of this discussion on how to narrow the choices to a few schools which are best for you, I'm sure you or your parents are still asking, "Yes, but which are the best schools?" There really is no way to say which are the best schools. Best for what? — For what you can afford? For the location you wish to be in? For the university you wish to go to? For the special interest you wish to focus on? In general, best should mean *best for you*.

Because of the diverse nature of architecture programs and the varied interests, aptitudes, and objectives of students, it is impossible to rank architecture schools. While some program aspects can be measured—e.g., number of library books, student/faculty ratio, scholarships, research facilities, studio space per student, faculty salaries—there is no method of assessing accurately the quality of instruction from one faculty to another or quantifying different points of view. Probably the most important factor in any educational endeavor is the student's motivation. Most architectural employers are far more interested in what you have

accomplished and can do as a person than in the "prestigiousness" of your degree. Despite the major differences and minor nuances in the programs of the professional schools in the United States and Canada, their graduates collectively have fundamentally similar attributes. And, in each graduating class from a single school the capabilities of the graduates are highly diverse. Most schools are excellent in their chosen areas of emphasis, but no school is excellent in all aspects of what you ought to learn. Undoubtedly, you will find many schools suited to your educational objectives. While you should seek as much information and as many opinions as possible, with a conscientious effort you will probably be in as good a position as anyone to make decisions regarding your own education and career. Besides, having faith in one's own ability to make non-quantifiable judgments is important to every successful professional. Your architecture education should be enjoyable, and we think your search will be, too.

AIA SCHOLARSHIPS

• **Minority/Disadvantaged Scholarship Program:** Twenty annual awards, renewable for two additional years, for recent high school graduates entering or in their first year in an accredited program in architecture. Candidates must be nominated by an architect, firm, community design center, guidance counselor/teacher, school of architecture dean/faculty member, or community, civic or religious organization; deadline for nominations (forms available from Scholarship Programs, The American Institute of Architects) is December 1; for applications, January 15. Awards vary according to need and are not intended to cover the full cost of a recipient's education.

• **AIA/AIAF Scholarship Program for First-Professional Degree Candidates:** Single-year awards for students in the final two years of an accredited professional degree program. Applications are allotted to schools based upon enrollment, and candidates must apply to the office of the school of architecture for forms, which have a postmark deadline of February 1. Awards range generally from $500 to $2,000, and considerations include academic performance, recommendations, and need.

• **AIA/AIAF Scholarship Program for Advanced Study or Research Beyond the First-Professional Degree:** Awards, ranging from $1,000 to $2,500 for a single year of advanced study or research, will be based upon the merit of the proposed program of study. Applications for graduates and professionals can be obtained directly from AIA Scholarship Programs for a February 15 postmark deadline.

AHA/AIA Fellowship in Health Facilities Design: One or more graduate fellowships totalling $6,000 for one year's study. Applications should be requested from The American Hospital Association, American Society for Hospital Engineering, 840 North Shore Drive, Chicago, IL 60611, and will be evaluated by a joint AHA/AIA committee based upon the proposed study program. Postmark deadline: March 15.

For more details on eligibility, conditions, procedures, and awards, write: Scholarship Programs, The American Institute of Architects, 1735 New York Avenue, NW, Washington, DC 20006, telephone (202) 626-7358.

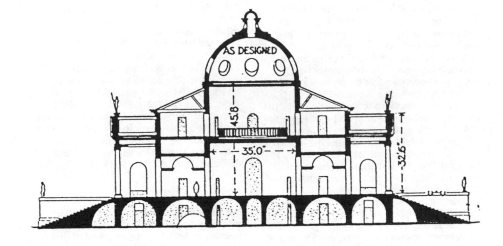

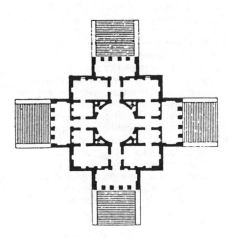

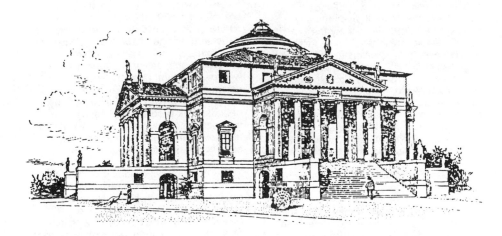

Section IV
Practicing
Architecture

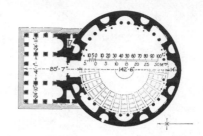 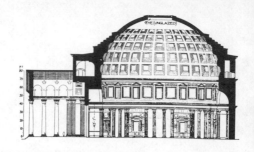

• Employment Opportunities

There are approximately 85,000 licensed architects in the United States today, including some who are retired and others who are not working as architects. Of course, substantial numbers of non-licensed people are working in architecture offices. An estimated 32,000 students are currently enrolled in schools of architecture in the United States; 17,000 are in 5-year professional degree programs, 4,400 in professional Master's degree programs and 10,600 in pre-professional four-year programs. In 1987, there were 3,100 5-year professional degrees awarded and 1,500 professional Master's degrees. The pre-professional programs awarded 2,300 degrees in 1987. In Canada, there are approximately 3,300 licensed practitioners who are members of the Royal Architectural Institute of Canada (RAIC); another 1,400 architects belong to the Order of Architects of Quebec. These figures have remained fairly constant over the past five years. However, the National Bureau of Labor Statistics' *Occupational Outlook* predicts an increase in architecturally related jobs over the next decade.

Determining the job market (or demand for new employees) is complicated by many factors, not the least of which is the apparent desire of many graduates to pursue a career other than one in an architecture office, and also by the lack of specific employment data. These factors, coupled with the cyclical nature of construction activity and the unpredictability of national and worldwide economics five to eight years hence, make an accurate assessment of the future needs for architects very difficult. A good source for predicting future needs is the *Occupational Outlook Handbook* published by the U.S. Government. This book should be in your local library.

The better graduates from professional programs historically have had little difficulty finding a professional job opportunity, particularly if they have acquired some summer experience in an office or in building construction and if they are willing to relocate. Often, various sectors of the country will be "booming" while other areas are in a state of near recession. Some cities (e.g., San Francisco) are notoriously overpopulated with architects, while in other areas they are chronically in short supply.

Beginning salaries for architecture interns also fluctuate widely, depending in part on geographical location, demand due to building activity, availability of applicants, and, most important, the capability of the individual applicant. An intern architect typically earns $20,000-22,000 per year. Since a new graduate must work as an intern architect for three years before taking the licensing exam and becoming a registered architect, the salaries are for interns, not registered architects. Remember, your entire educational experience requires approximately eight to nine years of combined formal schooling and apprenticeship and internship. Essentially, your internship salary allows you to earn an income while completing the last two or three years of your education. A 1987 survey of architectural firms indicated that the project managers in mid-sized firms earned an average of $38,000 annually. Partners earned between $41,000 and $88,000 depending on the size of the firm.

• Types of Offices

Both the public and the private sectors offer a wide range of opportunities for holders of architectural degrees. If you choose to practice in an architectural office, consider that the size and organization of the firm will affect the nature of your job. Offices are usually structured on one of two basic models; the first consists of a series of departmental specializations: designers, specification writers, structural experts, landscape designers, production draftsmen, etc. A job starts in one division and is passed to the next as work progresses. In such instances very few people will "see the job all the way through," but each performs a specific function for each job the office undertakes.

The other model divides the office into teams, each team being responsible for the project from start to finish. There may be various specialists on the team, or consultants may be employed. A team may be working on several jobs simultaneously, but will have little, if any, responsibility for other projects being undertaken by other teams. A small office, of course, will have only one team.

Few offices precisely fit these simplified models, and many have certain aspects of both. Some architectural firms subcontract with consultants and other firms for major portions of the contract, thus keeping their own staff to a minimal number. This has a decided advantage when construction activity drops off; the number of employees will not have to be reduced as quickly as in a large firm. Some firms have offices in several cities, and sometimes in other countries. The management and organization of any firm is a complex task; large architectural firms usually have their own personnel directors, accountants, office managers, etc. In fact, principals of large firms may spend little of their time on actual design or drawings for new buildings.

The architectural employee may be paid either an hourly wage or annual salary. Most firms expect more than forty hours per week during busy times, which can be frequent, and while hourly employees are paid overtime, salaried personnel often are not. Some firms have profit-sharing plans for those who are not partners, which provide incentive; but more often than not the architect will work more hours per week than many other professionals. Often these extra hours are spent at tedious and exacting tasks. Nearly every field includes work that is less than stimulating, and architecture is no exception. Many mundane tasks must be done carefully. Architecture is not quite what Ayn Rand's *Fountainhead* might have led you to believe.

Most architects working in larger firms have never been totally responsible for any building, must less a famous one. To expect instant success or recognition for building design is an unrealistic objective. Philip Johnson, one of the best known practicing architects in the world today, didn't even start architecture school until his late thirties. A large and complex building, such as a $100-million hospital, may require three to four years from preliminary programming to completion, with as many as forty people working nearly full-time on this one project.

An American Institute of Architects survey revealed that about 2% of the firms have one person, 56% have fewer than four, and 82% have nine or fewer. Thirteen percent of all firms have 1 to 24 employees, 3.6% have 25 to 74, and only 1.1% have more than 75 employees. But these large firms employ nearly 10% of all architects, while one-person firms account for 7.4% of all architects. About 75% of all

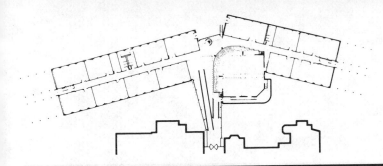

architects work in firms with fewer than 25 employees. Some experts suggest that the trend is toward more small firms (fewer than 5 persons) and large firms (over 75), but such is not the case today. There is considerable opportunity for architecture graduates to select both the type and size of office in which they will work.

• Other Architecture Career Opportunities

In government, at the federal level, 66% of the architects are at the Civil Service grade levels of GS-11, -12, and -13. They may be found in twenty different agencies. Probably even more often than in the private sector, persons holding degrees command considerably higher earnings than those without.

The Architects in Government Committee of the American Institute of Architects reported recently on a survey of over 2,000 architects employed by the federal, state, and local governments. A partial listing of the areas of specialization includes historic preservation, energy conservation, interior design, barrier-free architecture, land use planning, urban design, architectural design, architectural engineering, acoustical design, life safety, life-cycle costing, computer applications, seismic design, graphic design, post-construction evaluation, value management, environmental impact, quality control, social impact, economic impact, behavioral user studies, and master planning. Similarly, state and local agencies such as public works, health, education, building services, housing, and transportation as well as offices of architecture may employ architects.

Many employment options also exist outside of the traditional practice of architecture. Building and construction firms, development corporations, the Peace Corps, military services, real estate enterprises, landscape and planning firms, interior design firms, industrial and product design groups, building component manufacturers, and sales departments also employ architecture graduates in diverse jobs. And at least 3,000 people are primarily occupied in teaching architecture—a sizeable percentage of the profession.

• Registration

In the United States, licensing of architects is the legal prerogative of the individual state governments. However, due to the efforts of the National Council of Architectural Registration Boards (NCARB), guidelines for license examination eligibility and the exam itself are fairly uniform from state to state. Typically a minimum of three years' experience is required after receiving a professional NAAB-accredited degree in architecture before one can sit for the licensing exam.

In Canada, licensing of architects is the legal prerogative of each province, which delegates responsibility to a provincial association of architects. The requirements for registration/licensing in each province include a degree from a school of architecture, two or three years of professional experience and successful completion of a registration examination. The address of the association of architects in each province may be obtained from the Royal Architectural Institute of Canada.

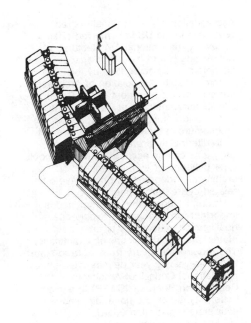

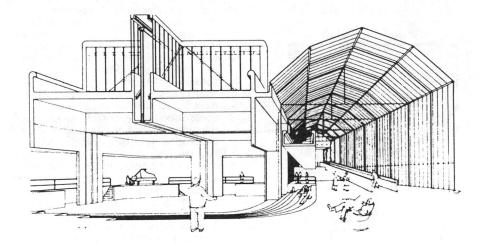

Accreditation

Accreditation of professional degree programs in the US is conferred after review by the National Architectural Accrediting Board (NAAB). Canadian schools may be accredited by the Commonwealth Association of Architects, the provincial component of the Royal Architectural Institute of Canada (RAIC).

It is worth emphasizing that *schools* of architecture in the United States are not accredited. Only *professional degree programs* can be accredited. Most schools offer only one or two accredited architectural degrees, but may have other related degree programs.

Having a degree that is accredited is important for meeting the experience qualifications necessary to take most states' architectural licensing examinations. The requirements vary from state to state and from year to year despite attempts by the National Council of Architectural Registration Boards (NCARB) to achieve uniformity. If you are uncertain, check with your state registration board. The schools will know the advantages or disadvantages of their degree programs relative to the law in their state.

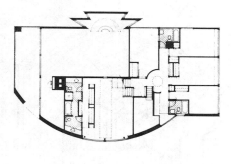

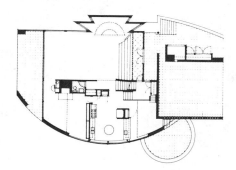

The following statement was prepared by John Maudlin-Jeronimo, executive director of the National Architectural Accrediting Board: The National Architectural Accrediting Board (NAAB) accredits programs which lead to a professional degree in architecture. Over one hundred programs in 93 schools are currently accredited. Graduation from an accredited program is important for registration as an architect and for employment, because accreditation is an indication of the quality of the education offered. Most states require a person to have graduated from an NAAB-accredited program, although some states allow experience to substitute for education. States require practical architectural experience (internship) prior to examination and registration.

Accreditation means more than help toward registration. The accreditation process provides independent evaluation of the quality of the professional program as assessed from a national perspective. It provides assurance that the program can adequately prepare students for internship prior to professional practice. Accreditation means that the school has prepared an Architecture Program Report (APR), which includes a statement of intentions, description of resources, a self-evaluation, strategies for improvement, and evidence that each student has completed NAAB's achievement-oriented performance criteria. Accreditation also means that a team consisting of an educator, architects, and a student has visited the school for three days of intensive discussion and observation and reported to NAAB about the program. Next, NAAB decides whether the program is to be accredited and for how long.

Accreditation does not mean that all schools are the same. Every program has its special features and room for growth. Some schools offer a choice of options while others have a more defined program. A single school may offer several accredited professional degree programs—for example, it may offer both the five-year undergraduate degree for high school graduates, and the three-and-one-half-year graduate degree intended for people who already have a degree in another field. A professional degree program is accredited by the same standards whether it leads to a Bachelor of Architecture or a Master of Architecture degree.

A new school of architecture cannot have a program accredited by NAAB until its first professional class has graduated. If the program is then accredited most state registration boards will consider the accreditation as retroactive for a year or two so that the first class can benefit from accreditation. Canadian and other foreign programs are not accredited by NAAB. If you are considering a school which is not accredited, check with the registration boards in the states in which you plan to practice about their rules. For more information about registration and internship write to your state board or the National Council of Architectural Registration Boards (NCARB, 1735 New York Avenue, NW, Washington, DC 20006).

For the most recent *List of Accredited Programs in Architecture,* write to NAAB (1735 New York Avenue, NW, Washington, DC 20006) for a free copy. For other information about any particular school, contact that school directly. Some schools make their Architecture Program Report and the NAAB Accreditation Report available for public inspection, usually through the school library.

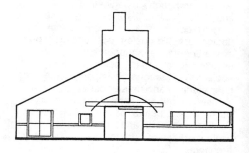

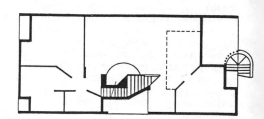

Abbreviations Used

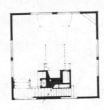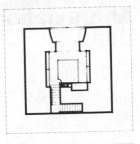

PROFESSIONAL ORGANIZATIONS

AAA—Alberta Association of Architects
ABET—Accreditation Board for Engineering and Technology
ACSA—Association of Collegiate Schools of Architecture
ACSP—Association of Collegiate Schools of Planning
AIA—American Institute of Architects
AIAS—American Institute of Architecture Students
AIP—American Institute of Planners
APA—American Planning Association
ASID—American Society of Interior Designers
ASLA—American Society of Landscape Architects
CAA—Commonwealth Association of Architects
CIP—Canadian Institute of Planning
CPUQ—Professional Corporation of Urbanists of Quebec
FIDER—Foundation for Interior Design Education Research
IDP—Intern-Architect Development Program
IDSA—Industrial Design Society of America, Inc.
LAAB—Landscape Architectural Accreditation Board
MAA—Manitoba Architectural Association
NAAB—National Architectural Accrediting Board
NCARB—National Council of Architectural Registration Boards
NASA—National Association of Schools of Art
NSAA—Nova Scotia Association of Architecture
OAA—Ontario Association of Architects
OAQ—Order of Architects of Quebec
RAIC—Royal Architectural Institute of Canada
RIBA—Royal Institute of British Architects

DEGREES

BA—Bachelor of Arts
BA(Arch)—BA in Architecture
BA(ED)—BA in Environmental Design
BA in Arch Sci—BA in Architectural Science
BA in ID (Int)—BA in Interior Design
BAA—BA in Art
B Arch—Bachelor of Architecture
B Arch Eng—Bachelor of Architectural Engineering
B Art—Bachelor of Art
BA/BS in Arch Stud—BA or BS in Architectural Studies
BBC—Bachelor of Building Construction
B Des—Bachelor of Design
BDIn—Baccalaureate en design industriel
BED—Bachelor of Environmental Design
BEDA—Bachelor of Environmental Design in Architecture
BE Des—Bachelor of Environmental Design
BES—Bachelor of Environmental Studies
BFA—Bachelor of Fine Arts
BID—Bachelor of Interior Design
B of Int Des—Bachelor of Interior Design
B Int Des—Bachelor of Interior Design
B Int Arch—Bachelor of Interior Architecture
B of Ind Des—Bachelor of Industrial Design
BLA—Bachelor of Landscape Architecture
B Prof Stds in Cons Mgt—Bachelor of Professional Studies in Construction Management
BPS—Bachelor of Professional Studies
BS—Bachelor of Science
BS(LA)—BS in Landscape Architecture
BS(Planning)—Bachelor of Science in Planning
BSAD—BS in Architectural Design
BSAE—BS in Architectural Engineering
BS Arch—BS in Architecture
BS Arch E—BS in Architectural Engineering
BSAS—BS in Architectural Studies
BSBC—BS in Building Construction
BSc—Bachelor of Science
B Sc Arch—Bachelor of Science in Architecture
B Sc Bldg Des—Bachelor of Science in Building Design
BSCE—BS in Construction Engineering
BS Con E—BS in Construction Engineering
BS Con Eng—BS in Construction Engineering
BS Cons Tech—BS in Construction Technology
BSCRP—Bachelor of Science in City and Regional Planning
BSED—BS in Environmental Design
BS in Bldg Sci—BS in Building Science
BS Int Arch—BS in Interior Architecture
BSL Arch—BS in Landscape Architecture
BSUP—BS in Urban Planning
B Urb—Baccalaureate en urbanisme
D Arch—Doctor of Architecture
DED—Doctor of Environmental Design
MA—Master of Arts
MA in URP—MA in Urban and Regional Planning
MAA—Master of Arts in Architecture
MA Int Des—MA in Interior Design
M Arch—Master of Architecture
M Arch UD—Master of Architecture and Urban Design
MAUD—MA in Urban Design
MBC—Master of Building Construction
MCP—Master of City Planning
MCRP—Master of City and Regional Planning
ME Des—Master of Environmental Design
MFA—Master of Fine Arts
MFA Int Des—MFA in Interior Design
MID—Master of Industrial Design
MLA—Master of Landscape Architecture
MLA in UD—Master of Landscape Architecture in Urban Design
MPCD—Master in Planning and Community Development
MPD—Master of Planning and Design
MRCP—Master of Regional and City Planning
MRP—Master of Regional Planning
MS—Master of Science
MS(UD)—MS in Urban Design
MS Arch Tech—MS in Architectural Technology
MS in Arch—MS in Architecture
MS Comm and Reg Plg—MS in Community and Regional Planning
MSCRP—MS in City and Regional Planning
MS Hist Pres—MS in Historic Preservation
MS Structures—Master of Science in Structures
MScA—Maitrise en sciences appliquées en amenagement
MSUP—MS in Urban Planning
MUD—Master of Urban Design
MUP—Master of Urban Planning
MUP Urb Des—Master of Urban Planning in Urban Design
M Urb—Maitrise en urbanisme
MURP—Master of Urban and Regional Planning
PhD—Doctor of Philosophy

TERMS & ABBREVIATIONS

ACT—American College Testing Exam
adm—admission
admin—administration
adv—advanced
app—applicant
arch—architecture or -al
ASAT—Architectural Scholastic Aptitude
   Test
assoc—associate
bacc—baccalaureate
bkgd—background
bldg—building
coll—college
comm—community
cr—credit(s)
curr—curriculum
des—design
dipl—diploma
educ—education
engr—engineer(ing)
Eng—English (except Engineer[ing] in
   degrees)
env—environment(al)
equiv—equivalent
ex—example(s)
exp—experience
FTE—full-time equivalent
for—foreign
fr—freshman
grad—graduate
GRE—Graduate Record Examination
GPA—grade point average
hr(s)—hour(s)
hs—high school
inc—including
ind—industrial
int—interior
lang—language(s)
mgt—management
na—not applicable
NA—not available
prof—professional
prog—program
pt—point
qtr—quarter
rec—recommendation
reg—regional
req—required
SAT—Scholastic Aptitude Test
sch—school
soc sci—social science
stg—standing
tech—technology
undgrd—undergraduate
univ—university
yr—year

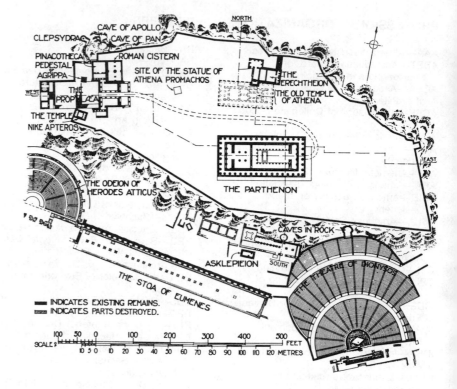

Organizations in Architecture and Related Fields

In the United States there are five major organizations fundamental to architecture. At present, all are located in the same building, and thus share the same address: 1735 New York Avenue, NW, Washington, DC 20006.

The American Institute of Architects (AIA) has as its principal membership registered architects in the US (about 50,000). Like ACSA, its membership is totally voluntary. While the thrust of the AIA is directed toward the practitioner, it has career information and scholarship programs in its Education Services Center. Many cities and all states have chapter organizations of the AIA. All are helpful resources. (202-626-7300)

The American Institute of Architecture Students (AIAS) is composed of student members at chapters established in 140 colleges and universities with architectural programs. Founded in 1957, AIAS hosts conferences, sponsors design competitions, coordinates student activities, and publishes both a monthly newsletter and a semi-annual journal specifically for member students. (202-626-7472)

The Association of Collegiate Schools of Architecture, Inc. (ACSA), as its name suggests, has as its principal membership the professional schools of architecture in both the United States and Canada. It exists for the purpose of improving the quality of architecture education. (202-785-2324)

The National Council of Architectural Registration Boards (NCARB) is comprised of all the individual state licensing boards of the United States. NCARB's mission is to assist its member boards by recommending guidelines covering rules, regulations and practice laws as well as standards for education, internship and examination for licensure. NCARB also serves the profession by granting certification to those architects who meet its standards. Certification facilitates reciprocal registration among the member boards. (202-783-6500)

The National Architectural Accrediting Board (NAAB) was co-founded in 1940 by ACSA, AIA, and NCARB for the purpose of accrediting professional architectural education programs. These three organizations continue today their sponsorship and support of NAAB as an independent agency. (202-783-2007)

In Canada, the **Royal Architectural Institute of Canada** (RAIC) is the national organization to which most practicing architects belong on a voluntary basis. Although the concerns of the RAIC are chiefly those of the architect in practice, its programs include research and scholarship. A representative of the student body is a member of the Governing Council of RAIC. Information on the profession may be obtained from each provincial association of architecture or from the RAIC at 328 Somerset West, Ottawa, Ontario, K2P 0J9. (613-232-7165)

Other organizations with helpful information:

American Planning Association (APA)
1776 Massachusetts Avenue, NW
Washington, DC 20036
(202-872-0611)

American Society of Interior Designers (ASID)
1430 Broadway
New York, NY 10018
(212-944-9220)

American Society of Landscape Architects (ASLA)
1733 Connecticut Avenue, NW
Washington, DC 20009
(202-466-7730)

National Institute for Architectural Education (NIAE)
30 West 22nd Street
New York, NY 10010
(212-924-7000)

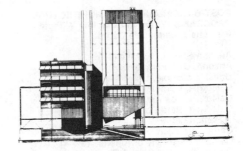

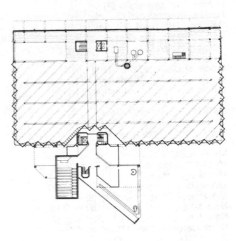

Specialized and Related Architecture Degrees

POST-BACCALAUREATE ARCHITECTURE PROGRAMS (Years to Complete Without Previous Architecture Degree)

Arizona State University (3+)
Arizona, University of (3½)
British Columbia, University of (3)
California, Berkeley, University of (3)
California, Los Angeles, University of (3)
California State Polytechnic University, Pomona (3)
Carnegie-Mellon University (3)
Catholic University of America (3½-4)
Cincinnati, University of (2)
Clemson University (4)
Colorado at Denver, University of (3½)
Columbia University (3)
Florida A&M University (4)
Florida, University of (3)
Georgia Institute of Technology (3½-4)
Harvard University (3½)
Houston, University of (3)
Howard University (3½)
Illinois at Chicago, University of (3)
Illinois at Urbana-Champaign, University of (3½)
Illinois Institute of Technology (3½)
Iowa State University (3+)
Kansas, University of (2¼+)
Louisiana Tech University (3½)
Manitoba, University of (4; 3 for environmental studies)
Maryland, University of (3½)
Massachusetts Institute of Technology (3)
Miami University (3+)
Miami, University of (3)
Mississippi State University (3)
Nevada, Las Vegas, University of (3+)
New Jersey Institute of Technology (2-3½)
North Carolina State University (3½-4)
Ohio State University (3+)
Oklahoma, University of (3)
Oregon, University of (3½)
Pennsylvania, University of (3)
Princeton University (3)
Rensselaer Polytechnic Institute (3)
Rice University (3½)
South Florida, University of (FAMU/USF architecture program) (2⅔)
Southern California Institute of Architecture (3½)
State University of New York at Buffalo (3½)
Syracuse University (3½)
Tennessee-Knoxville, University of (3)
Texas A&M University (3-4)
Texas at Arlington, University of (3)
Texas at Austin, University of (3½)
Texas Tech University (3)
Tulane University (3)
Utah, University of (3)
Virginia Polytechnic Institute and State University (3)
Virginia, University of (3½)
Washington State University (2-3)
Washington University (3½)
Washington, University of (3)
Wisconsin, Milwaukee, University of (3)

Yale University (3)

DOCTORAL PROGRAMS IN ARCHITECTURE

California, Berkeley, University of
California, Los Angeles, University of
Carnegie-Mellon University
Georgia Institute of Technology
Harvard University
Manitoba, University of
Massachusetts Institute of Technology
Michigan, University of
Montreal, Universite de
Pennsylvania State University (interdisciplinary environmental design only)
Pennsylvania, University of
Princeton University
Rice University
Texas A&M University
Virginia Polytechnic Institute and State University
Wisconsin-Milwaukee, University of

SPECIALIZATIONS WITHIN AN ARCHITECTURE DEGREE
(These specializations may be offered only in certain degree programs— contact the university for details)

Computer-Aided Design
Arizona State University
Arizona, University of
California, Los Angeles, University of
California Polytechnic State University, San Luis Obispo
Carnegie-Mellon University
Georgia Institute of Technology
Laval University
Minnesota, University of
Ohio State University
Pennsylvania State University
Texas at Austin, University of
Texas Tech University

Construction Management
Catholic University of America
Illinois at Urbana-Champaign, University of
Maryland, University of (proposed)
Nebraska-Lincoln, University of
Nevada, Las Vegas, University of
Oklahoma, University of
Pennsylvania State University
Pratt Institute
Texas A&M University
Washington, University of

Energy
Arizona State University (solar/energy design)
Arizona, University of (desert architecture)
California, Los Angeles, University of (technology, including energy-conserving design)
California Polytechnic State University, San Luis Obispo
Florida A&M University (energy)

Georgia Institute of Technology
Laval University
Michigan, University of
Minnesota, University of (energy-efficient design, technology transfer)
Ohio State University (passive solar design)
Southern California, University of (solar access, energy-conserving design)
Texas A&M University

Environment
Arizona, University of (environment/behavior)
California State Polytechnic University, Pomona (environmental studies)
Florida A&M University (environmental technology)
Florida, University of (environmental technology)
Kansas State University (environment/behavior)
Minnesota, University of (man-environment relations)
Tulane University (man-environment studies)
Wisconsin-Milwaukee, University of

Health and Hospital Facilities Design
Clemson University
Houston, University of (proposed)
Howard University
Texas A&M University

Interior Architecture
Hawaii, University of
Houston, University of (proposed)
Texas A&M University

Preservation
Arizona, University of
Ball State University
Cincinnati, University of
Columbia University
Florida, University of
Georgia Institute of Technology
Illinois at Urbana-Champaign, University of
Kansas State University
Kent State University
Laval University
Lawrence Institute of Technology
Maryland, University of
Michigan, University of
Minnesota, University of
Nebraska-Lincoln, University of
Ohio State University
Oklahoma, University of
Pennsylvania, University of
Pratt Institute
Texas A&M University
Texas at Austin, University of
Texas Tech University
Tulane University
Washington, University of

Technology
Arizona, University of (desert architecture)
California, Berkeley, University of
California, Los Angeles, University of

California Polytechnic State University, San Luis Obispo
Georgia Institute of Technology
Nevada, Las Vegas, University of
Oklahoma, University of (technology)
State University of New York at Buffalo (advanced building technology)
Texas A&M University (technologies, architectural and daylighting)
Wentworth Institute of Technology

Theory and History
California, Berkeley, University of (history, theory)
California, Los Angeles, University of (history, analysis, and criticism of architecture)
Catholic University of America (history)
Colorado at Denver, University of
Florida, University of
Georgia Institute of Technology
Houston, University of (graduate)
Laval University
Minnesota, University of
Ohio State University
Savannah College of Art and Design
Texas A&M University
Texas Tech University (history)
Tulane University (design and theory)

Urban Design
Arizona, University of (desert community design)
California, Los Angeles, University of
California State Polytechnic University, Pomona
City College of the City University of New York (urban landscape)
Colorado at Denver, University of
Georgia Institute of Technology
Howard University
Illinois at Urbana-Champaign, University of
Iowa State University (proposed)
Kansas State University (community/urban design)
Kansas, University of
Kent State University
Laval University
Manitoba, University of
Michigan, University of
Minnesota, University of
Nevada, Las Vegas, University of
Notre Dame, University of (architectural/urban design—Chicago and Rome)
Oklahoma, University of
Pennsylvania, University of
Rice University
Texas A&M University
Texas at Arlington, University of
Texas at Austin, University of
Texas Tech University
Toronto, University of
Washington, University of

Other
Arizona State University (professional practice and management)

Arizona, University of (design communications, arid lands architecture)
Auburn University (business/management)
California, Berkeley, University of (social concerns)
California, Los Angeles, University of (architectural design; policy, programming, and evaluation)
Catholic University of America (design, planning)
Cincinnati, University of (historic preservation)
Florida A&M University (management, architectural programming and evaluation)
Florida, University of (structural design, design)
Georgia Institute of Technology (behavioral studies)
Houston, University of (regional architecture, experimental architecture, design for space)
Howard University (tropical architecture, developing countries, urban design and research)
Iowa State University (business administration, housing, planning)
Illinois at Urbana-Champaign, University of (design, housing, history and preservation, structures, architectural practice, individual study)
Kansas, University of (built form and culture, architectural management)
Laval University (climate and design, architectural acoustics)
Louisiana State University (research-oriented MSArch)
McGill University (minimum-cost housing, architectural history and theory, architectural design)
Mississippi State University (small-town design)
Nevada, Las Vegas, University of (hotel and resort facilities design, tourism and planning development)
New Mexico, University of (emphasis in energy-conscious design, emphasis in behavior and design, emphasis in planning and design)
Pratt Institute (urban environmental systems management)
Savannah College of Art and Design (design with minor in history)
Southern California, University of (urban architecture)
Texas Tech University (design, structures)

RELATED DEGREE PROGRAMS*

Architectural Engineering
California Polytechnic State University, San Luis Obispo (B)
Drexel University (B)
Florida, University of (B)
Illinois at Chicago, University of (B,M)

* B=Bachelor; M=Master, D=Doctoral

Kansas State University (B)
Kansas, University of (B,M,D)
Lawrence Institute of Technology (B)
Miami, University of (B)
Oklahoma State University (B,M)
Pennsylvania State University (B,M)
Texas at Austin, University of (B,M)
Texas Tech University (B)
Wentworth Institute of Technology (B)

Construction Science/Management
Arizona State University (B)
Auburn University (B)
California Polytechnic State University, San Luis Obispo (B)
Clemson University (M)
Drexel University (B)
Florida, University of (B,M,D)
Georgia Institute of Technology (B)
Illinois at Urbana-Champaign, University of
Kansas, University of (M)
Louisiana Tech University (B,M)
Maryland, University of (proposed)
Montana State University (B)
Nevada, Las Vegas, University of (B,M)
North Dakota State University (B)
Oklahoma, University of (B,M)
Pratt Institute (B)
Spring Garden College (B)
Texas A&M University (B,M)
Tuskegee Institute (B)
Virginia Polytechnic Institute and State University (B)
Washington State University (B)
Wentworth Institute of Technology (B)

Industrial Design
Arizona State University (B)
Cincinnati, University of (B)
Georgia Institute of Technology (B)
Kansas, University of (B,M)
Montreal, Universite de (B,M)
Ohio State University (B,M)
Rhode Island School of Design (B,M)

Interior Design/Architecture
Andrews University (B)
Arizona State University (B)
Arizona, University of (B,M)
Auburn University (B,M)
Cincinnati, University of (B)
Colorado at Denver, University of (M)
Drexel University (B,M)
Florida, University of (B)
Idaho, University of (B)
Illinois at Urbana-Champaign, University of (B)
Iowa State University (B,M)
Kansas State University (B)
Kansas, University of (B,M)
Kent State University (B)
Kentucky, University of (B,M)
Lawrence Institute of Technology (B)
Louisiana State University
Louisiana Tech University (B,M)
Manitoba, University of (B)
Minnesota, University of (B,M)

Specialized and Related Architecture Degrees

Montana State University (B)
Nevada, Las Vegas, University of (B,M)
Ohio State University (B)
Oklahoma, University of (B)
Oregon, University of (B,M)
Rhode Island School of Design (B)
Savannah College of Art and Design (B,M)
Southwestern Louisiana, University of (B)
Spring Garden College (B)
Texas at Arlington, University of (B)
Texas at Austin, University of (B)
Wentworth Institute of Technology (B)

Landscape Architecture
Arizona State University (B)
Arizona, University of (B,M)
Arkansas, University of (B)
Auburn University (B)
Ball State University (B,M)
California, Berkeley, University of (M)
California Polytechnic State University, San
   Luis Obispo (B)
California State Polytechnic University,
   Pomona (B,M)
City College of the City University of New
   York (B)
Clemson University (B)
Colorado at Denver, University of (M)
Florida, University of (B)
Harvard University (M)
Idaho, University of (B)
Illinois at Urbana-Champaign, University of
   (B,M)
Iowa State University (B,M)
Kansas State University (B,M)
Kentucky, University of (B)
Louisiana State University (B,M)
Manitoba, University of (M)
Mississippi State University (B)
Montreal, Universite de (B)
Nevada, Las Vegas, University of (B,M)
North Carolina State University (B,M)
North Dakota State University (B)
Ohio State University (B,M)
Oklahoma, University of (M)
Oregon, University of (B,M)
Pennsylvania State University (B,M)
Pennsylvania, University of (M,D)
Rhode Island School of Design (B)
Southern California, University of (M)
Texas A&M University (B,M)
Texas at Arlington, University of (B,M)
Toronto, University of (M)
Virginia Polytechnic Institute and State
   University (B,M)
Washington, University of (B,M)

Planning
Arizona State University (B,M)
Arizona, University of (M)
Auburn University (M)
Ball State University (B,M)
California, Berkeley, University of
California, Los Angeles, University of (M,D)
California Polytechnic State University, San
   Luis Obispo (B,M)

California State Polytechnic University,
   Pomona (B,M)
Cincinnati, University of (M)
Clemson University (M)
Colorado at Denver, University of (M)
Columbia University (M)
Cornell University
Florida, University of (M,D)
Georgia Institute of Technology (M)
Illinois at Urbana-Champaign, University of
   (B,M)
Iowa State University (B,M)
Kansas State University (M)
Kansas, University of (M)
Laval University (M)
Lawrence Institute of Technology (B)
Manitoba, University of (M)
Massachusetts Institute of Technology (M)
McGill University (M)
Miami, University of (B)
Michigan, University of (M)
Montreal, Universite de (B,M)
Nebraska, University of (M)
Nevada, Las Vegas, University of (B,M)
North Carolina, Charlotte, University of
   (proposed M)
North Dakota State University (M)
Ohio State University (M,D)
Oklahoma, University of (M)
Oregon, University of (B,M)
Pennsylvania, University of (M,D)
Pratt Institute (M)
State University of New York at Buffalo (M)
Technical University of Nova Scotia (M)
Texas A&M University (M)
Texas at Austin, University of (M)
Toronto, University of (M)
Virginia Polytechnic Institute and State
   University (M)
Washington, University of (M)
Wisconsin-Milwaukee, University of (M)

Preservation
Ball State University (M)
Columbia University (M)
Montreal, Universite de (restoration,
   renovation, M)
Oregon, University of (M)
Pennsylvania, University of (M)
Savannah College of Art and Design (B,M)

Urban Design
Cincinnati, University of (B)
City College of the City University of New
   York (M)
Colorado at Denver, University of (M)
Columbia University (M)
Harvard University (M)
Kansas, University of (M)
Massachusetts Institute of Technology (M)
Minnesota, University of
Pennsylvania, University of (M)
Pratt Institute (urban environmental systems
   management, M)
Rice University (M)
Texas at Austin, University of (M)

Texas Tech University (B,M)
Virginia Polytechnic Institute and State
   University (M)
Washington University (M)
Washington, University of (M)

Other
Arizona State University (solar technology and
   planning, M)
Arizona, University of (environment/behavior,
   M,D; arid lands, D)
British Columbia, University of (advanced
   studies in architecture, M)
Catholic University of America (civil
   engineering, B)
Columbia University (master of science in
   architecture and building design)
Idaho, University of (art, B,M)
Illinois at Urbana-Champaign, University of
   (combined degrees with business
   administration, civil engineering, and urban
   planning, M)
Iowa State University (graphic design, B,M;
   art and design, B,M)
Kansas, University of (built form and culture,
   architectural management)
Laval University (regional planning and
   development, M)
Louisiana State University (graphic design, B;
   art, B,M)
Louisiana Tech University (history, M)
Massachusetts Institute of Technology
   (building technology, M)
Mississippi State University (small-town
   design, M)
New York Institute of Technology
   (architectural technology, B)
North Carolina State University (product
   design, B,M; visual design, M)
Notre Dame, University of (architectural/urban
   design—Chicago and Rome, M)
Ohio State University (construction
   management, B)
Rensselaer Polytechnic Institute (building
   sciences, B,M)
Spring Garden College (civil engineering
   technology, B)
State University of New York at Buffalo
   (combined degrees with management, civil
   engineering, and urban planning, M)
Texas A&M University (environmental design, B)
Virginia Polytechnic Institute and State
   University (urban affairs, B,M)
Wentworth Institute of Design (facilities
   management, B)

Regional Map of ACSA Members

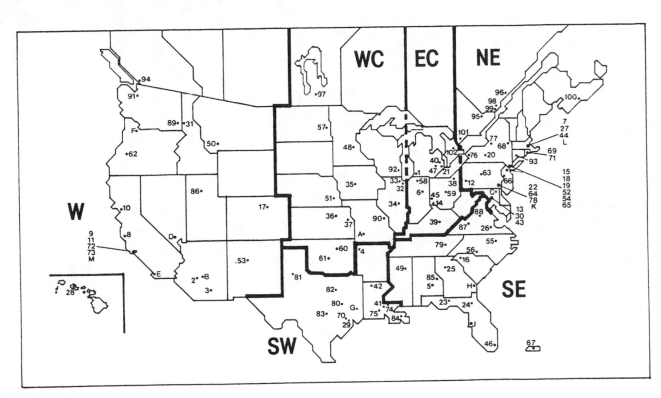

U.S. FULL MEMBERS

1 Andrews University (EC)
2 Arizona State University (W)
3 Arizona, University of (W)
4 Arkansas, University of (SW)
5 Auburn University (SE)
6 Ball State University (EC)
7 Boston Architectural Center (NE)
8 California Polytechnic State University, San Luis Obispo (W)
9 California State Polytechnic University, Pomona (W)
10 California, Berkeley, University of (W)
11 California, Los Angeles, University of (W)
12 Carnegie-Mellon University (NE)
13 Catholic University of America (NE)
14 Cincinnati, University of (EC)
15 City College of the City University of New York (NE)
16 Clemson University (SE)
17 Colorado, Denver, University of (W)
18 Columbia University (NE)
19 Cooper Union (NE)
20 Cornell University (NE)
21 Detroit, University of (EC)
22 Drexel University (NE)
23 Florida A&M University (SE)
24 Florida, University of (SE)
25 Georgia Institute of Technology (SE)
26 Hampton University (SE)
27 Harvard University (NE)
28 Hawaii at Manoa, University of (W)
29 Houston, University of (SW)
30 Howard University (NE)
31 Idaho, University of (W)
32 Illinois Institute of Technology (WC)
33 Illinois at Chicago, University of (WC)
34 Illinois at Urbana-Champaign, University of (WC)
35 Iowa State University (WC)
36 Kansas State University (WC)
37 Kansas, University of (WC)
38 Kent State University (EC)
39 Kentucky, University of (EC)
40 Lawrence Institute of Technology (EC)

41 Louisiana State University (SW)
42 Louisiana Tech University (SW)
43 Maryland, University of (NE)
44 Massachusetts Institute of Technology (NE)
45 Miami University (EC)
46 Miami, University of (SE)
47 Michigan, University of (EC)
48 Minnesota, University of (WC)
49 Mississippi State University (SE)
50 Montana State University (W)
51 Nebraska-Lincoln, University of (WC)
52 New Jersey Institute of Technology (NE)
53 New Mexico, University of (W)
54 New York Institute of Technology (NE)
55 North Carolina State University (SE)
56 North Carolina at Charlotte, University of (SE)
57 North Dakota State University (WC)
58 Notre Dame, University of (EC)
59 Ohio State University (EC)
60 Oklahoma State University (WC)
61 Oklahoma, University of (WC)
62 Oregon, University of (W)
63 Pennsylvania State University (NE)
64 Pennsylvania, University of (NE)
65 Pratt Institute (NE)
66 Princeton University (NE)
67 Puerto Rico, University of (SE)
68 Rensselaer Polytechnic Institute (NE)
69 Rhode Island School of Design (NE)
70 Rice University (SW)
71 Roger Williams College (NE)
72 Southern California Institute of Architecture (W)
73 Southern California, University of (W)
74 Southern University and A&M College (SW)
75 Southwestern Louisiana, University of (SW)
76 State University of New York at Buffalo (NE)
77 Syracuse University (NE)
78 Temple University (NE)
79 Tennessee-Knoxville, University of (SE)
80 Texas A&M University (SW)
81 Texas Tech University (SW)

82 Texas at Arlington, University of (SW)
83 Texas at Austin, University of (SW)
84 Tulane University (SW)
85 Tuskegee University (SE)
86 Utah, University of (W)
87 Virginia Polytechnic Institute and State University (SE)
88 Virginia, University of (SE)
89 Washington State University (W)
90 Washington University (WC)
91 Washington, University of (W)
92 Wisconsin-Milwaukee, University of (WC)
93 Yale University (NE)

CANADIAN FULL MEMBERS

94 British Columbia, University of (W)
95 Carleton University (NE)
96 Laval University (NE)
97 Manitoba, University of (WC)
98 McGill University (NE)
99 Montréal, Université de (NE)
100 Technical University of Nova Scotia (NE)
101 Toronto, University of (NE)
102 Waterloo, University of (EC)

U.S. CANDIDATE MEMBERS

A. Drury College (WC)
B. Frank Lloyd Wright School of Architecture (W)
C. Morgan State University (NE)
D. Nevada, Las Vegas, University of (W)
E. New School of Architecture (W)
F. Oregon School of Design (W)
G. Prairie View A&M University (SW)
H. Savannah College of Art & Design (SE)
J. South Florida, University of (SE)
K. Spring Garden College (NE)
L. Wentworth Institute of Technology (NE)
M. Woodbury University (W)

Descriptions of Schools, Colleges, and Departments of Architecture

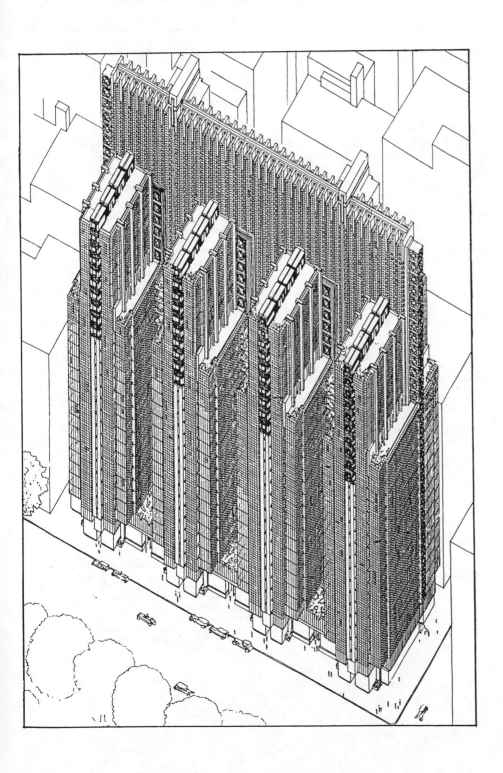

Andrews University

Department of Architecture
Andrews University
Berrien Springs, Michigan 49104
(616) 471-6003

Admissions:
Nationwide (800) 253-2874
In Michigan (800) 632-2248

Application Deadline(s): October 31, August 31
Tuition & Fees: Undgrd: $2100 per quarter
($138 per credit)
Endowment: Private

DEGREE PROGRAMS

Degree	Minimum Years for Degree	Accred.	Requirements for Admission	Full-Time Stdnts.	Part-Time Stdnts.	% of Applics. Accptd.	Stdnts. in 1st Year of Program	# of Degrees Conferred
B Arch	5	NAAB	HS Diploma	85	6	64%	30	8
BSAS	4		HS Diploma	27	3	80%	22	8

SCHOOL DEMOGRAPHICS (all degree programs)

Full-Time Faculty	Part-Time Faculty	Full-Time Students	Part-Time Students	Foreign Students	Out-of-State U.S. Stdnts.	Women Students	Minority Students
12	5	112	9	14%	58%	37%	40%

LIBRARY (Tel. No. 616-471-2417)

Type	No. of Volumes	No. of Slides
Architecture Resource Ctr	9,000	12,000

STUDENT OPPORTUNITIES AND RESOURCES

Andrews University is a residential university of approximately 3,000 students. Located between Grand Rapids, Michigan, and Chicago, Illinois, there are many opportunities for field trips and guest lectures. Students in architecture have close contact with other schools and programs within Andrews University, especially Computing and Engineering Technology in the College of Technology, Art and Behavioral Sciences in the College of Arts and Sciences, and the School of Business.

There are several 'small school' advantages for the study of architecture, with one-to-one contact in studios, and a faculty-to-student ratio of 1 to 12.

In addition to the interaction with students and faculty in other disciplines and other cultures, there are supper series, discussions, seminars, international clubs, extra-curricular lectures in archaeology, art, music, religion and off-campus involvements.

The diversity of cultural backgrounds and an holistic, integrative philosophy at Andrews University places emphasis on the individual. Each student has an advisor in his or her program of study. There are opportunities for cooperative work-study programs and foreign travel. Full-time faculty are committed to excellence in architecture and committed to values consistent with a Christian university setting.

Transfer students, with portfolios, are accepted on an individual basis.

SPECIAL ACTIVITIES AND PROGRAMS

Off-campus study programs are held in Europe, particularly Finland, and Australia. Within the campus and local community, architecture students and faculty participate in charrettes and workshops. The Andrews University Architecture Lecture Series brings outstanding guest lecturers to the Department of Architecture.

There is an active Andrews University Chapter of the American Institute of Architecture Students. The Society of Andrews Scholars provides intellectual and social activities for Honors students.

Career counselling and placement services are available within the Department of Architecture and the university generally. The Department of Architecture keeps records on alumni and has a 100% employment rate. Students and alumni from the B Arch and BSAS programs work in architects' offices as designers and members of production teams.

The Makielski Art Award for excellence in architectural presentation is presented annually to a student.

A Newsletter to professionals and a listing of weekly events are published by the Department of Architecture.

FACILITIES

The most recently constructed building on campus houses the Department of Architecture and provides accommodations for 125 students with crit alcoves. The building also houses an Architecture Resource Center, a materials center, amphitheater, lecture rooms, print room and storage for models, seminar and conference rooms, administrative and faculty offices.

A computer laboratory for word processing and computer graphics, including three-dimensional, is a high-use area within the building. A model shop is located in an adjacent building.

SCHOLARSHIPS/AID

Andrews University participates in all Federal Title 4 and State Assistance programs, and provides Institutional grants on the basis of need. Andrews University recognizes academic achievement through scholarships to incoming and continuing students.

A high percentage of students receive financial aid. In addition, there are many opportunities for student work on campus.

 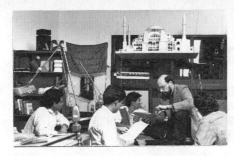 

UNDERGRADUATE PROGRAM
Philosophy Statement

The practice of architecture is considered as an endeavor to enhance meaningful human life by providing appropriate spaces for the various types of human activity, and by articulating and expressing cultural values and sentiments in architectural forms. Architecture is thus concerned with both science and art, function and form, activity and philosophy, society and the individual. The role of the architect is seen as defining spaces in culturally meaningful ways and thus facilitating the transformation of these spaces into places by the human activity that is to take place within them. Cultural and social input is thus seen as integral to the practice of architecture, making the universal application of architectural ideas possible only to the extent that there are cultural universals espoused within a society and by other societies.

In its theoretical and philosophical content, architecture is also viewed as an intellectual discipline. It concretizes the abstract aspirations of human intellect and applies theory to actual human situations. The process educates members of societies in new ways of expression within their cultures while endeavoring to facilitate the fulfillment of their physical, mental, social, and spiritual needs. The rigors of critical thinking and research methods are applied towards the profession's premises so as to best respond to all levels of human needs and aspiration.

The profession of architecture is also seen as incorporating environmental, technological and fiscal responsibility. While responsible use of technological progress for the betterment of human life is encouraged, harmony with nature is held as a goal. Conservation of energy, enhancement of health and safety, and preservation of natural resources are emphasized as integral aspects of responsible professional practice.

Appreciation of aesthetics is seen as an important aspect of the holistic view of human nature, and as closely akin to the spiritual dimension. Creativity in artistic expression is encouraged as an essential part of a responsible use of the gifts endowed to humans by their Creator. As the art and science of built environment, architecture not only adheres to the classical themes, *spiritus-mens-corpus*, but also helps provide the grounds for *societas*, thus enhancing human life in its various aspects.

FACULTY
Administration

Edward B Samuel, RA, Chair,
    Department of Architecture
Neville H Clouten, FRAIA, RA, Program Head,
    External Relations
Richard Powell, Director, Architecture Resource
    Center
Kathy Demsky, Architecture Librarian

Professors

Neville H Clouten, FRAIA, RA, B Arch, M Arch, PhD
William W Davidson, PE, BS, MS, PhD

Associate Professors

Stanley M Bell, AIA, RA, B Arch, M Arch
Edward B Samuel, RA, M Arch, PhD

Assistant Professors

John K Hopkins, IES, IALD, SBS, RA, B Arch
Cheryl J Jetter, BA, MA
Laurence M Mader, AIA, RA, B Arch
Arpad D Ronaszegi, B Arch, Grad Dipl
Bryan D Schnoor, B Arch
Sara Terian, BA, MA, PhD

Instructors

Laurie Segar, BS

Part-Time Faculty

Lilly Van Putten, IDS

Adjunct Faculty

Greg Constantine, BA, MFA
Peter Erhardt, BFA, MS
Robert Kingman, BS, MS
Laun Reinholtz, BS, MA, EdD
Dennis Woodland, BA, MA, PhD

Arizona State University

School of Architecture
Arizona State University
Tempe, Arizona 85287
(602) 965-3536

Graduate College
Arizona State University
Tempe, Arizona 85287
(602) 965-3521

Application Deadline(s): March 1,
November 15
Tuition & Fees: Undgrd: Ariz. Res:
$598/sem
Non-res: $2314/sem
Grad: Ariz. Res: $598/sem
Non-res: $2314/sem
Endowment: Public and Private

DEGREE PROGRAMS

Degree	Minimum Years for Degree	Accred.	Requirements for Admission	Full-Time Stdnts.	Part-Time Stdnts.	% of Applics. Accptd.	Stdnts. in 1st Year of Program	# of Degrees Conferred
BS Design	4		3.0 GPA Portfolio 2 yrs. selected preprof. coursework	444*	142	60%	47**	41
M Arch	2	NAAB	BS in Arch. Studies or equivalent - Portfolio	55	—	40%	28	23
MS	1		GRE - Portfolio BA, BS or B Arch	17	20	20%	9	—

*Includes 464 preprofessional architecture majors in first two years.
**In first year of professional program (third year).

SCHOOL DEMOGRAPHICS (all degree programs)

Full-Time Faculty	Part-Time Faculty	Full-Time Students	Part-Time Students	Foreign Students	Out-of-State U.S. Stdnts.	Women Students	Minority Students
27	26	516	162	7%	29%	24%	10%

LIBRARY (Tel. No. 602-965-6400)

Type	No. of Volumes	No. of Slides
Arch	20,000	70,000

STUDENT OPPORTUNITIES AND RESOURCES

Arizona State University, one of the largest urban universities in the Southwest, is located in the city of Tempe within the Phoenix metropolitan area. The area has a population of 1,600,000 and is growing by approximately 88,000 persons per year. The university had an on-campus enrollment in 1986-87 of 41,542. The university has three traditional colleges: Liberal Arts, Fine Arts, and Engineering and Applied Sciences; and seven professional colleges or schools: Business Administration, Education, Social Work, Law, Nursing, Public Programs, and Architecture and Environmental Design.

The region has a rich heritage of natural and cultural resources, including the Grand Canyon, the historic architecture of the Anasazi cliff dwellings and Spanish colonial missions, and contemporary buildings by Frank Lloyd Wright and Paolo Soleri. These and other attributes combine to create an ambiance that makes this area a mecca for architecture, planning, and design studies.

The program in architecture began thirty-eight years ago and was established as a separate college in 1964. The College of Architecture and Environmental Design is organized into three specific departments: Architecture, Design, and Planning. The combined full-time faculty numbers 46. The physical resources of the college include the Howe Architecture and Environmental Design Library, the Experimental Testing Station, photography laboratories, a workshop, a computer laboratory, a media center, a gallery, and a slide collection. The building and design science laboratories are augmented by structural testing, acoustical, lighting, human-factor, and solar experimental stations.

SPECIAL ACTIVITIES AND PROGRAMS

Summer Intern Program

Foreign Studies Program in London

Summer foreign travel programs

Distinguished visiting faculty and critics

Exhibits of student and professional work

Exchange programs in Germany and Mexico

Annual Design Excellence Awards Program

Inspection trips to San Francisco and Los Angeles

Short courses in various media techniques, including architectural photography and graphic design

Student Chapter of AIAS

Lecture Series

FACILITIES

The existing Architecture Building contains the Howe Architecture Library, slide library, studio and classroom spaces, wood/metal/plastics shop, media center, experimental research areas, a computer laboratory, advisement center, faculty offices and administration. A new 100,000 sq. ft. building addition will be under construction in the 1987-88 academic year. It will triple the facilities of the College and allow all classes to be offered at one location. The addition is being designed by the Hillier Group, winner of a national design competition.

SCHOLARSHIPS/AID

Financial aid, work-study employment, and long-term, short-term, and emergency loans are available to students in all programs of the College of Architecture and Environmental Design through the Arizona State University Financial Aids Office. Within the college, professional students may compete on the basis of scholastic standing and/or financial need for numerous scholarships, awards, and prizes specifically designated for architecture students. The School typically awards 20-25 graduate assistantships in teaching and/or research. The award is $1260 a semester for 1/4 time. Graduate assistants pay only in-state tuition at $1136. Out-of-state tuition waivers are also available for other highly qualified graduate students.

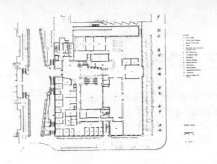
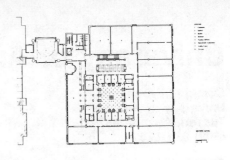

UNDERGRADUATE PROGRAM
Philosophy Statement
The undergraduate curriculum leads to the degree Bachelor of Science in Design with a major in Architectural Studies, and balances courses in general studies with architecture. The curriculum provides a firm base in university general studies and focuses on developing skills and understanding in communication, theory, technology, and design as preparation for completing studies leading to the professional degree, Master of Architecture.

Program Description
The undergraduate program consists of two 2-year sequences. In the first two lower-division years, the student takes a university general studies core consisting of courses in English, math, physical sciences, social sciences, humanities and art as well as introductory architectural history and theory courses, skills courses in drawing and sketching, and two courses in design fundamentals.

At the end of the two-year period, there is a screening process based on grade point average and a portfolio of creative work from which approximately 45 applicants are admitted into the final two upper-division years.

The upper-division focus is on design studios with the following sequence of emphasis: design methods, site and climate analysis, human determinants, and urban/cultural influences. These years also include sequential courses in environmental analysis, architectural programming, wood, steel and concrete structures, passive and active heating and cooling, materials and systems, architectural history, and professional electives.

GRADUATE PROGRAM
Philosophy Statement
The Master of Architecture program offers a challenging and integrated curriculum of professional studies in preparing the students for future leadership roles in the profession of architecture. It revolves around the integrating aspects of the design studio and advanced studies in building systems, history and theory, and architectural management and administration.

Program Description
The Master of Architecture program continues the design sequence of the earlier years with focus progressing from major public buildings in urban settings to high-rise buildings with systems emphasis in the first graduate year and optional and thesis studios in the final year. Other required courses include advanced structures, advanced building systems, professional practice, and theory and practice seminars. In addition, the student is required to develop an area of elective concentration. These areas are individually arranged. Current areas of concentration in which the faculty has particular strength include solar and energy efficient design, computer-aided architecture, architectural management, and urban design/housing.

FACULTY
Administration
John C C Meunier, Dean, College of Architecture & Environmental Design
Roger L Schluntz, AIA, Director, School of Architecture
Tim McGinty, RA, Assistant Dean
David G Saile, PhD, Graduate Coordinator
Richard Eribes, AIA, Master of Science Committee Chair
John R Peterson, AIA, Coordinator, Master of Architecture Committee Chair
James R Rapp, AIA, Upper Division Advisor
Barbara Colby, Lower Division Advisor
Berna Neal, Head, Architecture Librarian

Professors
B Michael Boyle, M Arch, PhD
Jeffrey R Cook, AIA, B Arch, M Arch
Richard Eribes, M Arch, PhD
Gerald McSheffrey, Dipl
John C C Meunier, AIA, B Arch, M Arch
John R Peterson, AIA, B Arch, M Arch
James R Rapp, AIA, B Arch, MS Arch
Roger L Schluntz, AIA, B Arch, M Arch

Associate Professors
Tim McGinty, AIA, B Arch, M Arch
David G Scheatzle, PE, AIA
E Yury Sheydayi, PE
K Paul Zygas, M Arch, PhD

Visiting Associate Professor
David G Saile, M Arch, PhD

Assistant Professors
Wendle R Bertelsen, B Arch, M Arch
George Christensen, FAIA, B Arch
Michael E Fifield, AIA, AICP, M Arch
Lisa Findley, M Arch
Mary Hardin, M Arch
Jong-Jim Kim, M Arch, PhD
Patricia G McIntosh, B Arch, Arch D
Max Underwood, BS Arch, M Arch
D Kristine Woolsey, M Arch
Hofu Wu, B Arch, M Arch

Visiting Assistant Professors
Reed A Kroloff, M Arch

Visiting Distinguished Professors
Barton Myers, FAIA
Fred Osmon
Antoine Predock, FAIA
Paolo Soleri

Part-Time Faculty
Kym Billington
Michael Borowski
Margy Chrisney
Kendall Dorman
David Eijadi
Kenneth Eller
Anthony Ellner
May Beth Hsich
Robert Hunt
Bruce Kimball
Paul Ladensack
Richard Perrell
Karin Pitman
Marley Porter
Bonnie Richardson
I Dale Sager
Young Smith
Phillip Tabb
John Westberg
Marcus Whiffen

Adjunct Faculty
Richard Close
Steve Dragos
James Elmore, FAIA
Michael Kroelinger
John McIntosh, PhD

University of Arizona

College of Architecture
University of Arizona
Tucson, Arizona 85721
(602) 621-6751

Office of Admissions
(602) 621-3237

Application Deadline(s): April 1 for priority
service
Tuition & Fees: Undgrd: AZ res: $1256/yr
Non-res: $4650/yr
Grad: Same
Endowment: Public

DEGREE PROGRAMS

Degree	Minimum Years for Degree	Accred.	Requirements for Admission	Full-Time Stdnts.	Part-Time Stdnts.	% of Applics. Accptd.	Stdnts. in 1st Year of Program	# of Degrees Conferred
B Arch	5	NAAB	Non-Res: top 20% or SAT 1100 or ACT 25 Res: top 50% or SAT 930 or ACT 21 Trans: 3.0 preferred	466	75	48%	250	72
M Arch	1		B Arch, 3.0 Portfolio	5		35%		
M Arch	2		BS in Arch or equiv, 3.0 Portfolio	13	2	25%		

SCHOOL DEMOGRAPHICS (all degree programs)

Full-Time Faculty	Part-Time Faculty	Full-Time Students	Part-Time Students	Foreign Students	Out-of-State U.S. Stdnts.	Women Students	Minority Students
21	11	484	77	9%	26%	26%	NA

LIBRARY (Tel. No. 602-621-2498)

Type	No. of Volumes	No. of Slides
Arch only	11,000	24,000

STUDENT OPPORTUNITIES AND RESOURCES

Tucson is located in southern Arizona's Sonoran Desert, an arid region of ideal climate and great natural beauty with a multicultural history. Both desert and mountain recreation areas are nearby, and Mexico is 65 miles to the south. Tucson is a decentralized metropolitan community of 650,000 people; the main campus of the university is near the old center of the city.

The University of Arizona is internationally recognized as a center for research. Its twelve colleges and thirty-nine research and service divisions offer diversified academic, cultural, social, and recreational opportunities. Enrollment is about 32,000 (including 7,200 graduate students) with every state and over 100 foreign countries represented. Thirty percent of entering students have an 'A' average in high school; fifty-eight percent have a 'B' average. Arizona is ranked 14th among public universities and 22nd among all institutions in the amount of research and development funding awarded. The University Library, with over two million items in the collection, is ranked 21st in the nation among research libraries.

The College of Architecture is located in the northwest quadrant of the campus, adjacent to the colleges of Fine Arts, Engineering and Business. Other colleges on the 325-acre campus include Medicine, Law, Pharmacy, Nursing, Education, Arts and Sciences, and Agriculture. Interdisciplinary opportunities are sought with these and other units on campus.

The Architecture Faculty is varied in academic and professional training and experience. Most are registered architects or engineers and have travelled, taught or studied abroad. The College has intentionally developed a faculty with a variety of interests, philosophies, experience and specializations. This diversity affords students the opportunity to be exposed to a variety of ways of thinking about and doing architecture and assures both breadth of preparation and opportunity for specialization in the upper years.

The College of Architecture student body is equally diverse with a rich mix of students from each region of the country, foreign lands, ethnic minorities, women and older students. Many entering students have previously completed two or more years of college. Some have already earned a degree and students 25 to 40 years of age are not uncommon. We believe this mix of eighteen-year-old freshmen and older, foreign, minority and women students provides a diversity which significantly enhances the learning experience.

SPECIAL ACTIVITIES AND PROGRAMS

Annual exchange program with students and faculty of the School of Architecture at LaSalle University in Mexico City

Study Abroad opportunities in Italy, Denmark, England, France

Summer Study opportunities in Boston and San Francisco

The Architecture Laboratory, a private nonprofit corporation, develops research and practice opportunities for faculty and internships for students

Computer laboratory

Internships in local offices

Annual lecture and exhibition program

Distinguished visiting faculty

Annual Beaux Arts Ball

Student Chapter of AIAS

Participation in competitions

Utilization of the community and region as a laboratory

Architects Registration Examination preparation seminars

Annual student publication "The Avenue"

Registration for classes may be completed at orientation sessions in New York, Chicago, or Los Angeles

Work-study program

Arizona Architectural Archives which houses drawings of significant southwestern architecture

FACILITIES

Architecture is housed in a single building constructed in 1964 and expanded in 1970 and 1978. The three-story structure has a central roofed courtyard (centrum) lighted and environmentally controlled by means of a large solar collector built as the State of Arizona solar demonstration project. Design studios provide 300 work stations each with a view to the adjacent Catalina Mountains. The Architecture Library, essential in developing the spirit of inquiry required of our students, is located within the building as are the computer laboratory, model shop, dark room, lecture hall and additional classroom and seminar spaces. Students also use classroom and other study and support facilities in many of the 132 buildings on the main campus.

SCHOLARSHIPS/AID

Applicants are encouraged to contact the Office of Student Financial Aid which annually administers the awarding of more than thirty million dollars in aid to over 12,000 students. Scholarships, grants and loans including Pell, NDL, GSL and work-study programs may be available. The College of Architecture also administers the award of approximately 35 scholarships to upper-division currently enrolled students. A limited number of teaching assistantships are available to graduate students.

UNDERGRADUATE PROGRAM
Philosophy Statement

Architecture is seen in perspective as a measure of society and in practice as both a social art and an applied science. The academic program is humanist in orientation and constructed to encourage a diverse but balanced educational experience. Development of an optimistic, ethical, nonstylistic attitude toward the design of the built environment is fostered. There is a strong commitment to general education and breadth outside of architecture and one-third of the coursework is in other disciplines. Students have opportunities to explore issues primary to architecture within a rapidly changing world. Self-discipline, motivation, and good academic preparation are required. Students are expected to cultivate well-developed abilities in critical thinking, analysis, evaluation, synthesis and communication. Architecture at Arizona is a demanding program of recognized excellence. Our goal is the preparation of national leaders for the next century.

Program Description

Five years of study are required for the Bachelor of Architecture degree. The program is of a 1-3-1 pattern; 1 year preprofessional, 3-year professional core and a fifth year of design options and a senior project. The preprofessional first year includes general education in English, History, Mathematics, Physics, Electives and architecture courses in graphic communication, concepts of structure, and architectural theory. Admission to the Professional Phase (second year) is selective and competitive.

Architecture courses in the 3-year Professional Phase core focus on four areas: Design/Communication, History/Theory, Technologies, and Practice/Management. Architectural studies are balanced by breadth electives in four general areas of knowledge: humanities, science, fine arts and business, plus open and architecture electives. Design options are offered in the first semester of fifth year. Option topics vary but typically include community design, entrepreneurial architecture, computer-aided design, preservation, energy-conscious design (including solar applications), lightweight or geodesic structures, arid lands architecture, interior architecture and behavioral aspects in design. Not all topics are offered each year. A senior project with a student-selected subject is required in the second semester of the fifth year. Students may develop an area of concentration in the fifth year by linking the design option, senior project and professional elective courses.

Professional studies are centered in the design studio, where the case study method is used. Successively more complex building problems, introduced in logical sequence for study, provide continuous opportunity for practice in design synthesis. Work in related lecture courses is coordinated with studio assignments.

The program aims to develop and strengthen individual abilities to understand context, observe carefully, think critically, design intelligently, communicate clearly, and recognize the responsibilities of professionalism.

GRADUATE PROGRAM
Philosophy Statement

In a complex society opportunities in architecture are many and varied. Issues and problems are equally so. The graduate program is structured to encourage the student with prior training and experience in architecture to investigate in depth an area or topic of particular personal interest and relevance. The program is primarily focused on individual studies and graduate students select their program of study using the extensive resources of the University and the College.

Program Description

A minimum study period of one year for five-year degree holders and two years for four-year degree holders is required. The latter are required to fulfill undergraduate as well as graduate requirements and are awarded both professional degrees upon successful completion of the master's program. The majority of candidates require more than the minimum time period to complete requirements.

All participants are involved in a workshop or practicum studio case study for one semester and a seminar in architectural theory for two semesters. Other specialized elective courses within the college are available. In addition, appropriate supporting courses in related fields are mandatory. A master's design thesis or report consisting of three parts—research, text, and graphic representation—completes the requirements.

The specific study program is developed in consultation with a graduate committee consisting of an adviser and three other faculty members. The committee monitors progress and conducts a final oral examination on the thesis and related subject matters.

The range of study areas is broad; a match is sought between individual choice of topics and faculty expertise. Emphases are offered in community design, arid lands architecture, preservation studies, architecture/behavior, and computer applications. Because of our desert environment, many theses have focused on arid lands, desert or energy-conscious architecture often utilizing the computer as a primary vehicle of study.

FACULTY
Administration

Robert G Hershberger, AIA, Dean
Franklin S Flint, AIA, Associate Dean
Kathryn Wayne, Librarian

Professors

Charles A Albanese, AIA, B Arch, M Arch
Kenneth Clark, RA, B Arch, M Arch
Franklin S Flint, AIA, B Arch, M Arch
Robert C Giebner, B Arch, M Arch
Ronald Gourley, FAIA, B Arch, M Arch
Ellery C Green, AIA, B Arch, M Arch
Robert G Hershberger, AIA, B Arch, M Arch, PhD
Kirby Lockard, FAIA, B Arch, M Arch
J Douglas MacNeil, RA, B Arch, M Arch
Fred S Matter, RA, BA, M Arch
Robert E McConnell, FAIA, B Arch, M Arch
R Larry Medlin, RA, B Arch, M Arch
Harris Sobin, RA, M Arch, JD
William P Stamm, RA, B Arch, M Arch

Associate Professors

Harry der Boghosian, RA, B Arch, M Arch
Dennis Doxtater, RA, B Arch, D Arch
Robert Dvorak, RA, B Arch, M Arch
Robert Nevins, AIA, B Arch, M Arch

Lecturer

Richard Ebeltoft, PE, B Arch, MSCE

Teaching Associate

John Dettloff, BS

Part-Time Faculty

Stanley Adams, PE, BS
Richard Brittain, BS, M Arch
Judith Chafee, FAIA, BA, M Arch
Warren Hampton, RA, B Arch, M Arch
Jurgen Hennecke, RA
Robert Holleman, PE, BS
Susan K E Moody, B Arch, M Arch
Lawrence Perkins, FAIA
Charles Poster, RA, BA, M Arch
A Richard Williams, FAIA

Adjunct Faculty

Sarah Dinham, MA, PhD

University of Arkansas

School of Architecture
VWH 209, University of Arkansas
Fayetteville, Arkansas 72701
(501) 575-4705

Application Deadline(s): Aug. 1, Dec. 1
Tuition & Fees: Undgrd: Ark. Res:
  $615/Semester
  Non-res: $1525/Semester
Endowment: Public

DEGREE PROGRAMS

Degree	Minimum Years for Degree	Accred.	Requirements for Admission	Full-Time Stdnts.	Part-Time Stdnts.	% of Applics. Accptd.	Stdnts. in 1st Year of Program	# of Degrees Conferred
B Arch	5	NAAB	18 ACT, 2.5 HS GPA	325	15	35%	150	45
BLA	5	LAAB	18 ACT, 2.5 HS GPA	50	5	65%	25	10

SCHOOL DEMOGRAPHICS (all degree programs)

Full-Time Faculty	Part-Time Faculty	Full-Time Students	Part-Time Students	Foreign Students	Out-of-State U.S. Stdnts.	Women Students	Minority Students
25	7	375	20	10%	25%	21%	3%

LIBRARY (Tel. No. 501-575-4708)

Type	No. of Volumes	No. of Slides
Art & Arch	40,000	75,000

STUDENT OPPORTUNITIES AND RESOURCES

The University of Arkansas Bachelor of Architecture program strives to combine professional education and general education to produce thinking professionals equipped to meet the challenges of a changing world. The design sequence is carefully orchestrated to provide a sequence of experiences that synthesizes theoretical and technical information. Analysis rather than intuition is stressed. Design-year teaching teams balance faculty primarily interested in conceptualization with faculty who stress pragmatic building design. Fayetteville's small size and the residential nature of the university fosters an extremely effective learning environment. The small size of the school and an extremely dedicated faculty assure that each student develops to the greatest degree possible. The rural location of the school is offset by an extensive program of visiting lecturers and design critics, structured field trips, and a mandatory urban-semester-away that can be selected from the school's Boston and Rome programs. The University of Arkansas is located in the beautiful Ozark Mountains; opportunities for all sorts of outdoor recreation abound. The university's size—14,000 students—is large enough to support a full range of social and cultural activities, including the very successful Razorback athletic programs, but small enough to avoid the anonymity often associated with large universities. The School of Architecture accepts at the freshman level all students accepted by the university. Freshman students compete on the basis of grade-point average for admission to the professional program at the sophomore level. Transfer students are accepted on the basis of portfolio review and grade-point average (2.5 minimum required) up to the beginning of the fourth year of the program; all students are required to complete the fourth and fifth year of their program from the offerings of this school.

SPECIAL ACTIVITIES AND PROGRAMS

The School of Architecture runs a two-week summer program for high school juniors and seniors to introduce them to the disciplines of architecture and landscape architecture. The cost of the program is approximately $500. Students undertake a design problem, are introduced to computer graphics, take several field trips, and experience what it is like to be a student in the school. All architecture students must participate in one of the school's urban-focused design semesters away from campus. These options include a summer fifth-year design studio offered in Cambridge, Massachusetts at the Harvard Graduate School of Design, a fourth-year design studio in Rome, and an exchange arrangement with Brighton Polytechnic Institute in the United Kingdom. Transfer students from other schools or other disciplines may take all of their first year architectural coursework in the summer session in order to be considered for admission to the sophomore professional program in the fall.

FACILITIES

Facilities of the school include dedicated work stations for all design students. Studios are an interesting work environment because students create work carrels "in the manner" of famous architects. The school has a comprehensive computer laboratory equipped with IBM-AT's complete with Auto-CADD, Mega-CADD, and various other software packages that are available to all students in the school. Courses from first year to fifth year include work to be done on computers. The school also has a completely equipped shop facility that is utilized by all students as part of their materials and methods of construction classwork and is available for special projects in furniture and cabinet design.

SCHOLARSHIPS/AID

Through various sources, the School currently awards some $35,000 in scholarships annually to its students. Although a scholarship based solely on academic performance is reserved for each design year, most awards are based on a combination of financial need and performance in both the design studio and academic coursework. Some awards are given as prizes for specific design projects and certain others are reserved for students in the Landscape Architecture program. In addition to the School-administered scholarship program, many students are recipients of financial aid through Pell Grants, National Direct Loans, Guaranteed Student Loans, College Work-Study, Supplemental Opportunity Educational Grants and the State scholarship program. In total, over fifty percent of the students in the School of Architecture receive scholarships and financial aid.

UNDERGRADUATE PROGRAM
Philosophy Statement

The principal aim of the architecture program is to equip its students with the analytical, technical, social, and cultural foundation necessary to define and solve architectural design problems after their formal educations are completed. Its intent is to prepare them to pursue their interests and develop their talents, and to respond effectively to the changing problems of the contemporary environment. Through exposure to fundamental principles and problem solving techniques, it tries to bring to each student the concept of architecture as a creative and relevant art—an art through which the student can ultimately enrich the broader community.

Program Description

The architecture program is a 167-credit-hour five-year Bachelor of Architecture degree program. The first year is a preprofessional year in which the student establishes an academic record upon which his admission to further work in the school is predicated. The first year course is divided between general education courses and basic professional courses that introduce architectural design and theory. Years two, three, and four are the core professional years. In these years the students develop a process to solve design problems and take all of their technical, history, and theory courses. Year five is organized to center around preparation and conduct of a terminal project designed to synthesize all skill and knowledge acquired in the previous four years. Years four and five include a strong focus on urban contextual issues. It is during these years that the urban-semester-away requirement must be satisfied. The final two years also include most of the professional and general education elective hours in the program in order that students may, with the assistance of their advisors, use these hours to develop a concentration of study in an area of special interest. Because the school has a strong commitment to liberal education, approximately thirty percent of the hours required for the degree are general education hours.

FACULTY
Administration

Clifton Murray Smart, Jr, AIA, Dean
Ernest E Jacks, Associate Dean
Michael J Buono, AIA, Architecture Program Director
John V Crone, ASLA, Landscape Architecture Program Director
H Gordon Brooks II, AIA, Recruiting Coordinator
Donna Daniels, Fine Arts Librarian
Christine Hilker, Media Supervisor & Slide Librarian

Professors

H Gordon Brooks II, AIA, B Arch, M Arch
Herbert K Fowler, BA, B Arch
Ernest E Jacks, B Arch
E Fay Jones, FAIA, B Arch, M Arch
Richard E Kellogg, AIA, B Arch, MS Arch
C Murray Smart, Jr, AIA, B Arch, MS City Plan
Cyrus Sutherland, AIA, M Arch
Jerry D Wall, B Arch Engr, SM Civil Engr, PhD

Associate Professors

Michael J Buono, AIA, B Arch, M Arch
Martha Dellinger, BA, MA, MFA
Elam L Denham, AIA, B Arch, MSc in Arch
Steven B Miller, AIA, B Arch, M Arch Urb Des
Patricia O'Leary, AIA, B Arch, M Arch
Graham F Shannon, AIA, B Arch, M Arch Urb Des
C Larry Tompkins, AIP, BS City Plan, M Urban Plan, PhD
Davide Vitali, Dipl Arch, M Arch

Assistant Professors

C A Debelius, AB, M Arch
Jeffrey Hartnett, BS Arch, M Arch
Martha S Sutherland, BFA, MA

Part-Time Faculty

Frank L Doughty, BA, B Arch
W Kim Fugitt, AIA, B Arch, M Arch
O Michael Green, BSEE
James E Snow, BSE, M ED
Don Spann, RA, B Arch

Visiting Assistant Professors

Mark Lockrin, BSc, B Arch
Doug Stanton, BEd, MA

Landscape Architecture

Frank B Burggraf, FASLA, BS, MLA
John V Crone, ASLA, BL Arch, M Reg Plan
Roger R Goddard, ASLA, BS, MLA
Karen Rollet, ASLA, BA, MS, MLA

Auburn University

School of Architecture
202 Dudley Commons
Auburn University, Alabama
36849-5316
(205) 826-4524

Office of Admissions
Martin Hall
Auburn University, Alabama
36849-3501
(205) 826-4080 (800) 392-8051

Application Deadline(s): May 1
Tuition & Fees: Undgrd: AL res: $1323;
 Non-res: $3969 per year
 Grad: Same as undgrd
Endowment: Public

DEGREE PROGRAMS

Degree	Minimum Years for Degree	Accred.	Requirements for Admission	Full-Time* Stdnts.	Part-Time Stdnts.	% of Applics. Accptd.	Stdnts. in 1st Year of Program	# of Degrees Conferred
B Arch	5	NAAB	SAT/ACT HS transcript	214	137	20%	88	58
B Sci BC	4		SAT/ACT HS transcript	254	127	35%	39	98
B of Int Des	4	FIDER	SAT/ACT HS transcript	45	26	40%	26	14
B of Ind Des	4		SAT/ACT HS transcript	67	71	60%	45	32
M of Ind Des	2		GRE-transcript	**				
B Land Arch	5		SAT/ACT HS transcript	21	21	75%	11	3
M Reg Plan	2		GRE-transcript	8		70%	4	2

*15 quarter hours or more   **applicants will be accepted Fall 1988

SCHOOL DEMOGRAPHICS (all degree programs)

Full-Time Faculty	Part-Time Faculty	Full-Time Students	Part-Time Students	Foreign Students	Out-of-State U.S. Stdnts.	Women Students	Minority Students
43	5	609	382	2%	30%	26%	2%

LIBRARY (Tel. No. 205-826-4510)

Type	No. of Volumes	No. of Slides
Arch	26,800	24,000

STUDENT OPPORTUNITIES AND RESOURCES

The School of Architecture at Auburn University offers programs in the Departments of Architecture, Building Science, and Industrial Design.

The Department of Architecture offers undergraduate programs in architecture, interior design, and landscape architecture. The department also administers the graduate program in regional planning. The department is committed to a high standard of professional education in design. Within the framework of a five-year professional undergraduate curriculum, the faculty seeks to prepare students primarily for the tasks for which society is dependent upon professional architects. Enrollment in the program in architecture is limited to a maximum of 400 students, which strikes a balance between the personalized educational needs of individual students and the provision of a broad range of faculty resources.

SPECIAL ACTIVITIES AND PROGRAMS

Study abroad program

Community service and regionally oriented projects

National, International, and local competitions

Fine Arts Week each spring (exhibits, speakers, musical and theatrical performances) Beaux Art Ball

Special summer program to enable students to join sophomore class in fall

Student Chapter of American Institute of Architects, actively involved in departmental affairs (student/faculty committees, planning new facilities for the department, research projects, construction, faculty/student teams consulting as architects in practice. Dean's Student Advisory Council)

Lecture series each quarter

Horizontal Studio (series of interdisciplinary interior, architecture, and landscape projects)

Tau Sigma Delta, national design honorary

FACILITIES

Architecture library
Computer laboratory
Shop facilities
Print room
Photographic darkroom
Audio Visual Center

SCHOLARSHIPS/AID

Auburn University awards approximately 800 scholarships totaling over $650,000 annually. In 1985-86, grants totaling approximately $3.5 million were made to over 2500 students. Architecture students are eligible for most and receive many of these awards, although no scholarships or grants are earmarked especially for architecture students. The university administers over $27 million through all types of student financial aid programs, including loans and work-study programs. (This figure excludes athletic scholarships and outside scholarships and fellowships.)

UNDERGRADUATE PROGRAM
Philosophy Statement

Historically, Auburn has been known for its excellence in architectural design education which has prepared its graduates for a creative role in the profession. The educational content of the undergraduate curriculum is divided approximately equally between four areas: (1) design, (2) technology and professional requirements, (3) humanities and science, and (4) electives. In addition, the student is provided with numerous resources, including interdisciplinary studies with interior design, landscape architecture, and building science, field trips, and the opportunity for study abroad. Auburn University offers a Business Minor for non-business majors which provides the student with a basic understanding of the foundations of business administration.

The School of Architecture offers a Dual-Degree Program of the Bachelor of Architecture and the Bachelor of Science in Building Construction.

GRADUATE PROGRAM
Philosophy Statement

The department offers a Master of Regional Planning degree in a two-year curriculum. The graduate program at Auburn is firmly based in physical planning, and is designed for the education of professional planners for smaller communities and non-metropolitan regions. The program (1) emphasizes physical planning and the related concerns of smaller communities, rural counties, and non-metropolitan regions; (2) provides the core of comprehensive planning knowledge plus opportunities in many specialty areas; and (3) provides practical planning experience directly through its curriculum. The Master of Regional Planning program is open to qualified students from a wide range of undergraduate fields. A bachelor's degree in one of the design professions, engineering, or the physical or social sciences is normally the best preparation for graduate study in planning at Auburn University.

FACULTY
Administration

Ray K Parker, FAIA, Dean
Daniel D Bennett, AIA, Head
Betty J Fendley, Academic Advisor
Sue Glaze, Interim Librarian

Professors

Daniel D Bennett, AIA, RA, B Arch, M Arch
Gaines T Blackwell, MFA
Nicholas D Davis, RA, AIA, BA, BS, MFA
Steffen R Doerstling, AIA Assoc, MA, Dr of Eng
Robert L Faust, AIA, RA, B Arch
William R Gwin, RA, AIA, B Arch, MVA, M Arch
Allan M Hing, IDEC, BFA, MA
Clark E Lundell, AIA, RA, NCARB, BED, M Arch
Peter Magyar, Assoc Member AIA, MAUD, Dipl.
E Keith McPheeters, FAIA, RA, B Arch, MFA in Arch
Darrell C Meyer, AICP, MRP
Richard G Millman, AIA, RA, B Arch, M Arch
Ray K Parker, FAIA, RA, BS, B Arch, M Arch

Associate Professors

Alan R Cook, RA, B of Env Des, M Arch
Tarik A Orgen, B Arch, PhD cand
Paul A Zorr, AIA, RA, BA Arch, MA Arch

Assistant Professors

David Braly, B Arch, M Arch
William S Briggs, BED, M Arch
J Douglas Burleson, RA, BED, M Arch
Cathryn S Campbell, Assoc Member ASLA, BLA, MLA
Scott J Finn, AIA, RA, BA, M Arch
Alan B LaFon, B Arch, M Arch
Brian J LaHaie, ASLA, MLA
Sheri L Schumacher, MFA, BA Int Des

Instructors

Scott E Fischer, AIA, B Arch
Mary Catherine Martin, BA

Part-Time Faculty

Alton C Keown, BA
Robert Frank McAlpine, B Arch, BID
William J. Peek, AIA, BSED, B Arch

Visiting Assistant Professors

Michael Hubbs, BA, BID
Behzad Nakhjavan, B Arch, M Arch
Mark Weaver, BLA, MLA

Adjunct Faculty

Robert W Aderholdt, PE, BS Mech Eng, MS Mech Eng, PhD Eng
Rebecca Burleson, BS
Patricia Cook, BA, BS
Thomas E Cooper, PE, BS Civil Eng, MS Sanitary Eng
William F Huston, PE, BSCE, MBA
Roger Killingsworth, AIC, CMAA, BS Arch Const, MS Const Mgmt
Norbert Lechner, RA, BS of Arch, M of Arch
Hendrick Mol, PE, BS Civil Eng, MS Civil Eng
Peter M Weiss, AIA, BA in Arch, B Arch, MA in Design
Steve Williams, PE, BS in Civil Eng, MS in Civil Eng

Ball State University

Department of Architecture
College of Architecture & Planning
Ball State University
Muncie, Indiana 47306
(317) 285-1900 (dept)
(317) 285-5861 (college)

Admissions Office
302 Administration Building
Ball State University
Muncie, Indiana 47306
317-285-8300

Application Deadline(s): Fall (undgrd): April 1
(transfers): June 13
(grad): June 1
Spring (undgrd):
December 1

Tuition & Fees: Undgrd: IN Res: $1767/yr;
non-res: $4074/yr
Grad: IN Res: $1743/yr;
non-res: $4074/yr

Endowment: Public

DEGREE PROGRAMS

Degree	Minimum Years for Degree	Accred.	Requirements for Admission	Full-Time Stdnts.	Part-Time Stdnts.	% of Applics. Accptd.	Stdnts. in 1st Year of Program	# of Degrees Conferred
BS Ed	4		sophomore standing in college	34		17%	104*	65
B Arch	5	NAAB	admission to university; high school rank, SAT	460		17%	104*	57
M Arch	1		B Arch, B average, portfolio, interview	2		60%	2	0
MSHP	2		bacc degree, B average	8		70%	4	3
MURP	2		bacc degree, B average, written statement	6	4	80%	3	2
BLA	5	ASLA	admission to university; high school rank, SAT	48		17%	104*	10
MLA	1-3**	ASLA	bacc degree, B average, portfolio, interview, written statement	27		60%	5	3
BUPD	5		admission to university; high school rank, SAT	3		17%	104*	(new program)

*College provides a common first-year curriculum required of all students in these degree programs

**1 w/5-yr BLA; 2 w/4-yr BSLA; 3 w/non-design degree.

SCHOOL DEMOGRAPHICS (all degree programs)

Full-Time Faculty	Part-Time Faculty	Full-Time Students	Part-Time Students	Foreign Students	Out-of-State U.S. Stdnts.	Women Students	Minority Students
45	5	575	85	5%	33%	25%	5%

LIBRARY (Tel. No. 317-285-5858)

Type	No. of Volumes	No. of Slides
College	26,700	60,000

STUDENT OPPORTUNITIES AND RESOURCES

Ball State University was selected in 1965 as the site for Indiana's first school of architecture. One of six colleges in a university of 18,000 undergraduate and 1000 graduate students, the College of Architecture and Planning now has over 500 students, of whom 33 percent are out-of-state residents or foreign. The college is comprised of three departments: Architecture, Landscape Architecture, and Urban Planning. The college enjoys an excellent relationship with the university and community at large. It is also located convenient to most of the major cities of the Midwest.

Architecture faculty hold degrees from some 42 institutions of higher learning. The department of architecture does not adhere to a particular dogma or limited philosophy; faculty have always been encouraged to develop and share individual interests and areas of specialization. Interdisciplinary programs with the college's two other departments are offered.

Ball State's main campus covers 946 acres. The facilities include the one-million-volume Bracken Library, the 3,600-seat Emens Auditorium, the Art Gallery and its growing permanent collection, the Science Complex, the Whitinger Business College, the Student Center, several large residence halls, the Wood Health Center, a sports complex and natatorium, and the College of Architecture and Planning itself. The last was realized during two building campaigns in the 1970s; designs for it were determined by competitions, and it now provides more than 120,000 square feet of space. The latest addition to the campus is the Bell Building, adjacent to the Architecture Building, which houses the departments of English, Mathematics, and Computer Science, as well as the university's computer services. Now under construction nearby is the new Center for Information and Communication Sciences.

SPECIAL ACTIVITIES AND PROGRAMS

Biennial "Polyark" London Lab: Spring quarter in Europe for full credit, open to 30+ students, second through fifth year; alternates with other trips to sites around the world (Middle East, 1985; Scandinavia and Russia, 1989).

Field trips to major American and Canadian cities each year for all students.

Nationally recognized guest lecture and exhibition series.

Six-month internships as a required part of the third year.

Highly successful community-based projects program, with a new mobile technical unit to support work at the sites.

Quarterly visiting faculty members from around the world.

Summer honors workshop for gifted high school students.

Special symposia on energy, leisure environments, environmental communications, historic preservation, etc.

Centers for Energy Research, Education, and Service (CERES) and Environmental Design, Research, and Service (CEDRS).

Active student chapters of AIA and ASLA.

Quarterly RE:CAP newsletter.

Writing in the Design Curriculum program to enhance verbal skills.

Accelerated entry program in the Summer to bring transfer students with 2 years of college credit up to the level of the second year of design.

FACILITIES

In the Architecture Building are:

Branches of the university library, slide library, and bookstore (Archeion).

Stations for INTERGRAPH and AUTOCAD computer graphics applications (soon to be expanded).

Workshops, photo labs, and video labs.

An historical archive of drawings by Indiana designers and of Indiana sites and structures.

Studio accommodations providing individual workspaces for students in all years.

Auditorium and exhibition spaces.

The college also has acquired a large motor home converted into a mobile studio for community-based projects throughout Indiana.

SCHOLARSHIPS/AID

A full range of scholarships, grants, grants-in-aid, loans, and employment is offered. The basis of selection is primarily financial need, but scholarships are awarded to freshmen admitted with honors. There is no closing date for applications, but priority is given to applications received by March 1. Institutional applications and the Financial Aid Form (FAF) are required. A $1000 student travel grant is awarded each year in architecture, and several other grants are made available each year to our students by professional organizations. Four graduate assistantships are also available in the Department of Architecture. Out-of-state students admitted to the university with distinction qualify for a waiver of the out-of-state portion of their tuition.

UNDERGRADUATE PROGRAM
Philosophy Statement

The undergraduate architecture program encourages the student to explore and expand his or her creative potential in design and to develop the basic professional skills of an architect. The faculty's diverse approaches and philosophies support a healthy balance between the technical and theoretical. Students build self-awareness and self-confidence through exposure to a variety of situations.

Program Description

The five-year undergraduate program leading to the B Arch degree is designed to prepare graduates for professional practice within the context of the dynamic and changing environmental design professions. Emphasis is placed on an interdisciplinary relationship with the Departments of Landscape Architecture and Urban Planning, which share the facilities and resources of the college. All three programs are

dedicated to the development of professional competence in the functional, aesthetic, and humane planning and design of natural and man-made environments.

The program uses the 14-quarter (9-semester starting 1988-89) sequence in the design studio, from the multidisciplinary freshman year to the fifth-year undergraduate thesis, as a forum in which the student develops an approach to design. Individual and team techniques are used in addressing problems in a real context. Diversity of faculty, philosophies, teaching methods, private practice, and research all combine to support this goal through the development of techniques in synthesis and problem solving. The studio is further supported by a strong coordinated effort in graphics, building technology, history, philosophy, and professional practice areas. Independent study opportunities are available in the upper years, and architecture electives, such as psychological aspects of environmental design, photography, medical facilities, sculpture, advanced rendering, theory and communications, solar skills, environmental graphics, archaeological applications, design for the elderly, human figure applications, brochure development, advanced programming, and historic preservation, give students an opportunity to pursue various aspects of the environmental design professions.

GRADUATE PROGRAM
Philosophy Statement

Graduate programs in architecture provide advanced training with a solid academic and professional base to prepare candidates for careers in architecture, urban design, and historic preservation. There is also a strong contextual interrelationship among these three areas, all dedicated to improving the quality of the physical environment.

Program Description

The Master of Architecture degree requires an additional year of academic work beyond the first professional degree (B Arch). The degree is described by its options; these include Architectural Design, Urban Design, Architectural History, Preservation and Restoration, Environmental Science and Technology, and Communication Technology and Design. The curriculum provides for a greater depth of specialization than is possible at the undergraduate level.

The Master of Science in Historic Preservation (MSHP) degree requires two years plus a summer internship, and is designed for students with backgrounds in areas other than architecture. Core courses include History, Philosophy and Theory of Preservation, History of Architecture and Urbanism, Preservation Technology, Contemporary Preservation Practice, and Documentation, plus electives. A thesis is required.

FACULTY
Administration

Robert A Fisher, RA, AIA, Dean of the College
Jeffrey L Hall, RLA, ASLA, Associate Dean
Marvin Rosenman, RA, AIA, Chairman for Architecture
Ronald L Spangler, CELA, ASLA, Chairman for Landscape Architecture
Francis H Parker, AICP, Chairman for Urban Planning
Gil R Smith, Administration Assistant for Architecture
Barbara Ballinger, Librarian
Phyllis Harland, Librarian
Connie Hittle, Slide Librarian

Professors

Anthony J Costello, RA, M Arch
Harry A Eggink, RA, M Arch
David R Hermansen, RA, SAH, NCPE, MS Arch
Uwe F Koehler, EDRA, M Arch
Paul A Laseau, RA, M Arch
Stanley B Mendelsohn, RIBA, PhD
Bruce F Meyer, RA, PhD
A E Palmer, RA, EDRA, M Arch
Marvin E Rosenman, RA, AIA, MS Arch
Charles M Sappenfield, RA, AIA, EDRA, Diploma
Arthur W Schaller, RA, B Arch
Andrew R Seager, RA, SAH, M Arch
J. Robert Taylor, RA, AIA, M Arch
James R Underwood, RA, B Arch
C Daniel Woodfin, RA, B Arch
John E Wyman, RA, AIA, B Arch

Associate Professors

Alfredo R Missair, Diploma

Assistant Professors

Carlos Casuscelli, M Arch
Daniel Doz, Diploma
David L Mackey, RA, M Arch
John McCreery, RA, AIA
Michel A Mounayar, M Arch
Gil R Smith, SAH, PhD
Andréa Urbas
Edward Wolner, MUP, PhD

Adjunct Faculty

Jeffrey D Culp, AIA, M Arch
Robert J Koester, RA, M Arch

Boston Architectural Center

Boston Architectural Center
320 Newbury Street
Boston, Massachusetts 02115
(617) 536-3170

Application Deadline(s): Rolling
Tuition & Fees: Undgrd: $1850/year
Endowment: Private

DEGREE PROGRAMS

Degree	Minimum Years for Degree	Accred.	Requirements for Admission	Full-Time Stdnts.	Part-Time Stdnts.	% of Applics. Accptd.	Stdnts. in 1st Year of Program	# of Degrees Conferred
B Arch	6	NAAB	High school diploma	644	69	100%	167	66

SCHOOL DEMOGRAPHICS (all degree programs)

Full-Time Faculty	Part-Time Faculty	Full-Time Students	Part-Time Students	Foreign Students	Out-of-State U.S. Stdnts.	Women Students	Minority Students
1	126	644	69	—	19%	20.1%	7%

LIBRARY (Tel. No. 617-536-9108)

Type	No. of Volumes	No. of Slides
Arch only	18,000	35,000

STUDENT OPPORTUNITIES AND RESOURCES

The Boston Architectural Center is in fact a small, independent college with 650 students. It offers an accredited professional degree program and an extensive continuing education program. The center was founded in 1889 as the Boston Architectural Club.

In 1966, the Center moved into its own building at the corner of Hereford and Newbury streets in Boston's historic Back Bay neighborhood.

Although its tuition is similar to those of state-subsidized institutions, the Boston Architectural Center is a private, nonprofit corporation that operates without public subsidy. It is able to accomplish this primarily because of its volunteer faculty.

BAC students tend to be clear-eyed about their career and role in society. They are all determined to practice the profession of architecture. They are relatively mature (the average age is 27). Many are pursuing their second careers with the dedication characteristic of late starters. About 85 percent of the students have had some prior college work before starting the BAC. More than one quarter of entering students have college degrees.

Demand for admission to the BAC is strong. Although 200 students are admitted each year, there is a waiting list. The fine reputation of the volunteer faculty is the basic reason for the program's sustained popularity. The required work-study, aided by a job-placement clearinghouse, is another.

The programs of the Center do not produce narrow specialists. The unusually large number of teachers and courses ensures that students have access to a varied and rounded view of the world of environmental design. A major objective of the curriculum is to teach many approaches to making the physical environment in ways that best serve the client and the user.

SPECIAL ACTIVITIES AND PROGRAMS

Active student organization, the Atelier, AIAS Chapter

Fifteen-week summer session for special courses and make-up

Scholarship program for travel

AIA Chapter Scholarship for travel or alternative programs

Foreign Study Tours

Merit Scholarships

Job placement office

Lecture series open to the public and students

Exhibition program

Student competitions

Inter-institutional programs with six other colleges

Community Design Center (CDC)-service-learning involving student volunteer assistance for local community groups

Summer program for high school students

FACILITIES

In addition to the usual design studios and classrooms, the BAC includes:
Computer classroom (10 stations)
Photo lab
Photo studio
Video center
Model shop
Student lounge
Rare book library

SCHOLARSHIPS/AID

The BAC awards approximately $30,000 per year in financial aid to students beyond the second semester at the Center. Awards are made each semester after interview with committee members. A large percentage of students receive Pell Grants (Basic Educational Opportunity Grants) and loans. Tuition at the school is low and it is usually within the capability of students (who work while attending classes at night) to pay. Scholarships and honorary awards are separate from financial aid and total over $20,000 per year.

UNDERGRADUATE PROGRAM
Philosophy Statement

Through all its years the BAC has been sustained by a clear and singular educational philosophy.

Its teaching program is maintained by an all-volunteer professional faculty, now numbering over 240 teachers.

BAC offers open access to its program: any student with at least a high school education can enter on a first-come, first-served basis.

Tuition is remarkably low. In 1903, students were charged $17.50 per year. In 1987, they paid $1850 a year.

The BAC maintains the oldest continuously operating architectural work-study program in the nation. All students are expected to engage in full-time professional work concurrently with their evening studies.

Program Description

The BAC offers a six-year program leading to the Bachelor of Architecture degree. To graduate, each student must complete 123 academic credits, document 36 months of work curriculum credits, and pass all reviews.

The BAC program covers approximately the same amount of material as a 5-year undergraduate program in architecture. Full-time students take 6 to 9 credits each term. If a student enrolls for 9 credits per term, then six years are required to complete the degree requirements.

A minimum residency of three years (six semesters) is required.

FACULTY
Administration

Arcangelo Cascieri, FAIA, Dean
Bernard P Spring, FAIA, President
Elsie Hurst, Hon AIA, Vice President for Administration
David Tobias, AIA, Vice President for Academic Affairs
Stephen Martin, Administrator of Student Services
Susan Lewis, Head Librarian

Maureen Mahoney, Registrar
Julia Seltz, Director of Media
  Services/Photography

Educators
Don Adams, BA, MBA
Kathy Adams
Kory Addis, BFA
Adolfo Albaisa, BFA, B Arch
Jennifer Aliber, BA, M Arch
Apostolos M Antonopoulos, PE, BSCE
Paula Aoki
Elie Atallah, B Arch
Robert Augustine, B Arch
Andrew Bank, BA, M Arch
Derek Barcinski, BA, B Arch
Rebecca Barnes, AB, M Arch
William Barry, B Arch
Hansel Bauman, BED
Ursula Beck, BA, MA, MS
Doug Bencks, BA, M Arch
Joyce Berman, BA, MA, B Arch
Seth Berman, BSCE, MSCE
Michael Bernard, AB, JD, MCP
Richard Bertone, Assoc Arch, B Arch
Christopher Blake, B Arch
Llewellyn Bley, BSCE, MSCE
H Lawrence Bluestone, AB, M Arch, MCP
Zane Bower, BA, BLA
Nina Brew, BA, B Arch, SM Arch S
Laura M Briggs, BFA, B Arch
Don Brown, B Arch, M Arch, MUD
Peter Byerly, BA, M Arch
Charles Callahan, Esq, BA, LLB
Steven B Canter, BA, B Arch
Gregory Carell, B Arch
Christine Carlyle, B Arch
Arcangelo Cascieri, BAC
Niccolo Casewit, BED, M Arch
Jeffrey B Causey, B Arch
Garth W Caylor, Jr, B Arch, MA
Yih-Ping Chang, B Arch, SM Arch S
Christopher Chiodo, BID
Corinne Chiogna, BS Art
Winston Chou, BFA, B Arch
Charles Cimino, AIA, Assoc Eng, MBA
James Clark, BA, B Arch
Scott Clark, BA, M Arch
Donald Coburn
Herb Cohen
Kevin Conway, BS, M Arch
James Cooper, BA, M Arch
Leslie Humm Cormier, MCRP, MA, PhD
Christopher M. Costanza, B Arch
Mark Cottle, BA, M Arch
Fred Cowen, BSCE
Greg Crawford, BED, B Arch
Ann Crew, BA
Shannon Criss, B Arch
Dennis Daly, BFA
John Dalzell, B Arch
John Dannecker, B Arch
Caroline Darbyshire, BLA
Michael R Davis, BS, M Arch
Robert Davis
Charles Deknatel, BA, MS, PhD
Norbert DeLacaze, Arch DPLG, Dipl
Manuel Delgado, Dipl
Gary Demele, BA

Douglas Dick, B Arch
Christopher D Diehl, BED
Christopher T Doktor, BED, M Arch
Paula Vaune Dugan, BA, M Arch
Rosalyn Elder, BA, M Arch, MAUD
Carlos Ferre, BA, BFA, M Arch
Carl Franceschi, B Arch
Laurie Friedman, BA, BS, M Arch
Gerard M Fuksa, BA, M Arch
Jeanne K Gang, BS
Pilar Garcia, BID
Marek A Garlicki, BPS
Russ Gerard, B Arch
Pamela Getz, BA
Michael Giardina, B Arch, M Arch
Statler Gilfillen, B Arch, MBA
James Gilmour, B Arch
Peter Goldstein, B Arch
Nils Gore, B Arch
Eric Gresla, B Env Design
William Hall
Christine Harvey, BFA, MFA
David Hatem, Esq, BA, JD
Timothy Haynes, BA, M Arch
Deleep Hazra, PE, B Eng, MS Eng
Adam Himber, BA
Jeff Hirsch, B Env Design, M Arch
James Hogan, B Arch
Jane Holden, B Env Design, M Arch
Andrea Homolac, B Arch
Tony Hoover, BA, MS
Patricia Horvath, BA
Hank Hughs
Donald Hunsicker, BA, M Arch
Joe Jakobowski
Walid E Jammal, BS
Todd Jersey, MA
Akel Ismail Kahera, B Arch, Dipl, SM Arch S
Sabir Kahn, BA, M Arch
Jonathan Kahn-Leavitt, BSE, M Arch
Anita Kercheval, B Arch
Fred Kimberk
Valdis Kirsis, AIA, B Arch
Eric Kirton, BS, M Arch
Jonathan R Knowles, Jr, BFA, B Arch
Lawrence Ko, B Arch
Andrea Kunst, BA, MA
Byron Dean Kuth, BFA, B Arch
Ron Laffely, B Arch
Cathleen Lange, B Arch
John Lawler, BA
Mary Lawton
Richard Leaf, BA, M Arch
Robert Levit, BA, M Arch
James E Loftus, B Arch
Daniel E Madru
Roland Malamuceanu, M Arch, SM Arch
Michael Marlow
Paul Marx, BA, MCP, PhD
Paul G May, BA, M Arch
Bill McIntosh, BS Mech Eng
Patricia Meehan, Dipl, B Arch
Stephen Mielke, BS, M Arch
Christopher Milford, B Arch, M Arch
Courtney Miller, BA, M Arch
Clifford Moller, B Arch
Amy L Murphy, BFA, B Arch
John Murphy, AIA, B Arch

Allan C Murray, BSC, B Arch, M Arch
Kristopher Musumano, BFA, B Arch
David Myers, BA, M Arch
Melvin Nash, Esq, BA, JD
Alan Natapoff, AB, PhD
Todd Neal, BED, B Arch
Gretchen Neely, BFA, B Arch
Daniel Ng, AB, M Arch
John O'Connell, BA, M Arch
Grace U Oh, BA, M Arch
Mike Panetta, B Arch
Clarence Passons, B Arch, M Arch
Allan Penn
Mary Anne Perkowski, BA, M Arch
Daphne Politis, MCP, SM Arch S
Louis Porcaro, B Arch
Le Proctor, B Arch
Tracy Quoidbach, B Arch
Elizabeth Ranieri, BFA, B Arch
Alice G Read, BA, M Arch
Steve Rich, AIA, PE, B Arch, BSCE
Paul Roberts, B Arch
Laura Robinson, BSE, M Arch
Joseph Rondinelli, BS
C R Rogers, BA
William Rowe, B Arch, BCE, MS
K H Schaeffer, BA, MA
Dan Schafer
Carl Scheidenhelm, BD, MAA
Julia Seltz, BFA
Susan Sheldon, B Arch
Richard Sherman, BA, MA
Owen Shows, BA, MA
Leigh Shutter, B Arch, MS
Robert Siegel, B Arch
Wayne E Siladi, BA, BSE
Cary L Siress, B Arch
Steven Sivak, BA, BS, M Arch
Edward Snow
Cynthia L Solarz, BA, M Arch
Laurence Spang, B Arch
John Spears, BA, M Arch
Bernard P Spring, AB, M Arch
Edwin J Steel
George Stephen, D Arch
Robert Sturgis, AB, M Arch
Marianne Takas, BA, JD
Bradbury W Taylor, BA, M Arch
Vladimir Taytslin, BS, MS
David Tobias, BED, B Arch
Ed Trafidlo, BS, B Arch
Joseph Tringale
Gerald L Valgora, B Arch, M Arch
Bradford Walker, BS Arch, M Arch
Ed Warner, BA, MA
George Warner, BA, M Arch
Clarence Washington, BS, MFA
Susan Weinz, BFA, Dipl
Jerry Weslar, AAS
Judy West
Elizabeth Whitbeck, BSCE
Jay Wickersham, BA, M Arch
John Williamson, B Arch
Thomas T Wilson, BID, B Arch
Michael Wright, AD, B Arch
Keith Yancey, B Arch, M Arch Eng
Paul Zanette, BA, B Arch
Imad A Zrein, BS, MS

University of British Columbia

School of Architecture
University of British Columbia
6333 Memorial Road
Vancouver, British Columbia V6T 1W5
Canada
(604) 228-2779

Application Deadline(s):
All application materials EXCEPT Portfolio -
March 31st; Portfolio - April 30th
Tuition & Fees: Undgrd: $1716/yr
              Grad: $1700/yr
Endowment: Public

DEGREE PROGRAMS

Degree	Minimum Years for Degree	Accred.	Requirements for Admission	Full-Time Stdnts.	Part-Time Stdnts.	% of Applics. Accptd.	Stdnts. in 1st Year of Program	# of Degrees Conferred
B Arch	3	CAA	BA/BSc/3 yrs in another school of Arch	130		60%	45	46
MASA*	1	N/A	Professional degree in Arch	9	2	—	7	—

*(Master of Advanced Studies in Architecture)

SCHOOL DEMOGRAPHICS (all degree programs)

Full-Time Faculty	Part-Time Faculty	Full-Time Students	Part-Time Students	Foreign Students	Out-of-State U.S. Stdnts.	Women Students	Minority Students
12	10	139	2	—	—	30%	—

LIBRARY (Tel. No. 604-228-3046)

Type	No. of Volumes	No. of Slides
Branch Library	3,000	25,000

STUDENT OPPORTUNITIES AND RESOURCES

The University of British Columbia is a large and diverse institution of some 30,000 students, located in Vancouver on a scenic headland overlooking the Straights of Georgia. The School of Architecture is relatively small, currently housing approximately 150 students in a three-year professional degree program. While it is administratively linked to the Faculty of Applied Science, the School is relatively autonomous in its academic affairs. Because the program is a second degree program, it is aimed at mature students who have made the decision to enter Architecture after sampling knowledge from other disciplines and acquiring the skills and critical attitude that a broad undergraduate education provides. Mature students make it possible to concentrate entirely on architectural matters during the three or more years of the professional B Arch program. As a result, the faculty is diverse in its professional interests and areas of specialization, the range including history and theory, social behavioural studies, science and technology, professional practice and design. Selective admission results in a diverse student body with high academic standing on entry, as well as demonstrable aptitudes and skills for architecture as revealed through portfolios and work experience. As the university has a general requirement for two years in residence in order to graduate, transfer students are accepted but only under exceptional circumstances.

SPECIAL ACTIVITIES AND PROGRAMS

The School program has several special features:

a) All students enter an introductory workshop. It lasts approximately 10 days and involves an expedition to one of the smaller communities in British Columbia. The students are housed in a camp situation and spend the day in the community or in a studio. They make a series of surveys of the community and assess opportunities for architectural interventions, for which they then develop proposals. In the process, they meet officials and members of the community and are supported by resource people drawn together by the faculty to provide particular information. The Workshop ends with a presentation of the results to the community and an appropriate celebration.

b) Every second year, the school runs a Study Abroad program. A section of approximately 20 students is taken abroad to a major city and sets up in a studio environment there, usually in conjunction with another School of Architecture. Using this base for a full term, they take a series of studio and lecture courses, and make field trips to important architectural monuments and projects. Design projects are focused on architectural interventions in those cities. Courses are provided by the faculty and professionals on location recruited as resource people. Over the past 15 years, this very popular and exacting program has been successfully undertaken in major cities such as Paris, Tokyo, Hong Kong, Amedabad, Athens, Jerusalem, and Venice.

c) The School provides a lecture series, bringing in visiting professors and professionals from the United States, Canada and Europe, and students and faculty have the opportunity to meet them in lecture, seminar, and more informal contexts. This program is run by ARCHUS, the student organization.

FACILITIES

The School is housed in the Lasserre Building, built in 1961 to house Fine Arts, Architecture, and Planning. All students in the B Arch program are provided with workstations on the third floor of this building. Other facilities are located elsewhere in this building or an annex, including a small microcomputer lab.

SCHOLARSHIPS/AID

The bulk of need-based financial assistance for students is provided through a student loan program, financed by the Federal and Provincial Governments. In addition, some scholarships are available for entering students, provided by private sources.

UNDERGRADUATE PROGRAM
Philosophy Statement

The intention of the B Arch Program is to provide educational preparation to meet national Certification standards in Canada which qualify the graduate to enter the registration process. They subsequently sit for the registration examinations which occur (usually) after a minimum of three years of work experience following certification. Because of the short duration of the B Arch program, there is a heavy emphasis on design as a creative enterprise, but also as a holistic integrative process. The design program is tutorial based, recognizing the diverse backgrounds of the students and their variable learning speeds which require individual attention. At the same time, the program fosters a sense of community in the School in various ways, encouraging students to learn from each other and to share their experiences as well as resources in a mutually supportive environment.

Program Description

Following the Introductory Workshop, described above, the incoming students undertake a variety of design projects together with introductory courses in technology, history and theory, techniques, and ideas in architecture. Through the second to fifth terms, inclusive, the studio program is vertically integrated and the first, second, and third-year students, with the advice of the faculty, select tutorials according to their needs. During their final terms they complete a graduation project consisting of a major design investigation. A full-time student takes three courses and one studio/tutorial every term. Students are free to reduce their load and complete the program on a part-time basis, so that many students take longer than three years to complete the program.

Of the total of 18 courses required in addition to the studio program, 12 are mandatory covering a range of history, socio-behavioural, technology, and professional subjects. Elective courses may be taken within the School or, in certain circumstances, in other departments in the University.

GRADUATE PROGRAM

The School offers a post-professional Master of Advanced Studies in Architecture (MASA) degree program. This is intended as a program of individual study leading to a research project and culminating in a written thesis or a major design investigation. The program is aimed at graduates, preferably with three to five years of professional experience, and may be undertaken on a full-time or part-time basis. Areas of concentration, both in research and in the thesis, are related to the availability of faculty and can include history and theory, housing, environments for special populations (e.g. children, elderly, mentally handicapped), and environmental technology.

FACULTY
Administration

Douglas Shadbolt, MAIBC, FRAIC, Director

Professors

Charles A Tiers, MAIBC/FRAIC, B Arch, M Arch

Associate Professors

Robin P A Clarke, MAIBC/RIBA, AA, M Arch
Raymond J Cole, BSc, PhD
Richard W Seaton, BA, PhD
Ronald B Walkey, MAIBC, B Arch, M Arch
Woodruff W Wood, MAIBC/FRAIC, B Arch

Assistant Professors

John A Gaitanakis, MAIBC/RA-US/MNAL, B Arch, M Arch
Andrew Gruft, MAIBC, B Arch
Dino P Rapanos, MAIBC, B Arch, M Arch
Joel Shack, MOAA, B Arch

Instructors

Michael Milojevic, B Arch, M Arch
Stephen I Taylor, P Eng, APEBC, BA Sc, MS

Part-Time Faculty

Richard W Seaton, BA, PhD

Adjunct Faculty

Michael Ernest, B Arch, MS
Patricia French, B Arch
David B Leaney, P Eng, BA Sc
Shelagh Lindsey, BA, MA
Eva Matsuzaki, B Arch
Chris Mattock, BED
Sherry McKay, BA, MA
Freda Pagani, B Arch
Moura Quayle, MBCSLA/MCSLA/MCFLA, BLA, MLA
Gerald Rolfsen, MAIBC, B Arch, PhD

California Polytechnic State University, San Luis Obispo

Architecture Department
School of Architecture and
Environmental Design
California Polytechnic State
University
San Luis Obispo, California 93407
(805) 756-1316 (dept)
(805) 756-1311 (school)

Admissions Office
California Polytechnic State
University
Admin Bldg 213
San Luis Obispo, California 93407
(805) 756-2311

Application Deadline(s): November 1-30 Fall
Quarter,
June 1-30 Winter
Quarter
Tuition & Fees: Undgrd: CA Res: $870/yr
Grad: CA Res: $870/yr
Non-Res: $870/yr + $98/
unit/qtr
Endowment: Public

DEGREE PROGRAMS

Degree	Minimum Years for Degree	Accred.	Requirements for Admission	Full-Time Stdnts.	Part-Time Stdnts.	% of Applics. Accptd.	Stdnts. in 1st Year of Program	# of Degrees Conferred
B Arch	5	NAAB	Top 1/3 of High School Class Supplemental Screening	826	0	13%	205	128
MS Arch	1		B Arch 3.0 GPA, GRE	20	0	60%	8	8
BSCRP	4	PAB		143	0	62%	61	27
MCRP	2		Four-Year Bachelor Degree 3.0 GPA, GRE	19	0	57%	7	6
BS L Arch	4	ASLA	Top 1/3 of High School Class Supplemental Screening	203	0	54%	58	43
BS Arch Eng	4	ABET	Top 1/3 of High School Class Supplemental Screening	198	0	25%	45	61
BS Const	4	ACCE	Top 1/3 of High School Class Supplemental Screening	176	0	52%	69	37

SCHOOL DEMOGRAPHICS (all degree programs)

Full-Time Faculty	Part-Time Faculty	Full-Time Students	Part-Time Students	Foreign Students	Out-of-State U.S. Stdnts.	Women Students	Minority Students
55	22	1533	0	2%	2%	27%	24%

LIBRARY (Tel. No. 805-546-1135)

Type	No. of Volumes	No. of Slides
University	16,700 Architecture	116,500 Architecture

STUDENT OPPORTUNITIES AND RESOURCES

The School of Architecture and Environmental Design enrolls approximately 1,500 students and has about 100 faculty members. It comprises the Department of Architecture and four other departments. In addition to the Bachelor of Architecture degree, four Bachelor of Science degree programs are offered: architectural engineering, city and regional planning, construction, and landscape architecture. The student is kept aware that all five programs have a common objective and that they are all aimed at the betterment of our physical environment.

The first two years of all five programs share several common courses which develop basic skills and background. Students who are unsure of their degree objective can consult with their advisors in order to maintain a flexible program of study that will keep their options open.

Two graduate programs are offered: the Master of Science, Architecture and the Master of City and Regional Planning. These programs are designed for students interested in advanced professional studies.

SPECIAL ACTIVITIES AND PROGRAMS

Articulation agreements with most community colleges in California

Poly Canyon: 15 acres on campus for on-site projects and experimental work

Summer quarter in operation

International programs through the university in Denmark and Italy

Large technical facilities available

School has own shops, photographic labs, print rooms, etc.

Participant in the Washington/Alexandria Center Consortium

High School Summer Workshop

Annual Design Village in Poly Canyon

Distinguished Visiting Lecture Series

FACILITIES

The excellent facilities include design laboratories, darkrooms, a soils laboratory, a stress laboratory, shops, a construction yard, a project yard, and grading galleries. An outlying area of 12 acres, known as "the Canyon," is available for extensive experimental construction. The location of the campus between the great population centers of San Francisco and Los Angeles is ideal for an environmental design school. Students are able to participate in environmental studies ranging from rural projects to large metropolitan complexes, and there is a continual stream of visiting instructors. Field trips to various parts of the state are arranged as part of students' required work.

SCHOLARSHIPS/AID

A number of scholarships are available specifically for architecture students. The following is a partial list of available awards. For more detailed information contact the Architecture Department Office.

Stephen O. Anderson Memorial Scholarship
Wallace W. Arendt Scholarship
Bechtel Affirmative Action Award
Black Students in School of Architecture and Environmental Design Scholarship
Thor Gulbrand Memorial Scholarship
D. Stewart Kerr Scholarships
Douglas W. Buzback Memorial Scholarship
George Agron Research Scholarship for

Graduate Study
 Joel Rottman Fellowship
 SGPA Research Scholarship
 Warren Ludvigsen Memorial Scholarship
 Julia Morgan/Phoebe Hearst Architecture
Scholarship
 Professional Architects Scholarship
 Wong-Brocchini Scholarships
 Frederick Peter Young Scholarships

UNDERGRADUATE PROGRAM
Philosophy Statement

The objective of this five-year Bachelor of
Architecture professional program is to develop
the design and technical skills necessary to
pursue a career in the field of architecture.
Architecture is concerned with man-made
environments and the people who use them. As
a result the architect is required to develop an
understanding of the sensitivity to human needs.
The Bachelor of Architecture degree is
accredited by the National Architectural
Accreditation Board and is the entry-level degree
leading to professional registration as an
architect.

Program Description

The curriculum in architecture includes, in
addition to university-wide general education
requirements, two years of courses in the
following four basic areas: structures, involving
sequences in calculus, physics, and strength of
materials; architectural practice, involving a
sequence in materials of construction and
practice; graphic visualization and presentation;
and design fundamentals. This is followed by the
three years of sequences in upper division
design studio, upper division architectural
practice, structures, architectural history, and
building support systems, together with a group
of general and technical elective courses.

GRADUATE PROGRAM
Philosophy Statement

The Master of Science in Architecture program
allows students to individualize their study plans
with limited special study areas. These areas
include:
 1. Computer Aided Design Applications
 2. Design, Energy, and Architectural Science
 3. Building Economics and Development
 Each area is intended to program the student
with the opportunity to undertake
post-professional studies.

Program Description

Candidates must hold a NAAB-Accredited
Bachelor of Architecture or Master of
Architecture degree or have significant
professional experience as a registered architect.
The curriculum involves a one-year sequence of
coursework (45 quarter units) designed to meet
the needs of the individual within the limits of the
areas of emphasis. The specific program of
study is determined by the candidate and his or
her graduate advisor. The program is appropriate
for recent graduates or mid-level practicing
professionals to pursue advanced studies with a
strong architectural practice orientation. The
curriculum includes 18 units of required theory,
methods, and emphasis area courses, supported
by 27 units of professional electives, support
electives and a comprehensive exam or thesis
project.

FACULTY
Administration

G Day Ding, FNZIA, FRAIA, FIE, AUST, Dean
W Mike Martin, AIA, RA, Department Head, Arch
James R Bagnall, Assoc. Dept. Head, Arch.
Patrick D Hill, Assoc. Dept. Head, Arch.
Kenneth M Kohlen, Assistant Dept Head, Arch

Professors

Joseph C Amanzio, AIA, RA, B Arch, M Arch, M
 Urban Design
Sharad P Atre, RA, B Arch, M Arch
James R Bagnall, BA Psych, M Arch
Ronald E Batterson, RA, BS Arch, M Arch, M
 Urban Design
David A Brodie, RA, B Arch, M Arch
William H Brown, AIA, RA, B Arch, M Arch
Arthur Chapman, BS Math, MS Math, B Arch
Allan R Cooper, AIA, RA, BA Arch, B Arch, M Arch
Mary P Cooper, RA, B Ed, MS Ed, M Arch, MLA
Mustafa Denel, BS CE, MFA Arch, PhD Arch
Merrill C Gaines, RA, B Bus Admin, M Arch
Donald P Grant, RA, BA Arch, M Arch, PhD Arch
Terry C Hargrave, RA, B Arch Eng, M Arch
John E Harrigan, BA Psych, MA Gen Psych, PhD
 Exper Psych
George J Hasslein, FAIA, RA, B Arch
Patrick P Hill, AIA, RA, MS Arch Eng
George K Ikenoyama, AIA, BS Arch, M Arch
Brian B Kesner, RA, BS Arch, M Arch
Donald J Koberg, RA, B Arch, M Arch
Kenneth M Kohlen, RA, B Arch, M Arch

Sandra P Lakeman, RA, BS Arch, M Arch
John H Lange, RA, BS Arch, M Arch, PhD Arch
Larry H Loh, AIA, RA, B Arch, M Arch
David Lord, RA, BS Arch, MS Arch, M Arch
W Mike Martin, AIA, RA, B Arch, M Arch, PhD Arch
Willard L McGonagill, RA, BS Arch Eng, BA Arch
Sandra Miller, AIA, RA, B Art Hist, M Arch
Sixto E Moreira, RA, BS Arch Eng, M Arch Des
Paul R Neel, FAIA, RA, BS Arch, B Arch, M Arch
Raymond E Nordquist, RA, BS Arch, M Arch
Jens G Pohl, B Arch, M Bldg Sci, PhD Arch Sci
Charles W Quinlan, AIA, RA, B Arch, M
 Arch-Town & Regional Planning
Marcel E Sedletzky, RA, BS Arch, M Arch
Vern Swansen, B Arch, M Arch
Don E Swearingen, RA, B Arch, M Arch
Paul M Wolff, AIA, RA, B Arch, M Arch
Donald S Woolard, RA, B Arch, MFA Arch

Associate Professors

Serim Denel, RA, B Arch, M Arch
Donna Duerk, B Arch, BA Arch, M Arch
Howard Weisenthal, B Arch, M Arch
Christopher Yip, BA, M Arch, PhD

Assistant Professor

Daniel L Panetta, AIA, BSLA, M Arch

Part-Time Faculty

Charles E Crotser, AIA, RA, B Arch
Randy C Dettmer, AIA, RA, B Arch
Rufus L Graves, BS
Henry Hammer, BS Arch, B Arch, M Arch
Curtis D Illingworth, BA Hist, BS Arch
Robert E Kitamura, AIA, RA, B Arch
Ralph J Lee, RA, B Arch, M Philosophy
Jim Maul, RA, B Arch
Frank M Seiple, RA, BS Arch
George Stewart, AIA, RA, B Arch
John Stuart, B Arch
Anne Vytlacil, AIA, M Arch
Wesley Ward, B Arch
Gregory J Wilhelm, AIA, RA, BS Arch, B Arch
Barry L Williams, AIA, RA, B Arch
Richard A Young, AIA, RA, B Arch

California State Polytechnic University, Pomona

Department of Architecture
College of Environmental Design
California State Polytechnic Univ.
3801 W. Temple Avenue
Pomona, California 91768
(714) 869-2680 (dept)
(714) 869-2666 (college)

Admissions Office
Bldg. 1, Room 105
California State Polytechnic Univ.
3801 W. Temple Avenue
Pomona, California 91768
(714) 869-2000

Application Deadline(s): Undgrd: Nov. 1 - Nov. 30 for admission for following Fall Qtr. Grad: Nov. 1 - March 1 (Fall Qtr.)
Tuition & Fees: Undgrd: CA Res: $250 per qtr. Grad: CA Res: $250 per qtr.; Non-res: $84 per unit
Endowment: State

DEGREE PROGRAMS

Degree	Minimum Years for Degree	Accred.	Requirements for Admission	Full-Time Stdnts.	Part-Time Stdnts.	% of Applics. Accptd.	Stdnts. in 1st Year of Program	# of Degrees Conferred
B Arch	5	NAAB	Calif. Resident, 3.0 min GPA, satisfactory SAT scores	452	64	12.5%	150	61
M Arch I	3	NAAB	BA in non-arch field, plus*					
M Arch I	2	NAAB	BA with major in arch or related field, plus*					
M Arch II	1		B Arch degree, plus*	33	12	20%	50	17
			*2.8 min GPA, portfolio, transcripts, statement of purpose, 3 letters of recommendation					
MLA	2 or 3		BA/BS, 3.0 GPA					
BSLA	4	LAAB	BA/BS, 2.0 GPA					
MURP	2		BA/BS, 3.0 GPA					
BSURP	4		BA/BS, 2.0 GPA					

SCHOOL DEMOGRAPHICS (all degree programs)

Full-Time Faculty	Part-Time Faculty	Full-Time Students	Part-Time Students	Foreign Students	Out-of-State U.S. Stdnts.	Women Students	Minority Students
22	10	500	76	2%	.5%	28%	41%

LIBRARY (Tel. No. 714-869-2665)

Type	No. of Volumes	No. of Slides
Univ	5,455	40,000

STUDENT OPPORTUNITIES AND RESOURCES

The Department of Architecture is one of four departments within the School of Environmental Design. About half of the School's 1100 students are in the Department of Architecture. The remaining students are divided between the departments of Environmental Studies, Landscape Architecture and Urban & Regional Planning. In addition to academic units, the School is organized with support units that include the Institute for International Studies, the Institute for Environmental Design Research, the Computer Aided Instruction Laboratory and the Admissions, Records and Advising Center.

The School of Environmental Design maintains its own Resource Center, archive, slide library and computer-aided instruction laboratory, (CAI Lab). The School also has an Instructional Services Center with a model shop, photo laboratory, audio visual equipment and general printing and copying services.

The School of Environmental Design is one of six schools within California State Polytechnic University, Pomona. The campus is located on approximately 1300 acres of the former Kellogg Ranch, the one-time winter residence of the Kellogg family of Battle Creek, Michigan.

While its campus has a rural flavor, Cal Poly's setting is a rich mix of diverse environments. The campus is located adjacent to a major freeway intersection connecting it to downtown Los Angeles 25 miles west, and the rapidly urbanizing areas of San Bernardino and Riverside Counties, the nation's fastest growing region, immediately to the east of campus.

The region is rich in architectural heritage as well, with significant works by Charles and Henry Greene, Irving Gill, Frank Lloyd Wright, Rudolf Schindler, Richard Neutra, Craig Ellwood, Charles Eames, Caesar Pelli, Charles Moore, Frank Gehry, Arata Isozaki and a host of contemporary designers spread throughout the greater Los Angeles area, providing ample opportunity for first-hand study. As an example of such resources the school maintains the Richard Neutra Family Home as a part of a family donation to the University. This facility is frequently used for seminars, tours and school events.

SPECIAL ACTIVITIES AND PROGRAMS

THE TOY PROJECT - A toy design project for about 40 mentally handicapped children at Lanterman State Hospital. The project is accomplished by first-year design students, scheduled during the Fall Quarter. The program is intended to heighten social awareness and involvement among design students.

FRIENDS OF POMONA - This program continues as a yearly event, as a public relations and articulation program with the community colleges. The one-day conference of instructors, from fifteen community colleges, is important to the Department's relationship with these schools.

SUMMER INTENSIVE ORIENTATION PROGRAM - High school minority students are invited to campus for a week-long orientation program in Environmental Design. The program, which began as an architecture minority project, has evolved into a School program with emphasis upon encouragement for university-level study. The program includes tours, seminars and studio work.

ARCHITECTURAL LICENSING WORKSHOP - This Workshop is offered each Spring for the Architectural Registration exam candidates.

ARCHITECTS WITHOUT DEGREES - This program has been developed with the office of Continuing Education. Support has been received from the State Board of Architectural Examiners, the C.C.A.I.A. and the C.C.A.E. As presently formulated, the program is available to those members of the profession who are short of credits for their professional degree. Course work is offered during evening sessions and weekends.

INSTITUTE FOR INTERNATIONAL STUDIES - The College of Environmental Design conducts a summer program which tours France and

Italy and terminates in formal coursework in Athens. In addition, special research projects are under way in Northern Italy.

FACILITIES

The School of Environmental Design maintains its own Resource Center with 6,000 books, technical reports and current periodicals related to the fields of environmental design. This collection is held in addition to the main library collection. Within the Resource Center, a slide library is maintained with a collection of 65,000 slides covering the history of architecture, urban design and planning, and landscape architecture from ancient times to the present. The Resource Center also includes a school archive which contains numerous donated items including material from the offices of Richard Neutra and Craig Ellwood and a contract documents and materials samples room. The computer-aided instruction laboratory (CAI lab) contains a mixture of Apple, IBM and Hewlett-Packard equipment with introductory and sophisticated CAD software, as well as a variety of other computer application software. A fully-equipped model shop and photography lab is available for student use. The Instructional Services Center offers reproduction services and audio-visual equipment check-out.

SCHOLARSHIPS/AID

There are a number of scholarships that students may apply for:

National AIA Scholarships

Producers' Council Scholarship

Pomona Chapter Women in Construction Scholarship

Pasadena/Foothill Chapter, AIA, Scholarships

Cashion, Horie, Cocke, Gonzalez, Inc. Scholarship

Women's Architectural League Los Angeles Chapter Scholarships

Women's Architectural League Orange County Chapter Scholarship

Stephen Hunt Memorial Scholarship

ALS Seminars Scholarship

These scholarships are offered once a year and are usually an award of $500.00.

UNDERGRADUATE PROGRAM
Philosophy Statement

The Bachelor of Architecture degree is offered in a five-year curriculum which is centered around the design laboratory. Students begin with exercises in drawing, graphics, and visual communication and progress toward comprehensive architectural projects that employ creative and analytic skills. The program within the Department of Architecture is directed toward the realities of architectural practice and decision-making processes as they relate to the profession of architecture. Designs are submitted in the form of drawings and models for review by instructors and invited guests. It is the intention of the Department to prepare individuals who will be able to conduct a thoughtful, socially responsible professional practice.

Program Description

Curriculum:

First Year:

Intro to Design; Intro to Env. Design; Intro to Architecture; Cities, Citizens & URP; Living with the Land; Freshman Composition; Am Civ or Am Govt; Am Civ or US Hist; Life Science (w/lab); Trigonometry; General Psych.

Second Year:

Arch Design; Arch History; Building Construction; College Physics; College Physics Lab; Intro to Philos; Advocacy & Argument; Prin of Economics.

Third Year:

Arch Design; Structures; Env. Controls; Building Construction; Prin Socio or Intro Cult Anthro; The Visual Arts.

Fourth Year:

Arch Design; Seismic Design in Arch; Arch Practice; Arch and Computers; Intro to Modern Fiction; Hist of Latin America or U.S. Since 1945; Information Admin; Unrestricted Electives.

Fifth Year:

Arch Design; American Architecture; Writing for Professions; Professional Electives*

(*must select minimum of 16 units).

GRADUATE PROGRAM
Philosophy Statement

The Master's Program in Architecture welcomes graduate students from a variety of academic backgrounds, including non-design disciplines. Like most architectural programs we emphasize design, but contrary to the general direction of other architectural curricula, our graduate program emphasizes issues of social responsibility, including the development of the ability to design buildings that sustain and enhance people's lives and their environment. All students prepare a thesis focused on issues of social responsibility or architectural theory. Within the School of Environmental Design, research activities are coordinated through the Institute for Environmental Design, which assists students and faculty in obtaining and managing research on community service projects. These projects are frequently funded by community groups and agencies which retain an active interest and participation in the results.

Program Description

The basic program is a three-and-one-quarter-year course of study or 10 quarters of full-time academic work. Students entering the program are placed at one of three basic levels depending upon their previous academic work.

LEVEL ONE: MASTER OF ARCHITECTURE–SECOND PROFESSIONAL DEGREE. Applicants holding a Bachelor of Architecture degree will normally enter the final year of the program. This requires four quarters of full-time work (64 units) culminating in a one-quarter thesis project.

LEVEL TWO: MASTER OF ARCHITECTURE–FIRST PROFESSIONAL DEGREE. Applicants holding a four-year Bachelor of Arts in Architecture, or an equivalent non-professional degree, will normally enter the second year of the program. This requires two-and-one-quarter years of full-time study (112 units) in which the final four quarters are taken with Level One students. A comprehensive design examination, given as part of the spring quarter design course, must be passed before students can advance to Level One.

LEVEL THREE: MASTER OF ARCHITECTURE–FIRST PROFESSIONAL DEGREE. Applicants holding a Bachelor's degree in a non-architectural field will normally enter the first year of the program. This requires three-and-one-quarter years of full-time study (160 units) including the comprehensive design examination at the end of the spring quarter of the second year and the final-quarter thesis project. Applicants with minimal preparation may also be asked to take additional pre-requisite courses including algebra, trigonometry, physics and graphics.

FACULTY
Administration

Marvin Malecha, AIA, Dean, College of Env Design
Patricia Belton Oliver, AIA, Associate Dean, College of Env Design
Barry L Wasserman, AIA, Chair, Department of Architecture
Kathy I Morgan, Librarian, Resource Center
Diane R Moe, Archives/Public Relations Coordinator

Professors

Spyros Amourgis, AIA, Dipl in Arch
Brooks Cavin III, AIA, M Arch
Richard Chylinski, AIA, M Arch
Paul N Helmle, AIA, B Arch
Frederick Koeper, PhD
Edward E Pickard, B Arch, M Env Design
Dariouche Showghi, Doctorate
Patrick M Sullivan, AIA, M Arch
Barry L Wasserman, AIA, M Arch
Bernard Zimmerman, AIA, B Arch

Associate Professors

William Adams, AIA, BA Arch
Arthur E Hacker, AIA, M Arch
Patricia Belton Oliver, AIA, M Arch

Assistant Professors

Hsin-Ming Fung, AIA, M Arch
Sigrid Pollin, M Arch

Lecturers

Michael W Folonis, B Arch
Maurice Herman, M Arch
Neil M T Jackson, PhD

Part-Time Faculty

Peggy J Bosley, M Arch
Charles M Calvo, BA Arch
Victoria Casasco, M Arch
Luis A Colasuonno, M Arch
Richard Corsini, M Arch
Catherine Cunningham, B Arch
Dorothy Danziger, BA, Fine Arts
Kip A Dickson, M Arch
Mark C Dillon, M Arch
Catherine A Garland, BS Arch
Christopher Genik, M Arch
Harold S Guida, M Arch
Denise L Lawrence, PhD
Michael J O'Sullivan, AIA, B Arch
Werner K Ruegger, M Arch
William M Taylor, M Arch

Adjunct Faculty

Ricardo Delle Sante
Craig Ellwood
Channing Gilson
Carol Newsom

University of California, Berkeley

College of Environmental Design
230 Wurster Hall
University of California, Berkeley
Berkeley, California 94720
(415) 642-0832

Admissions Office
Undergraduate Program:
(415) 642-0832
Graduate Program:
(415) 642-5577

Application Deadline(s): Grad: Jan 10 for
following Fall
Undgrd: November 30
for following Fall
July 31 for following
Spring
Tuition & Fees: Undgrd and Grad:
CA Res: approx. $738/sem
Non-res: approx. $2883/sem
Endowment: State

DEGREE PROGRAMS

Degree	Minimum Years for Degree	Accred.	Requirements for Admission	Full-Time Stdnts.	Part-Time Stdnts.	% of Applics. Accptd.	Stdnts. in 1st Year of Program	# of Degrees Conferred
BA	4		SAT, transcript, 4 yrs. math, 1 yr. biology or other natural science, 1 yr. physics	669	0	30%	150	200
M Arch	1-3	NAAB	GRE, TOEFL (foreign applicants from non-English speaking countries), transcript(s), min. 3 letters of application, exhibit of creative work	189	0	11%	72	118
PhD	3		GRE, TOEFL (as above), transcript(s), min. 4 letters of application, exhibit of research and professional work	38	0	20%	10	3

SCHOOL DEMOGRAPHICS (all degree programs)

Full-Time Faculty	Part-Time Faculty	Full-Time Students	Part-Time Students	Foreign Students	Out-of-State U.S. Stdnts.	Women Students	Minority Students
44	70	892	0		NA	35%	11%

LIBRARY (Tel. No. 415-642-4818)

Type	No. of Volumes	No. of Slides
Arch L Arch Planning	160,000	170,000

STUDENT OPPORTUNITIES AND RESOURCES

The University of California, Berkeley, has a very diverse student body of 30,000, of whom two-thirds are undergraduates. As the largest unit in the College of Environmental Design, the Department of Architecture provides many resources in Wurster Hall (see **Facilities**, below).

Architecture maintains close ties with the Departments of City and Regional Planning, Landscape Architecture, Structural Engineering, and Computer Science. Concurrent graduate degree programs are offered with several of these departments, and some faculty are shared among them. The faculty includes specialists in computer science, building science, building preservation, structural engineering, architectural history, sociology, planning, urban design, and

graphic design, as well as licensed architects. Research laboratories within the Department and elsewhere in the University and at Lawrence Berkeley National Laboratory provide students with opportunities for education and research. The Berkeley campus, located across the Bay from San Francisco, offers access to other institutions of higher learning, including Stanford University and the Davis, San Francisco, and Santa Cruz campuses of the University of California.

SPECIAL ACTIVITIES AND PROGRAMS

Lawrence Berkeley National Laboratory and Berkeley campus research programs in energy and the environment, indoor pollution, daylighting, and other topics.

Community-based planning and design activities.

Professional internship program drawing on some 80 architecture firms in the San Francisco Bay area.

University-wide computer network, including MicroVax and Sun workstations, MacIntosh and IBM personal computers located in the College, and access to all larger computers within the nine-Campus University system. CADD and a variety of other software programs are available.

Access to other Department, College, and University facilities, including the Building Science Lab, Environmental Simulation Lab, Computer Centers, Engineering Testing Labs, etc.

FACILITIES

Department of Architecture facilities include a computer center (MicroVax, Sun, MacIntosh, IBM hardware, CADD), shop, architectural detailing resources collection, building sciences laboratory (including artificial sky and thermal comfort laboratory), access to College's environmental simulation laboratory, design studios, library of 160,000 books, documents collection (rare drawings and papers), and visual-aids collection of 170,000 slides and 30,000 photographs. There are ample classrooms, seminar rooms, exhibit spaces, and an auditorium. A cafe and design store on the ground floor provide informal meeting places, food, and sustenance.

SCHOLARSHIPS/AID

Applicants are encouraged to contact the Financial Aid Office of the University for information on aid available (Financial Aid Office, 201 Sproul Hall, University of California, Berkeley, Berkeley, CA 94720). These include fellowship competitions, a special Graduate Minority Fellowship, and limited nonresidential tuition waivers.

UNDERGRADUATE PROGRAM
Philosophy Statement

Undergraduate study in the College of Environmental Design combines liberal and professional education in the environment of a great university. The four-year architecture major prepares students for either entry-level employment or admission with advanced standing to graduate study in this field. In addition, it provides general education to open a wide variety of study and career opportunities in business, government, and the other professions.

Program Description

The undergraduate Arts Bachelor (AB) degree with a major in architecture is normally awarded after four years of study. A quarter to a third of total coursework is concentrated in the major subject during the junior and senior years. Coursework in the major is distributed across several areas: design, community design, social aspects, theories and methods, energy management, structures, construction, architectural preservation, architectural history, and visual studies. About a third of the coursework is in breadth areas: English, math, the sciences, social science, the arts and humanities. About a sixth is in the College of Environmental Design core program, including drawing and introductory design. Remaining courses are electives.

GRADUATE PROGRAM
Philosophy Statement

The primary aim of the graduate program is professional education in architecture — the attainment of the M Arch degree, which is the basic professional degree accredited nationally for licensing or registration to practice architecture. The PhD program prepares students for research and teaching in architecture and environmental design.

Program Description

The size of the department and its affiliation with one of the major graduate universities of the world permit very considerable diversity and specialization among both students and teachers. Graduate students work independently with a faculty adviser to devise an individual study plan; course offerings in the department are structured around eight areas of study: Architectural Design, Social and Cultural Factors in Design, Practice of Design, Design Methods and Theories, Building Environments, Structures and Construction, History of Architecture, and Visual Studies. In addition to the M Arch and PhD degrees, the department offers concurrent degree programs with the Departments of City and Regional Planning and Structural Engineering.

FACULTY
Administration

Roger Montgomery, Acting Dean
Gary Brown, Acting Chair, Department of Architecture
Claude Stoller, FAIA, Vice-Chair
Raymond Lifchez, Chair, Department of Instruction in Environmental Design
Elizabeth Byrne, Head Architecture Librarian

Professors

Christopher Alexander, PhD
Edward Arens, PhD
Richard Bender, M Arch
Clare Cooper-Marcus, MA, MCP
Sam Davis, FAIA, MED
Margaret Dhaemers, MFA, MA
Russell Ellis, Jr, PhD
Norma Evenson, PhD
Sanford Hirshen, FAIA, B Arch
Spiro Kostof, PhD
Henry Lagorio, MA
Lars Lerup, M Arch
Raymond Lifchez, MS, MA, MCP
Richard Meier, PhD
Roger Montgomery, M Arch
Donald Olsen, FAIA, M Arch
Richard F. Peters, FAIA, M Arch
Jean-Pierre Protzen, Dipl Arch
Horst Rittel
Daniel Solomon, FAIA, M Arch
Claude Stoller, FAIA, M Arch
Marc Treib, M Arch, MA
Sim Van der Ryn, B Arch

Associate Professors

Charles Benton, M Arch
Jean-Paul Bourdier, DPLG, M Arch
Gary Brown, M Arch
Mary Comerio, M Arch, MSW
Galen Cranz, PhD
Anthony Dubovsky, MA
Richard Fernau, M Arch
Sara Ishikawa, B Arch
Mark Mack, M Arch
Stanley Saitowitz, M Arch
Kenneth Simmons, B Arch
Stephen Tobriner, PhD
Dell Upton, PhD

Assistant Professors

Paul Groth, PhD
Randolph Langenbach, M Arch
Gail Schiller, PhD
Mark Smith, M Arch
Jill Stoner, M Arch

University of California, Los Angeles

Graduate School of Architecture
and Urban Planning
University of California, Los Angeles
405 Hilgard Avenue
Los Angeles, California 90024
(213) 825-7857

Admissions Office
(213) 825-0525

Application Deadline(s): January 15 - PhD
February 1 - MA, M
Arch I, M Arch II
Tuition & Fees: Grad: Ca res: $449 per
quarter;
Non-res: $1811 per quarter
Endowment: State

DEGREE PROGRAMS

Degree	Minimum Years for Degree	Accred.	Requirements for Admission	Full-Time Stdnts.	Part-Time Stdnts.	% of Applics. Accptd.	Stdnts. in 1st Year of Program	# of Degrees Conferred
M Arch I	3	NAAB	BA/BS, portfolio & univ. reqts	122	0	30%	45	23
M Arch II	1		B Arch, portfolio & univ. reqts	59	0	46%	40	35
MA	2		BA/BS, portfolio & univ. reqts	19	0	44%	12	10
PhD	3		B Arch or M Arch univ. reqts	13	0	2%	6	1
MA Urban Planning	2	PAB of AICP & ASCP	BA or Eq., Univ Require.	126	0	50%	65	50
PhD in Urban Planning	4		MA in Planning or related field	30	0	35%	2	2

SCHOOL DEMOGRAPHICS (all degree programs)

Full-Time Faculty	Part-Time Faculty	Full-Time Students	Part-Time Students	Foreign Students	Out-of-State U.S. Stdnts.	Women Students	Minority Students
19	13	213 (Arch)	0	34%	66%	34%	17%

LIBRARY (Tel. No. 213-825-2747)

Type	No. of Volumes	No. of Slides
Arch & Urban Plng	23,200	65,000 75,000 Arch slides in Fine Arts Library

STUDENT OPPORTUNITIES AND RESOURCES

GSAUP at UCLA encompasses a diversity of graduate degree programs oriented toward different aspects of practice, research, and scholarship in the fields of architecture, urban design, and urban planning.

M Arch I is a first professional degree program that assumes no previous architecture background and from which graduates normally go on to professional registration and the practice of architecture.

M Arch II is a second professional degree program for students who already hold professional qualifications in architecture and wish to explore advanced and specialized work.

The MA program is oriented toward research and scholarship, rather than practice, in architecture and urban design.

The PhD in architecture is closely related to GSAUP's ongoing research efforts and offers students the opportunity to engage in original research work in the fields of design theory and methods; technology; history, analysis, and criticism; and policy, programming, and evaluation.

Both MA and PhD programs are offered in urban planning.

The Architecture/Urban Design faculty represents a wide range of backgrounds, interests, philosophical viewpoints, and research and professional activities. An appropriate balance is sought between senior and junior faculty, local practitioners who teach on a part-time basis, and distinguished visiting faculty from elsewhere in the US and abroad. The Visiting Faculty Program is intended not only to expose students to leaders in the field and to a wide diversity of approaches but also to maintain the program's relationship to the architectural profession in the area.

UCLA, one of the nine campuses of the University of California system, has a student body of about 31,000 (20,000 undergraduates and 11,000 graduates) and is able to provide a vast array of educational and cultural resources. The Architecture/Urban Planning Library is one of 16 special libraries on campus, which, together with the College Library and the University Research Library, give UCLA a total collection of over 5.5 million volumes. Extensive computer graphics facilities are located in the design studio and are available for students' use at any time. The school has good workshop and photographic facilities and an excellent slide library.

Urban Innovations Group, the independent, professionally managed practice arm of GSAUP, gives students the opportunity to work on real architectural, urban design, planning, and applied research projects under the direction of faculty members.

GSAUP is a small and flexible graduate school that regards special activities of various kinds as an essential complement to ongoing curricular, research, and practice activities. The themes and formats of these activities vary according to student and faculty interests and opportunities that present themselves.

SPECIAL ACTIVITIES AND PROGRAMS

Public lecture series

Exhibits

Intensive short courses, seminars and workshops on various topics

Conferences and symposia

Field trips

Exchanges with other University of California campuses

Overseas study (recently in Italy and Japan)

Participation in competitions

Publication activities

FACILITIES

The Grad School of Arch and Urban Planning occupies its own 36,000 square-foot building, Perloff Hall. The top floor of the building is the architecture studio in which most architecture students have their own drawing table and storage area. PhD students have their own designated study area in the building. The GSAUP shop is equipped with a large variety of tools, enabling students to build both model and full-scale projects in wood, metal, plastic and cardboard. The school maintains a complete photographic facility, consisting of a fully equipped dark room, film lab, map-o-graph area and a lighting studio. The computing system consists of an IBM 4361 group 5 computer equipped with 12 megabytes of memory, five gigabytes of on-line disc storage and an electrostatic plotter. A Computervision CV 5030 CAD System with 1.2 gigabytes of on-line disc storage and five high-resolution CAD workstations and a McDonnell Douglas GDS CAD system with 4 workstations are networked to the IBM computer. There is a completely integrated local area network which links over 20 IBM PC/XT/AT workstations equipped with color graphic input devices for CAD applications - all connected to the central campus computing facility via a high-speed fiber optic communication link.

SCHOLARSHIPS/AID

Several avenues of financial support are available to students. (1) The university provides financial assistance in the form of grants, loans, and work-study to students who can demonstrate sufficient monetary need, while the Graduate Division sponsors competitive grants based upon scholastic performance. (2) The Architecture/Urban Design Program offers a growing number of scholarships that are allocated on the basis of both financial need and academic merit. (3) Research assistantships are available under funded research projects in GSAUP. (4) Students have opportunities to work part-time at Urban Innovations Group.

More than half of our students receive some form of financial support.

GRADUATE PROGRAM
Philosophy Statement

The Architecture/Urban Design Program at UCLA was founded (in 1966) in an optimistic era, on a note of faith in the future of architecture and its chance to better serve humankind if theoretical advances in academic disciplines (especially in the social sciences) and the technical capabilities of the computer could be incorporated into an architectural education. Although the curriculum has been revised and clarified over the years (reflecting an increased confidence in the studio as a locus for effective learning), there has been no basic change in the school's philosophy. The school is committed to maintaining several complementary perspectives: those of the social sciences as applied to policy and design issues; the physical sciences as applied to building technology; formalization and computation as a foundation for design theory and methods; and the humanistic perspective of historical, analytical, and critical studies; and the interaction between these approaches is considered to be of the greatest importance. Beyond a fundamental concern with providing a thorough education in the basic professional sensitivities and skills, the school has chosen to develop intensive concentrations in important specialist areas in the environmental field, including history and criticism, human-environment relations, architectural theory and computer-aided design, energy-conserving design, housing, systems building, and urban design.

The faculty, which is characterized by a wide variety of backgrounds, viewpoints, and skills, has an active commitment to practice, research, and scholarship. In this small graduate school, a close network of direct relationships is built up between faculty and students, and the students' architectural education thus takes place in the context of a lively and diverse center of academic and professional activity.

Program Description

The three-year Master of Architecture (M Arch I) program is an accredited professional degree program for those holding a non-architecture bachelor's degree or a four-year degree in architecture. A series of design projects and courses of specialized instruction introduces a cross-section of approaches in which architecture may be conceptualized and practiced.

The one-year Master of Architecture (M Arch II) program is an advanced professional degree program in which the architectural graduate or experienced professional can study in specific areas to develop specialized conceptual and methodological skills and explore particular professional issues. This program is based on the concept of a combination of advanced theoretical studies and professional application.

The two-year Master of Arts (MA) program offers an academic degree and prepares students to do specialized research or teaching in the fields related to the architectural profession. Applicants are required to hold a bachelor's degree and should possess the experience and knowledge to allow them to do advanced research in whatever aspect of architecture they plan to explore within the context of the master's program.

FACULTY
Administration

Richard S Weinstein, Dean
Lionel J March, Head, Architecture/Urban Design Program
Anne Hartmere, Librarian

Professors

Marvin Adelson, PhD
Samuel Aroni, PhD
Charles Eastman, M Arch
Baruch Givoni, PhD
Lionel March, ScD
Murray Milne, RA, MS, M Arch
Barton Myers, RA, M Arch
Richard Schoen, FAIA, M Arch
George Stiny, PhD
Thomas Vreeland, FAIA, M Arch
Richard Weinstein, MA

Associate Professors

Frank Israel, RA, M Arch
Eugene Kupper, RA, M Arch
Jurg Lang, RA, Dipl Arch
Robin Liggett, PhD
George Rand, PhD

Assistant Professors

Diane Favro, PhD
Terry Knight, PhD
Patricia Patkau, M Arch
Ben Refuerzo, RA, D Arch Candidate

Part-Time Faculty

Berge Aran, PhD
Christine Cinciripini, M Arch
Charles Griggs, RA, B Arch
Cyril Harris, PhD
Kuppaswamy Iyengar, RA, M Arch
Charles Jencks, PhD
Rex Lotery, FAIA, B Arch
Anthony Lumsden, RA, B Arch
Charles Moore, FAIA, PhD
Barton Phelps, RA, AIA, M Arch
Robert Yudell, RA, M Arch

Adjunct Faculty

Thomas Hines, PhD

Carleton University

School of Architecture
Carleton University
Ottawa, Ontario, Canada K1S 5B6
(613) 564-6380

Admissions Committee
(613) 564-6380

Application Deadline(s): March 15
Tuition & Fees: Undgrd: Canadian students:
$1,515/yr
Visa students: $7,471/yr
Endowment: Provincial

DEGREE PROGRAMS

Degree	Minimum Years for Degree	Accred.	Requirements for Admission	Full-Time Stdnts.	Part-Time Stdnts.	% of Applics. Accptd.	Stdnts. in 1st Year of Program	# of Degrees Conferred
B Arch	5	CAA	University requirements	279	38	8%	75	54

SCHOOL DEMOGRAPHICS (all degree programs)

Full-Time Faculty	Part-Time Faculty	Full-Time Students	Part-Time Students	Foreign Students	Out-of-State U.S. Stdnts.	Women Students	Minority Students
18	9	279	38	10%	N/A	30%	N/A

LIBRARY (Tel. No. 613-564-6775)

Type	No. of Volumes	No. of Slides
University	10,000 (Arch)	100,000 (Arch)

STUDENT OPPORTUNITIES AND RESOURCES

The School of Architecture was started in 1968 in response to an increasing need in Ontario for the provision of architectural education. The school is an academically independent unit within the Faculty of Engineering. It has close and mutually beneficial links not only with Engineering but also with the School of Industrial Design, also a unit within the Faculty of Engineering. The School of Architecture enrolls about 320 undergraduate students and has 18 full-time faculty. It also has a number of part-time faculty, drawn from the profession, from other universities, and from federal government agencies and departments in the national capital region.

The school has its own building, which was completed in 1972. It has proved exceptionally successful as an environment for studying architecture.

SPECIAL ACTIVITIES AND PROGRAMS

Wide range of lectures, music, drama, athletics, and recreational events available to all students in the university.

Forum series of public lectures every two weeks.

Architecture Clinics for the public in conjunction with local architects.

Provision for students to do one term's study abroad.

Photographic studio, darkrooms, and equipment loan pool.

Workshops shared with students of Industrial Design.

Reproduction facilities.

Student materials shop.

Technical Data Room with AV facilities.

Computer graphics facilities.

Visiting Critics Studio.

SCHOLARSHIPS/AID

Carleton University awards $602,000 annually in entrance and in-course scholarships. There is bursary money in the amount of $150,000 that can be awarded on a need basis. There are emergency loan funds of $300,000 and long-term loan funds of $350,000. Architecture students are eligible for these funds though none are earmarked specifically for them. In addition, the School of Architecture has $5500 annually for in-course scholarships for architecture students.

UNDERGRADUATE PROGRAM
Philosophy Statement

The five-year undergraduate program in architecture leads to a professional degree which is recognized by the Ontario Association of Architects and accredited by the Commonwealth Association of Architects. Students may enter the program directly from high school, provided that they have obtained the Ontario Secondary School Honour Graduation Diploma (or equivalent) with a minimum 65 percent average (including functions, calculus, and physics). They may also enter the program as "mature" students, having either worked, travelled, or studied in other disciplines after high school; or, they may transfer into the program from other schools of architecture. Places in the program are limited and the number of applicants each year is large, so a good academic record and demonstrated interest in architecture are essential to be accepted. Although a majority of the students come from the province of Ontario, many come from elsewhere in Canada and a small number come from other countries. It is a policy of the school to accept students of diverse backgrounds, ages, and cultures.

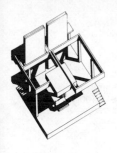
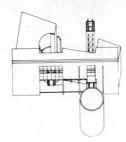
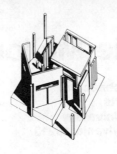

Program Description

The program has two major components: a core program, which is mandatory for all students, and an elective program, in which students may select courses or groups of courses which allow them to develop their own interests within the broad field of architecture. The first two years are made up almost exclusively of mandatory courses, and by the end of the second year students are expected to have mastered basic skills and knowledge. During the third and fourth years, the mandatory component of the program includes only design, theory and a half course in structures, and the elective program comes into full operation. During the fourth year, a Studies Abroad program and Visiting Critics' Studio are available to interested students. In the fifth year, students may choose from a number of program options, including a research and development project initiated by the student.

Ottawa, as the federal capital of Canada, is the base for many agencies and departments related to design, architecture, and the building industry. Thus Carleton's location is a significant advantage for the program, as a great deal of knowledge and expertise is accessible. It is also a significant factor in the development of faculty opportunities in research and professional consulting.

The School enjoys a good relationship with the rest of the university community, and increasingly in the elective program joint courses are being developed with other disciplines that are designed specifically for students in architecture, but that also attract students in other programs who have an interest in particular aspects of architecture and design. The school cooperates with the Department of Art History in offering combined BA and BA (Honours) degrees in Art History and Architecture.

GRADUATE PROGRAM
Philosophy Statement

A full graduate program is not yet offered by the School of Architecture. However, a number of directed reading courses are available as part of graduate programs offered by several other universities in Ontario and Quebec. It is anticipated that a full graduate program will evolve in specialized areas during the next few years. Approval in principle has been given to a Masters of Arts degree in Architectural Restoration and Preservation to be offered by the Institute of Canadian Studies at Carleton in cooperation with the School of Architecture. Enrollment is expected to start in the Fall of 1988.

FACULTY
Administration
Gilbert F Sutton, Director

Professors
R G Brand, MRAIC, B Arch, PhD
John Flanders, RIBA, FRAIC, Dipl Arch
S G Haider, B Sc, MS, B Arch, PhD
H S Loten, MRAIC, B Arch, M Arch, PhD
D Moizer, Dipl Arch
R E Osler, RIBA, MRAIC, Dipl Arch
H Sharon, MRAIC, MAAEI, B Arch

Associate Professors
K S Andonian, M Arch, MA Sc, PhD
Frank C Carter, B Arch, M Arch
Charles Gordon, BA, PhD
N Griffiths, Dipl Arch
E Kayari, MRAIC, B Arch, M Arch
G Milne, B Arch, M Arch
P Sharp, RIBA, Dipl Arch
Gilbert F Sutton, MRAIC, B Arch
M West, B Arch
D Westwood, RIBA, Dipl Arch

Assistant Professors
B Bell, M Phil
T Boddy, M Arch
M Bressani, B Arch, M Arch
Tom Dubicanac, B Arch, M Arch
L McNeur, B Arch, M Phil

Part-Time Faculty
R Botros, M Sc, Dr Ing
Y Cazabon, B Arch
J Cook, Dipl Arch, MA
William Dawson, B Eng
J Debanne, B Arch
S Hensel, B Arch
D Hoffman, B Arch
H Honegger, B Arch
B Kuwabara, B Arch
P Lambert, BA, MS
John Leaning, B Arch
S McKenna, B Arch
T Wolstenholme, B Eng

Adjunct Faculty
J Dalibard, FRAIC, B Arch, MSC
G MacDonald, BA, PhD
B Padolsky, OAA, FRAIC, B Arch, MSC
A Rankin, OAA, RAIC, RIBA, Dipl
J Smith, OAA, BA, M Arch
J Strutt, OAA, FRAIC, OAQ, B Arch

Carnegie Mellon University

Department of Architecture
College of Fine Arts
Carnegie Mellon University
Pittsburgh, Pennsylvania 15213
(412) 268-2355

Application Deadline(s): March 1
Tuition & Fees: Undgrd: $11,100/yr
Grad: $11,200/yr
Endowment: Private

DEGREE PROGRAMS

Degree	Minimum Years for Degree	Accred.	Requirements for Admission	Full-Time Stdnts.	Part-Time Stdnts.	% of Applics. Accptd.	Stdnts. in 1st Year of Program	# of Degrees Conferred
B Arch	5	NAAB	SAT/ACT scores	218	14	50%	78	32
MS	1-2		First Professional Degree, GRE	7	5	48%	12	6
M Arch	3	NAAB	BA/BS, portfolio, GRE	32	0	48%	9	14
PhD	3-5		Undgrd degree, GRE	8	5	30%	6	0

SCHOOL DEMOGRAPHICS (all degree programs)

Full-Time Faculty	Part-Time Faculty	Full-Time Students	Part-Time Students	Foreign Students	Out-of-State U.S. Stdnts.	Women Students	Minority Students
20	24	266	24	7%	72.4%	34%	4%

LIBRARY (Tel. No. 412-268-2451)

Type	No. of Volumes	No. of Slides
Arch	29,595	80,600

STUDENT OPPORTUNITIES AND RESOURCES

The Department of Architecture, along with the Departments of Drama, Music, Art and Design, comprise the College of Fine Arts. This intercollegial atmosphere exposes students to a stimulating mixture of events. The University also encourages this intercollegial atmosphere. Students are free to take classes in all Departments; faculty frequently hold joint positions, conduct joint classes, seminars and lectures.

The City of Pittsburgh provides an excellent location for the Department. A wide range of cultural opportunities are available including the Pittsburgh Symphony, the Pittsburgh Ballet, opera, theatre, the Three Rivers Art Festival, the Carnegie Institute and Museum and numerous art galleries. In addition, the city provides a wealth of design opportunities for students and faculty. Frequently, city officials and community groups work with the Department to explore solutions to projects, such as a new City-County building, booths for an art festival, renewal plans for the Garfield Community and many others.

The Department has particular strengths in a number of areas including: design, design theory, computer-aided design, energy conservation, and building performance.

SPECIAL ACTIVITIES AND PROGRAMS

Pre-College Program - offered in the summer, generally for high school students to explore the discipline of architecture.

Study Abroad Programs - summer study with faculty to various locations. Past trips have gone to China, Egypt and Turkey, England, Rome, France and North Africa.

Exchange Programs - CMU has a junior year abroad program established with the Ecole Polytechnique Federale de Lausanne in Switzerland.

Placement Programs - the University and Department run a series of seminars for resume and portfolio assistance. The Department also publishes a brochure listing available students' resumes.

Visiting Critics and Lecturers Series - distinguished guests present lectures and lead informal discussions.

Seminar Series - working program of presentation and informal discussion by faculty, graduate research assistants, and off-campus guests.

Student Awards:

PPG Industries Foundation Traveling Fellowship

Stewart L Brown AIA-Pittsburgh Chapter Scholarship Award

John Knox Shear Memorial Traveling Fellowship

Robert Burdett Assistantship

FACILITIES

Computer Aided Design Lab provides an environment for faculty, staff and graduate students to pursue their research.

Computer Studio is an undergraduate studio using IBM AT's set aside solely for the use of those students.

Woodshop supports a necessary and important part of student education.

Design and Information Processing Lab is set aside for the study of human problem-solving behavior.

Photography Lab is staffed and maintained by students.

SCHOLARSHIPS/AID

Students with demonstrated financial need and a satisfactory academic performance may be considered for support in varying amounts from a variety of resources including scholarship awards, approved loans, work/study aid, and research and teaching assistantships. The College Scholarship Services Financial Aid Form (FAF) CMU Application for Financial Aid is required of all students seeking aid from any source.

UNDERGRADUATE PROGRAM
Philosophy Statement

The heart of the architect's education at Carnegie-Mellon University has been and will continue to be design. Design is the vehicle through which the architect thinks, acts, and learns. The task of design entails many levels of expertise: creating as well as recognizing objects of quality; commanding processes suitable for the making of designs and buildings; and using superior technologies in undertaking these tasks.

The Department of Architecture, through its faculty and students, is committed to design, to excellence in design, and to advancement of knowledge in these areas. The Department is also committed to the principle of contributing to enhance the well-being of society. Architects have to function within a social context in order to create architecture. This context presents many constraints related to aesthetics, to function, to technology, and to economics. These constraints are the materials of the architect.

Program Description

The Bachelor of Architecture program is a five-year course of study in preparation for professional registration and practice. The core of the program is the design sequence where after the first year, groups of approximately 15 students work individually on design assignments ranging from comprehensive to specialized architectural problems. In addition, students are required to take courses in a variety of sequences:

The Technology Sequence is to prepare students to deal with materials, construction, engineering, energy and equipment problems encountered in buildings.

The History Sequence is taught as an integral part of the professional curriculum. These four courses are intended to contribute directly to the practice of architecture.

The Design Science Sequence introduces students to organizational and methodological aspects of architectural design.

University Electives allow students to choose from classes throughout the University.

Departmental Electives focus on philosophical questions, experiment with new techniques for architecture, or explore new subject matter.

Drawing Sequence is a four-course sequence where students learn representational skills.

GRADUATE PROGRAM
Philosophy Statement

The Graduate programs attempt to respond to specific expectations and experiences of students who are already at home in an academic environment, highly motivated, able to pursue studies in a self-directed manner and willing to commit themselves to a program with a higher than normal course-load and intensity.

Program Description

The Master of Architecture first professional degree program is a three-year curriculum of graduate study for students with a previous baccalaureate in another field. Students are required to have completed a course in calculus prior to entry. Students are required to devote one summer to work in a professional architectural office. A thesis is required in the final year of the program. Advanced standing, allowing completion of the program in one or two years, may be requested by students with previous backgrounds or degrees in architecture.

A Master of Science in the field of architecture and a PhD in architecture are post-professional degree programs which offer the opportunity to collaborate with other Carnegie-Mellon departments and expand the scope of education in the department.

The PhD program is directed to these students committed to a research career in an area of architectural sciences.

The MS and PhD programs support advanced study and specialization in a field that contributes to the student's professional career, such as building diagnostics or computer aided design.

FACULTY
Administration

Akram Midani, Dean
Irving Oppenheim, Acting Head
Henry Pisciota, Fine Arts Librarian

Professors

Omer Akin, AIA, PhD
Douglas Cooper, B Arch
Ulrich Flemming, PhD
Volker Hartkopf, M Arch
Delbert Highlands, M Arch
Howard Saalman, PhD
Robert Taylor, MFA

Associate Professors

Richard Becherer, PhD
Richard Cordts, M Arch
Irving Oppenheim, PhD
Gerhard Schmitt, PhD
Mete Turan, PhD

Assistant Professors

Walter Boykowycz, M Arch
Richard Cleary, PhD
Julie Cohen, PhD
Patrice Derrington, PhD
Mark English, M Arch
Bruce Lindsey, M Arch
Robert Woodbury, PhD

Instructor

Paul Rosenblatt, M Arch

Part-Time Faculty

Gerald Allen, M Arch
Michael Chirigos, B Arch
Robert Cole, RIBA, Dipl
Bharat Dave, MS
Jonathan Gray, M Arch
Michael Graybrook, B Arch
James K Griggs, M Arch
Janice Hart, MFA
Michael Hull, B Arch
Andrea Kahn, M Arch
Ann Ketterer, B Arch
Stephanie Ledewitz, M Arch
Steven Lee, M Arch
David Lewis, M Arch
Vivian Loftness, M Arch
Gerald Mattern, BSEE
Laura Nettleton, M Arch
Stephen Quick, M Arch
James Quinnan, MFA
Nino Saggio, MS
Scott Smith, MFA
Joseph Vaughan, M Arch
Pierre Zoelly, M Arch

The Catholic University of America

Department of Architecture and Planning
Pangborn Building
Catholic University of America
Washington, D.C. 20064
(202) 635-5188

Admissions Office
(202) 635-5305

Application Deadline(s): Undgrd: 1 February
Grad: 15 March
Tuition & Fees: Undgrd: $8,995/year
Grad: $8,995/year
Endowment: Private

DEGREE PROGRAMS

Degree	Minimum Years for Degree	Accred.	Requirements for Admission	Full-Time Stdnts.	Part-Time Stdnts.	% of Applics. Accptd.	Stdnts. in 1st Year of Program	# of Degrees Conferred
BS Arch	2 1/2		2 yr. Architectural Technology degree - 2.5 GPA	14	3	75%	8	4
BS Arch	4		1000 comb. Sat-top 1/2 of class TOEFL for foreign students	255	8	50%	71	54
B Arch	1	NAAB	BS or BA in Arch 2.5 GPA	21	23	80%	21	21
M Arch	3 1/2	NAAB	Undgr degree	32	9	80%	22	6

SCHOOL DEMOGRAPHICS (all degree programs)

Full-Time Faculty	Part-Time Faculty	Full-Time Students	Part-Time Students	Foreign Students	Out-of-State U.S. Stdnts.	Women Students	Minority Students
15	15-30	322	40	18%	85%	30%	17%

LIBRARY (Tel. No. 202-635-5167)

Type	No. of Volumes	No. of Slides
Dept	36,000	35,000

STUDENT OPPORTUNITIES AND RESOURCES

Located in the nation's capital, the Department of Architecture and Planning offers programs of study that actively benefit from the unparalleled resources of the city and the federal government. Some of the nation's most outstanding works of architecture, representing the full spectrum of American architectural history, are in the area. Both Washington and nearby Baltimore are undergoing exciting redevelopment, providing living case studies of urban growth. Students can utilize the repositories of the Smithsonian Institution and the libraries of the Library of Congress, the District of Columbia, the several other universities in the area, and the American Institute of Architects. Through the Consortium of Universities of the Washington Metropolitan Area, students have access to a very large number of courses. Proximity to one of the city's Metro stations provides immediate access to all of these resources.

The department's student body is composed of a rich variety of nationalities and races. Students come from the United States and many other parts of the world. They constitute about 40 percent of the enrollment in the School of Engineering and Architecture. The University has approximately 7,000 students, of which over half are graduate students.

The faculty is composed of individuals of varied and broad educational and professional backgrounds. Over two-thirds of the faculty carry on active practices.

SPECIAL ACTIVITIES AND PROGRAMS

The department conducts an extensive summer school program. All required undergraduate courses, all design studios at all levels, and numerous undergraduate and graduate courses are offered. Design faculty are drawn from other universities around the nation as well as from Catholic University.

The department conducts the Patrick Cardinal O'Boyle Foreign Studies Program in which 15 selected C.U. students spend 12 weeks in Europe, principally in Italy, Spain, and France.

Lecture series
Extended graduate field trips
Foreign Studies Program Competition for Seniors
Henry Adams Medal and Certificate
James O'Neil Memorial Award
Paul A. Goettelman Award
Annual Beaux Arts Ball
Active American Institute of Architects Student chapter

FACILITIES

The department is housed (beginning in Sept. 1987) in two buildings on campus:

Pangborn Hall houses the various departments of engineering of the School of Engineering and Architecture and the Administrative offices, computer lab, library and slide collection, faculty offices, and some design studios.

The Old Gym houses the graduate design studios, an undergraduate studio, a lecture/exhibition/reception space, and jury rooms. Plans are being developed to house all design studios in the Old Gym in the near future.

SCHOLARSHIPS/AID

Catholic University offers a wide variety of scholarships, grants, loans, and work appointments to new and continuing students at both the graduate and undergraduate levels. Federal funds are, by statute, awarded solely on the basis of financial need as determined by a federally approved needs analysis system. These funds are available to all as funding will allow. Awards of the university funds are based on the criterion of academic excellence in combination with financial need. Teaching assistantships and some scholarship funds are available through the department.

UNDERGRADUATE PROGRAM
Philosophy Statement

The goal of the undergraduate program is to provide the student with the knowledge, skills, and abilities fundamental to his or her training as a professional, enriched with a broad foundation in the humanities. The student's professional studies will include architectural design and graphic communication, structural and environmental control systems, building materials and methods of construction, and architectural history and theory. The full resources of the university are drawn upon to provide the student with exposure to the arts and humanities.

Program Description

The undergraduate program in architecture consists of 142 semester hours of study. A minimum cumulative grade point average of 2.0 and a C average in architectural design for the student's first two years of study is required for advancement from the second-year design studio to the third-year design studio. A minimum cumulative grade point ratio of 2.0 is required for graduation. Completion of the undergraduate program leads to the Bachelor of Science in Architecture degree. (This is a non-professional degree.)

Students who hold an associate degree in architectural science or an equivalent degree from a two-year community college may be eligible for the special program leading to the degree Bachelor of Science in Architecture. A minimum grade point average of 2.5 is required for admission. Students who are accepted for the program will be admitted with junior status.

In cooperation with the Department of Civil Engineering, the Department of Architecture and Planning offers dual degree programs in architecture and civil engineering. A concentration in civil engineering within the degree of Bachelor of Science in Architecture is also offered.

The curriculum for the first three years is required of all students in the core program. During their third year students elect one of the four subconcentration options for their fourth year of study. These options are design, building construction, history, and city and regional planning.

GRADUATE PROGRAM
Philosophy Statement

The first professional degree programs are oriented toward problem solving and design in the context of the real world, while exposing the student to the diversity of architectural experience. They are urban-oriented programs which draw upon the unique opportunities afforded by their location in the nation's capital.

Program Description

Central to the graduate programs are the design studios, where a variety of projects are presented for exploration and solution by student teams or the individual student. The studio experience is culminated by a thesis, based on an hypothesis developed by the student. This may be either a written thesis or a design thesis, either of which follows completion of comprehensive research and programming of the thesis topic. The design studios are directed by faculty members who have extensive experience in practice and teaching. Visiting critics, invited from the ranks of practitioners in architecture, engineering, urban design and planning, whose experience is relevant to the studio projects, are brought into the studios to provide richness and diversity in the students' design education.

Supporting the studio experience are advanced courses in architecture and related fields. These build upon and extend the basic knowledge gained by the student in the undergraduate curriculum. Lectures, seminars, and exhibitions are devised to introduce the student to the multitude of considerations faced by the practicing architect and to reveal differing philosophies and attitudes toward architectural design which have evolved to address these considerations. As in the studios, lecturers are invited from among the many outstanding professionals practicing in the Washington area to provide informal talks on their current work, to teach, or to add their particular insights to the support courses.

Through the Consortium of Universities of the Washington Metropolitan Area, students may earn credits from among the several other institutions of higher learning in the community.

FACULTY
Administration

Dr John J McCoy, Dean of School of Engineering & Architecture
Stanley I Hallet, AIA, Associate Dean and Chairman, Department of Architecture and Planning
James O'Hear III, RA, Assistant Chairman, Director, Undgrd Program
Joseph Miller, FAIA, Director, Grad Program

Professors

Seymour Auerbach, FAIA, B Arch, M Arch
Peter Blake, FAIA, B Arch
Stanley I Hallet, AIA, M Arch
Joseph Miller, FAIA, B Arch
Walter D Ramberg, AIA, B Arch, M Arch
Forrest H Wilson, Hon. AIA, PhD

Associate Professors

Julius Levine, APA, BSCE, MCP
George Marcou, APA, B Arch, MCP
Theodore Naos, AIA, B Arch, M Arch
James O'Hear III, RA, B Arch, M Arch
Thomas Walton, BS Arch, M Arch, PhD
John V Yanik, AIA, BS Arch, M Arch

Assistant Professors

Paul D C Chiasson, BED, M Arch
Marc Giaccardo, B FA, M Arch
R Jay Kabriel, B Arch, M Arch
Steven Kendall, BS, M Arch
Richard Loosle, RA, M Arch

Visiting Assistant Professors

Ann Cederna, B Arch, MAUD
Neil J Payton, RA, B Arch, M Arch

Part-Time Faculty

Kent Abraham, AIA, B Arch, M Arch
Robert Berg, AIA, CSI, BA, BS
James Binkley, AIA, BA, B Arch
Walter Geiger, AIA, M Arch, ML Arch
Vytenis Gureckas, RA, B Arch, MSBD
Barbara Hadley, BA
Arnold Kronstadt, B Mech Eng
William MacDonald
Iris Miller, AIA, M Arch
Diana Pardee, RA, BS Arch, M Arch
Milton Shinberg, AIA, B Arch
Samir Younes, M Arch

31

University of Cincinnati

**Department of Architecture
School of Architecture and
   Interior Design
College of Design, Architecture,
   Art and Planning
University of Cincinnati
Cincinnati, Ohio 45221-0016
(513) 556-6426**

**Office of Admissions
University of Cincinnati
Cincinnati, Ohio 45221-0091
(513) 556-3425**

Application Deadline(s): Freshmen - January 1
Transfers - May 1
Tuition & Fees: Undgrd: Ohio Res - $753/qtr
Non-Res - $1796/qtr
Grad: Ohio Res - $1171/qtr
Non-Res - $2303/qtr
Endowment: State

DEGREE PROGRAMS

Degree	Minimum Years for Degree	Accred.	Requirements for Admission	Full-Time Stdnts.	Part-Time Stdnts.	% of Applics. Accptd.	Stdnts. in 1st Year of Program	# of Degrees Conferred
B Arch	6	NAAB	*HS diploma, phys., pre-calculus, 2 yrs foreign lang., 1 yr fine arts, 4 yrs English SAT Verbal 500, Math 500, Total 1050, or ACT Eng 24, Math 24, Total 50	445	21	25%	73	65
BS Des Interior Design	5	FIDER	HS background as above SAT Verbal 450, Math 450, Total 1000, or ACT Eng 22, Math 22, Total 48	155	6	30%	38	23
MS Arch	2		Bacc grade req	9	3	20%	5	2
BUP	5		HS diploma, trig., 2 yrs foreign lang., 1 yr fine arts, 4 yrs English	66	4	80%	10	10
BS Des Indus Des	5		HS diploma, 3 yrs math, 2 yrs foreign lang., 1 yr fine arts, 4 yrs English	189	11	56.5%	35	30
BS Des Graph Des	5		Same as Industrial Design	228	6	49%	35	31
BS Des Fashion Des	5		Same as Industrial Design	209	8	64%	38	21

*Plus submittal of form showing evidence of creative ability, motivation, and serious interest

SCHOOL DEMOGRAPHICS (all degree programs)

Full-Time Faculty	Part-Time Faculty	Full-Time Students	Part-Time Students	Foreign Students	Out-of-State U.S. Stdnts.	Women Students	Minority Students
45	28	1622	70	0.8%	20%	52%	6%

*Includes School of Art

LIBRARY (Tel. No. 513-475-3238)

Type	No. of Volumes	No. of Slides
Design, Art, Architecture and Planning	48,100 (13,400 Arch)	212,000 (41,500 Arch)

STUDENT OPPORTUNITIES AND RESOURCES

The University of Cincinnati is well known for its Cooperative Education system which structures professional experience with academic studies. Organized into a schedule of three-month academic quarters alternating with three-month professional practice assignments, architecture students are working in most of the states in the U.S., with opportunities in major companies and cities and direct access to significant cultural activities and architecture.

Graduates from the Department of Architecture hold influential positions in the profession, as academics and principals in important architecture firms.

The Department of Architecture is in the School of Architecture and Interior Design and has a close relationship to the new professional discipline of interior design. Consequently, architecture students have access to courses that deal with space planning and behavioral studies and to the theory, history, and technology courses developed specifically for interior design. The School itself is part of the College of Design, Architecture, and Art, which offers degree programs in planning, urban administration health planning, industrial design, graphic design, fashion design, fine arts (including sculpture, ceramics, drawing, painting, and film), history of art and design, and art education. Courses from all these programs are available to architecture students who may substitute two design studios in a related discipline for two of the required middle-year studios. The College is part of a comprehensive university (35,000 students) located in the middle of a metropolitan region (1,500,000 inhabitants) of great historic interest and cultural richness.

SPECIAL ACTIVITIES AND PROGRAMS

Work/Study Program (required)
Historic Conservation Certificate Program
Foreign Study Program
Computer laboratory
Student Chapter of AIA
Community design projects
Co-op Newsletter (publication of the Professional Practice Division)
Full-scale design projects

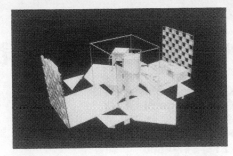

Historic building surveys
Guest lecture series
Student and faculty shows
Symposia and design workshops
Career counseling
Senior thesis exhibition
Summer studio program for transfer students

FACILITIES

The College is housed in the three contiguous buildings of the Wolfson Center for Environmental Design; some academic activities are located in other campus buildings, including the "car barns" facility for Architecture seniors. In the main complex are: a 40,000-volume library, classrooms, offices, design studios, ceramic laboratory, general shop, model shop, type and printing room, printmaking and lithography studios, photography and film labs, painting and sculpture studios, and a computer laboratory presently undergoing significant expansion. A $20 million building project for the College is to begin in the late 1980s.

SCHOLARSHIPS/AID

Undergraduate:
The University makes every effort to ensure that deserving students with limited resources are able to pursue their education. Most financial aid is awarded on the basis of two factors: scholastic ability and financial need. To assure consideration for the following academic year, an application should be filed with the Student Financial Aid Office by February 1, and a Financial Aid Form should be filed with the College Scholarship Service by February 1. Applicants are also considered for assistance offered through programs of the U.S. Department of Education: National Direct Student Loans, Educational Opportunity Grants, and Work-Study awards. General information about financial aid programs is available from the Student Financial Aid Office, 206 Beecher. Entering students may qualify for Vorheis or University Donor Scholarships. All students are eligible for a limited number of Departmental scholarships as well as AIA scholarships.

Graduate:
Graduate Assistantships, usually carrying teaching and/or research responsibilities, are awarded to approximately five full-time graduate students each year. These assistantships entail stipends up to $4,800, plus a University Graduate Scholarship and the general fee. University Graduate Scholarships pay all instructional fees except the general fee of $87 per quarter. Application for scholarship should be made to the Departmental office before February 15.

UNDERGRADUATE PROGRAM
Philosophy Statement

A six-year Cooperative Education Program provides sufficient time to deliver a comprehensive architectural education. It affords the opportunity to be theoretical and practical, aesthetic and technical, vocational and educational. The program is intended to educate architects who can design buildings (with all that that entails in terms of technical and professional knowledge) in a culturally responsible way (with all that that entails in terms of understanding the way members of a society think, know, and feel about the world around them).

Program Description

The four elements of the program are: (1) a two-year foundation program followed by a core program of required lectures which introduce the student to the essential knowledge and skills of the architect; (2) a series of topic packages (TOPACs) consisting of laboratories, seminars, and studios which are available on an elective basis to develop breadth or depth in the student's education as he or she may decide with the counsel of advisors; (3) the cooperative experience, with opportunities in a wide range of firms and geographic locations; (4) a culminating senior project in which the student demonstrates in a project of his or her own choosing the specific range of knowledge and skills gained during the preceding five years.

The Department of Architecture has been a member of the Association of Collegiate Schools of Architecture since 1924. It has been continuously accredited by the National Architectural Accrediting Board since 1948, and its courses satisfy the requirements maintained by the various state architectural registration boards.

GRADUATE PROGRAM
Philosophy Statement

The graduate program is intended for those who wish to develop a greater intellectual understanding of architecture as a discipline in order to be better equipped as educators, critics, or practitioners. The program is primarily concerned with research methodology and the development of theoretical understanding. It is an ideal complement to a first professional degree in architecture but has also been of value to those with backgrounds in art history, fine arts, psychology, landscape architecture, industrial design, and interior design.

Program Description

Much of the program is tailored to students' needs as they prepare themselves for the dissertations that culminate their studies. During the two years of study, required courses in statistical and historiographic research methodology, design theory, and a teaching/research seminar must be taken by all students.

Following admission to the program and prior to registration, the student (in consultation with an assigned advisor) will establish in detail the specific course pursuits to be taken each quarter. This program, which must be approved by the Director of the Graduate Program, will be reviewed quarterly by the student and his or her advisor for possible modification. At the conclusion of the dissertation, the student stands in oral defense of his or her findings before a thesis review committee.

It is possible to coordinate the master's program with the Bachelor of Architecture program, saving one year of study.

FACULTY
Administration

Jay Chatterjee, Dean, College of Design, Architecture, Art and Planning
Gordon B Simmons, Acting Director, School of Architecture and Interior Design
Robert L Williams, AIA, Associate Director, School of Architecture and Interior Design
Dennis A Mann, Chair, Department of Architecture

Professors

Dennis A Mann, RA, B Arch, M Arch
David L Niland, RA, B Arch, M Arch
John M Peterson, B Arch, M Arch
David L Smith, RA, M Arch
Richard A Stevens, BSME
William C Widdowson, B Arch, M Arch, PhD
Robert L Williams, AIA, M Arch

Associate Professors

Bruce Goetzman, AIA, B Arch, MS Arch, MCF
John E Hancock, RA, B Arch, M Arch
Gerald R Larson, M Arch
Gordon B Simmons, RA, B Arch, M Arch
Stephen J Vamosi, BSCE, MSCE

Assistant Professors

Diane Armpriest, MLA
Bradford Grant, RA, B Arch, M Arch
Bharati Jog, M Arch, M Comp Sci
Mary McAuliffe, B Arch, M Arch
Phillip Parker, RA, B Arch, M Arch
John Perkins, M Arch
Agus Rusli, B Arch, M Arch
Barry N Stedman, RA, B Arch, M Arch
Elysabeth Yates-Burns, M Arch

Part-Time Faculty

James Kalsbeek, B Arch
John Koverman, MS Arch
Nick Salmon, B Arch

Adjunct Faculty

Frank Fantauzzi, M Arch

City College of the City University of New York

School of Architecture
& Environmental Studies
City College of the CUNY
Convent Avenue at 138th Street
New York, New York 10031
(212) 690-4118 or 4119

Office of Admissions Services
City College of CUNY
101 West 31st Street
New York, New York 10031
(212) 947-4800

Application Deadline(s): January 15th for September, October 15th for February
Tuition & Fees: Undgrd: NY Res: $625/sem; Non-res: $1275/sem
Grad: NY Res: $950/sem; Non-res: $1600/sem
Endowment: Public

DEGREE PROGRAMS

Degree	Minimum Years for Degree	Accred.	Requirements for Admission	Full-Time Stdnts.	Part-Time Stdnts.	% of Applics. Accptd.	Stdnts. in 1st Year of Program	# of Degrees Conferred
BS Arch	4	NYSED	a) 80% or higher school average b) graduation in the top third of class (for current high school seniors only) or c) 900 or better combined total score SAT	485	149	NA	60.4	83
B Arch	1	NAAB	Grade point average of 2.50 in all courses taken in professional courses in architecture and in design workshop courses.	40	52	NA	NA	53
MUP	1	MSA	B Arch degree or equivalent	10	0	NA	NA	8
BSLA	4	ASLA	Same as BS Arch above	18	2	NA	28	7

SCHOOL DEMOGRAPHICS (all degree programs)

Full-Time Faculty	Part-Time Faculty	Full-Time Students	Part-Time Students	Foreign Students	Out-of-State U.S. Stdnts.	Women Students	Minority Students
22	26	551	203	8%	2%	25%	49%

LIBRARY (Tel. No. 212-690-5329)

Type	No. of Volumes	No. of Slides
Arch	24,800	55,701

STUDENT OPPORTUNITIES AND RESOURCES

Over 800 students, full and part time.

Located in Manhattan, accessible to major museums and world-prominent architecture and urban spaces.

Most culturally diverse student body with students from some eighty (80) countries, speaking over forty (40) different languages.

Students from all over the metropolitan area; recent high school graduates, transfer students from many other community colleges, colleges, and universities; significant number of previous degree students.

First two years of the five-year program are primarily liberal arts taught by other schools and departments of City College. Students are also encouraged to take additional courses as electives in art, history, economics, philosophy, industrial arts, international studies, computer sciences and urban design.

Faculty specializations include: professional design in the United States as well as in developing countries; renewable energies; computer-aided design; rehabilitation; preservation; urban planning in the United States and in Latin America; African architecture; technology, structures, theory, solar design, culture and the environment; film and media in architecture; visual literacy for primary and secondary school students (ongoing programs for primary and secondary school students to learn about architecture and the urban environment).

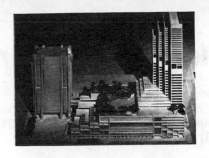

SPECIAL ACTIVITIES AND PROGRAMS

Summer study programs in: Italy, People's Republic of China, Cuba

*Fontainebleau School of Fine Arts - The City College Program:

An eight-week 6-credit comprehensive program in history-theory and research-independent study. Deadline for applying, May 16; April 15, if applying for scholarship aid.

Exchange programs in: Nigeria

Saturday Enrichment program for design reviews from young professionals, career counseling and seminars and dialogues on a variety of topics.

Cooperative work-study program where students achieve academic credit for working in architects' offices or through community service work in the City College Architectural Center.

Chapter of the AIAS and publication of student newsletter, "Pinup."

Joint degree program for students to achieve a dual degree in Architecture and Urban Landscape.

Job Placement service.

Lectures including: Aldo Giurgola on his prize-winning design for Canberra, Australia; Labelle Prussin on Culture and the Environment and The Architectural Heritage of Africa; Jim Morgan on the Architecture and Planning of Nicaragua; Helen Chung on the Architecture of China; Alan Feigenberg on the Architecture of Cuba; Jonathan Barnett on Design Guidelines; M. Paul Friedberg on Collaboration Between the Architect and the Landscape Architect; and Max Bond on Harlem Architecture in Urban Conflict.

FACILITIES

Fully-equipped model shop

Slide Library: slides, light tables, slide-duplicating equipment, copy-stand equipment.

Fully-equipped darkroom for developing and enlarging of black & white and color photography.

Architectural library

Computer lab for word processing, spread sheets and computer-aided design work

City College Architectural Center: community service work; research

SCHOLARSHIPS/AID

The City College School of Architecture & Environmental Studies has both merit and need-based financial assistance. Approximately sixty percent of our students are receiving financial aid.

We have the Tuition Assistance Program, Pell Grants, Guaranteed Student Loans and National Direct Student Loans. There are supplemental opportunity grants, the Seek Program, and College Work/Study Programs.

Professional organizations offer scholarships through the school and the New York State Regents offers Professional scholarships as well.

City College maintains a financial aid office; the other scholarships are posted in the school of architecture.

UNDERGRADUATE PROGRAM
Philosophy Statement

Architects, environmental designers, and planners have to be capable of synthesizing the needs of all those involved in the complex process of design to completion and management.

The School equally emphasizes the importance of good design, technical knowledge, and a clear understanding of times and context necessary to build.

The specific programs offered lead to professional degrees in Architecture, Urban Landscape and Urban Design.

Program Description

The educational program of the School is divided into three phases, each lasting two years. Each phase has a specific emphasis. In the first phase (first and second years), the student is offered a general education in liberal arts and sciences, as well as a series of lecture and workshop courses that serve as an introduction to the processes of change in the physical fabric of the urban environment of the past and present.

In the second phase (third and fourth years) course work is devoted to professional education in either architecture or urban landscape. In each semester, the student is required to take parallel courses in three areas: design workshops, history and theory, and construction technology for either architecture or urban landscape.

In the third phase, work is focused on advanced studies in architecture (fifth year) and on urban design (sixth year). The development of independent professional judgment is emphasized.

FACULTY
Administration

J Max Bond, Jr, RA, AIA, Dean
William Garrison McNeil, RA, Chairman
Jonathan Barnett, FAIA, AICP, Director, Graduate Program in Urban Design
M Paul Friedberg, FASLA, Director, Urban Landscape Program
Sylvia Wright, Librarian

Professors

Jonathan Barnett, RA, FAIA, AICP, B Arch
Jay Lance Brown, RA, M Arch
R Alan Cordingley, RA, M Arch
John Deans, RA, B Arch, MS
Giuseppe DeCampoli, PE, D Civ Eng, PhD
William Ellis, RA, B Arch, MCP
M Paul Friedberg, FASLA, RLA, BS, LLD(Hon)
Peter Gisolfi, ASLA, AIA, M Arch, MLA
David Guise, RA, B Arch
James R Jarrett, RA, M Arch
Wm Garrison McNeil, RA, B Arch, MSUD
Paul David Pearson, B Arch, MS, PhD
Rosaria Piomelli, AIA, RA, B Arch
Labelle Prussin, RA, B Arch, M Arch, PhD
Wm H Roehl, RA, MFA
Donald Ryder, FAIA, RA, BS
Norval White, FAIA, RA, MFA

Associate Professors

Carmi Bee, AIA, RA, B Arch, M Arch
Gordon Gebert, RA, B Arch, M Arch
Ghislaine Hermanuz, D d'Arch, MUSP
Cynthia Peterson, AIA, RA, B Arch, M Arch

Assistant Professor

John Loomis, M Arch

Clemson University

College of Architecture
Clemson University
Clemson, South Carolina 29631-0501
(803) 656-3081

Office of Admissions
Clemson University
Clemson, South Carolina 29631-4019
(803) 656-2287

Application Deadline(s): Open, but early fall recommended
Tuition & Fees: Undgrd: SC Res: $1045
Non-Res: $2565
Grad: SC Res: $1045
Non-Res: $1045
Per Semester
Endowment: State

DEGREE PROGRAMS

Degree	Minimum Years for Degree	Accred.	Requirements for Admission	Full-Time Stdnts.	Part-Time Stdnts.	% of Applics. Accptd.	Stdnts. in 1st Year of Program	# of Degrees Conferred
BA Design	4		SAT, Upper class rank, Interview	89	2	21%	35	25
BS Design				213	1		65	50
M Arch	2	NAAB	GRE, Portfolio, References, Interview	78		30%	39	31
MS Arch**	1		GRE, Study plan, References, Interview					
BS BL Sc & Mgt	4	ACCE	SAT, Upper class rank, Interview	103		40%	15	10
M BL Sc & Mgt*	2		GRE, Prerequisites, References, Interview	6	11		6	
BLA*	5		SAT, Upper class rank, Interview	6		30%	3	
BFA*	5		SAT, Upper class rank, Interview	13		30%	6	
MFA	2		GRE, Portfolio, References, Interview	16	1	25%	8	8
MCRP	2	APA	GRE, Prerequisites, References, Interview	30	3	35%	15	6

*New program   **Pending final approval

SCHOOL DEMOGRAPHICS (all degree programs)

Full-Time Faculty	Part-Time Faculty	Full-Time Students	Part-Time Students	Foreign Students	Out-of-State U.S. Stdnts.	Women Students	Minority Students
45	5	576	18	3%	37%	31%	3%

LIBRARY (Tel. No. 803-656-3932)

Type	No. of Volumes	No. of Slides
Arch	26,000 Vol 4,800 bound periodicals	70,000

STUDENT OPPORTUNITIES AND RESOURCES

Clemson University is located in the foothills of the Blue Ridge Mountains in upper South Carolina. Its Sylvan setting overlooking Lake Hartwell belies its strategic central location in the growth corridor extending from Atlanta to Charlotte, North Carolina. Clemson is a fully accredited state university founded a century ago on the family estate of Senator John C. Calhoun by his son-in-law Thomas Green Clemson. Originally chartered to educate agriculturalists, the school has expanded over the years in disciplines and degree programs while maintaining an intimacy of size and numbers.

The College of Architecture is one of nine academic units within the present university. It, in turn, is comprised of the Departments of Visual Arts and History, Planning Studies, Building Science and Architectural Studies. While administering their separate degree programs, a close association of these teaching areas, marked by cross disciplinary studies and faculty exchange, provide rich and varied learning opportunities for students of all levels and disciplines.

Regular updating of college curricula and the introduction of new programs respond to changing educational needs. An innovative sequence of post-baccalaureate studies for graduates of other than design disciplines seeking a professional architectural degree were introduced some years ago. Currently, a Master of Science program emphasizing architectural research is under development. The Department of Architectural Studies has joined forces with Planning Studies to implement a dual degree program, and has aided in the development of the new Landscape Architecture degree.

The approach to architectural education is based on the 4+2 organizational concept which employs both undergraduate and graduate degree programs. This system affords the beginning student an opportunity to achieve a sound general education while developing a base of career studies which may be applied to a range of professional programs at the graduate level. The separation into discrete curricula also permits advanced work to be taken at other institutions, and in like manner allows students from other schools to pursue their graduate studies at Clemson.

Architectural Studies, as well as those of other college programs, are located in Lee Hall, a building of contemporary demeanor which is steadily expanding to meet the multiple needs of a variety of disciplines. Serving to both complement and contrast the Clemson experience, resident study programs are conducted by the College of Architecture in Charleston, South Carolina and Genoa, Italy. These alternative learning opportunities are supported by the Clemson Architectural Foundation, which also makes possible a number of other college activities including gallery exhibits and a lecture series.

SPECIAL ACTIVITIES AND PROGRAMS

Summer orientation sessions for freshman students

Beginning-of-year schoolwide design fete

Monday evening lecture series and receptions

Undergraduate study program in Charleston, S.C.

Annual Homecoming Luncheon for College alumni

Traveling art and architectural exhibits in Lee Gallery

Traditional Beaux Arts Ball in the College courtyard

Field trips to Columbus, Indiana and New York City

Fall regional architectural symposium
Visiting distinguished critic program
Graduate study program in Genoa, Italy
ASC/AIA educational and social activities
Ongoing academic liaison with the US Air Force
Washington's birthday-inspired Cherry Cotillion
Honors Day recognition of student achievements
Spring Week of spontaneous creative activity
Career Day interviews with architectural
    practitioners

SCHOLARSHIPS/AID

The University Office of Financial Aid administers
and coordinates various types of undergraduate
financial aid including scholarships, loans and
part-time employment. A number of graduate
teaching and research assistantships are
available each year. In addition to paying a
salary, the assistantship entitles the student to a
reduction in academic fees. Alumni fellowships of
up to $10,000, awarded to outstanding graduate
students, require no services of the recipients.

UNDERGRADUATE PROGRAM
Philosophy Statement

Undergraduate study provides a broad based
general education and prepares the student for
professional level graduate work in architecture
or an allied discipline.

Program Description

The initial year of undergraduate study
emphasizes mathematics, science and language
while introducing the student to the bases of
design. Course work emphasizing general
knowledge continues in successive years
accompanied by studies in architectural history,
the visual arts, building science and an
increasingly rigorous exposure to design theory
and application. Advanced students have the
opportunity of spending a semester in
Charleston, South Carolina, where their regular
studies are enriched by the cultural ambience of
this 17th-century coastal city.

Entering students are expected to be
academically well qualified, as well as possessed
of creative potential and zeal for learning. A mix
of students with varied backgrounds both from
within and outside the state is encouraged.
Whenever possible, applicants are asked to visit
the campus and discuss career issues with
members of the architecture faculty. Each year's
freshman class is normally limited to one
hundred in order to assure that the close working
relationship that has existed between student
and teacher may be maintained.

GRADUATE PROGRAM
Philosophy Statement

Graduate study combines academic rigor with
creative challenge to prepare the student for
architectural practice and complements this
regimen with postprofessional research studies.

Program Description

The Master of Architecture program places major
emphasis on architectural design, accompanied
by courses in technology, theory and

professional practice, as well as elective
subjects. Studio design projects are both
complex and comprehensive, stressing social
awareness, contextual fit and intellectual clarity.
Practical office experience is a requisite part of
the overall program, which is concluded with a
thesis involving both problem identification and
resolution. A vital component of the graduate
program is the Charles E Daniel Center for
Building Research and Urban Studies in Genoa,
Italy, where studio and classroom work related to
this historic port city is invigorated by visiting
scholars and critics, and expanded by scheduled
field trips both in Italy and continental Europe.

The duration of study required for the Master
of Architecture degree is usually two academic
years. A concentration in Architecture and Health
Care is available to students who wish to study
the programming, planning and design issues
associated with physical and mental health care
delivery systems. Admission to the Master of
Architecture program is based on the student's
demonstrated ability to respond effectively to the
intellectual rigor and creative challenge integral to
advanced architecture studies. A personal
interview is normally required of candidates
whose application material has been favorably
reviewed by the Admissions Committee. As
referred to earlier, a post-baccalaureate program
to remedy deficiencies in course work required
for admission to the master's program is
available to otherwise qualified applicants.

The research-oriented Master of Science in
Architecture will be available to students who
have achieved the first professional degree in
architecture and wish to enrich their knowledge
and understanding through specialized study in
areas of architectural technology or theory.
Advanced work in Architecture and Health Care
will also be available through this academic
degree program.

FACULTY
Administration

James F Barker, Dean, College of Architecture
Lamar H Brown, Acting Associate Dean
John D Jacques, Head, Department of
    Architectural Studies
Peter R Lee, Director, Graduate Studies in
    Architecture
George C Means, Jr, Director, Graduate Studies
    in Architecture and Health Care
Samuel Wang, Director, Graduate Studies in
    Visual Arts
Cesare Fera, Director, Charles E Daniel Center,
    Genoa
Raymond Huff, Director, Charleston Program

Professors

John T Acorn, BA, MFA
Clarence L Addison, B Arch, M Arch
James F Barker, B Arch, M Arch
Norman L Book, BAE, M Eng, PhD
Lamar H Brown, B Arch
Jose R Caban, B Arch, M Civ Des
Donald L Collins, BLA, MLA
Martin A Davis, B Arch, M Phil
Teoman K Doruk, Dipl Eng, PhD
Cesare Fera, Laurea Arch, Lib Doc
Robert H Hunter, BS, MFA
John D Jacques, B Arch, M Phil

Yuji Kishimoto, B Arch, M Arch, MED
Peter R Lee, B Arch, M Arch
Roger W Liska, BS, MS, PhD
Barry C Nocks, BS, MRP, PhD
Richard B Norman, BS, B Arch, M Arch
Kenneth J Russo, B Arch, M Arch
Cecilia E Voelker, BA, MA, PhD
Samuel Wang, BA, MFA
Gayland B Witherspoon, B Arch, MS
Joseph L Young, B Arch, M Arch

Associate Professors

Lynn G Craig, B Arch, MS
Thomas W Dimond, BFA, MFA
Robert D Eflin, B Arch, M Arch
M David Egan, BS, MS
Francis M Eubanks, BS, MS
Robert Hogan, B Arch, M Arch
Mark R Hudson, BA, MFA
N Jane Hurt, M Arch, M Env Des, PhD
Dale J Hutton, B Arch, MS
Janet B Leblanc, BA, MA
James B London, BS, MA, PhD
Gordon W Patterson, BA, B Arch, M Arch
George M Polk, B Arch, M Arch
Stephen Schuette, BS, MS
James A Stockham, BFA, MFA
Lolly Tai, BS, MLA
Michael V Vatalaro, BFA, MFA
Gerald L Walker, B Arch, MCP, MS

Assistant Professors

Kerry R Brooks, BA, MUP
Sydney A Cross, BFA, MFA
Raymond Huff, B Arch
Jon Meyer, BS, MID, MFA
Herbert P Norman, Jr, BS, MA

Visiting Professors

Birsen Doruk, Dipl, PhD
Harlan E McClure, BA, B Arch, M Arch
George C Means, Jr, B Arch, M Arch

Visiting Associate Professor

Harry C Harritos, B Arch, M Arch

Visiting Assistant Professors

Gregg R Corley, BS, MS
Durham Crout, BS, M Arch
Terry Jarrard-Dimond, BA, MFA
Christian LeBlanc, BA, M Arch
John M Mumford, BS, MINED
Whitney Powers, B Arch, MS
Matthew H Rice, BA, M Arch
Robert Silance, BA, BFA, M Arch
Linda Varkonda, BA, MA, PhD

Adjunct Professors

Harold N Cooledge, Jr, BS, B Arch, MA, PhD
Robert D England, BA, MA
Edward L Falk, MA, MRP, DPA
Ralph E Knowland, B Arch, MBA, BISc & Mgt
Ireland G Regnier, BFA, MFA
Frederick G Roth, AB, B Arch, M Arch
Glenn E Varenhorst, BA, MPA, MS

University of Colorado at Denver

School of Architecture and Planning
University of Colorado
1200 Latimer Street
Campus Box 126
Denver, Colorado 80204-5300
(303) 556-2755

Admissions Office
(303) 556-2877

Application Deadline(s): March 15
Tuition & Fees: Grad: Co. res: $1758/yr.
Non-res: $5380/yr.
Endowment: Public

DEGREE PROGRAMS

Degree	Minimum Years for Degree	Accred.	Requirements for Admission	Full-Time Stdnts.	Part-Time Stdnts.	% of Applics. Accptd.	Stdnts. in 1st Year of Program	# of Degrees Conferred
M Arch	3½	NAAB	BA, BS	101	8	35%	45	25
M Arch	2		BA (Arch), BS (Arch)	60	6	65%	30	22
M Arch	1		B Arch, M Arch	2	1	97%	3	3
M Arch UD	1		B Arch, M Arch	7	3	95%	7	4
MID	3		BA, BS	22	8	80%	16	3
MID	2		B Arch, BID, BFA	6	4	85%	3	1
MLA	3	ASLA	BA, BS	28	2	76%	22	12
MLA	2		BLA, BSLA	8	2	84%	5	3
MURP	2	PAB	BA, BS	43	27	85%	18	28

SCHOOL DEMOGRAPHICS (all degree programs)

Full-Time Faculty	Part-Time Faculty	Full-Time Students	Part-Time Students	Foreign Students	Out-of-State U.S. Stdnts.	Women Students	Minority Students
30	25	267	56	12%	8%	51%	7%

LIBRARY (Tel. No. 303-556-2438)

Type	No. of Volumes	No. of Slides
Arch & Planning	12,000	12,000

STUDENT OPPORTUNITIES AND RESOURCES

The School of Architecture and Planning is composed of 300 full-time-equivalent students of whom 150 are in Architecture, 60 in Urban and Regional Planning, 15 in Urban Design, 45 in Landscape Architecture and 30 in Interior Design. The student body has an approximately 50/50 ratio of men to women and is comprised of about 80% in-state residents and 20% out-of-state, of which 12% are international students.

The School of Architecture and Planning is one of few design schools in the United States which offers five professional graduate degree programs in Architecture, Interior Design, Landscape Architecture, Urban Design and Urban and Regional Planning. This range of program offerings provides students with a wide range of educational experiences and access to a broad spectrum of courses in the above disciplines. The faculty of the School provide expertise in a variety of design and planning disciplines and are among nationally and internationally known scholars and practitioners.

The School is located in the heart of a sophisticated and growing urban area, the heart of downtown Denver, a magnificent laboratory for architecture, design and planning. The School has a Research Center which provides further opportunities for students.

SPECIAL ACTIVITIES AND PROGRAMS

The School offers the following special activities and programs:

Off-Campus study programs abroad

Architecture Mentor Program in cooperation with local practicing architects

The School Lecture Series features nationally and internationally recognized leaders in the design and planning fields

The Beta Lambda Chapter of Tau Sigma Delta honor society in Architecture is established in the School of Architecture and Planning. Each year distinguished students will be honored by selection to membership in the Chapter.

The School honors outstanding students with a variety of school awards in the fields of Architecture, Interior Design, Landscape Architecture, Urban Design and Urban and Regional Planning in addition to professional society student awards: AIA, APA, ASLA, ASID

The School honors one student with Alpha Rho Chi Medal

The School also offers several endowed scholarships to outstanding students: Temple Hoyne Buell Scholarship, AIA Scholarship and others.

The School has established student chapters of The American Institute of Architects, The American Planning Association, The American Society of Landscape Architecture, and The American Society of Interior Designers.

There is a school newsletter and several scholarly journals edited by the distinguished faculty: *Urban Design and Preservation Quarterly, Journal of American Planning Association,* and *Urbanism.*

Beaux Arts Ball is a traditional social event which takes place annually.

FACILITIES

The Architecture and Planning Library, a branch of the Auraria Library of the University of Colorado at Denver, serves as a learning resource center in the fields of architecture, design and planning. It contains the following collections to support the curricula of the College: 1) Reference - technical materials selected to support design and planning studio projects; 2) Circulating - material in the fields of architecture, landscape architecture, interior design, urban design and urban and regional planning; 3) Documentary - planning documents issued by local, regional, state and national agencies with an emphasis on planning materials pertaining to Colorado communities and concerns; 4) Periodical - current materials relating to architecture, design and planning; 5) Reserve - resource materials for required and supplemental class reading; 6) Nonprint - media, including architectural slides and microcomputer software.

The library is open 71 hours per week, including evenings and Sundays. The staff consists of a librarian, library assistant, and several student assistants. The library provides a number of services including reference and research assistance and library-use instruction. Additional services, such as interlibrary loan and computer-assisted research, are provided through the Auraria Library.

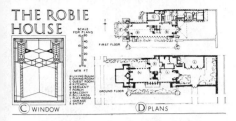

THE ROBIE HOUSE
C WINDOW   D PLANS
FIRST FLOOR
GROUND FLOOR

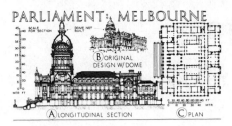

PARLIAMENT: MELBOURNE
B ORIGINAL DESIGN W/DOME
A LONGITUDINAL SECTION   C PLAN

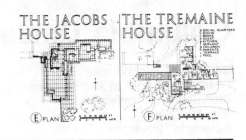

THE JACOBS HOUSE   THE TREMAINE HOUSE
E PLAN   F PLAN

Computer Laboratory

The Computer Laboratory of the School of Architecture and Planning is equipped for upscaled computer-aided design and drafting with a microcomputer based networking system. Six Zenith 2200 PC/ATs in addition to four IBM PC/XTs are now linked with a Novell central file server and 120 Megabyte hard disk drive for storage. This network and six additional PC/AT workstations are linked through the addition of AutoCAD compatible software that extends and enhances the ongoing use of AutoCAD and AE/CADD.

The School maintains a darkroom for student use as well as a variety of camera and audiovisual equipment. These facilities are valuable aids in preparing class presentations, design projects, portfolios, and in learning multimedia techniques for presentations. The model shop and photo lab is available for use in fabricating architectural models and in furniture design projects. A staff technician is on duty to assist students in the use of these facilities.

SCHOLARSHIPS/AID

The School of Architecture and Planning offers the following scholarships to graduate Architecture students:

Temple H Buell Scholarship	$2000
Robert K Fuller Scholarship	$2000
Fisher Traveling Scholarship I	$2200
Fisher Traveling Scholarship II	$1800
James M Hunter Scholarship	$1500

A limited number of Colorado grants are available to new students who are residents of Colorado and fulfill the University's criteria for financial need. Also available are Federal National Direct Student Loans (NDLS) and Federal Work-Study Assistance.

A.I.A. Colorado Educational Fund provides grants totaling from $2000 to $4000 for students and faculty to attend conventions, seminars and educational forums.

GRADUATE PROGRAM
Philosophy Statement

The Architecture Program philosophy is to offer a curriculum which is a blend of education and training and includes a variety of perspectives and views. Within this approach, various design ideologies and views are examined in respect to their historical context. This combined with critical review and design dialogues form the essential ingredient of design education. Students are introduced to fundamentals of design analysis and synthesis based on humanistic ideals as the means of meeting their personal aspirations. In this context, understanding of different design philosophies and constructs is the essence of the graduate design program. Furthermore, the School's teaching approaches are advanced by offering comprehensive design studios in which students learn how to think, analyze, synthesize, and be creative, combined with a variety of lectures and seminar courses in which students develop an intellectual framework in regard to the history, philosophies, theories and methods of design and planning.

Program Description

The Architecture Program at the School of Architecture and Planning is a professional curriculum founded on five major architectural components:

Architectural Design
History/Theory and Criticism
Environmental Context
Technology
Professional Practice

The primary objective of the Program is to prepare students to enter the professional practice of architecture with a thorough foundation in the bodies of knowledge and applied methods of planning and design in architecture. More specifically, the objectives of the Program are to develop:

Awareness of and sensitivity to the quality of the human environment, environmental context, and interrelationships of human behavior and the physical environment

Understanding the history, theory and criticism of architecture

Professional competence in architectural technology

Analytic problem-solving competence of synthesis and communication of the above knowledge into "physical form"

Understanding of the institutional framework within which architecture takes place

Skills and understanding of professional practice including management and professional conduct

The ultimate goals of the program are to provide the architecture student with a deep appreciation of physical and environmental quality while acquiring critical capacity, through comprehension of all facets of architecture.

The above objectives are achieved through five groups of courses organized in sequences of four coordinated modules.

The Program requires completion of 108 credit hours and three and one-half years of residency. The general requirements include:

Architectural Design Studio	48 credit hours
History, Theory and Criticism	15
Technology	18
Environmental Context	6
Professional Practice	6
Electives	21
Total	114

FACULTY
Administration

Hamid Shirvani, AIA, AICP, ASLA, Dean
Yuk Lee, Associate Dean
Robert W Kindig, AIA, Director of the Architecture Program
Marvin Hatami, ASID, Director of the Interior Design Program
Harry L Garnham, ASLA, Director of the Landscape Architecture Program
Peter Schaeffer, Director of the Urban and Regional Planning Program
Robert Wick, Librarian

Professors

John D Hoag, PhD
Robert W Kindig, AIA, M Arch
Yuk Lee, PhD
John M Prosser, AIA, M Arch
Hamid Shirvani, AIA, AICP, ASLA, Dipl Arch, M Arch, MLA, PhD

Associate Professors

Soontorn Boonyatikarn, M Arch
Lois Brink, MLA
M Gordon Brown, MBA, MS Arch
Thomas A Clark, PhD
Frances Downing, M Arch
Phillip Gallegos, AIA, M Arch
Harry L Garnham, ASLA, MLA
Marvin Hatami, FAIA, M Arch
David R Hill, AICP, PhD
Bernie Jones, PhD
Peter Schaeffer, PhD
Frederick R Steiner, PhD

Assistant Professors

Ned Collier, MS
Gary J Crowell, AIA, M Arch
Lauri M Johnson, MLA
Gail W Karn, AIA, M Arch, MCP
Taisto Makela, MA PhD
Bennett R Neiman, M Arch
Diane Wilk Shirvani, AIA, M Arch

Part-Time Faculty

Rhoda Bliss, MA
Robert Cox, M Arch
Emmet L Haywood, MCRP
Bruce Hazzard, MLA
Kenneth L Hoagland, MRP
Gregory Jameson, ASLA, MLA
Eric Kelley, AICP, MCP, JD
Claire Lanier, MID, MA
Gilbert McNeish, JD
Alan E Rollinger, BS
Stanley Specht, MLA, MA
Donato Stammiello, MA
F Scott Woodard, B Arch
Martin Zeller, MA

Adjunct Faculty

Cabell Childress, FAIA, B Arch
Mark Johnson, ASLA, MLA
Todd Johnson, ASLA, MLA
William Muchow, FAIA, M Arch
Anthony Pellecchia, AIA
Paul Saporito, B Arch

Columbia University

Division of Architecture
Graduate School of Architecture
Planning and Preservation
400 Avery Hall
Columbia University
New York, New York 10027
(212) 280-3414

Admissions
(212) 280-3510

Application Deadline(s): Master of Arch:
January 15
Building Design:
February 15
Urban Design:
February 15
Tuition & Fees: Grad: $11,970/yr
Endowment: Private

DEGREE PROGRAMS

Degree	Minimum Years for Degree	Accred.	Requirements for Admission	Full-Time Stdnts.	Part-Time Stdnts.	% of Applics. Accptd.	Stdnts. in 1st Year of Program	# of Degrees Conferred
M Arch	3	NAAB	Bacc degree	200	3	27%	64	62
MS Bldg Design	1		B Arch or M Arch	40	0	50%		38
MS Urban Design	1		B Arch or M Arch	20	0	50%		14
MSUP	2		Bacc degree	60	0	90%	42	18
MS Hist Pres	2		Bacc degree	60	0	80%	28	38
MS Real Estate Dev	1		Bacc degree	38	0	50%		38

SCHOOL DEMOGRAPHICS (all degree programs)

Full-Time Faculty	Part-Time Faculty	Full-Time Students	Part-Time Students	Foreign Students	Out-of-State U.S. Stdnts.	Women Students	Minority Students
36	83	418	3	10%	70%	40%	8%

LIBRARY (Tel. No. 212-280-3501)

Type	No. of Volumes	No. of Slides
Art & Arch (Slide Lib: Arch, HP, UP)	250,000	80,000

STUDENT OPPORTUNITIES AND RESOURCES

One of the greatest resources of the school is that so many members of the faculty carry on active professional practices in and around New York City. The faculty is diverse in terms of areas of practice, research, and study of history and theory.

Members of the design faculty are available to students for consultation and compiling portfolios. A job file is kept, listing job openings which are occasionally called into the office from architectural firms and related offices in and around the metropolitan area. These include full-time and temporary positions.

SPECIAL ACTIVITIES AND PROGRAMS

Traveling fellowship awards for 90% of students and for graduates with exceptional promise (for travel within a year after graduation)

Weekly public lecture series, attracting as speakers eminent architects, artists, and historians from all over the world

FACILITIES

The location of the Graduate School of Architecture is of enormous importance. New York City is the American culture capital. Its ethnic heterogeneity and artistic volatility, the local pool of visiting designers and critics, and the city's institutions, particularly the Museum of Modern Art, reinforce the educational apparatus and offer opportunities for research that are outstanding. The city's public agencies, such as the Urban Design Group of the City Planning Commission, offer other dimensions of design and practice. Students are encouraged to pursue personal objectives through the vehicle of research credits, which are given for community service and technical assistance activities, as well as for scholarly research.

The resources of the world's leading architectural library, Avery Library, are located in the school building and are fully available to students in the school. Physical facilities of the school and Avery Library have undergone a $5-million expansion program which provides two new lecture halls (one of 250 seats, the other of 80) and two new classrooms. Library space has expanded to 35,000 square feet and the university's Fine Arts Library has merged with Avery Library. The university-operated computer facility has hardware consisting of an IBM 360/91 and a 360/75 with a variety of terminal access facilities (including graphic terminals).

SCHOLARSHIPS/AID

Columbia's Graduate School of Architecture and Planning has $600,000 in scholarships. Students must borrow from Federally Insured Student Loan funds, if eligible. Perkins funds are available for all students who are unable to secure funds from the FISL loans or for those students who need supplemental loans. Teaching assistantships and readerships are available for second- and third-year students.

UNDERGRADUATE PROGRAM
Philosophy Statement

In regard to the teaching of design at Columbia, abstract "basic design" exercises are eschewed in favor of a mix of written and graphic analytical exercises involving historical works of architecture as well as problems in design. In these, the emphasis is not on exhaustive investigation by the student of the philosophical implications of a program, but on the student's direct response to a problem whose scope is clearly defined. In this way, students can achieve something substantive in the limited time allowed, given the overall academic priorities of the liberal arts college, and thereby gain in confidence.

Program Description

The undergraduate architecture program at Columbia is in Columbia College and open only to those students who have completed two years in the college. Students receive a BA degree with a major in architecture. Admission to the program is separate from the graduate school, and the program is administered by the dean of the college and the college's Committee on Instruction. The graduate school has a departmental representative who acts as a liaison between it and the college, who serves as faculty adviser to the undergraduate majors, and who coordinates the various components of the undergraduate curriculum in architecture.

The college major is staffed by faculty members from the architecture school and the art history department, and it is these interrelated spheres which define the philosophic character of the major. The curriculum consists of five terms of architectural history, a one-term course devoted to the investigation of the economic infrastructure of building as an activity, a term devoted to the principles of structure, a term course each of freehand drawing and architectural graphics, two terms of studio workshop, and a one-term senior seminar. Based on their overall academic performance, certain students may be admitted to a two-term Intermediate Studio in their senior year.

GRADUATE PROGRAM
Philosophy Statement

Columbia's Graduate School of Architecture is dedicated to the proposition that architectural design has always been and will continue to be the core of professional education. Anthropological, cultural, technological, and historical course work is offered as support for the design studio. It is the ability to synthesize vast, differentiated bodies of knowledge as they affect and modify the design decision-making process that is stressed. Centering the work of the studio are concepts of typology, topos, tectonics, and the hierarchy of public and private space.

The faculty of the school is diverse in its philosophical and ideological positions, including theoreticians, historians, and practitioners. What they have in common, however, is a belief that all architecture, the good and the great, is governed by sets of identifiable formal principles that transcend questions of culture, politics, and the economy.

Program Description

The budget of the Master of Architecture program is used to maintain a faculty-student ratio of 1:11 in the design studios. The design program constitutes about 50 percent of the total number of credits required for graduation. It is continuously evaluated and modified in order to better respond to the dynamic nature of the practice of architecture. Short or long design problems, case studies, historical and technological analyses, and research projects are utilized where deemed appropriate.

All school curricula are monitored and evaluated by an elected body of students and faculty. There are a minimum number of required courses, a large number of sectoral area courses (history, theory, technology, planning, social, scientific) and an extraordinary number of pure electives, many of which are drawn from sister schools and departments: law, engineering, and art history. Joint degree programs in the school lead to both the M Arch and MSUP. Other joint degree programs are with law, business, public health, and social work. However, the greatest educational asset is the set of programs that co-exist with the M Arch program: the country's oldest and most prestigious historic preservation program; an urban design program conceived and headed by one of the founders of New York City's influential Urban Design Group; and a new program in building design taught by world-renowned architects. There are also programs in urban planning and real estate development which complete the spectrum of professional programs that are available to the students.

FACULTY
Administration

Bernard Tschumi, Dean
Loes Schiller, Associate Dean
Kenneth Frampton, Chairman, Division of Architecture
Robert McCarter, Asst. Chairman, Architecture
Roy Strickland, Director,
    Columbia College Arch. Program
Angela Giral, Avery Librarian

Professors

Harold K Bell, BBA
Kenneth Frampton, Dipl Arch
Romaldo Giurgola, Arch, MS
Cyril Harris, PhD
Klaus Herdeg, M Arch
Richard Plunz, B Arch, M Arch
Jan Pokorny, Eng Arch, MS
James S Polshek, BS, M Arch
Robert A M Stern, M Arch
Bernard Tschumi

Associate Professors

Amy Anderson, M Arch
Joseph Connors, PhD
Marta Gutman, M Arch

Steven Holl, B Arch
William MacDonald, B Arch, MS
Alvaro Malo, B Arch, M Arch
Mary McLeod, M Arch, PhD
James Tice, B Arch, M Arch
Susana Torre, D Arch
Gwendolyn Wright, M Arch, PhD

Assistant Professors

Daniel M Bluestone, PhD
Zeynep Celik, M Arch, PhD
Edward Kaufman, PhD
Frank Matero, MS
Roy Strickland, M Arch

Lecturers

J Michael McCormick, MS, Eng ScD

Adjunct Faculty

Craig Barton
Kevin Bone
Jeffrey Bucholtz
Ann Buttenweiser
Peggy Deamer
Livio Dimitriu
Andrew Dolkart
Stan Eckstut
Deane Evans
James Gainforth
James Garrison
Gisue Hariri
Denis Hector
Jay Hibbs
Paola Iacucci
Rodolfo Imas
Kenneth Kaplan
Shulan Kolotan
Kunio Kudo
George Kunihiro
Alessandra Latour
Scott Marble
Robert Marino
Sandro Marpilero
Robert McCarter
Eden Muir
Paul Naecker
Guy Nordenson
Randall Ott
Ann Perl
Nicholas Quennell
Mario Salvadori
Eugene Santaomasso
Robert Silman
Andrew Tesoro
Christos Tountas
Karen Van Lengen
Lauretta Vinciarelli
Rafael Vinoly
Michael Webb
Tony Webster
Leonardo Zylberberg

The Cooper Union

Irwin S. Chanin
 School of Architecture
The Cooper Union
7 East 7th Street
New York, New York 10003
(212) 254-6397

The Cooper Union
Office of Admissions
41 Cooper Square
New York, New York 10003
(212) 254-2629

Application Deadline(s): Freshmen: January 1
Transfers: February 15
Tuition & Fees: Undgrd: $300 Student Fee (no tuition)
Endowment: Private

DEGREE PROGRAMS

Degree	Minimum Years for Degree	Accred.	Requirements for Admission	Full-Time Stdnts.	Part-Time Stdnts.	% of Applics. Accptd.	Stdnts. in 1st Year of Program	# of Degrees Conferred
B Arch	5	NAAB	HS Diploma, SAT scores Entrance exam (freshman) Portfolio and/or Bacc degree (transfer)	145	15	7.6%	28	21

SCHOOL DEMOGRAPHICS (all degree programs)

Full-Time Faculty	Part-Time Faculty	Full-Time Students	Part-Time Students	Foreign Students	Out-of-State U.S. Stdnts.	Women Students	Minority Students
10	28	145	15	8%	28%	33%	25%

LIBRARY (Tel. No. 212-254-6300 ext 360)

Type	No. of Volumes	No. of Slides
Arch	7,341	19,647

STUDENT OPPORTUNITIES AND RESOURCES

Cooper Union's location in the heart of New York City, in addition to providing a wealth of practicing professionals of the highest distinction as adjunct faculty, has a profound effect on many other features of the institution. There is the cosmopolitan character of a student body and faculty whose members live, work, and study in a world city. One of Cooper Union's major resources is an urban laboratory unparalleled in its stimulation and opportunities for research and community service for professionals who work and study in the fields of specialization it offers. New York's elaborate and unique social and cultural institutions are also a critical part of the educational ambience at The Cooper Union.

SPECIAL ACTIVITIES AND PROGRAMS

Lecture series
Annual Student Exhibition
Cooper Union Forum (lectures and performing arts)
Exhibitions
Study abroad or in US for credit
Continuing Education Program
Student representatives on standing committees
Saturday program for high school students

FACILITIES

8200SF Studio Space
9700SF (shared) Shop Facility: wood, metal, plastics, sculpture
Photography and Printmaking Studios, Film and Video Labs (also shared)
Computer Center (shared)
Arthur A Houghton, Jr Gallery of The Cooper Union

SCHOLARSHIPS/AID

All students admitted to The Cooper Union's degree-granting programs receive the equivalent of a full-tuition scholarship.
For information on other forms of financial assistance, contact:
The Office of Financial Aid and Career Counseling
41 Cooper Square
New York, NY 10003

UNDERGRADUATE PROGRAM
Philosophy Statement

Students of architecture are expected to have a deep personal involvement in their chosen profession. The faculty encourages students to develop their own understanding and recognition of basic principles. The stress on fundamentals is intended to equip the graduate with a lasting ability to produce an architecture responsive to the changing needs of society, one which reflects the potential of newly developed materials and building techniques.

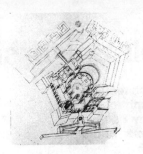

Program Description

The architecture curriculum is designed to prepare men and women for the professional practice of architecture. The program has been developed to equip graduates with a depth of understanding of human needs and a command of technology that will enable them to serve their community by shaping its man-made environment in a responsible and sensitive manner. The courses are related in a way that will focus the analytical powers of the student on the many problems involved in creating shelter and space for the complex needs of our society. Students learn to produce a meaningful synthesis of the social aesthetic, and technological needs for specific structures. Such syntheses are presented in the form of unified design proposals that include the building's setting in the community.

A combination of class lectures and personal discussions with a teaching staff composed of practicing architects guides students in their examination of both the intricacies of today's world and the still valid insights of past generations. By solving a series of design problems of increasing complexity, students are encouraged to develop an individual conviction about the kind of design contribution they must make. To do this, they draw on a growing understanding of their own inherent abilities, a deepening knowledge of principles governing the stucture of the physical environment, an enhanced sense for beauty, and an ever-increasing ability to crystallize and communicate their concepts.

FACULTY

Administration

John Q Hejduk, RA, FAIA, NCARB, Dean
Richard Henderson, RA, Associate Dean
Elizabeth Vajda, Head Librarian

Professors

Raimund J Abraham, Dipl Eng (MS)
Peter D Eisenman, RA, FAIA, NCARB, B Arch, MS Arch, MA, PhD
John Q Hejduk, RA, FAIA, NCARB, Certif in Arch, BS in Arch, M Arch
Richard Henderson, RA, B Arch
Josef Paul Kleihues, Dipl Ing (MS)
Ricardo M Scofidio, RA, NCARB, Certif in Arch, B Arch
Ysrael A Seinuk, PE, FACI, Deg in Civil Eng
Chester Wisniewski, RA, NCARB, B Arch

Associate Professors

Sue F Gussow, BS, MFA
Diane H Lewis, RA, B Arch

Part-Time Faculty

Diana Agrest, Dipl Arch
Mary Beth Betts, BA, PhD (in progress)
Kevin Bone, RA, B Arch
Christine Boyer, BA, MS, MCP, PhD
Arthur E Bye, RLA, FASLA, BS
Anthony Candido, B Arch
George Chaikin, B Arch, MS

Fred Chomowicz, RA, Certif in Arch
Elizabeth Diller, B Arch
Jay F Fellows, BA, MA, PhD
Robert James, RA, B Arch
Roderick L Knox, RA, NCARB, BFA, B Arch, M Arch
Toshiko Mori, RA, B Arch
Elizabeth O'Donnell, RA, B Arch
Sean W Sculley, RA, BA, B Arch
David J Shapiro, BA, MA, PhD
Joel Silverman, PE, BEE
Michael Sorkin, BA, MA, M Arch
Richard G Stein, RA, FAIA, NCARB, Certif, B Arch, M Arch
Michael Webb, Dipl
Regi Weile, RA, NCARB, B Arch
Tod C Williams, RA, NCARB, BA, MFA, LDS
Lebbeus Woods
Guido Zuliani, Dipl

Adjunct Faculty

Paul Bailyn, BME, MS, PhD
Alan Wolf, BS, MA, PhD

Cornell University

College of Architecture, Art and Planning
143 East Sibley Hall
Ithaca, New York 14853-6701
(607) 255-5236

Undergraduate Admissions
135 East Sibley Hall
Ithaca, New York 14853
(607) 255-4376

Application Deadline(s): Nov. 1 - Early decision applicants
Jan. 1 - Freshman applicants
Tuition & Fees: Undgrd: $11,500/yr
Grad: $11,500/yr
Endowment: Private

DEGREE PROGRAMS

Degree	Minimum Years for Degree	Accred.	Requirements for Admission	Full-Time Stdnts.	Part-Time Stdnts.	% of Applics. Accptd.	Stdnts. in 1st Year of Program	# of Degrees Conferred
B Arch	5	NAAB	4 units Eng and math, 1 unit physics, 3 units for lang rec.	300	0	21%	70	45
M Arch	2		B Arch grad standing	35	0	11%	17	13
BS Arch Hist	4		transfer after 2 years undgrd study	5	0	—	—	1

SCHOOL DEMOGRAPHICS (all degree programs)

Full-Time Faculty	Part-Time Faculty	Full-Time Students	Part-Time Students	Foreign Students	Out-of-State U.S. Stdnts.	Women Students	Minority Students
25	10	340	0	15%	68%	43%	26%

LIBRARY (Tel. No. 607-255-6719)

Type	No. of Volumes	No. of Slides
Fine Arts (Arch, Art and Planning)	116,000	300,200

STUDENT OPPORTUNITIES AND RESOURCES

The diverse programs in our college draw on the liberal arts to help students understand the present world and the accomplishments of the past as well as the concepts and tools of tomorrow. The development of technical skills is combined with the development of individual judgment and the confidence to make independent decisions. The most important aspects of our college are the quality of the faculty members and their dedication to students' individual growth. The small size of the college encourages strong interaction between the faculty and students as well as the special student relationships that are so important to the educational experience.

Students in our college have the opportunity to attend special lectures and exhibits, participate in programs in Rome and in Washington, D.C., take field trips to major cities to see buildings and visit art galleries and museums, and talk to major figures in the fields of art, architecture, and planning. Whether their interests are in the broad-based program in urban studies, the professional program in architecture, or the creative fields of fine arts, our college is dedicated to helping the students of today prepare for the world of tomorrow.

SPECIAL ACTIVITIES AND PROGRAMS

WASHINGTON PROGRAM. The Cornell-in-Washington program provides for architecture students a period of intensive exposure to the characteristics of urban development within the framework of a design studio. The concentration is on urban design issues, restraints relative to financing, zoning, development criteria, adaptive reuse, and multiuse developments.

ROME PROGRAM. The program offers architecture students a semester in Rome and access to academic facilities in the Palazzo Massimo. It is a special opportunity to observe, analyze, and speculate about the city in a direct, empirical way. The city, its architecture, painting, and sculpture, and the connections between those forms as well as the personal and cultural conditions of their creation are the subjects of the program.

SUMMER TERM IN ARCHITECTURAL DESIGN. The six-to-eight-week summer term in architectural design offers undergraduate and graduate students a concentrated period of design work. Undergraduate design-sequence courses are offered at the second- through fifth-year levels on the Ithaca campus. The Department of Architecture also provides a variety of opportunities for study abroad through the summer design studio, offered at the third-, fourth-, and fifth-year levels. Most recently, teams of faculty members conducted programs in Japan, Berlin, Paris-Veneto, the Aegean, and Norden (Scandinavia and Finland). Students from schools of architecture other than Cornell's are welcome to apply to the college for admission to any summer program in architecture.

OVERLAP PROGRAM. For qualified students, the department offers an option that combines the fifth year of the undergraduate B Arch program with the first year of the Master of Architecture program.

FACILITIES

The college occupies four buildings at the north end of the Arts Quadrangle. Students in the college work in physical proximity to one another, thereby gaining a broader understanding of other disciplines as well as of their own special areas of interest.

Departmental staff and faculty offices, college administrative offices, and architecture department studios and classrooms are housed in Sibley and Rand Halls. To assist students in preparation of plans and models, a blueprint machine and a woodworking and metal shop are located in Rand Hall.

In the past year the department has established a computer-aided design studio as part of the fourth-year architectural design sequence. The new CAD facility is stocked with state-of-the-art computer graphics display technology.

The college maintains the F.M. Wells Memorial Slide Collection. Its 300,000 slides include extensive holdings in architectural history and an increasingly comprehensive collection of slides on art and architecture from all parts of the world. The Fine Arts Library, in Sibley Dome, established in 1870 by Andrew D. White, Cornell's first president, has an outstanding 116,000-volume book collection.

SCHOLARSHIPS/AID

The College of Architecture, Art, and Planning is a privately endowed unit of the university. Tuition for the 1986-87 academic year is $11,500. The estimated cost of room and board is $3,825.

Personal expenses, including books, are estimated at $1,175. In addition, students in the college incur expenses for art and design supplies.

Financial-aid awards are made according to need, and financial need is not considered in the admission decision. To apply for financial assistance, applicants must complete the form included in the Cornell application packet and the Financial Aid Form of the College Scholarship Service. Awards include a combination of scholarship and loan funds and work-study employment.

UNDERGRADUATE PROGRAM
Philosophy Statement

If one could identify a singular philosophy for the architecture program at Cornell, it would be that architecture is a conceptual problem-solving discipline. The goal of the program is to produce conceptual thinkers, versed in the skills, history, theory, and science of their field.

The intention has always been to instruct architecture students in issues of basic and more sophisticated formal principles, developing an aptitude for functional and programmatic accommodation, structural and technological integration, energy-conscious design, and materials and methods of construction.

Rather than train architects who think of buildings as autonomous objects frozen in an assigned ideology, our goal is to produce architects who are capable of making independent judgments rooted in an ever-changing context of architectural thought.

Program Description

The first professional degree in architecture is the Bachelor of Architecture. This degree counts toward the professional registration requirements established by the various states and the National Council of Architectural Registration Boards. The professional program is normally five years in length and is designed particularly for people who, before they apply, have established their interest and motivation to enter the field. It therefore incorporates both a general and professional educational base.

The program is oriented toward developing the student's ability to deal creatively with architectural problems on analytical, conceptual, and developmental levels. The sequence courses in design, consisting of studio work augmented by lectures and seminars dealing with theory and method, are the core of the program. Sequences of studies in human behavior, environmental science, structures, and building technology provide a base for the work in design.

During the five-year program, the student has the opportunity to establish a foundation in the humanities and sciences through electives. This base may be expanded by further studies in these areas. Within the professional program, a basis for understanding architecture in its contemporary and historical cultural context is established.

The structure of the program incorporates considerable flexibility for the individual student to pursue his or her particular interest in the fourth and fifth years. By carefully planning options and electives in the fifth year, it is possible for a qualified student to apply the last year's work to the Bachelor of Architecture degree and to one of the graduate programs offered in the department. Some students are then able to complete the requirements for the master's degree in one additional year.

GRADUATE PROGRAM
Philosophy Statement

At Cornell University the uniqueness of the graduate program in Architecture is that it is a post-professional degree program requiring a first professional degree. Therefore, the program can assume a background in architecture, and can concentrate on the development of a critical attitude toward the profession and the production of architecture as a whole, and architectural education. This is done by means of the development of an integrative understanding of history, architectural theory and criticism and the development of sophistication of skills through design and research.

Program Description

The Master of Architecture degree program offers two areas of major concentration: architectural design and urban design. Both areas stress the integration of history, theory and practical skills, and design. The area of architectural design concentrates on the dialectic between architecture and the city. The area of urban design focuses on a distinct urban design methodology clearly complementing the current neo-positivistic urban planning practice. The program is not based on a set coursework and is individually tailored to the area of each student's thesis. Four terms of residence and a minimum of sixty credits are required to complete the program of study. Of these, thirty-six are in design studio work and between nine and twelve in an area of minor concentration within or outside the graduate field of architecture. The remaining twelve to fifteen credits are to be taken in general courses, of which at least six are to be taken outside the field of architecture, preferably outside the College of Architecture, Art and Planning, in order to ensure a broad course of study.

Students who are excelling in the undergraduate program of the Department of Architecture at Cornell and who wish to apply to the Graduate Program have the opportunity to have their fifth year of the undergraduate program overlap with their first year of the graduate program. The student is allowed to transfer a maximum of 30 credits toward the requirements for the Masters Degree which are in excess of the distribution requirements for the Bachelor of Architecture. The last year of studio work is done in the graduate design studio. After six years of study and upon successful completion of the requirements for both the undergraduate program as well as the Master's Thesis, the overlap student is awarded a Bachelor of Architecture as well as the Master of Architecture degrees.

FACULTY
Administration

William G McMinn, RA, FAIA, Dean
Val K Warke, RA, Chairman, Architecture
Judith Holliday, University Librarian

Professors

Donald Greenberg, BCE, PhD
Lee Hodgden, BS Arch Eng, M Arch
Alexander Kira, B Arch, MRP
Leonard Mirin, AB, MLA
Christian Otto, BA, MA, PhD
Charles Pearman, B Arch
Colin Rowe, MA
Mario Schack, Dipl Arch, M Arch in UD
John Shaw, B Arch, M Arch
Jerry A Wells, B Arch

Associate Professors

Werner Goehner, Dipl Ing ETH
George Hascup, B Arch
Martin Kubelik, BA Dipl Ing, MA, DR Ing
Archie Mackenzie, B Arch, M Arch
John Miller, B Arch, M Arch
Tom Peters, MTC Dipl Arch, DR Sc Techn
Henry Richardson, B Arch, M Arch, MRP
Val K Warke, B Arch, M Arch

Assistant Professors

Michael Cohen, B Sci, M Sci
Roy Hall, MS
Mark Jarzombek, BA, Dipl Arch, PhD
Bonnie MacDougall, PhD
Vincent Mulcahy, BA, M Arch
Jonathan Ochshorn, M Arch
John Ostlund, B Arch, M Arch
David Salmon, BS, MS, PhD
Andrea Simitch, B Arch
Mary Woods, BA, MA, M Phil, PhD
John Zissovici, B Arch, M Arch

Instructor

Arthur Ovaska, B Arch

Part-Time Faculty

Matthew Bell
Ralph Crump, B Arch
Michael Dennis, B Arch
Guillaume Jullian, BA, Dipl Arch
Ann Pendleton, M Arch
Pamela Scott, BA, MA

University of Detroit

School of Architecture
University of Detroit
4001 West McNichols Road
Detroit, Michigan 48221
(313) 927-1532

Admissions Office
(313) 927-1245

Application Deadline(s): Rolling admissions up to one month prior to the beginning of a term.
Tuition & Fees: Undgrd: $3450/term
Endowment: Private

DEGREE PROGRAMS

Degree	Minimum Years for Degree	Accred.	Requirements for Admission	Full-Time Stdnts.	Part-Time Stdnts.	% of Applics. Accptd.	Stdnts. in 1st Year of Program	# of Degrees Conferred
B Arch	5	NAAB	ACT or SAT, HS diploma, upper 1/3 of class (transfer: 3.00 Avg., Portfolio for transfer credit in design or graphics.)	185	26	N/A	70	30

SCHOOL DEMOGRAPHICS (all degree programs)

Full-Time Faculty	Part-Time Faculty	Full-Time Students	Part-Time Students	Foreign Students	Out-of-State U.S. Stdnts.	Women Students	Minority Students
8	10	185	26	14%	45%	24%	15%

LIBRARY (Tel. No. 313-927-1071)

Type	No. of Volumes	No. of Slides
Main Lib	441,176	21,075

STUDENT OPPORTUNITIES AND RESOURCES

Architecture begins with a basic understanding of human nature and of the relationship of people to their environment. Certain technical skills and special knowledge are also required by the architect to translate ideas into the documents that others will use to complete those ideas and turn them into concrete reality; places where people live, work, worship, study, shop, park, or play. To develop this competence in students, the School of Architecture at the University of Detroit offers a five-year professional degree program that leads to a Bachelor of Architecture degree.

To help students through these eventful years and ensure that they get the most from their educational experience, the school uses a personal advisory approach.

Students choose one of the architecture professors to act as adviser. The adviser can offer practical academic counseling based on professional knowledge of the field. This advisory relationship begins in the freshman year and continues through graduation.

The School of Architecture houses studios that provide an individual work station for each student, as well as such adjunct facilities as a model shop, photography darkroom, exhibition space, seminar rooms, and the Architecture Learning Resource Center containing slides, reference materials periodicals, and books.

The University of Detroit has one of the few architectural schools in the nation to integrate cooperative education into its professional degree program. Students alternate terms of classroom education with terms of co-op training assignments. Each student's employment must be related to some phase of the field of architecture, and the professional training normally increases in responsibility as a student progresses through the curriculum. This requirement offers important advantages. With the placement assistance of the co-op coordinator, students can test their aptitude for a particular segment of the field. The real-life situation gives students insight into the difference between theory and actual design practice. Under the supervision of a registered architect, they obtain practical experience that may also fulfill part of the internship requirement. Many are invited back to their co-op firms to complete the remainder of their cooperative training; students are frequently offered full-time positions in these firms after graduation. The five-year program enables a graduate to enter almost any area in the profession of architecture, from design to management.

The faculty has been selected on the basis of design excellence, diversity of opinion, and professional experience, as well as professional interest apart from design. All faculty members are involved on several levels of the educational program and are required to maintain sufficient involvement in professional practice to avoid academic narrowmindedness.

As important as the offerings within the School of Architecture are the opportunities provided by the greater school outside—the city of Detroit. This laboratory provides realistic case studies and planning problems. Detroit also offers students cultural activities, exhibitions, and lectures. Since this city is the hub of a great industrial complex, students become acquainted with social and historical forces that architects must understand in carrying out their responsibilities. Development of such understanding in students is one of the principal concerns of the School of Architecture.

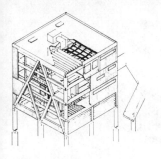

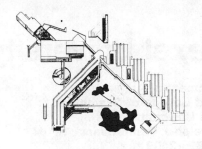

SPECIAL ACTIVITIES AND PROGRAMS

Architects' Day Program (each spring, student-faculty sketch problem)

Beaux Arts Ball

Kite-flying Contest (all-day design and construction of 3-D kite, most magnificent failure by specific standards receives the Charlie Brown award)

Community design activities (for credit)

Summer design studios for out-of-phase and/or transfer students

Dichotomy (journal of theory and criticism operated solely by students)

Exchange Program with the Technical University of Warsaw (for term 1 each year, open to fourth-year students)

Guest Lecture Series (invited guest lecturers of national or regional interest)

International study — summer term in Florence and Volterra, Italy

Co-operative Education Training — mandatory 3 terms beginning at the end of third term

Ictinus Design Awards for student work

AIAS-organized film program

FACILITIES

The University of Detroit is a private Jesuit institution of 6300 students located on an urban campus. The School of Architecture is housed in the Architecture Building which it shares with the University's Theater Department. In this building are studios, shops and lecture rooms. Residential facilities are available on campus.

SCHOLARSHIPS/AID

Students at the School of Architecture participate in every type of financial aid available at a private university. In 1985-86, 78% of the students enrolled in Architecture received financial aid totaling $798,646. This amount includes both Federal aid and State aid, as well as institutional scholarships in the amount of $278,017.

UNDERGRADUATE PROGRAM
Philosophy Statement

The aims of the School of Architecture are predicated upon the belief that there are universal principles in architecture that are valid because they derive from the nature of man, his psychology, his intellect, and his emotions. It is felt that architecture, or any other art form, is not something in and of itself but rather has a social responsibility.

Furthermore, the faculty of the school feels that the disciplines of architecture and the arts are means to an end, namely the expression of the spirit of man, and that this expression should be oriented toward a definition of the environment in such terms as to enlighten understanding of the unique values of life.

This is a design-oriented school; beauty is seen as a critical element in human existence. Neither design nor beauty is intended here to convey superficial cosmetics or styles. Indeed, the entire concept of style, whether derived from a movement or a single individual, is rejected, although the possible values derived therefrom are not deprecated. Simply, the school is totally concerned with the individual development of each student and with developing a meaningful problem-solving process devoid of superficial or spurious attributes.

Program Description

The undergraduate program has, as its purpose, the establishment of a solid base of professional skills as well as an appropriate background in the humanities. It is expected that this will provide the student with the perception of architecture as espoused in the school's philosophy rather than as a technical or artistic activity unrelated to man in the environment.

The undergraduate sequence, while providing the essential disciplines of design, structures, urbanism, and history and theory, also allows approximately 30 percent of the course content to be selected at the option of the student in the areas of electives and the humanities.

It is possible, but not necessary, for a student to focus these choices into either of two defined certificate programs: Business Certificate or Land Development Certificate. Both programs provide students with a solid foundation in economic issues relevant to the practice of architecture. Neither program extends the length of degree completion.

FACULTY
Administration

Bruno Leon, FAIA, Dean
Patricia A Martinico, Assistant Dean for Administration
Jonathon Gillham, Reference Librarian

Professors

Nicholas Chatas, RA, B Arch
Bruno Leon, FAIA, B Arch, RA
Robert Tucker, RA, B Arch

Associate Professors

Stephen LaGrassa, RA, B Arch, M Arch
John Mueller, RA, BS Arch

Assistant Professors

Robert Arens, RA, BSc, M Arch
Terrance Curry, B Arch
Frank Fantauzzi, M Arch
Anthony Martinico, AB, B Arch
Joseph Odoerfer, RA, M Arch

Part-Time Faculty

Frederick Bidigare, B Arch
Thomas O'Connor, BSAE
Paul Reehil, B Arch, JD
James Weeks, BFA, MA
Miriam Wisnewska, D Arch

Adjunct Faculty

Sarah Gravelle, PhD

Drexel University

Department of Architecture
Nesbitt College of Design Arts
Drexel University
Philadelphia, Pennsylvania 19104
(215) 895-2409

Office of Admissions
Drexel University
32nd and Chestnut Streets
Philadelphia, Pennsylvania 19104
(215) 895-2400

Application Deadline(s): Mid-August
Mid-November
Tuition & Fees: Undgrd: $3279/yr ($131/credit hour)
Endowment: Private

DEGREE PROGRAMS

Degree	Minimum Years for Degree	Accred.	Requirements for Admission	Full-Time Stdnts.	Part-Time Stdnts.	% of Applics. Accptd.	Stdnts. in 1st Year of Program	# of Degrees Conferred
B Arch	8*	NAAB	HS Diploma	—	227	75%	60	12

*Work-study program, evenings only

SCHOOL DEMOGRAPHICS (all degree programs)

Full-Time Faculty	Part-Time Faculty	Full-Time Students	Part-Time Students	Foreign Students	Out-of-State U.S. Stdnts.	Women Students	Minority Students
1	43	—	227	1%	28%	19%	5%

LIBRARY (Tel. No. 215-895-2768)

Type	No. of Volumes	No. of Slides
University	25,800 (Arch)	29,200 (Arch)

STUDENT OPPORTUNITIES AND RESOURCES

Drexel University has always been committed to part-time programs. Architecture has been offered continuously since 1895 at the University, and always in the evening. The work/study opportunity integrates the Department of Architecture into the University system of cooperative education and opens the study of architecture to a great diversity of students. In this program, students are older than most undergraduates; the average age is 23, and the average graduating age is 30. Over 75% of Drexel students have had previous college experience, and one third of the students already have a degree in another field. Transfer students are accepted from professional and pre-professional programs. While enrolled at Drexel, students often develop positions of responsibility in architectural firms. The students tend to be highly motivated since a part-time educational program, when combined with a full-time professional position, requires a significant personal commitment. Because of their work experience, it is not unusual for students to pass their registration exams immediately following graduation.

The evening format enables the Department to draw from the expertise and experience of the professional community in the Philadelphia area. Most of the faculty are in private practice, and some teach at other institutions. The faculty numbers 30 per quarter, all of whom teach part-time.

The Drexel campus is located on the edge of central Philadelphia. Students thus have ample opportunity for outside cultural, educational, and architectural experiences. Libraries, museums, theaters, and concert halls are within easy reach. Philadelphia's historical background and rich architectural tradition make the city an ideal laboratory for the study of architecture.

SPECIAL ACTIVITIES AND PROGRAMS

Guest Lecture Series

Tours of East Coast cities

Summer study tour abroad

Competitions and awards

Exhibits

Job placement services

Guest professionals from the Philadelphia region deliver supplemental lectures and serve as jurors for the critique of studio work

Drexel Architectural Society (student organization)

DAS Forum (student publication)

Fall, winter, and spring socials (students)

SCHOLARSHIPS/AID

Need-based financial assistance is offered in the form of remission of tuition. Student loans (Guaranteed Student Loans, PLUS Loans, and HELP Loans) and Pell Grants (Basic Educational Opportunity Grants) are also available through the Financial Aid Office. Partial scholarship awards are made for scholastic achievement to first, second, fourth, and fifth-year students. Certain architectural employers in the Philadelphia area offer tuition remission to their employees.

UNDERGRADUATE PROGRAM
Philosophy Statement

The graduates of this program should master the basic knowledge and skills of professional practice, as well as developing an awareness of the values and aspirations of contemporary society. The work/study opportunity offers a continuous dialogue between school and work; between theory and practice. Placing students in this dual position reinforces the notion that the practice of architecture is a continuous learning process.

Program Description

The Department of Architecture offers a single program leading to the degree of Bachelor of Architecture. This is a first professional degree and is recognized by the National Architectural Accrediting Board. The course of study usually takes 8 years to complete, but exceptional students can reduce its length to 6 years by meeting specific departmental requirements. The program is structured into three areas of study: (1) the studio design sequence (72 quarter credits); (2) required and elective architectural course work (66 quarter credits); and (3) general education requirements (54 quarter credits). Although the program permits students considerable choice in the selection and scheduling of course work, the studio sequence regulates the student's progress.

The lower level studios offer problems of increasing formal, social, and technical complexity ending in the 5th year Studio which emphasizes the integration of building systems into the design process. The upper level studios stress independence and development. The 6th year is built around architecture and the urban context. In the 7th and 8th years, students undertake year-long independent projects.

All classes meet once a week for 3 hour sessions. Most students take two or three courses per quarter. Attendance during the Summer Quarter is optional. Students are expected to supplement their academic work through full-time employment in architectural offices.

FACULTY
Administration

Dr J Michael Adams, Dean
Paul M Hirshorn, AIA, Head
Deborah F Sheesley, General College Librarian

Associate Professor

Paul M Hirshorn, AIA, MCP, MA, M Arch

Instructor

Robert B Ennis, BA, B Arch, MA

Adjunct Professors (Part-Time)

Peter F Arfaa, FAIA, M Arch
Sylvia Clark, RA, M Arch
Charles E Dagit, FAIA, M Arch
David C Hamme, B Arch
Marjorie Kriebel, RA, B Arch
Jon T Lang, PhD
Walter H Moleski, AIA, B Arch, MS
Mark Ueland, AIA, B Arch, M Arch

Adjunct Associate Professors (Part-Time)

Judith Bing, M Arch
John Dundon, AIA, B Arch, M Arch
Alan J Greenberger, AIA, B Arch
J Brooke Harrington, AIA, B Arch
Nadir Lahiji, B Arch, M Arch, PhD
Elizabeth W Lawson, AIA, B Arch
Arlene Matzkin, RA, B Arch
Donald Matzkin, RA, B Arch
Gilbert A Rosenthal, AIA, B Arch, M Arch
Otto Sperr, AIA, M Arch

Adjunct Assistant Professors (Part-Time)

Stephen Bonitatibus, AIA, M Arch
Richard E Brown, AIA, B Arch
Steven C Gatschet, AIA, B Arch
John O Higgins, B Arch, MS Urb Dsgn
Daniel O Kelley, AIA, M Arch
James Mitchell, AIA, M Arch
Kenneth J Mizerny, BSL Arch, ML Arch
Gray Read, M Arch
Joseph Scanlon, RA, B Arch
Jahan Sheikholeslami, AIA, M Arch

Instructors (Part-Time)

Sherman Aronson, M Arch
Faith Baum, RA, M Arch
Margaret Bemiss, M Arch
Andrew A Blanda, B Dsgn, M Arch
Alfred Borden, MFA
Alina Brajtberg, M Arch
Gianne Conard, AIA, BA, B Arch
James Dart, M Arch
Paul Halamar, BS
Don Jones, RA, M Arch
Jeffrey Krieger, RA, M Arch
Daniel K McCoubrey, RA, M Arch
Lawrence D McEwen, AIA, M Arch
Arthur Miller, AIA, B Arch
Jon Morrison, BS, MS
Serge Nalbantian, B Arch
Robert Nalls, AIA, M Arch
Terry Plater, M Arch
Rachel Schade, RA, M Arch
Douglas Seiler, RA, M Arch
Michael Stoneking, B Arch
Simon Tickell, RA, M Arch
James Williamson, M Arch
Michael Ytterberg, M Arch

Drury College

Hammons School of Architecture
Drury College
900 N. Benton Avenue
Springfield, Missouri 65802
(417) 865-8731 x288

Admissions Office
(417) 865-8731 x205

Application Deadline(s): August 1
Tuition & Fees: Undgrd: $5415 (excluding
 room & board)/yr
Endowment: Private

DEGREE PROGRAMS

Degree	Minimum Years for Degree	Accred.	Requirements for Admission	Full-Time Stdnts.	Part-Time Stdnts.	% of Applics. Accptd.	Stdnts. in 1st Year of Program	# of Degrees Conferred
B Arch	5	Candidacy Status	HS Diploma	92	15	80%	46	7

SCHOOL DEMOGRAPHICS (all degree programs)

Full-Time Faculty	Part-Time Faculty	Full-Time Students	Part-Time Students	Foreign Students	Out-of-State U.S. Stdnts.	Women Students	Minority Students
7	9	92	15	5%	15%	25%	10%

LIBRARY (Tel. No. 417-865-8731 x282)

Type	No. of Volumes	No. of Slides
College	300,000	32,000

STUDENT OPPORTUNITIES AND RESOURCES

Drury College is a small private liberal arts institution which was founded in 1873. Drury has an enrollment of 1100 day students and 1800 evening students. The college was founded as an undergraduate liberal arts institution and it has remained true to that mission while developing several high quality graduate and professional programs which are distinctive because of their liberal arts orientation (MBA, M Ed, and B Arch).

In recent years, through a very successful admissions effort, the college has improved the quality of the student body without a reduction in size. The student body's average ACT score of 23 is well above the national average, and it is anticipated that that average will continue to go up.

Through the generous support of Mr. John Q. Hammons, a local developer and member of the Drury College Board of Trustees, Drury College has been able to establish the Hammons School of Architecture. With Mr. Hammons' pledge to assist the college in building an $8.4 million endowment for the architecture program, the college is assured of the necessary resources required to establish a program of excellence. These funds will be used to construct the new architecture facility and provide for the program's long range financial support.

SPECIAL ACTIVITIES AND PROGRAMS

Architecture Lecture Series
Architecture Exhibition Series
Annual Cox Gallery Exhibition of Student Work
Architecture Awareness Week
Springfield Pre-Cast Concrete Company Competition
Architecture Field Trips
Sophomore and Junior Student Trip

Foreign Study Program
American Institute of Architecture Students (AIAS)
AIAS/AIA Professional Advisor Program
Student Awards Program:
 Outstanding Freshman Student
 Outstanding Sophomore Student
 Outstanding Junior Student
 Outstanding Senior Student
 Outstanding Fifth-Year Student
 Liberal Arts in Architecture Award
 American Institute of Architect's Book Award
Liberal Arts Lecture Series
Weekly Interdisciplinary Seminars
Center for Community Studies
Joint B Arch/MBA Program
Minors Available in 26 College Programs

FACILITIES

Drury College is currently planning the construction of a new 41,500 square foot architecture facility by the spring of 1989. This facility will accommodate 175 architecture students, 12 full-time and 6 part-time faculty, the combined art and architecture slide library, an environmental and structures technology lab, and a 40-workstation computer-aided design lab. This $4 million facility will be located at the entrance to the campus and symbolize the college's commitment to the integration of the architecture program into the liberal arts college.

The interim facilities provide adequate space for the architecture program. The college has made an initial investment of $500,000 for a 16-workstation mainframe computer-aided design system, $250,000 for the development of the base library collection, and $50,000 for the expansion of the combined art and architecture slide collection to 72,000 slides.

SCHOLARSHIPS/AID

Many types of scholarships and financial aid are available for Drury students. Forms can be obtained after Jan. 1 from a high school counselor or the Drury Financial Aid Office. An applicant should complete these forms and mail them as soon as possible; the earlier the forms are processed, the more possibilities for financial assistance. None of the programs reserve any funds for late applicants.

Financial aid up to the full amount of tuition may be awarded without respect to a student's need by use of certain academic and activity scholarships. Much of Drury's financial aid, however, is awarded on the basis of student need. A student's aid package may consist of federal and state grants, work-study (in which a student is paid for a campus job), loans, and a variety of Drury scholarships and grants.

UNDERGRADUATE PROGRAM
Philosophy Statement

The small liberal arts context of Drury College provides a positive framework for the development of a professional architecture program which seeks to help students to develop in the following areas: communication skills, critical thinking, the ability to make mature value judgments, empathy, self-confidence, and health and well-being. Clearly, the professional architectural program must effectively integrate the humanistic, moral, and ethical issues of the liberal arts with the technological requirements of design to achieve this mission. Since the strength of this architecture program is dependent upon the liberal arts context within which it exists, this professional program cannot be conceived or perceived in isolation of the college.

Program Description

The Bachelor of Architecture degree is a 2+3 program of study. The first two years constitute the Pre-Professional portion of the program and focus on the ideational aspects of architecture. Admission to the Pre-Professional portion of the program is open to all Drury College students.

The last three years of the curriculum are considered the Professional portion of the program and focus specifically on the quantitative aspects of architecture. Students apply for admission to the Professional Program at the end of the fall semester of their sophomore year. This application requires a written goal statement, transcript, and portfolio of work.

The five-year program requires 168 credit hours of instruction, a summer foreign study course, and a 12-week summer work experience. Included are 54 credit hours of general education course work, which is required of all Drury students, and 15 credit hours of free electives which may be used to develop a minor in any of the 26 programs of study at Drury College.

The Hammons School of Architecture is committed to the concept of personalized instruction. Towards this end, the school plans to maintain a low 12:1 student/teacher ratio, individual academic advisors, personalized assessment of professional development, and alternate career guidance. This will provide the students with an academic support system which is flexible and responsive to their particular needs and aspirations.

FACULTY
Administration

Jay G Garrott, AIA, Director
Judith Armstrong, Director of Library Services

Associate Professors

Jay G Garrott, AIA, M Arch
James B Griffin, AIA, M Arch

Assistant Professors

Martin Bailkey, MLA
Howard Iber, AIA, MS Arch
John McGuire, AIA, M Arch
Bruce E Moore, AIA, M Arch
Alkis Tsolakis, AIA, M Arch

Part-Time Faculty

Tom Beckley, BS
Charles C Hill, AIA, B Arch

Adjunct Faculty

Joyce Bonacker, MFA
Harriett Mears, BFA
Dudley Murphy, MFA
Tom Parker, MFA
Royle Vagle, M Ed
Jacqueline Warren, MFA

Special Instructor

Marcia Alscher, B Arch

Florida A&M University

School of Architecture
Florida A&M University
1936 So. Martin Luther King Blvd.
Tallahassee, Florida 32307
(904) 599-3244

Admissions Office
Foote-Hilyer Administration Building
Florida A&M University
Tallahassee, Florida 32307
(904) 599-2796

Application Deadline(s): For fall term: Mid-July
For spring term:
December 1
For summer term:
April 1
Tuition & Fees: Undgrd: Fla. Res: $1155 avg/yr
Non-Res: $2910 avg/yr
Grad: Fla. Res: $2754 avg/yr
Non-Res: $3948 avg/yr
Endowment: Public

DEGREE PROGRAMS

Degree	Minimum Years for Degree	Accred.	Requirements for Admission	Full-Time Stdnts.	Part-Time Stdnts.	% of Applics. Accptd.	Stdnts. in 1st Year of Program	# of Degrees Conferred
BS	4	—	2.5 GPA, 19/ACT, 900/SAT	205	21	57%	74	13
B Arch	5	NAAB	2.75 GPA in upper division courses	27	5	93%	25	39
MS	1½	—	3.0 GPA and/or 1000 GRE	10	3	22%	2	1
M Arch (4-semesters)	2	NAAB	3.0 GPA and/or 1000 GRE, 4-year BS Degree, Letter of Intent, Resume, Portfolio, 3 letters of reference, Admissions Exercise and Admission Information Form	16	4	22%	12	5

SCHOOL DEMOGRAPHICS (all degree programs)

Full-Time Faculty	Part-Time Faculty	Full-Time Students	Part-Time Students	Foreign Students	Out-of-State U.S. Stdnts.	Women Students	Minority Students
17	4	258	33	7%	7%	16%	40%

LIBRARY (Tel. No. 904-599-3244)

Type	No. of Volumes	No. of Slides
Arch	7,222	35,000

STUDENT OPPORTUNITIES AND RESOURCES

Founded in 1975, the Florida A&M School of Architecture is relatively small (approximately 300 students), offering a close relationship between faculty and students. The faculty and students form a highly diversified group of individuals with a wide range of ages, backgrounds, and knowledge. Students come from all parts of Florida and the United States and from various foreign countries.

In addition to being housed in a new, award-winning building (see section on "Facilities" below), students may also participate in the School's Washington, D.C. Architectural Study Center. Many students spend one or more semesters in residence in this highly urban setting. Students may also be involved with research through the School's Institute for Building Sciences, the research and service arm of the school. FAMU's resources are further enhanced by cooperative exchange programs with Florida State University and by the availability of many state government-connected facilities.

Forida A&M University, a member of the State University System, celebrates 100 years of operation in 1987. The campus is located near the downtown center of Tallahassee, Florida's capital, with a population of approximately 119,000.

SPECIAL ACTIVITIES AND PROGRAMS

Through the school's Lecture Series, distinguished men and women in the field of architecture and design are invited each semester to give their broad range of views on current architectural thought and practice. In addition to lecturing, the guest is asked to spend additional time to provide closer contact with students. A Visiting Minority Architect is in residence each year as a full-time faculty member.

The Exhibition Gallery sponsors 10-12 exhibitions per year including both traveling national and international exhibits and shows of student and faculty work.

Student field trips are encouraged and sponsored by the school. Students have traveled as a class to cities such as Atlanta, Boston, Savannah, New York, New Orleans, and Washington, D.C.

Students are encouraged to participate in one or both of the active student organizations—American Institute of

Architects/Students (AIAS) and the National Organization of Minority Architects (NOMA).

FACILITIES

The School moved into its specially designed facility in January, 1985. This unique, award-winning building encloses landscaped courtyards with outdoor conversation areas. In addition to office, studio, and classroom space, the building contains many special labs including: computer lab with CADD capabilities, photography lab, building construction lab with structural testing and demonstration equipment, model-making shop, and environmental technology lab. The building also contains a large Architectural Resources Center (print and non-print media), an Exhibition Gallery, a student lounge, and student association office.

SCHOLARSHIPS/AID

Florida A&M University offers financial aid to students in the form of scholarships, grants, loans, and part-time employment. Funding is from both university and outside sources. The School of Architecture currently has no separate financial aid available for undergraduates, but a few part-time jobs are sometimes available to those who qualify. Information on national, state, and local scholarships that are available to architecture students specifically is kept on reserve in the Architecture Library. Assistance in applying for scholarships is available through the Office of the Dean. Graduate students may receive assistance from the School through research assistantships.

 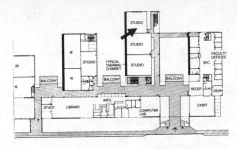 

UNDERGRADUATE PROGRAM
Philosophy Statement

The School of Architecture at Florida A&M University has maintained, from its beginning in 1975, a strong commitment to a balance of concern for the preparation of its students for the profession of architecture and the study of architecture as an academic discipline. Students are expected, upon graduation, to have well developed, entry level, professional skills as well as a philosophy regarding architecture and architectural design that forms the basis for life-long growth as an architect. The realm of architecture is considered inclusive, rather than exclusive; hence, the student acquires a broad range of scholarship while an undergraduate at the FAMU School of Architecture.

Program Description

The School offers professional and non-professional programs at the undergraduate level. The four-year non-professional program leads to a Bachelor of Science in Architectural Studies, and the five-year professional program confers a Bachelor of Architecture degree. The undergraduate curriculum provides a basic education in architecture and the built environment and includes requirements in mathematics, English, sciences, and humanities. Course sequences in architecture include architectural design, design methods, history, structures, environmental technology, building economics, construction, philosophy, and professional practice.

Applicants who wish to transfer into the School of Architecture are evaluated individually for admission and placement in the program. Only those applicants who have received an associate of arts degree from an approved "pre-architecture" program will be considered for direct admission into the junior year at FAMU. Other community college transfer students are required to complete pre-professional courses. These transferees are encouraged to take architecture coursework at FAMU during the summer prior to the fall when they expect to begin their normal coursework.

Admission into Upper Division (third and fourth years) and into the Bachelor of Architecture Program is by application only.

GRADUATE PROGRAM
Philosophy Statement

From its inception, the School of Architecture has attempted to address an expanded definition of architecture and the role of the architect in society. This concern has manifested itself through the areas of emphasis described below.

The overriding concern in each of the areas of emphasis is for people. The philosophy of the graduate program may be summarized as the balanced and careful consideration of both the art and science of architecture. Architecture is defined both as an area of study and as a profession—a dual emphasis that is appropriate to any first professional graduate degree program.

Program Description

At the graduate level, four different degree programs are offered which accommodate students from different backgrounds who may have varied educational and career goals. The four-semester Master of Architecture is designed for students with a four-year non-accredited degree in architecture who wish to earn a professional accredited degree. The program prepares students to practice architecture and provides opportunities to acquire additional skills in areas of specialization in the School. The three-semester Master of Architecture is designed as a second professional degree for students who already have an accredited degree in architecture. Students in this program may concentrate coursework in areas of specialization in the School electives. The eight-semester Master of Architecture is an accelerated curriculum designed for mature students with previous degrees in other fields who wish to earn a professional accredited degree in architecture. The three-semester Master of Science is designed for students who do not wish to earn a professional accredited degree but who desire to take coursework and acquire skills in areas of specialization in the school.

Applicants without architecture backgrounds will be advised regarding requisites to ensure maximum benefit from this program. Within the four graduate degree programs, five areas of curriculum emphasis are available to students: (1) architectural practice, (2) building science and technology, (3) low-cost construction, (4) architects in government and industry, and (5) architectural programming and design.

FACULTY
Administration

Roy F Knight, AIA, Dean
Larry L Peterson, Assistant Dean
Thomas R Martineau, AIA, Director, Institute for Building Sciences
Jeneice K Williams, SOA Librarian

Professors

Thorbjoern Mann, AIA(Assoc), PhD Arch
Ronald Shaeffer, P E, MS
Edward T White, AIA, MS

Associate Professors

Michael Alfano, Jr, AIA, MSUD
Lawrence E Birch, AIA, MS
Richard Crenshaw, ASTM, AIA, ASA, ASES, M Arch
George Dombek, B Arch, MFA
Keith H Grey, MUD
Enn E Ots, RA, M Arch
Larry L Peterson, M Arch
Thomas D Pugh, M Arch
Peter F Stone, RA, M Arch
William R Wiencke, MS

Assistant Professors

Peter Kaufman, BA, MA, MLS, PhD

Instructors

Ronald Lumpkin, M Arch
W Mack Rush, ASID, MS

Part-Time Faculty

Paul Anderson, AIA, B Arch
Bret Hammond, BLA
Craig D Huffman, B Arch
Mark A Lindquist, BA
Linda P Nolan, BFA, MS

University of Florida

College of Architecture
331 Architecture Building
University of Florida
Gainesville, Florida 32611
(904) 392-0205

Office of Admissions
135 Tigert Hall
University of Florida
Gainesville, Florida 32611
(904) 392-1365

Application Deadline(s): February 1
Tuition & Fees: Undgrd: $34-$37/credit hour
               Grad: $58/credit hour
Endowment: Public

DEGREE PROGRAMS

Degree	Minimum Years for Degree	Accred.	Requirements for Admission	Full-Time Stdnts.	Part-Time Stdnts.	% of Applics. Accptd.	Stdnts. in 1st Year of Program	# of Degrees Conferred
B Des	4		2.0 GPA at Junior level	800	50	40%	350	150
M Arch	2	NAAB	3.0 GPA, GRE of 1000, B Des	100	5	50%		50
MA in URP	2	PAB	3.0 GPA, GRE of 1000, bacc degree	60	5			
PhD*	3		3.0 GPA, GRE of 1000, M					
BLA	4	ASLA	2.7 GPA	150				
MLA	2	(New program)	3.0 GPA, GRE of 1000					
BBC	4	ACCE	2.0 GPA, comp of prereq.	350				
MBC/MSBC	1		3.0 GPA, GRE of 1000, bacc in bldg const, arch engr, engr, bus adm	50				
B Des (Int Des)	4	FIDER	2.0 GPA	175				

*Beginning Fall 1988

SCHOOL DEMOGRAPHICS (all degree programs)

Full-Time Faculty	Part-Time Faculty	Full-Time Students	Part-Time Students	Foreign Students	Out-of-State U.S. Stdnts.	Women Students	Minority Students
90	10	1685	60	5.8%	3.4%	25%	10.2%

LIBRARY (Tel. No. 904-392-0222)

Type	No. of Volumes	No. of Slides
Arch	5,000	90,000

STUDENT OPPORTUNITIES AND RESOURCES

Established in 1925, the UF is the oldest and largest of Florida's nine universities, making it the "flagship" institution in Florida. With 35,472 students, 13 colleges, 120 departments, and various research centers, UF provides resources, programs, and disciplines that help the architecture program flourish. Located on 2,200 acres in Gainesville, UF is one of five universities in the nation with all academic disciplines, including engineering, law and medicine. With 150,000 residents, Gainesville is centrally located in North Florida, easily accessible to the Atlantic Ocean and Gulf of Mexico.

The College of Architecture is composed of five programs: Architecture, Urban & Regional Planning, Interior Design, Landscape Architecture, and Building Construction. The Department of Architecture has a four-year program of general education in architecture, followed by a range of options in master's level work. The latter includes advanced design, structures, environmental technology, and historic preservation. The College also offers interdisciplinary participation in special studies courses.

The Department of Architecture maintains a close relationship to the architectural profession through professional organizations, with practicing architects participating in the teaching program.

Students are exposed to real-life problems through numerous research and service projects in the southeastern states and the Caribbean Basin.

SPECIAL ACTIVITIES AND PROGRAMS

Program of visiting critiques and lectures by professionals

Visiting lecture and exhibition series

Preservation Institute: Nantucket (Summer)

Preservation Institute: Caribbean (Summer)

VIA!/Italian Studies Program: Vicenza

Field trips to major cities

Mexico field trip

Work/Study and other Fellowships for selected graduate students

Teaching Assistantships for selected graduate students

Job Placement Program

Design Exploration Program (Summer 3-week session to introduce high school students to design fields)

Student publications and newsletters

Continuing education programs of professional interest

Architecture Advisory Council

Beaux Arts Ball, Arc Larc (Annual College Party)

Annual Spring Theory Symposium (sponsored by Graduate Program)

Annual Awards Program

AIAS, Tau Sigma Delta Chapter, Alpha Rho Chi, Gargoyle Society

FACILITIES

Micro-computer Lab
Intergraph Computer Lab
Photographic Lab
Soils & Concrete Lab
Steel/Welding Lab
Acoustical Modeling Research Lab
Woodworking Lab
Audiovisual/Slide Library
Architecture & Fine Arts Library

SCHOLARSHIPS/AID

The Department of Architecture offers financial assistance determined by various factors including scholastic ability, professional promise, and financial need. Education expenses and financial aid are discussed in the UF publication "Gator Aid," a brochure published by the Office of Student Financial Affairs.

The Graduate School offers the Graduate Council Fellowships as well as graduate fellowships for minorities with stipends ranging to $12,000 for 11 months to students entering for the first time.

Non-Florida Tuition Waivers are available for non-Florida students who hold fellowships or assistantships, or qualify through special programs.

Graduate assistantships up to one-half time are available to students who have sixth-year status.

Loans and Work-Study Financial Aid assistance are available to students who have demonstrated financial need.

UNDERGRADUATE PROGRAM
Philosophy Statement

The intent of the architecture program is to develop in students a desire for learning that will carry beyond their formal education; an attitude of responsibility for the welfare of their clients and the public; a truly professional attitude; the capability to perform in the practice of architecture as it exists today, an ability to discern change in the social, political, economic, and technological aspects of society that have impact on architecture; and an ability to make sound value judgments with respect to these changes.

Program Description

The Undergraduate Program provides the student with a sound foundation for a future career in the profession of architecture by providing a balance of course offerings to produce an architectural generalist, strong in design, who can respond to the present and future needs of society. An eight semester sequence of studio design courses is the backbone of the program. During the first two years, design is paired with the general education requirements necessary for an Associate of Arts degree (approx. 507 of course work), as well as introductory courses in History, Theory, Structures, and Environmental Technology. Admittance to the upper division is selective, based upon quality of studio work. Design studios in years three and four focus on

a wide range and scale of architectural building types in various contextual environments. Field trips to unique urban areas are part of the studio experience. Fall fourth-year design and history can be taken at our summer institute in Vicenza, Italy. Parallel courses in theory, the technologies, architectural practice, as well as electives, produces a student with a strong background in design as well as a solid foundation in the technical aspects of architecture.

GRADUATE PROGRAM
Philosophy Statement

The UF graduate program in architecture was established in 1972, and has become widely recognized as one of the most rigorous professional programs available. The central purpose of the program is to provide advanced professional training to enable architects to assume responsible roles solving complex planning and design problems, and to participate effectively in interdisciplinary development processes.

Since its beginning, the program has constantly evolved in response to change in architecture and urban design, and to a changing perception of educational needs. In 1981, the program requirements were changed to include an individual professional thesis. More recently, urban design has been increasingly emphasized within the Architecture Design Option, complemented by a new program specializing in developing urbanization within the Caribbean nations.

Program Description

The graduate program builds on a foundation of undergraduate studies in architecture. The first semester of study (the graduate professional core) assumes that students have the Bachelor of Design (Architecture) degree equivalent to the UF undergraduate program. In addition, graduate students often have experience working for architects. This strong background enables students to begin with intensive studies presented in the form of lectures, seminars, and studios. On completion of the first semester, students choose an area of special interest. These study paths are design, structures, preservation, and environmental technology.

Students with undergraduate degrees in non-architectural disciplines are eligible for graduate admission; however, they must complete all professional coursework before being granted a degree. These students should plan for three-and-one-half to four years of study to complete the master's program.

A joint graduate program with the Department of Urban & Regional Planning is available. Master's degrees in architecture and planning can be obtained in three years.

FACULTY
Administration

Dr Anthony James Catanese, AICP, Dean
Ralph B Johnson, Assistant Dean
Dr Richard E Schneider, AICP, Associate Dean
Robert T Segrest, Chairman
Gary D Ridgdill, RA, Graduate Program Director
Martin G Gunderson, Undergraduate Program Director
Edward H Teague, Associate University Librarian

Professors

Anthony James Catanese, PhD
Edward T Crain, M Arch
Anthony J Dasta, MS Arc Eng
Ronald W Haase, B Arch
Mark T Jaroszewicz, M Arch
Harold W Kemp, MS Arch
Bertram Y Kinzey, MS
Harry C Merritt, Jr, M Arch
Richard H Morse, M Arch
F Blair Reeves, M Arch
Gary D Ridgdill, M Arch
George Scheffer, MA Arch
Robert T Segrest, M Arch, MCP
Bernard F Voichysonk, MFA
William G Wagner, M Arch
Ira H Winarsky, MFA

Associate Professors

Jennifer Bloomer, M Arch
Francesco Cappellari, M Arch
Maelee T Foster, MFA
Martin G Gundersen, M Arch
Forrest F Lisle, Jr, MA Arch
Charles F Morgan, M Arch
Peter E Prugh, M Arch
Peter L Rumpel, B Arch
Herschel E Shepard, MFA in Arch
Gary D Siebein, M Arch
Manuel M Solis, MS Engr
Karl S Thorne, M Arch
Wiley L Tillman, M Arch
William L Tilson, M Arch
Tony R White, MAE
Thomas R Wood, M Arch

Assistant Professors

Orry W Hill, MA Arch
Mikal Kaul, M Arch
Robert McLeod, M Arch
Richard W Pohlman, M Arch
Thomas C Sammons, M Arch
Kim Tanzer, M Arch

The Frank Lloyd Wright School of Architecture

Taliesin West
Scottsdale, Arizona 85261
(602) 860-2700

Application Deadline(s): Open
Tuition & Fees: Undgrd: $4000/cal yr
Grad: $4000/cal yr
Endowment: Private

DEGREE PROGRAMS

Degree	Minimum Years for Degree	Accred.	Requirements for Admission	Full-Time Stdnts.	Part-Time Stdnts.	% of Applics. Accptd.	Stdnts. in 1st Year of Program	# of Degrees Conferred
Master of Architecture	7		H.S. Graduate/Aptitude	35	0	N/A		

SCHOOL DEMOGRAPHICS (all degree programs)

Full-Time Faculty	Part-Time Faculty	Full-Time Students	Part-Time Students	Foreign Students	Out-of-State U.S. Stdnts.	Women Students	Minority Students
31	—	35		25%	75%	25%	

LIBRARY (Tel. No. 602-860-2700)

Type	No. of Volumes	No. of Slides
Gen Acad	5,000	1,000

STUDENT OPPORTUNITIES AND RESOURCES

The Frank Lloyd Wright School of Architecture is the only one teaching the principles of Organic Architecture, the philosophy central to all learning activities at the school.

The school is small, totaling 35 faculty and a maximum of 35 students. The faculty-student ratio is approximately 1 to 1. The relationship is a master-apprentice one in the classical sense. Major financial support for the school comes from the professional practice of the faculty. The students participate as apprentices in the architectural work of the firm. Students and faculty, all of whom are members of the Taliesin Fellowship, live at Taliesin (Wisconsin) in the summer, and Taliesin West (Arizona) in the winter. All participate in social, esthetic, domestic and maintenance activities as well as work in all areas of architecture and construction. The total life style forms the basis of the experientially-based learning model.

Students are required to take control of their own learning activities, setting the direction and pattern for their work with advice from the faculty.

Both campuses are unique. Both are designated National Landmark properties. Buildings are all designed by Frank Lloyd Wright, and provide examples and demonstration of the philosophy and techniques fundamental to the mission of the institution. The Taliesin Fellowship, in these unique settings, provides a wholly integrated community of learners.

SCHOLARSHIPS/AID

A limited number of scholarships are available. These are usually reserved for students who have been in attendance more than one year and have demonstrated ability and talent in architecture and will not be able to continue without financial aid.

UNDERGRADUATE PROGRAM
Philosophy Statement

The purpose of the Frank Lloyd Wright School of Architecture is the education of students in the teaching of Frank Lloyd Wright in the field of Organic Architecture and to prepare students to enter the profession of architecture. The school aims to produce responsible, cultured, creative human beings who are capable of concentrating upon the obligations of professional life. The methods of teaching are based on learning by doing - traditionally associated with this school since its founding by Mr. and Mrs. Frank Lloyd Wright in 1932 at Taliesin, Spring Green, Wisconsin.

Program Description

Graduate and undergraduate programs are combined into seven years. A student entering from high school and working toward a masters degree will earn one in a minimum of seven years.

GRADUATE PROGRAM
Philosophy Statement

The school offers one degree, Master of Architecture (M Arch). The degree plan is structured to combine baccalaureate and masters level work and requires a minimum of seven years of post-high school experience. The degree plan encompasses a general education program which focuses on basic intellectual and social skills and the arts and professional level preparation in the field of architecture. The total program design involves the integration of five experiential activities and eight learning areas to achieve 38 specifically designated areas of knowledge and abilities. Hallmarks of the philosophy are learning by experience and the integration of all experience. The essence of this philosophy is that living is learning; thus one focus of the educational approach is to develop the skills to maximize learning and involvement in all experiences from the simplest and most mundane to the most complex and exotic. Based upon this philosophy the management of the curriculum is to provide an appropriate range of settings and experiences for the students. In so doing, faculty become co-learners.

Georgia Institute of Technology

College of Architecture
Georgia Institute of Technology
Atlanta, Georgia 30332-0155
(404) 894-4885

Undergraduate Admissions:
(404) 894-4154
Graduate Admissions:
(404) 894-4612

Application Deadline(s):
   Summer & Fall Qtrs: Feb 1;
   Winter Qtr: Oct 1;
   Spring Qtr: Jan 1
   Graduate: Aug 1
Tuition & Fees: Undgrd: GA Res: $602/qtr
   Non-Res: $1789/qtr
   Grad: GA Res: $602/qtr
   Non-Res: $1789/qtr
Endowment: Public

DEGREE PROGRAMS

Degree	Minimum Years for Degree	Accred.	Requirements for Admission	Full-Time Stdnts.	Part-Time Stdnts.	% of Applics. Accptd.	Stdnts. in 1st Year of Program	# of Degrees Conferred
BS*	4		SAT Scores, top 20% HS class	338	52	53%	137	82
M Arch	1		B Arch, Portfolio, Letters	7	0	17%	7	7
M Arch	2	NAAB	BS or B Arch, Portfolio, Letters	177	16	42%	63	64
M Arch/ MCP	2½		2 yr. w/B Arch or 2½ yr. w/BS	1	0	100%	0	1
MCP	2	AICP	BS/BA, Letters	49	5	40%	28	17
MS	2		BS/BA, Letters	0	0	—	0	0
PhD	3		MS, Portfolio, Letters	15	1	5%	4	0

*BS Degrees are also awarded in Building Construction and Industrial Design.

SCHOOL DEMOGRAPHICS (all degree programs)

Full-Time Faculty	Part-Time Faculty	Full-Time Students	Part-Time Students	Foreign Students	Out-of-State U.S. Stdnts.	Women Students	Minority Students
38	9	587	81	4%	28%	30%	8%

LIBRARY (Tel. No. 404-894-4877)

Type	No. of Volumes	No. of Slides
Arch	21,409	48,000

STUDENT OPPORTUNITIES AND RESOURCES

Georgia Tech is a co-educational institution offering study in the disciplines of architecture, engineering, management and science, complemented by a full set of liberal studies courses. A campus location near the heart of downtown Atlanta provides the College of Architecture with an excellent urban laboratory for its five programs in Architecture, Building Construction, Industrial Design, City Planning and the Doctoral Program in Architecture & City Planning. Atlanta, one of America's fastest growing cities and one of the most dynamic in urban growth, offers a diversity of social, cultural, and recreational opportunities in addition to outstanding examples of architecture.

With 11,000 students from all 50 states and 93 foreign countries, Tech is large enough to provide a complete range of student support services, yet small enough to enable an important sense of individuality. Student services include academic and personal counseling, single and married housing, fraternities and sororities, health services, food services, student center, GT bookstore and mall, student athletic complex, varsity and intramural sports, student organizations, yearbook, newspaper, and radio station.

Both freshmen and transfer students are accepted for academic quarters which begin in September, January, March, and June. Graduate Architecture students are admitted for study normally only at the beginning of each academic year.

Faculty of the College of Architecture represent a broad variety of backgrounds, interest and expertise. Over 50% of full-time faculty are active in professional practice. The remainder engage in research or scholarship. Visiting practitioners add an important dimension to the programs, participating in studio, seminar, and lecture courses.

SPECIAL ACTIVITIES AND PROGRAMS

Foreign Study Programs: Paris, France (academic year for fourth-year students), London, England (summer program for sixth-year students) and Cortona, Italy (summer program for all students).

Visiting Professor Program brings prominent practitioners, critics, and scholars to the College for seminars and studios.

Lecture Series by national and international leaders in architecture and related disciplines.

Annual SGF Studio: $7,500 in travel fellowships awarded to the best sixth year studio projects in the College.

Student Council: representation from first through sixth years.

Active chapter of the American Institute of Architecture Students (AIAS).

Student field trips to important architectural sites, e.g., Savannah, GA, Washington, D.C., and Columbus, Indiana.

Joint degree programs in City Planning, Management, and Landscape Architecture.

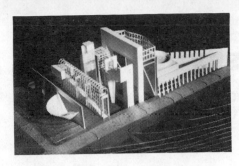

Sponsored research programs in Architectural Conservation, Environment and Behavior, Rehabilitation Technology, Construction, Energy, and Technology are integrated with instructional programs.

FACILITIES

Architecture Library: 21,409 volumes, 48,000 slides.

Research Laboratories located in College: Center for Architecture Conservation, Center for Rehabilitation Technology, and Construction Research Center.

Microcomputer Laboratory: computer graphics, studio applications, technology courses.

Photography Laboratory

Wood & Metal Shops

SCHOLARSHIPS/AID

The College of Architecture administers a number of financial aid opportunities for graduate students, including Fellowships, Research and Teaching Assistantship. The Office of Financial Aid will provide information on financial assistance for undergraduates, including loans and work-study programs.

UNDERGRADUATE PROGRAM
Philosophy Statement

The goal of the four-year undergraduate program is to provide basic architectural knowledge, verbal and design skills along with a broadly based general education. It is designed to prepare students for graduate study in the professional degree program. The design studio, required each quarter, has an important integrative role in the program, linking material from related courses in history, theory and technology to the activity of designing buildings and environments.

Program Description

The architectural component includes basic courses in science and mathematics, analysis and design of building components and environmental systems, urban planning, and architectural history. Design courses begin in the first year and continue through all four years. Studio projects are carefully sequenced to provide exposure to a range of issues, building types and scales appropriate to each level. The studio series culminates in a comprehensive project in the fourth year which is carried through the design development stage of production.

General education is distributed on an elective basis throughout the program with guidelines ensuring appropriate acquaintance with the social sciences and humanities. The curriculum structure encourages students to arrange the elective portion of their undergraduate program to follow individual interests while meeting requirements in professional and general studies.

Students may opt to participate in the nine-month foreign study program during their fourth year. Conducted by Georgia Tech faculty in cooperation with the Ecole d'Architecture Paris-Tolbiac in Paris, France, this program offers required fourth-year courses, including design, complemented by both individual and group travel opportunities in western Europe.

GRADUATE PROGRAM
Philosophy Statement

The two-year graduate professional degree program seeks to continue the development of professional capabilities initiated in the undergraduate program while responding to significant and ongoing shifts in the discipline of architecture. The program offers several areas of study grounded in knowledge, theories, methods, and skills related to the design and production of architecture, presents a diversity of positions which engage leading questions of our time, and encourages each student, within the limits of the resources of the College and Institute, to develop a specific focus in the broad continuum of architecture, consistent with individual interests and goals.

Program Description

Three different curriculum arrangements lead to the M. Arch degree: the two-year program for those holding a bachelor's degree in architecture from an accredited four-year program; the extended program, typically four years in duration, for those with degrees in fields other than architecture (two years of basic preparation leading to the regular two-year M. Arch Program); and the one-year post-professional degree program for students with a bachelor's degree in architecture from a five-year accredited program.

Presently, four major areas of study are available: Design Theory and Practice, Urban Design and Development, Behavioral Studies, and Architectural Technology. Each is characterized by a body of coursework, studios, and faculty with related interest and expertise. While these areas are specialized, they are each viewed in relation to design, with studio teaching as the most effective means of combining theory and application. Other emerging areas of study include Architectural History, Preservation/Construction, and Computers in Architecture.

The basic two-year curriculum has three components: a common core of courses with knowledge and skills related to the broad area of architecture and building; an elective curriculum focusing on the needs and interests of the individual student; and the thesis, an eighteen-credit-hour investigation which culminates the student's individual program of study.

A strong symbiotic relationship exists between the Graduate Programs in Architecture, the College's nationally known research program, and the Doctoral Program in Architecture and City Planning. These resources strengthen the character and enrich the diversity of opportunities for graduate study.

FACULTY
Administration

William L Fash, Dean
John A Kelly, AIA, Associate Dean
A Frank Beckum, Assistant Dean
John Myer, Assistant Dean for Research Administration
Giuseppe Zambonini, Director, Architecture Program
Richard Dagenhart, Associate Director, Architecture Graduate Program
Randal Roark, Associate Director, Architecture Undergraduate Program
Dr Catherine Ross, AIP, Acting Director, Doctoral Program
Kathryn Brackney, Architecture Librarian

Professors

Richard Aynsley, RA, MS Arch Eng, PhD
Alan Balfour, RIBA, Dipl Arch, MFA
A Frank Beckum, AIA (Assoc), B Arch, MFA
Arnall T Connell, BS Arch, MCP
Dale Durfee, AIA, B Arch, M Arch
William L Fash, AIA (Assoc), B Arch, M Arch
Rufus R Hughes II, AIA, B Arch
John A Kelly, AIA, M Arch E, M Arch
Anatoliusz Lesniewski, MS, PhD
Elliott Pavlos, AIA (Assoc), B Arch, MCP
John Templer, RIBA, MS Arch, PhD

Associate Professors

James M Akridge, ASHRAE, AEE, BME, ME
Douglas Allen, ASLA, BLA, MLA
Neal W Connah, BFA, MFA
Robert Craig, MA, PhD
Richard Dagenhart, RA, B Arch, M Arch, MCP
Thomas N Debo, PE, MCP, PhD CE
Lane M Duncan, AIA, B Arch, M Des
Lewis Lanter, AIA, B Arch, M Arch
Christian A. Nelson, AICP, MVS, PhD
Randal Roark, AIA, B Arch E, MCP, M Arch
Joan Templer, BA
Jean Wineman, MUP, Arch D
Craig Zimring, MA, PhD

Assistant Professors

John P Cleaveland, BCE, M Arch
Harris Dimitropoulos, M Arch, PhD
Elizabeth Dowling, AIA, M Arch, PhD
Michael Elliott, SPIDR, MCP, PhD
George B Johnston, B Arch, M Arch
E Larry Keating, AIP, MA, PhD
Nadir Lahiji, M Arch
Mark Linder, M Arch, MED
Peter Pittman, B Arch, M Arch
Albert Smith, BVA, MFA
James Williamson, B Arch, M Arch

Part-Time Faculty

Anthony Ames, B Arch, M Arch
Jennifer Bloomer, BS Arch, M Arch
Bettye Rose Connell, BSHE, MS
Merrill Elam, AIA, BA, MBA
Benjamin Erlitz, AIP, BA, JD
Marco Frascari, RA, M Arch, PhD
Michael Jones, RA, Dipl Arch
Rob Miller, AIA, BA, M Arch
Kempton Mooney, AIA, B Arch, M Arch
James Mount, AIA, B Arch, M Arch
Joseph Reshower
Stuart Romm, AIA, B Arch
William Russell, AIA, B Arch, MS
Mack Scogin, AIA, B Arch
Robert Segrest, AIA, M Arch, MCP
Joseph N Smith, FAIA, BS, B Arch

Adjunct Faculty

Stanley C Bailey, PhD
C Virgil Smith, Sc D

Hampton University

**Department of Architecture and
  Building Construction Technology**
Hampton University
Hampton, Virginia 23668
(804) 727-5440

Office of Admissions
(804) 727-5328

Application Deadline(s): June 30
Tuition & Fees: Undgrd: On Campus:
$6940/yr
Off Campus: $4740/yr
Endowment: Private

DEGREE PROGRAMS

Degree	Minimum Years for Degree	Accred.	Requirements for Admission	Full-Time Stdnts.	Part-Time Stdnts.	% of Applics. Accptd.	Stdnts. in 1st Year of Program	# of Degrees Conferred
B Arch	5	NAAB	Upper 1/2 HS class Comb SAT of 800 or equiv. ACT	156	6		75	16
BS in Bldg Const Tech	4	—	Upper 1/2 HS class Comb SAT of 800 or equiv. ACT	23	1		5	4

SCHOOL DEMOGRAPHICS (all degree programs)

Full-Time Faculty	Part-Time Faculty	Full-Time Students	Part-Time Students	Foreign Students	Out-of-State U.S. Stdnts.	Women Students	Minority Students
9	3	180	7	5%	74%	19%	88%

LIBRARY (Tel. No. 804-727-5443)

Type	No. of Volumes	No. of Slides
Arch	8,625	18,597

STUDENT OPPORTUNITIES AND RESOURCES

Enrollment in the Department of Architecture numbers approximately 150 students, with a full-time equivalent faculty of 8. This overall faculty-student ratio of 1:18 is indicative of the department's personal approach to teaching. Close ties are maintained to the Departments of Art, Building Construction, Housing, and Interior Design.

Hampton Institute is small (4,300 students) with students representing 35 states and 12 foreign countries. Located in historic Tidewater, Virginia, it is close to Williamsburg, Virginia, and Washington, D.C. The college's waterfront campus overlooks Hampton Roads and the Chesapeake Bay and is next to historic Fort Monroe.

SPECIAL ACTIVITIES AND PROGRAMS

Visiting Lecturers and Critics Program

Community involvement, community analysis and design

Summer Pre-Architecture Program for high school students

Interdisciplinary program with Department of Building Construction

Work-study/intern program

Student Chapter AIAS

Student Design Council

Annual "Spring Thing" week activities

Close ties to Hampton Roads Chapter AIA

FACILITIES

The physical facilities for all departmental and supportive functions are housed within the architecture building:

Studios
Classrooms
Library
Model shop
Photography darkroom

SCHOLARSHIPS/AID

Hampton Institute has $525,000 in college scholarships and grants. Also $3,200,000 is available through outside scholarships, loans, and federal and state work-study.

UNDERGRADUATE PROGRAM
Philosophy Statement

The department's location in a small liberal arts college enhances the program's relations with the humanities, social sciences, and physical sciences. The department is oriented to the dual pursuit of general education and professional education. The B Arch program provides a firm foundation for broad professional education that will direct the student into professional practice or into graduate studies as may be desired. The architect must be a scholar but must also have the technical and practical knowledge needed in today's technological society.

Program Description

Students enter directly into the department in their first year. The curriculum for the first two years is designed to introduce the student to the broad concepts and theory of architecture, and to the acquisition of skills necessary in the study and practice of architecture.

The core program then concentrates on the central function of the architect — the analysis of user requirements and the interpretation of these needs in terms of the built environment. The core curriculum includes required professional/technical course work and a substantial block of free electives. In addition, emphasis is placed on the solution of specifically urban problems and on the changing role of the architect as a major participant in multidisciplinary program development and as a member of the multiskilled design team.

The students in the first year are given special counseling on college life through the Freshman Studies area and also receive professional program counseling in the Department of Architecture.

The Department of Architecture enjoys excellent relationships with other departments within the college community. As a result, architecture students take many of their free electives in the Departments of Art, Business, Sociology, and Human Ecology (housing and Interior Design).

FACULTY
Administration

Dr Robert D Bonner, Dean
John H Spencer, FAIA, ASLA, RA, Chairman
Jocelyn Spratley, Librarian

Professors

James Hall III, AIA, B Arch, M Arch, MCP
John H Spencer, FAIA, ASLA, B Arch, BLA, MLA

Associate Professors

Solil Banerjee, B Arch
John Peter, AIA, B Arch, M Arch

Assistant Professors

Jay McClure, B Arch, M Arch
Oscar Northen, AIA, B Arch, M Arch

Lecturers

George Wallace, RA, B Arch

Visiting Instructors

Joel Chou, B Arch
David Vogan, B Arch

Harvard University

Graduate School of Design
Harvard University
48 Quincy Street
Cambridge, Massachusetts 02138
(617) 495-2591

Admissions Office
48 Quincy Street
Cambridge, Massachusetts 02138
(617) 495-5455

Application Deadline(s): January 15
Tuition & Fees: Grad: $11,500/yr.
Endowment: Private

DEGREE PROGRAMS

Degree	Minimum Years for Degree	Accred.	Requirements for Admission	Full-Time Stdnts.	Part-Time Stdnts.	% of Applics. Accptd.	Stdnts. in 1st Year of Program	# of Degrees Conferred
M Arch I	3½*	NAAB	BA or BS	299	9		95	85
M Arch II	1½		B Arch		included in above			
MLA I	3	ASLA	BA or BS	86	0		29	31
MLA II	2	ASLA			included in above			
MAUD	2		B Arch	37	1		17	19
MLAUD	2		BLA		included in above			
MDesS	1		Prof Degree	15	0		14	13
DrDes	2		Prof Master's Degree or MDesS	6	0		4	0

*2½ Years with advanced standing (e.g. BA in Arch.).

SCHOOL DEMOGRAPHICS (all degree programs)

Full-Time Faculty	Part-Time Faculty	Full-Time Students	Part-Time Students	Foreign Students	Out-of-State U.S. Stdnts.	Women Students	Minority Students
48	11	443	10	22%	63%	34%	13%

LIBRARY (Tel. No. 617-495-9164)

Type	No. of Volumes	No. of Slides
Arch	235,000+	100,000+

STUDENT OPPORTUNITIES AND RESOURCES

Research and Professional Studies
Student Teaching Positions
Career Advising and Placement Services
Alumni Association
Harvard Architecture Review
Student Forum
Various Prizes and Medals
Traveling Fellowships

SPECIAL ACTIVITIES AND PROGRAMS

Professional Development Programs
International Training Programs
Loeb Fellowship Program
Lectures and Exhibitions Program
Conferences
Career Discovery Program

FACILITIES

George Gund Hall
Frances Loeb Library
Library for Computer Graphics and Spatial Analysis
Laboratory for Construction Technology

SCHOLARSHIPS/AID

Assistance in planning for and securing adequate financing for attending graduate school is available to all GSD students; more than $1.4 million in financial aid is offered each year to those who could not afford otherwise to meet their expenses. The school provides three types of assistance programs: grants, employment opportunities and loans.
  For more information contact:
  Financial Aid Office
  Harvard University
  Graduate School of Design
  48 Quincy Street
  Cambridge, Massachusetts 02138
  617-495-5454

GRADUATE PROGRAM
Philosophy Statement

The program leading to the degree Master in Architecture as an accredited professional degree is intended for individuals who have completed the bachelor's degree with a major other than one of the design professions, or with a preprofessional undergraduate major in one of the design professions.

The course of study prepares persons for professional careers in architecture. The program is rigorous and comprehensive, preparing graduates for the full range of professional activities of the field. It provides a solid intellectual base of knowledge in history, theory, technology, the social environment and professional practice. Particular emphasis is given to developing mastery of design through an intensive series of design studio courses. As part of the process of developing independent thinking and resolving design issues, students are required to prepare a design thesis to serve as a transition from professional school to professional practice.

Program Description

The program leading to the degree Master in Architecture as a second professional degree is intended for individuals who have completed a five-year undergraduate professional program or its equivalent.

The course of study extends the base of knowledge of the professional field through graduate study with particular emphasis on mastery in design. Students advance their theoretical and analytical skills and expand their career opportunities in design. They are expected to demonstrate competence across the breadth of the field, developing a course of study that compensates for weaknesses and enhances areas of strength. An important requirement is the design thesis, which provides an opportunity to demonstrate mastery at the graduate level; only under special circumstances may the thesis be waived.

The program leading to the degree Master in Design Studies is intended for individuals who already hold the professional degree required for registration in a design field, and who seek a short, intense graduate program to advance their professional careers. This program may also serve as preparation for doctoral study.

The program leading to the degree Doctor of Design provides opportunities for advanced study in preparation for specialization in the practice and teaching of architecture, landscape architecture, and urban planning and design. The program is intended for persons who have already mastered professional skills and who now seek to make original contributions to these fields. Applicants are invited to define their own professionally oriented program of study. The program leading to the Doctor of Design differs from the Ph.D. program in its concern for the professions as fields of practice rather than academic disciplines.

FACULTY
Administration

Gerald M McCue, FAIA, Dean of the Faculty of Design
Jose Rafael Moneo, Chairman, Department of Architecture
Linda Jewell, Chairman, Department of Landscape Architecture
Peter G Rowe, Chairman, Department of Urban Planning & Design
Jorge Silvetti, Director, M Arch I and II Programs and Acting Director, Urban Design Programs
Michael van Valkenburgh, Director, Landscape Architecture Programs
William J Mitchell, Director, Special Programs and MDesS Program
Carl F Steinitz, B Arch, M Arch, PhD, AM (hon) Director, Dr Des Program
James S Hodgson, Librarian

Professors

Alan Altshuler, BA, MA, PhD
Howard Burns, BA MA
William A Doebele, AB, MCP, JD
Richard T Forman, BS, PhD, AM (hon)
José Gomez-Ibañez, AB, MPP, PhD
Gerald M McCue, FAIA, AB, AM Arch, AM (hon)
William J Mitchell, B Arch, MED, MA, AM (hon)
Jose Rafael Moneo, Dipl Arch, D Arch, AM (hon)
Peter G Rowe, B Arch, MAUD, AM (hon)
Daniel L Schodek, BS, MS, PhD, AM (hon)
Eduard F Sekler, Dipl Ing, PhD, AM (hon)
Jorge Silvetti, Dipl Arch, M Arch, AM (hon)
Carl F Steinitz, B Arch, M Arch, PhD, AM (hon)
John Stilgoe, AB, MA, PhD, AM (hon)
Albert Szabo, M Arch
Michael van Valkenburgh, MLA
François C D Vigier, B Arch, MCP, PhD

Adjunct Professors

J Miller Blew III, B Arch, MBA
Linda Jewell, B Arch, MLA
Alfred H Koetter, B Arch, M Arch
William J LeMessurier, AB, MS
Rodolfo Machado, Dipl Arch, M Arch
Moshe Safdie, B Arch, LLD (hon)
Carl M Sapers, AB, JD
John A Seiler, AB, M Arch, MBA, DBA
Peter E Walker, BSLA, MLA

Associate Professors

Harvey Bryan, M Arch, MS
Caroline Brown Constant, M Arch
Alex Krieger, MCPUD
Jonathan S Lane, B Arch, M Arch/MCP
Bruno D Pfister, M Arch

Assistant Professors

Miroslava M Benes, BA, MA
Michael W Binford, PhD
Carol J Burns, BA, M Arch
Ellen Harkins, BFA, B Arch, M Arch
K Michael Hays, B Arch, M Arch
Sheila Kennedy, BA, M Arch
Kevin Kieran, B Arch, M Arch
Bruce MacNelly, M Arch
Malcolm McCullough, BA, M Arch
Alistair McIntosh, B Arch, MLA
Elizabeth K Meyer, BS, MLA, MA
Spiro N Pollalis, PhD
Dagmar E Richter, Dipl
Alexander von Hoffman, BA, MA, PhD
George S Wagner, BA, M Arch
Wilfried Wang, Dipl Arch
John Whiteman, MCRP, PhD

University of Hawaii at Manoa

School of Architecture
University of Hawaii at Manoa
2560 Campus Road
George Annex 2-3
Honolulu, Hawaii 96822
(808) 948-7225; 948-7226

Application Deadline(s): Undgrd: Fall - April 1;
Spring - November 1
Grad: Fall - March 1;
Spring - September 1
Tuition & Fees: Undgrd: HI Res: $565/sem +
fees
Non-res: $1840/sem + fees
Grad: HI Res: $670/sem + fees
Non-res: $2190/sem + fees
Endowment: Public

DEGREE PROGRAMS

Degree	Minimum Years for Degree	Accred.	Requirements for Admission	Full-Time Stdnts.	Part-Time Stdnts.	% of Applics. Accptd.	Stdnts. in 1st Year of Program	# of Degrees Conferred
B Arch	5	NAAB	High School SAT of 1100	180		35%	60	25
M Arch	2	NAAB	B Arch	3				
M Arch	5	NAAB	Degree in other discipline	5				

SCHOOL DEMOGRAPHICS (all degree programs)

Full-Time Faculty	Part-Time Faculty	Full-Time Students	Part-Time Students	Foreign Students	Out-of-State U.S. Stdnts.	Women Students	Minority Students
11	24	190	0	NA	NA	NA	NA

LIBRARY (Tel. No. 808-948-8422)

Type	No. of Volumes	No. of Slides
Univ	50,000 (Arch & Design)	

STUDENT OPPORTUNITIES AND RESOURCES

Because of the intimate nature of the state of Hawaii, and particularly Oahu, the University of Hawaii's School of Architecture is ideally located to expose students to both a modern urban scene and the vestiges of a tranquil, rural past. Also, its location in the mid-Pacific opens up unique opportunities for communication with most of the Pacific Basin, which is one of the most rapidly changing areas in the world.

The School of Architecture is deliberately small and is pursuing a slow growth policy. Its size encourages a closely knit student body and a comradeship with faculty not often found in larger schools. On the other hand, its small size limits its offerings to the more traditional aspects of architecture at the undergraduate level and to only a few options at the graduate level.

FACILITIES

The School expects construction on its new facilities to start Summer of 1988 with completion probably Spring of 1990. The new facilities will include a computer lab, research and materials lab, graphics lab, in-house library, student lounge and other normal items.

SCHOLARSHIPS/AID

Student aid is handled by the campus and direct contact with that office is desirable. The School has several summer travel grants.

UNDERGRADUATE PROGRAM
Philosophy Statement

We believe that "Architecture is the creation of space that meets the needs of people and satisfies the yearnings of the human soul." With this in mind, we further believe that architecture should enhance its surroundings, be responsive to both physical and social localized conditions and, above all, strive for excellence.

Program Description

Hawaii offers the B Arch as its first professional degree, with two options. Both of these options are highly structured and require rigorous pursuit by the students if they are to be successful.

The first option is for students who wish to practice architecture in the more traditional roles. Students completing this option should be competently equipped to enter the field with a well-rounded background in the fundamentals of architecture and a solid base in one of the many developing subspecialties of architecture.

The second option is for students interested in interior design and renovation. Students completing this option will be equipped to practice in this rapidly changing field as professionals and to secure a license in either architecture or interior design. It should be noted that completion of this option will also furnish the student with a solid base for further professional development.

Many of the faculty for both of these options are practicing professionals, thus assuring the student body of continuing contact with the professional world.

GRADUATE PROGRAM
Program Description

The School of Architecture believes that a graduate degree should be a research-oriented degree that builds upon the solid foundation provided by a practice-oriented degree. The graduate program, therefore, is not an extension of the undergraduate program, but is instead a research-oriented study of extensive depth (48 semester credit hours) in selected areas of expertise. All entering graduate students must satisfy the professional core requirements of the undergraduate program in addition to the graduate requirements. Completion of this program furnishes the student with an M Arch degree, which may be a first or second professional degree. More importantly, this program should expose the student to architectural research and furnish a high level of expertise in a given architectural specialty.

Areas of study in this degree are limited to the areas of expertise of the program's faculty. Students who wish to pursue any of the more unusual architectural frontiers should contact the school prior to application to ensure that such interests can be accommodated in the program.

FACULTY
Administration

Elmer E Botsai, FAIA, HFRAIA, HFNZIA, HFRCIA, Dean
Barry J Baker, AIA, FRAIA, Associate Dean and Graduate Chairman
J Peter Jordan, AIA, Undergraduate Chairman
Wil Frost, Reference Librarian

Professors

Elmer E Botsai, FAIA, HFRAIA, HFNZIA, HFRCIA, AB Arch
Bruce Etherington, AIA, B Arch, M Arch, PhD

Associate Professors

Barbara Allen, MS
Barry J Baker, AIA, FRAIA, Dipl Arch
Fred Creager, AIA, BS
Lewis Ingleson, AIA, B Arch
J Peter Jordan, AIA, B Arch
Leighton Liu, MFA
Joyce Noe, AIA
Don Shaw, AIA, BA Arch, B Arch
Gordon Tyau, AIA, B Arch, MSc (Arch)

Part-Time Faculty

Walter Bell, AIA
Evan Cruthers, AIA
Wesley Deguchi, AIA
Donald Dugal
John Gilje, PhD
Frank Haines, FAIA
John Hara, AIA
Michael Kawaharada, PE
Alan Leitner
Richard Malmgren
Patrick Onishi, AIA, B Arch
James Reinhardt, AIA
Crystal Rose, D Law
Theodore Suzuki, PE
Gerald Takano, B Arch
Calvin Yonamine

University of Houston

College of Architecture
122 ARC
University of Houston
Houston, Texas 77004-4431
(713) 749-1181

Undergraduate Admissions:
(713) 749-2321
Graduate Admissions:
handled by the College

Application Deadline(s): Undgrd: July 15
Grad: April 15
Tuition & Fees: Undgrd: TX Res: $16/Sem Hr.
Non-res: $120/Sem Hr.
$180/Sem Fees
Grad: (Same)

Endowment: Public

DEGREE PROGRAMS

Degree	Minimum Years for Degree	Accred.	Requirements for Admission	Full-Time Stdnts.	Part-Time Stdnts.	% of Applics. Accptd.	Stdnts. in 1st Year of Program	# of Degrees Conferred
BSED	4		HS Diploma SAT	12	6	80%	2	6
B Arch	5	NAAB	HS Diploma SAT	416	45	60%	135	57
M Arch	1		B Arch, 3.0 GPA, GRE, Portfolio	32	6	30%	32	38
M Arch	2	NAAB	BS Arch, 3.0 GPA, GRE, Portfolio	10	2	40%	5	4
M Arch	3	NAAB	Non-Arch Degree, 3.0 GPA, GRE	48	3	60%	18	18

SCHOOL DEMOGRAPHICS (all degree programs)

Full-Time Faculty	Part-Time Faculty	Full-Time Students	Part-Time Students	Foreign Students	Out-of-State U.S. Stdnts.	Women Students	Minority Students
26	15	518	62	13%	9%	26%	7%

LIBRARY (Tel. No. 713-749-7551)

Type	No. of Volumes	No. of Slides
Arch & Art	42,360	58,790

STUDENT OPPORTUNITIES AND RESOURCES

Located three miles from downtown Houston, the University of Houston is a large, state-supported urban university with approximately 30,000 students enrolled in 13 academic and professional colleges. The size and scope of the university coupled with the city and the greater Houston region provides students with a wide variety of learning, employment, and cultural opportunities.

The College of Architecture at the University of Houston had its beginnings in 1946 and has grown in 40 years to a college of approximately 550 students with a total of about 30 full-time faculty supported by a large number of adjunct, part-time, and visiting faculty. These faculty, active in the profession in the greater Houston area, bring to the college the resources and knowledge that are available only in large, urban university settings.

The student body is composed of a quite diverse mix of students with most backgrounds, ages, and nationalities being represented and, while most of the students come from the South Texas area, a significant number are from out of state and foreign countries.

The greatest strength of the college is its design faculty. Most are actively engaged in architectural practice and the majority have been recognized for design excellence through design awards at the local, state, and national levels. Supplementing these quality faculty are numerous visiting critics and noted architects who regularly visit and participate in the programs of the College.

SPECIAL ACTIVITIES AND PROGRAMS

Center for Experimental Architecture - an endowed research and study center within the College with a strong emphasis on NASA and other space-related projects.

Environmental Center of Houston - the research arm of the college which manages architectural and urban design-related research and community service activities.

Visiting Critics Programs - bring renowned architects to the campus for participation in selected classes.

Foreign Study Programs - presently operating summer study programs in France and Rome.

Also under development are institutes in health care facilities design and in interior architecture, which are intended to offer advanced research and study opportunities to upper-division and graduate students.

FACILITIES

The College of Architecture is located in a new (completed 1986) building designed by Philip Johnson which has quickly become a campus and city landmark. Housed within the facility are the Architecture and Art Library, a fully equipped shop, gallery and display space, a computer center and enough class and studio space to more than adequately house the needs of the program.

SCHOLARSHIPS/AID

Over $25,000 in scholarships and loans are available annually for upper-division and graduate students through the college supported by the Texas Architectural Foundation, the American Institute of Architects Foundation, and individual donors. University-wide support in grants, loans, and work-study are available through the Office of Financial Aid. Graduate students are eligible for teaching and research stipends within the college and its institutes and there are many part-time and summer work opportunities in the city during the school year and summers.

UNDERGRADUATE PROGRAM
Philosophy Statement

The college seeks to prepare students for eventual active practice in the environmental design professions. The program's goal is to have students develop topflight ability and skills in architectural design by providing them with a thorough understanding of current and historic architectural theory and the technologies of architecture.

Program Description

The curriculum core in the Bachelor of Architecture program consists of a group of cognate blocks, dealing with substantive knowledge and process areas of development, and a series of studio, analytical, and design experiences. In the beginning years, there is a focus on broad awareness and skill development objectives providing a comprehensive overview of environmental design and related issues. Design explorations at this level are intended to familiarize the student with the language, the forms, and the forces influencing architectural design and to reinforce the student's interest and confidence in his or her developing abilities. In the intermediate years the program emphasizes the refinement and extension of analytical and design skills and the development of a more specific knowledge base particularly in the areas of building technology, historical perspective, and cultural meaning. The final year of the program promotes the further refinement of selected skills and capabilities, and may culminate in a thesis project that consists of a research phase in the first semester and an execution phase in the second. While the majority of the students elect a building design for the thesis, there has been an increasing number of research theses and projects dealing with issues of planning and experimental environments.

Students have access to the entire faculty as a resource team, and part of the goal of the foundation program is to introduce students to the faculty and to the material resources of the college. As students progress through the program they are expected to assume a greater responsibility for seeking out the kind of assistance they need in their work. In the upper-level studios in particular, the faculty acts primarily in a resource role for the student in his or her project work. In this sense an important goal of the program is to liberate students from the need for faculty guidance and to bring them to a point where they can act responsibly and independently, using their own initiative, self-determination, and resourcefulness. During the spring semester there is a general review by the faculty of all students in the third year of design, and students are counseled as to which of the undergraduate degree programs they should pursue. At that time they must develop a guided program of elected study in another discipline which will help them in achieving their goals and objectives.

GRADUATE PROGRAM
Philosophy Statement

The graduate program seeks to examine theoretical issues in design and urban design and to contribute to the development of new knowledge and understanding through research, design investigations, and critical thought. The program provides well-educated, generalist professionals with a strong preparation in design so that they will be able to assume responsible positions in diverse professional and academic roles.

Program Description

The Graduate Division offers students with a baccalaureate degree in any of a variety of disciplines an opportunity to pursue a program of advanced study leading to the Master of Architecture degree in one to three years.

Three programs of study are available: a one-year program for students holding a professional, five-year degree from an accredited school of architecture: a two-year program for students holding a four-year degree in environmental design or a related design discipline; and a three-year program for students with a degree in another field.

All three programs emphasize theory-based design with special opportunities for advanced study in urban design, history-theory, regional architecture, and experimental architecture with an emphasis on design for space. In addition, the college has developed support for advanced study opportunities in health care facilities design and interior architecture.

FACULTY
Administration

William R Jenkins, FAIA, Dean
Peter J Wood, Associate Dean
Thomas M Colbert, RA, Assistant to the Dean
Robert H Timme, Director, Graduate Studies
Larry Bell, Director, Sasakawa International
    Center for Space Architecture (SICSA)
Margaret Culbertson, Librarian

Professors

Myron Anderson, BSME, MSCE
Larry Bell, B Arch, MFA
William R Jenkins, B Arch, M Arch
Burdette Keeland, BS Arch, M Arch
John Perry, B Arch, M Arch
Robert H Timme, BA, B Arch, M Arch
Bruce C Webb, BA, B Arch, M Arch

Associate Professors

Michel Bezman, Dipl Arch, Dipl Eng
Elizabeth Bollinger, BS, M Arch
Robert E Griffin, B Arch
Robert Lindsey, BS Arch, B Arch, M Arch
Shafik I Rifaat, BS Arch, M Arch, MCP
Peter J Wood, BA, M Arch
John Zemanek, BS Arch, B Arch, M Arch, MCP
Peter J Zweig, BA, B Arch, M Arch

Assistant Professors

Leonard Bachman, B Arch, M Arch
Thomas M Colbert, B Arch, Honors Dipl
Veronica Dorian-Becnel, B Art, M Arch
Howard S Gartner, B Arch, M Arch
Philip R Goyert, Jr, B Arch, M Arch
Lewis D Hodnett, Jr, B Arch
Lannis Kirkland, B Arch, M Arch
Paul Lodholz, B Arch
Patrick A Peters, B Arch, M Arch

Adjunct Faculty

David Andrews, B Arch
Richard Buday, B Arch
Joseph Colaco, BS, MS, PhD
Tom Diehl, B Arch, Grad Dipl
James G Easter, Jr, B Arch, M Arch
Leslie Elkins, BA, M Arch
Ed Eubanks, BA, M Arch
Fredric Fleshman, BBA, B Arch, M Arch
Wilhelm Hahn, B Arch
Mark Hoistad, BS, M Arch
Suzanne Labarthe, BA, B Arch
John Lemr, BA, B Arch, M Arch
Rafael Longoria, BA, B Arch, MBA
Joseph McManus, Jr, BA, B Arch, M Arch
Barry M Moore, FAIA, B Hist, B Arch, M Arch
Deborah Morris, BFA, M Arch
Donald Olson, BLA
Richard Payne, B Arch
A Ray Pentecost, III, B Arts, B Arch, M Pub
    Health, PhD
Anthony Salvaggio
Catherine Spellman, BA, B Arch
William Stern, B Arts, M Arch
David Thaddeus, BCE
T Gerald Treece, BA, JD
Guillermo Trotti, B Arch, M Arch
Scott Waugh, B Arch

Instructor

Geoffrey John Brune, B Arch

Howard University

School of Architecture and Planning
Howard University
2366 6th Street N.W.
Washington, D.C. 20059
(202) 636-7420/21

Admissions:
M. W. Johnson Administration
 Building, Room G-30
2400 6th Street N.W.
Washington, D.C. 20059
(202) 636-6200

Application Deadline(s): June 1st for Fall
admission
Tuition & Fees: Undgrd: $2,713/sem
Grad: $2,873/sem
Endowment: Private and Public

DEGREE PROGRAMS

Degree	Minimum Years for Degree	Accred.	Requirements for Admission	Full-Time Stdnts.	Part-Time Stdnts.	% of Applics. Accptd.	Stdnts. in 1st Year of Program	# of Degrees Conferred
B Arch	5	NAAB	HS Grad/SAT combined 800	230	18	25%	73	40
M Arch	2-3½	—	Bachelors in any field other than Arch/or non-Professional in Arch	*	—	—	—	30
MS Arch	1	N/A	Five-Year B Arch	6	—	25%	6	4

*Degree being reorganized to be offered in Fall 1987.

SCHOOL DEMOGRAPHICS (all degree programs)

Full-Time Faculty	Part-Time Faculty	Full-Time Students	Part-Time Students	Foreign Students	Out-of-State U.S. Stdnts.	Women Students	Minority Students
23	6	236	18	41%	55%	25%	98%

LIBRARY (Tel. No. 202-636-7773)

Type	No. of Volumes	No. of Slides
Arch	23,210	33,600

STUDENT OPPORTUNITIES AND RESOURCES

The School of Architecture and Planning is one of seventeen academic units within a major urban University. Located in the nation's capital, the school benefits from interaction with an active national and international community. The student body reflects the school's international environment.

The school's facilities include individually partitioned studio spaces for each design student, an in-house computer laboratory, a fully equipped photographic laboratory, and a fully equipped carpentry/model shop.

The newly developed exhibition gallery displays the work of notable firms and individuals, competitions, and public sector projects. Most recent among the exhibits have been the winning entries of the Vietnam Veterans Memorial Competition, the history/development of the Pennsylvania Avenue Development Corporation, the work of Aga Khan Awardee Hassan Fathy, SOM 50th Anniversary, Richard Neutra's Traveling Sketches, and Mies van der Rohe as the Teacher. The lecture series, too, provides an exposure that is in support of the several curricula. Recent visiting lecturers have included Hugh Newell Jacobsen, E. Fay Jones, Dean Robert Maxwell, Christian Noberg-Schulz, Don Hisaka, Edgar Tafel, Stanley Tigerman, et al.

The Department of Architecture is fortunate to have within its parent academic unit the Department of City and Regional Planning. Faculty teach between the departments, and every effort is made to provide a broad view of the built environment through joint seminars, cross-registration, etc. Mechanical Engineering, Civil Engineering, Electrical Engineering, and Environmental Systems Engineering departments provide the student with access to a range of engineering support.

SPECIAL ACTIVITIES AND PROGRAMS

Study trips to foreign countries have been institutionalized during both the summer and winter recesses. Purposes of the trips have ranged from the study of architectural form in Europe to historical restoration in Haiti to design and culture in Japan.

Field trips to domestic environments of architectural significance (conducted on a continuing basis during the academic year).

The School's internal awards program includes medals for design excellence, scholarships and traveling fellowships.

FACILITIES

The School of Architecture and Planning is housed in its own facility that includes extensive studio space, an independent library, a construction laboratory, classrooms, faculty and student assistant offices, a 250-seat auditorium, a carpentry shop, an exhibition gallery, administrative offices and appropriate "soft places"/lounges.

SCHOLARSHIPS/AID

The School has a range of scholarships, grants, and loans available to students in architecture. For financial aid information, applicants should write to the Office of Financial Aid, Room 211, Howard University, 2400 6th Street N.W., Washington, D.C. 20059.

UNDERGRADUATE PROGRAM
Philosophy Statement

The five-year professional degree, Bachelor of Architecture, is the major academic program offered in architecture. Throughout the five years of study, the design studio serves as the synthesizing element of the curriculum. Work in the design studio is introduced in the first semester of residence and continues through the final year with a design thesis.

The program emphasizes the view that design is both a process and a product. The problems of people in an urbanizing society are given central consideration within this perspective.

Program Description

The initial years of the program are highly structured around a core of courses designed to develop skills, values, and processes related to design of the built environment.

The first year of study involves courses in elements of architectural design, graphics, communications theory, and man and his environment, together with supporting course work in English and mathematics.

At the beginning of the second year, students are formally introduced to the design studio sequence, construction techniques, and structures. This year not only involves the student in the development of the physical space of the architectural envelope but also introduces the student to the concept of the architect's responsibility to the role of physical form in urban places.

Throughout the educational sequence, courses in graphics, building construction, history and theory, urban design engineering, structures, landscape architecture, construction documents, and management support the design studio. Studio experiences are structured to expose the student to increasingly complex problems of diverse building types, environmental conditions, and structural systems.

Students are encouraged to cross-register in other programs offered at the university, such as planning, business and engineering.

GRADUATE PROGRAM
Philosophy Statement

The one-year Master of Science in Architecture program is designed for the highly motivated student who seeks to pursue advanced study/research in an area of his or her selection. Graduate students have access to the entire faculty while pursuing their studies in selected topics, such as urban design, tropical architecture, Third World development, and historic preservation.

The Master of Architecture degree program exists to accommodate holders of bachelor's degree in a field other than architecture. This first professional degree is developed with the studio as the central forum for exploration and discovery. Supporting courses are recommended on an individual basis.

Program Description

The MS Arch is a one-year advanced degree for students who hold the B Arch degree from an accredited school. Requirements for the degree include two 6-credit-hour studio/research courses, 18 hours of electives chosen to support the student's areas of studio work/research and 6 hours of required professional electives.

The M Arch is a two to three-and-one-half year program depending on prior academic work and progress within the curriculum. Normal semester loads are 18 credit hours.

Applicants to the program must have developed a statement of interest that indicates the area to be studied and the expected methodology to be used. Students are encouraged to pursue supporting course work in other academic components of the university.

FACULTY
Administration

Harry G Robinson III, AIA, Dean
Victor A Adegbite, AICP, Associate Dean
Victor Dzidzienyo, CW, Chairman
Margaret Dorsey-Jones, Librarian

Professors

O Glean Chase, BS Arch
John Chen, M Arch
Ahmed Elnaggar, D Arch
Patrick K Jadin, RA, M Arch
Harry G Robinson III, AIA, AICP, B Arch
Sam Z Simaika, AIA, D Arch

Associate Professors

Raj Barr-Kumar, AIA, M Arch
Victor Dzidzienyo, B Arch
Thomas Heggans, M Arch
William S Hicks, AIA, B Arch
Jose Mapily, RA, B Arch
Asghar Minai, RA, PhD
Khosrow Moradian, B Arch
Donald H Roberts, RA, B Arch
Harry L Siler, B Arch

Assistant Professors

Ralph J Belton, RA, M Arch
Angel Clarens, AIA, B Arch

Part-Time Faculty

Hector Alvarez, AIA, M Arch
Robert Beathea, B Arch
Outram Hussey, B Arch
Edward Pinkard, MBA, MCP
Benjamin Skyles, RA, B Arch
Joseph Taylor, RA, M Arch

Adjunct Faculty

John Gattuso, ASLA, BLA

University of Idaho

Department of Architecture
College of Art and Architecture
University of Idaho
Moscow, Idaho 83843
(208) 885-6272

Application Deadline(s): April 1st for Fall;
November 1st for Spring;
May 1st for Summer
Tuition & Fees: Undgrd: ID Res: $520/sem
Non-res: $1520/sem
Grad: ID Res: $687/sem
Non-res: $1687/sem
Endowment: Public

DEGREE PROGRAMS

Degree	Minimum Years for Degree	Accred.	Requirements for Admission	Full-Time Stdnts.	Part-Time Stdnts.	% of Applics. Accptd.	Stdnts. in 1st Year of Program	# of Degrees Conferred
B Arch	5	NAAB	Univ. Req. (transfers-portfolio)	225	11	80%	57	54
M Arch	1		Univ. Req. + portfolio	6		50%		3
MA Arch	1		Univ. Req. + portfolio	3		30%		1
BFA Int Des	4	FIDER (antic. 1988)	Univ. Req.	49		95%	17	12
MA Int Des	1		Univ. Req. + portfolio	2		50%		1

SCHOOL DEMOGRAPHICS (all degree programs)

Full-Time Faculty	Part-Time Faculty	Full-Time Students	Part-Time Students	Foreign Students	Out-of-State U.S. Stdnts.	Women Students	Minority Students
12	7	285	11	2.3%	25%	38%	3.5%

LIBRARY (Tel. No. 208-885-6272)

Type	No. of Volumes	No. of Slides
Art & Arch	9,500	35,000

STUDENT OPPORTUNITIES AND RESOURCES

The Department of Architecture participates in the state, regional, and national activities of the American Institute of Architects and other environmental design organizations, is fully accredited by the National Architectural Accrediting Board, and is a full member of the Association of Collegiate Schools of Architecture.

Students of architecture and interior design are encouraged to broaden their experience through participation in the activities of the college and the university.

The American Institute of Architect Students chapter is active in professional programs for the architecture students. Likewise, members of the Student Chapter of the American Society of Interior Designers are actively involved in professional interior design programs. Representatives from these student organizations are encouraged to consult with the faculty in matters related to the conduct of departmental programs. In addition to taking advantage of departmental opportunities, many students participate in college and university-wide student government, student publications, intramural and intercollegiate athletics, and other interest groups.

SPECIAL ACTIVITIES AND PROGRAMS

Students participate in field trips to locations such as San Francisco, Portland, Seattle and Vancouver, British Columbia. There is a visiting lecture series, and an annual workshop sponsored jointly with Washington State University's School of Architecture. The workshops feature two nationally known architects. There is on-going research in the use of computer-aided design and other computer applications in architecture. International programs are offered in Rome and London, in cooperation with Washington State University. There is a student chapter of Tau Sigma Delta Honorary Society. Public service projects are sometimes accomplished with small towns in Idaho.

FACILITIES

The Department of Architecture is housed in a three-building complex with the total design studio space of 21,148 square feet. In addition, there are administrative offices, faculty offices, complete computer center with two computer systems, photography laboratory, shop, white printing room, reference library, slide library, and two main critique spaces. The College occupies area in seven buildings with a total of approximately 85,000 square feet. Along with architecture are housed landscape architecture, art, interior design as well as a university gallery and a downtown gallery. The University Library houses the architecture book collection.

SCHOLARSHIPS/AID

UI awards approximately $43,948 in general student scholarships and $426,826 in student loans per year to architecture majors. Several teaching assistantships are available to M Arch graduate students each year. About $2000 in scholarships is awarded directly to architecture majors each year through competitions.

UNDERGRADUATE PROGRAM
Philosophy Statement

Architects and interior designers are concerned with environmental design and are dedicated to the creation of a more effective and responsive human environment. In order to prepare students to meet this challenge, a variety of disciplines are encompassed by the college design program, bringing the interdisciplinary team approach to the educational experience.

Program Description

The Department of Architecture offers two undergraduate options in disciplines that are fundamental for the design of the human environment and are linked together by a common core in design and allied fields. The undergraduate may elect to pursue specialized programs leading to the five-year degree of Bachelor of Architecture (B Arch) or the four-year degree of Bachelor of Fine Arts in Interior Design (BFA). Both are professional programs that combine a specialized core curriculum with a breadth of opportunities in elective and general educations.

GRADUATE PROGRAM
Philosophy Statement

Graduate degree programs are offered to meet the needs of individuals interested in specialized advanced study. Graduate study in art and architecture involves independent and creative effort in the search for new knowledge and understanding.

Program Description

The M Arch program is the professional degree program in architecture. The thesis shall be one or more comprehensive, architecturally oriented projects presented in written and visual form. Admission to this program requires the five-year professional Bachelor of Architecture degree.

The program leading to the MA in Interior Design is an extended program for persons with undergraduate degree backgrounds in interior design, architecture, or other design-oriented fields. Special emphasis is placed on the sociological and psychological implications of the interior environment.

FACULTY
Administration

Paul L Blanton, FAIA, RA, Dean, College of Art and Architecture
Ronald D Bevans, AIA, RA, Associate Dean, College of Art and Architecture
Gifford Pierce, Chair, Department of Architecture
Frank Cronk, Chair, Department of Art
James Kuska, Chair, Department of Landscape Architecture

Professors

Robert Baron, RA, B Arch, M Arch
Ronald D Bevans, AIA, B Arch, M Arch
Paul L Blanton, FAIA, BS, M Arch
R G Nelson, B Arch

Associate Professors

Cynthia Blue-Blanton, BA, MA
William Bowler, B Arch, M Arch
Brian Sumption, B Arch, M Arch

Assistant Professors

Bruce Haglund, BS, M Arch
Wendy McClure, B Arch, M Arch
M Joseph Numbers, B Arch, M Arch
John Pulliam, B Arch, MBA
D Nels Reese, B Arch

Part-Time Faculty

Kenneth L Carper, B Arch, MS
Larry G Fisher, RA, BS, MS

Adjunct Faculty

David F Giese, BA, MFA
James Kuska, BS, ML Arch
Willard L'Hote, BFA, MFA
George Roberts, BS, MS

Illinois Institute of Technology

College of Architecture, Planning
  and Design
Department of Architecture
Illinois Institute of Technology
Crown Hall, 3360 S State Street
Chicago, Illinois 60616
(312) 567-3260

Office of Admissions
10 W. 33rd Street
Room 101, Perlstein Hall
Illinois Institute of Technology
Chicago, Illinois 60616-3793
Illinois toll-free: 1-800/572-1587
Out-of-state toll-free: 1-800/448-2329

Application Deadline(s): Rolling Admission,
  although early
  application is
  encouraged.
Tuition & Fees: Undgrd: $8850/yr
  Grad: $8850/yr
Endowment: Private and Public

DEGREE PROGRAMS

Degree	Minimum Years for Degree	Accred.	Requirements for Admission	Full-Time Stdnts.	Part-Time Stdnts.	% of Applics. Accptd.	Stdnts. in 1st Year of Program	# of Degrees Conferred
B Arch	5	NAAB	HS diploma-SAT or ACT	258	16	68%	65	44
M Arch	3½ 2 1		BS or BA B Arch or equivalent; TOEFL B Arch	45	11	70%	10	8

SCHOOL DEMOGRAPHICS (all degree programs)

Full-Time Faculty	Part-Time Faculty	Full-Time Students	Part-Time Students	Foreign Students	Out-of-State U.S. Stdnts.	Women Students	Minority Students
15	13	303	27	20%	—	19%	16%

LIBRARY (Tel. No. 312-567-3355)

Type	No. of Volumes	No. of Slides
Arch	11,000	15,000

STUDENT OPPORTUNITIES AND RESOURCES

The closely knit IIT campus of approximately 6500 students is located about three miles south of Chicago's Loop, an area rich in cultural and other resources for scholarship and research. The campus is conveniently located close to public transportation making it possible to easily reach all points in the city and suburbs. In addition, IIT's minibus provides free transportation between the main campus and IIT's downtown campus and suburban commuter train lines. As a world-famous center of modern architecture, Chicago is a great and unique resource for the study of architecture. Chicago is also the home of many distinguished architectural firms that are a source of summer and part-time jobs as well as permanent positions. The architecture program's reputation for a high standard of quality and a demanding curriculum provide strong credentials for students in the job market. IIT graduates are recognized for their ability to assume responsibility for their work and contribute to the profession. Students interested in transferring to the architecture program may apply in the Fall Semester only. A portfolio review is required if transferring from another architecture program, although students are not placed above the second-year level.

SPECIAL ACTIVITIES AND PROGRAMS

The College of Architecture, Planning and Design has special programs and activities available to its architecture students. Throughout the year the college sponsors lectures and slide presentations by prominent architects, designers, professors and students who have had the opportunity to be a recipient of one of the various traveling fellowships awarded. In addition, IIT is engaged in an exchange program with the Scot Sutherland School of Architecture RGIT in Aberdeen, Scotland. Each year two third-year architecture students are selected to spend their junior year abroad. Students can also take advantage of the joint degree program and obtain a B Arch/MBA degree in six rather than the normal seven years.

FACILITIES

Mies van der Rohe's S.R. Crown Hall is the home of the College of Architecture, Planning and Design. It holds the facilities for all the architecture, planning and design students, including a well-equipped and staffed shop for model making and a complete photo lab. A wide variety of large-scale and personal computers are available within both the university and the college.

SCHOLARSHIPS/AID

Students with outstanding scholastic credentials qualify for Presidential Leadership Scholarships and Dean's Scholarships. Additional merit scholarships are also available within the Department of Architecture: Crown Scholarships; Edgar and Ellen Higgins Foundation; Ludwig K. Hilberseimer Memorial; John A Holabird Summer Study Fellowship; Samuel Horwitz Memorial Scholarships; Jerrold Loebl Travelling Fellowship; Mies van der Rohe Scholarship; Vernon Spencer Watson Scholarship Fund. Need-based grants and loans are available through the Financial Aid Office. About 70% of IIT's full-time undergraduates receive some financial assistance.

UNDERGRADUATE PROGRAM
Philosophy Statement

The College of Architecture, Planning and Design at IIT has a rich heritage. The College's strength lies both in the adherence to a strong philosophical base and a commitment to the advancement of the profession it serves. There is a continuous tradition of innovation, experimentation, and achievement which reaches for the potential of our future.

Program Description

IIT's five year Bachelor of Architecture program is structured to provide the technical background and cultural education necessary for the professional practice of architecture. The educational objective is to establish a solid foundation of the skills and discipline required for unlimited problem-solving challenges. The curriculum, as initially established by Mies van der Rohe, is based on a sequenced educational program. The student's first years focus on learning the required professional skills and are combined with the later experience of developing refined advanced level projects and the study of architecture as an art. The faculty, comprised of practicing architects recognized for their individual contributions to architecture, work directly with each student. The studio learning process, an important part of architectural education from the very first year, provides the opportunity to test and apply the fundamental principles studied. Students work in small groups with professors, learning to analyze problems and generate solutions.

GRADUATE PROGRAM
Philosophy Statement

The Department of Architecture offers programs of graduate study which prepare students to meet the many professional responsibilities faced by architects of today.

The curriculum for the graduate programs is developed on the principles of architectural education established by Mies van der Rohe here at IIT. These principles demand not only consummate mastery of the skills and knowledge of the practice of architecture but also an understanding of the architect's role within today's economically and culturally complex society. The goals of the programs, founded in a rational method of work, are to refine the students' organizing, evaluating, and problem-solving abilities.

Program Description

There are several courses of study within the architectural program that are related to Chicago and the issues confronting its community of practicing architects, each leading to a Master of Architecture degree. Program One, a 1-year program for holders of a Bachelor of Architecture degree, leads to the Master of Architecture as a second professional degree. Program Two is a 2-year program leading to the Master of Architecture as a first professional degree for holders of a 4-year preprofessional bachelor's degree in architectural studies or a Bachelor of Architecture degree from a foreign university. Program Three is a 3½-year program for holders of a bachelor's degree in areas other than architecture and also leads to the Master of Architecture as a first professional degree. These programs recognize that a major portion of new construction within the city must be profit-oriented and sponsored by the private sector, examine the potential economic and political variables affecting the built environment, analyze the relationship of architecture to the production and delivery systems of the construction industry, attempt to improve accepted practices by exploring current trends and the decision-making process, and seek to provide for leadership in the architectural profession.

FACULTY
Administration

George Schipporeit, AIA, RA, Dean and
  Chairman
San Utsunomiya, AIA, RA, Assistant Dean
Anita Anderson, Reference Librarian

Associate Professors

Pao-Chi Chang, AIA, RA, BS Arch, MS Arch
David C Hovey, AIA, RA, B Arch, MS Arch
Louis Johnson, AIA, RA, B Arch, MS Arch
George Schipporeit, AIA, RA
David Sharpe, AIA, RA, B Arch, MS Arch
Alfred Swenson, AIA, RA, B Arch, MS Arch
Arthur Takeuchi, AIA, RA, B Arch, MS Arch
San Utsunomiya, AIA, RA, B Arch

Studio Professors

Alfred Caldwell, AIA, RA, BS
Myron Goldsmith, AIA, RA, BS Arch, MS Arch
Gilbert Gorski, AIA, RA, B Arch
John Heinrich, AIA, RA, B Arch
Gerald Horn, AIA, RA
Peter Roesch, AIA, RA, MS Arch
Burton Samuels, AIA, RA, B Arch

Part-Time Faculty

James Baird, AIA, RA, B Arch, MS Arch
Leonard Bihler
Dirk Denison, AIA, RA, B Arch MS Arch
Majoub Elnimeiri
John Hartray Jr, AIA, RA, B Arch
Robert Krawczyk, B Arch
Janet Krehbiel, AIA, RA, B Arch
Randy Long
Corey Postiglione
Christopher Rudolph, AIA, RA, B Arch
Paul Shaver, AIA, RA
Walter Sobel, AIA, RA
John Vinci, AIA, RA, BS Arch
Max Willig, AIA, RA, B Arch

University of Illinois at Chicago

School of Architecture
University of Illinois at Chicago
Box 4348 m/c 030
Chicago, Illinois 60680
(312) 996-3335

Application Deadline(s): B Arch, July 1 (Feb. 1
suggested)
M Arch, March 1 (earlier
encouraged)
Tuition & Fees: Undgrd: IL Res: Approx. $2385/yr
Non-res: Approx. $5700/yr
Grad: IL Res: Approx. $2700/yr
Non-res: Approx. $6609/yr
Endowment: Public

DEGREE PROGRAMS

Degree	Minimum Years for Degree	Accred.	Requirements for Admission	Full-Time Stdnts.	Part-Time Stdnts.	% of Applics. Accptd.	Stdnts. in 1st Year of Program	# of Degrees Conferred
B Arch	5	NAAB	Univ. req. for Freshmen, 3.25 out of 5.0 GPA for transfers	460			108	60
M Arch	1		B Arch, letters, statement of intent, portfolio, 4.0 out of 5.0 GPA, GRE	1		40%	1	5
M Arch	2	NAAB	BS in Arch studies, letters, statement of intent, portfolio, 4.0 out of 5.0 GPA, GRE	20		59%	11	5
M Arch	3	NAAB	bacc, 4.0 out of 5.0 GPA, letters, statement of intent, GRE	86		66%	36	23

SCHOOL DEMOGRAPHICS (all degree programs)

Full-Time Faculty	Part-Time Faculty	Full-Time Students	Part-Time Students	Foreign Students	Out-of-State U.S. Stdnts.	Women Students	Minority Students
27	19	567	0	6%		20%	14%

LIBRARY (Tel. No. 312-996-4588)

Type	No. of Volumes	No. of Slides
Arch & Art	9,600	224,000

STUDENT OPPORTUNITIES AND RESOURCES

The University of Illinois at Chicago began its undergraduate program in architecture as a two-year preparatory program at Chicago's "Navy Pier" as a part of that institution's evolving out of the US Navy V-2 officer training during World War Two. By 1965, the University of Illinois at Chicago Circle had blossomed into its new campus on the City's near west side, within view of Chicago's historic skyline. The study of architecture was expanded to a fully accredited five-year undergraduate program leading to a first professional degree (B Arch). By 1977, a three-year first professional Master's degree program was instituted for entering students having an undergraduate degree in a discipline other than architecture. That was quickly followed by a two-year first professional degree Master's program for candidates having a four-year undergraduate architectural degree (MS in Arch). By 1980, a second professional Master's degree program was put into place for those candidates having a first professional degree (B Arch).

The School of Architecture at the University of Illinois is a part of the College of Architecture, Art and Urban Planning. Interdisciplinary offerings are encouraged with these sister departments, though the administration of each of these units is completely independent.

The proximity of the School of Architecture (within the setting of the University) to the rich architectural heritage of Chicago cannot be overlooked. Chicago's seminal architectural tradition is well known internationally, and the city is thought by many to be the "Mecca" of America's central architectural tradition. That tradition forms the basis of architectural education at UIC, and the proximity to that history forms a "living laboratory" for students. Adjunct faculty and jurors at the architecture school regularly come from within the front ranks of Chicago's leading architectural practitioners who are the cutting edge of that continuously moving American architectural tradition.

SPECIAL ACTIVITIES AND PROGRAMS

Program Abroad For Undergraduate Students:
The School, in cooperation with the Department of Architecture in Urbana-Champaign and the Unite Pedagogique No. 3, offers a study-abroad program. Home base is Versailles, France. Course work parallels offerings in Chicago and Urbana while emphasizing the culture, landmarks, ambience, and opportunities of Europe. Formal course work is enriched by guided or informal field study and trips.
Program Abroad For Graduate Students:
The graduate program, in cooperation with the University of Washington, offers a one-quarter, ten-week program in Rome at the Palazzo Pio in the Campo di Fiori.
Eight-week Summer Program (regular and special class work).

Special Awards:
The Adrian Smith Fellowship in Architecture
The School of Architecture Faculty Traveling Fellowship
The Helen Hano Morgante Scholarship Fund
The Pella Prize
Endowed Lectures:
The Eva Maddox Endowed Lecture
The Gordon Crabtree Endowed Lecture
Public Lecture Series. Speakers in 1986-87 have included:
Terry Brown, architect, visiting critic-University of Cincinnati
Francois Bucher, professor-Florida State University
Douglas Davis, artist, author, architecture critic-Newsweek
Judith DiMaio, architect
Susan Handelman, associate professor-University of Maryland
Paul Jay, professor-Loyola University-Chicago
Jeffrey Kipnis, writer, lecturer, UIC visiting professor
Martin Kleinman, architect, UIC visiting professor
Daniel Liebeskind, Director Architecture Intermundium, Milan
Ross Miller, architecture critic
David Niland, architect, UIC visiting professor
Thomas Gordon Smith, architect, UIC visiting professor
Patrick Pinnell, architect, UIC visiting professor
Anthony Vidler, professor of architecture-Princeton
Public Lecture Series 1987-88
Fall Speakers include:
David Spaeth, architect, visiting professor, University of Kentucky

John Whiteman, architectural educator, Harvard University; director, Skidmore, Owings & Merrill Foundation
John Blatteau, architect, visiting professor, University of Pennsylvania
Diane Favro, PhD, architectural educator, University of California
Dr Richard Selzer, surgeon, Yale Medical School, author
Publications:

The NEWSLETTER is published three times a year by the School of Architecture. It contains a forum for faculty; reviews of preceding quarters' lecturers; faculty, alumni and student notes; updates on our overseas programs; and a detailed calendar of University and Chicago architectural events.

Threshold is the Journal of the School of Architecture, published once each year by Rizzoli, International.

Published annually, The Bulletin is the catalog of the School of Architecture, listing faculty, staff, graduate and undergraduate students, course structure, lecture series, and other vital information about the School.

FACILITIES

The School of Architecture Computer Lab offers students the opportunity to explore computer-aided design through its IBM-PC based systems running various CAD, spreadsheet and word processing programs, all of which are menu driven and can be interfaced. Peripherals include digitizing pads with Autocad templates, mouses, a 14-color high-resolution printer, a H-P plotter and 24" wide IBM proprinters. Classes are currently being taught in computer basics and Autocad.

The College of Architecture, Art and Urban Planning provides the School of Architecture with the services of two well-equipped fabrication shops. These facilities offer students and faculty alike the opportunity to model space and form in either wood, metal, or plaster.

In addition, students of the School have access to many photo darkrooms. Experiments in light modelling form can be easily set up and the results documented in these on-campus facilities.

SCHOLARSHIPS/AID

Financial aid is administered through the Office of Financial Aid and includes grants, scholarships, tuition waivers, loans, and employment. In addition, there are a

few grants and prizes specifically for students in the School of Architecture. A limited number of tuition waivers and teaching and research assistantships are available for graduate students.

PHILOSOPHY STATEMENT

Architecture is reflective of the aspirations of a culture, while simultaneously understanding of the continuous need for change through leadership. The study of architecture is, therefore, necessarily a civilizing discipline so as to train those who would mirror, as well as those who would lead their society. Cultural, as well as technological capability is crucial to those who would build in response to the needs of their epoch as well as for those who would discover new directions. Students of architecture at the University of Illinois at Chicago focus on the subject of the making of buildings as a synthetic response to the many forces acting on the form such buildings take. Therefore, the architecture studio is the center of activity at the School of Architecture at UIC.

The philosophy of the School is that the study of architecture is pluralistic in its intentions, establishing precedent as well as invention as not mutually exclusive, but ultimately interdependent, pursuits. Dialectically engaged, UIC's architecture program offers the extremes as well as the means for pursuing architecture in a pluralistic society.

Both the undergraduate and graduate programs in architecture share the following mission:

(1) to develop aesthetic sensibility and establish connoisseurship as a reasonable goal.

(2) to foster intellectual inquiry in order to cope with rapidly changing societal imperatives, and

(3) to assist the student in acquiring the necessary capabilities to engage in the practice of architecture.

It is important to stress the pluralistic nature of architectural education at the University of Illinois at Chicago. Both undergraduate and graduate curricula are structured so as to encourage debate such that the student is offered the many opportunities pedagogically available to engage in individual decision-making.

Courses in architectural theory, structures, environmental controls, computer-aided studies, urban planning, interiors, criticism, landscape design and visual studies are offered as a basis for decision-making which is then synthesized in the core of the program, the architectural studio.

Offerings in the architectural studios are diverse and wide-ranging. Individual buildings, as well as large urban planning problems, define some of the boundaries of the work offered in studio. The tradition of building, so common to the roots of Chicago architecture, forms a reassuring basis for the making of architecture at UIC. That tradition both informs as well as measures the work of the student in architectural studio at the University.

Undergraduate Program Description

The undergraduate curriculum is organized as a five-year sequential program of study leading to the professional Bachelor of Architecture degree with four areas of specialization: architectural design, building technology, structures, and humanities. The Bachelor of Architecture curriculum requires 252-259 quarter hours for graduation.

The program requires that the student complete work in each of the following interrelated areas: general education, studio, professional electives, and general electives.

General education provides the student with a balanced background in the liberal arts and sciences, including 44 credit hours in the humanities and social sciences and 12 credit hours in natural sciences, in addition to the development of skills in English composition and mathematics.

The studio is the core to the architectural curriculum, beginning in the first year with problems that are scaled to the student's personal and immediate experience and expanding as the student's vocabulary, technical skill, and maturity increase to allow consideration of complex building and urban design problems.

Professional electives provide access to knowledge in the environmental design field and develop the skills necessary to apply that knowledge.

General electives, coupled with the general education requirements, enable the student to develop breadth in subject areas outside the school and to explore individual interests. Since architecture must depend on the ideas and understandings developed in many disciplines, students are encouraged to use these electives to provide a mix of university-wide courses that relate to and support their architectural studies.

Graduate Program Description

The School of Architecture of the University of Illinois at Chicago offers three graduate programs leading to the professional Master of Architecture degree. Each of these separate programs is designed to provide both professional training in architecture and the opportunity for exploration into more specialized areas and topics of the built environment.

Option 1

The one-year Option One graduate program is designed for holders of a first professional degree in architecture. This program is an intensive course of study developed to further the students' critical skills and analytical abilities while expanding their areas of architectural expertise. Students in the program, which leads to the second professional degree, are required to take a minimum of 48 quarter hours in design, architectural theory and advanced elective courses in related fields.

Option 2

The two-year Option Two graduate program is designed for holders of a four-year pre-professional degree in architectural studies or environmental design. This curriculum is for those students who have already chosen to pursue a career in architecture and wish to gain the specialized knowledge and skills necessary to attain the first professional degree. Students are required to take from 48 to 101 quarter hours depending upon their level of preparation for advanced study. The program includes coursework in design, building science, structural engineering, architectural history and theory, planning and related elective courses. In the spring quarter of their first year, students have the option of participating in the School's Rome Program.

Option 3

The three-year Option Three graduate program is designed for holders of baccalaureate degrees in fields other than architecture. This is an accelerated curriculum that provides the specialized knowledge and skills that lead to the professional degree in architecture. Students are required to take from 102 to 156 quarter hours depending upon their level of preparation. The program consists of coursework in design, building science, structural engineering, architectural history and theory, planning and related elective courses. Students may participate in the Rome Program in the Spring Quarter of their second year.

FACULTY

Administration

Stanley Tigerman, FAIA, RA, Director, School of Architecture
Kenneth Dale Isaacs, Director, Graduate Studies, School of Architecture
Richard R Whitaker, Jr, AIA, RA, Dean of College of Architecture, Art & Urban Planning
Donald Ehresmann, Acting Associate Dean
Teresa Cann, Assistant Dean for Operations
Vince Paglione, Assistant Dean of Students
David Austin, Architecture & Art Librarian

Professors

Rene Amon, FASCE, RE, PhD
Edward Deam, AIA, RA, M Arch
Elliott Dudnik, AIA, RA, PhD
Michael Gelick, AIA, RA, M Arch
Robert Gerstner, ASCE, RE, PhD
Ezra Gordon, FAIA, RA, B Arch
R. Thomas Jaeger, AIA, RA, M Arch
Phillip Kupritz, AIA, RA, M Arch
John Macsai, FAIA, RA, B Arch
Stanley Tigerman, FAIA, RA, M Arch
Richard Whitaker, AIA, RA, B Arch

Associate Professors

Bruno Ast, AIA, RA, M Arch
Stuart Cohen, FAIA, RA, M Arch
Lloyd Gadau, AIA, RA, B Arch
Kenneth Isaacs, MFA
Hinman Kealy, MCP
Sidney Robinson, AIA, RA, D Arch
Louis Rocah, AIA, RA, MSc Arch
Kenneth Schroeder, AIA, RA, M Arch
Thomas Gordon Smith, RA, M Arch
Roger Whitmer, AIA, RA, MS

Assistant Professors

David Fanella, PhD
Roberta Feldman, PhD
Jon Liljequist, RE, JD
John Naughton, AIA, RA, M Arch
Anders Nereim, AIA, RA, B Arch
Martha Pollak, PhD

Part-Time Faculty

Roula Alakiotou, M Arch
Andrea Clark Brown, M Arch
Julian Dawson, MS Civil Engr
Deborah Doyle, Dipl
Paul Florian, Dipl
Bryan Fuermann, PhD
Douglas Garofalo
David Greenspan, M Arch
John Hartray, Jr, B Arch
Edward Hoffman, Jr, B Arch
Catherine Ingraham, PhD
Ronald Krueck, BS Arch
Tannys Langdon
Michael Lustig
Michel Mossessian, MA
William Murphy, B Arch
James Nagle, FAIA, RA
Benjamin Nicholson, M Arch
Michel Paillet, M Arch
Thomas Rajkovich, B Arch
Wallace Rappe, M Arch
Norberto Rosenstein, M Arch
Molla Selassie, MSc
Richard Solomon, M Env Des
John Tittman
Diane Travis, M Arch

Adjunct Faculty

Thomas Beeby, AIA, RA
Laurence Booth, FAIA, RA
Helmut Jahn, FAIA, RA
Lawrence Perkins, FAIA, RA
John Vinci, FAIA, RA
Ben Weese, FAIA, RA
Cynthia Weese, AIA, RA

Visiting Distinguished Professors

David Bell
Peter Eisenman
Mario Gandelsonas
Allan Greenberg
David Handlin
Jeffrey Kipnis
Michael Sorkin
David Spaeth

University of Illinois at Urbana-Champaign

School of Architecture
University of Illinois
608 East Lorado Taft Drive
Champaign, Illinois 61820
(217) 333-1330

Graduate Admissions Office
(217) 244-4723
Undergraduate Affairs Office
(217) 333-7720

Application Deadline(s): Undgrd: Nov 1 for Fall
Grad: Feb 15 for Fall
Tuition & Fees: Undgrd: IL Res: $1,960/yr
Non-res: $4772/yr
Grad: IL Res: $2514/yr
Non-Res: $6434/yr
(All tuition and fees are
subject to change.)
Endowment: Public

DEGREE PROGRAMS

Degree	Minimum Years for Degree	Accred.	Requirements for Admission	Full-Time Stdnts.	Part-Time Stdnts.	% of Applics. Accptd.	Stdnts. in 1st Year of Program	# of Degrees Conferred
BS Arch Studies	4		HS class rank, ACT or SAT	598	0	65%	177	129
M Arch	1		B Arch, GPA, letters, statement of purpose, portfolio	20	0	50%	20	6
M Arch	2	NAAB	Nonprofessional arch degree, GPA, letters, statement of purpose, portfolio	132	0	70%	62	68
M Arch	varies	NAAB	Degree in any discipline, GPA letters, statement of purpose, portfolio	54	0	80%	21	**
M Arch/MBA	2½	NAAB*	Nonprof arch degree, GPA, MBA admission, letters, statement of purpose, portfolio					
M Arch/MSF	2½	NAAB*	Nonprof arch degree, GPA, MSF admission, letters, statement of purpose, portfolio					
M Arch/MCS	2½	NAAB*	Nonprof arch degree, GPA, MCS admission, letters, statement of purpose, portfolio					
M Arch/MSCE	2½	NAAB*	Nonprof arch degree, GPA, CE admission, letters, statement of purpose, portfolio					
M Arch/MUP	2½	NAAB*	Nonprof arch degree, GPA, MUP admission, letters, statement of purpose, portfolio					

*M Arch degree only.

**After 2 years Track 3 students are included in Track 2 numbers.

SCHOOL DEMOGRAPHICS (all degree programs)

Full-Time Faculty	Part-Time Faculty	Full-Time Students	Part-Time Students	Foreign Students	Out-of-State U.S. Stdnts.	Women Students	Minority Students
47	10	804	0	3.3%	12.3%	25.2%	4.9%

LIBRARY (Tel. No. 217-333-0224)

Type	No. of Volumes	No. of Slides
Arch & Art	42,000*	225,000

*(24,000 Arch only, plus 45,000 Arch in main library stacks)

Lecture and Exhibition series
Plym Distinguished Professorship (Past recipients - Gunnar Birkerts, Paul Rudolph, and Joseph Esherick)
Limited summer school program
Annual Architecture Awards (A³) Banquet
Job Placement Office
Student organizations:
Gargoyle, national architecture honorary
Student Advisory Council (SAC)
Student Publications Office
American Institute of Architecture Students (AIAS)
Construction Specifications Institute (CSI)
Computers in Architecture (CIA)
Architects in Management (AIM)
Society of Architectural Historians (SAH)
Illuminating Engineering Society (IES)
Black Architectural Students Association (BASA)
Women in Architecture (WIA)
Alpha Rho Chi (APX)
School publications:
RICKERNOTES - Student weekly newsletter
REFLECTIONS - School of Architecture Journal
REFLECTIONS MONOGRAPH SERIES
ARCHITECTURE AT ILLINOIS - Alumni   newsletter

STUDENT OPPORTUNITIES AND RESOURCES

Within the College of Fine and Applied Arts, other degree programs allied to architecture are offered as follows: School of Art and Design, BFA and MFA in Industrial Design; Department of Landscape Architecture, BLA and MLA; and the Department of Urban and Regional Planning, BAUP and MUP. The College of Agriculture offers a BS in Interior Design.

Resident undergraduate architecture students in good academic standing and meeting all curriculum requirements may apply during their sophomore year for acceptance to the junior year Study Abroad Program in Versailles, France. The two-semester program fulfills the course requirements of the junior year. Versailles faculty are selected from the faculty at the Urbana-Champaign campus on a rotating basis.

Initiated in 1986, the architectural design thesis studio adjunct critic program provides design thesis students an opportunity to work with internationally known Chicago architects. Students meet with their adjunct critic several times during the year, in Chicago or on campus.

The School of Architecture Professional Advisory Council is composed of fifteen architects who convene from time to time at the request of the School Director to discuss, advise, and interact with faculty of the School on topics of interest relative to the practice of architecture and the educational program in architecture at the University of Illinois at Urbana-Champaign.

The Council members are all registered architects and/or architectural engineers and include some alumni, professionals from large and smaller practices from the Chicago metropolitan area, as well as downstate and out-of-state locations.

Research units include: the Architecture Research Center (ARC), the Small Homes Council-Building Research Council, the Housing Research and Development Program (HR&D), and the US Army Construction Engineering Research Laboratory (CERL).

SPECIAL ACTIVITIES AND PROGRAMS

Junior-year Study Abroad Program in Versailles, France
Undergraduate academic counseling system
Computer applications in architecture

FACILITIES

The Architecture Building:
    College of Fine and Applied Arts administrative offices
    School of Architecture administrative offices
    Graduate admissions office
    Temple Buell Architecture Gallery
    Ricker Library of Architecture and Art
    Slide Library
    Graduate architectural design studios
    Lecture rooms/seminar rooms
    Structures labs
    Faculty offices
    Computer lab
    Photographic studio
    Photographic darkroom
    Model shop

Flagg Hall:
    Undergraduate Affairs Office
    Undergraduate architectural design studios
    Seminar rooms
    Lighting lab
    Computer labs
    Faculty offices

Noble Hall:
    Undergraduate architectural design studios
    Photographic studio
    Faculty offices

Architecture Research Center:
    Offices for School of Architecture research faculty and
    research assistants

SCHOLARSHIPS/AID

Information on fellowships, scholarships, teaching
assistantships, research assistantships, and resource
assistantships is available from the School of Architecture
graduate admissions office or the office of undergraduate
affairs. Approximately 50 percent of the graduate
students receive financial support from the School.

For additional scholarship and loan information, please
refer to university catalogs and direct inquiries to the
Director, Student Financial Aids Office, 420 Student
Services Building, 610 East John Street, Champaign,
Illinois 61820.

UNDERGRADUATE PROGRAM
Philosophy Statement

From its inception in 1867, the professional program in
architecture has been built on the interdependence of
professional practice and architectural education. In 1893
the program was divided into two branches, design and
engineering, the latter being the first of its kind in the
United States. The impetus for the division came from
architects in Chicago, the home of the early skyscraper.
From early ties to engineering, through the waxing and
waning infuence of the Ecole des Beaux Arts, the
necessary contents of an architect's knowledge have
been ever increasing, leading, by 1950, to an expension
in the curriculum from four to five years, and again, in
1969, to the six-year (4+2) program with eight options for
the professional Master of Architecture as the terminal
degree.

The School respects the traditions of architecture and
its own past without being locked into them. It looks to
the future of the profession with optimism. It keeps a
close watch for changing conditions and new
opportunities.

The School sees the scope of architecture to be so
vast that no individual is likely to master it all, that all
aspects of life and nature are of significance to
architecture and that, with few exceptions in practice,
teamwork is indispensable. Yet the architect can ill afford
to be unacquainted with any of the major components of
architecture, ranging from art, history and design to
economics, engineering, computer-aided design and
management.

As conditions for practice and needs of the public
have changed, the School has made adjustments and
changes in the curriculum's contents and emphasis. The
School attracts and strives to continue to attract creative
talent, to foster creative skills, provide the best possible

core of theory and knowledge, instill disciplined ways of
thinking about problems, and to send forth well-equipped
individuals ready to enter and effectively serve the
profession and the public well into the next century.

In the final analysis, the expectation of graduates is to
prepare themselves for an active professional role; to
gain knowledge of architectural problems and ways to
address them; to become familiar with the language of
the many disciplines which contribute to the shaping of
the built environment; to become aware of the past,
current and new applications of information and
knowledge; to become aware of the influences of change
affecting architecture; to become sensitive to the needs
of society and its link with the natural environment; to
acquire ability to solve architectural problems; and to
develop a sense of confidence in their personal
interpretation of the role of the profession in society and
in their ability to become a vital part of the practice of
architecture as they individually perceive it.

Program Description

The School of Architecture offers a four-year
undergraduate preprofessional curriculum leading to the
Bachelor of Science in Architectural Studies degree.

The undergraduate curriculum offers an appropriate
balance of basic professional studies in architectural
design, architectural history, construction, environmental
technology, structures, and studies in the arts and
sciences.

The university recommends that students whose goals
include establishment of professional standing attain the
M Arch degree. The two-year graduate program at Illinois
leads to this professional degree.

GRADUATE PROGRAM
Program Description

For applicants who have attained a four-year BS Arch
Studies or a similar degree in architecture from a school
of architecture, the two-year graduate professional
degree program (Track 2) emphasizes further study in
architectural disciplines. In the first year, all candidates
select an area of concentration and are required to enroll
in a core of advanced studies in design, professional
practice, structures, and electives. The second year is
devoted to an optional area of concentration selected
from architectural design, architectural history and
historic preservation, architectural management/business
administration, architectural practice, housing
environments, structures, urban design, and individual
study.

For applicants who have attained the five-year B Arch
professional degree, the one-year M Arch professional
degree (Track 1) provides the opportunity to concentrate
in a specific area of study, comparable to the second
year of the Track 2 program.

The Track 3 M Arch professional degree program is
designed for applicants who have a bachelor's degree in
a field other than architecture. Prior education and
professional experience may affect the time required to
complete this program.

Double degree programs offered by the School are: M
Arch/MBA (Business Administration); M Arch/MSF
(Finance); M Arch/MCS (Computer Science); M Arch/MCE
(Civil Engineering in Construction Management); M
Arch/MUP (Urban Planning).

FACULTY
Administration

R Alan Forrester, RIBA, RAIC, Director, School of
    Architecture
Ingvar Schousboe, FSCE, FACI, Associate Director, S of A
Arthur L Kaha, RA, Assistant Director and Coordinator for
    Undergraduate Affairs, S of A
Jane Block, Architecture Librarian

Professors

James R Anderson, B Arch, MUP
Jack S Baker, FAIA, M Arch
William Eng, AIA, M Arch, MS Urban Design
John S Garner, B Arch, M Arch, PhD
Bruce L Hutchings, AIA, ASCA, M Arch, MLA
Michael Kim, AIA, M Arch, PhD
Samuel T Lanford, AIA, B Arch, M Arch
Walter H Lewis, AIA, MS Arch
H James Miller, AIA, PE, B Arch, M Arch
Alec Notaras, RA, Dipl
William J O'Connell, AIA, B Arch, M Arch
Shivnath Prasad, RA, Dipl
Ingvar Schousboe, PE, SE, MS ENG
Jack H Swing, RA, BLA, BS Arch
Richard L Tavis, RA, B Arch, M Arch
James P Warfield, RA, B Arch, M Arch
David J Wickersheimer, NSPE, AIA, B Arch, MS Arch
Claude A Winkelhake, M Arch, PhD

Associate Professors

Johann G Albrecht, MA PhD
Mir M Ali, ASCE, MASC U, PhD U
Donald E Bergeson, RA, M Arch
Richard J Betts, PhD
Botond Bognar, RA, M Arch, MA
Ernest H Clay, RA, B Arch, M Arch
Carolyn Dry, RA, B Arch, M Arch
William H Erwin, RA, SE, B Arch, MS Arch
Lloyd A Leffers, AIA, B Arch, MS Arch
Robert T Mooney, AIA, B Arch, M Arch
Robert G Ousterhout, MA, PhD
Henry S Plummer, M Arch
Ronald E Schmitt, RA, B Arch, M Arch
Robert I Selby, AIA, B Arch, M Arch
James E Simon, AIA, B Arch, MS Arch
Robert L Smith, PE, BS
William J Voelker III, AIA, B Arch, M Arch, MBA
Hubert White, AIA, B Arch

Assistant Professors

Michael J Andrejasich, AIA, M Arch
Kathryn H Anthony, PhD
Paul J Armstrong, M Arch
Clark T Baurer, M Arch
Charles D Knight, M Arch
Dale B Poynter
Charles R Reifsteck, M Arch
Lydia M Soo, M Arch, MA

Lecturers

Arthur L Kaha, RA, B Arch, M Arch
Paul Kruty, MA

Instructors

Ellen Dickson, M Arch
Karen Gans-Piazza, M Arch
Patrick McLane, BA
Michael Rabens, M Arch

Part-Time Faculty

Kurt P Froehlich, M Ed, JD
John B Hackler, FAIA, B Arch
Raymond H Lytle, AIA, B Arch, M Arch
Edward P Perry, AIA, B Arch, M Arch
Robert B Riley, PhB, B Arch
A Richard Williams, FAIA, M Arch

Iowa State University

Department of Architecture
156 College of Design
Iowa State University
Ames, Iowa 50011
(515) 294-4717

Admissions and Records
109 Beardshear
Iowa State University
Ames, Iowa 50011
(515) 294-5836

Application Deadline(s): Undgrd: August 15
Grad: February 1
Tuition & Fees: Undgrd: Iowa Res: $852/sem
(≥12 hours)   Non-res: $2744/sem
Grad: Iowa Res: $1009/sem
Non-res: $2859/sem
Endowment: Public

DEGREE PROGRAMS

Degree	Minimum Years for Degree	Accred.	Requirements for Admission	Full-Time Stdnts.	Part-Time Stdnts.	% of Applics. Accptd.	Stdnts. in 1st Year of Program	# of Degrees Conferred
B Arch	5	NAAB	Upper ½ of class ACT 24, SAT 980	48	0	27%	242	20
M Arch	1		B Arch, portfolio GRE TOEFL, upper ½ of class	7	1	32%	5	3
M Arch	2	NAAB	BA in Arch or Env Des, portfolio GRE, TOEFL, upper ½ of class	22	5	34%	10	3
M Arch	3.5	NAAB	Bacc. in other than Arch GRE, TOEFL	17	0	31%	8	1
M SAS	1.5		Bacc. upper ½ of class	0	2	0%	0	1
BS in CRP*	4	PAB	Upper ½ of class in ACT 24, SAT 980	70	8	95%	12	20
MCRP*	2	PAB	Bacc. in Urb. Pl., Arch or related field, upper ½ class	20	5	75%	6	10
BLA+	5	LAAB	Upper ½ class in ACT 24, SAT 980	144		58%	45	29
MLA+	1⅓		Bacc. in Lands Arch or related field, upper ½ class	6		30%	5	3

*Dept. of Community & Regional Planning + Dept. of Landscape Architecture.

SCHOOL DEMOGRAPHICS (all degree programs)*

Full-Time Faculty	Part-Time Faculty	Full-Time Students	Part-Time Students	Foreign Students	Out-of-State U.S. Stdnts.	Women Students	Minority Students
22	9	617	47	10%	41%	18%	7%

*Note: Figures include BA program, currently being phased out.

LIBRARY (Tel. No. 515-294-7102)

Type	No. of Volumes	No. of Slides
Arch & Art	11,000	110,000

STUDENT OPPORTUNITIES AND RESOURCES

The College of Design includes the Departments of Architecture, Landscape Architecture, Art and Design, and Community and Regional Planning and programs in Interior Design, Graphic Design and Art and Crafts. All departments are housed in the same building, which was built in 1978.

Students in the college must satisfy a common core of 45 credits. Advanced students have opportunities for interdisciplinary study in the college and the university as well as an opportunity to study on campuses abroad through the department's Foreign Study Program.

The architecture faculty come from diverse backgrounds and educational institutions. They have interests in relating architecture to computer applications, man and environment relations, design methods, historic preservation, the handicapped and elderly, solar design, building systems, programming, housing, energy systems, and many other areas.

Faculty and students have access to the facilities of the university library, the computation center, the College of Design Research Institute and to media services.

SPECIAL ACTIVITIES AND PROGRAMS

AIAS Student Chapter
Field trips to urban centers
Foreign Study program
Intern Development program
Visiting lectures program
Exhibits program
Faculty Seminars
Tau Sigma Delta national architecture honorary society
Student Awards
College Symposia
Placement Office

FACILITIES

The department is housed in a single building with the three other departments of the college (Art & Design, Landscape Architecture, and Community & Regional Planning). Design studios, faculty offices, a lecture room and a daylighting laboratory make up department spaces. Shared facilities include a library/reading room, a slide library, gallery and exhibit rooms, drawing studios, seminar room, computer laboratory and a photography laboratory.

SCHOLARSHIP/AID

The University offers financial assistance with grants, scholarships, loans and part time employment opportunities, either singly or in combination. Scholarship recipients are selected on the basis of academic merit or other demonstrated talent. Financial aid need is determined on the basis of the Family Financial Statement on the Financial Aid Form. Approximately 150 students in architecture receive financial aid totaling $584,000 from the University.

In addition, the department awards a very few scholarships from department funds to advanced students on the basis of merit. Several teaching and research assistantships of approximately $5300 per year are available to graduate students.

UNDERGRADUATE PROGRAM
Philosophy Statement

The program is structured to take advantage of the interdisciplinary nature of the colleges and to prepare the student for a professional career in architecture.

Program Description

The undergraduate professional program of 134 credits is preceded by a 32.5 credit pre-professional program and leads to the first professional degree, Bachelor of Architecture. Admission to the professional program is based upon the applicant's performance in the completed pre-professional program, and on available resources in the department.

GRADUATE PROGRAM
Philosophy Statement

The M Arch program is designed to provide professional education in the practice of architecture as well as a graduate concentration, utilizing university-wide resources, in one of four areas: Community, including town, neighborhood, and urban design; Resources, including appropriate technology and energy conscious design; Design Methods, including practice, environmental evaluation, and computer applications; and Management, including business, development, and construction.

The MSAS program is designed to enable students to conduct scholarly work and research in architecture.

Program Description

The first of two graduate programs the department offers leads to the professional degree, master of architecture. It is a three-part program serving students with a variety of backgrounds. Applicants holding BA or BS degrees in architecture or environmental design and applicants with B Arch degrees are given advanced standing in the program. Applicants with undergraduate degrees in fields other than the above may receive advanced standing or may be required to complete additional prerequisite work as part of the program, depending upon their prior education and experience. Students holding B Arch degrees must complete a minimum of 30 graduate credits; other students must complete a minimum of 60 credits including 40 graduate credits.

A second graduate program leads to the degree of master of science in architectural studies. It is a 40 graduate credit nonprofessional program and is for applicants holding degrees in architecture or other disciplines.

FACULTY
Administration

Thomas D Galloway, Dean and Director, College of Design
Michael Underhill, RA, AIA, B Arch, MCP, Chairman, Department of Architecture
Diane K Childs, Library Assistant

Professors

David A Block, RA, AIA, B Arch, M Arch
Herbert W Gottfried, AB, PhD
Howard C Heemstra, RA, AIS, B Arch, M Arch
Eino O Kainlauri, RA, AIA, B Arch, M Arch
Marion J Kitzman, BFA, MA
Karol J Kocimski, RA, AIA, Dipl, M Arch
Donald I McKeown, RA, BS, MS
Rabindra Mukerjea, RA, AIA, B Arch, MAS
Lawton M Patten, B Arch
Wesley I Shank, RA, AIA, BA, M Arch
Paul Shao, MFA, ED D
Vernon F Stone, RA, AIA, B Arch

Associate Professors

Robert A Findlay, RA, B Arch, M Arch
Jamie L Horwitz, BFA, PhD
Peter Orleans, RA, M Arch
Arvid E Osterberg, RA, B Arch, M Arch, D Arch
James R Patterson, RA, B Arch, MS
Walter J Toporek, B Arch, M Arch
Edmund R Young, RA, AIA, B Arch, M Arch

Assistant Professors

Christopher N Bardt, B Arch, M Arch
Bruce L Bassler, RA, AIA, BS, M Arch
Clare Cardinal-Pett, M Arch
Kyna J Leski, B Arch, M Arch
John H Maves, B Arch, M Arch
Mark B Orlowski, BS, M Arch, D Arch

Instructors

Mary J Ververka, BA, MS

Part-Time Faculty

Joseph W Chauncey, RA, AIA, AB, PhD
Thomas R Clause, RA, AIA, B Arch
Mark C Englebrecht, RA, AIA, B Arch, M Arch
Douglas A Frey, RA, AIA, BS
Calvin F Lewis, RA, AIA, B Arch
Charles Masterson, M Arch
Robert K Olson, RA, AIA, B Arch, M Arch
Charles T Overton, RA, B Arch, M Arch
John S Rice, RA, AIA, B Arch
Richard J Roseland, RA, AIA, B Arch
Steven Strassburg, AIA, BA, M Arch
Douglas A Wells, RA, AIA, BA

Kansas State University

Department of Architecture
College of Architecture
 and Design
211 Seaton
Kansas State University
Manhattan, Kansas 66506
(913) 532-5950 (college)
(913) 532-5953 (dept)

Director of Admissions
119 Anderson Hall
Manhattan, Kansas 66506
(913) 532-6250

Application Deadline(s): Undgrd: None
                        Grad: 1 December for
                        fall term;
                        1 March for spring
                        term
Tuition & Fees: Undgrd: KS res: $666/sem;
                Non-res: $1751/sem
                Grad: KS res: $726/sem;
                Non-res: $1811/sem
Endowment: Public

DEGREE PROGRAMS

Degree	Minimum Years for Degree	Accred.	Requirements for Admission	Full-Time Stdnts.	Part-Time Stdnts.	% of Applics. Accptd.	Stdnts. in 1st Year of Program	# of Degrees Conferred
B Arch	5	NAAB	successful completion of environmental design curriculum; 2.50 GPA	240	12	*	80	87
BLA	5	LAAB	successful completion of environmental design curriculum; 2.50 GPA	43	5	*	25	21
BIA	5	FIDER	successful completion of environmental design curriculum; 2.50 GPA	69	0	*	21	20
M Arch	1.5		undergraduate degree and transcripts; references; admission to Graduate School	28	0	40%	12	6
MRCP	2	APA/ACSP	undergraduate degree; admission to Graduate School	16	4	40%		7

*Kansas State University is an open admissions university. All students from Kansas and Missouri are accepted in the freshman year; after successful completion of the two year environmental design curriculum, students apply for admission to one of the professional programs.

SCHOOL DEMOGRAPHICS (all degree programs)

Full-Time Faculty	Part-Time Faculty	Full-Time Students	Part-Time Students	Foreign Students	Out-of-State U.S. Stdnts.	Women Students	Minority Students
34	3	396	21	6%	46%	24%	8%

LIBRARY (Tel. No. 913-532-5968)

Type	No. of Volumes	No. of Slides
Arch	35,000	45,000

STUDENT OPPORTUNITIES AND RESOURCES

At Kansas State University, architecture students from the Kansas/Missouri region, many parts of the U.S., and various foreign countries, develop academically and professionally in cooperation with students preparing for careers in regional and community planning, interior architecture, and landscape architecture. Students spend the first two years of undergraduate study in the Department of Environmental Design. In this interdisciplinary department they have the opportunity to gain an understanding of broad concepts and issues related to the design professions and to begin acquisition of skills common to them. The faculty's varied experience and educational preparation help to ensure a lively academic environment with ample opportunity to pursue individual interests in architecture. Many architecture students choose significant elective course work offered by other colleges in the university, including art, business, computer science, and social science.

Design studios, where most students spend a great deal of time pursuing individual and group study, are the symbolic "living room" of the department. The studio areas are complemented by specialized facilities for computer graphics, photography, architectural ornament, sun and wind studies, seminars, displays, and design reviews. The College library and audiovisual collections, as well as several copy centers, are conveniently located and well staffed to meet the special needs of architecture students.

The department makes full use of the community and the region as a laboratory for learning. In cooperation with civic and government groups, academic studies are carried out by students in rural and urban settings from Manhattan to Kansas City to Chicago.

SPECIAL ACTIVITIES AND PROGRAMS

Ekdahl Lecture Series
Fine Arts Lecture Series
Faculty Seminars
University Convocation Speakers
Landon Lectures on Public Affairs
Auditorium Performing Arts Program
Internship Program (optional during fourth year for credit and paid employment in the profession)

Intersession
Oz Journal
AIAS Chapter
Design Council
Tau Sigma Delta Honorary Society
Design Weekend
Chicago Trip
Design Discovery Program
Boston Architecture and Design Summer
Architecture from the Plains Exhibits/Lectures
Exchange Program w/School of Architecture, Aarhus, Denmark
Bryant Lectureship
Beaux Arts Ball
Architecture and Design BlitzFest
Alumni Fellow Program
Kansas City Program
Collaboration Studio
Architecture Update Monthly Newsletter

FACILITIES

Computer-Aided Design Lab
Micro-Computer Lab

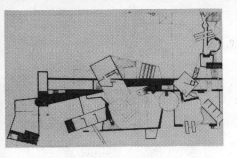
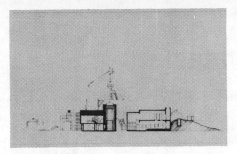
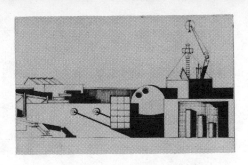

Heliodon
Wind Tunnel
Artificial Sky
Photo Lab
Audio-Visual Aids Collection
Technology Information Collection
Weigel Library

SCHOLARSHIPS/AID

At Kansas State University more than 1,500 students received scholarship aid in 1986/87. More than 7,000 were recipients of loans, and more than 5,000 were employed on the University campus. A total of almost $32 million was received by students through these programs. In addition to eligibility for most University aid programs, students in the College of Architecture and Design qualify for several special scholarship awards, and for a variety of prizes.

Graduate students may qualify for teaching and research assistantships carrying up to $4,000 in salary and a substantial reduction in tuition.

UNDERGRADUATE PROGRAM
Philosophy Statement

The boundaries of professional practice have swiftly expanded and few architectural firms render only those services they did a decade ago. Variety and change characterize the profession, yet there remains a core of activity and concern that architects share. The five-year architecture curriculum was developed in response to these circumstances and in the belief that architectural education should accommodate a broad range of student interests and areas of aptitude.

Program Description

Students entering the Department of Architecture have completed a two-year program of study in the Department of Environmental Design. The Department of Environmental Design offers the interdisciplinary graduate and undergraduate course work in the College. Students in the first two years are introduced to the knowledge, concerns, attitudes, methods, and skills common to the environmental design professions of architecture, interior architecture, landscape architecture, and regional and community planning. Students undertake a curriculum in architecture after successful completion of an interdisciplinary curriculum in the Department of Environmental Design. The curriculum in the third, fourth, and fifth year in the Department of Architecture includes a central body of professional and technical course work, an array of design studio courses from which students make a selection each semester, and substantial blocks of professional support and free electives. Fully 50% of the course work during the final three years of study offers the students significant choice.

The faculty is committed to a program of broadly-based professional education in architecture. Thus, undergraduate specialization is discouraged, but students are helped to define and pursue special interests or abilities within the curricular framework. Through participation in an elective thirty-week internship program, students may gain first-hand experience in private professional offices, public agencies, or other organizations In the design and building industry field while earning academic credit.

GRADUATE PROGRAM
Philosophy Statement

Development of specialized knowledge and skills after completion of baccalaureate studies is the central purpose of the Master of Architecture program. Graduate study strengthens preparation for creative professional roles and responses to increasingly complex problems in the physical and social environment. The program addresses areas of specialization in which the school possesses unusually extensive faculty and curricular resources.

Program Description

Students who have a first professional degree in architecture, a non-professionally accredited degree in architecture, or a baccalaureate in certain other fields, may be accommodated in the College's post-professional or non-professional graduate program. A minimum of 30 semester hours, usually one and one-half years in residence, are required. However, the duration of individual programs varies with personal goals and academic and professional preparation.

Faculty members participating in the Master of Architecture program currently offer special expertise in the following areas. The area of environment/behavior and place studies affords opportunity for study and research in behavioral programming and evaluation design for special users and place studies. The second area of specialization, preservation and community design, affords opportunities to gain knowledge required in making effective decisions about the design of towns and cities, and to relate the role of the designer to other disciplines and to the concepts and policies of community and urban development within a historical perspective. Students study preservation and adaptive use of significant structures and revitalization of historic neighborhoods and urban fabric in Plains States communities. Emphasis is placed on interdisciplinary collaboration.

FACULTY
Administration

Mark Lapping, CP, RF, Dean
William Jahnke, PE, Assistant Dean
Robert Burnham, RA, AIA, Head, Department of Architecture
Richard Hoag, Head, Department of Environmental Design
Eugene Kremer, FAIA, RA, Director, Program Development
Paul Windley, Director of Graduate Studies
Patricia Weisenburger, Director of Architectural Branch Library

Architecture Faculty
Professors

Gary Coates, B Env Des, M Arch
Edward De Vilbiss, AIA, RA, B Arch
F Gene Ernst, AIA, RA, B Arch, M Arch (UD)
Eugene Kremer, FAIA, RA, B Arch, M Arch
William Miller, AIA, RA, B Arch, M Arch
Sidney Stotesbury, BS, MA, PhD
Paul Windley, BS, B Arch, M Arch, D Arch

Associate Professors

Dale Bryant, RA, B Arch, M Arch
Robert Burnham, AIA, RA, B Arch, M Arch
Keith Christensen, RA, B Arch, M Arch
William Jahnke, BSME
James Jones, RA, B Bus Adm, M Arch
Carolyn Norris-Baker, B Arch, MA, PhD
David Seamon, BA, MA, PhD
Donald Watts, B Arch, M Arch

Assistant Professors

Martha Abbott, BA, M Arch
Daniel Faoro, B Arch, M Arch
Vladimir Krstic, M Eng/Arch, Dipl
Douglass Lundman, B Art, B Arch
Michael McNamara, B Arch, M Arch
Llewellyn Seibold, BS, M Arch
Raymond Streeter, RA, B Arch, M Arch

Instructors

David Brown, B Arch

Environmental Design Faculty
Professors

Bernd Foerster, FAIA, BS Arch, M Arch
Richard Hoag, BA, M Arch

Associate Professors

Anthony Chelz, B Art Ed, MFA
Gary Haycock, AIA, BFA, M Arch
Fayez Husseini, B Arch, M Arch, MFA
Richard McDonald, BS, M Arch
Eugene Wendt, B Arch, M Arch

Assistant Professors

Robert Bullock, BFA, MFA
Lorn Clement, BS, BLA, MLA
Gwen Owens-Wilson, AIA, RA, BA, B Arch, MS, PhD
Susanne Siepl-Coates, Dipl, M Arch

Part-Time Faculty

Bruce McMillan, B Arch, M Arch
Ifan Payne, B Arch, PhD
Carol Watts, BA, M Arch, PhD

University of Kansas

School of Architecture and Urban Design
205 Marvin Hall
University of Kansas
Lawrence, Kansas 66045-2250
(913) 864-5126

Admissions Office:
(913) 864-4281

Application Deadline(s): December 1 for early decision
February 1 for late decision

Tuition & Fees: Undgrd: KS Res: $1325/yr.
Non-res: $3495/yr.
Grad: KS Res: $1440/yr.
Non-res: $3610/yr.

Endowment: Public

DEGREE PROGRAMS

Degree	Minimum Years for Degree	Accred.	Requirements for Admission	Full-Time Stdnts.	Part-Time Stdnts.	% of Applics. Accptd.	Stdnts. in 1st Year of Program	# of Degrees Conferred
B Arch	5	NAAB	KS Students upper ½ of HS MO Students upper ⅓ of HS Other Students upper 1/10 of HS	520	0	45%	135	80
BS Arch E	5	ABET	KS Students upper ½ of HS MO Students upper ⅓ of HS Other Students upper 1/10 of HS	147	0	58%	40	29
B Arch (Career Change)	2.5	NAAB	Bachelor's degree with 3.0 GPA	24	0	70%	12	10
M Arch	1.5		Bachelor's degree with 3.0 GPA	34	44	75%	50	23
MS Arch E	1		Engineering degree with 3.0 GPA	20	10	52%	14	4
MUP	2	AIP	Bachelor's degree with 3.0 GPA	34	10	81%	16	13
DE	3		Master in Eng. with 3.0 GPA	3	0	-	0	2

SCHOOL DEMOGRAPHICS (all degree programs)

Full-Time Faculty	Part-Time Faculty	Full-Time Students	Part-Time Students	Foreign Students	Out-of-State U.S. Stdnts.	Women Students	Minority Students
32	23	782	64	3%	10%	25%	3%

LIBRARY (Tel. No. 913-864-3244)

Type	No. of Volumes	No. of Slides
Art & Arch	75,000	56,000

STUDENT OPPORTUNITIES AND RESOURCES

The New York Times *Selective Guide to Colleges* calls KU "a cornbelt Berkeley that in selected areas offers some of the finest programs in the country. Standout areas include architecture...." The campus, atop Mount Oread, is one of the most beautiful in America, and one of the most affordable. The University is a comprehensive research and teaching institution with a large College of Liberal Arts & Sciences, a graduate school, and eleven professional schools. This comprehensiveness provides a broad range of diverse educational opportunities for freshmen and transfer students who are interested in excellent undergraduate programs in Architecture and Architectural Engineering.

The University has 26,000 students, 780 of whom are students in undergraduate or graduate programs in the School of Architecture & Urban Design. The University is in Lawrence, Kansas, about 40 miles west of Kansas City, a major metropolitan area. Lawrence is a traditional university town with 75,000 inhabitants.

Faculty in the School of Architecture & Urban Design represent a balanced mix of expertise in the theory and practice of Architecture, Architectural Engineering, and Urban Planning. A selective admissions process assures a student body representative of in-state and out-of-state students without regard to race, sex, age, or national origin.

SPECIAL ACTIVITIES AND PROGRAMS

The School of Architecture & Urban Design has especially strong junior-year-abroad programs in Scotland and Germany, semester-long programs in Copenhagen, and summer programs in Italy. All of these study-abroad programs are supported in part by scholarships. Shorter study trips led by faculty each year during the summer provide opportunities elsewhere in Europe and the Far East.

Career Counseling and Placement services are offered in the school and at the university level. Internships are available to fifth-year students during the summer and first semester of the fifth year.

Major student awards are the Thayer Medal for Design, the Alpha Rho Chi Medal for Service, the AIA Award for Design, and the top senior GPA Award. All qualified students are encouraged to enroll in the University Honors Program. Students may be elected to Tau Sigma Delta and Phi Alpha Epsilon.

FACILITIES

The school is in newly renovated Marvin Hall, which has outstanding studio and support equipment.

Within the school there are beginning and advanced computer laboratories, a photographic lab, a model shop, a construction lab, a solar lab, a lighting lab, and a builder's yard.

A technical reference with 3,350 books and periodicals is accessible to all students in the school, as well as a slide library with 56,000 slides. A publishing center provides the most advanced image-setting technology available.

SCHOLARSHIPS/AID

The School of Architecture and Urban Design has a limited number of scholarships for entering freshmen that are administered directly by the school. Additional awards and scholarships are available to students at all year levels.

All students who wish to be considered for the university's financial aid or for the scholarships available to architecture and architectural engineering students must complete applications at the Office of Student Financial Aid, 26 Strong Hall.

Each year three to five sophomores are chosen to receive scholarships to spend the third year at selected universities in Europe. Exchange programs are in place with Heriot-Watt University in Edinburgh, Scotland, and the University of Dortmund, Germany. Up to five students may be selected to spend the fall semester of the fourth year in Copenhagen, Denmark, through the Danish International Study Program. Approximately 16 students receive awards to attend classes on historic preservation during the summer near Siena, Italy.

UNDERGRADUATE PROGRAM
Philosophy Statement

As a field of study, architecture is considered both an art and a science. As a method of practice, it is a complex interdisciplinary professional activity. The Bachelor of Architecture curriculum responds to both of these considerations by offering a series of overlapping sequences in both professional and academic course work.

The Bachelor of Science in Architectural Engineering is offered jointly by the Schools of Architecture and Urban Design and Engineering. Architectural engineers are concerned with the scientific, technical, and mechanical aspects of buildings. They may be called upon to design the structure of buildings or to design and correlate other engineering components in building design. The curriculum in architectural engineering emphasizes the technological aspects of design, while providing the student with a firm understanding of the architectural design process.

Program Description

The core of the curriculum in architecture is a sequence of design studios comprising one-third of the total degree requirements. In addition, students complete sequences in graphics, structures, building construction, environmental technology, and architectural history. Course work in site planning, urban design, and professional practice completes the professional content of the program.

In addition to the professional courses offered within the school, students are expected to complete course work in a variety of academic disciplines within the university. Beyond mathematics, physics, and English, the student is expected to fulfill breadth and depth requirements through a distribution of elective course work in fine arts, the humanities, and the natural and social sciences.

In the fifth year of the program, students elect to complete the year in residence or apply for admission to the internship option, in which the student works full-time in a professional architectural office and completes an independent study project in the fall semester, then returns to the university to complete the degree requirements in the spring semester.

GRADUATE PROGRAM
Philosophy Statement

Graduate study in architecture leads to the Master of Architecture degree with options for specialized study in Built Form and Culture, Environmental Technology, Architectural Management, and Urban Design. This is an advanced, post-professional or academic degree depending upon the student's previous educational background. Each option is structured to provide the student with coursework in theory, methods, values, techniques of anaysis, and a workshop. The M Arch program is planned to be completed in three full semesters. Regardless of the option selected, the degree requirements consist of 36 credit hours of course work including a thesis, final project, or comprehensive exam.

Program Description

The Built Form and Culture emphasis focuses on study and research into the relationships between built environments at many scales and socio-cultural processes and contexts. It includes exploration of design implications and applications of building/culture interactions. The option is open to students with undergraduate degrees in a wide range of fields, from architecture and design to anthropology and philosophy.

The Urban Design emphasis enables a graduate student to acquire the skills and understanding necessary to assume professional practice or public sector responsibilities for complex or large-scale design problems. The course of study is directed toward students who wish to practice in a traditional architectural role and obtain a greater understanding of contextual influences in design, who wish to pursue an urban design consulting career, or who wish to influence urban environmental decisions in a variety of professional and non-professional roles.

The Architectural Management emphasis in Kansas City is oriented to the administration of the practice of architecture and related disciplines. The objectives of the program are to provide participants the skills and knowledge necessary to become effective participants in the management of an organization, to provide information related to the management of planning, design and construction projects, and to expose students to major issues facing design professions.

FACULTY
Administration

W Max Lucas, PE, Dean
Dennis E Domer, Associate Dean
Lois E Clark, Assistant Dean
René F Diaz, Chair of Architecture
Eric Strauss, Chair of Urban Planning
Ronald N Helms, PE, Chair of Architectural Engineering
Michael Swann, Director, Regents Center for Architectural Studies
Ursula Stammler, Director, Architectural Resource Center

Professors

Bezaleel Benjamin, MSC, PhD
Alan Black, MCP, PhD
Thomas Dean, AIA, PE, RA, PhD
Dimitrios Dendrinos, Dipl, MUP, PhD
René F Diaz, B Arch, M Arch
Stephen Grabow, B Arch, M Arch, PhD
Ronald N Helms, PE, B Arch, MS Arch E, PhD
Charles Kahn, FAIA, PE, RA, B Arch, MS Civil
Wojciech Lesnikowski, M Arch/Plan
W Max Lucas, PE, BS Arch E, MS Arch E, PhD
James Mayo, B Arch, MUP, PhD
Louis F Michel, BA, MA
Victor Papanek, PhD (Hon)

Associate Professors

William Carswell, RA, MUP
Hobart Jackson, BA, MS
Glenn LeRoy, AIA, RA, B Arch, M Arch, MCP
Thomas McCoy, AIA, RA, B Arch
Barry Newton, RA, Dipl Arch
Steve Padget, RA, B ED MSC
Gaylord Richardson, RA, B Arch, BS Arch, M Arch
Dan Rockhill, B Arch, M Arch
Dennis Sander, RA, B Arch, M Arch
Kent Spreckelmeyer, AIA, RA, Dipl, B Arch, D Arch
Harris Stone, RA, M Arch
Eric Strauss, JD, PhD

Assistant Professors

Clay Belcher, BS Arch E, MBA, PhD
Fwu-Shiun Liou, PhD
Donna Luckey, M Arch, PhD
Judith Major, BS, MLA, MS Arch
Kirk McClure, B Arch, MCP, PhD

Part-Time Faculty

Richard Findlay, RA, BSAS, M Arch
Mark Gardner, BLA
David Griffin, AIA, RA, B Arch, M Arch
John Lee, RA
Robert Messmer, BED, B Arch
Ralph H Ochsner, BA, MRCP
Mark Peters, BA, M Arch
Hugo Reissner, BA
Marc Richardson, BS Eng
Mary Rickel, BA, BFA, B Arch
Antoine Roumanous, ENSBA, DPLG
Jim Scott, BED, B Arch, M Arch
Janet Smalter, B Arch
David Van Sickle, B Arch

Adjunct Faculty

Kent Cripin, MBA
Bruce Culley, CPA, MBA
William Douglas, PE
Allen Garner, PhD
Dean Graves, AIA, BS, M Arch
Ginny Graves, BA
Ted A Murray, BA, MRP, MBA
Viki Noteis, B Arch, M Arch
G William Quatman II, AIA, BED, B Arch, JD
Tom Roberts, PhD
Jim Surber, M Ind Eng
Frank Zilm, AIA, RA, B Arch, D Arch

Kent State University

School of Architecture and Environmental Design
200 Taylor Hall
Kent State University
Kent, Ohio 44242
(216) 672-2917

Admissions
(216) 672-2444

Application Deadline(s): Late January is advised
Tuition & Fees: Undgrd: $1052/sem
Grad: $1179/sem
Endowment: State

DEGREE PROGRAMS

Degree	Minimum Years for Degree	Accred.	Requirements for Admission	Full-Time Stdnts.	Part-Time Stdnts.	% of Applics. Accptd.	Stdnts. in 1st Year of Program	# of Degrees Conferred
BS	4	—	ACT Comp. 24, HS GPA 3.0, upper 25% of class (early admissions)	325	25	20%	100	50
B Arch	1	NAAB	BS in Arch, 2.5 GPA	50	5	50%	50	42
M Arch (Track One)2	2	NAAB	BS in Arch, 2.75 GPA	20	2	35%	12	10
M Arch (Track Two)1	1	—	B Arch, 2.75 GPA	7	2	30%	7	5

SCHOOL DEMOGRAPHICS (all degree programs)

Full-Time Faculty	Part-Time Faculty	Full-Time Students	Part-Time Students	Foreign Students	Out-of-State U.S. Stdnts.	Women Students	Minority Students
19	8	402	34	7%	35%	32%	1%

LIBRARY (Tel. No. 216-672-2876)

Type	No. of Volumes	No. of Slides
Arch	12,000	13,000

STUDENT OPPORTUNITIES AND RESOURCES

Kent State University strives to create optimal conditions for intellectual discovery, human development, and responsible social change in its commitment to provide learning opportunities for the population served by its campuses. Currently, the more than 25,000 students on the Kent Campus and the seven Regional Campuses have a choice of some 170 undergraduate degree programs, 18 Doctoral level programs, and 12 degrees in 33 Masters level programs in the arts, sciences, and professions.

The University is centrally located in northeastern Ohio. Over 4,500,000 people reside within an hour's drive of the University. Metropolitan centers such as Cleveland, Akron, Canton, and Youngstown provide many resources for architectural students.

There are 100 buildings on the scenic 1,200 acre Kent campus. The focal point of the campus is the University Student Center with its corresponding plaza. On one side of the plaza is a 12-story, open stack library which houses more than 1,000,000 volumes and a complete learning resource center. On the other side of the plaza is the Student Center which houses dining facilities, meeting and conference rooms, recreational areas, a ballroom, a bookstore, and a cinema.

The School of Architecture and Environmental Design, administered through the College of Fine and Professional Arts, is located in Taylor Hall near the center of campus. Over 400 students are enrolled in the programs available through the School of Architecture. These programs include a four-year general pre-professional program in architecture, a five-year undergraduate professional program, and a six-year graduate professional program with options in urban design or preservation of the built environment.

SPECIAL ACTIVITIES AND PROGRAMS

A spring semester architectural study program is offered each year in Florence, Italy. Kent State University's Center for International and Comparative Programs, which co-sponsors the program, helps with travel arrangements, health services, insurance, international student I.D.'s, legal documents, and other planning details. The curriculum corresponds to the regular four-year program and is offered by a staff of Italian architects and members of the School of Architecture faculty. The Italian instructors are Adolfo Natalini and Christiano Toraldo di Francia.

Upper level students have the opportunity to work with community groups and institutions interested in improving the physical environment. Recent projects have included the Lakefront Development, Flats District, Warehouse District, and Theatre District of Cleveland, Ohio; the Central Business Districts for Canton and Youngstown; and the long-range campus plan for the University of Akron.

The School of Architecture and Environmental Design at Kent State University has recently formed the Urban Design Center of Northeast Ohio. The Urban Design Center complements its public activities by facilitating linkages between the school and other resources for urban study including Cleveland State University, Akron, and Youngstown State University. The Urban Design Center serves as a resource for the public and private interest by gathering, analyzing, and disseminating information related to the design of the urban environment. It initiates the research, design, and implementation of projects appropriate for the environment of a given site, district, community, and region. The Center seeks to develop Urban Design expertise and provide broader education experiences for the students, faculty, and area design professionals while providing community service and educating the public about the benefits to be derived from good design of the physical environment. The Urban Design Center is currently funded by the Ohio Board of Regents and the communities it serves.

The School of Architecture offers an extensive lecture series featuring international architects

and urban designers. The School lecture series program is also enhanced by lecturer series from both the Cleveland and Akron Chapters of the American Institute of Architects.

Kent State University's School of Architecture has an extensive annual award program. Opportunities also exist for design awards provided through the Architects Society of Ohio.

The Student Chapter of the American Institute of Architects is open to all students in the school. The group plans social and educational activities for the students and faculty, including the annual Beaux Arts Ball and a lecture series. The Student Chapter has recently been named the outstanding student organization on Kent State University's campus.

Tau Sigma Delta, an honorary architectural fraternity, is open to upper level students who achieve a level of excellence in scholarship. The organization recognizes outstanding scholarship and outstanding professional achievements by students and/or area architects.

FACILITIES

The School of Architecture and Environmental Design at Kent State University is housed in Taylor Hall in the central part of the campus. Each student has an individual drafting work station and storage area. Studios for the second through fifth year of the Bachelor of Architecture program are located on the fourth floor of Taylor Hall; freshmen are located in an adjacent building, Lake/Olson; and graduate studios are located in an adjacent building, Stopher Hall. Taylor Hall is well equipped and houses an auditorium for approximately 150 architectural students, a gallery for the exhibit of student and professional work, an architectural library, classrooms, seminar spaces, and a computer graphics laboratory.

SCHOLARSHIPS/AID

Kent State University has developed a financial aid program to assist students who lack the necessary funds for a college education. This program, consisting of scholarships, loans, grants, and part-time employment is administered by the Office of Student Financial Aid, located in Rockwell Hall. The Honors College also offers a number of scholarships to distinguished high school scholars and creative artists. Scholarships supported by the American Institute of Architects and the Architects Society of Ohio are available for selected fourth- and fifth-year students. In addition, there are a number of Abbott Bryant Scholarships available for students with demonstrated need.

UNDERGRADUATE PROGRAM
Philosophy Statement

The four-year general program in Architecture leads to a pre-professional degree, Bachelor of Science. The first two years of this program emphasize coursework in the College of Arts and Sciences, with one or two courses in architecture each semester. The third and fourth years of the program emphasize studies in architecture. This program is designed for students who wish to pursue more advanced study in architecture or related fields, or students who wish to enter the workforce in fields related to architecture, or

students who wish to be employed in an architecture firm at a paraprofessional level. The degree of Bachelor of Science with a major in Architecture is granted upon completion of the four-year program of studies. The degree requires a total of 129 semester credit hours including 75 in architectural courses. Students must attain a 2.25 grade point average in architecture courses and a 2.00 overall grade point average.

The five-year undergraduate program leads to the degree of Bachelor of Architecture. The curriculum for the four years is the same as for students pursuing the BS degree. During the fifth year, students pursue additional study in the areas of design, structures, specifications, and professional practice. A minimum of 32 credit hours of study with a 2.50 grade point average is required in this additional year. Students successfully completing this course of study are eligible to take the State Board Examination for Architects after a three-year apprenticeship in an architect's office. This program is designed for students who desire to become professional practicing architects and is accredited by the NAAB.

GRADUATE PROGRAM
Philosophy Statement

The six-year program of study leads to the degree of Master of Architecture. The program involves completion of the four-year Bachelor of Science degree program described above plus completion of a two-year graduate program (Track One), or completion of the five-year professional degree plus a one-year graduate program (Track Two). This program is designed for students who wish to explore subject material in greater depth or to pursue a special interest not covered in regular coursework. The Masters programs are particularly appropriate for students who are interested in becoming researchers, teachers, or consultants in a particular aspect of architecture. The two-year, Track One Masters program is focused toward graduate options in either urban design or preservation of the built environment. This two-year Masters program is accredited by the NAAB.

Program Description

Track One is open to students who possess a four-year Bachelors degree with a major in architecture or environmental design and a minimum undergraduate grade point average of 2.75. Completion of this track normally requires two years of full-time study. The degree Master of Architecture is granted upon completion of the 54 semester credit hours of work. Students must maintain a 3.00 grade point average; failure to do so makes the student liable to dismissal. Track Two is open to students who possess a five-year professional degree in architecture from an

accredited architectural school and a minimum undergraduate grade point average of 2.75. Completion of this track normally requires one year plus one summer of full-time study. The degree Master of Architecture is granted upon completion of 32 semester credit hours of work. Students must maintain a 3.00 grade point average; failure to do so makes the student liable to dismissal.

FACULTY
Administration

Thomas Barber, Dean, School of Architecture & Environmental Design
James E Dalton, AIA, Director, School of Architecture
Rebecca J Mayne, Architectural Librarian

Professors

Foster Armstrong, AIA, B Arch, M Arch
Elmer Bjerregaard, AIA, B Arch, M Arch
James E Dalton, AIA, B Arch, M Arch
Jack Kremers, AIA, B Arch, M Arch
Osyp Martyniuk, AIA, M Arch, PhD
Conrad McWilliams, AIA, B Arch, M Arch
Joseph Schidlowski, B Arch, M Arch
Robert Shively, PE, BSCE, MA

Associate Professors

Glen Dreyer, AIA, B Arch, M Arch
Neil Guda, AIA, B Arch, M Arch
David Hughes, AIA, B Arch, M Planning
James Montalto, B Arch
William Ross, AIA, B Arch, M Arch
Thomas Stauffer, AIA, M Arch, M City Planning

Assistant Professors

Charles Graves, Jr, B Arch, M Arch
Charles Harker, AIA, B Arch, M Arch
Elwin Robison, BA, PhD
Daniel Vieyra, AIA, B Arch, MS

Part-Time Faculty

Priscilla Graham
Vincent Leskosky, AIA, M Arch
Eric Pempus, MS, JD
Herbert Slone, AIA, M Arch
Athene Tarrant, RIBA, B Arch
Paul Westlake, AIA, M Arch

Adjunct Faculty

Thomas Korllos

University of Kentucky

College of Architecture
117 Pence Hall
University of Kentucky
Lexington, Kentucky 40506-0041
(606) 257-7617

Admissions:
(606) 257-7623

Application Deadline(s): February 1
Tuition & Fees: Undgrd: In-State: $1332/year;
Out-of-State: $3812/year
Endowment: Public

DEGREE PROGRAMS

Degree	Minimum Years for Degree	Accred.	Requirements for Admission	Full-Time Stdnts.	Part-Time Stdnts.	% of Applics. Accptd.	Stdnts. in 1st Year of Program	# of Degrees Conferred
B Arch	5 years	NAAB	University Requirements+ Aptitude test (competitive) ACT or SAT	232	17	36%	74	38

SCHOOL DEMOGRAPHICS (all degree programs)

Full-Time Faculty	Part-Time Faculty	Full-Time Students	Part-Time Students	Foreign Students	Out-of-State U.S. Stdnts.	Women Students	Minority Students
21	13	232	17	.4%	19.58%	18%	6%

LIBRARY (Tel. No. 606-257-4305)

Type	No. of Volumes	No. of Slides
Arch	27,395	90,000

STUDENT OPPORTUNITIES AND RESOURCES

One of the most distinctive attributes of the program at Kentucky is the emphasis that it places on establishing conditions and circumstances in which the tutorial relationship between student and teacher — a relationship so essential to the student architect — can be maintained. All classes are small, and a student-faculty ratio of 12:1 is the norm in the design studios.

An important corollary to this emphasis is the postulate that regardless of its teaching and space resources, the population of a school of architecture should never grow so large that a student's identity becomes jeopardized with effacement by sheer numbers, this if only for the reason that student architects, more so than other young people entering the professions, must learn from, criticize, debate with, and collaborate with each other.

Hence, the size of the student body in the College of Architecture is regulated by means of a carefully formulated, competitive admissions procedure and thorough reviews of students' portfolios and performance during their progress through the first three years of the program. Total enrollments are maintained at not more than 300. Of this number, 15 percent are out-of-state and foreign students. The steadily increasing numbers of women and ethnic minority students now stand at 46 and 15 respectively. A substantial majority of new students are transfer students who have completed 30 or more hours of college credit.

Kentucky's selective admissions procedure is a little more elaborate than most in that it is not solely, or even chiefly, concerned with a candidate's academic record or standardized measures of his or her academic potential, but rather with indications of "effective intelligence" as an architect. Many young people excel academically but prove inadequate and unhappy as architects, while for a variety of reasons, significant numbers of quite gifted architects do not distinguish themselves academically. Hence, though not omniscient, the College Admissions Committee seeks to identify students with a demonstrable aptitude and motivation for architecture or, failing this, exhibiting characteristics of some latent potential for architecture. One indication that this admissions strategy is effective is that the level of student attrition in the architecture program is lower than in any other undergraduate program at Kentucky, while, at the same time, the College of Architecture's grading practices are among the least liberal.

The university is located in Lexington, a growing city of approximately 200,000 people in the heart of the famous Bluegrass region of Kentucky. Lexington, Louisville and Cincinnati form an approximate equilateral triangle, about 80 miles on each side, with each city within a 1-1/2-hour drive of the others. Chicago, Washington, Atlanta and St. Louis are all within a day's drive. The university, the city, and the surrounding region together offer many cultural and recreational opportunities.

The College of Architecture has a sound collaborative relationship with many academic units in the university, in particular with the College of Engineering, the Department of Art, the University Art Museum, and the other design disciplines on campus.

The college's faculty is a deliberately diversified group who represent a number of ideological positions in architecture. Faculty members enjoy a very high level of autonomy in what they teach and how they teach it and are freely and continuously engaged in a dialogue with both their colleagues and their students, using their teaching and scholarly and creative work as the stimuli for this debate.

SPECIAL ACTIVITIES AND PROGRAMS

Introduction to Architecture: a two-week summer program for young (and not so young) people contemplating career options.

Work-study Opportunities

International Workshops: Typically one international program is conducted each spring and two each summer. Two or more regular faculty members, foreign visiting critics and lecturers, and 15-20 students participate in each program. Students who have completed the first two years of studio and architectural history and theory are eligible to enroll in these programs, which are accompanied by a mandatory preparatory seminar in the preceding semester. The Spring Program is located in Venice.

Field trips to major US cities such as Boston, New York, and Chicago are run informally by interested faculty, generally during the spring vacation.

Exhibition and visiting lecturer series bring nationally and internationally recognized architects and teachers to Lexington on a regular basis. Three or four such speakers are co-sponsored each year by the local chapter of the Kentucky Society of Architects.

Visiting Professors come to Lexington for a semester for a year or two from distinguished practices and schools of architecture in this country and abroad.

Visiting critics routinely serve on major student project reviews throughout the program and on all final design-thesis juries.

Annual graduate recruitment visits by several of the nation's most distinguished offices.

Active Student Council and Tau Sigma Delta honorary society.

FACILITIES

The College of Architecture is currently housed in two older buildings on campus. Pence Hall houses the college library, audio-visual center, workshop, computer graphics and photographic facilities, and 60 percent of the design studio space. The remaining 40 percent of the design studios and some faculty offices are housed about 150 yards away from Pence in a building shared with other disciplines. The need for a new College of Architecture building has been recognized by the Board of Trustees as the highest priority need in Academic Affairs since 1974. The college is hopeful that funding for the project will become available before the present decade is out.

SCHOLARSHIPS/AID

Scholarship, loan, and work-study opportunities are available through the Student Financial Aid Office. In addition, the College Assembly Committee on Admissions, Advising and Scholarships, with the aid of the College Alumni Association and the Kentucky Society of Architects, raises about $30,000 per year, which provides maintenance and travel scholarships for many students. Eligibility for most College of Architecture scholarships is based on merit and demonstrated financial need.

UNDERGRADUATE PROGRAM
Philosophy Statement

A deliberately traditional five-year program is offered, with distinct emphasis on architecture as a rigorous academic and cultural endeavor. The underlying assumption is that the responsibility of a school is to concentrate on the discipline while the responsibility of the profession is to furnish an adequate postgraduate internship. The major program components comprise the architectural design sequence (58 credit hours in ten semesters), the architectural and urban history and theory sequences (a minimum of 22 hours in eight semesters—and perhaps as much as double the normal expectation in four- and five-year undergraduate programs), and the technical and professional practice sequences (25 hours in seven semesters). These sequences and the professional elective offerings amount to 120 of the 176 hours required for the degree. Proposed curriculum changes are intended to give additional emphasis to these areas of the program. Studio will increase by 2 credit hours, history and theory by 2 hours, and the technical sequences by 7 hours, while elective requirements will diminish from 15 hours to 12. The overall degree requirements will increase by 1 hour.

Within these rather simply stated curricular emphases, which make no concessions to the specialist options that have come to characterize the degree programs of many other schools (e.g. building technology, construction management, planning, etc.), the school has espoused the intent of stipulating course content and expectations of student performance in sufficiently general terms to preserve a maximum of individual teaching autonomy and responsibility for each member of the faculty and to provide each student with opportunities for assuming an increasing responsibility for the

determination of his or her direction and development as an architect. In addition to the diversity of approach, process, and product provided by the 20 or so studio section design critics, the elective options in the advanced history and theory sequence support this intent, as do the International Workship program options, the professional elective offerings, and the vertical studio critic options in the fourth and fifth years of the program. Thus the curriculum develops design as the central focus of study, but allows for significant individual variation in students' experience and development.

FACULTY
Administration

José Oubrerie, Dean and Chairman
Clyde R Carpenter, AIA, Associate Dean, Student Affairs
Paul M Pinney, Associate Dean, Administration
Daniel Hodge, Librarian

Professors

Clyde R Carpenter, M Arch
Maria G Dallerba-Ricci, D Arch Plan
Charles P Graves, M Arch
Richard S Levine, M Arch
J P Noffsinger, D Arch
David A Spaeth, MS Arch

Associate Professors

Stephen C Deger, MS Arch Eng
J Russell Groves, B Arch
Michael D Kennedy, MS
Paul Pinney, MS Arch
Anthony Roccanova, M Arch
Jerzy Rozenberg, MA
Julia Smyth-Pinney, M Arch

Part-Time Faculty

Larry Bender, B Arch
Stephen P Bennett, BA
Ellen Doble-Smith, M Arch
Robert Gillig, BS Arch
Leslie G Hennessey, PhD
Charles P Jolly, B Arch
Robert Kelly, M Arch
R Michelle Lambson, B Arch
Jeffrey T Pearson, B Arch
Leonardo Ricci, PhD Arch

Adjunct Faculty

Hans Gesund, PhD

Visiting Professors

Mark Clary, B Arch
David Leary, M Arch
Keith Plymale, MS Arch
Rob Rothblat, M Arch

Laval University

Ecole d'architecture
Université Laval
Vieux Séminaire
Quebec, PQ
G1K 7P4, Canada
(418) 656-2543/2544

Bureau du Registraire:
(418) 656-3080

Application Deadline(s): Undgrd & grad
studies - Fall: May 1st
Winter session:
November 1st
Tuition & Fees: Undgrd: $250 - $300/semester
Foreign student: $2948/
semester
Endowment: Provincial

DEGREE PROGRAMS

Degree	Minimum Years for Degree	Accred.	Requirements for Admission	Full-Time Stdnts.	Part-Time Stdnts.	% of Applics. Accptd.	Stdnts. in 1st Year of Program	# of Degrees Conferred
B Arch	4	OAQ, CAA	PROVINCE OF QUEBEC - High School diploma (with a science major) OTHER PROVINCES - Grade 13 with a science major or 12th grade + 1 year of University with a science major AMERICAN STUDENTS: High School diploma and a year of university FOREIGN STUDENTS: Baccalaureate with major in science and a year of university or the equivalent	290	11	40%	86	45
M Arch	2		Bachelor's Degree in Arch or equiv	10	9	70%	4	5

SCHOOL DEMOGRAPHICS (all degree programs)

Full-Time Faculty	Part-Time Faculty	Full-Time Students	Part-Time Students	Foreign Students	Out-of-State U.S. Stdnts.	Women Students	Minority Students
22	5	300	20	8%	—	38%	—

LIBRARY (Tel. No. 418-656-3542)

Type	No. of Volumes	No. of Slides
Art & Arch	2,000	10,000

STUDENT OPPORTUNITIES AND RESOURCES

The walled city of Quebec is one of the oldest settlements on the North American continent and has a rich heritage in buildings, including very good examples of restoration and adaptive use. The unique character of the city and its geographic location make it an ideal setting for the study of architecture. Quebec City is also the capital of the province and, with a population of 470,000, constitutes one of the political and cultural centers of Canada.

Laval University is the oldest francophone university on the continent. It has an enrollment of approximately 30,000 undergraduate students and 5,000 graduate students. There are about 2,500 faculty members. The university offers a wide variety of recreational, cultural, and leisure-time opportunities. Public lectures, special-interest clubs, concerts, films, theater, conferences, and conventions add an important dimension to life on the campus, which is located in Ste Foy, a suburban area 5 miles from the old city. The language of instruction is French.

SPECIAL ACTIVITIES AND PROGRAMS

Exhibits program

Lecture program

Field trips to urban centers in Canada and the USA

Foreign study program: Turkey, England, France

Exchange program with Universidad de Guanajuato, Mexico

Center of Nordic Studies

Photography darkrooms and studio

FACILITIES

The School of Architecture has a total enrollment of 300, of which 3 percent are graduate students. Its many facilities are accessible to both graduate and undergraduate students. These include the Architectural and Urban Acoustics Laboratory, the Computer-aided Architectural Design Laboratory, the Climate Simulation Laboratory, the Energy Laboratory, the Construction Laboratory, the Architectural Documentation Center, and the Models Workshop.

In the autumn of 1988, the School of Architecture is to be housed in one of the most historic and oldest buildings in the old city, in a complex of buildings to become the downtown campus.

SCHOLARSHIPS/AID

Organizations offering scholarship programs to Canadian students include Design Canada, Parks Canada, the Quebec Ministry of Education, the Central Mortgage and Housing Corporation, and the National Research Council in Natural Sciences and Engineering.

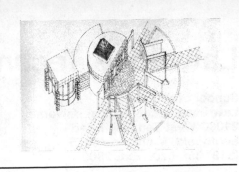

UNDERGRADUATE PROGRAM
Program Description

A four-year Bachelor of Architecture degree program is offered. The curriculum provides a design studio education that is enriched throughout the eight semesters by complementary course work in the areas of theory and history of architecture, social sciences, environmental studies, building and construction sciences, and architectural media.

The basic themes addressed in the design studios are architecture and environment, in the first and second semesters; space/materialization, in the third and fourth semesters; and programming and building technology, in the fifth and sixth semesters. The seventh semester is concerned with theme exploration. The focus in the eighth semester (diploma) is on the synthesis of previous design experiences and theoretical course work through a project initiated and developed by the student.

The B Arch degree offered at Laval prepares students for graduate studies or for professional practice after a two-year period of professional training.

GRADUATE PROGRAM
Program Description

The Graduate School at Laval offers a Master of Architecture degree in collaboration with the School of Architecture. This program provides advanced education in architecture and related fields in accordance with the particular interests of the faculty and the nature of the research projects initiated every year by faculty and students.

Two types of curricula lead to the degree. The A option is designed for those students who already hold professional degrees in architecture. This option emphasizes the development of in-depth inquiries within a specific area of concern in one of the professional activities of architecture.

The B option is designed for those students who hold degrees in disciplines other than architecture as well as for those with professional degrees. This option emphasizes research activity in architecture and related fields.

FACULTY
Administration

Léo R Zrudlo, Director of the School
Alexis Ligougne, Academic Secretary (Vice Director)
Pierre Jampen, Director, undergraduate program
Denise Piche, Director, graduate program

Professors

Joseph Baker, B Arch
Paul N Bourque, B Ed, MSc Civ Eng
Pierre Guertin, B Arch, MURB, Doct Urb
Z Jarnuskiewicz, B Arch
Jean-Gabriel Migneron, MURB, PhD URB
Takashi Nakajima, B Arch, M Arch, PhD
André Robitaille, Dipl Arch
Léo Zrudlo, B Arch, M Arch, PhD

Associate Professors

Benoît Bernier, B Arch
Claude Dube, B Arch, MURB
Maurice Gauthier, Dipl Arch
Pierre Jampen, Arch Eng, M Arch
Pierre Larochelle, B Arch
Jean-Claude Leclerc, B Arch
Raymond Levesque, B Arch
Alexis Ligougne, B Arch, M Arch
Jean Michaud, B Arch
Denise Piche, BSc, MURB, PhD
Jiri Prochazka, Dipl Arch

Aygen Toruner, Dipl Arch
Gilles Tremblay, B Arch
Emilien Vachon, B Arch
Douglas Wren, Dipl Arch

Assistant Professor

Jan B Zwiejski, Dipl, M Arch, D Arch

Part-Time Faculty

Claude Belzile
Philippe Watson

Adjunct Faculty

Guy Duchesneau
Gerard Roger

Lawrence Technological University

School of Architecture
Lawrence Technological University
21000 West Ten Mile Road
Southfield, Michigan 48075
(313) 356-0200 Ext. 2800

Admissions:
(313) 356-0200 Ext. 3166

Application Deadline(s): Three months prior to the beginning of each term.
Tuition & Fees: Undgrd: $3315 (1987-88)
Grad: $4410 (1987-88)
Endowment: Private

DEGREE PROGRAMS

Degree	Minimum Years for Degree	Accred.	Requirements for Admission	Full-Time Stdnts.	Part-Time Stdnts.	% of Applics. Accptd.	Stdnts. in 1st Year of Program	# of Degrees Conferred
BS Arch	4		HS Diploma, Min. 2.50 HS GPA, ACT/SAT Scores	403	208	70%	270	63
B Arch	1	NAAB	Min. 2.50-2.72 GPA, BS Arch, Portfolio	20	23	59%	43	18
BS Int Arch	4	FIDER	HS Diploma, Min. 2.50 HS GPA, ACT/SAT Scores	95	36	70%	42	6
M Arch	2		Undergraduate architecture degree, Min. 2.50 GPA	15	5	45%	22	0

SCHOOL DEMOGRAPHICS (all degree programs)

Full-Time Faculty	Part-Time Faculty	Full-Time Students	Part-Time Students	Foreign Students	Out-of-State U.S. Stdnts.	Women Students	Minority Students
21	63	503	262	4.1%	18.0%	25.1%	8.1%

LIBRARY (Tel. No. 313-356-0200 x3000)

Type	No. of Volumes	No. of Slides
University	65,000	45,000

STUDENT OPPORTUNITIES AND RESOURCES

Lawrence Technological University has enjoyed an outstanding reputation since its founding in 1932. It is Michigan's largest private college with a co-ed enrollment of more than 6,200 students from throughout the state, the nation, and 30 foreign countries. With over 700 students enrolled in the School of Architecture, Lawrence Institute of Technology has one of the nation's largest architectural programs and is among the 30 oldest in the country.

Lawrence is known and highly respected for offering one of the most comprehensive programs in architecture and interior architecture/interior design at affordable tuition rates (which are the same for both residents and non-residents). Lawrence is accredited by the North Central Association of Colleges and Schools, and the professional degree is accredited by the National Architectural Accrediting Board.

State-of-the-art facilities, including multiple computer resources, and an outstanding, dedicated faculty who offer personalized attention to talented, committed students, combine to create an exceptional educational environment. Located in Southfield, Michigan, a progressive residential/office suburb of 90,000 people, the modern park-like campus provides a comfortable, attractive, and convenient suburban environment in which to live and study.

Transfer students are encouraged to enter any of the degree programs in which they have the interest and qualifications.

SPECIAL ACTIVITIES AND PROGRAMS

ArchLECTURE: The esteemed visiting professional lecture series which brings the academic and professional communities together at least once a month with distinguished personalities of national and international reputations for excellence on significant work in architecture. Over 100 ArchiLECTURES have been presented by such luminaries as: Helmut Jahn, Chicago; John Portman, Atlanta; Eberhard Zeidler, Toronto; James Sterling, London, England; Robert Venturi, Philadelphia; Harry Weese, Chicago; William Caudil, Houston; Hugh Stubbins, Cambridge; Paolo Soleri, Scottsdale; Oscar Newman, New York; Raymond Moriyama, Toronto; Hugh Newell Jacobsen, Washington, D.C.; Joan Goody, Boston; Barton Myers, Toronto; James Luckman, Los Angeles; and Charles Gwathmey, New York.

Visiting Critics: Highly acclaimed commentators and design leaders from within the profession, with special insights on the contemporary scene, provide a regular forum for the exchange of ideas, dialogue, and critical commentary of student work. Critics, among others, have included: Paul Rudolph, New York; Paul Goldberger, New York; Wolf Von Eckardt, Washington, D.C.; Peter Eisenmen, New York; and Arthur Drexler, New York.

Visiting Professorships: At least once a year, a noted authority and practicing professional of national esteem from another campus or city is invited to teach within the architecture program. Personalities have ranged in scope from Edmund Bacon, nationally respected urban planner, to Bruce Goff, well-known for his imaginative and non-traditional approach to architecture, and from architectural historian Kenneth Frampton, to retired SOM principal Walter Netch and corporate design leader Vincent Kling.

Art & Design Awareness: Art, design and architectural awareness is heightened through a weekly series of presentations known as "The Design Lecture Series" which provides for student interaction with a variety of regional artists, designers, and architects.

Building Science & Technology Lecture Series: Presents technical information related to component manufacturing, the building process, and the construction industry. (Held every week in a regularly scheduled sequence.)

Exhibition Series: Significant exhibits of art, furniture, photography, sculpture, building design, and faculty and student work are displayed in the Architecture Gallery on a scheduled basis throughout the year to further increase the student's exposure to the fine arts.

European Study Program: The "Grand Tour" is a faculty-guided travel adventure of selected European countries. Specifically planned for architecture students, the focus of this travel program is on first-hand exploration and discovery of Europe's rich architectural heritage. Museums, monuments, gardens, urban spaces and buildings of historical and architectural significance are emphasized.

Pre-College and Design Discovery Programs: Focused courses for talented high school students and adults considering mid-career changes are conducted on Saturdays throughout the spring term. Studio and seminar courses in design and visual communications enable high school students to earn college credit prior to admittance to the degree program.

FACILITIES

The School of Architecture houses 16 design studios, a 300-seat auditorium, numerous lecture, jury, and seminar rooms, an exhibition gallery, audio/visual resource center and slide library, student lounge, and faculty and administrative offices. A model shop, graphics laboratory, photographic dark room, construction systems materials resource center, and an interior design (contract furnishing & finishes) resource center are available to students within the building.

In addition, the School of Architecture also contains two specialized computer laboratories dedicated to architectural studies. One is equipped with microcomputers primarily used for programming, word processing, and statistical applications. Electronic mail terminals which interconnect all campus facilities and departments via 3 Digital VAX mainframe computers is also used extensively. The second architectural computer laboratory offers more advanced studies in computer aided design and features work stations equipped with color monitors, terminals, and digitizing menus which are linked to two PRIME 9950/Mod 2 and 9655 mainframes. Medusa software supports the system, enabling undergraduate as well as graduate students to explore two-dimensional design and drafting applications and advanced three-dimensional, solid modeling and design processes.

The Gregor S. and Elizabeth B. Affleck House, designed by Frank Lloyd Wright was given to the College in 1978. Located in Bloomfield Hills, Michigan, this exceptional gift, unique to the resources of any school of architecture, is used as a conference center and classroom laboratory. The home provides an excellent means of acquainting Lawrence students and the public with a first-hand experience of Wright's architectural genius.

Among the notable resources housed in the Lawrence library is the private and professional library of the late, renowned architect, Albert Kahn. The collection consists of nearly 3,000 books acquired by Mr. Kahn from around the world. Available for student use, the collection is housed in the original walnut library removed from the offices of Albert Kahn & Associates.

In contrast to many other colleges' typical dormitories, Lawrence offers economical, on-campus housing which is available in the college-owned and operated 142-unit apartment building. Each unit consists of a one- or two-bedroom, attractively furnished apartment which includes a private bath and full-sized kitchen with modern appliances. Many also include a private balcony or patio.

90

SCHOLARSHIPS/AID

Nearly two-thirds of the students at Lawrence defray part of their educational costs through some form of financial assistance. Over $4.7 million in scholarships, grants, loans, and work-study jobs were awarded during the 1985-86 academic year. Both need-based and academic-based scholarships and financial aids are available.

The School of Architecture is fortunate to have a number of scholarships available exclusively to architectural and interior design students. Many are offered through the generosity of notable national architectural firms. The Minoru Yamasaki Scholarship, Troy, MI; Edward D. Stone Memorial Scholarship, Ft. Lauderdale, FL; John Portman Scholarship, Atlanta, GA; Smith, Hinchman & Grylls Scholarship, Detroit, MI; Giffels & Assoc. Scholarship, Southfield, MI; the Gerre Jones Scholarship, Washington, D.C.; the Skidmore, Owings, & Merril Scholarship, Chicago, IL; and the Masonry Institute of Michigan Scholarships are among the many distinguished firms and institutions recognized by this program of financial assistance.

UNDERGRADUATE PROGRAM
Philosophy Statement

The undergraduate architecture program at Lawrence is based on a balanced curriculum establishing a broad inter-disciplinary foundation for the undergraduate and professional pursuit of architecture, interior architecture, planning and environmental disciplines. The program integrates the sciences, mathematics, and humanities with the design process in a creative relationship which recognizes human concerns, social responsibilities and the technological disciplines controlling the built environment. Due to the wide sweep of skills and insights required by the architect in the "contemporary world", the program includes studies in law, economics, structures, business, energy matters, environmental systems, and landscape, graphic and urban design, as well as architectural practice, management, and land development. Special emphasis is given to art, architectural and cultural history. A wide range of architectural electives is offered which provide an opportunity for the student to gain specialized in-depth knowledge.

Program Description

Students in the Lawrence architectural sequence begin their pursuit of architectural studies immediately on entering their freshman year. This is a deliberate program distinction from some other schools where architectural classes often do not begin until the third year of studies.

Students in the Lawrence architectural program pursuing the professional degree, Bachelor of Architecture, receive one year of basic design education, followed by four intense years of architectural design including the development of a thesis within six years of study. This is in sharp contrast to many schools which provide for one year of basic design at the third-year level which is followed by three years of architectural design. The Lawrence approach allows for study in all major areas of architectural education as well as the liberal arts within a concentrated but flexible time period that begins with the student's first day on campus.

The Bachelor of Science programs in architecture and interior design are planned to provide a broad foundation for the full development of a student's skill and his/her social and environmental awareness with the goal of maximizing the student's personal creativity. The fundamental objective is to produce young professionals capable of clear thinking. The program is rooted in the rational, subjective mastery of basic knowledge as the foundation of a profound intuitive skill. Dual Bachelor of Science degrees may be earned in Architecture/Interior Architecture. The Bachelor of Science in Architecture and the Bachelor of Science in Interior Architecture generally require four years of study. Generally, only five years are required to complete the requirements for both degrees.

GRADUATE PROGRAM
Philosophy Statement

Architecture—the art, science, and technology of the constructed environment—can no longer be spoken of in the uncertain terms of "design." For nearly a century, the artistic illusions surrounding the traditional image of the architect have been fading away in favor of an identity capable of satisfying the full range of human aspirations. In that sense, we have returned to the insight of Vitruvius who, nearly two thousand years ago, challenged architecture to provide ". . .commodity, firmness and delight."

Put in modern terms of convenience, comfort, safety and beauty, today's architectural education must prepare architects to employ their full creative instincts and learn to fulfill the needs of society for an all-embracing environment that is satisfying, uplifting and accepts human existence as its responsibility and not as its servant.

The Professional Degree Program (PDP) at Lawrence Institute is firmly committed to an education meeting this challenge.

The PDP is the culmination of an architecture student's examination of creative, professional, and social problems. The goal is for the student to contribute original, creative, and useful ideas toward the responsible solution of a selected architectural problem.

Program Description

The Professional Degree Program provides exceptional students, with demonstrated professional potential, the opportunity to expand their talents and career interests. This is accomplished through the identification of, and solution to, a specific contemporary architectural problem of the student's selection. The year-long thesis carefully documents the various stages of research, analysis, conceptualization, alternative generation and design solution. This entire process is carried out in small groups of students working under the direction of selected thesis moderators. Additional specialized courses which focus on design theory and philosophy, management, development, practice, technology, and computers may be selected as electives.

Upon successful completion of these studies, the student is granted the first professional degree, Bachelor of Architecture, which is accredited by the National Architectural Accrediting Board.

In addition to four-year graduates, the Professional Degree Program attracts qualified and talented students from throughout the United States and many foreign countries who have successfully completed similar undergraduate programs of study in architecture.

FACULTY
Administration

Karl H Greimel, FAIA, RA, Dean
Gary A Kecskes, Assoc AIA, Associate Academic Administrator
John Sheoris, FAIA, Graduate Thesis Coordinator
Gary Cocozzoli, Director of Library

Professors

James Abernethy, B Arch, M Urb Pl
Karl H Greimel, AS, BA, MBA
Harold Linton, BFA, MFA
Joseph Olivieri, BME, MS

Associate Professors

Robert Carr, BFA, MA
Robert Champlin, BS Arch, M Urb Pl
Thomas Nashlen, BS Arch
Daniel Price, M Urb Pl, BS Ntl Res, B Arch
Betty-Lee Seydler-Sweatt, B Arch, M City Design
John V Sheoris, B Arch, M Arch
Joseph Varga, BSCE, MSCE

Assistant Professors

William Allen, BLA
Gordon Bugbee, BS, M Arch
Robert Fearon, B Ar E
Thomas Klausmeyer, BSME, BS Arch, BSAE

Jean LaMarche, BS Arch, B Arch
Robert Lynch, BS, M Arch
Rochelle Martin, B Arch, D Arch
Thomas Regenbogen, BS, MFA
Steven Rost, BS, BA, MFA
Ian Taberner, B Arch

Instructors

Maryanne Clink, BS Arch, B Arch

Part-Time Faculty

Nancy Agarwal, MA
Eugene R Baker, BFA
William J Beitz, Jr, BS Arch, B Arch
Francis Bennett, BS Arch
John L Berbiglia, BSEE
Lester Berman, BSCE, MSCE
Robert M Bernhard, B Arch E, MSCE
Harold Binder, AB Arch, M Arch
Russ E Boltz, BA, JD
Thomas M Brady, BS Civ E, MBA
Kenneth A Breisch, BA, MA
Donald Carter, B Arch
David M Chasco, BA Arch, M Arch
Garnet R Cousins, BS Arch, B Arch
Russell W Dixon, BS, MA
Ann Eaton, BFA, MA
Ted Ewald, BEE
Miklos Ferber, BS Civ E
Harvey Ferrero, BS Civ E
James J Giachino, B Arch E, MUP
Paul H Goldsmith, BS Arch
Don J Gonzalez, AB, MA
Jon Greenberg, B Eng
Gary Grobson, BS
John K Grylls, BSE, JD
Richard Hall, BS, B Arch, M Arch
Ernest Hickson, B Ind Ed, BEE
Norman Hughes, BS
Gary Jelin, BS, B Arch
Dane Johnson, BS, B Arch
Sandra Johnstone, BS Int Des
Gary A Kecskes, BS Arch, B Arch
Aleksis A Lahti, BS
Russell C Lewis, BS, MA
Gretchen Maricak, BS Arch, B Arch
Janice Means, BA Ed, SS, BS Eng
Keith G Mickelson, B Arch, MUP
Philip Nicholas, BA, B Arch E
Virginia North, ID
Dale Northup, BA, MA
Timothy O'Connor, BSME
Dominic J Pastore, BAE
Earl W Pellerin, BS
Robert B Powell, B Arch
Elliot Rappaport, BSEE, MSEE
Robert J Reinhard, BSEE, MBA
Charles T Robinson, BSCE, MSCE
Richard Rochon
Larry M Rockind, B Arch, M Arch
James Rundquist, BS, B Arch
Joseph Savin, B Arch
Gerald D Scherr, BA, JD, MBA
Ruth A Schnee, MFA Int Des
David Scholfield, BA, JD
Ralph C Schwartz, JD
Victor Shrem, BA, MUP
Clifford H Snyder, BES, M Arch
Douglas J Sordyl, BCE, ME
Ralph Stevenson, BSME, MSCE
Roy J Strickfaden, FA Arch
Benedetto Tiseo, BS
Karl Tropf
Zeyn Uzman, PE, MSCE
Roger Vanderklok, BS, B Arch
S B Vora, MS
Sandra Walters, ID
Robert A L Williams, B Arch
Edward Willoughby, BS Civ E
Stanley Wyre, BS Arch, JD
Daniel Zechmeister, BSCE
George B Zonars, M Arch

Louisiana State University

School of Architecture
102 Design Building
Louisiana State University
Baton Rouge, Louisiana 70803
(504) 388-6885 (school)
(504) 388-5400 (college)

Office of Admissions
110 Thomas Boyd Hall
Louisiana State University
Baton Rouge, Louisiana 70803
(504) 388-1686

Application Deadline(s): June 1 for
professional program
in architecture.
July 1 and December
1 for University

Tuition & Fees: Undgrd: La Res: $865/sem
Non-res: $2265/sem
Grad: La Res: $865/sem
Non-res: $2265/sem

Endowment: Public

DEGREE PROGRAMS

Degree	Minimum Years for Degree	Accred.	Requirements for Admission	Full-Time Stdnts.	Part-Time Stdnts.	% of Applics. Accptd.	Stdnts. in 1st Year of Program	# of Degrees Conferred
B Arch	5	NAAB	completion of all 1st year required courses and minimum GPA (on 4.0 scale) of 2.25	380		50%	180	55/yr
MS Arch*	3		prior degree in architecture or related fields, GRE and TOEFL scores, portfolio review					
BLA	5	ALSA	completion of all 1st year required courses and interview					
MLA*	3.5		undergraduate degree, GRE and TOEFL scores, portfolio review					
BID	4	FIDER	completion of all 1st year required courses, minimum GPA (on 4.0 scale) of 2.25, interview					

*MS Arch from School of Architecture; MLA from School of Landscape Architecture.

SCHOOL DEMOGRAPHICS (all degree programs)

Full-Time Faculty	Part-Time Faculty	Full-Time Students	Part-Time Students	Foreign Students	Out-of-State U.S. Stdnts.	Women Students	Minority Students
12	11	380		28%	14%	33%	3%

Figures shown for School of Architecture only.

LIBRARY (Tel. No. 504-388-2665)

Type	No. of Volumes	No. of Slides
Design Resource Center*	10,000	20,000

*Includes architecture, landscape architecture, art and interior design.

STUDENT OPPORTUNITIES AND RESOURCES

Louisiana State University is a major university located in the State Capital, Baton Rouge. Its location is in an area of significant growth potential with a unique climatological, geographical and cultural character. The School of Architecture at LSU offers a professional baccalaureate degree. There are 200 students enrolled in the professional program (years 2-5) and approximately 180 students in the preprofessional first-year program. The School of Architecture is one of three in the College of Design which includes the School of Art and the School of Landscape Architecture. A program in interior design is offered within the School of Architecture. In the College of Arts and Sciences are the related fields of mathematics and sociology. Physics is offered in the College of Basic Sciences, and management and economics in the College of Business Administration. A related curriculum in construction technology is offered in the General College. Several departments in the College of Engineering, such as Civil Engineering and Mechanical Engineering, offer instruction in other technological areas. All of these support areas are in place and available for architecture majors to broaden their education. The breadth of LSU's offerings in related fields allows students greater flexibility in placing personal emphasis on their roles in the profession. Strong linkages also exist between the school and the local, state and national professional associations. As a means of strengthening relationships with the profession, frequent interactions occur between local and regional professionals and the student body.

SPECIAL ACTIVITIES AND PROGRAMS

Combined B Arch/MBA program offered to qualified students by the School of Architecture and the College of Business Administration

Master of Science in Architecture program

Academic Programs Abroad (travel/study electives such as the London program and the Yucatan in Mexico program)

Annual lecture series

Participation in national design competitions

Active student chapter of the AIAS

School of Architecture Office of Building Research

School of Architecture Alumni Association

Collaborative studios with interior design and landscape architecture

Design Career Day (opportunity to interview with architectural firms for graduating seniors and to secure summer employment for upperclassmen)

Recruitment of high ACT score students and high quality minority students

Annual O. J. Baker Competition and Awards Luncheon hosted by local chapter of A.I.A. and School of Architecture

Access through LSU's membership in the Research Libraries Group to the collections of 35 other major institutions and 19 museums

FACILITIES

The School of Architecture is housed in Atkinson Hall located on the southern terminus of the main campus quadrangle. The program utilizes 15 design studios, a teaching support lab, a general workroom, a 694 sq. ft. exhibition gallery/jury space, and general classroom in Atkinson Hall. The College of Design Building offers two design studios to accommodate 180 preprofessional program students, an auditorium with a seating capacity of 150, seminar rooms and a Design Workshop. The Design Resource Center is available 73 hrs. per week and has specialized resources of 10,000 volumes, 20,000 slides, 85 serials and more than 800 master's theses and fifth-year projects. The Computer Aided Design and Geographic Information System (CADGIS) Lab is open 78 hrs. per week and includes an Intergraph VAX 730 CAD system, 3 IBM XT and AT terminals, a microcomputer lab with 19 Apple IIe's and 18 MacIntosh terminals. A MacIntosh Office Design Exploration (MODE) lab which replicates a small design office environment is also available.

SCHOLARSHIPS/AID

LSU awards more than 500 substantial merit scholarships each year to Louisiana freshmen. Financial assistance to students is administered by LSU's Student Aid and Scholarship Office. The School of Architecture awards $4,400 in scholarships each year to selected upperclassmen: Terry Devine Scholarship ($500), M. N. Davidson Scholarship ($375/2), Southwest La. Architects Scholarship ($500), Mississippi-Louisiana Brick Manufacturers Assoc. Scholarship ($2,000), Stanley and Craig Routh Scholarship ($300), AIA Auxiliary Travel ($300), Louisiana Architects Assoc. Travel Fellowship ($1,000), Charles Durand Scholarship ($500), and 5 students per year are nominated for AIA/AIAF Scholarships ($500-$2,000). Annual competitions include: O. J. Baker ($300), Hill Veterinary Clinic ($1,000), Acme Brick ($300) and Fourth Year Portfolio Award ($300). Some teaching assistantships are also available for fourth- and fifth-year students for $400/semester.

UNDERGRADUATE PROGRAM
Philosophy Statement

The School of Architecture is dedicated to preparing students to develop those professional capabilities needed to enter the profession of architecture as an effective apprentice to a qualified practicing architect, with the end view of achieving the augmenting experience necessary to become a fully qualified professional architect; to those basic intellectual disciplines which will allow future development of other capabilities which may be necessitated by changes in the profession and/or society; and to those insights and perceptions necessary to develop a receptiveness and understanding of beauty and human feelings. The program focuses on practicality and scholarship, benefits from a strong and diverse faculty, and has a commitment to reflect the opportunities offered in the region.

Program Description

The curriculum in architecture is a five-year curriculum leading to a Bachelor of Architecture degree. The curriculum is organized around four horizontal "streams": design, management, technology and humanities. The design stream is the major focus and synthesizing element of the program. Humanities provides insight into and awareness of human needs and resources in terms of culture, tradition, histories, contemporary mores and social constraints. Management entails the organization of interdependent activities and the direction of resources to the achievement of specified objectives. Technology involves the application of technical knowledge to the resolution of problems which are encountered in creating a physical element in the environment. Design is viewed as the art and science of synthesizing the preceding into physical reality, while accommodating human activities and aspirations. Students are required to earn 39 credits in specified courses providing a solid core of general education and a sound liberal arts foundation. The 39 "core" credit hours are part of the total number of 170 credit hours required to earn the Bachelor of Architecture degree.

GRADUATE PROGRAM
Philosophy Statement

The Master of Science degree program is a research-oriented, multidisciplinary program designed to provide its graduates with those capabilities needed to offer developmental leadership in their particular areas of interest in the profession of architecture and the broader construction industry. The location of the program may be utilized to provide an applications focus on the problems of warm-humid climates. However, the research and developmental capabilities around which the program is organized are oriented toward more universal applicability.

Program Description

Applicants accepted into the program will follow an individually prescribed, multidisciplinary curriculum selected by the student and the student's graduate committee to meet the student's needs and career objectives. The degree program requires a minimum of 36 semester hours of graduate credit, including a research-oriented, individual thesis project which may vary from 3 to 9 semester hours of credit. In addition to a basic group of required core courses, a broad range of support courses and other resources are available through the university. Completion of the program will require a minimum of 3 semesters of work for full-time students and may require longer for students receiving research or teaching assistantships or for those requiring additional preparatory work involving nongraduate credit.

General areas of concentration in the program include, but are not necessarily limited to:

building systems/forms; community design/development; energy conservation/management; facility planning/project management; historic preservation/restoration; information systems/computer applications; and solar design/applications.

The School of Architecture's Office of Building Research is an adjunct to the program. Through funded research and other contacts with various agencies of national, state and local government and with private industry, the Office of Building Research offers the potential for sponsorship, research assistantships and other support for the student's research activities and thesis.

FACULTY
Administration

Ken Carpenter, AIA, Dean, College of Design
Christopher C Theis, AIA, RA, Director, School of Architecture
Jason C Shih, PE, Coordinator, Office of Building Research
Sandra Mooney, Acting Head, Design Resource Center

Professors

Ken Carpenter, AIA, M Arch
A Peters Oppermann, AIA, M Arch
Jason C Shih, PE, PhD
Fount T Smothers, AIA, MS Sys Eng
Christopher C Theis, AIA, RA, M Arch

Associate Professors

Ali Chowdhury, PhD
Edmund J Glenny, RA, M Arch
J Micheal Pitts, RA, M Arch
Julian T White, AIA, M Arch

Assistant Professors

Jill Bambury, RA, M Phil
Rodolphe Elkhoury
John F Leaver, RA, M Arch

Part-Time Faculty

Edward Barbier, MFA
William Brockway, FAIA, B Arch
David Brinson, AIA, B Arch
William Burks, AIA, M Arch
Charles Colbert, FAIA, MS Arch
Bobbie Crump, AIA, B Arch
Kevin Harris, AIA, M Arch
Agi Vajna, MFA
Sammy Vincent, B Arch

Louisiana Tech University

Department of Architecture
School of Art and Architecture
Louisiana Tech University
P.O. Box 3175 T.S.
Ruston, Louisiana 71272-3175
(318) 257-2816

Admissions Office
Louisiana Tech University
P.O. Box 3178 T.S.
Ruston, Louisiana 71272
(318) 257-3036

Application Deadline(s): 30 days prior to
commencement of
academic quarter
Tuition & Fees: Undgrd: La Res: $472;
Non-res: $787/qtr
Endowment: Public

DEGREE PROGRAMS

Degree	Minimum Years for Degree	Accred.	Requirements for Admission	Full-Time Stdnts.	Part-Time Stdnts.	% of Applics. Accptd.	Stdnts. in 1st Year of Program	# of Degrees Conferred
B Arch	5	NAAB	HS Diploma, ACT	247	2	70%	60	28
BFA Int Des	4	FIDER	HS Diploma, ACT	40	4	85%	20	8

SCHOOL DEMOGRAPHICS (all degree programs)

Full-Time Faculty	Part-Time Faculty	Full-Time Students	Part-Time Students	Foreign Students	Out-of-State U.S. Stdnts.	Women Students	Minority Students
14	2	247	2	11%	16%	23%	10%

LIBRARY (Tel. No. 318-257-3555)

Type	No. of Volumes	No. of Slides
University	12,000 (Arch)	25,000 (Arch)

STUDENT OPPORTUNITIES AND RESOURCES

Louisiana Tech University is a comprehensive university, offering a wide range of curricula and degrees at the undergraduate, graduate and doctoral levels. It is located in the north-central region of the state of Louisiana, in the city of Ruston. The town possesses many of the qualities and characteristics associated with the southern small town, but is in many respects atypical. The contradiction existing between the small-town image and its almost metropolitan level of amenity has consequently provided the university with a fertile environment for its development and growth - both quantitatively and qualitatively.

The Department of Architecture is an academic department within the School of Art and Architecture, which is in turn a division of the College of Arts and Sciences. The School is the largest division in the College, providing educational opportunities for majors in the fields of fine art, graphic design, interior design, studio, photography and architecture. The various curricula within the School of Art and Architecture interact to a high degree, with the result that the significant links between architecture and the fine arts have played, and will continue to play, a dominant role in the structure of the program.

The program is characterized by the existence of an exceptionally fine and stable faculty representing a wide range of viewpoints, and demonstrating a great deal of interactive expertise. The personal and educational interactions which the faculty supports have had a great influence on the quality of the program and the learning experiences it generates. The differing understandings of and attitudes toward architecture, professionalism and the current and future role of the architect have supported and enhanced the basic direction of the program, and have served to give it both added strength and progressively greater depth.

The University, through its reputation for academic excellence, attracts students of exceptionally high calibre, and student enrollment in the program is broad and diverse. Their general attitude toward their education is marked by a strong desire to learn and a firm commitment to personal growth and the expansion of their knowledge of their world. Students graduating from the architecture program therefore tend to be strongly committed to their roles as young professionals, highly motivated in their pursuit of design and professional excellence, enthusiastic about their abilities and their potential for continued learning, and feeling a high degree of responsibility for their personal actions and interventions in the environment. All students graduating from the program are active participants in the Intern Development Program, and the performance of the program's graduates in the Architectural Registration Examination is consistently well above national averages, as is their record of initial placement and subsequent advancement in professional offices and practices, where they quickly assume leadership roles and responsibilities.

SPECIAL ACTIVITIES AND PROGRAMS

Travel Abroad: Tech Rome, Tech Mexico and Tech China are Louisiana Tech University's travel-study programs. The programs offer a wide range of academic coursework, including offerings in the field of art, architecture, urban design, urban history and landscape studies.

Field Trips: The program has established an annual series of field trips for its students. Generally speaking, one regional trip is offered each quarter, and one trip to a major urban center outside the region is offered over one of the quarter breaks.

Lecture Series: The program supports an active and well-rounded lecture series, and this serves to greatly enhance its educational opportunities. Students in the program in addition participate in a diverse range of lectures offered in the fields of fine art, sculpture, interior design, graphic design and photography.

Exhibition Series: The School of Art and Architecture supports an annual exhibition series which brings both travelling and curated exhibits to the campus.

Student Organizations: The program is characterized by highly effective and very active chapters of the AIAS and Tau Sigma Delta. These student organizations participate directly in all of the affairs of the program, organize a wide range of special activities, and contribute to both the quality of the program and the motivation and commitment of the student body.

Honors Program: An Honors Program is available for exceptional students.

FACILITIES

The major studio, lecture, seminar, audio-visual, computer and office spaces for the architecture program at Louisiana Tech University are located on the twelfth, thirteenth, and fifteenth floors of the Wyly Tower of Learning. The quality of these spaces is excellent, and their location at the center of the campus, adjacent to the Prescott Memorial Library, the Bookstore, the Quadrangle and the other facilities occupied by the School of Art and Architecture is of significant benefit to the program.

In addition to the areas specifically allocated to the program, the Department has access to the ceramics, woodworking and metalworking shops and photographic and graphics facilities and studios which are a part of the facilities allocated to the Department of Art. The specialized facilities and equipment used in the entire range of the engineering disciplines are available for use by the students and faculty in the program as a result of the interdisciplinary character of the program's technology sequence.

SCHOLARSHIPS/AID

Financial support to students is provided at the institutional level by the Financial Aid Office. This office administers state and federal Educational Grants and Loans, Scholarships and Work/Study Funding. The services of the Financial Aid Office are available on an equal opportunity basis to all qualified students enrolled in the program.

Freshmen entering the program may compete for academic scholarships offered by the institution, the College and the Louisiana Tech Alumni Foundation. These scholarships are administered by the Office of Admissions, and are awarded on the basis of high school performance and academic merit.

The Department of Architecture annually awards the F. Jay Taylor Architecture Scholarship of $1,000 to a student in the program, and competes at the national level for scholarship awards from the AIA/AIA Foundation, and at the state level in the Louisiana Architects Association Fellowship Program. Four Graduate Assistantships are, in addition, available to students in the fifth year of the program. These assistantships represent a significant source of financial support for exceptional students in the program.

UNDERGRADUATE PROGRAM
Philosophy Statement

The fundamental goal of the program at Louisiana Tech University is that of providing a professional architectural education of excellence, and of developing the research and service components necessary for the support and enhancement of its basic educational program. The program intends to prepare its graduates for ultimate entry into independent practice in the profession, as recognized specialists in the creation of significant buildings and places for people's enjoyment and use.

To achieve this goal, the program provides its students with a comprehensive, balanced and rigorous set of educational experiences. Through these the inter-related influences of history, theory, context, pragma, technology and practice on the form of the built environment are investigated and ultimately understood, and the significant traditions, concerns and processes of the architect are accepted, valued and extended.

Program Description

The five-year curriculum in architecture offered by the Department is a professional degree program, and is consequently comprehensive, rigorous and demanding. The program leads to the award of the degree of Bachelor of Architecture on completion of its curricular requirements, and this degree is accredited by the National Architecture Accrediting Board. As such the program prepares the student for professional internship and, after completion of the required internship period, the Architects Registration Examination.

The structure, sequence form and content of both required courses and elective options which make up the curriculum leading to the award of the professional Bachelor of Architecture degree have been intentionally designed by the Department to provide a rigorous education in design, theory, history, technology, practice and the liberal arts as these relate to the profession and practice of architecture. The curriculum has been specifically tailored to meet the needs of a professional program aspiring to excellence.

The course structure is based on the 4+1 model, and follows the general pattern of the quarter system of instructional periods used at Louisiana Tech University. Academic credit is, however, earned in semester hour units, which is among the unique features of the institution. The academic year is divided into Fall, Winter and Spring quarters, with two additional six-week-long summer sessions available to the students for additional course work.

Each student majoring in architecture must complete a curriculum which consists of 173 semester hours of credit spread over a five-year or 20-quarter period. Students transferring into the program from another accredited institution are required to earn a minimum of 31 credit hours from Louisiana Tech to be eligible for the award of the Bachelor of Architecture degree, and additional coursework beyond the 173 hours stipulated in the curriculum may be required in order to meet equivalency requirements. Students transferring into the program with a baccalaureate degree in another discipline typically require a minimum of 100 semester hours of credit earned in the program to qualify for the award of the professional degree.

GRADUATE PROGRAM
Philosophy Statement

While the program does not itself offer a degree program at the graduate level, several opportunities for cooperative and interdisciplinary study at the graduate level are available. Cooperative programs focusing on studies at the graduate level in which the program participates are the Master of Arts in History in the College of Arts and Sciences, the Master of Science in Civil Engineering in the College of Engineering, the Master of Business Administration in the College of Administration and Business and, with Grambling State University, the Master of Arts in Liberal Studies in the College of Liberal Arts.

FACULTY
Administration

Joseph W Strother, Director, School of Art & Architecture
Peter Schneider, AIA, RIBA, Head, Department of Architecture

Professors

Phoebe Allen, MFA
Edward V Kemp, FAIA, RA, M Arch
F Lestar Martin, AIA, RA, M Arch
Peter Schneider, AIA, RIBA, RA, B Arch

Associate Professors

Charles Harrington, RA, M Arch
Ian K Macaskill, RIBA, RA, B Arch
Mary K Morse, MFA
Kenneth W Schaar, PhD
Henry V Stout, AIA, RA, M Arch

Assistant Professors

Robert Fakelmann, AIA, RA, M Arch
Tim Hayes, RA, M Arch
Robert Moran, RA, M Arch

Instructors

Elise Moentmann, B Arch

Adjunct Faculty

Les Guice, PhD
David Holz, PhD
Reginald Jeter, PE, MSC
Gary E Milford, PhD

University of Manitoba

Faculty of Architecture
University of Manitoba
201 Russell Bldg.
Winnipeg, Manitoba, Canada, R3T 2N2
(204) 474-9458 (Graduate)
(204) 474-9268 (Undergraduate)

Admissions Office:
(204) 474-8814

Application Deadline(s): Graduate Program:
May 15th for Fall
Oct 15th for Spring
Tuition & Fees: Undgrd: $1250
Canadian/academic year
Grad: $1300
Canadian/academic year
Endowment: Public

DEGREE PROGRAMS

Degree	Minimum Years for Degree	Accred.	Requirements for Admission	Full-Time Stdnts.	Part-Time Stdnts.	% of Applics. Accptd.	Stdnts. in 1st Year of Program	# of Degrees Conferred
M Arch	4	MAA & CAA	Non-design 1st degree, 2.5 Min GPA	93	4	30%	14	27
M Arch	3	MAA & CAA	BES, 2.5 min GPA			included in above		
M Arch	1	MAA & CAA	Prof Arch degree			included in above		
BES	3		High School Diploma, 2.5 min GPA	135	58	10%	63	50

MAA: Manitoba Association of Architects   CAA: Commonwealth Association of Architects   BES: Bachelor of Environmental Studies

SCHOOL DEMOGRAPHICS (all degree programs)

Full-Time Faculty	Part-Time Faculty	Full-Time Students	Part-Time Students	Foreign Students	Out-of-State U.S. Stdnts.	Women Students	Minority Students
20	26	228	62	No distinction is made for these categories.			

LIBRARY (Tel. No. 204-474-9217)

Type	No. of Volumes	No. of Slides
Arch & Fine Arts Slide Library	57,380	130,000

STUDENT OPPORTUNITIES AND RESOURCES

Graduates with a baccalaureate in Environmental Studies are employed with architectural and landscape architecture firms, with building contractors, and at all levels of government and the building industry. A small percentage of graduates go into business for themselves as carpenters, photographers, painters and sculptors, and architectural model makers and by providing drafting services for professional design firms and graphic design services. The majority of graduates pursue graduate studies in architecture, landscape architecture, or city planning.

Students are assigned individual space in the design studio. They have access to a workshop, a darkroom, and a library of 130,000 slides and 57,380 books and journals in the J.A. Russell Building, which houses the Faculty of Architecture, in addition to all the library and other facilities of a comprehensive university. The University of Manitoba currently has a full-time student enrollment of approximately 24,000.

The above description relates largely but not exclusively to the Department of Environmental Studies.

SPECIAL ACTIVITIES AND PROGRAMS

Faculty Visiting Lectures/Exhibition Series. Joint Urban Design Seminar/Studio with City Planning and Landscape Architecture. Special academic programs that financially support graduate students as teaching and research assistants.

Graphics Workshop: in the week preceding the beginning of term, the second-year students in Environmental Studies spend approximately 50 hours at a remote site, in workshops comprising intensive skill-building sessions in methods and techniques in graphic communications.

Chicago Field Trip: third-year students in Environmental Studies spend ten days in Chicago. The group, supervised by 2 staff members, is given intensive briefings on the history of Chicago and its architecture through visits to key buildings both in Chicago and en route. The group meets with architects and the Chicago Planning Commission.

Studio 4 in the Department of Architecture spends one term in Montreal, in association with Schools of Architecture in that city.

A term spent in China is a recent innovation, involving students from the three Graduate Departments of Architecture, Landscape Architecture and City Planning.

The Faculty supports a lecture series that is presented throughout the academic year.

A number of prizes and awards are available for students in all Departments.

FACILITIES

Computer Labs
Photographic Labs
Environmental Control Labs
Workshop

SCHOLARSHIPS/AID

To request a copy of the University of Manitoba's "Awards Bulletin," write to: Awards Office, Room 401, The University of Manitoba, Winnipeg, Manitoba, R3T 2N2 Canada (204 - 474-9531).

UNDERGRADUATE PROGRAM
Philosophy Statement

It is the objective of the Department of Environmental Studies to provide students with a broad base of knowledge and understanding of the interrelationships of man and his environment as well as a basis for developing the fundamental design methodology and technique needed to respond to those needs and aspirations of society that demand some form of design product.

Program Description

The Department of Environmental Studies provides a preprofessional education basic to the succeeding graduate disciplines of architecture, landscape architecture, and city planning at the University of Manitoba. The curriculum is structured around a design sequence that

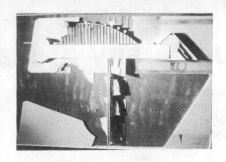

provides opportunities for examining and responding to the socioeconomic aspects of man in community as well as the complex relationships between man and his environment that demand some form of artifact.

The design studio and project reviews are therefore fundamental didactic methods through which students broaden and demonstrate their understanding of a sense of community and the consequences of intervention. The overall objective is the development of confidence in one's ability to resolve problems with economy and elegance and a respect for land as a community of biotic and abiotic things, all within a context of societal values. Accordingly, the design sequence is supported by tutorials, lectures, and workshops in graphics, design methods and theories, history of culture, and building technology. Electives in the social sciences serve not only to question value systems and attitudes but also to guide the development of practical and technical proficiency and refine analytical, discursive, and conceptual skills.

The third year of the program is structured into Middle School Options. These options provide students with opportunities for in-depth study of the concepts, ideologies, and professional requirements particular to architecture, landscape architecture, and city planning. The options are jointly administered by Environmental Studies and the parent graduate program.

PHILOSOPHY STATEMENT

The mission of the Faculty of Architecture is to recognize its responsibility to society involving man and environment, by dedication to excellence in design education and creative works. The Department of Architecture is concerned with first, the education and training of professionals who are to resolve our needs for physical shelter in harmony with the environment; and second, the broadening of the profession's knowledge, methodology, and skills in order to contribute to the development of our cultural heritage.

PROGRAM DESCRIPTION

The Department of Architecture offers a professional program leading to the degree of Master of Architecture (M Arch).

The program is divided into three phases: Pre-Master, Masters and Practicum; with major evaluation occurring between each phase in accordance with the requirements of the Faculty of Graduate Studies and the supplementary regulations of the Department.

Seven term-length Studio Courses, with input lectures, seminars, site visits, and consultation form the core of the curriculum, followed by the Practicum. The Pre-Masters phase, consisting of Studios One through Four, provides instruction, demonstration, and exercises with criticism on various aspects of the design process in solving problems in architecture and related design disciplines. The Masters phase, Studios Five through Seven, identifies and explores multi-function building projects, form-stimulating qualities of site and extreme climatic factors, and urban design disciplines and constraints. Upon completion and major evaluation of the Studio Courses, students undertake the Practicum as an

independent work of an approved program to demonstrate professional knowledge and skills culminating in a public presentation.

Support Courses, in lecture and seminar format, are required to complement the Studio Courses to provide professional knowledge and specialized disciplines necessary in the architectural profession.

Elective Courses on architecture, theory, preservation, and other selected topics and issues of the profession are offered by the Department to provide diverse opportunities to pursue concentrated exploration of specialized knowledge to supplement the required Studio and Support Courses. Students are encouraged to take additional electives offered by other departments of the University to gain access to the many resources available in a major university.

The program is supplemented with lectures and presentations by visiting architects and related professionals from the city, across Canada, the United States and abroad; with assistance from the Faculty Endowment Fund, the Manitoba Association of Architects, and other supporting bodies and organizations.

Students are admitted into the Department of Architecture at varying levels of the program. Baccalaureates with non-design degrees are admitted to Studio One and undertake the full four-year program. A majority of students, with Environmental Studies or Interior Design degrees from the University of Manitoba, are admitted to Studio Three, and normally complete the courses in three years. Students with non-professional or professional degrees in architecture are admitted into the appropriate level according to academic background, technical knowledge and skills, and professional experience.

Upon receiving the M Arch degree, the architectural graduate from the University of Manitoba is entitled to become an associate member of the Manitoba Association of Architects, the provincial component of the Royal Architectural Institute of Canada. After completion of three years qualified practice, the graduate is eligible to apply for license to practice architecture in Manitoba. Other provincial architectural associations recognize the University of Manitoba degree in architecture and require similar postgraduate practice before eligibility for application for a license to practice. The program is accredited by the Commonwealth Association of Architects and graduates are exempt from all final examinations of the Royal Institute of British Architects, with the exception of the examination in Professional Practice. The Department of Architecture is an active member of the Association of Collegiate Schools of Architecture.

The Department of Architecture shares with the departments of Environmental Studies, Interior Design, City Planning and Landscape Architecture the rich and diverse resources of the Faculty of Architecture. With an overall enrollment of five hundred plus students served by forty-two full-time and thirty-eight part-time members from the professions, the Faculty provides unique opportunities to develop an awareness and understanding of related design professions leading to collaborative and

multi-disciplinary work and studies. The resources of this design Faculty include an extensive architecture and fine arts library, an exceptionally large and growing slide collection, fully-equipped workshops, building materials and resources centre, climatological studies equipment, and work stations of the university's computer system.

FACULTY
Administration

Thomas H Hodne, FAIA, Dean, Faculty of Architecture
Jonas Lehrman, MAA
Gustavo Da Roza, FRAIC, Head, Department of Architecture
Ian MacDonald, Acting Head, Department of Environmental Studies
Michele Laing, Head, Architecture and Fine Arts Library

Professors

Gordon Adaskin, RCA, Dipl
Jacques Collin, MAA, Dipl
Gustavo Da Roza, FRAIC, B Arch
Claude De Forest, MAA, M Arch
Don Ellis, MAA, M Arch
Ozdemir Erginsav, MAA, MAR, MAUD
Rory Fonseca, M Arch, PhD
Peter Forster, AA Dipl
Thomas Hodne, FAIA, M Arch
Denis Jesson, MAA, B Arch
Jonas Lehrman, MAA, M Arch
Harlyn Thompson, MAA, M Arch
John Welch, MAA, AA Dipl

Associate Professors

Benjamin Harnish, B Arch, M Sc
Winston Leathers, RCA, Dipl Art
Ian MacDonald, MAA, B Arch
Dieter Roger, Architekt
Octavio Tivoli, Arch

Assistant Professor

Knut Haugsoen, MAA, M Arch

Part-Time Faculty

Wayne Bissky, MA, M Arch
Judith Bruun, M Arch
Steve Cohlmeyer, MAA, M Arch
Etienne Gaboury, B Arch
Richard Perron, B Sc
Douglas Regelous, LLB
Ben Wasylyshen, BID
David Whetter, B Arch, M Arch
Jim Yamashita, MAA, B Arch
Lea Zeppetelli, B Arch

Adjunct Faculty

Mario Carvalho, PhD
Kent Gereke, PhD
John Glanville, M Sc, P Eng
Robert Madill, BA, MSA
Ken McLachlan, PhD
Carl Nelson, M Arch
Alex Rattray, MLA
William P Thompson, PhD
Charles Thomsen, BFA

University of Maryland

School of Architecture
University of Maryland
College Park, Maryland 20742-1411
(301) 454-3427

Application Deadline(s): Undgrd – Feb 1; Grad – March 1; Foreign students – Feb 1
Tuition & Fees: Undgrd: MD Res: $1600; Non-res: $4477
Grad: MD Res: $2760; Non-res: $4890
Endowment: State

DEGREE PROGRAMS

Degree	Minimum Years for Degree	Accred.	Requirements for Admission	Full-Time Stdnts.	Part-Time Stdnts.	% of Applics. Accptd.	Stdnts. in 1st Year of Program	# of Degrees Conferred
BS Arch	4		Spec. app.; portfolio; 56 cr. hrs.; Direct Admit.: 3.5 GPA, 1200+SAT	97	10	33%	44	43
BS Urb Studies	4		Spec. app.; portfolio/56 cr. hrs.	4	0	54%	3	1
M Arch	2	NAAB	BS Arch or equiv; GRE: 3.0 GPA; Spec. app.; portfolio	36	18	35%	17	20
M Arch	3+	NAAB	BA or BS; GRE; 3.0 GPA spec. app.; portfolio	35	19	33%	17	16
M Arch	1		1st prof. degree: B Arch or M Arch	0	1	45%	1	0

SCHOOL DEMOGRAPHICS (all degree programs)

Full-Time Faculty	Part-Time Faculty	Full-Time Students	Part-Time Students	Foreign Students	Out-of-State U.S. Stdnts.	Women Students	Minority Students
21	3	172	48	6%	24%	39%	7%

LIBRARY (Tel. No. 301-454-4316)

Type	No. of Volumes	No. of Slides
Arch Only	36,000	220,000

STUDENT OPPORTUNITIES AND RESOURCES

In location, faculty and students at the University of Maryland School of Architecture enjoy the best of all possible worlds. Situated on 1,300 acres, the College Park Campus is a part of the larger metropolitan area of Washington, DC, which is rapidly becoming the nation's capital in cultural and intellectual activity as well as political power. The Kennedy Center for the Performing Arts, the Filene Center, and the many fine area theaters regularly present performances by the world's most exciting and renowned artists. The Smithsonian Museums and the National Gallery of Art, among others, sponsor standing collections and special exhibits that attract national attention. In addition to cultural activities, the Nation's Capital, home of the AIA national headquarters, provides the finest laboratory for architectural research and urban studies with its L'Enfant Plan and monuments. The possibilities for personal and professional enrichment offered in this exciting cosmopolitan area are indeed enormous.

Outside the metropolitan area, and just minutes from the campus, the scene in the Maryland countryside is pleasantly rural. Historic Annapolis, the state capital, is only a short drive away, and the city of Baltimore, with its rich variety of ethnic heritages, its cultural and educational institutions, and its impressive urban transformation, is only 30 miles from College Park.

SPECIAL ACTIVITIES AND PROGRAMS

Kea Distinguished Professorship (Visiting Professional)

Studio projects focus on issues of the Washington-Baltimore metropolitan region and Maryland communities

Visiting studio critics

Summer field work involving underwater and land excavations in Israel, Tunisia, Turkey, Jordan, and Sri Lanka

Summer studios in Europe

Summer Preservation Programs in Cape May, New Jersey, and Kiplin Hall, Yorkshire, England

CADRE (Center for Architectural Design and Research) projects with faculty-student participation

Research opportunities with AEPIC (Architecture and Engineering Performance Information Center)

School of Architecture Exhibition Program

Special lecture/seminar program at the Smithsonian and National Gallery of Art

Joint Architecture (Regional) Design Competition

Annual School of Architecture public lecture series

Student Government Association and Student AIA Chapter

Community Service Projects

Students' Beaux Arts Ball and fall barbecue and football game

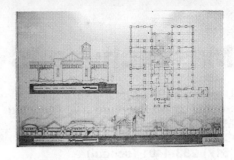

FACILITIES

The School is housed in a modern air-conditioned building which provides design work stations for each student, a large auditorium, seminar and classroom facilities. A well-equipped woodworking and model shop, an environmental testing laboratory, computer-aided design facility, and a darkroom are also provided.

The Architectural Library and Slide and Visual Resources collection provide rare opportunities for research with the entire library of the National Trust for Historic Preservation; video and photographic equipment; rare books, special collections and slides and photographs on architecture, architectural technology, planning and preservation.

SCHOLARSHIPS/AID

Financial assistance is available to graduate students in the form of Graduate School Fellowships, Graduate Assistantships, Dean's scholarship, Work Study Grants, and loans. For information on these and other forms of aid, contact the Graduate School.

Undergraduate financial assistance includes work-study and loan programs. For information on these and other forms of aid, contact the University Financial Aid Office, Undergraduate Program.

UNDERGRADUATE PROGRAM
Philosophy Statement

Although the changing patterns of world and national problems can be expected to have major impacts on the practice of architecture and urban planning in the coming decades, it is clear that well-prepared environmental designers and architects will continue to be in demand as the physical environment in which we live and work is adapted to suit new circumstances. Architecture as a field of activity will continue to provide personal challenges of the highest order, the opportunity for varied work and for public service, and the chance to see others benefiting from and enjoying the products of one's efforts.

The School's basic mission is to provide the general education and professional training to develop the skills required by the graduate architect. Its curriculum in architecture is organized around courses in architectural and urban design, architectural history and theory, and architectural science and technology. Although its program is demanding, many electives, both in architecture and related fields and in the sciences and humanities, are also available. Courses in design studio involve the student in a series of design case studies, often drawn from actual situations in the surrounding environment. Both science/technology and design courses utilize field trips, "hands on" experience, and the expertise of visiting critics and lecturers as well as regular faculty.

Program Description

The four-year undergraduate program leads to Bachelor of Science degrees in two major fields of study, architecture and urban studies.

The undergraduate major in architecture is designed to minimize the time required to complete the curriculum leading to the professional degree, Master of Architecture. The urban studies program is designed for students admitted to the school who desire strong academic preparation in architecture and urban studies subjects at the undergraduate level, but who plan to pursue careers other than architecture, such as urban planning or public administration.

The first two years of the program are primarily general university studies but include an introduction to the built environment, the history of architecture, and drawing. Study in the third and fourth years is concentrated in architectural design (analysis and synthesis), architectural structures, environmental control systems, construction and materials, urban studies, history of architecture, site analysis, and more drawing. The emphasis is on developing and maintaining a reasonable balance among the theoretical, practical, technical, and aesthetic aspects of architecture.

GRADUATE PROGRAM
Graduate Program Description

The graduate program emphasizes the design studio as the center of creative activity and integration of the total curriculum: design and urban design, science-technology, history and theory, and other university studies. The courses in structures, environmental technologies, construction, and materials are related to architectural design practice and theory.

A thesis is required in which the student must present the research, analysis, and design of a building or building complex within a given context and comprehensive environment.

The following M Arch options are available: a two-year first professional degree program following the BS or BA with major in architecture; a three-year-plus, first professional degree program for those students with a baccalaureate in fields other than architecture; a one-year program for those who wish to pursue specialized studies in architecture and already possess the first professional degree (B Arch or M Arch); and a Master's Certificate in Historic Preservation.

FACULTY
Administration

John Ames Steffian, AIA, Dean
Stephen F Sachs, AIA, Associate Dean
Nancy K Lapanne, Assistant to the Dean
Sally Sims, Acting Architecture Librarian

Professors

Ralph Bennett, MFA Arch
John W Hill, FAIA, MA
Roger Lewis, FAIA, M Arch
John Loss, AIA, M Arch
Paul Lu, AIA, ASLA, APA, MLA
B Frank Schlesinger, FAIA, M Arch
John Ames Steffian, AIA, M Arch

Associate Professors

William Bechhoefer, AIA, M Arch
Karl Du Puy, M Arch
Richard Etlin, PhD, FAAR, M Arch
David Fogle, AIP, MRCP
Thomas Schumacher, AIA, FAAR, M Arch
R Lindley Vann, PhD

Assistant Professors

Brian Kelly, M Arch
Sombat Thiratrakoolchai, D Arch
Marion Weiss, M Arch

Lecturers

Uwe Prost
Stephen Sachs, AIA, B Arch

Part-Time Faculty

Jonathan Barnett, M Arch
Alan Dynerman, M Arch
William Loerke, MFA, PhD
Mark McInturff, B Arch
William Murtagh, PhD
Victoria Rixey, M Arch
Ellen Sands, M Arch
Gregory Wiedemann, M Arch
Joseph Wilkes, B Arch
Forrest Wilson, PhD

Massachusetts Institute of Technology

Department of Architecture
School of Architecture and Planning
MIT, 77 Massachusetts Avenue
Cambridge, Massachusetts 02139
(617) 253-4401 (school)
(617) 253-7791 (dept)

Application Deadline(s): January 1
Tuition & Fees: Undgrd: $12,500/yr.
Grad: $12,500/yr.
Endowment: Private

DEGREE PROGRAMS

Degree	Minimum Years for Degree	Accred.	Requirements for Admission	Full-Time Stdnts.	Part-Time Stdnts.	% of Applics. Accptd.	Stdnts. in 1st Year of Program	# of Degrees Conferred
BSAD	4	—	Institute req.	90	0	na	na	26
M Arch	2	NAAB	BSAD or equiv - portfolio	98	na	20%	20	39
M Arch	3½	NAAB	BA or BS - portfolio					
SM Arch Studies	2	—	B Arch, M Arch, BA or BS - portfolio	64	na	30%	38	25
SM Visual Studies	2	—	BA or BS - portfolio	47	na	18%	24	7
SM	2	—	BA or BS - portfolio					
PhD	—		MA	46		15%	11	5
SM Real Estate Development	1		BA or BS - GMAT - related work exp.	36	na	46%	36	35

SCHOOL DEMOGRAPHICS (all degree programs)

Full-Time Faculty	Part-Time Faculty	Full-Time Students	Part-Time Students	Foreign Students	Out-of-State U.S. Stdnts.	Women Students	Minority Students
33	34	255	2	29%	no inf	29%	1%

(student #s represent *grads* only)

LIBRARY (Tel. No. 617-253-7053)

Type	No. of Volumes	No. of Slides
Arch & planning	175,000	359,000

STUDENT OPPORTUNITIES AND RESOURCES

Architecture is one of two academic departments that make up the School of Architecture and Planning. The department enrolls approximately 300 students each year, of whom 25-30 percent are undergraduates. International students constitute approximately 25 percent of the enrollment, comparable to 20 percent for all of MIT.

Architecture students have access to the academic resources of the entire Institute. The Department's own curriculum, in addition to providing study in professional subjects and related areas, includes opportunities for study and research in environmental design, design for Islamic cultures, building technology, and media technology. Instructional ties are maintained with the Departments of Urban Studies and Planning and Civil Engineering. Students may choose to pursue relevant study in other units of the

Institute, such as the Departments of Economics, Political Science, and Humanities, and the Sloan School of Management. MIT also maintains a cooperative relationship with other institutions in the Boston area. Graduate students may cross-register at Harvard University and Wellesley College.

The Boston metropolitan area, with its concentration of cultural and intellectual activities, is a major resource for students. Professional study draws on the strong, varied character of Boston's urban neighborhoods, which makes them natural settings for the study of architectural design problems.

SPECIAL ACTIVITIES AND PROGRAMS

Center for Real Estate Development

Aga Khan Program for Islamic Architecture

Special Interest Group in Urban Settlement (SIGUS)

Research in design methods, energy, construction management

Internship for professional program students

Membership in International Laboratory for Architecture and Urban Design, Siena, Italy

East Asian Architecture and Planning Program

FACILITIES

The Media Laboratory - studies in the invention and creative use of modern electronic media - primary areas of application include education, electronic publishing, and the arts

Laboratory for Architecture and Planning

Center for Advanced Visual Studies

Computer Resource Laboratory

SCHOLARSHIPS/AID

Financial support is available to graduate students in a number of forms. Partial scholarships are awarded from department funds on the basis of need; incoming students receive a disproportionate number of these awards. Many continuing students receive research and teaching assistantships in the department. Scholarships for undergraduates and loans are awarded from institute funds through the MIT Student Financial Aid Office.

UNDERGRADUATE PROGRAM
Philosophy Statement

The concern of the School of Architecture and Planning is for a more humane environment, one which supports the needs of everyday life and satisfies the full range of human experience. There is a shared commitment to exploration in all aspects of architecture and to respond to the demands of an increasingly diffuse and complex profession. Faculty and students are interested in examining alternative ways of designing and seeing and alternative technologies. There is continued focus on research, both academic and applied.

Educational programs are offered that will prepare students for practice, research and further study on the frontiers of professions that determine the form and quality of the physical environment and shape environmental policies and opportunities. It is essential, therefore, to select students who will exercise a high degree of responsibility and initiative in the formulation of their career plans.

Program Description

The department offers two undergraduate courses of study: Course IV, leading to the Bachelor of Science in Art and Design, and Course IV-B, leading to the Bachelor of Science.

Course IV is a flexible program for students whose primary interest falls within the subject areas of the department. There are four possible areas of concentration: visual arts; architectural design; building technology; and history, theory and criticism of art and architecture. Within a broad framework, students develop individual courses of study best suited to their needs and interests. Students whose area of concentration is architectural design complete the first half of the requirements for the M Arch degree.

Course IV-B is for students who find that their basic intellectual commitments are to subjects within the department but whose educational interests and goals cut across departmental boundaries. These students may, with the approval of the department, plan a course of study that directly suits their interests while including the fundamental areas within the department.

GRADUATE PROGRAM
Program Description

The Master of Architecture (M Arch) is awarded after completion of a 2 to 3-1/2 year accredited program combining intensive training in architectural design with a broad range of other subjects, providing preparation for certification and practice.

The Master of Science in Architecture Studies (SMArchS) is a two-year post-professional program offering the opportunity to do research and study in one of the following areas of investigation of the building environment: environmental design; design and housing; design and building technology; history, theory and criticism; and design for Islamic cultures.

A two-year MS program in Media Arts and Sciences is offered in the department through MIT's Media Laboratory. Areas of study include computational video and telecommunications; computer graphics and animation; computer music, epistemology and learning; film/video; graphic imaging; human systems interface; or spatial imaging. The SM Visual Studies (SMVisS) degree is awarded for work in visual design and environmental art at the Center for Advanced Visual Studies.

The PhD program is meant for students interested in research in areas represented in the department: history, theory and criticism of Western (19th and 20th centuries) and Islamic architecture and urbanism; design methods; building technology; and media arts and sciences.

FACULTY
Administration

John de Monchaux, RIBA, Dean, School of Architecture & Planning
William L Porter, FAIA, Head, Department of Architecture
Leon B Groisser, Executive Officer, Department of Architecture
Margaret DePopolo, Rotch Librarian, School of Architecture & Planning

Professors

Stanford Anderson, M Arch, PhD
Julian Beinart, M Arch, MCP
Leon Glicksman, BS, MS, PhD
Leon Groisser, ScD
N John Habraken, BI
Imre Halasz, DA
Ronald Lewcock, B Arch, PhD
John R Myer, FAIA, B Arch
Otto Piene, MA
William Porter, M Arch, PhD
Maurice Smith, B Arch
Waclaw Zalewski, DTS

Associate Professors

James Axley, BS, M Arch, MS, PhD
Ranko Bon, PhD
Eric Dluhosch, M Arch, PhD
David Friedman, PhD
Sandra Howell, PhD
Jan Wampler, M Arch

Assistant Professors

Benjamin Buchloh
Rosemary Grimshaw, M Arch
William Hubbard, B Arch, SM Arch S
Leila Kinney, BA, MA, M Phil
Frank Miller, M Arch
Leslie Norford, BS, MA
Francesco Passanti, MA

Lecturers

Fernando Domeyko
Dennis Frenchman
Nabeel Hamdi
Shun Kanda

Part-Time Faculty

Henry Millon, PhD
Patrick Purcell, M Des
Carl Rosenberg, M Arch
Erich Schneider-Wessling

Adjunct Faculty

Richard Tremaglio, M Arch

McGill University

School of Architecture
McGill University
815 Sherbrooke Street West
Montreal, QC H3A 2K6
Canada
(514) 398-6704

Application Deadline(s): BSc (Arch) + B Arch:
March 1st
M Arch + Graduate
Diploma: February 1st
Tuition & Services Fees: Undgrd: Canadian:
approx. $950/yr
Foreign: approx.
$6625/yr
Grad: Canadian:
approx. $450/sem.
Foreign: approx.
$3400/sem.
Endowment: Private

DEGREE PROGRAMS

Degree	Minimum Years for Degree	Accred.	Requirements for Admission	Full-Time Stdnts.	Part-Time Stdnts.	% of Applics. Accptd.	Stdnts. in 1st Year of Program	# of Degrees Conferred
BSc (Arch)	3		Quebec DCS or equiv.*	141	1	25%	48	42
B Arch	1**	OAQ, CAA, RAIC, RIBA		49	31	98%	35	57
M Arch	1½		McGill B Arch or equiv.***	25	15	30%	18	6

*Quebec Diploma of Collegial Studies in Pure and Applied Science, or equivalent, i.e., 2 years post-secondary studies in science and engineering.

**After McGill BSc (Arch); for other candidates, a minimum of 2 years.

***Candidates with a degree in a related field may be considered.

SCHOOL DEMOGRAPHICS (all degree programs)

Full-Time Faculty	Part-Time Faculty	Full-Time Students	Part-Time Students	Foreign Students	Out-of-State U.S. Stdnts.	Women Students	Minority Students
11	18	215	47	10%	NA	42.6%	NA

LIBRARY (Tel. No. 514-398-4742)

Type	No. of Volumes	No. of Slides
Arch and Art	61,235	40,000

STUDENT OPPORTUNITIES AND RESOURCES

McGill University is situated in downtown Montreal, a French-language city known for its agreeable ambiance, its cultural, social and athletic activities, and its friendliness. There is an excellent transportation system, and some affordable housing within easy walking distance of the University.

Moreover, McGill students have access to residence and dining facilities on campus, and university-sponsored clubs and societies of every kind. Students also have access to a wide variety of courses in other faculties over and above the requirements of the architecture curriculum. The Dean of Students Office sponsors a "buddy system" and offers other assistance to students, including a loans and bursaries program.

Students in Architecture benefit from an active undergraduate society which organizes social and athletic events as well as a Visiting Lecturer series. The School conducts an annual week-long sketching school outside Montreal and offers an annual summer course in Venice. Fifteen travelling scholarships in the amount of $2,500 each are awarded every year. The Blackader-Lauterman Library of Architecture and Art is one of the best in Canada in its specialty.

SPECIAL ACTIVITIES AND PROGRAMS

Academic
Summer Course Abroad: Annual 4-week supervised course in Venice.
Wilfred Truman Shaver Scholarship program: 10 annual awards of $2500 each for supervised student travel.
Annual Summer Sketching School outside Montreal.
Field trips to local sites and other cities such as: New York, Boston, Philadelphia, Washington, Chicago, and Toronto.
Alcan Lecture Series: Annual series of lectures by prominent architects from North America and abroad.

Student
The Fifth Column: Journal of Canadian Students in Architecture; edited and published at McGill University.

Architectural Undergraduate Society: social, cultural, and athletic activities.

Research
Canadian Architecture Collection: Unique collection of plans, drawings, photographs, and monographs of Canadian Architects.
Centre for Minimum Cost Housing: Research and publication in Minimum Cost Housing.
Research in History and Theory

FACILITIES

Blackader-Lauterman Library of Architecture and Art
61,235 physical volumes (39,288 titles + 17,613 volumes of serials) plus 743 periodical titles, of which 280 are current subscriptions.

Canadian Architecture Collection
40,000 items (drawings, photographs, monographs, etc.) in Canadian Architecture.

Visual Resources Library
40,000 slides plus 500 maps and other reference material.

Communications Laboratory
Photographic studio and labs; silk screen, studio film apparatus, film editing, 16mm. movie equipment; lino cut and wood cut printing.

CAD Laboratory - 6 micro computer work stations, plus plotters and printers.

Architectural Workshop - Equipment for wood and metal work mock-ups, model making, etc.

SCHOLARSHIPS/AID

Undergraduate

The School of Architecture annually offers prizes and scholarships in a total amount of $50,000. This includes 10 Wilfred Truman Shaver Travelling Scholarships of $2,500 each. All awards are made on the basis of academic merit.

Also available is a loan and bursary fund.

McGill University offers a number of entrance scholarships for which Canadian citizens are eligible to apply. These are awarded in a university-wide competition.

Graduate

The School of Architecture annually offers fellowships and teaching assistantships in a total amount of $18,500. Students may also apply for University Fellowships.

UNDERGRADUATE PROGRAM
Philosophy Statement

The principal objective of the McGill School of Architecture is to impart to its students competence in both the art and the science of building design and building construction.

Students receive a comprehensive background in engineering subjects such as Strength of Materials, Structures, Surveying, Mechanical and Electrical Services, etc., and in architectural subjects such as History/Theory, Freehand Drawing, Civic Design and Computer Aided Design. In Design, the School does not subscribe to only one philosophy, but through the diversity of its teaching staff exposes students to a variety of approaches to problem solving.

Program Description

The McGill undergraduate architectural program is divided into two parts. The first leads to a non-professional degree, the Bachelor of Science (Architecture), as a preparation for professional studies. The second, consisting of a minimum of two semesters for those with the McGill BSc (Arch) degree, leads to the professional degree, Bachelor of Architecture, which has long been recognized by the Order of Architects of Quebec and the Royal Institute of British Architects as representing completion of their educational requirements for membership. The B Arch degree is also recognized by the Commonwealth Association of Architects. Candidates in the first part of the program who plan to go on to the professional degree in Architecture must follow the series of required and elective courses stipulated for professional studies and achieve an acceptable standing in both Design and Construction courses and in their cumulative grade point average. Students must also have had a total of 6 months related professional experience before applying to the B Arch program.

GRADUATE PROGRAM
Philosophy Statement

The School of Architecture at McGill University offers a Master of Architecture and a Graduate Diploma program for study beyond the first professional degree in architecture. These programs have been conceived to respond to the needs of the graduate with some experience in the field who wishes to acquire more specialized knowledge in architecture.

The M Arch program reflects a tradition at McGill University of academic inquiry and research, and provides an opportunity for a small number of students and staff to work together. The program is organized in such a way as to meet the needs of the professional practitioner and the research specialist, and is intended to extend traditional architectural education as well as address new issues.

Program Description

The M Arch program is a three-semester program in which there are three options: Minimum Cost Housing, Architectural Design, and Architectural History/Theory.

The program is open to applicants who have a professional degree in architecture; in special cases, however, candidates with a degree in a related field may be considered for the Minimum Cost Housing option or the History/Theory option. The residence requirement is three academic semesters and students should complete their studies within the prescribed time. The M Arch degree is awarded upon fulfillment of the required program of study and the successful completion of a written thesis based on research which the student has undertaken throughout the course of studies. The thesis is thus considered the core activity of the program. During the first semester, students in all three options are required to take the Graduate Research Seminar, and to decide on a research topic for the M Arch thesis with the approval of the Program Coordinator. Thesis Supervisors are also assigned at this time. In the second semester, as part of the thesis research course sequence, a significant start on the thesis is undertaken, and students are required to make a presentation of work in progress to the class.

FACULTY
Administration

Bruce Anderson, FRAIC, Director
Derek Drummond, FRAIC, Macdonald Chair
Alberto Perez-Gomez, FMAA, Bronfman Chair
Irena Murray, Head Librarian

Professors

Bruce Anderson, FRAIC, OAQ, B Arch, M Arch
Derek Drummond, OAQ, FRAIC, B Arch
Alberto Perez-Gomez, Dipl Eng Arch, MA, PhD
Witold Rybczynski, B Arch, M Arch
Radoslav Zuk, OAQ, FRAIC, B Arch, M Arch

Associate Professors

Vikram Bhatt, Dipl Arch, M Arch
Ricardo Castro, B Arch, M Arch, MA
David Covo, OAQ, MRAIC, BSc (Arch), B Arch
Adrian Sheppard, OAQ, MRAIC, B Arch, M Arch
Pieter Sijpkes, BSc (Arch), B Arch

Part-Time Faculty

Gavin Affleck
Raymond Affleck
George Baird
George Bassett
Jean-François Bédard
John Bland
Joseph Cadloff
Howard Davies
Gordon Edwards
Lucie Fontein
Abraham Friedman
Julia Gersovitz
Dan Hanganu
Jeffrey Hannigan
Peter Jacobs
Alka Jain
Shun-Min Ko
Phyllis Lambert
Roy LeMoyne
Seymour Levine
John Lingley
Harry Mayerovitch
Serge Melanson
John Pastier
Mark Pimlott
Mark Poddubiok
Roger Richard
Norbert Schoenauer
Duncan Swain
Gentile Tondino
Martin Troy
Philip Webster
Stuart Wilson
Lea Zeppetelli
Jozef Zorko

Miami University

Department of Architecture
Miami University
125 Alumni Hall
Oxford, Ohio 45056
(513) 529-6426

Admissions Office
Grey Gables
Miami University
Oxford, Ohio 45056
(513) 529-2531

Application Deadline(s): March 1
Tuition & Fees: Undgrd: Ohio res: $2584/yr
Non-res: $4021/yr
Grad: Ohio res: $2734/yr
Non-res: $4171/yr
Endowment: State

DEGREE PROGRAMS

Degree	Minimum Years for Degree	Accred.	Requirements for Admission	Full-Time Stdnts.	Part-Time Stdnts.	% of Applics. Accptd.	Stdnts. in 1st Year of Program	# of Degrees Conferred
BED	4		HS Diploma/Optional Portfolio	200	0	35%	55	35
M Arch	1½*		B Arch/Portfolio Statement of Objectives/3 references	2	0	50%	—	2
M Arch	2	NAAB	BED or Equiv./Portfolio/Statement of Objectives/3 references	30	0	30%	15	12
M Arch	3†	NAAB	Bachelor's Degree Statement of Objectives/3 references	12	2	35%	10	6

*36 semester hours, one academic yr + 1 summer   †8 semesters; 3 yrs + 2 summer terms

SCHOOL DEMOGRAPHICS (all degree programs)

Full-Time Faculty	Part-Time Faculty	Full-Time Students	Part-Time Students	Foreign Students	Out-of-State U.S. Stdnts.	Women Students	Minority Students
15	6	244	2	10%	45%	35%	10%

LIBRARY (Tel. No. 513-529-6650)

Type	No. of Volumes	No. of Slides
Arch and Art	40,000	42,000

STUDENT OPPORTUNITIES AND RESOURCES

The programs at Miami University operate under the belief that design is both a fundamental issue and an appropriate focus for an interdisciplinary, liberal university education. For this reason students enroll in design studio courses every one of the four undergraduate years. These studio courses serve as the core of a series of theoretical, technical and liberal arts courses which afford the student a broad exposure not only to architecture, but to many related fields. This exposure prepares the student with the understanding that architecture does not exist in a vacuum, but rather, is a constituent part of the social, political and cultural fabric of society.

To further this fundamental goal, freshmen take not only two studio classes, but three interdisciplinary courses as part of their basic education. These courses—Creativity and Culture; Natural Systems; and Social Systems—are part of the basic curriculum of the School of Interdisciplinary Studies. Often these courses are team-taught with faculty from the Department of Architecture. In the sophomore through senior years students have the option of pursuing these interests to a minor in philosophy, or enrolling in other courses to achieve minors in landscape architecture, art and architectural history, or specially tailored studies in other curricula.

Miami University has a deep and important commitment to undergraduate teaching. This is achieved through small class size and the presence of senior faculty in almost all courses. The faculty is supplemented by nationally known critics and regional practitioners to provide a comprehensive mix of theoretical and professional instruction.

SPECIAL ACTIVITIES AND PROGRAMS

In addition to the aforenoted visiting critics program, Miami has two continually active off-campus programs. The Miami University European Center in Luxembourg has a student enrollment of one hundred juniors studying a wide range of topics at our Luxembourg campus. The Department of Architecture maintains a presence in Alexandria, Virginia, where each semester fifteen students and one faculty member join resources with students and faculty from four or five other programs around the world to study architecture and the urban issues raised in the greater Washington, D.C. metropolitan area.

These off-campus programs add tremendously to the breadth of a Miami education.

The University maintains a very active Honor's Program which offers wide-ranging coursework for qualifying freshmen. An ever-changing series of courses is taught by many of the University's most talented senior faculty. All disciplines are covered and successful completion of a requisite number of courses at graduation is recognized with a special certification.

In addition to the continuing off-campus programs, the Department sponsors numerous field trips and summer workshops both in the U.S. and abroad. In recent years these have included the study of vernacular architecture in Spain and a workshop to prepare a series of measured drawings of the Cathedral at Metz.

Twice recognized by the Ohio Board of Regents as an outstanding academic unit, the Department of Architecture has been given substantial financial support from the State over and above standard funding levels. These additional monies have allowed the Department to equip and staff a computer lab and a research center.

FACILITIES

The Department of Architecture is housed in Alumni Hall, the former University Library. The central portion of the building dates to 1907, when it was the "most lavish building" ever undertaken by the University. It remains among the most exciting and historically significant buildings on campus. Through a series of additions and renovations it now houses all studio and seminar courses, faculty offices, the Art and Architecture Library, computer lab and gallery spaces.

SCHOLARSHIPS/AID

Student aid opportunities at Miami University are generous and extensive. All students are eligible for funds administered through the Student Financial Aid Office. In 1986-87 architecture students received $94,307 in grants and scholarships, $138,587 in loans, and $15,957 in workstudy positions. Approximately 90 percent of graduate students received financial support through stipends and fee waivers.

UNDERGRADUATE PROGRAM
Philosophy Statement

The emphasis of the undergraduate program is to provide students with a broad basis for environmental design. The first two years stress a comprehensive and interdisciplinary approach in all classes. The final two years allow a more focused investigation into any one of a number of design disciplines. The design studio is stressed as the major vehicle for synthesizing all other courses.

Program Description

The undergraduate curriculum provides a broad basic structure common to all students and at the same time encourages diversity through guided electives.

The freshman and sophomore years are designed to provide an introduction to and basic understanding of design—at different scales and with different emphases. The freshman courses develop communication and design skills and provide ways of understanding environments, a necessary foundation for all designers. The sophomore courses are designed to expose students to varying design problems, the significance of history, concepts of structures, design process, thermal environments, and humane relations. The goal of these two years is to develop in students an understanding of the range of opportunities in design and a knowledge of their own abilities so that intelligent choices about directions within design may be made, and appropriate academic programs developed. A concentrated effort is made to counsel and advise students in the process of making these decisions.

The junior and senior years allow students to elect courses consistent with their own direction. A balanced program is maintained by requiring each student to select courses in the following areas: design studios, communication skills, design process, history, theory, and environmental systems. Additional elective time is reserved for courses of the student's choice.

The four-year program in design provides a strong base for a subsequent professional degree in architecture, and in conjunction with other departments in Miami University provides an equally strong base for professional degrees in related design professions.

GRADUATE PROGRAM
Philosophy Statement

The Master of Architecture program has as its goal a balance between practical concerns and theoretical issues. The fifth-year studio problem requires a student to integrate functional and aesthetic design concepts and to develop all major physical systems (structural, environmental, and mechanical) in an integrative and supportive manner. The sixth-year self-directed design studio (thesis) requires the student to explore design issues in greater depth.

Program Description

The Master of Architecture is designed primarily as the concluding two-year professional degree to follow the four-year undergraduate Bachelor of Environmental Design curriculum. The graduate program also provides courses of study for graduates holding the five-year Bachelor of Architecture degree. Applicants with undergraduate degrees in fields other than architecture are also accepted as graduate students, and extended programs of study leading to the Master of Architecture degree are designed to build on their previous academic experience.

The graduate studio experience at Miami offers a unique opportunity for working with internationally recognized visiting studio critics as well as full-time faculty and consultants from other disciplines. The design studio is a working laboratory in which analysis and synthesis become real and meaningful activities to students. The first year of graduate studio is faculty-directed to provide the student with a comprehensive building design experience. The year is divided evenly between working with full-time faculty on a long-term project and with the visiting critics on short-term projects.

The second year of graduate studio is student-directed in consultation with a team of faculty advisers. The year is also divided evenly between working on the self-directed program and working with the visiting critics. Individual creativity and analytical development are strongly emphasized as is the interdependence of the architect with related professionals.

The graduate program requires courses in structural design, environmental controls, architectural materials, and professional practice. Electives are sufficiently broad to provide the student with a wide sampling from many design-related fields and at the same time offer an in-depth study in one of several fields: social and cultural factors, programming and analytical methods, technological issues, energy-efficient design, urban design and planning, visual studies, management, and natural systems.

The framework of the graduate program is designed to provide an intensive dialogue between a small group of graduate students and faculty. It prepares participants for a self-motivated, significant involvement in the field of architecture as practitioners, researchers, teachers, or specialists.

FACULTY
Administration

Hayden B May, RA, Dean, School of Fine Arts
Robert Zwirn, RA, Chair, Department of Architecture
Robert A Benson, PhD, Director, Graduate Program
Thomas A Dutton, Director, Undergraduate Studies
Joann Olson, Humanities Librarian/Art/Architecture

Professors

Gerardo Brown-Manrique, B Arch, M Arch
Hayden B May, BS Arch, MCP
Fuller Moore, B Arch, M Arch

Associate Professors

Robert Benson, MA Art, PhD
Thomas Briner, B Arch, M Arch
Ann Cline, B Arch, M Arch
Thomas A Dutton, B Arch, M Arch
Robert Zwirn, AIA, B Arch, M Arch, JD

Assistant Professors

Bertram C Alexander, BS Arch, M Urb Pl
Paul Clarke, B Arch, M Arch
Catherine Cresswell, BA, M Arch
Craig Hinrichs, BS Arch, M Phil Arch
Scott Johnston, BED, M Arch
Sergio Sanabria, B Arch, PhD

Part-Time Faculty

C H Barcus
Terry Brown, B Arch, M Arch
Steve Carter, BS Arch
Gerald S Hammond, AB, B Arch
James R Miller, BS Engr, MS Engr
Tim E Montgomery, BS, M Arch
William G Owsley, BS Art, MA Art Hist
Charles E Stousland

University of Miami

School of Architecture
University of Miami
1223 Dickinson Dr.
P.O. Box 249178
Coral Gables, Florida 33124
(305) 284-3438, 284-3731

Admissions Office
University of Miami
1342 Ashe Building
P.O. Box 248025
Coral Gables, Florida 33124
(305) 284-4323

Application Deadline(s): March 1st
Tuition & Fees: Undgrd: Tuition - $9787/yr
Room & Board - Approx.
$4100/yr
Grad: 9 Credits @ $395:
$3555/yr
Endowment: Private

DEGREE PROGRAMS

Degree	Minimum Years for Degree	Accred.	Requirements for Admission	Full-Time Stdnts.	Part-Time Stdnts.	% of Applics. Accptd.	Stdnts. in 1st Year of Program	# of Degrees Conferred
B Arch	5	NAAB	3.0 GPA, 1,000 SAT	340	28	n/a	64	91
MURP	2	PAB	3.0 GPA, 1,000 GRE	21	3	40%	9	2
M Arch	1.5/2.0	n/a	3.0 GPA, 1,000 GRE and portfolio	10	0	10%	7	2

SCHOOL DEMOGRAPHICS (all degree programs)

Full-Time Faculty	Part-Time Faculty	Full-Time Students	Part-Time Students	Foreign Students	Out-of-State U.S. Stdnts.	Women Students	Minority Students
22	22	371	31	26%	21%	30%	37%

LIBRARY (Tel. No.   )

Type	No. of Volumes	No. of Slides
Arch	40,000	30,000

STUDENT OPPORTUNITIES AND RESOURCES

The University of Miami is a private, independent, international university composed of fourteen schools and colleges. The main campus is located in Coral Gables, a unique city designed by George Merrick and Denman Fink, one of the founders of the University's architecture program. The School of Architecture's sub-tropical setting in one of America's first planned communities adjacent to metropolitan Miami, the center of tremendous growth and development, provides excellent opportunities for students and faculty to observe and influence dynamic changes in architecture and urbanism.

The School enrolls approximately 400 students from throughout the United States and the world. The diversity of the student body, including a significant percentage of women students, assures the broad range of perspectives and experiences necessary for the serious study of architecture. The faculty includes nationally known practicing professionals and research architects. Variety of ideas and currency of practice is stimulated through a regular Visiting Critics Program and guest lecturers. The curriculum structure emphasizing the design studio guarantees close collaboration between students and faculty in developing traditional and future directions in architectural thought.

SPECIAL ACTIVITIES AND PROGRAMS

Academic year Visiting Critics Program
Academic year Study Abroad Programs in London and Venice
Summer Study Abroad Programs in Italy, Greece, and Colombia

Summer Program for Gifted High School Students
Annual Beaux Arts Ball
Image Processing and Computer-Aided Design Research and Development Units
Continuing Education Courses and Workshops
Student Chapters of AIAS, APA, and Tau Sigma Delta

FACILITIES

The School of Architecture is housed in a complex of five buildings with a total square footage of 43,000. Included are:
Architecture studios
Lecture and seminar rooms
Jury rooms
Image processing/video laboratory
Computer-aided design laboratory
Wood/metal workshop
Slide library
Reference library

SCHOLARSHIPS/AID

The University of Miami offers direct scholarship funds through the Scholarship programs and the John F. Kennedy and Martin Luther King Grants. Different donor loans and outside loans including federal loans such as Perkins Loan Program (formerly NDSL) are also available. Scholarships limited to architecture students include the James E. Branch Scholarship and the Robert Fitch Smith Fund.

UNDERGRADUATE PROGRAM

Bachelor of Architecture

The purpose of the five-year curriculum leading to the B Arch degree is to educate skilled architecture professionals who are committed to responsible stewardship of both the built and the natural environments. Emphasis is placed on the practice of architecture as a process of decision-making and design; hence the structure, content, and method of the B Arch program aim toward educating students capable of generating solutions to environmental problems ranging from the individual to the urban scale.

Bachelor of Science in Land Development & Planning

This planning program is designed to prepare students to enter the private sector in the field of land development and to plan the physical environment. The program is oriented toward the preparation of students interested in the field of urban development including both private and public sector planning and implementation.

GRADUATE PROGRAM
Philosophy Statement

Master of Architecture Program

This program is designed to provide an environment for serious inquiry into the nature of architecture. The program is intended for students holding an accredited degree in architecture (or its equivalent) who wish to develop an individual interest or specialty in architectural theory and practice. It offers students the opportunity to investigate specific aspects of architecture and to elaborate their understanding through teaching, research, publications, and professional practice.

Master of Urban and Regional Planning

The planning program derives direction from South Florida's special opportunities for students and planning professionals. The impact of rapid population growth on a fragile national environment, a multi-ethnic population, a unique and strong area-wide governance, and South Florida's role as a gateway to the Caribbean and Latin America are reflected in the diversity of the program.

Program Description

The Master of Architecture program has two separate tracks:

Track 1: The objective of this track is to explore in depth the architectural design process. This is accomplished by an intensive approach to architecture project development and by the study of a wide range of theoretical issues as context and complement of the design process. A minimum of 30 semester-hour credits is required to be completed over 3 semesters.

Track 2: The objective of this track is to allow the student to specialize in one specific academic area within the context of the discipline. Completing approximately 42 semester-hour credits over a two-year period is required. The program is largely based on individual interest within the field of architecture.

Students with a previous degree from other disciplines: Students entering this option will complete the undergraduate requirements leading to the NAAB-accredited professional Bachelor of Architecture degree and will then work in one of the two tracks for the Master of Architecture.

The two-year Master of Urban and Regional Planning program utilizes the total range of university resources in order to provide an understanding of the physical, social, economic, and political processes that generate growth and change in contemporary human settlements. Areas of concentration include urban design, urbanization in developing countries, environmental planning, community development planning, transportation planning, and others such as health-care delivery services.

FACULTY
Administration

J Thomas Regan, Dean
Felipe J Prestamo, AIA, Interim Associate Dean
Tomas Lopez-Gottardi, Director, Undergraduate Architecture Program
Elizabeth Plater-Zyberk, RA, AIA, Director, Graduate Architecture Program
Ralph Warburton, AICP, FAIA, Director, Graduate Planning Program
Carol Wolf, Librarian

Professors

Paul Buisson, ACSA, RA, Dipl
Rocco Ceo, B Arch, M Arch
Gary Greenan, AICP, RLA, BLA, MCRP
Basil Honikman, RA, A Arch, PhD
Richard Langendorf, AICP, B Arch
Jean-François LeJeune, M Arch
Tomas Lopez-Gottardi, AICP, RA, AIA, B Arch, M Arch
John Medina, M Arch
Joseph Middlebrooks, AIA, RA, B Arch, M Arch
Nicholas Patricios, RA(UK), AICP, BA, PhD
Felipe J Prestamo, AIA, Arch, MCP

J Thomas Regan, ACSA, B Arch, PhD
Stephen Schreiber, M Arch
Thomas A Spain, RA, AIA, B Arch, MA
Michael Stanton, B Art Ed, M Arch
Ralph Warburton, AICP, PA, AIA, RA, B Arch, M Arch

Associate Professors

Jose A Gelabert-Navia, AIA, RA, B Arch, MFA
Jan Hochstim, AIA, RA, BS, B Arch
Joanna Lombard, AIA, RA, B Arch, M Arch
Aristides Millas, NCARB, RA, B Arch, M Arch
Elizabeth Plater-Zyberk, RA, AIA, B Arch, M Arch

Assistant Professors

Jorge Hernandez, M Arch
Teofilo Victoria, B Arch, M Arch

Part-Time Faculty

Maria Abreu
Roberto Behar
Marina Blanco
Juan Caruncho
Maria Fleites
Ana Gelabert-Navia
Oliver Kerr
Joseph LaRocca
Rolando Llanes
Frank Martinez
Luisa Murai
Marilys Nepomechie
Deborah Neve
Claudio Noriega
Daniel Tinney
Jorge Trelles
Luis Trelles
Sanford Youkilis

Visiting Critics

Javier Cenicacelaya, Dipl, MA
Maurice Culot
Inigo Salona, Dipl
Ann Tate
Jerry Wells

University of Michigan

College of Architecture and Urban Planning
University of Michigan
2000 Bonisteel Blvd
Room 2150
Ann Arbor, Michigan 48109-2069
(313) 764-1300

Application Deadline(s): January 15 - Grad;
February 1 - Undgr
Tuition & Fees: Undgrd: Mich. Res: - $2744/yr;
Non-res: - $8640/yr
Grad: Mich. Res: - $4180/yr
Non-res: - $8748/yr
Endowment: Public

DEGREE PROGRAMS

Degree	Minimum Years for Degree	Accred.	Requirements for Admission	Full-Time Stdnts.	Part-Time Stdnts.	% of Applics. Accptd.	Stdnts. in 1st Year of Program	# of Degrees Conferred
BS	2+2		junior standing	174	11	64%	89	80
M Arch	2	NAAB	BS or BA in Arch, portfolio	169	6	68%	98	81
MUP	2	ACSP	bacc, min. 3.0 GPA	42	4	86%	13	20
M Arch/MUP	3		see M Arch & MUP above	*	*			
M Arch/MBA	3		see M Arch above + GMAT	*	*			
M Arch/MSE	2½		see M Arch above	*	*			
Arch D	3		master's or equiv	43	8	35%	14	6

*Enrollment in this program is included in the figure given above for M Arch.

SCHOOL DEMOGRAPHICS (all degree programs)

Full-Time Faculty	Part-Time Faculty	Full-Time Students	Part-Time Students	Foreign Students	Out-of-State U.S. Stdnts.	Women Students	Minority Students
33	12	428	29	25.6%	14%	24.5%	5.9%

LIBRARY (Tel. No. 313-764-1303)

Type	No. of Volumes	No. of Slides
Arch/UP/Art	50,000	44,000

STUDENT OPPORTUNITIES AND RESOURCES

The University of Michigan is located in Ann Arbor, a dynamic community of 110,000 people in Southeastern Michigan. The community is a center for research and high technology. Nearby is Detroit, the nation's fifth-largest city. One of a small number of state universities consistently ranked among the top ten American universities, the university consists of seventeen schools and colleges and has a total enrollment of 34,847 students. The College of Architecture and Urban Planning, with 457 students, is one of the smaller academic units. The extensive eduational resources of the entire university are available to each student.

Instruction in architecture has been continuous at Michigan for eighty-one years. In the College of Architecture and Urban Planning, faculty and students engage in a cooperative learning process. Available knowledge about the built environment is assembled and transmitted, while new knowledge is generated through scholarly inquiry in research and design activities. The College has a basic commitment to the expansion of knowledge and to the maintenance of its programs at the leading edge of new developments in its areas of competence.

The Art and Architecture Building, completed in the fall of 1974, is shared with the School of Art and provides several innovative teaching spaces, including the Visual Simulation Laboratory, the Building Technology Laboratory, the Computer Laboratory, the Wood and Metal Shop, and the Copy Center. The Architecture Library, with an extensive collection of resources, is conveniently located in the building.

There is a broad diversity among the faculty in background, education and experience. Of the 49 faculty, 12 are foreign born. Forty faculty hold a professional license, including 28 architects, 3 structural engineers, 2 mechanical engineers, 2 landscape architects and 3 planners. Other disciplines represented by at least one person include ergonomics, economics, anthropology, sociology, psychology, physics and history. The architecture program has maintained a student-faculty ratio of approximately 11:1 for many years.

The Architecture Research Laboratory, the first of its kind when established in 1948, and now the Architecture and Planning Research Laboratory, has substantial influence on the architecture program and provides opportunities for student research and employment on a comprehensive range of issues dealing with physical and operational environments. During the last seven years, the research volume has averaged $1 million per year.

SPECIAL ACTIVITIES AND PROGRAMS

Raoul Wallenberg Lecture

Ongoing lecture series which is open to the University at large and to the public

Student-organized "brown-bag" lectures

The Thomas S Monaghan Distinguished Professorship and the Charles Eames Lectureship, both bringing well-known professionals to the College to act as visiting studio teachers and scholars.

The Muschenheim Fellowship and the Sanders Fellowship, awarded to young professionals to teach in the studio program and to pursue their own creative activities at the College.

Annual Willeke Design Prize Competition - Provides students with the opportunity to enter a school-wide competition, written and juried by an internationally known architect. The generous sum of $3,000 is awarded to the winner.

The Denmark International Study Program

The Vienna Exchange Program

Student publication, DIMENSIONS

Local chapter of national student organization, AIAS

FACILITIES

College accommodations include classrooms, a 150-seat lecture hall, conference and seminar rooms, faculty and administrative offices, and a complete wood/metal/plastics shop, as well as specialized facilities.

The building conforms to all barrier-free design regulations. Parking space adjacent to the building has been reserved for handicapped persons.

A microcomputer lab room with 52 graphic workstations will be completed in the near future.

The architecture/planning studio, a 90' x 360' space, contains 450 work stations.

SCHOLARSHIPS/AID

Architecture students whose resources are inadequate to meet reasonable educational expenses may request financial aid and seek the advice and counsel of the Office of Financial Aid. Three types of assistance are available: grants, loans, and part-time employment. These are offered on the basis of need, as determined by the Office of Financial Aid. In addition, architecture students are considered for grants within the College. No financial assistance is available through the Office of Financial Aid for entering foreign students.

UNDERGRADUATE PROGRAM
Philosophy Statement

The College of Architecture and Urban Planning engages in teaching and research in architecture and urban planning. The College is a place of professional education where knowledge is transmitted and generated through scholarly inquiry. The promulgation of new knowledge in the fields of planning and architecture is a responsibility of the College. In pursuit of this objective, the College supports research and scholarly activities and continually develops ties between the research and teaching programs. A goal of the College is to maintain its educational programs at the forefront of new knowledge.

Teaching and research in both architecture and urban planning are undertaken with full consideration of their aesthetic, social, political, economic, cultural, and ecological responsibilities. The goals of the College are directed toward the attainment of a humane and responsive environment. Such an environment we believe is essential to support and enhance the daily activities of people, and to help them achieve well-being, growth, and self-realization. Accordingly, the College seeks to foster recognition that human needs and aspirations are intimately related to the environment, and flow from the quality of interaction of people with their environment.

The College strives to foster a nurturous environment in three ways: through its graduates as they pursue their professional careers; through new knowledge made available to the professions and to society; and through its actions in service to society.

Program Description

The undergraduate degree program requires a minimum of four years of higher education. The first two-year segment, Years 1 and 2, includes a broad range of liberal arts courses. The Pre-Professional Studies may be taken either at The University of Michigan or at any other accredited university or community college, and are prerequisite to admission to the professional program. The second two-year segment, Years 3 and 4, consists primarily of required core courses in architecture, which the student takes while enrolled in the College of Architecture and Urban Planning. The Bachelor of Science (BS) degree, a non-professional baccalaureate degree, is awarded upon completion of all of the requirements of Years 1 through 4.

The objectives of Years 1 and 2 are: (1) to increase the student's ability to understand, evaluate, and communicate ideas; (2) to prepare students to make informed decisions regarding their academic and career goals; and (3) to provide a broad academic foundation of principles in subject areas considered essential to subsequent study in architecture.

Objectives of Years 3 and 4 are: (1) to provide a firm foundation in the vocabularies, principles, and interrelationships of a broad range of environmental design determinants essential to professional work in architecture; and (2) to provide opportunities for the students to develop their basic skills, knowledge, perceptions, and insights in areas related to the built environment.

GRADUATE PROGRAM
Philosophy Statement

The professional programs of the College provide students with knowledge and skills for clarifying and solving problems pertaining to architecture, urban planning, and the built environment; educates students to apply their knowledge and skills with full consideration of the context and the needs of client/user groups; and fosters student's creativity and strengthens their interest, motivation, and commitment to improve the human environment. While respecting the need for students to develop their individual aspirations and technical competence, the College seeks also to aid them in developing a clarity of purpose and a broad sense of responsibility for their judgments and actions as professionals.

The diversity of the teaching program of the College is intended to prepare students to pursue both a variety of traditional and non-traditional careers in architecture and urban planning, and to assume positions of leadership within a wide spectrum of public and private organizations and institutions. Programs are designed to be flexible and to respond readily to changes in the fields of architecture and urban planning, but they are sufficiently structured to safeguard against topicality and poor coordination.

Each of the major programs of the College has distinct spheres of concern pursued independently. The College also recognizes and supports the contributions made by other academic areas to the educational environment important to our students and faculty. Accordingly, the College provides and encourages both formal and informal settings for interdisciplinary teaching, research, and service activities.

Program Description

The graduate degree program normally requires two years of study. The student has considerable freedom in planning a program, electing courses and choosing an area of emphasis for intensive work. To be eligible for admission to Year 5 a student must have received either a BS degree from the College of Architecture and Urban Planning or a four year (minimum) baccalaureate degree from another university in a program equivalent in content to Years 1 through 4.

Years 5 and 6 consist of graduate level course work in architecture and related fields. The first professional degree offered by the College, Master of Architecture (M Arch), is awarded upon satisfactory completion of these two years. This phase of the program builds upon fundamentals established in the previous years of undergraduate studies.

Each student focuses a significant amount of study in one of several defined problem areas. These areas of emphasis include, but are not limited to: formal and symbolic issues, functional and behavioral issues, urban design, historic preservation, community design, professional practice, housing, energy efficiency, structural and construction issues.

FACULTY
Administration

Robert M Beckley, FAIA, Dean
Kent L Hubbell, Head, Architecture Program
Linda N Groat, Associate Dean
Mitchell J Rycus, Head, Urban Planning Program
Robert E Johnson, Interim Head, Doctor of Arch Program
Colin W Clipson, Head, Research Program
Peg Kusnerz, Librarian

Professors

Norman E Barnett
Robert M Beckley, FAIA, M Arch
Harold J Borkin, AIA, B Arch
Kurt Brandle, AIA, Dipl Ing, Dr Ing
James A Chaffers, AIA, M Arch, Arch D
Colin W Clipson, AIA
J Sterling Crandall, M Arch
Gerald E Crane, AIA
Robert M Darvas, AIA
Lester Fader, AIA, B Arch
Allan G Feldt
Kent L Hubbell, AIA, B Arch, MFA
Henry S Kowalewski, AIA, B Arch
Kingsbury Marzolf, AIA, M Arch
Gerhard Olving, AIA, M Arch
Leon Pastalan
William A Werner, AIA, M Arch

Associate Professors

Linda N Groat, MFA
Robert E Johnson, AIA, M Arch, Arch D
Mitchell J Rycus
William J Scott Jr, M Arch
Anatole Senkevitch Jr, M Arch
Sharon E Sutton, AIA, M Arch
James A Turner, M Arch

Assistant Professors

Yung-Ho Chang
Mojtaba Navvab, M Arch
Emmanuel-George Vakalo, M Arch

Part-Time Faculty

Gunnar G Birkerts, AIA, Dipl Ing
Keith A Brown, AIA, B Arch
Robert W Marans
Robert C Metcalf, FAIA, B Arch
Christopher Wzacny, AIA, B Arch

Adjunct Faculty

Tivadar Balogh, AIA, B Arch
Thomas R Fitzpatrick, B Arch
William R Jarratt, AIA, B Arch
William B Looney, AIA, M Arch

University of Minnesota

**School of Architecture
and Landscape Architecture
110 Architecture Building
89 Church Street SE
University of Minnesota
Minneapolis, Minnesota 55455
(612) 624-7866**

Application Deadline(s): Undgrd: April 1 for following fall quarter; Grad: February 15 for fall

Tuition & Fees: *Undgrd: MN Res: $52/credit
Non-res: $129/credit
**Grad: MN Res: $799;
Non-res: $1598
*per credit
**full-time rate (7- to 15-credit)

Endowment: Public

DEGREE PROGRAMS

Degree	Minimum Years for Degree	Accred.	Requirements for Admission	Full-Time Stdnts.	Part-Time Stdnts.	% of Applics. Accptd.	Stdnts. in 1st Year of Program	# of Degrees Conferred
BA	4		Univ req, hs diploma	268	5	15%	20	20
BED	4		Univ req, hs diploma	6	0	1%	1	5
BLA	5	LAAB	Univ req, portfolio, letters, pre-LA completion interview	116	5	80%	25	20
B Arch	5	NAAB	1 yr college, GPA 2.75, design problem, portfolio optional	280	20	30%	40	55
M Arch	1		B Arch	6		20%		4
M Arch	2	NAAB	Pre-professional, etc.	40	4	30%		20
MLA	2			13	2	75%		2

*Figures include students who are enrolled for the first two years of architectural studies in the BA or BED program; most students also plan to receive the B Arch degree, the first professional degree offered through the school.

SCHOOL DEMOGRAPHICS (all degree programs)

Full-Time Faculty	Part-Time Faculty	Full-Time Students	Part-Time Students	Foreign Students	Out-of-State U.S. Stdnts.	Women Students	Minority Students
16	28	729	36	10%	40%	33%	2%

LIBRARY (Tel. No. 612-624-6383)

Type	No. of Volumes	No. of Slides
Arch/L Arch	42,426	130,600

STUDENT OPPORTUNITIES AND RESOURCES

The University of Minnesota School of Architecture and Landscape Architecture offers both undergraduate and graduate degree programs in architecture and landscape architecture. A Master of Arts in Urban Design is under development. Total enrollment is roughly 765, including 390 undergraduates in the architecture programs, 116 undergrads in landscape architecture, 50 graduate students in architecture and 15 graduate students in landscape architecture. While perhaps 40 percent of the enrollment is drawn from Minnesota, Wisconsin, and elsewhere within the Upper Midwest, a steadily increasing proportion of the degree candidates come from other parts of the United States, and some 10 percent are from other countries. The rich variety of cultural, recreational, and architectural resources of the Twin Cities and the region offers an increasingly attractive complement to the international reputation of the school and university, making admission a challenge.

Architectural education at Minnesota provides students ready access both to active practitioners (most of the faculty have a major involvement in professional practice) and to scholar-researchers within the full-time faculty of the school and elsewhere throughout the university. Man-environment relations, energy efficiency in design, historic preservation/restoration, architectural history and theory, and urban design/planning are all well served by the school's faculty as part of the design generalist strength of a Minnesota architectural education. Fine engineering programs, in addition to outstanding departments in the liberal arts, business, public policy, etc., give great breadth of opportunity to architecture students at Minnesota.

SPECIAL ACTIVITIES AND PROGRAMS

Foreign study program for third-year undergrads and first-year grad students in the first professional degree programs

Field trips, including a yearly visit to Chicago

Lecture series at the school and at related institutions, such as the Walker Art Center

Direct affiliation with the Underground Space Center and the Minnesota Building Energy Research Center

Annual Summer Session (classes in architectural design, graphics and history)

Materials supply co-op facility (maintained by students)

Two student publications

Involvement in Intern Development Program with fine job opportunities for students

Collaborative learning with students in landscape architecture as well as joint degree opportunities

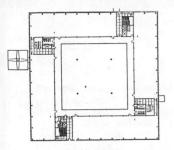

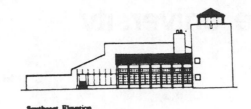

Southeast Elevation

Northeast Elevation

FACILITIES

Steadily expanding program in computer-aided design including a 35-station CAAD studio.

Student access to the school's Built Environment Communications Center (which employs various forms of audiovisual media for educational and documentary use) and to the school photo lab and shop.

Major new addition anticipated during 1988-89, increasing gross space by close to fifty percent and housing new Urban Design Center.

SCHOLARSHIPS/AID

Within limits of federal and state allocations, the University Office of Financial Aid administers loans and grants for all students who apply and can demonstrate need.

In addition, students in architecture and landscape architecture compete for scholarships and for prize money through design competitions. Graduate students may seek university-wide fellowships and awards. These range from $250 with no tuition reduction to $12,000 plus full tuition rebate. Finally, the School has funding for roughly 70 quarters of teaching assistant and research assistant positions at one-quarter time with hopes of moderate increases in future years; nonresident students who receive these appointments have the additional advantage of paying in-state tuition (a saving of $1200 per quarter in 1986-87 when tuition fellowship are figured in). There are also other fellowships accessible only to SALA students. Roughly 60 percent of all graduate students receive assistantships and/or fellowships.

UNDERGRADUATE PROGRAM
Philosophy Statement

Education of the design generalist remains the primary thrust of undergraduate education at Minnesota, but the degree programs also encourage the choice of an area of concentration, and all students undertake a thesis of one quarter's duration as the capstone of their education. Encouragement of vitality and variety within the student body is evidenced by an admissions policy under which more than 30 percent of the entering design students already have degrees in areas other than architecture. Many from this group gain graduate student status later in their studies with considerable savings in total educational costs.

Program Description

Undergraduates who wish to pursue the four-year preprofessional degree may earn either the BA with a major in architecture through the College of Liberal Arts or the Bachelor of Environmental Design through the Institute of Technology. The professional degree, Bachelor of Architecture, requires five years of study. The first year in both the preprofessional and professional degree programs includes physics, calculus, and English composition. Drawing and an introductory architectural history sequence are also recommended. Those who successfully complete the prerequisite courses must survive a challenging admission competition before being allowed to start the two- or four-year sequences of architectural design courses for the

preprofessional or professional degrees. B Arch students take eleven quarters of design plus one quarter of thesis coupled with six quarters of history and theory, twelve courses in various areas of technology and practice, six to eight required classes in drawing and planning, and 35 or more elective credits. The BA involves 180 credits, the BED 192 and the B Arch 244.

GRADUATE PROGRAM
Philosophy Statement

Graduate architectural education in the two- to four-year M Arch program shares much of the design generalist orientation of the B Arch but with somewhat greater flexibility in certain course choices and greater encouragement for concentrations and research. Joint design studios in the final two years of study benefit both grad and undergrad students, with each grad student choosing a faculty mentor before starting the two-quarter M. Arch thesis. This approach is meant to help graduate students pursue a more personalized mix of scholarship, research and design as a basis for further education and/or leadership roles in practice and/or teaching.

Program Description

Three types of students are encouraged to seek the Master of Architecture degree at Minnesota: (1) those holding a B Arch; (2) those who have a preprofessional degree; and (3) those who have earned a baccalaureate but have had little or no experience with architectural studies or practice. Those in the first two categories may apply immediately to the Graduate School; those in the third category normally require one to two years as pre-grad architecture majors taking prerequisite courses before Graduate School application can be endorsed.

The two-year Master of Architecture follows a preprofessional degree or its equivalent period of study and involves 78 credits counting the thesis; the 78 credits normally include 30 in design (on top of 36 in two earlier years), 16 in thesis and 32 in a mix of required and elective courses from inside and outside the School of Architecture and Landscape Architecture. Students typically select an area of concentration, and some even seek a second master's degree in a related area such as business, American studies, journalism, etc. Roughly 20 percent of the graduate group of 50 are from other countries, providing opportunity for cross-cultural contact in seminars and design studios. A high level of professional skill is promoted by the combination of practitioner faculty members and the large percentage of students who have had two to five years of office experience. All students are counseled to select courses demanding significant levels of individual scholarship and inquiry. Students pursuing the four-quarter M Arch tailor programs to their particular needs in consultation with the Director of Graduate Studies and the faculty.

FACULTY
Administration

Harrison Fraker, AIA, RA, Professor and Head
A Kristine Johnson, Librarian

Professors

Roger D Clemence, ASLA, M Arch, MLA
Harrison Fraker, AIA, MFA
Roger Martin, FASLA, MLA

Associate Professors

Gunter Dittmar, M Arch
Mary Alice Dixon Hinson, M Phil
Lance LaVine, RA, M Arch, MCP
Julia W Robinson, AIA, B Arch, MA
Garth Rockcastle, AIA, M Arch
Leon Satkowski, PhD
Robert D Sykes, ASLA, MLA
Susan Ubbelohde, M Arch
J Stephen Weeks, AIA, B Arch

Assistant Professors

Lee B Anderson, M Arch
Joseph Burton, PhD Arch
Patrick Condon, ASLA, BSED, MLA
Cynthia Jara, RA, M Arch

Part-Time Faculty

John Cummings, MBA
Tom DeAngelo, AIA, M Arch
Foster Dunwiddie, AIA, B Arch, M Arch
David Graham, AIA, M Arch
Dennis Grebner, AIA, M Arch
Craig Johnson, MA
Edward Kodet, AIA, M Arch
James Lammers, AIA, MS Arch Tech
Kay Lockhart, RA, M Arch
Thomas Meyer, B Arch
Richard Morrill, RA, M Arch
Dale Mulfinger, AIA, B Arch
John Myers, M Arch
Oliver Ng, M Arch
Leonard Parker, FAIA, M Arch
John Rauma, FAIA, M Arch
Jeffrey Scherer, B Arch
Michael Shekner, MSCE
James Stageberg, FAIA, M Arch
Marshall Tanick, JD
Milo Thompson, FAIA, M Arch
Duane Thorbeck, FAIA, M Arch
Lee Tollefson, AIA, M Arch

Adjunct Faculty

Ladislav Cerny, PhD
William Moorish, MAUD
Joan Nassauer, MLA
Lance Neckar, MLA
David Pitt, PhD

Mississippi State University

School of Architecture
Mississippi State University
P. O. Drawer AQ
MS State, Mississippi 39762
(601) 325-2202

Application Deadline(s): Undgrd: March 1
Grad: April 1
Tuition & Fees: Undgrd: Miss res: $1788/yr
Non-res: $2970/yr
Grad: Miss res: $1788/yr
Non-res: $2970/yr
Endowment: Public

DEGREE PROGRAMS

Degree	Minimum Years for Degree	Accred.	Requirements for Admission	Full-Time Stdnts.	Part-Time Stdnts.	% of Applics. Accptd.	Stdnts. in 1st Year of Program	# of Degrees Conferred
B Arch	5	NAAB	High School Diploma, ACT or SAT scores	250	0	95%	100	33
BLA*	5	LAAB of ASLA						
M Arch	12 mos.		B Arch portfolio	8	0	75%	4	6
MS Small Town Studies	12 mos.		BS or BA portfolio	4	0	75%	1	2

*Offered by College of Agriculture

SCHOOL DEMOGRAPHICS (all degree programs)

Full-Time Faculty	Part-Time Faculty	Full-Time Students	Part-Time Students	Foreign Students	Out-of-State U.S. Stdnts.	Women Students	Minority Students
17	14	262	0	8%	50%	30%	6%

LIBRARY (Tel. No. 601-325-2204)

Type	No. of Volumes	No. of Slides
Arch	12,183	30,304

STUDENT OPPORTUNITIES AND RESOURCES

Mississippi's School of Architecture is relatively new, and intent on maintaining its newness. Established in 1973, the school takes its mission from the land-grant concept and accepts as its role the development of professional education, service, and research in architecture. Guided by an advisory council composed of architects throughout the state, the school has developed rapidly and has been encouraged by the profession, the public, and most important, its students.

Current enrollment in the school is held to 250 students to permit maximum interaction of students and faculty, yet allow for diversity of programs and personalities. As the school of architecture for the state of Mississippi, and an important force in the region, the school seeks to take advantage of the unique qualities of the state as a laboratory for architectural investigation. This includes its rural, small town, and urban environments. Mississippi State University is the largest of the comprehensive state universities and offers a genuine diversity of programs that interact within the architectural curriculum, including engineering, art, landscape architecture, and the humanities.

Because of its rural location, the school has developed an outstanding visiting lecturer and critic program, inviting leaders in the field to the campus, as well as a comprehensive program of travel to major urban centers that is basic to architectural education. Travel is reinforced through organized field trips during each of the five years, a summer European Study Program, and a Student and Faculty Exchange Program with Plymouth Polytechnic Institute in England.

SPECIAL ACTIVITIES AND PROGRAMS

Advisory Council, Mississippi Chapter AIA

Off-campus design center in Jackson, Mississippi

Architecture Tuesday (evening visiting lecture series)

Center for Small Town Research and Design

ASC/AIA Student Chapter

Beaux Arts Ball

Tau Sigma Delta, National Honor Society in Architecture and the Allied Arts

Dean's Council of Students

Summer Design Camp (one-week orientation for high school students)

Summer session studio for transfer students

Second degree three-year program for students with degrees in other fields

Student travel as part of the curriculum

History of Southern Architecture

Chautauqua in Mississippi, annual national symposium focusing on small town design

Student and faculty exchange program with Plymouth Polytechnic Institute

European travel program

Arts in the School of Architecture Series (Architecture, Music, Film, and Art)

Friday Forum Program sponsored by Tau Sigma Delta

FACILITIES

In 1977, the School of Architecture saved from imminent destruction and rehabilitated a 1930's cattle-judging pavilion. A lantern-like symbol at night, the award-winning renovation houses the undergraduate design studios and the Center for Small Town Research and Design. In 1982 the School completed an award-winning addition which houses graduate studios, faculty and administrative offices, the library and gallery, jury room, an auditorium which supports music and film as well as the architecture lecture series, computer laboratories, photographic studios, materials-testing facilities, and a metal and woodworking shop.

SCHOLARSHIPS/AID

Mississippi State University awards approximately $16 million in financial aid each year. The University awards $4,000 to $8,000 scholarships, along with waiver of out-of-state tuition, scholarships to students with ACT scores of 27 or higher. Approximately 40% of the class to enter architecture in the Fall of 1987 will have these scholarships, representing a sum of about $85,000. Within the School of Architecture, special design competitions and scholarships totaling $10,000 provide aid for architecture students. These include the Robert V.M. Harrison High School Design Competition Scholarship (1st year tuition), the Mississippi Chapter of AIA Scholarship ($1,000), the Mississippi Forest Association/Mississippi Lumber Manufacturers Association Competition ($1,500), the Mississippi Concrete Industries Association Competition ($750), the Delta Brick and Tile Co., Inc. Competition ($500), Mississippi/Louisiana Brick Manufacturers Scholarship ($2,000), the Pella Traveling Fellowship ($2,000), and the Alumni Scholarship ($250).

UNDERGRADUATE PROGRAM
Philosophy Statement

The school believes that architectural education can best be accomplished in an environment that stimulates the search for ideas by faculty and students. The size of the school and its small-town setting make possible a highly personal yet intense academic experience.

Travel, visiting critics and lecturers, foreign exchange programs, symposia, and diverse student activities provide richness within a highly ordered educational setting.

The aspirations which motivate all activities are those of excellence and maximum creative effort. Students who graduate possess the ability to confront all scales and types of modern architectural problems in diverse circumstances.

Program Description

The School of Architecture offers an intensive, five-year, course sequence leading to the professional Bachelor of Architecture degree. The program consists of a preprofessional year coupled with the professional program of three years on campus and then one year at its off-campus Jackson Center.

The first part of the program is highly structured, providing the core of experience for developing necessary basic skills, methods, attitudes, and understanding. The second part is somewhat more flexible, recognizing the individual student's abilities, interests, goals, and direction toward professional development. The school is committed to the concept that physical form is a responsibility of the architect and that the understanding of its development is the essence of the educational experience.

Students move to the Jackson Center in their fifth year for a program divided among specialized studies, research, and design at the urban scale. The student is in residence for a minimum of one year to provide a transition from the university to the professional world. Special opportunities for case-study evaluation, on-site studies, and public awareness are available at the Jackson Center.

Normally students enter the program as freshmen and are involved immediately in architecture studio. Required courses, with coordinated studio experiences each term, continue throughout the five-year undergraduate experience. Students with lower ACT scores will be expected to defer first-year design until the summer between their freshman and sophomore years. Transfers are not encouraged but are possible. Transfer students are accepted into a summer design studio in preparation for the professional architectural curriculum.

Students with bachelor's degrees in other fields are encouraged to apply for admission into a special accelerated-studies option. By attending three summers and three normal academic years, the student may qualify for the professional Bachelor of Architecture degree.

GRADUATE PROGRAM
Philosophy Statement

The American small town offers an exciting environment for study of town planning and design and interdisciplinary research. Its physical and social character are an arena for meaningful scholarship at the graduate level. Mississippi and the other states of the southern region possess an important heritage, one of interest to students concerned with the preservation and enhancement of the quality of life in the American small town.

Program Description

The Graduate Program in Town Planning Design is a unique, twelve-month, interdisciplinary course of study which emphasizes the small town. It is a response to the growing need for design expertise in the management and planning of small towns, neighborhoods, small cities and planned developments. Classes explore the history of urban settlement, the analysis of town form, town design methods, and planning and implementation strategies, and provide the opportunity for individual research. Students may also choose to associate with a faculty expert in the areas of computer-aided design, energy systems, housing, and architectural history.

The School of Architecture offers two non-professional graduate degrees: the Master of Science in Architecture for students having a previous professional degree in architecture and for specialized architectural studies, and the Master of Science in Small Town Studies for students having degrees from other disciplines. Each student's program of study is determined in consultation with the graduate adviser. In addition to necessary course work, a written comprehensive examination and a thesis is required. Stipends and research and teaching assistantships are available, and the Center for Small Town Research and Design offers internship grants.

FACULTY
Administration

John M McRae, AIA, Dean
Christos A Saccopoulos, AIA, Associate Dean
Thomas W Henderson, Architecture Librarian

Professors

Arnold J Aho, AIA, RA, BS, B Arch, M Arch
Robert C Craycroft, AIA, RA, B Arch, M Arch & Urban Design
Michael W Fazio, AIA, RA, B Arch, M Arch, PhD
Robert M Ford, AIA, RA, B Arch, M Arch
John M McRae, AIA, Professor

Associate Professors

Ian G. Banner, ARCUK, RIBA, BA, Dipl Arch
Thomas W Henderson
George W Parsons, AICP, BS, MS Landscape Arch
Kathleen Saccopoulos, BSc, MS
Gary A Shafer, AIA, RA, B Arch, M Arch
Rodner B Wright, AIA, RA, BS, M Arch

Assistant Professors

Sheri Daniel, BA
Bruce Grulke, M Arch
David Lewis, BS
Rachel McCann, BA, MS
Martin Schwartz, RA, BA, M Arch

Adjunct Faculty

Charles C Barlow, Jr, B Arch
Phillip D Hardwick, BS, MBA
Robert V M Harrison, FAIA, RA, B Arch, M Arch, MBA
Ryland Hemphill, BA
Michael Mitias, BA, MA, PhD
David W Mockbee, BA, JD
Samuel Mockbee, BA
Joanne S Pritchard, BA
Chris Risher, Jr, AIA, RA, B Arch, M Arch
Wayne F Timmer, AIA, RA, B Arch, M Arch & Urban Design, M Arch

Montana State University

School of Architecture
Montana State University
Bozeman, Montana 59717
(406) 994-4255

Office of Admissions
(406) 994-2452

Application Deadline(s): September 1
Tuition & Fees: Undgrd: MT Res: $1652/yr.
Non-Res: $3470/yr.
Endowment: Public

DEGREE PROGRAMS

Degree	Minimum Years for Degree	Accred.	Requirements for Admission	Full-Time Stdnts.	Part-Time Stdnts.	% of Applics. Accptd.	Stdnts. in 1st Year of Program	# of Degrees Conferred
B Arch	5	NAAB	HS Diploma for Mont. app., Upper ½ of class out-of-state	295		95%	121	45
BA Int Des	4		HS Diploma for Mont. app., Upper ½ of class out-of-state	30		95%	15	5

SCHOOL DEMOGRAPHICS (all degree programs)

Full-Time Faculty	Part-Time Faculty	Full-Time Students	Part-Time Students	Foreign Students	Out-of-State U.S. Stdnts.	Women Students	Minority Students
13	4	325		16%	16%	31%	2%

LIBRARY (Tel. No. 406-994-4091)

Type	No. of Volumes	No. of Slides
Arch	17,200	39,000

STUDENT OPPORTUNITIES AND RESOURCES

Montana State is a comprehensive multipurpose institution with over 10,000 students enrolled in seven colleges and schools. The size of the enrollment allows for closer student-faculty relations than are possible at many larger universities. Montana State's beautiful setting offers unlimited opportunities for combining academics and outdoor recreation, including hiking, fishing, and cross-country and downhill skiing. The 1,170-acre campus with more than forty major buildings is on the outskirts of Bozeman, a city of 29,000 near many outstanding scenic and recreational areas, such as Yellowstone and Grand Teton national parks, Jackson Hole and Bridger Bowl and Big Sky ski areas.

Architectural education began at Montana State in 1913 and the School of Architecture was formed in 1924. At present, there are more than 320 students enrolled in the programs. Approximately two-thirds of the students are from Montana and one-third come from other states and Canada. There is an active student organization that sponsors social events, films, lectures, trips and design competitions. Students are involved broadly in the affairs of the School and serve on committees that govern the

conduct of the School. The program in Interior Design is a recent addition to the School and it maintains a close working relationship with architecture.

The faculty, while diverse in educational backgrounds and viewpoints, remains enthusiastic about regional and environmental concerns as a basis for architectural design. Faculty members have won major design competitions or awards, written texts and articles, and conducted significant research and practice. All regard themselves as full-time educators. Some maintain part-time architectural practices and others are engaged in a variety of professional and public service activities.

SPECIAL ACTIVITIES AND PROGRAMS

An internship option is available to qualified students between the fourth and fifth years of the curriculum. A student may elect to spend one quarter and a summer as an intern in an architect's office in place of a quarter in school. This internship can be served anywhere in the United States or abroad.

A summer European field trip is conducted every other year if there is sufficient student interest. Accompanied by a faculty adviser, students visit, draw, and study historic buildings and sites, as well as investigate modern architecture and planning.

The school maintains a Community Design Center that is available to third-, fourth-, and fifth-year students. Projects focus on design solutions for actual regional problems. Students deal with real clients representing public, quasi-public, and philanthropic groups.

The Visiting Lecturer Series brings outstanding design professionals and academicians to lecture

to the student body on current theory and practice. Lecturers during the past two years have included such well-known architects and historians as Gunnar Birkerts, Arne Bystrom, William Jordy, William Turnbull, E. Fay Jones, Taft Architects, Peter Eisenman, J.B. Jackson, Paul Friedberg, Paul Rudolph, Reyner Banham, and David Gebhard, as well as lecturers from Japan, England and Austria.

The School's Exhibit Hall has continuous shows of student, faculty, and professional work as well as selected traveling exhibits.

Each year the School publishes a periodical containing articles by faculty and well-known architects and educators and current student work. A faculty member and a student committee are responsible for selecting and editing projects and articles for this journal.

In conjunction with the State AIA, the School holds an annual Honor Awards Banquet where all of the graduating seniors are recognized, and scholarships and student recognition are awarded to the student body.

During Spring, Summer and Autumn Quarters the Field School on Early American Building is conducted on an eleven-acre mountain site twelve miles from Bozeman. Students in the program reconstruct early examples of American architecture using authentic tools and construction techniques and effectively translate history into practice.

FACILITIES

The School of Architecture is located in a complex of buildings that includes the School of Art and the Department of Music and Film & TV. The Architecture Building contains the art and architecture library, a photographic slide room, a blueprint room, a photographic darkroom and a model-making shop in addition to design studios, exhibition and jury rooms, lecture classrooms, seminar rooms and faculty offices. A computer graphics laboratory with 10 complete micro-computer stations and plotters is also contained in the building.

SCHOLARSHIPS/AID

An average of twenty scholarships each year are awarded on the basis of scholastic excellence to students continuing in the architecture program. These scholarships range from $100 to $750 and total approximately $7,500. High School seniors intending to enroll at MSU are eligible to apply for one of the twenty available $1,250 University Presidential Scholarships. Application deadline for these scholarships is in January. Students attending High School Week also are eligible on a competitive basis for scholarships ranging up to $1,000. Financial aid and loan programs are available to qualified students through the University Financial Aid Office.

UNDERGRADUATE PROGRAM
Philosophy Statement

The architectural program at MSU is a design-oriented, professional, and regionally based curriculum that regards architecture as the art and science of building, an endeavor that must provide appropriate accommodations for human activities. Architecture has its roots in the geology, topography, vegetative cover, climate, and culture of the region, and each problem and regional site must be regarded as unique.

The faculty is made up of individuals who come from a variety of backgrounds and philosophical viewpoints and enjoy teaching and a close informal relationship with undergraduate students. The School intends that graduates have confidence in their skills and abilities and have a fundamental understanding and working knowledge of all of the basic concerns influencing architecture.

Program Description

The five-year program leading to the Bachelor of Architecture degree takes a balanced approach to architectural education and provides instruction in theory, technical understanding, professional knowledge and basic skills. The educational intent of the program can be described by the three generalized areas that make up the curriculum. These areas are design, the professional core and the general education core.

The School views architectural design as central to the process and thinking that separates the practice of architecture from other professions. A high level of design studio education is considered essential for all students and the design studio experience is a major vehicle for integrating all of the elements of an architectural education. The student takes a design studio each quarter and each year of the sequence has a set of objectives, an emphasis, a scale and complexity, and a range of projects. The sequence begins with basic two- and three-dimensional design and then takes the

student through a series of architectural design projects that range from small individual buildings to large-scale multibuilding complexes in urban locations. The last two quarters of design are spent on a thesis project of the student's own choosing.

In addition to the design sequence, students take a professional set of courses made up of architectural history and preservation; structural analysis and design; architectural theory; computer applications; architectural graphics; heating, ventilating and air conditioning; climate and energy; acoustics; illumination and electrical systems; construction materials and practices; professional practice and documents; planning theory and practice. Electives in architectural history, structures, delineation, and energy systems provide additional courses for those students who wish to study a particular area in greater depth.

Also required is a general education core curriculum. Viewed as fundamental to a university education, this part of the curriculum ensures that each student is exposed to the study of human civilization and the natural world. This reflects the belief that a university education should not only develop an area of specialization, such as architecture, but also significantly broaden each student's understanding of cultural and natural phenomena. The requirement is divided into the following areas:

1) communications - college level competence in the areas of writing and speaking; 2) mathematics - concepts and modern techniques of mathematical thought and critical reasoning; 3) fine arts and humanities - exploration of the visual and performing arts, literature, language, philosophy, history and religious study; 4) natural sciences - an understanding of the methods of scientific inquiry and the fundamental principles and knowledge accepted in the physical and life sciences; 5) social science - exploration of basic social disciplines such as anthropology, economics, geography, political science, psychology and sociology; 6) technology - manipulation of our physical environment and our response to its constraints. Each student selects one to four courses in each of these six

groupings from a wide variety of university offerings.

Within these curricular groupings, Montana State University is dedicated to providing a well-rounded professional education for students preparing to enter the practice of architecture.

FACULTY
Administration

Robert C Utzinger, AIA, Acting Dean
Jerry A Bancroft, Acting Director

Professors

Ronald Hess, AIA, B Arch, M Arch
George S McClure, PE, BS, MS, PhD
Robert C Utzinger, AIA, PE, BS, BS Arch, M Arch

Associate Professors

Jerry A Bancroft, RA, B Arch, MS Arch
Dale A Brentrup, RA, B Arch, M Arch
Paul Gleye, BA, MA, PhD
Peter C Kommers, AIA, B Arch, M Arch
Clark E Llewellyn, RA, B Arch, M Arch

Assistant Professors

Pamela J Bancroft, RA, B Arch, M Arch
Ralph Johnson, AIA, B Arch, MS Arch
Henry E Sorenson, Jr, B Arch, M Arch

Part-Time Faculty

Linda Brock, AIA, BA, M Arch
Jonathan Foote, AIA, B Arch, M Arch
Donald J McLaughlin, AIA, B Arch

Adjunct Faculty

Scott D Chartier, B Arch, MBA, M Arch
Jacob Meyer
William Miller, BS
Michael Shepherd, BDA, M Arch

Université de Montréal

Ecole d'Architecture
Faculté de l'Aménagement
Université de Montréal
C.P. 6128, Succ. "A"
Montréal, Québec, Canada H3C 3J7
(514) 343-6007

Application Deadline(s): Undgrd: March 1
Grad: February 1
Tuition & Fees: Undgrd: Canadian Students:
$700/year
Foreign students: $6000/year
Grad: Approximately the same
as for undgrd.
Endowment: Public

DEGREE PROGRAMS

Degree	Minimum Years for Degree	Accred.	Requirements for Admission	Full-Time Stdnts.	Part-Time Stdnts.	% of Applics. Accptd.	Stdnts. in 1st Year of Program	# of Degrees Conferred
B Arch	4	British Commonwealth Accred. Board	Diplôme collégial d'enseignement général et professionnel*	264	18	10%	80	61

*All courses and lectures are given in French. Students whose native language is not French may be required to pass a French language proficiency test.

SCHOOL DEMOGRAPHICS (all degree programs)

Full-Time Faculty	Part-Time Faculty	Full-Time Students	Part-Time Students	Foreign Students	Out-of-State U.S. Stdnts.	Women Students	Minority Students
21	14	264	18	5%	—	45%	—

LIBRARY (Tel. No. 514-343-6009)

Type	No. of Volumes	No. of Slides
Arch, Indus, Des, LA, UP	46,464	

STUDENT OPPORTUNITIES AND RESOURCES

The school of Architecture is part of the Faculté de l'aménagement (Faculty of Environmental Design). The other departments of the faculty are:
- the school of landscape architecture;
- the school of industrial design; and
- the town planning institute.

Students in the school of architecture are offered the possibility of an extensive choice of optional and elective courses in the different departments of the faculty.

Through the Quebec interuniversity collaboration agreement, students have the opportunity to take elective courses in other Quebec universities.

In Montreal there are three other universities:
- Concordia
- McGill
- l'Université du Québec à Montréal.

SPECIAL ACTIVITIES AND PROGRAMS

ACADEMIC

As a department of Faculté de l'aménagement, the school works closely with departments of urban planning, landscape architecture, and industrial design at the bachelor's degree level.

Concentrated summer course on renovation, recycling and restoration in collaboration with the Heritage Montreal Corporation.

Hydro-Aménagement lecture series with recognised lecturers from Canada, USA and abroad.

STUDENT

Undergraduate students association in architecture.

Various academic, social, and sport activities.

FACILITIES

FACULTE DE L'AMENAGEMENT LIBRARY

More than 60,000 books and a wide selection of periodicals in the field of architecture, landscape architecture, industrial design, and town planning.

PHOTOGRAPHY LAB

A specialized full-time photography technician is available to help students in their projects.

SCHOLARSHIPS/AID

The ALCAN-ARCOP Prize offered to a final year student.

The Cardinal-Hardy Traveling Scholarship in Housing awarded to a final-year student.

The FRANCOU Traveling Scholarship for studies in France awarded to a final-year student.

UNDERGRADUATE PROGRAM
Philosophy Statement

L'Ecole d'architecture offre un programme d'études de premier cycle conduisant au baccalauréat professionnel et donnant accès à l'ordre des architectes du Québec.

L'Ecole vise la formation de professionnels capables d'assumer les tâches traditionnelles d'analyse, de conception et de réalisation des édifices, en accord avec les besoins et les ressources des individus et des groupes.

L'Ecole vise également la formation de professionnels susceptibles d'accéder aux nouvelles pratiques rendues nécessaires par le ralentissement de la croissance démographique et économique, par les crises écologique et énergétique et par l'aspiration de la société à une meilleure qualification culturelle de l'environnement physique.

Program Description

L'Ecole propose dans son programme de baccalauréat un ensemble de cours théoriques, méthodologiques, techniques, économiques et sociologiques impliqués dans le processus de design. Elle propose également, dans le cadre de ses unités, des activités pédagogiques destinées à développer la capacité de synthèse de ces connaissances par un éventail de travaux reflétant des tâches qui attendent le futur professionnel. Enfin, l'Ecole vise à offrir des programmes diversifiés permettant aux architectes de s'insérer ultérieurement dans les différents niveaux et secteurs d'activité où émergent les nouvelles formes de pratique de l'architecture.

Le programme du baccalauréat en architecture comporte deux secteurs d'enseignement:

1) La formation de base

Elle vise à développer la réflexion, l'intuition, les capacités d'évaluation, les outils et le processus de design ainsi que la connaissance des différents contextes d'intervention.

Elle comprend obligatoirement:
- Une initiation au milieu de l'aménagement et les projets de sensibilisation et de synthèse de la première année;
- cinq trimestres d'atelier dans au moins trois unités distinctes;
- seize crédits (c'est-à-dire de six à huit cours) dans chacun des trois champs d'étude de l'Ecole, à savoir: sciences humaines appliquées à l'architecture, technologie et sciences du bâtiment, méthodologie et communication.

Cette formation de base comporte déjà une certaine diversification puisqu'elle permet des choix en ce qui concerne tant les unités que les cours.

2) Approfondissement

Il est assuré pare les cours à option et les cours au choix. Les premiers permettent d'approfondir les connaissances de base dans chacun des trois champs d'étude; ils sont, ou régulièrement inscrits à l'horaire (cours à option proprement dits), ou offerts uniquement en fonction de besoins spécifiques et d'une clientèle suffisante (cours sur demande).

L'étudiant peut également acquérir jusqu'à douze crédits de cours au choix dans l'ensemble des cours universitaires. Ce choix est toutefois sujet à l'approbation de la direction de l'Ecole.

Le programme d'architecture est reconnu par l'Association des Architectes du Commonwealth.

GRADUATE PROGRAM
Philosophy Statement

Les études de 2e et 3e cycles (master and PhD programs) sont données par la Faculté de l'aménagement avec la participation des quatre départements. Ces programmes d'études sont offerts aux étudiants détenant un baccalauréat de l'un des quatre départements de la Faculté et de la pluparet des autres départements de l'Université ou l'équivalent.

Program Description

1) *Maîtrise*

Deux programmes de MScA (maîtrise en sciences appliquées en aménagement) sont offerts:

MScA option "aménagement"
Un minimum de 18 crédits de cours de 2e cycle et 30 crédits attribués à la recherche et à la rédaction d'un mémoire.

MScA option "Restauration, rénovation, recyclage"
Un minimum de 36 crédits de cours dont au moins 27 de 2e cycle et 12 crédits de travaux dirigés.

NOTE: Si la préparation d'un étudiant n'est pas jugée suffisante pour les études qu'il veut entreprendre, le doyen peut exiger de lui des cours de préparation dont le total ne peut dépasser 24 crédits.

2) *PhD*

Un programme de doctorat (PhD) est aussi offert dans les divers domaines de l'aménagement.

FACULTY
Administration

Jean-Claude Marsan, Doyen, Faculte de l'amenagement
Louis C Pretty, OAQ, FIRAC, Directeur
Vesna Blazina, Librarian

Professeur Titulaire

Janos Baracs, Ing Dipl
Melvin Charney, B Arch, M Arch
Jean Cousin, Arch Dipl
Colin H Davidson, M Arch
Jean-Jacques Lipp, Ing Dipl
Jean-Claude Marsan, MSc, PhD
Claude Parisel, B Arch, M Arch
Harry Parnass, M Arch (UD)
Jean-Luc Poulin, Arch Dipl
Pierre Teasdale, B Arch, MSCA
Ricardo Verges, Arch DPLG, Dipl CH
Leonard Warshaw, B Arch

Professeur Agrégé

Jules Auger, B Arch
P Richard Bisson, B Arch, M Urb, D IEP, DEA
Jacques Derome, B Arch, MScEd
Alan John Knight, AA, D Arch
Denys Marchand, BA, DFAM
Pierre Morisset, B Arch
Jean Ouellet, DEAM
Romedi Passini, ETH, PhD
Louis C Pretty, B Arch

Part-Time Faculty

Jean-Claude Boisvert, B Arch
Yvon Boyer, B Arch
Mario Brodeur, B Arch
Dinu Bumbaru, B Arch
Sophie Charlebois, B Arch
Renée Daoust, B Arch, M Urb
Christian DeConinck, B Arch
François Deslauriers, Ing Dipl
P Ladia Falta, B Arch, M Arch
Julia Gersovitz, B Arch, M Arch
Yolaine Gourd, BA
Jacques Lachapelle, B Arch, MScA
Iréna Latek, M Arch
Maryse Leduc, B Arch
Claude Lemieux, B Arch
Louis Martin, B Arch
Serge Mélanson, B Arch
Alena Prochazka, B Arch, M Arch
Roger Richard, M Arch
Léa Zeppetelli, B Arch

Morgan State University

Program In Architecture
Morgan State University
Hillen Road and Cold Spring Lane
Baltimore, Maryland 21239
(301) 444-3225

Graduate Admissions
School of Graduate Studies
Morgan State University
Baltimore, Maryland 21239
(301) 444-3185

Application Deadline(s): Fall: May 1st
Spring: October 1st
Tuition & Fees: Undgrd: Md res: $769/sem
Non-Res: $1531/sem
Grad: Per Credit: Md res:
$55/sem; Non-Res: $65/sem
Fees: $58
Endowment: State

DEGREE PROGRAMS

Degree	Minimum Years for Degree	Accred.	Requirements for Admission	Full-Time Stdnts.	Part-Time Stdnts.	% of Applics. Accptd.	Stdnts. in 1st Year of Program	# of Degrees Conferred
M Arch (First professional)	3	Cand	90 hrs	35	3	60%	12	5
M Arch (Academic)	1		30 hrs	3	1	50%	—	1

SCHOOL DEMOGRAPHICS (all degree programs)

Full-Time Faculty	Part-Time Faculty	Full-Time Students	Part-Time Students	Foreign Students	Out-of-State U.S. Stdnts.	Women Students	Minority Students
3	3	38	4	70%	4%	12%	10%

LIBRARY (Tel. No. 301-444-3450)

Type	No. of Volumes	No. of Slides
University	287,936 (total)	2,000 (total)

STUDENT OPPORTUNITIES AND RESOURCES

The Program in Architecture is housed in the Jenkins Building along with the Departments of Social Work, Urban Studies, Transportation and Education. Design studios and classes in general are small, ranging from 5 to 12 students. Each student is assured an unusual amount of faculty supervision. Located in the City of Baltimore, and 35 miles from Washington, D.C., students have immediate access to the many architectural treasures of the region on an individual basis and by means of class-related field trips.

Faculty members are actively engaged in the practice of architecture and engineering in and around the Baltimore region. When appropriate, students are involved with the faculty in executing projects in their professional offices.

SPECIAL ACTIVITIES AND PROGRAMS

Freshman Year — Field Trip
Sophomore Year — Field Trip
Architectural Lecture Series
Community Design Task

FACILITIES

Architectural Design Studios
Jury Room

Exhibit Walls
Reference/Study Room
Computer Center
Graphics Studio
Technical Laboratory
Faculty Offices
Reproduction Center
Department Office

SCHOLARSHIPS/AID

The University provides scholarships for all departments based on merit and need. Students are eligible to apply for Pell Grants, National Direct Student Loans, and the Work Study program. Applications are available from the Office of Financial Aid. Deadline for applications is February 15.

GRADUATE PROGRAM
Philosophy Statement

The program is devoted to developing multidisciplinary thinkers capable of understanding and interrelating the processes, activities and values which influence built form, land use decisions, and the quality of environmental design.

Program Description

Two degree programs are offered. The Master of Architecture (First Professional Degree), and the Master of Architecture (Academic Degree). The First Professional Degree Program is open to students with no prior architectural education who possess a Bachelor's degree from an accredited institution. The Academic Degree program is open to holders of the Bachelor of Architecture degree.

Course work in the First Professional Degree program includes: Architectural Design, Building Technology, History and Theory, Practice, Management, Graphic Communication and selected electives.

The Academic Degree program is designed to allow flexibility for professionally mature students interested in pursuing advanced work of their own selection. Two design studios and six elective courses constitute the requirements.

FACULTY
Administration

Andrew Stevenson, PhD, Dean
Anthony N Johns, Jr, AIA, Chair

Professors

Anthony Johns, Jr, BS, B Arch, M Arch

Associate Professors

Mahendra Parekh, B Arch, MCRP

Assistant Professors

Gilbert Cooke, AIA, B Arch, M Arch

Part-Time Faculty

Leon Bridges, FAIA, B Arch
Ramesh Desai, BE, ME
Bernard Madison, B Arch

Adjunct Faculty

Suzanne Garriques, BA, MA, PhD

University of Nebraska-Lincoln

College of Architecture
University of Nebraska-Lincoln
210 Arch Hall
Lincoln, Nebraska 68588-0106
(402) 472-3592

Undergraduate Admissions
University of Nebraska-Lincoln
Administration 12
Lincoln, Nebraska 68588-0415
(402) 472-3620

Application Deadline(s): Undgrds - August 15
& January 1
Grads - March 15
Tuition & Fees: Undgrds: NE Res: $43/cr. hr.
Non-res: $119/cr. hr.
Grad: NE Res: $60/cr. hr.
Non-res: $142/cr. hr.
Fees: 1-3 cr. hr.=$37.16;
4-6=$82.36; 7+more=$100.36
Endowment: Public

DEGREE PROGRAMS

Degree	Minimum Years for Degree	Accred.	Requirements for Admission	Full-Time Stdnts.	Part-Time Stdnts.	% of Applics. Accptd.	Stdnts. in 1st Year of Program	# of Degrees Conferred
BSAS	4		ACT-21 upper ½ of class SAT-970 —2.6 GTA (Transfer)	357	32	48%	145	59
M Arch	2	NAAB	3.0 GPA	54	3	60%	33	18
MCRP	2	AICP	2.75 GPA	18	12	75%	12	12

SCHOOL DEMOGRAPHICS (all degree programs)

Full-Time Faculty	Part-Time Faculty	Full-Time Students	Part-Time Students	Foreign Students	Out-of-State U.S. Stdnts.	Women Students	Minority Students
22	14	447	47	25%	25%	20%	3%

LIBRARY (Tel. No. 402-472-1208)

Type	No. of Volumes	No. of Slides
College	32,500	43,000

STUDENT OPPORTUNITIES AND RESOURCES

A student body numbering approximately 450 and composed not only of Nebraska residents but also of students from Mexico, Germany, Africa, the Middle East, and Asia provides a stimulating cultural mix. At least four of the larger architectural firms in the United States are located in nearby Omaha, Nebraska. These firms design work worldwide and take an active interest in the school and the employment of its graduating students. The city of Lincoln, as well as the university, provides numerous cultural activities that bring outstanding performers, artists, and personalities of national and international repute to the area. Numerous additional benefits accrue to the students and citizens of the area from Lincoln's function as the capital city of Nebraska.

Within the College of Architecture two departments function on an interactive basis. The Department of Community and Regional Planning, and the Department of Architecture provide opportunities for students to become involved in a wide range of projects outside the normal classroom setting.

Course work in the Architecture Department includes classes coordinated with the engineering, art, agriculture, geography, and psychology departments and colleges. This provides numerous interdisciplinary contacts during a student's course of study.

The Hyde Chair of Excellence allows the College to attract visiting faculty of national and international distinction. Through this endowment, renowned scholars and practitioners are invited to spend a semester or more in residence at the College, teaching and working with architecture and planning students in lectures, seminars, studios, and in an informal mentor role.

Faculty interests and specializations range from Asian architecture, energy-conscious design, and historic preservation to environment and behavior. Practicing architects serve on the adjunct faculty, and this helps to maintain a strong tie between the department and the professional community.

SPECIAL ACTIVITIES AND PROGRAMS

Ampersand student newsletter (biweekly)

Dimensions Magazine, published quarterly, jointly with Nebraska Society of Architects

The Nebraska Community Improvement Program (cosponsored annually by College of Architecture and State Department of Economic Development)

Specially funded projects

Summer make-up and special courses

Job placement assistance

Professional internship program for advanced architecture and planning students

Professional Continuing Education in cooperation with Nebraska Society of Architects

Foreign studies program in London, England; Dublin, Ireland; Guadalajara, Mexico and Xian, China

Participating organization in the Center for Great Plains Studies, UNL

Annual visits by prominent lecturers and studio critics (Hyde Lecture Series)

Student Advisory Board

Professional Student Organizations

Tau Sigma Delta Honorary Society

Field Trips

Charettes

Summer High School Workshop

FACILITIES

The College of Architecture provides the most remarkable educational facilities offered anywhere in the Midwest. A recent $4.35 million renovation of the college facilities offers a new Computer Lab, Materials Shop, and Media Center Complex, which includes equipment rooms, photography studio, and darkroom. The college also houses a 35,000 volume Architecture Library, a slide library with over 10,000 slides, a materials library, graduate student offices, student organization offices, student lounge facilities, and the most unique design studios found anywhere in the United States.

SCHOLARSHIPS/AID

The College of Architecture has a number of scholarships and fellowships available for graduate and undergraduate students in Architecture. The College of Architecture has established a Student Loan Fund of $400 to help students in emergencies. Interest-free loans are available to students on a short-term basis.

The University Office of Scholarships and Financial Aid offers support with National Merit Scholarships, Regents Scholarships, Pell Grants, National Direct Student Loans, College Work-Study Programs, and Guaranteed Student Loans.

UNDERGRADUATE PROGRAM
Philosophy Statement

It is the goal of the department to provide the maximum opportunity for undergraduates to develop their interest and fundamental education in the design professions. This foundation should enable the undergraduate to select a specific design discipline to pursue as a profession. Students are expected to become visually literate and skilled in solving problems by the time they complete their undergraduate work. Such skills will then be applicable in the professional architecture degree program as well as in alternative design fields that a student may choose to pursue.

Program Description

The undergraduate degree program is a four-year course of study consisting of two years of pre-architecture study and two years of preprofessional study.

Every attempt is made through a strong student advisory program to keep the student's options for career alternatives open throughout the BSAS program. Students often will study two, three, or even four years of the BSAS program and learn that their interests and talents may lead more to environmental design disciplines than to architecture—planning, urban design, landscape architecture, interior design, product design, graphic arts, etc. The BSAS program is considered excellent preparation for those fields, and students have found most credits to be transferable.

The emphasis of the BSAS curriculum is on the development of problem-solving abilities. The context is "designs for mankind" and the concentration is on the development of the essential graphic, analytical, and intellectual skills necessary to solve and communicate design; both the curriculum and the experiential studies serve to sensitize students to environmental and humanitarian concerns.

The first two years of the program, the pre-architecture phase, may be taken in the College of Architecture or in equivalent studies at another university, community college, or four-year college. The objective of the pre-architecture program is to develop a diversified and mature student with good basic design and graphics skills. Following successful completion of the pre-architecture phase, qualified students may apply to the Department of Architecture for admission to the two-year preprofessional program. The preprofessional curriculum is organized to provide both a solid foundation for the subsequent specialized study of architecture and a sound general education in the humanities.

Students may, with adequate advanced language preparation, complete the fall semester of their fourth year in Guadalajara, Mexico, in an exchange program with the Universidad Autonoma de Guadalajara.

GRADUATE PROGRAM
Philosophy Statement

The graduate programs are oriented toward developing basic architectural skills to a high level of competence. It is the program's goal to develop the leadership qualities of its graduate students so they may direct the course of the profession to meet the needs of the future as well as the present.

Program Description

The third twp-year segment of the six-year professional curriculum, leading to the Master of Architecture degree, is highly professional and specialized. The curriculum is essentially directed toward the study of building design and encompasses advanced architectural design studies, structural and environmental control design, professional practice methods and principles, elective courses, and research. An organized professional internship program, providing academic credit for professional field experience, is available to the students during these two years.

Students may choose, for one required semester of urban-context studies, to study with the faculty conducting the London Studies Program during each spring semester.

A traditional one-year graduate program is also available for individuals who have completed a five-year professional degree program; completion of this program also qualifies the individual for the M Arch degree.

A two-year degree program in community and regional planning leads to the Master of Community and Regional Planning degree. Candidates for the MCRP are admitted from any baccalaureate degree program.

FACULTY
Administration

W Cecil Steward, FAIA, RA, Dean
Joseph Luther, Assistant Dean
James Potter, RA, Architecture Department Chair
Gordon Scholz, Comm. & Regional Planning Department Chair
Robert Duncan, Architecture Department Vice Chair
William Borner, RA, Architecture Department Graduate Chair
Kay Logan-Peters, Librarian

Professors

William Borner, RA, B Arch, M Arch
Dale Gibbs, FAIA, RA, B Arch, M Arch
Robert Guenter, RA, BS, M Arch
Tom Laging, RA, B Arch, M Arch
Ernest Moore, RA, BS, D Arch
Homer Puderbaugh, RA, B Arch, MS
Keith Sawyers, B Arch, M Arch
W Cecil Steward, RA, FAIA, B Arch, MS

Associate Professors

Robert Duncan, B Arch, M Arch
Ted Ertl, RA, B Arch, M Arch
Alexander Maller, BS, M Arch
James Potter, RA, BS, M Arch, PhD
Ted Wright, B Arch, M Arch, PhD

Assistant Professor

Sharon Kuska, EIT, BS, MS

Part-Time Faculty

Scott D Beman, RA, B Arch, M Arch
Phil Corkill, RA, PE, BS, MS
Bruce C D Helwig, B Arch
King K Little, PE, BSCS, BSCE, MSCE
Honora H Pritchard, BS, M Arch
Michael S Roach, BSAS, M Arch
Dennis Scheer, B Arch, M Arch
Robert A Schoenleber, BSAS, M Arch
Lee Schriever, RA, B Arch
Richard K Sutton, BS, MLA

Adjunct Faculty

Richard Austin, RLA, BS, MS
M Marie Fischer, BS, MA
John K Hulvershorn, RPRA, BS, MS, PhD
Joseph Luther, BA, MUP, PhD
James McGraw, BA, MA, MRP
N Brito Mutunayagam, BS, MS, DEDP
Gordon Scholz, RA, AICP, B Arch, MUP, M Arch, MBA
Kim Todd, RLA, BS

University of Nevada, Las Vegas

Architecture and Allied Studies
University of Nevada, Las Vegas
4505 South Maryland Parkway
Las Vegas, Nevada 89154
(702) 739-3031
(702) 739-0960

Office of Admissions
(702) 739-3443 (Admissions)
(702) 739-3031 (Architecture
Studies)

Application Deadline(s): Rolling basis.
Tuition & Fees: Undgrd: NV Res: $36/cred hr
Non-res: $36/cred hr +
$1,100/sem
Grad: NV Res: $41/cred hr
Non-res: $41/cred hr +
$1100/sem
Endowment: State

DEGREE PROGRAMS

Degree	Minimum Years for Degree	Accred.	Requirements for Admission	Full-Time Stdnts.	Part-Time Stdnts.	% of Applics. Accptd.	Stdnts. in 1st Year of Program	# of Degrees Conferred
BS Arch Architectural Design	4		Univ Adm	60	20	*	40	(6) '88
Construction Administration	4		Univ Adm	15	0	*	15	(10) '91
Interior Arch/ Design	4		Univ Adm	15	5	*	15	(10) '91
Landscape Arch	4		Univ Adm	10	5	*	10	(6) '91
Urban Planning/ Design	4		Univ Adm	8	3	*	8	(5) '91
M Arch	1½	initiate (1989–90)	Arch Selective Adm	(estimated) 45	—	—	15	(15) '91
M Const Admin	1½	initiate (1990–91)	Arch Selective Adm	(estimated) 45	—	—	15	(15) '92
M Int Arch	1½	initiate (1991–92)	Arch Selective Adm	(estimated) 45	—	—	15	(15) '92
M Landsc Arch	1½	initiate (1991–92)	Arch Selective Adm	(estimated) 30	—	—	10	(10) '93
M Urban Plan	1½	initiate (1992–93)	Arch Selective Adm	(estimated) 24	—	—	8	(8) '93

* 100% for the first 2 years; selective admission to upper division courses.

SCHOOL DEMOGRAPHICS (all degree programs)

Full-Time Faculty	Part-Time Faculty	Full-Time Students	Part-Time Students	Foreign Students	Out-of-State U.S. Stdnts.	Women Students	Minority Students
4	14	60	20	10%	20%	20%	10%

LIBRARY (Tel. No. 702-739-3280)

Type	No. of Volumes	No. of Slides
Central	2,500	80,000 Arch
Professional	1,500	20,000 Arch

STUDENT OPPORTUNITIES AND RESOURCES

Las Vegas is an exceptionally exciting environment for the study of Architecture, Construction, Design and Planning. A boom town city of contrasts, it is known internationally as an entertainment capital of the world. Despite the common perception of Las Vegas as a resort city, it is one of the nation's most rapidly developing communities of approximately 650,000 residents. As a cosmopolitan metropolis in the tradition of the West, Las Vegas is a brand new city with the imagery of a neon desert, which carries career advantages for prospective architects, constructors, designers and planners.

Surrounding La Vegas is one of the most picturesque areas of the entire southwest, offering students unlimited outdoor recreation year round. Within a 50-mile radius lie the shores of Lake Mead, the colorful Red Rock Canyon, the massive Hoover Dam, and the Colorado River Recreation Area; the Valley of Fire; skiing at 12,000-ft. Mt. Charleston—1 hour drive from the campus; and a panorama of eroded sandstone landscapes and forgotten ghost towns. Nearby also is the historical Death Valley Monument. In addition, the city is only four to five hours by car from Southern California's beaches, theaters and amusement parks, and Southern Utah's ski slopes and national parks such as Zion, Bryce, Cedar Breaks and the Grand Canyon. Such a locale presents an exciting place for architectural studies.

The University of Nevada, Las Vegas, is a young, growing and proud institution. Founded in 1957, UNLV today offers 50 undergraduate and 30 graduate degree programs to a student population of 14,000 which is growing at the rate of more than 1,000 new students each year. The University's 335-acre campus is located in metropolitan Las Vegas.

Architecture and allied studies, the newest professional program at UNLV, is the only program for the State of Nevada. Like the University, it is growing rapidly as degree programs are being put in place to keep pace with its students. The student body of 80 in 1988 is expected to reach three times that figure within the next five years and offers the advantage of individualized instruction from both practicing professionals and academic faculty. Internships and work opportunities are especially good with many students being able to gain considerable professional experience while attending classes. Students who seek a dynamic, challenging environment in an exciting, unique locale will find ample career opportunities in architecture, construction administration, interior architecture and design, landscape architecture and urban planning.

SPECIAL ACTIVITIES AND PROGRAMS

There are a number of activities of interest to students such as: student professional associations, clinical internships, international study, field study programs, design competitions, special lectures and exhibitions.

Student professional associations assist students with the transition into professional life and acquaint them with the profession relating to their program of study. These include:

- American Institute of Architecture Students
- Student Association of Interior Designers
- Associated General Contractors, Student Chapter
- Associated Builders and Constructors, Student Chapter
- National Association of Home Builders, Student Chapter
- American Society of Landscape Architects, Student Chapter
- American Planning Association, Student Chapter

All students admitted to upper division and graduate professional study will be required to complete one internship program during a summer prior to graduation. A second internship or international study is also required. Normally, these are taken between the third and fourth year and between the fourth and fifth year.

International summer study is currently offered through the school of Fine Arts at Fountainebleau, France. As the program develops, additional options in Europe, Asia, Mexico and Canada will be implemented.

FACILITIES

Facilities include design studios, lecture and seminar rooms, and technical laboratories, as well as offices for the faculty and administration. A professional periodical and reference library, slide collection and computer drafting laboratory are available for faculty and students. Expansion of current facilities, now dispersed at various locations on the UNLV campus, will continue until a new central facility is completed.

SCHOLARSHIPS/AID

A wide variety of financial aid and loan programs are available to students with demonstrated need or exceptional promise without regard to race, creed, color, national origin or sex. For further details, prospective students should contact the University Financial Aid Office.

UNDERGRADUATE PROGRAM
Philosophy Statement

The central function of the undergraduate program is to prepare students for entry into professional levels of instruction for careers in: Architecture, Construction Administration, Interior Architecture and Design, Landscape Architecture, and Urban Planning and Design.

After completion of two years of basic Liberal Arts, Science studies, and skill development for Design, students may apply for admission to upper division undergraduate coursework or to the early admissions program leading to the Professional Masters Degree. Since Architecture and allied studies are new programs at UNLV, graduate professional study is not expected to

be initiated before the 1989–90 academic year when the first graduates of the undergraduate program will have completed the B.S. Degree. N.A.A.B. accreditation will be sought for students completing the professional degree at the graduate level. The undergraduate program fully prepares students for entry into graduate or professional study at other institutions as well as the graduate program at UNLV.

Program Description

Students seeking the Bachelor of Science in Architecture Degree must satisfactorily complete a curriculum of a minimum of 131-138 credits depending upon the concentration selected. Coursework concentrations are offered relating to the following disciplines: Architectural Design, Construction Administration, Interior Architecture and Design, Landscape Architecture, and Urban Planning and Design.

New and transfer students who have been admitted to the University and select Architecture as a major are admitted to the lower-division program. A separate application/admission procedure is required for entry to upper division concentrations and graduate programs. Acceptance into the lower division program does not guarantee acceptance to upper-division programs. While UNLV accepts credits transferred from other institutions, transfer credits are not applied to specific degree programs until reviewed and accepted by appropriate academic units. Transfer coursework must be equivalent in both content and level of offering. Additionally, a review of samples of design projects completed from previous studio classes is required.

Admissions to upper-division programs is competitive. Transfer applications into upper-division programs are considered only if vacancies occur. Admission is limited to students with equivalent coursework who are competitive with continuing UNLV students.

GRADUATE PROGRAM
Philosophy Statement

Our philosophy of Graduate Architectural and Allied Professional education is based on four general premises: First, upon an informed administration and public, capable of distinguishing between the minimally trained and the highly educated professional; second, upon the provision of course work, requiring all professional level students to be grounded in the fundamentals of Design, Technology and Management; third, upon the provision of adequate fiscal support for professional education programs in order to provide adequate laboratory and research facilities, together with the specialized faculty trained to conduct aesthetic, social and physical scientific research; and finally, upon the attitudes of the students, faculty, and administrators of the program toward the standards of their curriculum and upon their sense of ethics and respect for their own profession.

Program Description

As UNLV is currently developing graduate degrees for architecture and allied studies, it is

not expected that the Master of Architecture Degree will be in place before the 1989–90 academic year. However, certain features of the first professional degree are established and the following description is intended to guide those considering making application for graduate architectural studies to this university at that time.

The proposed Master of Architecture Degree will be 1-1/2 years in length for full-time students. Early admission to exceptionally well-qualified students will be granted after two years of undergraduate preparatory study. Subsequent admission may be granted after three or four years of undergraduate study and the 3-1/2 year period may be reduced according to individual evaluation of credits earned and the level of preparation. Thus, the total number of years required for the Master of Architecture Degree will range from a minimum of 5-1/2 years to a maximum of 7-1/2 years. Students from other institutions who have earned a Bachelor of Architecture as the first professional degree can complete the Masters program in one academic year.

FACULTY
Administration

J Hugh Burgess, AIA, Arch D, Head
Camille S Clark, MLS, Architecture Reference Librarian

Professor

J Hugh Burgess, AIA, BS, MS Arch, Arch D

Associate Professor

Attila E Lawrence, ASID, BFA, MA

Assistant Professors

Richard M Beckman, AIA, B Arch, M Arch
Raymond J Lucchesi, AIA, B Arch

Part-Time Faculty

Ronald R Bennett, PE, BSCE
Stefanie Bradie, RA, B Arch, M Arch
Steven P Carr, AIA, BED
Craig S Galati, AIA, B Arch
George Garlock, AIA, B Arch
Ronald J Gomes, BA, JD
Floyd T Harris, PE, BS
Charles Kajkowski, PE, BSE
Patrick Klenk, AIA, B Arch
Lyndon L Meeks, BSCE
Ted Rexing, AIA, BFA
Frank E Reynolds, AICP, BS Arch Engr, MUP
Rene A Rolin, ASID, BS
Thomas J Schoeman, BFA, M Arch
Sandra Streiby, BA
David Wallister, AIA, B Arch
Jack W Zunino, ASLA, MLA

Adjunct Faculty

James A Cardle, BSCE, PhD
Thomas J Holder, MFA
Cathie C Kelly, PhD
Douglas D. Reynolds, BS, MS, PhD
Robert H Tracy, MA, PhD
Herbert C Wells, BA, MS
Richard V Wyman, BS, MS, PhD

New Jersey Institute of Technology

School of Architecture
New Jersey Institute of Technology
323 Dr. Martin Luther King Boulevard
Newark, New Jersey 07102
(201) 596-3080

Admissions Office
Undgrd: (201) 596-3300
Grad: (201) 596-3460
Toll-Free (800-200-NJIT)

Application Deadline(s): Freshman: Spring
Nov 1; Fall May 1
Transfer: Spring Nov 1; Fall June 1
Graduate: Spring Nov 1; Fall June 5
Tuition & Fees: Undgrd: NJ Res: $1356/sem
Non-Res: $2422/sem
Grad: NJ Res: $131/credit;
Non-Res: $185/credit
Endowment: Public

DEGREE PROGRAMS

Degree	Minimum Years for Degree	Accred.	Requirements for Admission	Full-Time Stdnts.	Part-Time Stdnts.	% of Applics. Accptd.	Stdnts. in 1st Year of Program	# of Degrees Conferred
B Arch	5	NAAB	HS Diploma - Transcripts SAT, Math Achievement I or II, Portfolio	378		25%	135	51
M Arch	1		B Arch, 3.0 GPA, Portfolio Three letters of recommendation	8				
M Arch	3½	(pending)*	BA or BS Degree, 3.0 GPA, Portfolio, Three letters of Recommendation (BA or BS in Architecture for advanced standing)	34	6			
MSAS	1½		B Arch or equiv., 3.0 GPA Portfolio		2			

*Program began in 1985

SCHOOL DEMOGRAPHICS (all degree programs)

Full-Time Faculty	Part-Time Faculty	Full-Time Students	Part-Time Students	Foreign Students	Out-of-State U.S. Stdnts.	Women Students	Minority Students
24	32	420	53	4.7%		20.9%	24%

LIBRARY (Tel. No. 201-596-3083)

Type	No. of Volumes	No. of Slides
Arch Info Ctr		63,000

STUDENT OPPORTUNITIES AND RESOURCES

The school's location allows for diverse educational settings for studio problems, architectural analysis and historical study. Newark and New York are great store-houses of architecture and urbanism. Smaller New Jersey cities and towns are examples of Main Street America. Directly to the north and south, along routes 78 and 1, among others, explosive growth corridors of high tech industries and suburban garden cities are developing from farmland.

The region also offers opportunities for architectural culture in its museums, exhibits of historic and current design work, gallery shows, lectures, etc. New York City, only minutes away from campus by subway also provides the opportunity for theatre, music, and other general cultural activities.

Recent work at the SOA has drawn upon these resources in studies of high-rise buildings in Manhattan; studies for alternative life styles; theatres in Newark; and studies for waterfronts on the ocean, rivers and bays of New Jersey.

SOA faculty members have broad experience in teaching, design, planning, research, building, lecturing, consulting, and writing. They are active professionals, known for their contributions and commitment to environmental quality and architectural design.

A growing expertise in computer use in design puts the NJIT faculty at the forefront of this field. Computer graphic studios are in place in the school and each student receives a personal-computer for his/her own use.

The SOA/NJIT program is recognized by the State Board for Examiners of Architecture as meeting their requirements for licensing. The NJSA offers several financial assistance programs to students at the school, including scholarships, fellowships and grants.

SPECIAL ACTIVITIES AND PROGRAMS

Special Lecture Series: Well-known speakers bring innovative, provocative ideas about modifying the human environment.

Visiting Lecturers and Critics Program

AIA Student Center

Student supply store

Community involvement projects

Summer travel opportunities for eligible students through awards from the Fund for Educational Enrichment

Field trips to Toronto, Boston, Chicago, Philadelphia and other cities

Faculty lecture series

Exhibits

School Socials

Participation in competitions

Beaux Art Ball

Institute Honors Program

Summer abroad studio and course work

Student lecture series

FACILITIES
Public transportation
Photography darkroom
Computer graphics
Architectural Information Center
Woodworking shop

SCHOLARSHIPS/AID
The School of Architecture/NJIT currently has a variety of scholarships and grants available. At present, scholarships have been awarded to third, fourth and fifth-year students from the New Jersey Society of Architects Foundation: State and federal financial aid programs are available through NJIT; National Direct Student Loans are available to students who attend at least half-time.

A summer travel grant program is funded by SOA's Fund for Educational Enrichment.

Part-time college work study program and graduate assistantships are also available.

UNDERGRADUATE PROGRAM
Philosophy Statement
The School of Architecture seeks to educate students to assume positions of responsibility and leadership in the architectural profession and in developing areas of opportunity in technology and community design related to the discipline of Architecture. An emphasis on studio design in the curriculum is reinforced by courses in history, building science and social concerns. A diverse faculty brings its expertise to bear on issues of architecture - technology - culture that challenges students to prepare them for their productive years as practitioners, scholars and researchers. Attention is paid to fulfilling the mission of the Institute as a premier technological institution in the nation with extensive capacity in computer graphics and design directed towards the traditional human-centered values of architecture. These values, historically expressed by Vitruvius in the reign of Caesar Augustus as fitness for use (Utilitas), meaningful technical correctness (Firmitas), and the generation of aesthetic satisfaction (Venustas), still challenge us at the SOA today. In an era when demographic and technological changes create both a threat of environmental stress and a promise of human deliverance, we believe architecture provides for a synthesis of human and technical expertise.

Program Description
The total time needed to earn a Bachelor of Architecture degree (the first professional degree) at NJIT is five years. The curriculum consists of an introductory year in design followed by four years of professional curriculum. Credits for the Bachelor of Architecture degree must be distributed as follows: required architecture credits, 100 credits; architecture electives from Building Sciences, community and urban design, and history and theory, 12 credits; unrestricted electives, 10 credits; freehand drawing, 3 credits; general university requirements, 44 credits.

GRADUATE PROGRAM
Philosophy Statement
The graduate program in the School of Architecture seeks to provide a context and atmosphere for advanced learning that enables graduates with the M Arch to assume leadership roles in architectural design. Building sciences, and community and urban design are important areas of research and scholarship in the MSAS Program. The New Jersey-New York Metropolitan Region offers graduate students a laboratory in which to develop innovative responses to problems of communities and cities. The NJIT institutional setting affords students an opportunity to bring the potentials of advanced technologies to bear on problems of buildings and the built environment. The faculty represents a broad set of academic and professional experiences that combine a humanistic appreciation of the timeless with an artistic and scientific quest for continual improvement.

Program Description
MASTER OF ARCHITECTURE
The Master of Architecture Program is offered for students qualified for advanced study in architectural design and professional practice. Candidates are placed in two groups, according to their previous degree(s), courses and experience.

MASTER OF SCIENCE IN ARCHITECTURAL STUDIES
The Master of Science in Architectural Studies is intended for those seeking new direction in their careers, as well as opportunity for scholarly inquiry and research. It is a one year, non-design program of advanced technical studies in areas such as computer-aided design, energy conservation in buildings and communities, and architecturally related consulting, engineering and planning. Applicants must have a professional degree in architecture or a related discipline.

FACULTY
Administration
Sanford R Greenfield, FAIA, Dean
G Michael Mostoller, AIA, Associate Dean
David Hawk, AIA (Assoc.), Coordinator of Graduate Programs

Professors
Sanford R Greenfield, FAIA, B Arch, M Arch, Ed M
C Richard Hatch, AIA, M Arch
David L Hawk, B Arch, M Arch, M City Planning, PhD
Bridgett Knowles, AIA, B Arch, M Arch
G Michael Mostoller, AIA, B Arch, M Arch

Associate Professors
David Elwell, RA, MFA
Karen Franck, PhD
Glenn Goldman, AIA, M Arch

Barry Jackson, AIA, B Arch, M Arch
Sandra V Moore, Ed D
Donald Wall, B Arch, M Arch, D Arch
Leslie Weisman, MA
Troy West, RA, B Arch, M Arch
M Steven Zdepski, RA, B Arch, M Arch

Assistant Professors
Bharat Gami, RA, B Arch, M Arch
Susan Henderson, SAH, CAA, M Arch
Felize Ozel, B Arch, M Arch
Anthony Schuman, RA, M Arch

Special Lecturers
David Buege, RA, M Arch
Douglas Darden, RA, MA
Kunio Kudo, M Arch
Brian McGrath, RA, B Arch, M Arch
David Spiker, B Arch, M Arch

Part-Time Faculty
Frank Arvan, M Arch
Christine Boyer, PhD
David Diamond, RA, M Arch
Juanita Ellias, PhD
Manouchehr Eslami, RA, PhD
Georgia Goldberg, RA, M Arch
Cleveland Harp, RA, M Arch
Robert Henry, MS
Everardo Jefferson, RA, M Arch
Nadir Lahiji, M Arch
John Lebduska, RA, B Arch
Peter McCleary, M Arch
James McGlumphy, RA, B Arch
Thomas Navin, M Arch
Taeg Nishimoto, M Arch
Elizabeth O'Donnell, B Arch
Peter Papademetriou, RA, M Arch
Nina Prantis, BFA
Peter Rees, RA, B Arch, M Arch
John Shuttleworth, BA, BS Arch
Jeri Smith, M Arch
Charles Thanhauser, RA, M Arch
Fred Travisano, AIA, B Arch
Julian Weiss, RA, B Arch, M Arch
Kevin Wilkes, B Arch
Timothy Wood, RA, B Arch, MCA
Wilson Woodridge, B Arch
John Zoldos, BCE

Adjunct Faculty
Erv Bales, ASME, AEE, PhD
Dennis Gibbins, M Arch
Eugene Stamper, MS

University of New Mexico

**School of Architecture
and Planning**
University of New Mexico
2414 Central Avenue SE
Albuquerque, New Mexico 87131
(505) 277-2903

Admissions Office
(505) 277-2903

Application Deadline(s): Undgrd: Mar 1
Grad: 3½-year
program - Mar 1
2-year program and
Post-Professional
Masters: Mar 1 and
Nov 1
Tuition & Fees: Undgrd: NM Res: $576/sem;
Non-res: $2187/sem;
Grad: NM Res: $576/sem;
Non-res: $2187/sem
Endowment: Public

DEGREE PROGRAMS

Degree	Minimum Years for Degree	Accred.	Requirements for Admission	Full-Time Stdnts.	Part-Time Stdnts.	% of Applics. Accptd.	Stdnts. in 1st Year of Program	# of Degrees Conferred
BA Arch	4		1 year college, 2.5 GPA letters, portfolio	98	22	65%	55	(86/87) 34
BA Env D	4		1 year college, 2.5 GPA letters, portfolio	9	1	85%	4	6
M Arch	3½	NAAB	BA or BS, 3.0 GPA	35	8	35%	15	4
M Arch	2	NAAB	BA Arch, 3.0 GPA	34	22	75	17	10
M Arch	1½		B Arch, 3.0 GPA	5	2	70	3	3
MCRP	2	PAB	BA or BS, 3.0 GPA	15	24	70	9	8

SCHOOL DEMOGRAPHICS (all degree programs)

Full-Time Faculty	Part-Time Faculty	Full-Time Students	Part-Time Students	Foreign Students	Out-of-State U.S. Stdnts.	Women Students	Minority Students
16	18	185	90	5%	35%	35%	25%

LIBRARY (Tel. No. 505-277-2357)

Type	No. of Volumes	No. of Slides
Multiple discipline	18,000	90,000

STUDENT OPPORTUNITIES AND RESOURCES

The School of Architecture and Planning has a student body of 275, including graduates and undergraduates. There is a stimulating mix of ethnic groups and students who come from diverse economic backgrounds. Approximately 40 percent of the students come to New Mexico from out of state and from abroad. The architecture programs are committed to the creation of a supportive physical and cultural environment and have strong ties with the planning program at the School, the College of Fine Arts and the College of Engineering.

The faculty of the school consists of over 30 full- and part-time members. It includes practicing architects, historians, and research architects with a broad range of competencies from solar technology to post-occupancy evaluation, as well as allied professionals such as planners, social scientists, landscape architects, and engineers. The faculty is involved in teaching, research, and public service linked to the academic concerns of the school.

The University of New Mexico in Albuquerque, with over 23,000 students, is the major university for the state. In addition to the School of Architecture, the University houses the following professional Schools: Education, Engineering, Fine Arts, Law, Management, Nursing and Medicine, as well as the College of Arts and Sciences.

The Albuquerque area, in addition to its natural beauty and fine climate, has many environmental and technical resources. Nearby mountains and deserts offer a variety of architectural applications and environmental experiences. Energy research is undertaken at Sandia Laboratory and the Los Alamos Laboratory.

The School accepts transfer students with special emphasis on those wishing to complete the final two graduate years leading to the professional degree of master of architecture.

SPECIAL ACTIVITIES AND PROGRAMS

The Design and Planning Assistance Center provides service to New Mexico communities and to those in need. The Research and Development Center coordinates such activities within the school.

The Institute of Environmental Education focuses on the education of elementary, junior and high school students in the areas of architecture and the environment.

A Summer workshop "Genesis of Form" deals with the traditions of New Mexico and their effect on contemporary design.

A Continuing education program offers 4 to 5 evening courses per semester.

Architectural Exhibitions (2 to 3 per semester).

An extensive Monday lecture series (11 lectures per semester).

A special program of visiting architects from abroad teaching in graduate studios.

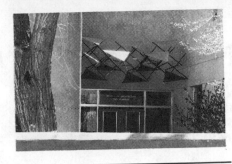

Three annual publications are produced by the School: *The News*, the School's newsletter, *MASS*, a journal of opinion and *Portfolio*, showing student work.

The AIAS student chapter organizes a variety of student activities.

FACILITIES

The School, its studios, faculty offices, administrative office and lecture rooms are housed in two adjacent buildings facing the main entrance to the university. The Design and Planning Assistance Center, the social outreach arm of the School, operates out of a store-front facility within walking distance of the school. A computer lab is located in the School, as well as a well-equipped woodworking and model shop.

The architecture library and slide collection are integrated with those of the College of Fine Arts, and a special Resource Center within the School houses further basic books, tapes and slides.

AIAS, the student organization, operates a student facility within the School.

SCHOLARSHIPS/AID

The university offers a complete array of financial aid programs ranging from federally funded student loans to special university scholarships. The school itself offers about thirteen stipends for graduate and teaching assistants, each ranging from $1275 to $2050 plus some tuition waivers. Workstudy jobs are also available.

A number of merit awards are offered annually by the School supported by the "Friends" of the School, the local AIA chapters, Women in Construction, and other Associations. Students are also eligible for National AIA awards and scholarships.

72% of students get aid.

UNDERGRADUATE PROGRAM
Philosophy Statement

The curriculum recognizes the broad range of knowledge and skills needed by students preparing themselves for roles in the creation of a humane and responsive physical environment.

The curriculum is flexible to permit students to chose between a pre-professional course of study in architecture, which prepares them for graduate work in architecture leading to a professional degree, or a more generalized environmental design program, which prepares them for further graduate studies in such areas as planning or landscape architecture.

Program Description

The preprofessional program leading to the Bachelor of Arts in Architecture is the first four years of the school's six-year program leading to the professional degree of Master of Architecture. This program, as well as the one leading to the Bachelor of Arts in Environmental Design, enables students to develop the basic abilities of analysis and synthesis and provides them with a set of attitudes and a foundation of skills through studios linked to courses and seminars. Upon graduation, students should be able to play an effective, if beginning, role working within real-world constraints but able to formulate constructive proposals for better environments.

They will also have a wide array of educational and career choices open and known to them.

Students apply for acceptance into either program at the end of their first year at the university. During that year they should have completed the prerequisite courses required for acceptance into the School of Architecture. Both programs include a wide range of required and elective courses. The four-year program leading to the degree of Bachelor of Arts in Architecture consists of 66 semester credit hours in architecture and 62 hours in arts and sciences or other fields. The four-year program leading to the Bachelor of Arts in Environmental Design consists of 50 credit hours in architecture and 78 hours in other fields, of which 21 must constitute a concentration in a single discipline outside architecture.

GRADUATE PROGRAM
Philosophy Statement

The graduate programs prepare students for diverse roles as architects in shaping the physical environment and provide the environmental, cultural, and technical insights and skills that lead to a responsive and adaptive architecture. The programs attempt to balance these concerns while allowing for the development of the students' individual interests.

Program Description

Programs leading to the professional degree of Master of Architecture are open to two groups: 1) Graduate students who hold bachelor's degrees in other fields and wish to blend previous education with studies in architecture can complete the degree in three to three-and-one-half years; 2) Graduate students who hold a four-year preprofessional degree from a school of architecture can obtain the Master of Architecture in two years.

The Master of Architecture programs are built around studios, and consist of required and elective courses, seminars, and independent work, which together address the aesthetic, environmental, behavioral, historical, technical, programmatic, and managerial aspects of building design and construction.

Three "Emphasis" programs are available within the final two years of the graduate program leading to the degree of Master of Architecture: 1) Energy Conscious Design, 2) Behavior and Design, and 3) Planning and Design.

A special post professional degree program is available to graduate students who hold the professional degree of Bachelor of Architecture and who can obtain the Master of Architecture in one and a half years. This program accommodates the special interests of the student within the bounds of the expertise of faculty members in the school and the university.

A two-year graduate program leading to the Master of Community and Regional Planning is also offered. The program's broad range of courses are open to all students in the school.

FACULTY
Administration

George Anselevicius, FAIA, RA, Dean
Nicholas Markovich, Assistant Dean
Nancy Pistorius, Librarianship (College of Fine Arts)

Professors

George Anselevicius, FAIA, RA, Dipl Arch
Richard Nordhaus, M Arch
Wolfgang Preiser, BDA, PhD
Don Schlegel, FAIA, RA, M Arch
Anne Taylor, Assoc AIA, PhD

Associate Professors

Richard Anderson, MUP, PhD
Edith Cherry, AIA, RA, M Arch
Stephen Dent, AIA, RA, M Arch
Nicholas Markovich, AIA, M Arch
William Siembieda, PhD Urb Plan
Robert Walters, RA, B Fine Arts

Assistant Professors

Steve Borbas, APA, MS City & Reg Plan
Ted Jojola, MA City Plng, PhD
James Richardson, M Arch, M City Plng
Kramer Woodard, MS

Lecturers

Paul Lusk, M Arch
Ed Norris, AIA, B Arch

Part-Time Faculty

Terry Conrad, MA Art
Ed Fitzgerald, B Arch
Kirk Gittings, MA
Bob Habiger, M Arch
David Henkle, PhD
G Robert Johns, BSLA
Min Kantrowitz, M Arch
Paul McHenry, AIA, RA, M Arch
Baker Morrow, BA
Don Peterson, M City Plng, JD
Michel Pillet, Dplg
V B Price, BA
Toby Pugh, AIA, RA, M Arch
Jose Rivera, PhD
Paul Robinson, M Arch
Stanley Sager, BA
Lawrence Shuster, MSME
Maria Varela, MA
Chris Wilson, MA

Adjunct Faculty

Bill Harris, PhD
Christopher Mead, PhD

New School of Architecture

New School of Architecture
1249 "F" Street
San Diego, CA 92101
(619) 235-4100

Application Deadline(s): April 1
Tuition & Fees: Undgrd: $125 per unit
Endowment: Private

DEGREE PROGRAMS

Degree	Minimum Years for Degree	Accred.	Requirements for Admission	Full-Time Stdnts.	Part-Time Stdnts.	% of Applics. Accptd.	Stdnts. in 1st Year of Program	# of Degrees Conferred
B Arch	5		HS degree portfolio, letter of intent	85	30	80%	20	60

SCHOOL DEMOGRAPHICS (all degree programs)

Full-Time Faculty	Part-Time Faculty	Full-Time Students	Part-Time Students	Foreign Students	Out-of-State U.S. Stdnts.	Women Students	Minority Students
11	21	85	30	5%	5%	30%	30%

LIBRARY (Tel. No. 619-429-6000)

Type	No. of Volumes	No. of Slides
Arch & General	4,000	2,000

STUDENT OPPORTUNITIES AND RESOURCES

The New School of Architecture is a private school, without the numerous regulations imposed on public institutions. Architecture is the only course of instruction offered.

Design studios are taught by outstanding San Diego architects who have an excellent variety of experiences and expertise to offer students. Studios are limited to 18 students and are held 12 hours per week. Each student has ample opportunity for individual assistance from the instructor.

Both day and evening classes are offered, therefore enabling students to work in local architectural offices while attending school, if they desire.

Faculty have been selected for their expertise and also for the diversity of their backgrounds. As a result students are exposed to a wide variety of architectural philosophies.

NSA works closely with the local AIA chapter in assisting them with local projects. Students have participated in urban design projects with border communities, as well as working with local elementary students in an ongoing career-oriented program.

SPECIAL ACTIVITIES AND PROGRAMS

The school's AIAS chapter schedules numerous activities during the year including: visits to many local architectural offices; lectures by outstanding architects, interior designers and others in the design community; field trips to renowned architectural sites, such as Taliesin West; a softball team that challenges local architectural office teams; and a number of social events.

The school publishes a magazine entitled "Cartouche" four times each year. Students not only contribute articles, but gain experience in graphic layout and design.

NSA sponsors a lecture series each Fall, bringing well-known Southern California architects to San Diego to talk not only to students, but the general public.

FACILITIES

Located in downtown San Diego, near the hub of urban activity, the facilities of the New School of Architecture consist of 18,000 square feet of space in the Ratner Art Center. Housed in a large studio are spaces equipped with drawing boards and layout areas for each student in each year. Each student is assigned an individual work space.

Several classrooms are used for lecture classes and design reviews (crits), many of which are video-taped for future use by students.

A large, comprehensive library, a bookstore, a computer lab, several galleries, an audio-visual lab, a model and graphics art workshop, and office space complete the educational environment available to students.

The urban location of the college promotes interaction between local architects and the students. "Brown bag" discussions in the gallery area of the school occur on a regular basis. Several local architects have their offices in the loft space which is located above the school. The college is easily accessible by public transportation as well as having easy freeway access for commuters.

SCHOLARSHIPS/AID

FINANCIAL AID

The New School of Architecture has been approved by the Veterans Administration for its students, who qualify, to receive educational benefits. Veterans should obtain information specifically for them from the Business Office.

Until the school receives accreditation from NAAB, Guaranteed Student Loans and other government-sponsored financial aid is not available. Until that time, students will need to make other arrangements.

SCHOLARSHIPS AND AWARDS
Condia-Ornelas
Fourth- or fifth-year female student with highest GPA in Design.
Buss-Silver-Hughes & Associates
Scholarship to a student, based on design ability, grade point average and financial need.
Construction Specification Institute (CSI) Scholarship
Awarded during Winter Quarter to fifth-year student with highest grade in Specification Writing.
Women in Architecture (WIA) Scholarship
An annual award to an outstanding female student with financial need.

The New School of Architecture provides each year the awards to the graduating class for superior achievement in Design, Architectural Technologies, and academic excellence.

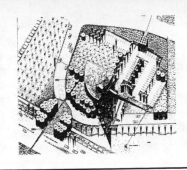

UNDERGRADUATE PROGRAM
Philosophy Statement

The New School of Architecture is committed to excellence in education and in fulfilling its mission to serve the San Diego professional architectural community. NSA has a distinctive educational program with selected broad liberal arts and general education courses to produce practicing architects who also possess the intellectual foundations of liberal arts graduates.

OBJECTIVES
To Develop:
- Skills of problem recognition, formulation and solution.
- Skills of analysis.
- Professional competence.
- Awareness of the contribution of allied disciplines to the design process.
- Awareness of the architectural profession's past, present, and future in a pragmatic framework of communication skills as they relate to the architectural profession in society.
- Motivation and to encourage attitudes for continued professional and personal learning.

Program Description

The program is divided into a five-year sequence of courses, each year building on the previous years.

Architectural drafting techniques are taught in the first year. These courses develop the skills necessary to support the students' creativity and problem solving abilities. Math and physics are taught to provide the necessary tools to solve the structure problems that students will encounter in the upper-division classes. Written communication is a very important factor in the success of an architect. This skill is strongly stressed. English courses including report writing and specification writing will be taught in the first, third, and fifth years.

Upper-division students spend a good portion of their time in design-lab classes. Lectures are held to a minimum, with the major emphasis placed on learning by doing. Instructors give students individual help.

The straight lecture classes, such as a course on structures, will be taught with the use of the latest audiovisual methods. Students will have the use of videotapes of class lectures.

The school provides the student with the type of education that will make him or her employable upon graduation.

FACULTY
Administration

Jeffrey Shorn, AIA, Dean, Architecture & Design
Allen Dueber, AIA, Dean of Admissions & Guidance
James P Brown, AIA, Chairman, Architectonics
Sheila McQuillan, Librarian

Professors

R Gary Allen, AIA, B Arch
Allen Dueber, AIA, B Arch
Jeffrey Shorn, AIA, M Arch

Assistant Professors

Ralph Roesling, AIA, B Arch
Charles Slert, AIA, M Arch

Part-Time Faculty

Arthur Balourdas, AIA, BA, M Arch
James P Brown, AIA, M Arch
Anthony Cutri, AIA, M Arch
John Desch, AIA, M Arch
Eric Fotiadi, RCE, SE, MS
C W Kim, AIA, M Arch
Angeles Leira, APA, MA
Susan Luzzaro, MA
Joe C Nicholson, MA
John Nicita, RCE, BS
Patrick O'Connor, APA, MCPUD
Manuel Rodriguez, AIA, M Arch
Stephen S Wallet, AIA, M Arch
Coulter Winn, AIA, M Arch

129

New York Institute of Technology

School of Architecture
New York Institute of Technology
Old Westbury, New York 11568
(516) 686-7593

Admissions Office
(516) 686-7520

Tuition & Fees: Undgrd: $2495 per semester
(Frshmn & Soph)
$2831 per semester
(Upper-classmen)
Endowment: Private

DEGREE PROGRAMS

Degree	Minimum Years for Degree	Accred.	Requirements for Admission	Full-Time Stdnts.	Part-Time Stdnts.	% of Applics. Accptd.	Stdnts. in 1st Year of Program	# of Degrees Conferred
BS Arch Tech	4		HS Diploma - SAT Scores	1139	243	95%	290	141
BSAT Energy Management	4		Common 2-yr. BSAT core, 2.75 GPA	12	0	50%	8	4
BSAT Bus Admin	4		Common 2-yr. BSAT core, 2.75 GPA	6	0	50%	6	New Program
BSAT EM MEM (Combined)	5		BSAT EM, 3.00 GPA	2			2	New Program
B Arch	5	NAAB	Common 2-yr. BSAT core, 2.75 GPA, 3.0 in Arch, Portfolio	125	35	30%	70	68

SCHOOL DEMOGRAPHICS (all degree programs)

Full-Time Faculty	Part-Time Faculty	Full-Time Students	Part-Time Students	Foreign Students	Out-of-State U.S. Stdnts.	Women Students	Minority Students
30	59	1284	278	15%	15%	20%	20%

LIBRARY (Tel. No. 516-686-7579)

Type	No. of Volumes	No. of Slides
Art, Arch, Int Design	13,565	26,144

STUDENT OPPORTUNITIES AND RESOURCES

Architecture is a leading component of the New York Institute of Technology, which also offers study in the arts, business, engineering and the computer field. Student enrollment in architecture has continued to increase. This steady flow of incoming students can be attributed in large part to the attraction of a diverse faculty consisting of professional architects, engineers and related experts, many of whom are adjuncts teaching in specialized areas of the curriculum.

The student body is a diversified group representing the many different outlooks of a college that has both urban and suburban campuses.

All students in the Center for Architecture are first admitted to the four-year BS in Architectural Technology degree program. They may be accepted for the five-year B Arch degree program after completion of two years (one year for advanced transfers) with a cumulative grade index of 2.75 or an index of 3.0 in the major area and a review of their professional portfolios. Completion of at least 60 credits of study at the Old Westbury campus is required of all transfer students for the Bachelor of Architecture degree.

The Center encourages student and faculty involvement in related urban and suburban communities. Both groups are also encouraged to participate in bringing visiting experts to the Center. Students attend meetings of the local chapter of the American Institute of Architects, which also conducts professional development programs that may be attended by faculty and students. Student chapters at the Old Westbury, New York City and Central Islip campuses conduct fall and spring lecture series, inviting leading architects and theorists in the field. Members of the faculty present informal lectures on their practice, travel and special expertise. Annual meetings are also held with the Construction Specifications Institute and the Producers' Council.

Graduates place well in the New York State qualifying examinations for licensure. They are filling responsible positions in leading offices and many have opened their own offices.

SPECIAL ACTIVITIES AND PROGRAMS

Suburban community design studies for Hempstead, Bayville, Westbury, Babylon. Urban studies with focus on New York City.

Center for Energy Policy and Research. Computer simulation and graphics laboratory. Annual summer program abroad.

Elective special studies courses, including solar conservation, landscape architecture, advanced rendering, sketching, interior architecture.

School participation in local high schools (teaching, exhibits, competitions).

Extensive, varied field trips to sites to study design problems and site planning; trips organized by students to Washington, Boston, New Haven, Chicago, etc. Evening and late afternoon courses. Coop & IDP programs.

Five-year combined Bachelor of Science and Master's degree programs.

FACILITIES

New York Institute of Technology's three campuses offer a rich variety of environments that include the dense urbanism of the Metropolitan Center in New York City, the suburban atmosphere of the Dorothy Schure Old Westbury campus on Long Island, and the almost rural surroundings of Central Islip, Long Island. All three campuses benefit from the cultural richness of the New York metropolitan region.

Computer simulation and graphics laboratory.

The Central Islip campus offers residential halls with diverse living arrangements.

SCHOLARSHIPS/AID

The Office of Admissions at New York Institute of Technology offers merit scholarships to all qualified high school and transfer students. For the academic year 1985-86, architecture students at the Old Westbury campus received scholarship awards of $275,200.

For the same period the college's Financial Aid Office administered $322,800 in state and federal loans to architecture students on the basis of financial need. Upper-level students participated in local and national AIA scholarship programs with awards ranging from $200 - $1500.

UNDERGRADUATE PROGRAM
Philosophy Statement

New York Institute of Technology's Center for Architecture is a career-oriented college where students are educated to participate in the task of providing shelter that fulfills human needs and aspirations. Architecture is an art which responds to programmatic necessities, its physical context, and material exigencies, as well as invention and precedent. It requires a generalist position, which is not limited to a singular outlook concerning architectural education, theory, and practice.

The Center for Architecture's faculty reflects both the diversity required of today's architectural profession and the needs of our students. The faculty are registered in their professional specialties and maintain active practices. Many of them employ the Center for Architecture's graduates and thus provide their initial experiences in the professional world.

Program Description

The four-year Bachelor of Science in Architectural Technology program and the accredited five-year Bachelor of Architecture program constitute the foundation of the Center's offerings. Both programs have a common two-year core after which the students enter professional level studies where they may choose to pursue the following options:

1. A Bachelor of Science in Architectural Technology. This degree focuses on the significant areas of knowledge needed in the architectural profession with an emphasis on construction and engineering.

2. A four-year Bachelor of Science in Architectural Technology with a minor in Energy Management.

This program equips students in the theoretical and practical aspects of technology and construction with an emphasis on management and energy policy analysis.

3. A Bachelor of Science in Architectural Technology with a minor in Business Administration.

This degree enables students to complement an expertise in construction and engineering with the organizational and managerial skills required in today's development and real estate markets.

4. An accredited five-year first-professional Bachelor of Architecture degree.

Students take architectural design also in the four professional years and an architectural design thesis in the fifth year. The main components of this program are architectural design and humanities in addition to a sound exposure to the technologies. Elective courses enable students to reinforce any of the program's components or branch off into another skill.

5. A combined five-year BSAT in Energy Management and a Master's in Energy Management degree.

Students take eighteen credits of graduate level Energy Management courses in their fifth year.

GRADUATE PROGRAM
Philosophy Statement

The combined five-year Master's and Bachelor's degree programs, offered through the Center for Architecture and other Schools and Centers at the Institute, provide a scholarly and career equivalent to the five-year first professional degree in areas of architectural practice other than design.

The specific area of expertise now offered at the master's level is Energy Management with Business Administration and Computer Science following very shortly.

Program Description

Coursework toward the combined degree program begins to differentiate from standard BSAT work only when 66 credits have been completed. Participation in the program normally begins in the third year of undergraduate study. Entrance requirements into the combined degrees are:

1. Completion of 66 credits of the BSAT curriculum

2. Achievement of cumulative index of 2.85

3. 18 credits of "free" electives still available

Within the Master's in Energy Management combined degree program, the foundation of the program is an eighteen-credit energy management set of courses focusing on energy conservation, generation, management and policy development.

The program prepares students to enter a career in architecture addressing the needs of energy efficient design and development.

FACULTY
Administration

Anthony J DiSanto, Acting Dean
Stuart Furman, Chairman
Joan Bassin, Assistant to the Dean
Clare Cohn, Branch Librarian

Professors

Frederick Bentel, RA, M Arch, D Arch
Aly Dadras, RA, BS Arch Eng, MS
Anthony DiSanto, RA, BA, M Arch
Dean Goss, PE, BSCE, MCE

Associate Professors

Paul Amatuzzo, RA, B Arch
Robert Battipaglia, PE, B Mgt E, BCE
Robert Beattie, RA, B Arch
Maria Bentel, RA, B Arch
John diDomenico, RA, B Arch, M Arch
Livio Dimitriu, RA, B Arch
Kadri ElAraby, RA, MSc (Plan), DrPA
Jonathan Friedman, RA, BA, M Arch, Dipl Arch
Percy Griffin, RA, B Arch, M Urb Plan
Gary Hess, MA, PhD
Rodolfo Imas, RA, M Arch
Robert Jensen, RA, B Arch, MA
Robert King, RA, BA, M Arch
Quentin Munier, RA, MSCE, B Arch
Arthur Pettorino, RA, B Arch
Alan Sayles, RA, B Arch
J Michael Schwarting, RA, B Arch, M Arch
Terry Sideris, PE, BS
William Walther, RA, B Arch, M Arch

Assistant Professors

Ralph Albanese, RA, BS, M Arch
Michele Bertomen, RA, B Arch
Beyhan Karahan, RA, BS, M Arch
Marvin Mitchell, RA, B Arch, MS Arch
James Wiesenfeld, PE, BSCE

Part-Time Faculty

Joan Bassin, BA, MA, PhD
Stuart Furman, RA, B Arch
Alyce Knight, B Arch, MA
Julio M San Jose, FTPI, M Arch, D Arch

Adjunct Faculty

Frank Bellantoni, PE, BCE
Michael Berthold, RA, B Arch
Phyllis Birkby, RA, M Arch
Robert Braun, B Arch
Gary Bruno, RA, B Arch
Louis Buscemi, RA, B Arch
Robert Campagna, RA, B Arch
Salvator Caradonna, PE, BSCE
Christopher Chimera, RA, BA, MFA
Murray Cohen, RA, B Arch
Benjamin Copito, PE, BSCE
Nicholas DeFelice, PE, MCE
David Diamond, B Arch, M Arch
Anthony DiProperzio, RA, BS
John Finnie, PE, BME
Heiko Folkerts, APA, BS Ed
William Gati, MS
Lloyd Goldfarb, RA, M Arch
Judy O'Buck Gordon, Dipl, BED, M Arch
Pascal Hofstein, RA, DplgUP
Deborah Huff, MFA
Carl Karas, M Arch
John Keenen, M Arch
Paul Koch, PE, PhD
Katherine Krizek, B Arch
Dennis Kuhn, RA, B Arch
Arthur Kunz, ASPO, MS Arch
Stephen Leet, B Arch
Edward Lockley, PE, MS
Robert Madey, RA, B Arch
Michael McNerney, B Arch
George Meltzer, RA, B Arch
Michael Michel, RLA, BLA
Philip Monastero, RA, B Arch
Vladimir Morosov, Dipl.
Diane Neff, BS, M Arch
Theresa O'Leary, B Arch
Stan Orens, PE, BSME
Thomas Pepper, BFA
Peter Pran, RA, MS Arch
Robert Rivielle, RA
Richard Rode, RA, Ctf
Joseph Scarpulla, RA, MS
Arthur Schiller, RA, M Arch
Frank Scicchitano, PE, MCE
Lindsay Shapiro, M Arch
Rudolph Shatarah, BSCE
Judith Sheine, RA, M Arch
Gregory Shoemaker, RA, B Arch
Christopher Sideris, IPE, BS
Benjamin Silberstein, PE, BSME
Michael Szerbaty, B Arch, M Arch
Peter Thaler, BA, B Arch, M Arch
Ann Tichich, RA, B Arch
Douglas Wilke, RA, PE, B Arch
Carlos Zapata, B Arch

North Carolina State University

Architecture Department
School of Design, Box 7701
North Carolina State University
Raleigh, North Carolina 27695-7701
(919) 737-2204/2205/2206

Application Deadline(s): January 1 (BEDA)
February 1 (B Arch and M Arch)
Tuition & Fees: Undgrd: NC Res: $880/yr
Non-res: $4220/yr
Grad: Same
Endowment: Public

DEGREE PROGRAMS

Degree	Minimum Years for Degree	Accred.	Requirements for Admission	Full-Time Stdnts.	Part-Time Stdnts.	% of Applics. Accptd.	Stdnts. in 1st Year of Program	# of Degrees Conferred
BEDA	4		HS Dipl, Interview, Portfolio	195	8	20%	55	36
B Arch	1	NAAB	BEDA or Equiv, Portfolio	13	1	40%	14	13
M Arch	2	NAAB	BEDA or Equiv, Portfolio, 3.0 GPA	22	2	30%	12	8
M Arch	1½		B Arch (NAAB accred), 3.0 GPA	0	0	30%	0	0
M Arch	4	NAAB	Non-Arch BA or BS, Portfolio, GRE, 3.0 GPA	50	4	30%	15	14

SCHOOL DEMOGRAPHICS (all degree programs)

Full-Time Faculty	Part-Time Faculty	Full-Time Students	Part-Time Students	Foreign Students	Out-of-State U.S. Stdnts.	Women Students	Minority Students
16	4	280	15	3%	20%	35%	7%

LIBRARY (Tel. No. 919-737-2207)

Type	No. of Volumes	No. of Slides
Design/Arch	26,000	55,000

STUDENT OPPORTUNITIES AND RESOURCES

North Carolina State University is the state's land-grant institution and has a total enrollment of 23,000. There are nine schools on campus. The School of Design has approximately 600 students. By statute 85 percent of the undergraduate population is from North Carolina. The remaining 15 percent and students in the graduate programs are currently drawn from 28 states and 10 foreign countries.

Raleigh, the state capital, is the governmental and commercial focus of the Research Triangle region - an area defined by Chapel Hill, home of the University of North Carolina, and Durham, home of Duke University. In the middle is the Research Triangle Park, a unique complex of public and private research installations. These institutions, along with the many agencies of state and local government, make the Triangle community a rich learning resource and a cosmopolitan environment for the study of architecture.

The School of Design faculty numbers approximately 45 and represents a wide spectrum of backgrounds in design disciplines.

The full-time Architecture faculty of 16 includes both those who conduct architectural practices and those engaged in scholarly research and other creative activities.

In addition to architecture, there are undergraduate and graduate programs in landscape architecture and product and visual design.

SPECIAL ACTIVITIES AND PROGRAMS

CDRS - Center for Design Research and Service

Design Council (student governmental organization)

American Institute of Architecture Students chapter

Architecture Graduate Student Association

Student Publication of the School of Design (longest continuously-published student journal in U.S.)

Outstanding program of exhibitions on all aspects of design

Public lecture programs with prominent speakers

Annual Distinguished Visiting Critic Studio (M Arch)

Opportunities for study at other U.S. architecture schools and overseas programs (Vienna, Copenhagen, Leicester, etc.)

Courses available at UNC-Chapel Hill and Duke University as well as other Raleigh colleges

Commencement awards and recognitions

"Competition Studios" offered regularly

FACILITIES

Architecture students have access to the excellent physical resources of the School of Design which include a permanent studio work station for each student. The various resource centers are well-equipped and managed by skilled staff: the Design Library located in the heart of the school; the Media Resources Center with extensive photographic, printing and other media equipment; the Materials Processing Center for model fabrication in wood, metal, plastics and fabric; the Physical Systems Lab for structural, construction, and ECS experimentation and display; and the Environmental Simulation Laboratory which contains rapidly growing graphics and computer resources.

SCHOLARSHIPS/AID

Financial aid in the form of scholarships, fellowships and teaching assistantships has increased significantly in recent years. Scholarships awarded by the Department to undergraduate students totaled $10,000, and a number of students qualified for other need-based university grants. Approximately $16,000 is now available annually for graduate fellowships. In addition, ten teaching assistantships valued at $2500+ annually are awarded to qualified graduate students. Out-of-state students appointed to assistantships may receive remission of out-of-state tuition, which represents an additional $3300 benefit.

UNDERGRADUATE PROGRAM
Philosophy Statement

The undergraduate program is a broadly-based, four-year curriculum leading to the degree of Bachelor of Environmental Design in Architecture. University requirements and electives provide a broad base of liberal education. Architecture courses focus on design process, history and theory, technological systems, and environmental context. They have been structured to provide a foundation for advanced study in professional Bachelor's and Master's programs in Architecture, but also provide a sound background for students who wish to pursue other educational and career objectives. A diversity of design experiences is also available in the School's other departments - Landscape Architecture, Product/Visual Design, and Design.

Program Description

The first year is common to all students in the School of Design, with university course requirements and an intensive course in Design Fundamentals. In the second year, the student selects a degree program (architecture, landscape architecture, product or visual design) and begins the studio/design experience and the information-based courses of the selected major. Six consecutive intermediate level studios are required. Elective core courses in architecture and related design disciplines are accompanied by university requirements in a variety of subject areas such as science, mathematics, humanities and social sciences.

BACHELOR OF ARCHITECTURE
Philosophy Statement

The Bachelor of Architecture Program prepares students for professional practice and related roles in architecture.

Vitruvius' statement regarding the goal of architecture serves as a guide: "In architecture as in all other operative arts, the end must direct the operation. The end is to build well. Well-building hath three conditions: commodity, firmness and delight." Our intention is to expose the students to and develop their understanding of these conditions. We also intend to provide Bachelor of Architecture students with the skills necessary to meet Vitruvius' conditions of good building. The faculty embraces a broad definition of the practice of architecture and is therefore free of a singular, dogmatic, or stylistic approach. The curriculum offers exposure to a diversity of ideas which surround architecture and related disciplines.

Program Description

The Bachelor of Architecture curriculum is a one-year program of 30 credit hours which builds upon a four-year pre-professional curriculum such as NCSU's BEDA program.

The focus of this intensive, professional experience is the design of buildings, but the curriculum addresses all aspects of practice. The assumption is that specialization within architecture must be built upon solid foundations. The curriculum provides these foundations, preparing students for specialization through further education or involvement in practice.

The ultimate goal of the Bachelor of Architecture Program is to make it possible for the student to acquire the knowledge, skill, and sensitivity necessary to be an architect who builds well.

The first-semester studio is faculty-directed and typically involves the design of a programmatic and technical complexity. The second-semester studio consists of a student-initiated final project which has been selected, programmed and researched in the prior semester. Required and elective professional courses in practice, history, technology, theory and other subjects complement the studios and provide a sound intellectual framework for future professional work.

GRADUATE PROGRAM
Philosophy Statement

The Master of Architecture program prepares students to assume responsible professional roles in architecture.

The primary goals of the program are to help students (1) achieve a high level of competence in architectural design by building knowledge and skills necessary for professional activity; (2) develop a commitment to professional values and responsibilities; (3) understand the variety of roles for architects in practice and related fields; and (4) develop as unique, autonomous individuals who accept responsibility for their professional, intellectual and creative development.

Program Description

The Department of Architecture offers three tracks to the Master of Architecture degree. Track 1 is for applicants with a four-year undergraduate degree in architecture and may be completed in two years of full-time study. Track 2 is for applicants holding a five-year NAAB-accredited Bachelor of Architecture degree and normally requires three semesters in residence. Track 3 is for students with degrees in fields other than architecture. This track normally requires four semesters of preparatory work but can be completed in less than four semesters; each case is evaluated individually.

In the Master of Architecture program, students encounter architectural problems at a variety of scales, requiring analytic, conceptual and developmental abilities. The design studio is the focus of this activity, enabling students to test ideas and theories about design in the context of both 'real life' and idealized problems. The final studio is devoted to a self-initiated, detailed architectural project that is carried out under the guidance of the student's graduate advisory committee.

Other course work supplements and amplifies these experiences. A wide variety of courses are available within the School of Design in urban and community design, architectural history and theory, methods and programming, architectural conservation, management and professional practice, and building technology. The program's flexible curriculum offers the student considerable freedom to individualize his or her plan of study, based on personal, educational and professional goals.

The majority of recent graduates have chosen to enter private architectural practice, undertaking the rich professional challenges it offers. While acknowledging the primacy of the practice orientation, the Master of Architecture program enlarges the professional framework to include alternative, non-traditional career roles as well.

FACULTY
Administration

Deborah W Dalton, Interim Dean
Robert P Burns, FAIA, Associate Dean and Department Head
Linda W Sanders, AIA, Assistant Department Head
Caroline Carlton, Design Librarian

Professors

Peter Batchelor, AIA, M Arch, MCP
Robert P Burns, FAIA, M Arch
Roger H Clark, FAIA, M Arch
Henry L Kamphoefner, FAIA, M Arch
John P Reuer, PhD
Henry Sanoff, AIA, M Arch
Vernon Shogren, M Arch
Ignazio Zubizarreta

Associate Professors

Georgia Bizios, AIA, M Arch
Frank Harmon, AIA, Dipl
Wayne Place, PhD
Patrick J Rand, AIA, M Arch
Linda W Sanders, AIA, M Arch
Paul Tesar, M Arch

Assistant Professors

Cristina Barrios-Cader, MAUD
Fatih Rifki, M Arch
John O Tector, MS, PhD (Pending)

Adjunct Faculty

Susan Cole Cannon, M Arch
Phil Freelon, AIA, M Arch
Edwin F Harris, Jr, FAIA, B Arch
Harwell H Harris, FAIA, DFA (HON)
Thomas C Howard, B Engr
Jeffrey Lee, M Arch

University of North Carolina at Charlotte

College of Architecture
University of North Carolina at Charlotte
Charlotte, North Carolina 28223
(704) 547-2357, 58, 59

Admissions Office:
(704) 547-2213

Application Deadline(s): Freshman: March 15
Fifth Year: February 1
Tuition & Fees: Undgrd: NC Res: $850/yr
Non-res: $4310/yr
Grad: NC Res: $850/yr
Non-res: $4310/yr
Endowment: Public

DEGREE PROGRAMS

Degree	Minimum Years for Degree	Accred.	Requirements for Admission	Full-Time Stdnts.	Part-Time Stdnts.	% of Applics. Accptd.	Stdnts. in 1st Year of Program	# of Degrees Conferred
BA Arch	4		400 verbal, 450 Math SAT, Letter of Intent	239	47	20%	73	35
B Arch	1	NAAB	BA Arch, BED, or equil. degree, portfolio, Letter of Intent	9	0	44%	9	9

SCHOOL DEMOGRAPHICS (all degree programs)

Full-Time Faculty	Part-Time Faculty	Full-Time Students	Part-Time Students	Foreign Students	Out-of-State U.S. Stdnts.	Women Students	Minority Students
19	10	248	47	6%	28%	23%	2%

LIBRARY (Tel. No. 704-547-4025)

Type	No. of Volumes	No. of Slides
Central Arch	17,444	55,000

STUDENT OPPORTUNITIES AND RESOURCES

The college's location in a rapidly growing area of the Carolinas provides a laboratory for the study of major architectural and societal issues, especially those related to urbanization and the development of a new Southern city. Since the campus is reasonably near major East coast cities and because the COA values architectural and educational pluralism, numerous field trips occur.

The highly diversified full-time faculty, together with the part-time faculty, provide a rich variety of architectural thoughts, inquiry, and expertise. The school's substantial visiting architects program expands the faculty resources and encourages study of significant architectural ideas. Part-time faculty may direct courses or they may be part of a teaching team. At the same time, the college maintains its moderate enrollment so that students may become familiar with each other and the faculty.

To support the goal of providing a comprehensive architectural and general education, many special innovative activities are made an integral part of the program. Students are provided opportunities to develop individual interest and skills while acquiring commonly required knowledge and skills.

The program is further enriched by the offerings of other disciplines in the university and by excellent relationships with the architectural community and the general Charlotte community.

SPECIAL ACTIVITIES AND PROGRAMS

Visiting Architects Studio: at least annually an upper-year studio is directed by two nationally significant visiting architects.

Visiting Lecturer Program: an extensive number of guest lecturers and visiting part-time faculty participate in the program.

The Spring Experience: each spring a two-day program of lectures, workshops, and seminars focuses upon a major architectural topic and related issues.

Exhibitions by distinguished architects.

Distinguished Visiting Professorship.

Study Abroad Program: UNCC is a coordinating institution for the US for one- or two-semester structured architectural study in Copenhagen, Denmark. Students from all schools in North America can participate. Summer programs in London and in Copenhagen are being initiated.

Summer Architectural Traveling Scholarship: each spring an outstanding upper-year student is awarded a scholarship for a self-organized summer architectural study.

Community Assistance Program.

Student architectural publication, Student Chapter of the AIA, and Architectural Student Council initiate and coordinate field trips, special design competitions, and annual social events.

Summer Session Studies.

North Carolina Architects Advisory Committee.

Adjunct Professor Program: Charlotte architects and business/political leaders serve as guest critics, lecturers, or advisers.

Materials Laboratory.

Student Study Field Trips to major US cities.

Job Placement Services.

FACILITIES

Construction of the COA's new building will commence in early 1988. It is designed by the collaborative efforts of Ferebee-Walters of Charlotte and Gwathmey-Siegel of New York. The 86,000-sq.-ft. building will include major materials/technical/computer/photo labs as well as galleries, studios, classrooms and offices. It is to be a demonstration of visual and environmental design inquiry.

SCHOLARSHIPS/AID

UNCC's Financial Aid Office has a comprehensive financial assistance program of scholarships, fellowships, work-study funds, and loans. The College of Architecture awards a series of small, competitive study and traveling fellowships, and fifth-year fellowships.

UNDERGRADUATE PROGRAM
Philosophy Statement

The College of Architecture recognizes the architect's fundamental concern for ordering the built environment in a manner that relates to the natural environment, making optimum use of resources and serving the social, physical, and spiritual needs of people. Thus, students are encouraged to understand the what, why, and how of a problem related to the physical environment, to examine alternatives and their consequences, and to provide the most suitable solution.

Students are educated to be both thoughtful and skillful, balancing analytical and synthetic experiences and achieving both graphic and problem-solving competence. The college is concerned that students learn to deal with complexity, understand major issues of our society, and become active participants in their solution. The program strives for students to understand the visual, functional, environmental, and technical aspects of architectural order. Therefore, the COA encourages both individual expression through valuing design pluralism and a holistic approach.

Program Description

Studies are organized into the Foundation Program (first and second years), the Development Program (third and fourth years), and the Advanced Program (fifth year). During the first two years, emphasis is upon development of graphic skills and problem-solving techniques as well as upon visual ordering, qualitative structures-environmental systems, human behavioral needs, and historic studies.

The third and fourth years are devoted to building design and optional architectural studies. In addition, there are quantitative studies in technology. A series of elective seminar-lecture studies are available in such areas as theory, acoustics, lighting, solar energy, housing, development, computers, landscape architecture, and preservation. The extensive general elective program encourages study in other disciplines, such as engineering, geography, earth science, business administration, behavioral sciences and natural sciences. The Bachelor of Arts in Architecture degree is awarded at the end of the fourth year, and the Bachelor of Architecture degree upon completion of the fifth year.

GRADUATE PROGRAM
Philosophy Statement

The college believes that students in the fifth-year B Arch program, who already hold an undergraduate architecture-related degree, should have the opportunity for individual exploration of major architectural issues of their specific interest, while at the same time, developing the knowledge and skills common to all architects. Because the college supports a holistic attitude, studies seek to intimately relate the visual, physical, behavioral, and technical aspects of architectural design. Application of students from other schools is encouraged.

Program Description

The first semester of the fifth-year B Arch program is primarily one of common architectural studies with the examination of important architectural issues and the development of major areas of knowledge and important skills through studios and seminars. In addition, each student identifies a set of issues and topics to individually explore in preparation for the thesis project, which is executed in the spring semester. The thesis advisory team includes a college faculty member, a non-college advisor who has expertise in the thesis subject, and the fifth-year faculty.

To encourage students to pursue collaborative studies while working on the thesis, an architectural issues seminar and professional practice course are incorporated into the second semester. Students are exposed to a breadth of architectural thought through the number of visiting architects/teachers who serve in a variety of capacities, such as resource persons for specialized areas and general design critics.

FACULTY
Administration

Charles C Hight, AIA, PE, Dean
Robert J MacLean, Chair of Instruction

Professors

Charles C Hight, AIA, PE, BSCE, B Arch
Michele Melaragno, Lic Classica, DCE
Charlie Mitchell, PE, MSCE

Associate Professors

Nelson S Benzing, BS Arch, M Arch
Michael A Gallis, B Arch, MCP
Kingston Heath, PhD
Richard Hill
Robert J MacLean, B Arch, M Arch
Christopher C Morgan, B Arch, M Arch
John A Nelson, B Arch, M Arch
Eric J Sauda, B Arch, M Arch
Dean B Vollendorf, B Arch, M Arch

Assistant Professors

Craig Jameson, B Arch, M Arch
Kenneth Lambla, BED, M Arch
Deborah Ryan, MLA
Robert G Venn, BA, MFA
Gregory Weiss, MFA
Peter Wong, B Arch, M Arch

Lecturers

Lindsay Daniel, BA, B Arch

Part-Time Faculty

Graham Adams
Gerald Allen
Kirk Bodick
Robert Campbell
David Egan
Gary Gumz
Charles Gwathmey
Dennis Hall
James Story

Adjunct Faculty

Jory Johnson, BA, MLA
Michael Swisher, AB, MFA

North Dakota State University

Department of Architecture
North Dakota State University
Box 5285
Fargo, North Dakota 58105-5285
(701) 237-8614

Office of Admissions
North Dakota State University
Box 5596
Fargo, North Dakota 58105
(701) 237-8643

Application Deadline(s): May 15
Tuition & Fees: Undgrd: ND Res:
$398/quarter
Non-res: $796/quarter
Endowment: Public

DEGREE PROGRAMS

Degree	Minimum Years for Degree	Accred.	Requirements for Admission	Full-Time Stdnts.	Part-Time Stdnts.	% of Applics. Accptd.	Stdnts. in 1st Year of Program	# of Degrees Conferred
BS Env Des	4		Univ. Req., ACT	194	16	30%	54	55
B Arch	1	NAAB	BS Env Des	50	5	—	—	49

SCHOOL DEMOGRAPHICS (all degree programs)

Full-Time Faculty	Part-Time Faculty	Full-Time Students	Part-Time Students	Foreign Students	Out-of-State U.S. Stdnts.	Women Students	Minority Students
13	2	235	21	4%	54%	20%	5%

LIBRARY (Tel. No. 701-237-8616)

Type	No. of Volumes	No. of Slides
Arch	9,750	33,550

STUDENT OPPORTUNITIES AND RESOURCES

North Dakota State University offers students the chance to study architecture as members of a small and close-knit group whose members have been selected for their academic and professional promise. While students and faculty have interests that may range through the theoretical, technological, historical, and sociological areas of study, all combine these interests with a basic concern for the professional practice of architecture.

Ours is a relatively small campus, but the university is a member of a consortium of three colleges, located close together and offering a rich variety of courses, extensive library holdings, and student activities. Within the Department, architecture students may choose to enroll in courses in the Landscape Architecture program. Close ties are maintained between the Department of Architecture and programs in art, construction management, horticulture, interior design, city planning, and several fields of engineering. Each student is required to prepare an individual program of elective courses that complement the professional curriculum.

The faculty includes specialists in many fields, including historical restoration and preservation, illumination, industrialized building methods, urban design, and the integration of architectural technologies. Because of the close association of students and faculty, students can draw on this diverse expertise in pursuing their own interests and formulating their own approaches to architecture and the profession.

SPECIAL ACTIVITIES AND PROGRAMS

Active student organizations: American Institute of Architecture Students; Tau Sigma Delta; American Society of Landscape Architects.

Summer foreign study program (in recent years, travel to England, Germany, Netherlands, Spain, and Italy).

Student-organized field trips (in recent years, to Chicago, Minneapolis, and New York).

Student participation in standing and special committees of the Department.

Brown-bag seminars and weekend workshops organized by American Institute of Architecture Students.

Annual Architects' Week of student events with lectures, social events, and an awards ceremony, held in conjunction with a meeting of the North Dakota Chapter, American Institute of Architects.

Joint degree program with the Department of Community and Regional Planning.

FACILITIES

Photographic darkroom; a broad range of reproduction facilities; low-velocity wind tunnel; machine to duplicate sun angles; artificial sky; temperature recording equipment; demonstration and testing equipment in illumination and acoustics; and other facilities are available.

(Students are encouraged to use the available equipment to further their own interests in technical and general topics of their study.)

SCHOLARSHIPS/AID

Four awards and twelve scholarships (totaling about $5,000) are administered within the Department, and additional scholarships are available through the College of Engineering and Architecture. Entering students are eligible for Helgason Scholarships, awarded on the basis of financial need as well as merit without need. Students are also eligible for university-wide scholarships, loan funds, and awards. At least two student competitions, conducted within the Department, reward students who display unusual talent in architectural design. Outstanding students in the fourth- or fifth-year of the architecture program are employed as teaching assistants.

UNDERGRADUATE PROGRAM
Philosophy Statement

Here the subject of architecture is considered sufficiently broad to accommodate many points of view and many theories of design among our faculty and students. Architecture is viewed as a distinct pursuit in itself, combining aspects of art, science, and business. Instead of compartmentalizing the study of different aspects of the profession of architecture, at North Dakota State University we stress the interrelationships among subjects. It is this unity of purpose that bridges the diversity of opinion and expression that are presented in the program. At the undergraduate level we believe a sound and broad professional education is more meaningful than narrow specializations.

Program Description

The program of the Department of Architecture is focused on the five-year curriculum leading to the degree of Bachelor of Architecture. Students are provided with opportunities to acquire the general education that is a necessary foundation for the professional practice of architecture, to develop architectural skills and knowledge (technological, problem-solving, and creative) that lead to professional competence and understanding, and to become capable in related topics, selected by the student according to his or her interests and abilities. The study of environmental conditions and climatic adaptation has become a principal concern of many courses.

In completing their elective courses, students develop a specialized study of some area outside architecture but related to it, with the possibilities ranging from philosophy to construction.

Applicants who are not admitted to the Department may enroll in the General Program of the College of Engineering and Architecture and pursue the first-year program in architecture. During the year vacancies in the beginning class are filled from the General Program on the basis of the students' university performance. Students transferring from other post-secondary institutions are not granted advanced standing in the architecture program, although many courses may be applicable to curriculum requirements.

FACULTY
Administration

Harold L Jenkinson, RA, Acting Chair, Department of Architecture and Landscape Architecture
Dennis C Colliton, RLA, ASLA, CSI, Director, Landscape Architecture Program
Susan J Wee, AAL, Library Associate

Professors

Cecil D Elliott, RA, AIA, B Arch, M Arch
Vincen W Hatlen, RA, B Arch, M Arch
Harold L Jenkinson, RA, B Arch, M Arch

Associate Professors

Dennis C Colliton, RLA, ASLA, MLA
Nate Krug, RA, AIA, M Arch
Romolo Martemucci, RA, B Arch, MS Urban Design

Assistant Professors

Barbara Andersen, BSLA
Donald C Faulkner, RA, AIA, BS, M Arch
Steve Martens, RA, BA, M Arch
Ronald Ramsay, LM, B Arch
Randy Swanson, RA, M Arch, MS Arch

Instructors

Brian E Pecka, BLA
Milton Yergens, RA, AIA, B Arch

Part-Time Faculty

Harlan K Ormbreck, RA, AIA
Mark Shaul, RA, AIA, CSI, B Arch, M Arch
Michael St Marie, ASID, BA
Earl E Stewart, RA, AICP, APA, MS
Harold A Thompsen, RA, AIA, B Arch

Adjunct Faculty

James Penuel, AS

University of Notre Dame

School of Architecture
University of Notre Dame
Notre Dame, Indiana 46556
(219) 239-6137/6138

Office of Admissions
113 Administration Building
University of Notre Dame
Notre Dame, Indiana 46556
(219) 239-7505

Application Deadline(s): Fall: Freshmen,
February 1
Transfers, April 15
Tuition & Fees: Undgrd: $11,500 per year
*($360/cr)
Grad: $8,545 per year
($473/cr)
*housing included
Endowment: Private

DEGREE PROGRAMS

Degree	Minimum Years for Degree	Accred.	Requirements for Admission	Full-Time Stdnts.	Part-Time Stdnts.	% of Applics. Accptd.	Stdnts. in 1st Year of Program	# of Degrees Conferred
B Arch	5	NAAB	Completed application, Official transcript of HS, Letter of eval. from sec. school teacher, Official report of scores on SAT and CEEB	219	2	%	58	34
M Arch	1-1/2		Undergraduate NAAB accredited, Professional Degree in Arch. or equiv., Min. of two to three years of practice pref. Letters of Recom. Portfolio of Creative Work					

SCHOOL DEMOGRAPHICS (all degree programs)

Full-Time Faculty	Part-Time Faculty	Full-Time Students	Part-Time Students	Foreign Students	Out-of-State U.S. Stdnts.	Women Students	Minority Students
10	7	219	2	2%	45	32	1%

LIBRARY (Tel. No. 219-239-6654)

Type	No. of Volumes	No. of Slides
Arch	15,500	19,000

STUDENT OPPORTUNITIES AND RESOURCES

Notre Dame is an internationally recognized coeducational university of Catholic origin and character founded in 1842; its size and nature foster collegiality, community, and a close relationship between departments. The Architecture program was begun in 1898, the first Catholic architecture program in the United States. Architecture became a Department in the College of Engineering in 1919 and in 1983 it was made the School of Architecture. The graduate degree program in architecture was established in 1984. Each program has strong ties to other departments, particularly art, art history, American studies, anthropology, and philosophy.

Both programs derive special opportunities from their locations in Rome and near Chicago. A Chicago design focus began in 1982 in the professional program's fourth year, and in 1984 in the graduate program's fall term. The professional program's junior year and the graduate program's spring term are offered in Rome; the undergraduate program began there in 1969, and graduate studies started in 1985. In 1986 the Rome Architecture Center was established in completely renovated facilities. Collectively these programs provide learning opportunities to study the architecture and urban environment in Rome and much of Western Europe and the wealth of contemporary American architecture in Chicago.

SPECIAL ACTIVITIES AND PROGRAMS

Career Discovery Program: a two-week residential summer program for high school students interested in architecture.

Rome Architecture Center: European base for the study of architecture and urbanism.

Visitors in Architecture: the distinguished lecture program initiated in 1981 numbers 50

professionals to date including three AIA Gold Medalists, 22 AIA Fellows, one Allied Arts Medalist and two Honorary members; a series with six universities is annually held in Rome; and over 40 guests serve on design reviews.

Awards: a comprehensive recognition of academic successes are formally made to over 20 students at the annual Awards Ceremony and Commencement.

Organizations: nationally honored as the 1984 Outstanding Chapter, the students of the American Institute of Architects conduct a full professional and social program each year including field trips, lecture series, Beaux Arts Ball, and Career Day.

Publications: periodically produced by the School and by students including The Notre Dame Architecture Review, Central, Journal and Rome Album.

FACILITIES

The professional and graduate degree programs in architecture are housed in a historic building on the Notre Dame campus devoted entirely to the School of Architecture and in Rome in a 17th-century palazzo located in the heart of the historic city. Both buildings contain studio, classroom, lecture, library, exhibition, and office facilities. Computer, shop and reproduction facilities are available to students and faculty on campus and are planned for inclusion in the renovation of the campus Architecture Building.

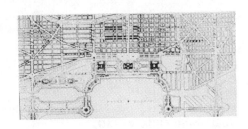

SCHOLARSHIPS/AID

All financial aid for the professional degree program in architecture is based on merit or projected merit and the need of the student as determined by the financial need analysis of the College Scholarship Service. 67% of the undergraduate students receive some type of financial assistance.

The graduate degree program in architecture is endowed through the Montedonico/Bond Fellowships, Joseph Z. Burgee and Joseph Z. Burgee, Jr., Fellowships, and funds provided by other benefactors and the University. Graduate aid is determined by the School of Architecture and almost all candidates receive some form of assistance. Substantial support is awarded to those candidates deemed outstanding.

UNDERGRADUATE PROGRAM
Philosophy Statement

The undergraduate program is focused on the development of well-rounded creative, sensitive, thinking professionals and responsible citizens and it provides a balanced professional and general studies curriculum.

The program prepares students for practice internship in architecture, allied fields, or graduate studies. Emphasis is placed on the preparation of the architect as: leader, with a capability of working with different disciplines in the environmental professions; communicator, with an understanding of the basic concerns that govern architecture; and person, with a commitment to serving society to gain a more just and humane environment.

Program Description

The first professional degree program, Bachelor of Architecture, is a 162-credit, five-year NAAB-accredited curriculum; also offered is a 164-credit engineering option and joint programs with concentrations in Art, Art History and Philosophy. The programs concentrate on fundamental professional education with courses in design, history, technology, and environmental studies, supplemented by theology, humanities, social and physical sciences, and recommended or free electives.

The programs begin with a structured freshman year of coursework and guidance common to all Notre Dame students including architectural introduction and communication courses. The second and fourth years contain the core courses in design, technology, history and environmental studies. The design sequence is central to the program starting with design process in the second year and continuing through the fifth year's thesis and advanced studios. The design concentration is enhanced by programs in Rome and in Chicago. The third year is a mandatory period of studies abroad in Rome including design, architectural, urban and visual studies courses. The fourth year builds on the Rome experience with a design program focused on Chicago as a study laboratory. The fifth year concludes the design sequence with professional practice and recommended or free electives in related disciplines.

GRADUATE PROGRAM
Philosophy Statement

The graduate program is focused on design with respect to architecture and urbanism. The city, its architecture and architects, past and present, are studied to provide a commentary on existing conditions and are used as a basis for design investigations. Emphasis is placed upon the fundamental relationship between architectural history, theory and design in all areas of investigation. History and theory are called upon to provide the basis for value judgments in design and to provide substance for design criticism. Culture and societal needs are seen in historical perspective as they influence theory and, ultimately, architectural and urban form.

Program Description

In 1984 the University of Notre Dame School of Architecture established a 30-semester-credit-hour postprofessional graduate degree, the Master of Architecture. The course of studies is intended for candidates who hold a first professional degree in architecture from an accredited program or the equivalent. Preference is given to those applicants who have a minimum of two or three years of professional practice experience and architect's registration.

The area of study is architecture and advanced architectural and urban design with directed studio work and individual thesis projects forming the core of the program. Courses in graduate elective study supplement the program's core. The studies focus on physical design, specifically the architecture and urbanism of Chicago and Rome. Field studies are conducted in Rome and other Italian cities as well as in Paris and in Chicago and its metropolitan area.

The program is typically three semesters long and it begins every fall: the first semester's twelve credits concentrate on Chicago and are taken in residence at Notre Dame, the second semester's twelve credits center on Rome and are pursued abroad, and the third semester's six credits focus on the thesis and other remaining work and are completed back on campus.

FACULTY
Administration

Robert L Amico, RA, AIA, Chairman
Linda L Messersmith, Library Specialist

Professors

Robert L Amico, RA, AIA, B Arch, M Arch
Brian J Crumlish, RA, AIA, BS, MS
Kenneth A Featherstone, RA, RIBA, Dipl Assoc, M Arch
Donald E Sporleder, RA, AIA, BS, MS

Associate Professors

Norman A Crowe, RA, B Arch, M Arch
Steven W Hurtt, RA, AB, MFA, M Arch

Assistant Professor

John W Stamper, RA, BS, MA, PhD

Part-Time Faculty

Esmee C Bellalta, RLA, ASLA, BLA, MLA
Jaime J Bellalta, CCAC, BS Arch, Cert

Adjunct Faculty

John A Bertoniere Jr, BA
Jeffrey N Blanchard, BA, MA
Edward W Jerger, BSME, MS, PhD
Kenneth R Lauer, PE, BSCE, MCE, PhD
Paul McGinn, BSMSE, MSMSE, PhD MSE
Piero Meogrossi, PhD
Leonard Morse-Fortier, BS, MSE
Richard A Piccolo, BID, MFA
Gloria L Sama, B Arch, MA Arch, M Bldg Science

Visiting Faculty

Bernard R Boylan, PE, BS
Stuart E Cohen, RA, FAIA, B Arch, M Arch
Martin R Kleinman, RA, M Arch
James F Yerges, PE, BS, MS, PhD

The Ohio State University

Department of Architecture
Ohio State University
189 Brown Hall/
190 W. 17th Avenue
Columbus, Ohio 43210
(614) 292-5567

Admissions Office
Ohio State University
3rd Floor Lincoln Tower
1800 Cannon Drive
Columbus, Ohio 43210
(614) 292-3980

Application Deadline(s): Undgrd: 1 March
(subject to change)
Grad: 1 February
Tuition & Fees: Undgrd: OH res: $630/qtr.
Non-res: $1660/qtr.
Grad: OH res: $801/qtr.
Non-res: $1998/qtr.
Endowment: Public

DEGREE PROGRAMS

Degree	Minimum Years for Degree	Accred.	Requirements for Admission	Full-Time Stdnts.	Part-Time Stdnts.	% of Applics. Accptd.	Stdnts. in 1st Year of Program	# of Degrees Conferred
BS Arch	4		Sophomore Standing Architectural prerequisites	220	60	NA	90	60
M Arch	2	NAAB	BA or BS in Arch; Portfolio; GRE or TEOFL; Transcripts; Letters	60	2	20%	25	25
M Arch	3	NAAB	BA or BS; Portfolio; GRE or TOEFL; Transcript; Letters	24	0	20%	10	6
M Arch	1		B Arch; Portfolio, GRE; Transcripts; Letters	6	0	20%	6	6

SCHOOL DEMOGRAPHICS (all degree programs)

Full-Time Faculty	Part-Time Faculty	Full-Time Students	Part-Time Students	Foreign Students	Out-of-State U.S. Stdnts.	Women Students	Minority Students
22	18	310	62	15%	27%	25%	3%

LIBRARY (Tel. No. 614-292-2852)

Type	No. of Volumes	No. of Slides
Arch	20,000	50,000
Fine Arts	80,000	230,000

STUDENT OPPORTUNITIES AND RESOURCES

As a land grant institution, The Ohio State University is committed to a full range of academic endeavors. Each year the faculty of the University offer more than 7000 courses in 202 academic career areas. Graduate programs include master's degree work in 116 disciplines and doctoral studies in 86 subjects. Programs range from traditional subjects such as philosophy and economics to more specialized areas such as Disaster Research and Medieval and Renaissance Studies.

The University library system, one of the largest in North America, has a completely computerized catalog that gives students access to 3.7 million volumes.

Ohio State is a city within a city, containing municipal-type amenities such as two golf courses and an airport. Students are offered a wide range of opportunities for extracurricular enrichment such as public lectures, musical performances, drama productions, and cinema.

Located in Columbus, Ohio, the University is within 600 miles of two-thirds of the population of the United States. Further, the city offers valuable resources such as a strong professional architectural community, the Ohio Historical Society, Battelle Memorial Institute, the Columbus Museum of Art, the Columbus Symphony Orchestra, and a readily available laboratory of historic renovations and contemporary

architecture such as German Village, the Ohio Theater, and the forthcoming Visual Arts Center.

The Department of Architecture is combined with the Departments of Landscape Architecture and City & Regional Planning to form the School of Architecture. The School is a separate entity within the College of Engineering. Within this framework, the Department of Architecture is well situated both to take advantage of the diversity of the University and to provide an enriching and nurturing environment.

In addition to the general architectural curriculum, the faculty of the Department offer specializations in Computer-Aided Architectural Design, Architectural Preservation Design, and Passive Solar Design. With some additional time in residence, second degree opportunities are available in related disciplines such as Computer & Information Sciences, Civil Engineering, Business Administration, History of Art, City & Regional Planning, and Landscape Architecture.

Both undergraduate and graduate admissions are generally for the autumn quarter only. Undergraduate transfer applications are accepted but are encouraged only from exceptionally qualified students.

SPECIAL ACTIVITIES AND PROGRAMS

Summer Academy offers introductory architecture courses to junior and senior high school students.

Lecture Series promotes a broader educational experience for students by bringing noted

architects such as Michael Graves, Frank Gehry, Cesar Pelli, Gunnar Birkerts, and Mario Botta to the University.

Distinguished Visiting Professors offer at least one graduate design studio each quarter —Peter Eisenman, Charles Gwathmey, and James Stirling and Hans Hollein were the appointments from 1986 to 1988.

Columbus Neighborhood Design Assistance Center exposes students to real working situations while helping to revitalize the city's commercial districts.

Oxford Program allows students to travel in England and study with tutors at Oxford University for a summer quarter.

Rome Program permits students to tour Italy while being centered in Rome.

Summer Jobs Program provides entry level job opportunities for students during the Summer Quarter.

Student Organizations encourage greater camaraderie and student initiative: the Department boasts strong chapters of the American Institute of Architecture Students and Alpha Rho Chi.

Chic (student prepared journal) fosters investigation and research into critical theory.

Continuing Education permits career development for non-traditional students (especially in CAAD) and a further awareness of architecture to the general public.

FACILITIES

Learning Resources Center with 24 IBM personal computers.

Computer-Aided Architectural Design Laboratory containing a dedicated IBM 4341 host computer, four microcomputers, over 20 monochromatic and color computer graphic stations, and a variety of other peripherals such as plotters, printers, and tablets.

Photography Studio with photographic and video equipment, darkroom laboratory, and shooting studio.

Environmental Simulation Laboratory containing a wind tunnel and various daylighting and acoustic simulators.

Workshop with large and small woodworking tools, paint-spray booth, and hand tools.

Print Shop with an ozalid print machine, multilith printer, and binding equipment.

The Baumer Collection of 500 historical architectural books.

The American Architecture Books and the *Fowler* microfilm collection of the significant architectural books in print between 1485 and 1900.

SCHOLARSHIPS/AID

The Department awards at least ten prize scholarships ranging from $750-$2500 each year. In addition, undergraduate and graduate students are eligible for financial aid through the University in the form of student loans, the work study program, and other grants and scholarships. Entering graduate students with outstanding records may apply (by 1 February) for University Fellowships with stipends of $785/month and tuition and fee waivers. The Department also awards fifteen to twenty graduate associateships with monthly stipends of $350 to $700 plus one-half or full tuition and fee waivers for 10 or 20 hours of work per week.

UNDERGRADUATE PROGRAM
Philosophy Statement

The undergraduate program in architecture offers a strong curriculum in architectural design, theory, and technology within the larger framework of a broad liberal arts education. Students concentrate equally on the development of knowledge and the refinement of skills. The goal is to provide an education in which a sophisticated intellectual and cultural focus on architecture is combined with a general education in the humanities and sciences. An emphasis is placed on developing an understanding of architecture's relationship to and dependence on the larger world. The role of architectural education at The Ohio State University is to prepare students for a lifelong process of intellectual exploration, reflection, and development.

Program Description

The undergraduate architectural curriculum provides a liberal arts education for the general pursuit of knowledge and the beginning of a professional education for the general practice of architecture. The freshman year is comprised primarily of general education courses and a selection of introductory and prerequisite courses for architecture. The sophomore and junior years are focused on a design studio sequence and integrated courses in architectural history/theory, graphics, structures, and construction. The senior year is devoted to selective studios, elective seminars, and general electives within the University. The studios allow the investigation of design from a broad range of methodological and program options; the seminars permit an in-depth study of specific architectural issues; and the general electives encourage the development of relationships to other disciplines.

GRADUATE PROGRAM
Philosophy Statement

The goal of graduate architectural education at The Ohio State University is to prepare students for professional practice. The emphasis is placed on design and, in particular, how it is influenced by theory and technology. A principal objective is to develop a familiarity with the structures of criticism and the strategies of critical interpretation. The faculty offer diverse perspectives but share a common expectation of rigor in the pursuit of the meaning of architectural form. The focus of instruction is the use of formal analysis to strengthen intellectual growth, to stimulate creative and analytical powers, and to foster the development of the skills necessary for significant performance within the profession.

Program Description

The graduate curriculum provides a professional education for the student who plans to pursue a career in architecture. It is divided into two components. For two quarters the basic course of instruction is in architectural design and the concurrent study of theory, building technology, and professional practice. The following four quarters offer selective studios and seminars from a series of options offered by regular and visiting faculty. In addition to the standard program, specializations are offered in computer-aided architectural design, preservation design, and passive solar design.

Three programs lead to a Master of Architecture degree: a three-year-plus program for students who have completed a four-year undergraduate program with a major in a discipline other than architecture; a two-year program for students who have completed a four-year undergraduate program with a major in architecture from an NAAB accredited program; and a one-year program for students who hold a professional Bachelor of Architecture degree from an NAAB-accredited school.

A notable feature of instruction within the Department of Architecture at The Ohio State University is the small class size and the close tutorial relationship established between faculty and students.

FACULTY
Administration

Jerrold R Voss, AICP, Director
Robert S Livesey, AIA, Chairman
Jane McMaster, Architectural Librarian

Professors

Masao Kinoshita, AIA, B Arch, M Arch
Robert S Livesey, AIA, AB Arch, M Arch
Richard A Miller, FAIA, M Arch
Michael Passe, EE, RE, BEE
Christos I Yessios, Arch Dipl, PhD
Paul E Young, Jr, AIA, B Arch, M Arch

Associate Professors

Douglas Graf, RA, AB Arch, M Arch
Kenneth S Lee, B Arch, M Arch, D Arch
Yousef Marzeki, Arch Dipl, MCP
Robert E Samuelson, AIA, B Arch, M Arch

Assistant Professors

Jacqueline Gargus, RA, BA, M Arch
J Benjamin Gianni, RA, BA, M Arch
Kay Bea Jones, M Arch
Jeffrey Kipnis, BA, MS
Bruce E Lonnman, B Arch, M Civil Eng
Geoffrey K Nishi, RA, B Arch, M Arch
Mark O'Bryan, B Arch, M Arch
John J Reagan, RA, BS Arch, M Arch
Cornelius Van Wyk, BS, M Arch, MS
Robert D Vuyosevich, RA, AB Arch, M Arch

Part-Time Faculty

Gary Alexander, BS, M Arch
Robert Bates, BS, M Arch
David Goth, M Arch
Timothy A Harvey, PE, MS Civ Eng
Judith L Kitchen, B Arch, M Arch Hist
Dean Neuenswander, M Arch
Michael Paplow, AB Art, M Arch
Thomas Schnell, AIA, B Arch, M Arch
Richard W Trott, FAIA, B Arch, MS
George Van Neil, AIA, B Arch
Robert N Wandel, AIA, B Arch

Adjunct Faculty

Tadao Ando
Perry E Borchers, Dipl Arch, B Arch, MS Arch
Gilbert H Coddington, FAIA, B Arch, MS Arch
Wayne Dipner, AIA, B Arch
Peter Eisenman, FAIA, B Arch, PhD
Hans Hollein
Daniel Libeskind, B Arch, MA
Fumihiko Maki, M Arch
James Morganstern, M Arch, M Art Hist, PhD
Richard Parent, BS, MS, PhD
Burkhard von Rabenau, Dipl, PhD

Oklahoma State University

School of Architecture
Oklahoma State University
Stillwater, Oklahoma 74078-0185
(405) 744-6043

Undergraduate - Admissions Office,
103 Whitehurst: (405) 744-6876
Graduate - Graduate College,
202 Whitehurst: (405) 744-6368

Application Deadline(s): Undgrd: none
                       Grad: February 15
Tuition & Fees: Undgrd: OK Res:
    $26-30/credit hour
    Non-res: $81-95/credit hour
    Grad: OK Res: $35/credit hour
    Non-res: $116/credit hour
Endowment: State

DEGREE PROGRAMS

Degree	Minimum Years for Degree	Accred.	Requirements for Admission	Full-Time Stdnts.	Part-Time Stdnts.	% of Applics. Accptd.	Stdnts. in 1st Year of Program	# of Degrees Conferred
B Arch	5	NAAB	Univ. Req.	212	0	90%	79*	28
B Arch Engr	5	ABET	Univ. Req.	82		90%		8
M Arch	1		B Arch, portfolio, 3 letters	6		40%		3
M Arch Engr	1		B Arch Engr, 3 letters	4		50%		3

*Includes Architecture & Arch. Engr.

SCHOOL DEMOGRAPHICS (all degree programs)

Full-Time Faculty	Part-Time Faculty	Full-Time Students	Part-Time Students	Foreign Students	Out-of-State U.S. Stdnts.	Women Students	Minority Students
18	0	304	0	21%	9%	20%	27%

LIBRARY (Tel. No. 405-624-7089)

Type	No. of Volumes	No. of Slides
Arch	10,806	4,876

STUDENT OPPORTUNITIES AND RESOURCES

The School of Architecture, founded in 1909, offers professionally-oriented undergraduate and graduate degree programs in architecture and architectural engineering/structures. The School's parallel program emphasis on architectural design and architectural engineering is unique in the sharing of faculty, course work and facilities. This sharing, under one roof, is a major strength of the School and makes it the only such integrated program in the United States.

Average enrollment is approximately 300 students. The School maintains a controlled admissions policy into the upper-division and graduate programs. The School is a part of the College of Engineering, Architecture and Technology, which facilitates access to state-of-the-art electives and graduate course work. The School also maintains affiliations with the Departments of Art, Interior Design and Landscape Architecture in order to provide students and faculty the opportunity for a rich and diverse blend of educational experiences.

The faculty, in keeping with the School's professionally-oriented program, have distinguished educational and professional experience, as well as diverse professional and public service backgrounds. The majority are licensed architects or engineers with national or international experience. Many of the faculty are active and in leadership roles in the various professional societies. The scholarly record of the faculty is equally strong: four are past Fulbright Scholars, one of the most prestigious academic awards in any field. Many have received recognition for their teaching excellence.

The School has all of its major course work within its own building, providing a single, centralized location of all major instruction. Included in the new facility are the Cunningham Resource Center containing all of the university's collection of materials on architecture and related subjects and the Architectural Computer Center equipped with a variety of equipment for the use of students in architecture and architectural engineering. Emphasis is on the use of the computer in the design process and on engineering analysis in the technical disciplines.

SPECIAL ACTIVITIES AND PROGRAMS

Ten-week annual summer study program in Europe; ten-week bi-annual summer study program in China.

Summer Option Program for transfer students; summer program for high-school students.

Student chapters of AIAS, NSAE and CSI.

Annual distinguished lecture series.

Spring "Architecture & Design Week" in conjunction with other university design-oriented programs.

National and international student architectural design competitions.

Energy-related courses available to both curricula.

Summer and graduate job assistance program.

Collaboration with practicing architects and architectural engineers state-wide and regionally as visiting jury critics and lecturers.

FACILITIES

The Architecture Building, renovated in 1975 to accommodate all of the physical requirements of the School, allows all major classroom and studio instruction to be held in a single location. All faculty offices are also located in the building. The Cunningham Resource Center provides access to all university materials on architecture and related subjects. Each student is assigned a permanent studio desk and area from the freshman year through the graduate program. This organization allows a close and important interaction between faculty and students throughout the program at all levels.

SCHOLARSHIPS/AID

Oklahoma State University makes available approximately $2.5 million in student loans, $3 million in student grants, and $500,000 in scholarships annually. Architecture students are eligible for all of these funds. The university also operates an extensive work-study employment program open to architecture students. An additional $15,000 in scholarships is restricted to students enrolled in the College of Engineering, Architecture and Technology. The School of Architecture administers several fellowships for students within the School, including the William Caudill Fellowship, R.E. Means Fellowship, and several supported grants from industry. Upper-division and graduate students are eligible for teaching and administrative assistantships, including non-resident tuition waiver grants.

UNDERGRADUATE PROGRAM
Philosophy Statement

The School of Architecture is dedicated to providing the highest quality program of higher education to students whose career goals are to enter the professional practice of architecture and architectural engineering. This educational goal allows the School to focus its resources towards the specific needs of the vast majority of its students at a level of excellence not otherwise achievable.

In preparing its students, the School understands that the professions of architecture and architectural engineering will change significantly over time. The professional degree, therefore, is not seen as an end in itself, but as the beginning of a lifelong process of professional growth which properly includes individual continuing education and professional development.

Program Description

The undergraduate programs are professional-degree granting programs, leading to either the Bachelor of Architecture or Bachelor of Architectural Engineering degree. The individual programs are each five years in length, or they may be combined for a dual-degree in six years. The two programs are accredited by NAAB and ABET respectively. The first two years of each program are virtually identical, allowing the student to become familiar with each field of study before making a final choice between programs.

The Architecture program places strong emphasis on applied conceptual design skills, with the design studio as the central focus around which are organized courses in history, theory, practice, management, technical and general education subjects. The Architectural Engineering program places strong emphasis on creative structural analysis and design skills, with a combination of design studio and technical analysis courses as the program core, supported by courses in environmental controls, advanced structural systems, mathematics, sciences, technical and general education course offerings.

All students meeting the general entrance requirements of the university are accepted into the first two-year segment of the program. Admission into the upper-division of the program is based upon academic selection criteria established by the School.

Both programs prepare graduates to function as professionals, in one case as licensed architects, in the other as licensed engineers. The architecture program develops in greater depth the student's understanding, knowledge and skills related to the subjective and aesthetic qualities of architecture. The architectural engineering program develops in greater depth the student's understanding, knowledge and skills related to the objective, technical qualities of architecture.

GRADUATE PROGRAM
Philosophy Statement

A one-year, post-professional degree program is offered leading to either the Master of Architecture or Master of Architectural Engineering degree. This program is for students who possess a five-year professional degree in the field in which advanced study is desired. Applicants who do not meet this requirement may apply for admission to the undergraduate program as a means of fulfilling the requirement prior to application for the one-year Master's program.

The School does not offer a two-year professional degree program leading to a Master of Architecture degree for students possessing four-year non-professional degrees.

Program Description

The one-year M Arch program permits students to pursue studies in greater depth or to concentrate on a more focused area than is possible during undergraduate study. The Master of Architecture program offers opportunities in three areas: 1) architectural design, 2) practice & management, 3) architectural education.

Admission to the graduate program is limited and subject to the regulations and procedures of the Graduate College and the School. A minimum 2.5 GPA for the last 60 credit hours is required, together with a portfolio of photographic examples of student work (M Arch program only) and 3 letters of recommendation. All admission materials must be received by February 15 for full consideration.

FACULTY
Administration

Virgil R Carter, FAIA, Head
Teresa A Fehlig, Architecture Librarian

Educators

Eric Angevine, BS Arch Engr, MS Engr
Louis O Bass, PE, B Arch Engr, M Arch Engr
Alan W Brunken, AIA, B Arch, M Arch
John H Bryant, AIA, B Arch, M Arch
Virgil R Carter, FAIA, B Arch, M Arch
Robert B Condia, AIA, B Arch, MS Arch & Bldg Des
William H Haire, AIA, B Arch, MS Mgmt
David A Hanser, B Arch, M Arch
Bob Heatly, B Arch, M Arch
Nigel Jones, RIBA, BA, B Arch
James F Knight, AIA, B Arch, M Arch
Steve O'Hara, PE, B Arch Studies, M Arch Eng
Arlyn A Orr, PE, B Arch Engr, M Arch Engr
Richard L Tredway, AIA, B Arch, M Arch
Jeffrey K Williams, BS Arch, M Arch
Robert Wright, B Arch, M Arch

University of Oklahoma

College of Architecture
University of Oklahoma
180 West Brooks, Room 252
Norman, Oklahoma 73019
(405) 325-2444

Office of Admissions
(405) 325-2251

Application Deadline(s): October 1 - June 1
for fall;
December 1 for
spring;
April 1 for summer
Tuition & Fees: Undgrd: OK Res:
$395/semester
Non-res: $1298/semester
Grad: OK Res: $509/semester
Non-res: $1716/semester
Endowment: Public

DEGREE PROGRAMS

Degree	Minimum Years for Degree	Accred.	Requirements for Admission	Full-Time Stdnts.	Part-Time Stdnts.	% of Applics. Accptd.	Stdnts. in 1st Year of Program	# of Degrees Conferred
M Arch (1)	1		B Arch, 3.00 gpa in last 60 hrs., port., 3 letters/rec, int.	7	4	—	8	8
M Arch (2 yr)	2	NAAB	Pre-Arch, 3.00/last 60 hrs., portfolio, 3 rec, letter of int.	8	2	—	6	1
M Arch (3+yr)	3	NAAB	Bachelor's, 3.00 gpa/last 60 hrs., Evid./creat., 3 rec., int.	7	7	—	6	3
B Arch	5	NAAB	Portfolio, 2.50 gpa	93	54	—	0	54
PreArch (BSED)	4		2.00 gpa	132	99	—	(140)	26
General (BSED)	4		2.00 gpa	4	8	—	6	8
Pre-LA (BSED)	4		2.00 gpa	16	16	—	7	3
Int. Des (BID)	4	FIDER	2.00 gpa	46	42	—	39	17
Con Sci (BSCS)	4	ACCE accred. pending	2.00 gpa	48	41	—	25	21
M Sci in CS	1		3.00 gpa last 60 hrs., letter of intent	3	1	—	1	4
MLA	2		3.00 gpa last 60 hrs., portfol., 3 rec., letter of intent	4	4	—	8	0
MRCP	2	APA-ACSP-ACIP	3.00 last 60 hrs.	13	2	—	12	10

SCHOOL DEMOGRAPHICS (all degree programs)

Full-Time Faculty	Part-Time Faculty	Full-Time Students	Part-Time Students	Foreign Students	Out-of-State U.S. Stdnts.	Women Students	Minority Students
29	18	381	280	19%	15%	25%	7%

LIBRARY (Tel. No. 405-325-5521)

Type	No. of Volumes	No. of Slides
Branch	14,000	20,000

STUDENT OPPORTUNITIES AND RESOURCES

The campus is located in Norman, twenty miles south of Oklahoma City, the state's largest city and its capital. Its location on the edge of the Oklahoma City metropolitan area helps to preserve a small college-town atmosphere and gives students the opportunity for hands-on experience for both rural and urban scale projects.

As one of five divisions of the College of Architecture, the Division of Architecture provides students with the opportunity to take course work in Construction Science, Interior Design, Landscape Architecture, and Urban Planning along with the closely allied discipline of engineering.

Architecture majors constitute 413 of the 661 students in the College. One of the strengths of the Division of Architecture is the diversity in its student body. Students come from 27 states and 30 foreign countries. The variety of backgrounds is unusual for a state university and illustrates that the Architecture Program is well-known in the United States as well as in foreign countries. Transfer students are accepted.

The Faculty is very diverse in academic and professional backgrounds. All full-time faculty members of the Division are either licensed architects or possess doctorates in a specialized area. The faculty has substantial professional office practice experience.

SPECIAL ACTIVITIES AND PROGRAMS

The College of Architecture student body is governed by the Student Board of Representatives, which helps establish school policy and sponsors "Architecture Week" each spring. Professional and honorary societies active within the college include Student Chapter of the American Institute of Architects, Student Chapter of Associated General Contractors of America, Student Chapter of American Society of Interior Designers, Alpha Rho Chi, Tau Sigma Delta, and Women in Architecture.

Architecture has an active lecture series of nationally known speakers sponsored through the University of Oklahoma Speakers Bureau. A regularly published faculty and student newsletter informs them of important activities.

A preceptorship program permits selected students to earn credit in a professional office. The London Study Abroad Program is available each spring or summer semester to selected students, accompanied by a senior professor. Each year a group of urban design students accompanied by a faculty member tours the Chicago area. Other tours are conducted to sites in Oklahoma and the Dallas/Fort Worth area.

FACILITIES

Located within the College:
Branch Architecture Library
Architecture Bookstore with textbooks and art, model, and drafting supplies
Photography lab with provisions for color and black-and-white developing, enlarging and printing
Workshop with facilities for woodworking, welding and model-making
Computer lab with 5 fully independent CAD stations, 3 main-frame graphics terminals, and 28 micro-computers, all capable of CAD.
Design/Research Center for experience in research and in experimental design for faculty and graduate students.

SCHOLARSHIPS/AID

Several scholarships and awards are provided by the professional societies, the building industry and patrons of architecture and the allied arts. Annual awards include:

American Institute of Architects/Henry Adams Medal
American Institute of Architects/Henry Adams Certificate of Merit
American Institute of Architects Foundation Scholarships
Alpha Rho Chi Medal
Tulsa Women's Architectural League Travel Scholarship
Hudgins, Thompson, and Ball, Incorporated Scholarship
Masonry Advancement Fund Scholarships
Construction Science Award
Oklahoma Garden Club Scholarship
Awards for Outstanding Performance
Acme Brick Competition Awards

Four types of financial assistance are available through the Office of Financial Aids: scholarships, grants, loans, and work-study employment.

UNDERGRADUATE PROGRAM
Philosophy Statement

The educational mission of the Architecture program is twofold:

To provide the opportunity for a broad, interdisciplinary educational experience which will enable our graduates to deal effectively with the greatly increasing complexity of our future design and planning problems.

To prepare students to successfully enter the profession of architecture with adequate skills and knowledge in order to demonstrate immediate value and long-term leadership capabilities.

To accomplish this goal, the curriculum has several major emphases:

Seek a balanced architectural response to nature, man and technology.

Explore the interaction between art and science, form and substance, aesthetics and technology.

Promote a multidisciplinary pursuit of the quality environment.

Develop an understanding of the creative process and design approach.

Encourage a commitment or value system which will support a life-long professional effort.

Program Description

The Architecture programs at the University of Oklahoma include a four-year pre-architecture degree (Bachelor of Science in Environmental Design), a five-year professional undergraduate degree (Bachelor of Architecture) and a six-year Master of Architecture degree.

Undergraduate students are admitted into the BSED degree program through the University College after completing prescribed University requirements (generally one year of college coursework). Upon completion of 75 credit hours in the pre-architecture program, each student's portfolio and academic coursework is reviewed. Students are then advised into various programs in the College, including the professional architecture programs.

In essence, the degree structure offered at the University of Oklahoma is a "4-1-1" system. The first four years of the five year B Arch program is identical to the four-year BSED degree program. The fifth year of the B Arch program is identical to the first year of the two-year M Arch program.

The BSED pre-professional program in Architecture is composed of three major curricular components: general education requirements; the Environmental Design core program; and the basic architectural design program. The five-year B Arch degree program adds to this foundation an emphasis on the practice aspects of the architecture profession.

GRADUATE PROGRAM
Philosophy Statement

A professionally accredited Master's degree program in Architecture is offered by the Division of Architecture which operates within the multidisciplinary framework and philosophy of the College of Architecture. The objectives of this program are threefold:

1. To insure mental and ethical readiness to successfully enter the professions of architectural practice or architectural education with advanced knowledge in a specialized field of interest.

2. To develop functional competency in the application of basic research methods and advanced architectural programming techniques.

3. To develop a comprehensive understanding of issues related to either Urban Design/ Preservation, Architectural Design/ Technology or some other specialized field of knowledge closely related to the practice of Architecture.

Program Description

A one-year Master of Architecture program is offered to students who have completed a 5-year professional degree program in architecture. A two-year Master's program is available for graduates of a pre-architecture baccalaureate degree at an institution accredited by the profession. A "3½" year of variable-length Master's degree is available for students with undergraduate degrees in areas other than architecture. Regardless of educational background and professional experience, all students are required to complete the same course requirements to obtain the same degree.

The sixth year of any of three M Arch programs is identical and encourages the development of a specialization in one of the two structured options: "Urban Design/Preservation" or "Architectural Design/Technology." The individualized development of other specializations is also possible in the "Architectural Studies" option. A thesis option, instead of a professional project option, is available in any of the areas of specialization. In this case, the thesis and related research take the place of the professional project studio.

FACULTY
Administration

W H Raymond Yeh, RA, FAIA, Dean
Thomas H Selland, Associate Dean; Director of Design/Research Center; Director, Regional and City Planning Division
James L Kudrna, RA, AIA, Director, Architecture Division
Robert L Jones, FAIA, Director, Urban Design Program at Tulsa
Dortha L Killian, Director, Interior Design Division
Harold W Conner, R Engr, Director, Construction Science Division
Edmund N Hilliard, ASLA, Director, Landscape Architecture Division
Ilse Davis, Library Technician

Professors

Wayland W Bowser, RA, B Arch, MS
Robert Goins, B Arch, MRCP
Arn Henderson, RA, AIA, B Arch, BS Arch Engr, MS
Murlin R Hodgell, RA, FAIA, BS Arch, MS Arch, MRP, PhD
Robert Lehr, BA, MRCP
Thomas L Sorey, RA, AIA, B Arch, M Arch
W H Raymond Yeh, RA, FAIA, BS, B Arch, M Arch

Associate Professors

William C Bauman, RA, BA, B Arch, MS
P Mack Caldwell, RA, AIA, BA, M Arch, Post-Grad Dipl
Harold W Conner, AIC, R Engr, BS, MS
Joel K Dietrich, RA, AIA, BED, M Arch
Patricia L Eidson, AIA, ASID, BS, B Arch
E Gene Emery, RA, AIA, B Arch, M Arch
Edmund N Hilliard, ASLA, BLA, MS
Bobby R Hunter, AIC, BS, MS, PhD
Robert L Jones, FAIA, B Arch, MS
Dortha L Killian, BFA, MFA
James L Kudrna, AIA, B Arch, M Arch
Richard S Marshment, AICP, BS, M Arch
Terry L Patterson, AIA, B Arch, M Arch
Jay W Randle, BA, ML Arch
Jerlene A Reynolds, ASID, BA, MCP
Thomas H Selland, B Arch, M Arch, PhD
Russell E Ushick, AICP, BA, MA, DED, JD
M Iver Wahl, AIA, B Arch, M Arch, MLA
David R Walters, RA, RIBA, BA, B Arch

Assistant Professors

Eren Erdener, RA, Dipl, MS, PhD
Anne Hoover Henderson, BA, MA, MLA
William W McManus, Jr, AIC, BS, MS
Thomas A Taylor, AICP, BA, MS
J Bruce Thomas, BS, M Arch

Part-Time Faculty

Ross Bell, RA, AIA, B Arch
Baron Bieber, BSED, M Arch
Robert E Busch, BSED
Floyd O Calvert, R Engr, BSME, MME, D Engr
Fred Erdman, R Engt, BS, MBA
Stan W Gralla, RA, AIA, B Arch
Steven Hill, BA, MLA
John Lotti, RA, AIA, B Arch
Richard Lueb, BS, B Arch
Sally A Mahaffey, BA
Maryjo Meacham, BA, M Arch
Fran Oden, ASID, BA
Linda Rice Price, BA, MRCP
J Lee Rodgers, BS, MRCP
Fred Shellabarger, RA, AIA, AB, BS Arch
Donna Thompson, ASID, BS
Diane Tucker, BS, MBA
Larry Wofford, BA, MBA, PhD

Adjunct Faculty

Arthur N Tuttle, RA, AIA, BS, MFA, MRP

Oregon School of Design

Oregon School of Design
734 NW 14th Avenue
Portland, Oregon 97209
(503) 222-3727

Application Deadline(s): March 1 for following
September; apps.
considered until fall
semester if space
available.
Tuition & Fees: Undgrd: $4270/yr
Endowment: Private

DEGREE PROGRAMS

Degree	Minimum Years for Degree	Accred.	Requirements for Admission	Full-Time Stdnts.	Part-Time Stdnts.	% of Applics. Accptd.	Stdnts. in 1st Year of Program	# of Degrees Conferred
B Arch	10 semesters		HS diploma, ref, statement, interview	70%	30%	—	15	22

SCHOOL DEMOGRAPHICS (all degree programs)

Full-Time Faculty	Part-Time Faculty	Full-Time Students	Part-Time Students	Foreign Students	Out-of-State U.S. Stdnts.	Women Students	Minority Students
1	12	70%	30%	13%	13%	38%	18%

LIBRARY (Tel. No. 503-222-3727)

Type	No. of Volumes	No. of Slides
Arch	1,750 3,000 journals	10,000

STUDENT OPPORTUNITIES AND RESOURCES

In 1981, Portland area design professionals established Oregon School of Design, the only independent institution in the Pacific Northwest to offer the Bachelor of Architecture degree. Founders of the school had three goals:

To offer an opportunity to study architecture in a unique urban setting;

To provide a comprehensive and integrated architectural curriculum; and

To provide a center for public discussion of architectural issues of importance to the city of Portland and its citizens.

The school relies on and is enriched by the continued support of the design community which founded it. Local design professionals are involved as trustees, adjunct faculty, jurors, donors and advocates, and provide employment opportunities for students and graduates.

OSD's maximum enrollment is 75 students (an average of 15 per class), thus ensuring a low student-teacher ratio and individual design instruction and criticism. Students range in age from 19-40 years. The average age is 28, and 40% are women. Many of these students have attended other post-secondary institutions, and about one-third have previous degrees in another field. From 1981-1985, OSD graduated 17 students. All have been employed by local or regional design or engineering firms or are attending graduate school.

Placement of transfer students is evaluated on a case-by-case basis by the Director of Academic Affairs. Student visas are available, also.

Students benefit from the resources of Portland's community of higher education facilities, which include Lewis and Clark College, Maryhurst College, Oregon School of Arts and Crafts, Pacific Northwest College of Art, Portland State University, Reed College, and University of Portland, as well as a number of community colleges and business and professional schools.

Excellent architectural resource collections are available at Reed College, Portland State University, the Oregon Historical Society, Pacific Northwest College of Art, and the Multnomah County Public Library.

OSD has gathered its faculty from a wide range of sources, including Europe and South America, and has employed graduates of Columbia University, Princeton University, University of Oregon, University of Virginia, Reed College, Harvard University, University of Florida, Washington State University, Yale University, University of Southern California at San Diego, University of Pennsylvania, and Willamette University. All studio and history/theory faculty are design professionals who have teaching experience in the United States or abroad. Many of these are visiting and adjunct faculty who practice in Portland's design and construction community.

SPECIAL ACTIVITIES AND PROGRAMS

In cooperation with The Architecture Foundation and the OSD Chapter of the American Institute of Architecture Students, OSD sponsors lectures at which locally, nationally, and internationally known architects and scholars are invited to speak. These lecturers have included Kenneth Frampton, Peter Eisenman, Charles Moore, Frank Gehry, Charles Gwathmey, Anthony Vidler, Kurt Forster, Moshe Safdie, Daniel Solomon, Susanna Torre, and many others.

Raphael Moneo and Leon Krier have presented Van Evera Bailey Memorial Lectures, a program OSD began in 1986 through the Oregon Community Foundation, in conjunction with the University of Oregon and under the administration of The Architecture Foundation.

A week-long charrette is held each semester to focus student and faculty research on a topic of high public interest and visibility. The 1985-87 topics were public open spaces and civic art, issues related to the proposed convention center in Portland, and a proposal for an urban public space on the new light rail line. OSD makes a public presentation of findings at the conclusion of each charrette and has published the results of the Portland Convention Center Proposal study, as well as a summary of the proposals for an urban space. Substantial representation of student work has been included in the school's latest catalog.

Thesis projects of the fifth-year students consider issues which affect the city of Portland and are presented for public review at the end of each academic year.

A series of monthly debates regarding controversial issues in architectural practice is scheduled each semester. These debates are oriented toward design professionals and address such topics as the value of architectural competitions, the autonomy of the architect in the design process, consideration of contemporary building, and the issue of style.

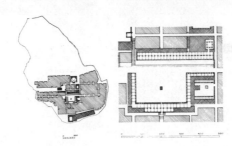

FACILITIES

Portland is an ideal laboratory for the study of architecture and urban design. Its architectural history is rich and diverse. With a metropolitan population of over one million, the area provides a variety of opportunities to observe and participate in developing solutions to urban challenges. Portland's city planning reflects a high level of public involvement and concern for historic preservation, downtown improvement, urban squares and parks, neighborhood quality, and modern mass transit. And OSD, situated in Northwest Portland within walking distance of downtown, takes advantage of these opportunities throughout its curriculum. The school's classrooms, studio space, and research library are located in a load-bearing brick warehouse with a timber post and beam support system. The building itself is one of the many beautiful converted buildings in the city's Pearl District.

SCHOLARSHIPS/AID

Please check with the school regarding federal and state financial aid programs. Third, fourth and fifth-year students may apply for loans through a private student loan program. Several scholarships are awarded to upper division students each year. Part-time employment is available with local design firms during the school year and summer months.

UNDERGRADUATE PROGRAM
Philosophy Statement

Oregon School of Design has four broad philosophical concerns which have determined the content of the curriculum.

Optimism

We uncompromisingly affirm the dignity of life. This position is based on the knowledge that buildings and cities which affirm the dignity of life have been built in the past, and on the conviction that a methodology for creating more of them can be learned and practiced, reaffirming historic principles that have been considered no longer relevant in a technological society.

Integration of Scales

There are five primary scales of architecture: material, interior space, building, landscape, and city. What affects one scale affects all the others; therefore, all scales must be examined systematically, thoroughly, and simultaneously. Such rigorous examinations lead to the creation of environments which best reflect human needs and aspirations.

Urban Advocacy

The city is one of the most profound reflections of a society's success or failure to meet the basic collective needs and aspirations of its people, and its form is the most complex expression of architecture. OSD is located in the city of Portland and is involved in research and public discussion of principles of responsible urban design and projects which affect the city's vitality.

Public Language

As a public and permanent art, architecture must use public language—that is, conventions. The use of conventions—those traditions of design and building which have stood the test of time, which people understand, and which reflect cultural values most successfully—assures permanence.

Program Description

A highly structured curriculum prepares students for professional practice by providing intense coursework in design, history/theory, technology, and visual studies. It reflects a natural and logical hierarchy of coursework which proceeds from general principles (first and second years) to specific applications (third and fourth years) and culminates in a fifth-year Thesis, which requires students to synthesize the curriculum's objectives in a major project. The core coursework of years one and two establishes fundamental principles of urban design, building design, the relationship between building and landscape, the design of interior space, and materials and construction, while third and fourth-year coursework tests the thorough application of these principles in conjunction with advanced study in technology and history/theory. Thesis work is to demonstrate a mastery of all five scales of architectural design based upon a thorough knowledge of the fundamentals of architecture as they have been manifested throughout the discipline's history.

In addition, OSD believes that the quality of architectural design depends on a solid understanding of the major areas of knowledge of our culture. Therefore, OSD requires that students have a well-balanced foundation in the liberal arts. These requirements can be met at other easily accessible colleges and universities in the Portland area or transferred from previous post-secondary course work.

FACULTY
Administration

Norman C Zimmer, FAIA, Director
David Rockwood, RA, Director of Academic Affairs

Full-Time Faculty

David Rockwood, AIA, M Arch

Part-Time Faculty

Harold Bahls, RA, M Arch
John Cava, RA, M Arch
John Czarnecki, RA, M Arch
Mary Czarnecki, M Arch
Bob Gulick, BS
Thom Hacker, M Arch
David Inkpen, BA
Don Ross, RA, B Arch
William Tripp, RA, B Arch
Leila Whittemore, BA

University of Oregon

**Department of Architecture
School of Architecture
 and Allied Arts
107 Lawrence Hall
University of Oregon
Eugene, Oregon 97403
(503) 686-3656**

Application Deadline(s): February 1
Tuition & Fees: *Undgrd: OR Res: $1487/yr.
             Non-res: $4190/yr.
             Grad: OR Res: $2318/yr.
             Non-res: $3455/yr.
*A $50.00 deposit, payable at
 registration, is required.
Endowment: Public

DEGREE PROGRAMS

Degree	Minimum Years for Degree	Accred.	Requirements for Admission	Full-Time Stdnts.	Part-Time Stdnts.	% of Applics. Accptd.	Stdnts. in 1st Year of Program	# of Degrees Conferred
B Arch	5	NAAB	Univ. Req., Personal Statement Portfolio, Standard Test Scores	408	NA	66%	99	77
M Arch (Post Prof)	1⅓		B Arch, Personal Statement Portfolio, References	5	NA	19%	4	3
M Arch (First Prof)	2-3⅓	NAAB	Personal Statement, Portfolio, References	104	NA	73%	50	22
B Int Arch	5	FIDER	Personal Statement, Portfolio, Refs.	82	NA	77%	30	22
M Int Arch (Post Prof)	1⅓		Personal Statement, Portfolio, References	0	0	—	0	0
M Int Arch (First Prof)	2-3⅓		Personal Statement, Portfolio, References	17	NA	60%	10	2
MS in Historic Preservation	2		Personal Statement, Portfolio, References	12	NA	70%	6	2
BLA	5	ASLA	Personal Statement, Portfolio, Refs.	72	NA	90%	15	30
MLA	2		Personal Statement, Portfolio, Refs.	61	NA	80%	22	6
BA/BS in PPPM(Planning)	2+2		Personal Statement, Portfolio, References	52	NA	80%	30	25
MPA (Public Affairs)	2	NASPA	Personal Statement, Portfolio, References	42	NA	60%	21	11
MURP (Urban Planning)	2	APA	Personal Statement, Portfolio, References	22	NA	75%	11	11

SCHOOL DEMOGRAPHICS (all degree programs)

Full-Time Faculty	Part-Time Faculty	Full-Time Students	Part-Time Students	Foreign Students	Out-of-State U.S. Stdnts.	Women Students	Minority Students
83 (28 Arch)	24 (11 Arch)	1440 (550 Arch)	N/A	14.4%	24.8%	47.1%	10.1%

LIBRARY (Tel. No. 503-686-3637)

Type	No. of Volumes	No. of Slides
Arch & Allied Arts	42,000	200,000

STUDENT OPPORTUNITIES AND RESOURCES

The Department of Architecture is one of six departments in the School of Architecture and Allied Arts, which includes Landscape Architecture; Planning, Public Policy and Management; Art History; Art Education; and Fine and Applied Arts. A FIDER-accredited program in interior architecture is offered by the department. Students are encouraged to take studio coursework in other environmental design disciplines and to participate in lecture and lab courses of special interest. A major strength of the department's program lies in the broad range of coursework offered in the school. The program offers both undergraduate and graduate degrees in architecture.

The faculty of the department are particularly committed to excellence in design education. Over the years exceptional strength has developed in the areas of environmental control systems, design theory, and historic preservation. A program of guest lecturers ensures outstanding visitors, and the University of Oregon Museum of Art provides excellent art exhibits.

SPECIAL ACTIVITIES AND PROGRAMS

Historic Preservation Program (at the graduate level)

Urban Spring (participants live in an urban area, engage urban design issues)

AIAS (student chapter affiliated with AIA)

Student newspaper *AVENU* (published monthly by students, has been in continuous operation for fifteen years)

The Oregon Coast Program (students live and study at the Oregon Institute of Marine Biology for one term)

Summer Studio in Rome

Foreign study opportunities (Japan, Greece, England, Denmark, West Germany)

Architecture and Allied Arts lecture series (visiting lecturers from throughout the U.S. and abroad)

Solar Energy Center (conducted jointly with the Physics Department, a major research center in the western U.S.)

Professional Practicum Program (with area architectural firms)

Terminal Studio class (two-term intensive design class for graduating students)

Field trips (Portland, Seattle, and San Francisco)

Visual Language Program (with the Department of Fine Arts)

Summer program for high school students

FACILITIES

Three microcomputer labs, each with computer graphics capabilities

Photographic labs

Woodshop

SCHOLARSHIPS/AID

Undergraduate and graduate students have access to several regularly recurring departmental scholarships, most of which are awarded on the basis of need and scholastic achievement. Awards generally cover in-state tuition costs for one to three terms. Students may also apply for a number of grants and loans on a university-wide basis.

UNDERGRADUATE PROGRAM
Philosophy Statement

The program in architecture places the design studio at the center of architectural education. Supporting courses are designed to contribute to the studio experience. There is a long tradition of noncompetitive design education at Oregon as well as the expectation that students will take responsibility for planning their own education.

Program Description

The first two years of the five-year B Arch professional degree program are structured to provide students with a coordinated introduction to architectural design. Studio courses begin in the first year and deal directly with architectural design. Study sequences beginning in the third year are sufficiently flexible to accommodate students' individual interests and needs. The architecture program's close association with programs in interior architecture, landscape architecture, planning, public policy and management, art history, and the fine arts provides a supportive environment with opportunities for collaborative work.

The curriculum is organized into four major areas: general university requirements (45 credits), architectural design (64 credits), subject or supportive courses (80 credits), and electives (42 credits). These distribution requirements total the 231 credits needed for the B Arch degree. The design area provides students with opportunities to engage in comprehensive and integrative design of the physical environment. Students work closely in studio groups of about

16, two out of three terms per year. Emphasis is on the development of design process skills and on the appropriateness of proposals as they satisfy issues of place, human activity support, construction (and structure), environmental control, and spatial ordering. Subject area courses provide basic knowledge in all of these areas as well as in media, design process (and methods), and the context of the profession. Students have a good deal of choice concerning the kinds of subject area courses that are taken, although all students must satisfy a breadth requirement.

GRADUATE PROGRAM
Philosophy Statement

The graduate program provides study opportunities both for those seeking a first professional degree and for those seeking an advanced professional degree. Students pursuing an advanced degree have the opportunity to design their own programs based on the wide-ranging interests of faculty in the department. At this level, architectural education is highly individualized, placing stress on the student's original research contributions to the field.

Program Description

There are four active programs of graduate study in architecture and interior architecture. The post-professional program leading to the Master of Architecture degree (Option I) and the corresponding program leading to the Master of Interior Architecture degree normally take from four to six terms to complete. Applicants must have a professional degree in their area of study. A final thesis project is a requirement for these programs. Thesis study should involve work with significant theoretical issues in architecture or design.

The first professional master's degree program (Options II and III) is available to students holding non-professional degrees in architecture or degrees in other fields, respectively. Option II allows students to be admitted to the first professional master's program with advanced standing. A non-professional degree in architecture is prerequisite. This option is usually completed in six terms (the minimum residency).

Option III is for students with degrees outside architecture. Students in this option complete the entire first professional master's program requirements in residence. Opportunities are available for study abroad. Students in Option III normally complete their work in ten terms. There are corresponding Options II and III in interior architecture.

The Master of Historic Preservation degree is jointly administered by the departments of Architecture and Art History. Students may apply to this six-term program from a background in any field.

In addition, there are substantive programs at the graduate level in landscape architecture; planning, public policy and management; and the history of art and architecture. Opportunities for interdisciplinary graduate work are good; several

students have received combined master's degrees.

FACULTY
Administration

Wilmot G Gilland, AIA, RA, Dean
George M Hodge, Reg Struct Eng, Associate Dean
Donald B Corner, RA, Department Head
Sheila M Klos, Head AAA Librarian

Professors

Jerry Finrow, AIA, RA, B Arch, M Arch
Wilmot Gilland, AIA, RA, MFA
Arthur Hawn, IDEC, MA
George Hodge, Reg Struct Eng, MS Arch Eng
Lyman Johnson, FIDEC, MA
William Kleinsasser, RA, MFA
Guntis Plesums, RA, B Arch, M Arch
John Reynolds, RA, B Arch, M Arch
Charles Rusch, AB, M Arch

Associate Professors

G Z Brown, RA, M Arch
Donald Corner, RA, M Arch
Gunilla Finrow, RA, Dipl Arch, M Arch
Donald Genasci, RA, B Arch, Arch Assoc Dipl Urban Des, MA
Rosaria Hodgdon, RA, Dott Arch
Gary Moye, RA, B Arch, M Arch
Donald Peting, RA, B Arch, M Arch
James Pettinari, RA, B Arch, M Arch
Hans-Joachim Schock, PhD
Michael Shellenbarger, RA, B Arch, MS
Michael Utsey, RA, B Arch, M Ev D

Assistant Professors

Elizabeth Cahn, B Arch, MS
Virginia Cartwright, M Arch
Howard Davis, M Arch
Terrance Goode, RA, M Arch
Ronald Kellett, RA, BES, M Arch
Peter Wilcox, B Arch, M Arch

Instructors

Wayne Jewett, MFA

Part-Time Faculty

John Briscoe, AIA, RA, B Arch Eng
Stanley Bryan, RA, B Arch, M Arch
Philip Dole, RA, B Arch, MS
Earl Moursund, RA, M Arch
Pasquale Piccioni, RA, B Arch
Stephen Tang, Reg Struct Engr, MS, PhD
Glenda Utsey, B Arch, MLA

Adjunct Faculty

Dan Herbert, RA, BFA, B Arch Eng
Barbara-Jo Novitski, M Arch
Otto Poticha, AIA, RA, BS
Robert Thallon, RA, BA, M Arch
Jenny Young, M Arch

The Pennsylvania State University

Department of Architecture
The Pennsylvania State University
206 Engineering Unit C
University Park, Pennsylvania 16802
(814) 865-9535

Admissions Office
The Pennsylvania State University
201 Shields Building
University Park, Pennsylvania 16802
(814) 865-5471

Application Deadline(s): November 30 for
following fall
Tuition & Fees: Undgrd: PA res: $1498/sem
Non-res: $3009/sem
Grad: PA res: $1232/sem
Non-res: $2463/sem
Endowment: Public

DEGREE PROGRAMS

Degree	Minimum Years for Degree	Accred.	Requirements for Admission	Full-Time Stdnts.	Part-Time Stdnts.	% of Applics. Accptd.	Stdnts. in 1st Year of Program	# of Degrees Conferred
B Arch	(4)+1	NAAB	SAT or ACT scores, HS diploma	28				27
BS Arch	4		SAT or ACT scores, HS diploma	207		10%	80	14
MS in Arch	1		Prof. degree, grad. adm. portfolio, transcripts, letters of reference	8				2

SCHOOL DEMOGRAPHICS (all degree programs)

Full-Time Faculty	Part-Time Faculty	Full-Time Students	Part-Time Students	Foreign Students	Out-of-State U.S. Stdnts.	Women Students	Minority Students
20	0	243		2%	32%	30%	6%

LIBRARY (Tel. No. 814-863-0511)

Type	No. of Volumes	No. of Slides
Arch	15,000	250,000

STUDENT OPPORTUNITIES AND RESOURCES

The university occupies a beautiful campus in State College, in a rural area of central Pennsylvania that is within convenient travel distance of major metropolitan centers.

Students take courses in related departments such as Art, Art History, Landscape Architecture, and Engineering. The Department has its own interactive Computer-Aided Design Laboratory available to all students. Transfer students are admitted upon portfolio and transcript review. Students also benefit from the innumerable opportunities for diverse educational, cultural, and recreational activities that a large and comprehensive state university provides. The relatively small size of the program encourages intense and informal interaction between students and a committed, energetic faculty. The studio is often the setting for such interaction. Studio facilities are available on a 24-hour basis. Each student is assigned a permanent work station in the facilities, which are centrally located on the campus.

SPECIAL ACTIVITIES AND PROGRAMS

Laboratory for Environmental Design and Planning
Computer Lab (VAX 11/750, VAX 8200, Evans and Sutherland interactive graphics system, plotter, digitizer, laser printer, and other peripherals) with 20 stations in central lab and near studio areas.
Work-study semester with practicing architects
Semester abroad in England, Italy, and Germany
Annual Visiting Lecturer Series
Field Trips
Awards programs
Summer program for interested students (non-majors)
Professional societies
Annual Beaux Arts Ball

FACILITIES

Computer lab with 20 stations in central lab and near studio areas
Photographic darkroom
Model shop
Individual work stations for every student
Departmental library

 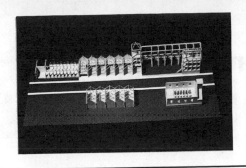 

SCHOLARSHIPS/AID

A number of loans, grants, and scholarships are available through the NDSL, GSL, and university loan programs and the SEOP, EOP, Pell (BEOG), and PHEAA grant programs. Approximately $12,000 is available in university and Senatorial scholarships. The department annually awards four half-time graduate assistantships of $2,500 per semester to candidates for the MS degree.

UNDERGRADUATE PROGRAM
Philosophy Statement

The objectives of the Department of Architecture are to provide excellence in professional, resident instruction in the field of architecture and opportunities for service and research related to the areas of theory and practice in architecture, design, and planning. The focus is on the content of design, namely the acquisition of knowledge and skills through studio education and the acquisition of professional values, perspectives, and attitudes.

Program Description

The curriculum consists of a five-year period of undergraduate studies leading to the first professional degree of Bachelor of Architecture for students holding a high school diploma. The department also offers a Bachelor of Science in Architecture (preprofessional).

The first four-year phase provides courses leading to the Bachelor of Science degree through a foundation core of design, introductory studies in architecture and environmental design, programming and implementation techniques, architectural data systems, design theories, methodologies, and research. The fifth-year phase leading to the first professional degree of Bachelor of Architecture is available to students who have satisfactorily completed the first four-year phase and have been accepted for continuance of their studies toward the professional degree.

GRADUATE PROGRAM
Philosophy Statement

The MS post-professional degree places upon self-directed candidates the responsibility to establish their own priorities in terms of a course of studies leading toward recognized strengths and/or areas of specialization in the profession. The program intends to enhance the students' qualifications as professional architects, teachers, consultants, or researchers.

Program Description

The post-professional degree, Master of Science, is an academic degree available to students holding a professional degree in architecture. The program for the Master of Science degree is strongly oriented toward individualized studies and specialized research.

Areas of possible emphasis include architectural design, programming, computer applications to architecture, and technology and the program encourages students to take full advantage of the university-wide resources. An interdisciplinary PhD administered through the Graduate School is available to qualified students.

FACULTY
Administration

Arthur K Anderson, Jr, Acting Head of Department

Professors

Sidney Cohn, B Arch, MUP, PhD
Gideon Golany, BA, Dipl CP, MSc, MA, PhD
Louis Inserra, B Arch, M Arch

Associate Professors

Arthur Anderson, B Arch, MFA Arch
Pier Bandini, MS Arch, Dr Arch
Don Leon, B Arch, MS Arch
John Lucas, B Arch, M Arch
Dennis Playdon, B Arch, M Arch
Wladyslaw Strumillo, B Arch, M Arch, PhD
Wesley Wei, B Arch, M Arch
Lawrence Wolfe, B Arch

Assistant Professors

Richard Alden, B Arch, M Arch
Andrzej Bulanda, B Arch, M Arch, MCE
Karen Dominguez, BA, M Arch
Denson Groenendaal
Jawaid Haider, B Arch, PhD
Loukas Kalisperis, BS
Donald Kunze, B Arch
Howard Ray Lawrence, B Arch
Katsuhiko Muramoto, B Arch, M Arch
Alan Popovich, BS-B Arch, MS

Instructors

Daniel Willis, B Arch

Adjunct Faculty

Roland Fleischer, BA, MA, PhD
Moses Ling, BAE, MS
M Kevin Parfitt, BAE, MS
Elizabeth Smith, MA, PhD
Luis Summers, B Arch, MS, PhD
Elizabeth Walters, BA, MA, PhD
Barbara Wollesen-Wisch, AB, MA, PhD
Craig Zabel, BA, AM, PhD

University of Pennsylvania

Department of Architecture
Graduate School of Fine Arts
110 Meyerson Hall
University of Pennsylvania
Philadelphia, Pennsylvania 19104
(215) 898-5728/9

Admissions Office
(215) 898-6520

Application Deadline(s): January 15
Tuition & Fees: Undgrd: N/A
Grad: $11,936 Tuition/yr
$744 General Fee
Endowment: Private

DEGREE PROGRAMS

Degree	Minimum Years for Degree	Accred.	Requirements for Admission*	Full-Time Stdnts.	Part-Time Stdnts.	% of Applics. Accptd.	Stdnts. in 1st Year of Program	# of Degrees Conferred
M Arch I	3	NAAB	drawing, design, physics, history, baac (any field)	117	2	43%	44	37
M Arch I	2	NAAB	BA or BS, BSed (grad. of 4 yr. pre-professional prog)	38		36%	18	18
M Arch	1		B Arch	17		39%	17	17
M Arch/MLA	3½			3			1	1
M Arch/MCP	2		BA or BS, Req'd Courses	21	2		12	7
MCP	2		incl. above					
MLA	2/3		B Arch, BLA, BA or BS, Req'd Courses	85	5		43	28
MRP	2		B Arch, BLA, BA or BS, Req'd Courses	6			3	3
MS Arch	1	n/a	BS Arch, B Arch or M Arch	2			2	6
PhD	3	n/a	B Arch or M Arch	7	7**		6	4

*Applicants to all programs must present portfolios, GRE results, letters.

**38 on dissertation.

SCHOOL DEMOGRAPHICS (all degree programs)*

Full-Time Faculty	Part-Time Faculty	Full-Time Students	Part-Time Students	Foreign Students	Out-of-State U.S. Stdnts.	Women Students	Minority Students
10	25	194	9	15%	8%	35%	4%

*Figures for Architecture Masters Programs only

LIBRARY (Tel. No. 215-898-8325)

Type	No. of Volumes	No. of Slides
Fine Arts	60,000	275,000+ 60,000 photograph

STUDENT OPPORTUNITIES AND RESOURCES

Because we maintain a relatively small-sized student body and the student-faculty ratio for studio is usually 12:1 or lower, students are able to benefit from individual attention. The acceptance ratio is good, and the students are of a high calibre academically. The Graduate School of Fine Arts includes, besides the Department of Architecture, the departments of Fine Arts (painting and sculpture), Landscape Architecture, Regional Planning, and programs in Urban Design and Historic Preservation. Interdepartmental collaboration is encouraged, providing students opportunities for interdisciplinary study and work; joint degrees and certificates are possible. The student lecture series features prominent professionals in all of these disciplines. The larger University setting offers numerous resources. Founded by Benjamin Franklin in 1740, it is a private institution that has been a pioneer in the development of many professional fields of higher education, culminating in such recognized centers as the Wharton School and the Hospital of the University of Pennsylvania. The School contributes to decisions regarding architectural development of the campus, as well as joining with it in leading the way in urban renewal of surrounding areas. Philadelphia, founded and planned by William Penn in the 17th century, has undergone a remarkable renewal and revitalization. It is a world leader in urban planning. Its renowned orchestra, its Museum of Art and its historical heritage are just a few of the city's cultural offerings. Internationally-known architects enjoy coming to this mid-way point between New York and Washington, allowing for a diverse and prestigious group of visiting critics. The regular faculty are predominantly practicing architects who combine a good theoretical basis with the realities of building.

SPECIAL ACTIVITIES AND PROGRAMS

Architectural Rare Book Room: approximately 1,400 books

Archives of Paul Phillipe Cret, Friedrich Weinbrenner, Louis I. Kahn, and G. Robert Le Ricolais

VIA: architectural journal, edited by students

Bi-Annual Newsletter

Student Annual Review of Work

Travelling exhibitions and annual shows of student/faculty work

Student Lecture Series (chosen and invited by students)

Studios and Courses Abroad: these have included Ahmedabad, Bogota, Venice, Rome, Paris

European Travelling Fellowships (15 at $1500 each annually)

Summer Preparatory Program for candidates for the Graduate Program in Architecture who have not completed the necessary prerequisites or are required to have additional design experience

Computer Studies related to design

Elective Week: mid-term menu of mini-courses

Design Week: a week's charrette with one of five guest architects chosen for their philosophical diversity

Certificates offered in Urban Design, Landscape Architecture and Historic Preservation

FACILITIES

Large studios, a computer center, a structures lab, the galleries of the Institute of Contemporary Art are all available within Meyerson Hall, the building of Graduate School of Fine Arts. Meyerson is, itself, located in the heart of one of the finest urban campuses in the country. The University's well-known museum is close at hand, and the extensive Library of the GSFA is housed in the original 19th-century Landmark Building designed by Frank Furness and currently under elaborate renovation by the neighboring firm of Venturi, Rauch, Scott-Brown.

SCHOLARSHIPS/AID

Of the 172 students in architecture, approximately 100 apply for financial aid by submitting the Graduate and Professional School Financial Aid Service (GAPSFAS) form. After taking federally insured loans (GSL, Supplemental Loan, Perkins National Direct Student Loan), students demonstrating financial need are considered eligible for $264,000 in university scholarships and departmental endowed scholarships and for possible graduate work-study funds. Several other loan programs, not federally insured, are available. A further $20,000 in stipends and $50,000 in tuition remission is available for students granted teaching assistantships.

Each year, approximately $22,500 (endowed) is awarded for traveling fellowships to Europe based on open design competitions.

Financial Aid awards from the Department are need-based. A typical financial aid package is a combination of loans ($5,000-$12,000), scholarship ($1,000-$3,500) and work-study ($1,000-$1,600) or part-time employment for those showing substantial need. Awards are contingent upon federal funding. Teaching Assistantships are awarded in the $2,000-$4,000 range.

GRADUATE PROGRAM
Philosophy Statement

The long-established humanistic tradition of the school continues. The search for appropriate architectural form is the underlying philosophy of the architectural program. It thus emphasizes the importance of social, cultural and physical contexts (both natural and built). In addition, the department gives value to architectural principles and experience, techniques of representation, current technology and economics. The integration of such data requires a strong theoretical framework and a well-developed architectural vocabulary. These are ensured by a mandatory core program - theory, technology, studio - offered in the first three semesters of the M Arch program. Studio problems tend to embody contemporary reality and are generic in nature. The architectural process is broadened and enriched by interdepartmental collaboration.

Program Description

The Master of Architecture degree may be earned in one to four years, depending on professional experience and academic background. College graduates who have not had basic design or any of the other prerequisite courses for admission to the three-year graduate program must enroll in a preliminary year in the school. The program for such students is four years. Graduates with a baccalaureate in any field who fully satisfy the prerequisites for admission, but who have had no professional education, may complete the program in three years. Students who have had advanced academic work in architecture (eg., a BS Arch degree) can normally complete the program in two or two and a half years. The one-year program is open only to holders of a Bachelor of Architecture degree and is three semesters (fall, spring, and summer) in length.

FACULTY
Administration

Lee G Copeland, FAIA, Dean, Graduate School of Fine Arts
Alan Levy, FAIA, Chairman, Department of Architecture
Joseph Rykwert, Chairman, PhD, Architecture
David G DeLong, Chairman, Graduate Program in Historic Preservation
Alan Morrison, Head Librarian, Furness Library

Professors

Lee G Copeland, FAIA, M Arch, MCP
Peter McCleary, M Arch
Joseph Rykwert, AA
Adele Naude Santos, M Arch, MCP, MUD

Associate Professors

David DeLong, M Arch, PhD
Marco Frascari, M Arch, PhD
Richard Wesley, B Arch, M Arch

Assistant Professors

Homa Fardjadi, M Arch
David Leatherbarrow, B Arch, PhD
Donald Prowler, AB, M Arch

Part-Time Faculty

Mark Aseltine, M Arch
Madge Bemiss, BA, M Arch
John Blatteau, M Arch
Bill Braham, BSE, M Arch
Adriano Cornoldi, M Arch
Weld Coxe
Richard Farley, M Arch, M Eng
Nicholas Gianopulos, BS Arch Eng
Robert Gutman, BA, PhD
Denis Hector, B Arch
Stephen Izenour, B Arch, MED
James Kruhly, B Arch, M Arch
Kinya Maruyama, MS
Chris Matheu, M Arch
Walter Moleski, B Arch, MS
Rocco Pace, BSME
Robert Quigley, B Arch
Miles Ritter, M Arch
Susan Snyder, M Arch
Herman Vinokur, BSME

Adjunct Faculty

John Bower, FAIA, B Arch
Gilbert Cass, M Arch, MUD
Lindsay Falck, B Arch, M Urb & Reg Plan
Jose Forjaz, MS Arch
Craig Hodgetts, M Arch
Yves Lepere, B Arch
Alan Levy, FAIA, B Arch
Mohsen Mostafavi, Dipl
David Polk, B Arch
George Qualls, FAIA, M Arch
Jack Thrower, M Arch
Ann Tyng, FAIA, PhD
Terry Vaughan, M Arch

Prairie View A&M University

Department of Architecture
Prairie View A&M University
PO Box 2072
Prairie View, Texas 77446
(409) 857-2014

Application Deadline(s): Fall term - Apr 1
Spring term - Nov 1
Tuition & Fees: Undgrd: TX Res: $240 + fees/yr;
Non-res: $1800 + fees/yr
Endowment: State

DEGREE PROGRAMS

Degree	Minimum Years for Degree	Accred.	Requirements for Admission	Full-Time Stdnts.	Part-Time Stdnts.	% of Applics. Accptd.	Stdnts. in 1st Year of Program	# of Degrees Conferred
B Arch	5		University Requirements	144	0	%	42	25

SCHOOL DEMOGRAPHICS (all degree programs)

Full-Time Faculty	Part-Time Faculty	Full-Time Students	Part-Time Students	Foreign Students	Out-of-State U.S. Stdnts.	Women Students	Minority Students
5	0	144	0	13%	15%	8%	87%

LIBRARY (Tel. No. 409-857-2012)

Type	No. of Volumes	No. of Slides
University	5,400 (Arch)	9,500 (Arch)

STUDENT OPPORTUNITIES AND RESOURCES

The Department of Architecture enjoys its location in the College of Engineering which makes possible very fruitful associations with engineers. This location also makes available to the architecture students several key technical electives in the engineering disciplines.

The location of the university only 50 miles away from downtown Houston permits the observation, by the faculty and students, of several important buildings by locally and nationally acclaimed architects such as: Johnson and Burgee (Transco Tower, Penzoil Place, Republic Bank, University of Houston College of Architecture Owings Building); Skidmore, and Merrill (One Shell Plaza, Allied Bank); Cesar Pelli (Rice University-Herring Hall); I.M. Pei (Texas Tower); James Stirling (Rice University School of Architecture); and Taft Architects (Y.W.C.A. Downtown Branch).

The student body size is small, ranging from 150 to 170 persons in recent years, yet it has a rich mixture of persons from Africa, Asia, the Caribbean, Illinois, Kansas, Missouri, California, Nevada, Pennsylvania, Virginia, Maryland, Georgia, Oklahoma, and Louisiana, as well as Texas.

The Learning Resource Center of the University Library has available several 16mm architectural films including the "Pride of Place" Series and from the series produced by the Fogg Museum: "Chicago's Modern Architecture," "The Architecture of Isfahan," and "Pioneers of Modern Architecture."

There is a young, energetic, and concerned faculty with varied and diverse training from Texas A&M University, Rice University, University of Houston, M.I.T., and Kansas State. Faculty specialities include: Building Design, City Planning, Urban Design, Computer-Aided Design, and Energy Conservation.

SPECIAL ACTIVITIES AND PROGRAMS

Visiting critics and lecture series with distinguished speakers and informal discussions

Student Organizations: AIAS, Architectural Honors Club

Extensive activities in community service in Architectural and Urban Design

Outstanding Computer-Aided Design Laboratory (Hewlett-Packard A900 w/Holguin ADC400 Software)

Undergraduate research opportunities in Urban Design, and Alternative Energy Design

Internship or Cooperative Education Program

Yearly field trips to one or more major cities

Annual All-College Student/Faculty Picnic and Honors Awards Banquet

Student Design Competition

Special summer program for high school students and high school graduates

Career counseling and placement services

FACILITIES

The Department of Architecture is located in the
Engineering Center which has two buildings
joined at the entrance lobby. The architecture
facilities occupy approximately 14,000 square
feet of floor area, which includes:

Design Studios, Seminar and Jury Room

Slide Library, Reference Room and Blue Print Room

Computer-Aided Design Lab (HP-A-900 Main
Frame)

Photography Lab, Model Shop and Materials Lab

Computational Lab (HP 3000 Main Frame)

Display Room

Faculty and Administration Offices

SCHOLARSHIPS/AID

A full range of scholarships, grants, loans, and
employment opportunities are offered through
the University Financial Aid Office.

Scholarships are from a variety of sources
including: University, Honors Program, College,
Foundations, and Corporations. An average of
85% to 90% of all students in architecture
receive some form of assistance.

UNDERGRADUATE PROGRAM
Philosophy Statement

The Department of Architecture strives to provide
for the dual pursuit of general and professional
education. The fostering of professional ethics,
standards, and practices, and the development of
analytical and conceptual skills in problem
solving, as well as the further development of the
powers of perception and creative faculties, are
also departmental goals.

The professionally oriented program provides
a positive framework to effectively integrate
humanistic issues with the strong technological
coursework.

There are opportunities for students to
become involved with Energy Design Research
or to pursue special interest by taking
architectural electives in the areas of Planning,
History, and Structural Design.

Program Description

The curriculum is a five-year professional
program leading to the Bachelor of Architecture
Degree. The first two years of the curriculum
provide the students with general education and
preparatory courses for the upper professional
division of the program.

In the upper division the primary objective is to
provide professional-level training in Architectural
Design, Environmental Design, Drawing
Techniques, Methodologies, Structural Design,
Computer-Aided Design, Programming, History,
Planning, and Research. Students are introduced
to the broad concepts and theories of
architecture, environmental controls, building
construction, urban planning, and computer-aided
design. The program is designed to provide
professional training of the highest quality which
will enable the graduate to practice architecture
with a high level of competence within the
broadest spectrum of responsibility to the client
and society.

FACULTY
Administration

Marshall V Brown, Department Chairman

Associate Professors

C K Andoh, B Arch, MP
M V Brown, PE, BS, M Arch
H S Yang, BA, M Arch, PhD

Assistant Professors

D B Kerl, AIA, BA
B S McMillan, B Arch, M Arch
S R Wiltz, AIA, BA, M Arch

Pratt Institute

School of Architecture
Pratt Institute
200 Willoughby Avenue
Brooklyn, New York 11205
(718) 636-3402/3403/3404/3405

Admissions Office
(718) 636-3669/3670

Application Deadline(s): March 1 FALL
November 15
SPRING
Tuition & Fees: Undgrd: $265 per credit
$4075/12-18 credits
Grad: $300 per credit
$4200/14 credits
Endowment: Private

DEGREE PROGRAMS

Degree	Minimum Years for Degree	Accred.	Requirements for Admission	Full-Time Stdnts.	Part-Time Stdnts.	% of Applics. Accptd.	Stdnts. in 1st Year of Program	# of Degrees Conferred
B Arch	5	NAAB	Academic Transcripts; Portfolio SAT's Recommendation	520	51	50%	152	120
BS Const Mgmt	4		Academic Transcripts; Recommendation	25	44	66%	16	5
BPS Const Mgmt	4		Academic Transcripts; Recommendation	25	44	66%	16	5
B Arch/MSUD	6		Prior acceptance to B Arch	5	0	NA	NA	NA
B Arch/MSCRP	6½		Prior acceptance to B Arch	5	0	NA	NA	NA
M Arch	1½		B Arch; Portfolio; 3 Recommendations	18	12	45%	17	17
MSCRP	2	PAB	BA/BS; Writing sample; 3 Recommendations	18	39	75%	13	10
MSUD	1½		B Arch or equivalent; Portfolio; 3 Recommendations	14	7	75%	10	6
MS Urban Env Syst Mgmt	1½		BA/BS; 3 Recommendations; Writing sample and/or Portfolio	1	1	NA	2	

NA = Not available.

SCHOOL DEMOGRAPHICS (all degree programs)

Full-Time Faculty	Part-Time Faculty	Full-Time Students	Part-Time Students	Foreign Students	Out-of-State U.S. Stdnts.	Women Students	Minority Students
16	84	601	177	13%	NA	33%	25%

LIBRARY (Tel. No. Arch: 718-636-3412
Institute: 718-636-3684)

Type	No. of Volumes	No. of Slides
Arch Resource Ctr	2,000	5,000
Inst Library	31,500	18,000

STUDENT OPPORTUNITIES AND RESOURCES

Set within the context of metropolitan New York, architectural education at Pratt is enriched by the interplay of the social, cultural, economic, and political forces that shape the city and dictate the requirements of responsible architectural practice.

The school's greatest resource remains its faculty, composed primarily of actively practicing New York architects and distinguished foreign visitors. The student-faculty ratio is 8:1. Students have the opportunity to experience highly diverse teaching styles, design orientations, areas of specialization, and research interests. The pleasant environment of a small urban school with active campus life is enhanced by the opportunity of associating with students in diverse professional programs such as fine arts, design, fashion, information and computer science, and engineering.

Pratt Center for Community and Environmental Development, the oldest, largest, and most successful community advocacy service in the country, offers technical assistance to neighborhood revitalization groups, and serves as a valuable resource for applied practice for architecture and planning students.

SPECIAL ACTIVITIES AND PROGRAMS

Semester-long foreign programs for credit: Rome, Copenhagen.

Pratt Journal of Architecture, a student publication providing a forum for the discussion of substantive issues. It is distributed internationally and has been critically acclaimed.

Exhibitions which are shown both in the School and at other institutions.

Several international travel/study field trips.

Extensive lecture series featuring the dominant national and international figures in architecture today.

Summer and winter intensive courses enable students to accelerate their academic progress.

Summer program for high school students.

The Cooperative Work/Study (Co-op) program provides on-the-job professional experience in engineering. In Co-op, students can earn money to help pay for their education.

An excellent Placement Office provides opportunities for on campus interviews as well as assistance in every phase of professional placement. There is no limit to the number of interviews for which a student may register. The office has a record of over 90% placement. Summer jobs are also coordinated by the placement office.

FACILITIES

Pratt is located on a 25-acre, tree-lined campus, in a pleasant, landmarked brownstone section of Brooklyn. Parking facilities are ample and the campus is easily reached by subway, bus or car.

Pratt provides on-campus housing for all students who request it. Accommodations are modern and offer a variety of choices.

The library offers on-line access to many data sources as well as an extensive collection of books and periodicals and an inter-library exchange program.

Computer facilities and supporting software are extensive and state of the art. Clusters of computer terminals are located in the dorms, and several other convenient sites on campus. Easy access to computers means that students are not required to purchase their own computer.

SCHOLARSHIPS/AID

In 1984-85, 6890 undergraduate architecture students received grants, loans, and/or on-campus jobs. A total of $2,111,729 in aid was awarded to 408 students. Thirty-seven students received restricted scholarships amounting to $36,000. Pratt participates in all state and federal financial aid programs as well as offering institute programs. The Pratt Architecture/ National Talent Search offers $460,000 in scholarships. National Talent Search is open to all students in public and private high schools who are U.S. citizens or permanent residents. Scholarship Awards are: Four $40,000 five-year full tuition awards; ten $15,000 five-year, $3,000/yr. awards; fifteen $10,000 five-year, $2,000/yr. awards.

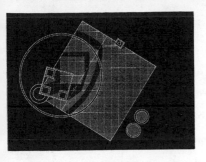

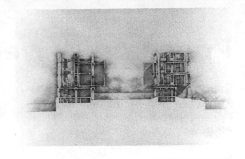

UNDERGRADUATE PROGRAM
Philosophy Statement
Within the context of a heavily design-oriented program, students are encouraged to pursue their own interests by choosing from a wide range of technical and theoretical electives offered by a highly diverse faculty. The Bachelor of Architecture degree, requiring 175 credits, is organized into three main categories: a core of 97 credits of required architectural courses, 44 credits of liberal arts, and 34 credits of free electives. The core of 97 credits is concentrated primarily in the first three years and is structured to give a basic professional preparation in architectural design, construction technology, graphic communications, and the humanistic aspects of design. The elective area is composed of 17 credits of professional electives offered by the School of Architecture's undergraduate and graduate programs and 17 credits that may be selected from the offerings of any school in the Institute. Elective options are generally exercised during the later years, allowing students to develop their own architectural education in accord with their particular needs and goals.

The Construction Management program offers a balance of technology and business management with less emphasis on architectural design and engineering science. It is a four-year full-time or eight-year part-time evening program. This permits students to hold jobs while seeking the degree. All faculty are directly involved in the construction process.

GRADUATE PROGRAM
Philosophy Statement
The Graduate Program in Architecture is organized to respond to the diverse backgrounds and needs of the students and to prepare them to meet the continually advancing standards of performance in design. Pratt's internationally renowned faculty represent a broad range of academic and professional approaches to architecture as it relates to varying socioeconomic and technological contexts in different world regions.

Program Description
The 36-credit program in Graduate Architecture is based on a strong developmental design stage with emphasis upon context and methodology of building. Worldwide urban development and renewal problems are studied both in principle and in connection with building design.

The Graduate Urban Design Program focuses on the urban development process and includes courses that deal with the historical, social, and economic implications of planning and architectural activities. A total of 41 credits is required for the MS in Urban Design. Students with undergraduate degrees in architecture or related design disciplines such as environmental design, interior design, geography or urban studies are eligible on the basis of undergraduate grades, portfolio, and an interview. Many students with undergraduate degrees or work experience are eligible for advanced standing.

The Graduate Program in City and Regional Planning offers a professionally oriented interdisciplinary course of study that emphasizes the pragmatic application of planning theory and expertise. Students in the 63-credit program may specialize in comprehensive physical planning, historic preservation, public policy analysis, economic development, real estate development, or community planning; enter joint programs in law and planning (with Brooklyn Law School) or business administration and planning (with Pace University); or design a curriculum to suit their particular needs.

Courses are offered on an evening and daytime schedule to allow individualized full-time and part-time programs.

FACULTY
Administration
Paul Heyer, RA, AIA/RIBA, Dean
Sidney Shelov, RA, AIA, NCARB, Associate Dean

Donald Cromley, RA, Chairperson, Undergraduate Architecture
Lyman Piersma, Administrator of Student Affairs
Peter Mannello, RA, NCARB, Chairperson, Construction Management
Theo David, RA, AIA, CAA, Chairperson, Graduate Architecture
Stuart Pertz, RA, AIA, AICP, Chairperson, Urban Design
Frank DeGiovanni, APA, Acting Chairperson, City & Regional Planning
Roberta Greenberg, MLS, Coordinator, Architecture Resource Center

Professors
Theoharis David, RA, NCARB, B Arch, M Arch
Gamal El-Zoghby, B Arch, M Arch
Warren Gran, RA, NCARB, B Arch, MS Design
William Katavolos, BID
Haresh Lalvani, B Arch, MS Trop Arch, PhD
John Lobell, BA, M Arch, M Arch, Theory
Mimi Lobell, RA, BA, M Arch
Albert Lorenz, B Arch, MS Media
Stanley Salzman, RA, NCARB, B Arch, M Arch
Ronald Shiffman, AICP, BA Arch, MS City Plan
Michael Trencher, RA, BA Eng, B Arch, M Arch
Hanford Yang, RA, NCARB, BA, B Arch, M Arch
Ayse Yonder, B Arch, MCP

Associate Professors
Frank DeGiovanni, BA, MRP, PhD
Constantine Karalis, RA, NCARB, BS, M Arch, MSCP

Part-Time Faculty
Professors
Raimund Abraham, Dipl Eng
Barbara Carr, BFA
Sam DeSanto, RA, NCARB, B Arch, M Arch
Vittorio Giorgini, Doctorate in Arch
Michael Louis Goodman, NCARB, B Arch
John Johansen, RA, NCARB, BS, B Arch, M Arch, PhD
Y S Lee, BS CE, MS, MCE
Felix Martorano, B Arch, MS Design
Larry Mersel, RA, B Arch
Nancy Miao, RA, NCARB, BA, MS, M Arch
Barbara Neski, RA, BA
Stuart Pertz, RA, AIA, AICP
Sidney Shelov, RA, AIA, NCARB, BFA
William Shopsin, RA, NCARB, BA
Charles Thornton, BCE, MCE, PhD

Associate Professors
Robert Alpern, N/A
Bill Bedford, RA, B Arch, M Arch, MCP UD
Christine Bevington, RA, B Arch
Alton Burton, BSCE, MCE
Carol Clark, BA, MS
Donald Cromley, B Arch, M Arch
Daniel Cuoco, BCE, MSCE, MBA
Ronald DiDonno, B Arch
Livio Dimitriu, BA
Juan Downey, B Arch
Frank Fish, MSCRP
Stephen Friedman, BA, MA, PhD
James R Gainfort, BA, B Arch
Alex Goldfine, RA, BS Arch, M Arch
Michael Hollander, RA, BA, M Arch
Ernest Hutton
Tian-Fang Jing, BSCE
Floyd Lapp, BA, MPA UP
Joseph Larocca, PE, BCE CM
Jim Maeda, RA, BS, MS
Robert Mayers, RA, B Arch, M Arch
Susan Motley, BA
Brent Porter, RA, BS Arch, MS Arch & Urban Design
Theodore Prudon, MS
Harvey Schultz
Bert Sherman, Cert of Des, BCE
John Shuttleworth, BFA, MFA, BS Arch, BA Arch
Norbert Turkel, AIA, RA, Arch Eng
Joan Wallick, B Arch, MCP
Michael Webb, Poly Dipl
Joel Weinstein, B Arch Eng
Sarelle Weisberg, RA, BA, M Arch
Arthur Zabarkes, MS

Assistant Professors
Richard Anderson, BA, MCRP, City & RP
Louis Aponte-Pares, B Arch, MS

Edward Benevengo, BS, M Arch
Gail Benjamin, AB
William Bobenhausen, RA, AIA, BA
Francoise Bollack, M Arch
Lynne Breslin, AB, M Arch
Dan Bucsescu, RA, B Arch, MSC
George Cakiades, BS (CE), MS (CE)
Eduardo Castro, BSCE, MSCE
Keith Clarke, MS
Christopher Compton, RA, B Arch
Rex Curry, BA, MCRP, City & RP
Arthur Edwards, BA, M Arch
Helen Englehardt, BA, MES
Peter Federman, NCARB, BA, M Arch
Giuliano Fiorenzoli, Dipl FA, M Arch, M Arch & US
Dennis Gallagher, BA, JD
Deborah Gans, RA, BA, M Arch
Raymond Gordon, B Arch, MSRP
Margaret Guarino, BFA, MS CRP
Ken Halpern, B Arch, M Arch
Ira Hirschman, BA, MCRP
Howard Horii, RA, B Arch Design, Cert of Arch
James Howie, B Arch
Igal, B Arch, M Arch
Georges Jacquemart, B Arch
Jan Kalas, RA, NCARB, B Arch
Sergei Kanevsky, B ME, M ME, PE
Nicholas Koutsomitis, BA
Stephen Lamb, BS, Con Mgmt
Thomas Leeser, B Arch, M Arch
Yevsey Lenchner, MSME
M Emanuel Levy, RA, AIA, B Arch, M Arch
Christian Lischewski, DPL ING, M Arch AS
Kathleen Madden, BA, BFA
Walter Mahony, BA, B Arch, MFA
Paul Mankiewicz, BA, MA, M Ph
Peter Mannello, RA, B Arch
Frank Manzo, BS
Katherine Mathews, BFA, MLA
John McNanie
Norman Mintz, BA, MS
John Nambu, BA, MA, B Arch
Signe Nielsen, ASLA, BA, BS
Taeg Nishimoto, B Arch, M Arch, RA
Pascal Ouintard-Hofstein, RA, DPLG
Robert Pelosi, BA
Hani Rashid, BA, M Arch
Lester Rivelis, BS, JD
David L Rodriguez, BS
Jeff Rotenberg, MSME
Michael Rubenstein, B Arch, MCP/M Arch, RA, AIA
John Schuyler
Robert Schwartz, B Arch
John Shapiro, MS, BA
Ted Sherman, RA, BA, B Arch
Mark Shoemaker, BS, M Arch
Harry Simmons, RA, NCARB, B Arch, M Arch
William Valletto, BS, JD, MSUP
Gerard Wall, B Arch, MSUP

Instructors
Dennis Bator, RA, B Arch
Madeline Burke-Vigeland, BA, B Arch
Norman Cox, RA
Michael Dexter, BSME, MSME, PE
Keller Easterling, BA, M Arch
Lambert Egbuchulam, BE (ME), ME (ME)
Edward Eliason, RA, NCARB, AIA
Jack Esterson, B Arch
Michael Flynn, BFA
Roland Goodman, BA
Michael Greenberg, BCE, MSCE
Christopher Guerra, B Arch
Tobias Guggenheimer, BA, M Arch
Cindy Harden, BS, M Arch, RA
Ann Koll, B Arch, MA
Benjamin Kracauer, BA, M Arch
Leonard Lizak, M Arch
Christian Mathieu-Zatrec
Anne Raleigh Perkins, BA, B Arch
Richard Pollack, B Arch, M Arch
Susan Reynolds, BA, MSUP
Paul Sionas, BS, B Arch
Orestes Valella, B Arch

Princeton University

School of Architecture
Princeton University
Princeton, New Jersey 08544
(609) 452-3741

Graduate Admissions
Princeton University
307 Nassau Hall
Princeton, New Jersey 08544
(609) 452-3034

Application Deadline(s): January 7: Grad
January 15: Undgrd
Tuition & Fees: Undgrd: $12,550/yr.
Grad: $12,650/yr.
Endowment: Private

DEGREE PROGRAMS

Degree	Minimum Years for Degree	Accred.	Requirements for Admission	Full-Time Stdnts.	Part-Time Stdnts.	% of Applics. Accptd.	Stdnts. in 1st Year of Program	# of Degrees Conferred
AB	4	—	University Requirements	74	—	NA	40	24
M Arch	1½	—	B Arch	6	0	10%	3	3
M Arch	2	NAAB	Univ Requirements, portfolio	26	0	17%	14	20
M Arch	3	NAAB	Univ Requirements, portfolio	23	0	14%	7	20
Arch/PhD	4	—	Univ Requirements, portfolio	8	0	19%	4	1

SCHOOL DEMOGRAPHICS (all degree programs)

Full-Time Faculty	Part-Time Faculty	Full-Time Students	Part-Time Students	Foreign Students	Out-of-State U.S. Stdnts.	Women Students	Minority Students
12	20	133	0	10%	—	38%	NA

LIBRARY (Tel. No. 609-452-3128)

Type	No. of Volumes	No. of Slides
Arch	25,100	22,000

STUDENT OPPORTUNITIES AND RESOURCES

Students in the School of Architecture enjoy the benefits of its small size and full integration into the larger Princeton University community. In recent years the school has had an enrollment of approximately 60-70 graduate students and 60-70 undergraduates. Graduate studios and seminars range in size from 10 to 20 students; all lecture courses are structured according to Princeton's preceptorial system to include small discussion groups. Interaction between students and faculty is encouraged at all levels. In addition, shared faculty and extensive cross-listed course offerings with other departments in the university encourage students to pursue their architectural education through a wide range of related disciplines, including art and archaeology, civil engineering, urban and regional affairs, history, sociology, and European cultural studies. Graduate and undergraduate programs in the School of Architecture share faculty, course offerings, resources, and facilities.

SPECIAL ACTIVITIES AND PROGRAMS

Work-study opportunities for undergraduate and graduate students
Public lecture programs run by students and faculty
Public exhibition programs run by the students and faculty
Student publications
Committee of Student Representatives (elected representatives assist in curriculum development and policy making in the school)
Assistantships-in-Instruction for qualified graduate students
Extensive program of visitors for design reviews
Intensive, semester-long visiting critic (graduate-level)
Undergraduate award for travel: the Shanley Prize
Graduate travelling fellowship: the Butler Fellowship; the William Norton Travelling Grant

FACILITIES

Facilities are housed primarily in the architecture building, in the center of campus. The building houses undergraduate and graduate studios, seminar rooms, the Hobart Betts Lecture Hall, exhibition space, and faculty offices, as well as the school's library, its slide collection, the Visual Studies Laboratory, and a computer-graphics laboratory. Additional facilities for work related to building and construction technologies are located nearby in the Princeton Architectural Laboratory, which contains equipment for wood and metal work, a model shop, and measuring equipment for structural testing.

SCHOLARSHIPS/AID

At the undergraduate level, Princeton University provides financial aid to all students on the basis of need. For current information concerning financial assistance at the undergraduate level, contact the Office of Financial Aid, 205 West College, Princeton University, Princeton, New Jersey 08544.

At the graduate level, Princeton University provides many fellowships and scholarships to entering and continuing graduate students. Fellowships and scholarships are grants-in-aid to enable excellent students to carry out their graduate studies; they require no services in return and are not taxable under present law and policy. Assistantships-in-instruction and research are granted on the basis of merit and need. These are normally awarded after one year of study. Compensation usually includes remission of a portion of tuition along with a stipend at a rate set annually by the Graduate School. In addition to the Federally Insured Student Loan Program, short-term contingency loans of up to $500 are available to assist students in emergencies.

UNDERGRADUATE PROGRAM
Philosophy Statement

Within a liberal arts university, the study of architecture is not an independent study: it is rooted in the humanities, social sciences, engineering and the sciences. From these related studies, architecture gains its sense of history, its definition of contemporary problems, its technologies, its value structure, and its basis for studies of the future of the built environment. At Princeton, the four-year undergraduate program leading to the AB degree offers a broad liberal education in which architecture is an area of concentration.

Program Description

Undergraduates are admitted to the undergraduate college through the Undergraduate Office of Admissions, not through the School of Architecture. In the freshman and sophomore years, students take a wide variety of courses in the college and a selection of prerequisite courses in architecture in preparation for a concentration in architecture in the upperclass years. Extensive advising programs are available to assist students in planning their course of study. In the two upperclass years there are two programs of study in architecture, permitting students to concentrate either in architecture and design or in the history and theory of architecture. The Program in Architecture and Design is for students who wish to concentrate in the design and theory of architecture and provides strong preparation for subsequent professional study in architecture (and urban design) at the graduate level, often with advanced standing. The Program in History and Theory of Architecture is for students who wish to concentrate on historical and theoretical problems within the discipline of architecture, either as preparation for further study in this area or as preparation for graduate professional study in architecture. For students interested in pursuing studies both in architecture and engineering, a joint program in architecture and engineering is available through the Department of Civil Engineering in the School of Engineering and Applied Science. This program leads to a BSE degree. All undergraduate students conclude their studies at Princeton with an independent thesis project. For students in the Program in Architecture and Design, this is a semester-long design project and comprehensive essay. For students in the Program in History and Theory, it is a year-long written thesis. Each student has an individual faculty adviser for the thesis.

GRADUATE PROGRAM
Philosophy Statement

The graduate programs emphasize the development of knowledge and abilities in the traditional pursuits of the design and orderly development of buildings, landscapes, and cities. In the context of an increasingly urban society and the complexity of its values, it is the responsibility of the school to investigate and to embrace the physical, social, political, technical, and aesthetic issues that affect society in the making of its physical developments that accommodate our society.

Program Description

The Master of Architecture program is the professional degree program offered by the school. Its purpose is to educate students whose careers will be in the professional practice of architecture. The program is recognized by the National Architectural Accrediting Board as qualifying graduates for examination for professional state licensing after an internship. The program provides opportunities for study in the related fields of urban planning, public affairs, building technology, the social sciences, and architectural history and theory. Three programs lead to the M. Arch degree: a three-year program for students who have completed a four-year undergraduate program with a major in a field other than architecture; a two-year program for students who have completed a four-year undergraduate program with a major in architecture (these students are admitted with a year of advanced standing); and a one-and-one-half year program for students who hold a professional B. Arch degree (or its equivalent for foreign students). Course work consists of studios and seminars in design, history, analysis and theory, building technology, landscape, urban studies, and social and behavioral studies. Instruction introduces students to theories, bodies of knowledge and the design of buildings, landscapes and components of the urban fabric.

Students already enrolled in the M. Arch program may apply to the Director of Graduate Studies for permission to enter the Ph.D. program in architecture after one year of residence. This program is offered for students whose careers are likely to be in teaching, scholarship, and research in architecture. It does not lead to a professional degree. The program is focused on specialized advanced study and original research in a specific area of architecture. It provides a core of studies leading to the general examination and a range of studies in support of an individual's scholarship and research. The Ph.D. program is open to applicants holding an appropriate bachelor's or master's degree in architecture, planning, engineering, and social and behavioral sciences, as well as in selected fields in the humanities, environmental sciences, and public affairs. The Ph.D. in architecture is granted in three fields of study: History and Theory of Architecture; Social and Behavioral Studies in Architecture; and Technical Studies in Historic Architecture.

FACULTY
Administration

Robert M Maxwell, RIBA, Dean
Ralph Lerner, Director of Graduate Studies
Anthony Vidler, Departmental Representative (Undgrd)
Frances M Chen, Librarian, School of Architecture

Professors

Alan Colquhoun, Dipl
Robert Geddes, M Arch
Michael Graves, M Arch
Robert Mark, CE
Robert Maxwell, B Arch
Chester Rapkin, PhD
Anthony Vidler, Dipl

Associate Professors

Ralph Lerner, M Arch

Lecturers

Beatriz Colomina, Dipl
Juliet Richardson-Smith, M Arch
Joel Sanders, M Arch
Terence Smith, M Arch
Mark Wigley, PhD

Part-Time Faculty

Robert Dripps, M Arch
Edward Jones, Dipl
Stephen Kieran, M Arch
Jerry Kugler, M Arch
Robert Ponte, PhD
Donald Prowler, M Arch
Carl Rosenberg, M Arch
David Stillman, MSME
James Timberlake, M Arch
Carles Vallhonrat, M Arch

Adjunct Faculty

Robert Gutman, PhD

159

University of Puerto Rico

School of Architecture
University of Puerto Rico
P.O. Box 21909 - U.P.R. Station
Río Piedras, P.R. 00931
(809) 764-0000 Ext. 2102

Application Deadline(s): BED - Jan 31; M
Arch, - 1st Monday
of Mar for Fall,
1st Monday of
Nov for Spring
Tuition & Fees: Undgrd: PR Res: $700/yr.
Non-res: $2150/yr.
Grad: PR Res: $1,700/yr.
Non-res: $3150/yr.
Endowment: State

DEGREE PROGRAMS

Degree	Minimum Years for Degree	Accred.	Requirements for Admission	Full-Time Stdnts.	Part-Time Stdnts.	% of Applics. Accptd.	Stdnts. in 1st Year of Program	# of Degrees Conferred
BED	4	-	H.S. diploma, interview, apt. exam	200	12	25%	60	25
M Arch	2	NAAB	Bacc. diploma, 2.5 gen. average, portfolio	54	25	80%	20	12

SCHOOL DEMOGRAPHICS (all degree programs)

Full-Time Faculty	Part-Time Faculty	Full-Time Students	Part-Time Students	Foreign Students	Out-of-State U.S. Stdnts.	Women Students	Minority Students
25	4	254	42	2%	-%	37%	-%

LIBRARY (Tel. No. 809-764-0000 X2122)

Type	No. of Volumes	No. of Slides
Arch	21,227	87,602

STUDENT OPPORTUNITIES AND RESOURCES

The University of Puerto Rico is the major government-supported institution of higher learning of the Commonwealth of Puerto Rico. Comprising eleven campuses with a total of 50,000 students, it provides education in the arts and sciences, architecture, planning, engineering, agriculture, law, medicine, business administration, communications, and other fields. The School of Architecture is located on the main campus in Río Piedras, a subdivision of San Juan, the island's largest and most cosmopolitan city.

The Río Piedras campus, with a luxuriant tropical setting of local flora, has an extensive complex of buildings that represent the various stylistic developments of Puerto Rican architecture. A large student center provides a social nucleus for daily student life. The General University Library contains nearly 2,400,000 volumes.

The School of Architecture occupies its own buildings, not far from the Student Center. Over 250 students are enrolled in the school's professional programs, which include a four-year Bachelor of Environmental Design curriculum that combines basic professional studies with the arts and sciences and a first professional degree in architecture, the Master of Architecture. The M Arch program also accommodates students who have the equivalent of the BED degree or who already possess a first professional degree, but wish to continue their studies with emphasis on research and advanced design.

The school works closely with other schools, such as fine arts, planning, and natural sciences, on research and community-oriented projects and collaborates with many governmental agencies on specific projects. Many faculty members have served as advisors for agencies such as the Planning Board and the Departments of Natural Resources, Health, and Education, and the Office of Preservation. The school also maintains a close working relationship with the local community of architecture professionals.

The school draws visiting professors from as far north as Canada and as far south as Argentina, from Europe and from the Orient. Yet, the school is committed to analyzing problems and creating design solutions for the tropical Caribbean. The school is currently involved with research in the history of Puerto Rican architecture, tropical climate technology, and historical preservation.

SPECIAL ACTIVITIES AND PROGRAMS

In order to encourage student participation in the community, the school has been participating in historical preservation research of various towns in Puerto Rico. Much of the students' work has been influential in shaping the development policies of these towns.

As a means of facilitating architectural research, the school has established the Architecture and Construction Archives where more than 50,000 architectural documents are being catalogued.

The school sponsors research in well equipped labs in acoustics and wind tunnel technology.

The summers are spent in Vicenza or in the Archives cataloguing and researching architectural drawings.

Students in the Graduate Program are encouraged to participate in local and international design competitions. Outstanding graduating students are presented with awards and medals by the local AIA Chapter, the "Colegio de Arquitectos de Puerto Rico" and the Alpha Rho Chi Fraternity.

FACILITIES

The school has the following facilities: computer lab, photography lab, student photography lab, graphic arts studio (with a resident artist), model making studio, acoustics lab, technology labs (climate, materials and structure), architectural library, slide library, architecture and construction archive.

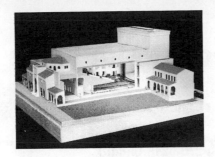

SCHOLARSHIPS/AID

Available through the University of Puerto Rico:
Pell Grant
Work/study
Honor Student Grants

UNDERGRADUATE PROGRAM
Philosophy Statement

The School of Architecture is committed to developing professionals with a holistic view of the built and natural environments and a dedication to serving the human community. The school seeks a balance in the development of design talent, technical knowledge, and appreciation of user perceived needs and aspirations, especially in the context of Puerto Rico and the Caribbean. Emphasis is given to the identification, analysis, and solution of real problems and the documentation of decision making in the design process. Tropical climatology, town and country design, and the special environmental concerns of islands and developing countries are focal areas.

The undergraduate BED program offers basic studies in the arts and sciences, a strong design studio experience, and basic professional preparation in structures, technology, and history of Architecture.

Program Description

The four-year undergraduate program leads to the degree of Bachelor of Environmental Design. The first two years of the program combine a continuous design studio experience with basic courses in the arts and sciences and introductory work in architectural studies. The third and fourth years combine more advanced studio work in architectural design with basic and intermediate professional studies in structures, technology, climatology, and architectural history.

To obtain the BED degree, the student must complete 144 credit hours with a 2.00 grade point average. To be considered for admission to the graduate M Arch program, the student must have a grade point average of 2.50 or higher.

GRADUATE PROGRAM
Philosophy Statement

The Graduate Program provides study opportunities for those seeking a first professional degree. Because of the privileged location in the Caribbean Tropics, the search for an appropriate form and content is the underlying philosophy of the Graduate Program. This involves a rigorous, self-checking approach to design and research.

The school gives emphasis to design with social implications, environmental and cultural context, and technological influences.

Program Description

Admission to the graduate program requires completion of the school's undergraduate program with a 2.50 grade point average or equivalent preparation at another university. Students enter the advanced phase of professional study by completing required work in practice-oriented courses and several advanced courses in theory, structures, technology, and design. They choose among a variety of free electives in faculty specialty fields or in topics of their own choosing. The final year of the two-year program involves a thesis to demonstrate the student's competence for functioning at a self-disciplined, comprehensive, and integrative professional level. In consultation with the thesis advisers, the student identifies a relevant problem to be solved by architectural design, carries out a well-documented research process, and then programs and presents a viable design solution.

Students who already possess a first professional degree may receive up to 50 percent of the required 74 graduate-level credit hours by transferring credits or through advanced standing and may pursue an M Arch program tailored to their individual needs.

FACULTY
Administration

Juan Marqués, RA, CAPR, Dean
Enrique Vivoni, RA, CAPR, Assistant Dean
Sylvia Muñiz de Olmos, Library Director

Professors

Eugene Crommett, RA, ThD
Norberto Dávila, MSCE
Darío González, RA, B Arch
Antonio Miró, RA, B Arch
Efrer Morales, RA, B Arch
Efraín Pérez-Chanis, RA, M Arch
Jaime Zeno, BSME, CAAM, MEME

Associate Professors

Aureo Andino, RA, B Arch
Rafael Crespo, MFA
Carlos Lavandero, RA, B Arch, MCP, MLA
Oscar Marty, RA, M Arch
Arleen Pabón, M Arch, PhD
Edwin Quiles, RA, M Arch
Jorge Rocafort, BSEE, MS, PhD

Assistant Professors

Lope Max Díaz, MA
Pedro Muñiz, M Arch, PhD
Enrique Vivoni, RA, M Arch, PhD

Instructors

Héctor Arce, RA, M Arch
Eduardo Bermúdez, M Arch
Jośe González, MET
Pablo Ojeda, M Arch, Dipl
Sylvia Ramos, RA, B Arch

Part-Time Faculty

Humberto Betancourt, B Arch
Samuel Corchado, M Arch, MUD
Ricardo Jiménez, RA, M Arch
Lillian D López, M Arch
Emilio Martínez, M Arch
Thomas Marvel, M Arch
Esteban Sennyey, B Arch/UDes
Eduardo Sobrino, M Arch, PhD
Raúl Zurinaga, B Arch, MRP

Rensselaer Polytechnic Institute

School of Architecture
RPI
Troy, New York 12180-3590
(518) 276-6460

**Office of Admissions
and Financial Aid**
RPI
Troy, New York 12180-3590
(518) 276-6216 Undgrd
(518) 276-6789 Grad

Application Deadline(s): January 15 (Undgrd)
Tuition & Fees: Undgrd: $11,500/academic year
Grad: $356/credit hour
Endowment: Private

DEGREE PROGRAMS

Degree	Minimum Years for Degree	Accred.	Requirements for Admission	Full-Time Stdnts.	Part-Time Stdnts.	% of Applics. Accptd.	Stdnts. in 1st Year of Program	# of Degrees Conferred
BS (Bldg Sci)	4		Students may transfer from B Arch program	10	0			35*
B Arch	5	NAAB	University requirements; portfolio	187	5	50%	46	30
M Arch	1½	NAAB	Completion of RPI core or equivalent	1	1	100%	1	1
M Arch	3½	NAAB	Baccalaureate any field; portfolio	16	2	50	8	5
M Arch	1½		Accredited architecture degree; portfolio	5	2	33	1	5
MS (Bldg Sci)	1½		Degree in a related field	1	1	33	1	1

*Degree is awarded to all students at end of 4 years; some students choose this as their final degree from Rensselaer.

SCHOOL DEMOGRAPHICS (all degree programs)

Full-Time Faculty	Part-Time Faculty	Full-Time Students	Part-Time Students	Foreign Students	Out-of-State U.S. Stdnts.	Women Students	Minority Students
18	12	219	10	5%	50%	25%	11%

LIBRARY (Tel. No. 518-276-6465)

Type	No. of Volumes	No. of Slides
Arch	30,776	63,669

STUDENT OPPORTUNITIES AND RESOURCES

The School of Architecture focuses on the design of places. RPI seeks to influence the development of architectural thought and practice through the work and ideas pursued in the school, and through the work of its graduates.

Design is approached as critical inquiry, using in-depth exploration into the situation at hand to raise issues, establish priorities, pose questions, produce appropriate responses, and to learn something about all similar situations. In this way, design and the research involved in design are seen as opportunities for discovering how building, thinking and living perpetually intersect, influence and reciprocate with each other. Each project incorporates exploration of the cultural, social, communal, aesthetic contexts within which it is set and to which it will contribute. This inquiry is conducted through design—by making and critically assessing proposals for new and rehabilitated places and buildings.

Working within this framework, RPI offers a small (250 students) program, a faculty of 30 active in scholarship through practice and research, an exciting and growing institution, and a strong commitment to exploration and risk-taking.

SPECIAL ACTIVITIES AND PROGRAMS

Students are admitted directly to professional studies in accredited programs; there are no later admissions points.

Immediate (first semester) immersion in serious architectural studies, including design, theory, history, technology and computing.

Roman Studies program and other overseas opportunities for students who have completed the first five semesters.

Summer design studio for students at all levels; a special 12-week studio for transfer and graduate professional students.

Co-op work experience opportunities for interested students.

Transfer applications are encouraged.

RPI is located in a rejuvenated Victorian city; access to New York City and New England, including a number of outstanding architecture schools and interesting cities. Many projects are set in New York, Boston, Philadelphia and Montreal.

FACILITIES

The School of Architecture is housed in the Greene Building, located in the center of the RPI campus, open 24 hours a day, and including all essential facilities: studios, architecture library, wood shop, coffee shop, exhibition, dark room, reproduction, computing and computer-aided design facilities.

SCHOLARSHIPS/AID

RPI offers financial assistance to undergraduate students in the form of scholarships, loans, and employment; this assistance is based on the family's financial need as demonstrated by the Financial Aid Form of the College Scholarship Service. Graduate financial aid is available in the form of tuition scholarships and teaching assistantships; graduate aid is awarded on the basis of merit.

UNDERGRADUATE PROGRAM
Philosophy Statement

The intent of the professional program is to cause students to engage in critical thinking, continuous inquiry, and the pursuit of significance in thinking and doing. These three processes are seen as interrelated and always informed by the cultural, social, political, economic, technological and historical contexts within which architects work. While formal architectural education assists in the development of specific architectural competencies, it is seen as but the beginning of a lifetime of exploration and learning.

Program Description

Students are enrolled in studio in each semester and begin serious design work immediately. After five semester-long core studios, students in the B Arch program exercise choice of studio, project and critic for the next four semesters. The program ends with an individually developed and executed thesis project.

Technological issues are introduced as essential to the conception, design and making of architecture in the first year. Formal sequences in structures, materials, construction, energy and environmental controls begin in the second year.

Computing is also introduced as integral to design exploration in the first-year studio. A series of elective courses follows.

A four-course sequence in history and theory is required. The faculty offer a series of upper-division electives in theory, history, technology, computing, management and practice.

Students who matriculate in the B Arch program and who decide not to pursue an architecture degree may, any time after the second year, transfer to a 4-year BS program and then enter the building industry or do graduate study in law, finance, development, construction, planning or another related discipline.

GRADUATE PROGRAM
Philosophy Statement

RPI offers two graduate programs: the Master of Architecture as a first professional degree for students who have bachelors degrees in other disciplines, and a 30-credit postprofessional research-oriented program leading to the Master of Architecture (as a second professional degree) or to the Master of Science (for students who do not have a professional architecture degree). It is also possible to earn the M Arch (as the first professional degree) in six years, after matriculating at RPI as a freshman.

The 3-1/2 year M Arch program provides a balanced education in architectural design, history, theory and technology. The existence of this graduate professional program is an acknowledgment of the importance of the notion of the architect as an educated generalist. Its purpose is to support, nurture and develop this fragile construct in a world enamoured with specialization. The M Arch can be seen as both the extension and the raision d'etre of an individual's general education.

The postprofessional M Arch and MS programs offer the opportunity for advanced, focused and intellectually rigorous architectural studies. While the faculty does not limit the range of possible exploration, the building (making) of architecture, and the place of technology in architectural thought and production serve as a common thread through postprofessional studies at RPI. Students are encouraged to concentrate their work within one or more of these realms of inquiry: philosophy of technology in architecture, emerging technologies, computer-aided architectural design. These are not seen as distinct and separate realms; rather they represent points of entry into, and centers of intensity within, the discourses of interest within the program.

Program Description

The M Arch (first professional degree) program begins with a 12-week summer design studio and then continues through six regular academic semesters. The program includes parallel coursework in design, history, theory, technology and professional electives; it culminates in an individually conceived and executed master's thesis.

The post-professional program includes 30 credit hours of project and coursework arranged in close collaboration with a faculty mentor. A thesis is required. A common intellectual framework and critical perspective is developed in required seminar courses, and interchange among students and work is maintained in a graduate colloquium. It normally takes three semesters to complete.

FACULTY
Administration

David S Haviland, Dean
Walter M Kroner, AIA, Director, Center for Architectural Research
Mark S Rea, Director, Lighting Research Center
Virginia S Bailey, Architecture Librarian

Professors

Dora P Crouch, PhD
David S Haviland, B Arch, M Arch
Roland L Hummel, PE, MSCE
Walter M Kroner, AIA, B Arch, M Arch
Patrick J Quinn, FAIA, B Arch, M Arch
Graham Williams, AIA, B Arch, M Arch
Robert F Winne, B Arch, M Arch

Associate Professors

David H Bell, RA, M Arch
Caren Canier, BFA, MFA
Peter W Parsons, AIA, B Arch, PhD (cand)
Mark S Rea, BS, MS, PhD
Kenneth L Warriner, RA, B Arch, Dipl Arch (cand)

Assistant Professors

Sibel Bozdogan, B Arch, M Arch, PhD
Frances Bronet, BSCE, B Arch, MS
William L Glennie, AB Arch, MSCE
Eduard Hueber, Dipl Arch
Thomas Kinslow, B Arch
Nicole F Pertuiset, Dipl Arch
Rajmohan Shetty, B Arch, SM
John M Tobin, B Arch, M Arch

Part-Time Faculty

Cinzia Abbate
Thomas Bartels, M Arch
Robert F Bristol, MLA
Anthony Garner, BA, M Arch
Jason Harper, B Arch
Susan Lewis, MA
Jaimini Mehta, M Arch
Carmela Merola, MS, PhD
Mark Mistur, B Arch
Scott Parker, B Arch
Rodney Place
Simon Ungers, RA, B Arch
Terence Van Elslander, B Arch, M Arch
Marc Worsdale, BA
Anna B Zaffanella, MA

Adjunct Faculty

Michael J O'Rourke, PE, PhD

Rhode Island School of Design

Division of Architectural Studies
Rhode Island School of Design
2 College Street
Providence, Rhode Island 02903
(401) 331-3511 ext. 148

Office of Admissions
Rhode Island School of Design
2 College Street
Providence, Rhode Island 02903
(401) 331-3511 ext. 125

Application Deadline(s): January 21
(freshmen)
March 7 (transfer)
Tuition & Fees: Undgrd: $13,835/yr
Grad: $13,835/yr
Endowment: Private

DEGREE PROGRAMS

Degree	Minimum Years for Degree	Accred.	Requirements for Admission	Full-Time Stdnts.	Part-Time Stdnts.	% of Applics. Accptd.	Stdnts. in 1st Year of Program	# of Degrees Conferred
B Arch	5	NAAB	2 yr, algebra, 1 sem trig, 1 yr science, transcript, SAT, Statement	268	—	40%	85	80
BLA	5	ASLA		19	—	56%	7	5
B Int Arch	5	FIDER		59	—	46%	26	5
BID	5	IDSA		103	—	20%	49	11
MID	2	IDSA		9	—	29%	5	2

SCHOOL DEMOGRAPHICS (all degree programs)

Full-Time Faculty	Part-Time Faculty	Full-Time Students	Part-Time Students	Foreign Students	Out-of-State U.S. Stdnts.	Women Students	Minority Students
23	13	458	—	16%	73%	38%	7%

LIBRARY (Tel. No. 401-331-3511 ext 293)

Type	No. of Volumes	No. of Slides
Univ	65,750	86,686

STUDENT OPPORTUNITIES AND RESOURCES

The department has approximately 280 students representing almost every state in the country. Neighboring countries as well as South American and European nations are also represented. Providence's location on the New York-Boston axis facilitates interaction between critics and students.

Architecture is part of the Division of Architectural Studies integrated with the Departments of Interior Architecture, Landscape Architecture, and Industrial Design. There are close ties among the four departments as well as among the school divisions.

The faculty is characterized by a great diversity of backgrounds and, equally important, a variety of areas of specialization.

SPECIAL ACTIVITIES AND PROGRAMS

Cross-registration with neighboring Brown University; students may enroll for one course each academic year at Brown University

Each year eminent professionals are invited to offer visiting critic studios in each department

Visiting lecturer series

Endowed lectureships: the Haffenreffer Lecture in Landscape Architecture and the Colin Shoemaker Memorial Lecture in Architecture

Opportunity to study for one year at the institution's headquarters in Rome; RISD's European Honors Program is among the nation's oldest overseas study programs in architecture, art, and design

Six-week "Wintersession" period between semesters, designed to encourage students in the Division of Architectural Studies to take courses in the areas of fine arts and design or pursue independent studies

FACILITIES

The Division of Architectural Studies is housed in the Bayard Ewing Building, with additional studio space and access to wood, metal, and model shops. A CADD-equipped computer lab has moved to the main architecture building. The RISD Museum of Art is another resource available to students. In addition to the RISD library, the Brown University library is accessible for students.

SCHOLARSHIPS/AID

Scholarship aid is not available to first-year students or foreign students. Aid is available in the form of RISD scholarships ($200-$8000), Pell Grants (up to $2100), Supplemental Education Opportunity Grants ($200-$2000) and various loan and work-study programs. Students with a previous bachelor's degree are eligible for only loans or work-study aid.

UNDERGRADUATE PROGRAM
Philosophy Statement

A professional, five-year undergraduate program is offered in which architecture is viewed as both an artistic and technical discipline, shaped by its intrinsic rules as well as by the forces of society at large. The school seeks to provide a healthy balance of practical and theoretical issues in the curriculum.

Program Description

The principal concern of the program is to provide a curriculum leading to the Bachelor of Architecture degree that is firmly based on the classical foundations of architecture education: architectural design, the history and theory of architecture, and building technologies.

The close proximity of professional programs in landscape architecture, interior architecture, and industrial design provides for a wealth of exposure to other design-related disciplines. This, together with optional cross-registration at neighboring Brown University, makes for a special intellectual context in which the learning and teaching of architecture is to occur.

Founded upon English models of the arts and crafts movement over one hundred years ago, Rhode Island School of Design has traditionally given emphasis to the craft and design components in its pedagogical activities. Thus, the training of the mind is carefully balanced by the acquisition of skills, including the necessary understanding of structure and technology. Together with solid history and theory of architecture courses, these are the foundations that will allow students to be responsible professionals, intellectually equipped to deal with the complexities of the cultural situation of our time.

GRADUATE PROGRAM
Philosophy Statement

The only graduate program currently available is in the Department of Industrial Design.

FACULTY
Administration

Samuel B Frank, Chair, Division of Architectural Studies
Timothy Culvahoose, Acting Head, Department of Architecture

Professors

Derek Bradford, AIA, ASLA, RA, RIBA, Dipl Arch, M Arch
Charles Fink, AIA, RA, B Arch
Marc Harrison, IDSA, BID, MID
Kenneth Hunnibell, IDSA, BFA, MAE
Charles W Luther, FAIA, RA, BS Arch, EdM
Friedrich St Florian, AIA, FAAR, M Arch, MS
Merlin Szosz, BFA, MFA
Harold Washburn, RA, BS Arch
Wilbur Yoder, AIA, RA, BS Arch, MS

Associate Professors

James Barnes, AIA, RA, B Arch, MS
John Behringer, Dipl
J Michael Everett, ASLA, B Arch, M Arch, MLA
Leonard Newcomb, RLA, BA
Robert O'Neal, BS-ID, MA
Colgate Searle, BLA, MLA
Judith Wolin, B Arch, MED

Assistant Professors

Mitchell Ackerman, MID
Samuel Frank, RA, M Arch
Margaret McAvin, MLA, M Arch
C Shayne O'Neil, M Arch
Paul Pawlowski, FAAR, ASLA, B Arch, MLA
Seth Stem, BA
George Wagner, M Arch

Part-Time Faculty

F Douglas Adams, AIA, RA, M Arch
Jeffrey Berg, RA, M Arch
Sara Bradford, MA
Steven Caney, BFA
William Cavenaugh, B Arch
Tim Culvahouse, MED, B Arch
John Dunnigan, MFA
Peter Guimond, Reg Eng, MS
Robert Harper, M Arch
Donald Leighton, BLA
Roseanne Somerson, BFA
Peter Tagiuri, RA, M Arch
T Kelly Wilson, M Arch

Rice University

School of Architecture
Rice University
P.O. Box 1892
Houston, Texas 77251-1892
(713) 527-4864

Admissions Office
(713) 527-4036

Application Deadline(s): February 1
Tuition & Fees: Undgrd: $4,900/yr
                Grad: $4,900/yr
Endowment: Private

DEGREE PROGRAMS

Degree	Minimum Years for Degree	Accred.	Requirements for Admission	Full-Time Stdnts.	Part-Time Stdnts.	% of Applics. Accptd.	Stdnts. in 1st Year of Program	# of Degrees Conferred
BA	4		univ. req.	100	0	27%	27	18
B Arch	5+1 yr. preceptorship	NAAB	BA (arch) from Rice	28	0		14	14
M Arch	1½		B Arch	11	0	12%	5	6
M Arch	2	NAAB	BA (arch)	15	0	14%	7	8
M Arch	3½	NAAB	BA or BS	44	0	20%	12	11
M Arch UD	1½		B Arch or BA in Arch	5	0	20%	2	3
D Arch	2		M Arch or M Arch UD	0	0	5%	0	0

SCHOOL DEMOGRAPHICS (all degree programs)

Full-Time Faculty	Part-Time Faculty	Full-Time Students	Part-Time Students	Foreign Students	Out-of-State U.S. Stdnts.	Women Students	Minority Students
12	21	200	0	25%	65%	38%	6%

LIBRARY (Tel. No. 713-527-4800)

Type	No. of Volumes	No. of Slides
Art and Arch	49,000	200,000

STUDENT OPPORTUNITIES AND RESOURCES

Architecture has been a course of study at Rice since the University opened in 1912. The School of Architecture seeks to contribute to the realization of a more humane built environment through teaching, research and public service. It offers seven different degree programs to accommodate students of various backgrounds and interests: undergraduate and graduate; pre-professional, professional and post-professional.

The curriculum emphasizes preparation for the general practice of architectural design within a humanistic frame of reference. The core and elective courses of the School are enriched by those elsewhere in the University in art, art history and classical archaeology, public policy, management and environmental studies. The curriculum maintains sufficient flexibility to allow for individualized programs of instruction where appropriate. It also provides for "mainstreaming" of students in advanced design studios at both undergraduate and graduate levels and, in the case of the Bachelor of Architecture program, a year-long practicum (preceptorship) in leading architectural offices in the United States and abroad.

The enrollment of the School is relatively small, as is that of the University, and contributes to a sense of community among students and faculty. The campus was laid out by Cram, Goodhue, and Ferguson who designed its first buildings in a distinctive, eclectic manner incorporating Venetian Gothic, Byzantine and southern Romanesque elements. It is located within walking distance of Houston's principal museums, medical center, Hermann Park and several of its most attractive neighborhoods. The city supports diverse offerings in the visual and performing arts, and is itself a stimulating architectural and urban environment.

SPECIAL ACTIVITIES AND PROGRAMS

Sophomore field trip

Preceptor program (two-semester practicum in leading architectural offices for approved students who have received the BA from Rice)

School lecture series

Rice Design Alliance lecture series at the Museum of Fine Arts, Houston

Cullinan Lectures and Papers in Architecture

CITE, quarterly review of architecture and design of the Rice Design Alliance

Jury week (fall and spring)

Traveling fellowships

Special visiting critics studios at both the graduate and undergraduate levels

Architectural exhibitions in the Farish Gallery

Student organization, including representation at ACSA functions

Summer program in Paris and Barcelona

FACILITIES

The School of Architecture occupies quarters renovated and expanded by James Stirling, Michael Wilford and Associates in 1981. These include an advanced computer graphics laboratory and the Farish Gallery, which mounts a full schedule of architecture and design exhibitions each year. The School adjoins the Alice Pratt Brown Art and Architecture Library, completed in 1986, which consolidates the University's holdings in art history, architecture, city planning, landscape and classical archaeology.

SCHOLARSHIPS/AID

The financial aid program at Rice University seeks to provide assistance as needed to all students who are admitted. Through low-interest loans, grants, campus work opportunities, or a combination of these programs, Rice attempts to give the students sufficient aid to meet educational expenses.

Approximately 70 percent of architecture graduate students receive some kind of financial aid from the university, in the form of either scholarship or a stipend.

UNDERGRADUATE PROGRAM
Philosophy Statement

The undergraduate programs are intended to provide an intensive preparation in fundamental aspects of architectural theory and professional practice consistent with the broader objectives of a liberal arts education. The School adheres to no single design approach but rather is process-oriented and endeavors to maintain balanced diversity within its faculty and student body. Students are encouraged to pursue individual interests and to undertake independent study with faculty guidance where appropriate.

Program Description

The undergraduate program in architecture is designed around a basic professional framework allowing options for individual student growth and exploration. The first four years are structured to serve the needs of both students who wish to study for an undergraduate professional degree in architecture and those who intend to earn a graduate professional degree. However, options exist for those students who may decide to pursue a general education with an emphasis on architecture, with the Bachelor of Arts as a terminal degree.

Students in the undergraduate program pursuing a Bachelor of Arts degree can choose between two majors during their second year of study: Architecture or Architectural Studies. Architecture is a preprofessional program of concentration with four years of design studios, related lecture courses, and a liberal component of free electives that use the resources of the entire university. Architectural Studies offers early concentration in architecture for two-and-a-half years followed by a wide selection of free electives, allowing the student a broadly based education with a possible second major.

Students who have successfully completed the four-year program with a major in architecture may apply for the first professional degree program, leading to a Bachelor of Architecture degree. This is a two-year program with the first year spent in the Preceptorship Program, which places students in the offices of leading architects and planners for one academic year of practical experience. A tuition of $200 is charged during this year. The second year is spent at Rice completing requirements for the Bachelor of Architecture degree.

GRADUATE PROGRAM
Philosophy Statement

The graduate programs presuppose an adequate grounding in the liberal arts and focus on professional and post-professional instruction, including research. The curriculum is sufficiently flexible to accommodate varying backgrounds and interests, and individualized courses of study can be arranged once basic analytical and design skills are acquired. Students are encouraged to undertake preparation of a master's thesis in theory or design and to otherwise demonstrate the capacity for independent study and research.

Program Description

The Master of Architecture program, leading to an accredited first or second professional degree, provides three curriculum tracks: a track for students already holding a Bachelor of Architecture degree; a track for students holding a non-professional bachelor's degree that represents a four-year major in architecture; and the Qualifying Graduate Program for students with at least a bachelor's degree in an area other than architecture.

The curriculum track for students holding a Bachelor of Architecture degree, titled the Architecture and Environmental Research Track, requires three semesters of study, including the preparation of a thesis. In addition to the thesis, students normally take two studios and nine courses. The curriculum is highly structured at the beginning, particularly during the first semester, becoming less structured to allow students to pursue their own areas of interest.

Students holding a bachelor's degree with a major in architecture enter the Building Design and Technology Track where they are required to complete four academic semesters of study consisting of four studios, three of which are in architecture, and twelve elective courses. While at Rice students in both tracks will be eligible to take the same elective courses and some of the same studios, particularly those offered by visiting critics.

The Qualifying Graduate Program has been specifically developed to allow students with degrees in other areas to receive an accredited M Arch degree upon successful completion of at least seven semesters of academic study. For the first four semesters students in the program pursue their studies largely independently from other graduate students in the school. The first two semesters of the program involve an intensive weekly schedule in which most instruction takes place within the studio. The studios follow a workshop format with exercises covering a variety of pursuits in basic design, architectural design, building, and environmental technology. The third and fourth semesters of the program are more conventional with respect to studio and course requirements. The final three semesters are completed within the normal framework of the Master of Architecture program. In all, a student must successfully complete at least seven semesters of studio and twenty additional courses. Students with sufficient architectural background may be admitted into the program at the third-semester level.

The program leading to a Master of Architecture in Urban Design is typically taken as a second professional degree. A normal program of study involves three studios, two of which must be in urban design, and nine elective courses. The curriculum is highly structured at the beginning and then becomes less structured to allow students to pursue their own areas of interest.

For a limited number of students interested in advanced graduate education, the school offers a course of study leading to the degree of Doctor of Architecture.

FACULTY
Administration

O Jack Mitchell, FAIA, Dean
Gordon Wittenberg, Acting Director
Jet Prendeville, Librarian

Professors

William T Cannady, FAIA, RA, B Arch, M Arch
John J Casbarian, AIA, RA, B Arch, MFA
O Jack Mitchell, FAIA, RA, B Arch, M Arch, MCP
Peter C Papademetriou, RA, AIA, M Arch
Anderson Todd, FAIA, RA, MFA

Associate Professors

Spencer Parsons, RA, M Arch
Peter D Waldman, RA, BA, MFA
Gordon Wittenberg, RA, M Arch

Assistant Professors

Richard Ingersoll, PhD
Albert Pope, RA, B Arch, M Arch
William Sherman, RA, M Arch
Scott Wall, M Arch

Part-Time Faculty

Josiah Baker, M Arch
Bill A Bavinger, B Arch
James B Blackburn, Jr, MS, JD
Joseph P Colaco, PE, PhD
R George Cunningham, PE, BS
Wally B Ford, PE, MCE
John Mixon, LLM, JD
Eric O Moss, RA, M Arch
M A Reiner, PhD
Eduardo Robles, M Arch
Danny Samuels, AIA, RA, B Arch
Frank S White, BS
Judith Wolin, MED

Adjunct Faculty

Chester A Boterf
Karen Broker
Walter Widrig

Roger Williams College

Architecture Division
Roger Williams College
Bristol, Rhode Island 02809
(401) 253-1040

Application Deadline(s): February 1
Tuition & Fees: Undgrd: Tuition: $7000/yr
Room & Board: $4210/yr
Studio Fee: $1170/yr
Endowment: Private

DEGREE PROGRAMS

Degree	Minimum Years for Degree	Accred.	Requirements for Admission	Full-Time Stdnts.	Part-Time Stdnts.	% of Applics. Accptd.	Stdnts. in 1st Year of Program	# of Degrees Conferred
B Arch	5	NAAB	HS Diploma	226		44%	95	19

SCHOOL DEMOGRAPHICS (all degree programs)

Full-Time Faculty	Part-Time Faculty	Full-Time Students	Part-Time Students	Foreign Students	Out-of-State U.S. Stdnts.	Women Students	Minority Students
10	25	280	—	6%	78%	31%	NA

LIBRARY (Tel. No. 401-253-1040)

Type	No. of Volumes	No. of Slides
Arch	6,000	11,000

STUDENT OPPORTUNITIES AND RESOURCES

Roger Williams College is a coeducational undergraduate institution of approximately 2000 full-time students which provides a curriculum designed to encourage the development of critical and independent thought while preparing students for careers and for life-long learning. The faculty and the courses reflect a rare combination of the elements of a traditional liberal arts college with a rich variety of professional and artistic programs normally found in larger institutions.

Roger Williams College is located on an eighty-acre, contemporary campus, overlooking a bay of the Atlantic Ocean. The relatively small size of the college, its semi-rural setting, and its emphasis on the teaching role of the faculty foster an atmosphere encouraging close interaction among students, faculty and staff. At the same time, the educational and cultural opportunities of nearby cities are easily accessible. Providence, the state capital, is 18 miles away and Boston, 62 miles.

The College is composed of nine Divisions, or schools:
Architecture
Business
Engineering Technology
Fine Arts
Humanities
Mathematics & Computer Science
Natural Science
Social Science
Open Division

Of the approximately 2000 full-time students, 1280 board in school residences. The ratio of men to women is 3:2. The college enrolls students from 25 states. Most students come from New England, New York, Pennsylvania and New Jersey. The International students number 175 representing 35 nations.

The Architecture Division presently enrolls approximately 200 students, of which 25% are women. The percentage of women continues to rise. Women represent 35% of the acceptances for the Fall 87 class.

Transfer credit for major courses will be considered for courses taken at another accredited college or university provided a grade of "C" or better was earned and that the course is considered equivalent in subject matter to courses offered at Roger Williams College.

SPECIAL ACTIVITIES AND PROGRAMS

Each year the Architecture Division sponsors a distinguished Lecturer Series. The lectures introduce students to the work and ideas of people celebrated in their fields and help set a standard of excellence for students to follow. In the past the series has brought to the campus such notable architects as Paul Rudolph and Michael McKinnell, renowned landscape architect Laurie Olin; structural engineer William LeMessurier; architectural historians William Curtis, Stanford Anderson and Malcolm Quantrill.

Visiting Critics from Rhode Island and Boston routinely provide a forum for dialogue and critical commentary of student work.

The nearby cities of Providence, Newport, Boston, New York and New Haven are excellent "laboratories" of architectural design. Each semester faculty members schedule field trips as part of studio time or on weekends.

There is an ACS/AIAS chapter at Roger Williams College. The club arranges programs for the students, including field trips and receptions for lecture series speakers. The student body president regularly meets with the Director to discuss student concerns and attends important faculty meetings.

FACILITIES

Roger Williams College has just completed the construction of a new "state of the art" building to house the Architecture Division on campus. The 46,000 square-foot structure contains design studios, review rooms, the architecture library, a computer laboratory, an exhibition gallery, a photo studio and a model-making shop.

The building's design is the result of a national design competition jointly sponsored by the college and the National Endowment for the Arts which attracted 152 designs from 41 states.

SCHOLARSHIPS/AID

Roger Williams College strives to maintain an active and equitable program of financial assistance for students who would otherwise not be able to attend the institution. The sole criterion for financial assistance is demonstrated need, and aid is awarded without regard to age, sex, race, creed, national origin, or handicap, if any.

Basically, there are three types of financial aid: loans, employment and grants-in-aid, frequently named scholarships by some organizations. Assistance may consist of one, or any combination of these types of financial aid, and might come from a variety of sources.

UNDERGRADUATE PROGRAM
Philosophy Statement

The primary goal of our educational program is to prepare students for the practice of architecture at the professional level, to prepare for licensure, and to provide for a sufficient depth of understanding of the components of architectural practice. This means preparing to design buildings that take into account the needs of the people and the physical, social and cultural context of the building. In accomplishing these objectives, the architecture program develops or teaches the necessary visual and communication skills, the knowledge of building techniques, and an understanding of human problems in an environmental context.

Program Description

The Architecture program at Roger Williams College is one of six architecture programs in New England, one of two full-time undergraduate programs, and the only accredited Bachelor of Architecture program in a small, private, liberal arts college. It fulfills a regional need in an area which does not have an adequate number of undergraduate opportunities for those who are prepared to undertake the study of the profession immediately after high school, or within one or two years after graduation.

The Architecture program gives students a strong sense of design, a rigorous technical background, and the breadth of a liberal arts education over the five-year course of study which leads to the Bachelor of Architecture degree.

The program also teaches and nurtures the artistic skills, visual acuity, and formal and organizational dexterity which is necessary in the creative solution of the visual nature of architecture.

At the same time, in consonance with the overall goals of the educational program at Roger Williams College, the Architecture Division is committed to the development of the "whole person" in society through thorough professional training combined with the undertaking of a required sequence of general education courses. These courses expose the student to a range of study in areas of Moral and Ethical Reasoning, Behavioral Studies, Historical Studies, Social Analysis, Literature and the Arts, and Science and Technology. This general education sequence is designed not only to acquaint the student with the range of concerns of the educated person in society, but to enable the student to develop the critical and analytical faculties necessary for the more in-depth study of the constituent components of the architecture profession.

FACULTY
Administration

Dr. Malcom Forbes, Dean of the College
Raj Saksena, AIA, Director, Architecture Division
Elizabeth Peck-Learned, Architecture Librarian

Teaching Faculty

Zane Anderson, AIA, RA, NCARB, AB, M Arch
Richard Chafee, AB, MA, PhD
Andrew Cohen, AIA, RA, NCARB, B Arch, M Arch
Ulker Copur, B Arch, M Arch, PhD
Paul Donnelly, AIA, PE, RA, B Arch, MS
Roseann B Evans, RA, BA, M Arch
Grattan Gill, RA
Americo Mallozzi, AIA, RA, NCARB, BS
William L McQueen, RA, B Arch
Robert T Meeker, RA, NCARB, B Arch, M Arch
Eleftherios Pavlides, BA, M Arch, PhD
Raj Saksena, AIA, RA, NCARB, B Arch, M Arch

Part-Time Faculty

Ethan Anthony, NCARB, B Arch
Mauricio Barreto, AIA, NCARB, BFA, B Arch
Jeffrey T Berg, RA, AIA, BA
Douglas Brownlow, BA
William J Cavanaugh, FASA, B Arch
Mark Chuddy, PE, BS
Raymond A DeCesare, RA, NCARB, AIA, BS
Christine DelVecchio, AAIA, BSA, B Arch
Joseph DelVecchio, AAIA, BFA, B Arch
Katharine A Field, BA, BA Arch/Fine Arts
Timothy J Foulkes, BS Eng
John Holmes, RA, NCARB, BA, B Arch
Thomas A Incze, BA, M Arch
Gregory Laramie, B Arch, BFA
Ron Mitchell, BA, M Arch
Sheikh Rahman, PE, RA, BS, MS
John Riley, RA, NCARB, B Arch
Jeffrey Staats, RA, NCARB, AIA, AICP, B Arch, M Arch
Susan Stuebing, BBA, M Arch
Clement T Van Buren, BA, M Arch
Harvey Allen Wagner, RA, BS Arch
Bradford Walker, BS, M Arch

Adjunct Faculty

Khalid Al-Hamdouni, Dipl, BS, MS
Pen Fang, BS, MS, PhD

University of South Florida

FAMU/USF Cooperative Master of
Architecture Program
10770 N 46th Street
Suite A-800
Tampa, Florida 33617
(813) 974-4031

USF Office of Admissions
University of South Florida
4202 Fowler Avenue
Tampa, Florida 33620-6900
(813) 974-3350

Application Deadline(s): June 29 for Fall
Nov 9 for Spring
Mar 14 for Summer
NOTE: these dates do
not apply for int'l
students.
Tuition & Fees: Grad: FL Res: $69/credit hour
Non-res: $194/credit hour
Application Fee: $15
Endowment: Public

DEGREE PROGRAMS

Degree	Minimum Years for Degree	Accred.	Requirements for Admission	Full-Time Stdnts.	Part-Time Stdnts.	% of Applics. Accptd.	Stdnts. in 1st Year of Program	# of Degrees Conferred
M Arch	2 2/3	candidacy status	Baccalaureate Degree from regionally accredited institution, GRE score of 1000 or more or a "B" average or better in upper division (on 4 point scale), Physics, Calculus & Basic computer courses at under-graduate level; Portfolio, Personal interview	7	41	n/a	23	None

SCHOOL DEMOGRAPHICS (all degree programs)

Full-Time Faculty	Part-Time Faculty	Full-Time Students	Part-Time Students	Foreign Students	Out-of-State U.S. Stdnts.	Women Students	Minority Students
3	12	7	41	—	—	32%	7%

LIBRARY (Tel. No. 813-974-2047)

Type	No. of Volumes	No. of Slides
Main	5,500 (Arch)	7,025 (Arch)

STUDENT OPPORTUNITIES AND RESOURCES

The FAMU/USF Cooperative Master of Architecture Program has just been founded by the state government. Although in its infancy, this cooperative program between Florida A&M University and the University of South Florida is allied with both a major multi-disciplinary research university and The Florida Center for Urban Design and Research. The architecture program provides students with unlimited possibilities for study in a major metropolitan area with a diverse economic base, maritime edges, subtropical climate, and high growth rate.

The program has two endowed chairs to be filled next year, one for Architecture, the other for Urban Design and Architecture. The occupants of the endowed chairs will be specialists in a field relating to the unique aspects of this region. Students will have opportunities to increase their knowledge of gerontological, vernacular, tropical environment, urban design, and maritime edge matters while studying with these specialists.

The Florida Center for Urban Design and Research will function as a graduate institute offering internships for one or two semesters of work/study in urban design and development issues related to real jobs and problems. The work will be performed under supervision of faculty and professionals. It will earn graduate semester-hour credit. The Center will also employ students from other graduate programs around the country, who will mingle with in-program students, enriching their perspectives.

Through FAMU's School of Architecture, the architecture program has access to a Small Towns Assistance Clearinghouse. The activity of this Center, focusing on the Florida panhandle town of Apalachicola, provides rural experience and opportunity.

The program is expected to grow to approximately 200 students with a full-time faculty of 20. This faculty is supplemented by adjunct faculty of practicing architects, and by the expertise of the faculty of the School of Architecture at FAMU in Tallahassee. Graduate students in the Florida University System may take part in the Traveling Scholar Program, utilizing resources on other campuses in the state system.

Candidacy for accreditation by the NAAB (National Architectural Accrediting Board) has been applied for.

SPECIAL ACTIVITIES AND PROGRAMS

Lecture Series: Respected designers and researchers will be invited to the campus year round. The lectures given by these persons will be open to the public. Members of the local A.I.A. chapters and other allied professions will be specifically invited.

Award Programs: Special events will be held to which the public will be invited that will introduce the persons who will occupy the two endowed chairs. Other events will be held to honor the recipients of the scholarships that the program has to offer.

Off-Campus Study: It is planned that at least one international study program will be offered each year. Initially, this study program will visit the United Kingdom, but plans are being formulated to arrange study programs in other areas of the world. These programs will be cooperative in nature, using both the faculty and facilities of programs located in the host country.

The State University System owns overseas centers in London, England, and in Florence, Italy.

Student Organization: The originating class of 1986 has begun a chapter of the AIAS. Activities have included field trips out of state, social activities, and hosting a meeting of the local chapter of the AIA.

FACILITIES

Computer Facilities: Eight stations of AutoCAD-equipped computers exist for student use in a laboratory facility. Each faculty member has a microcomputer and the administrative facilities are computer supported.

Photographic Labs: A range of photographic equipment has been purchased for student use both to take and process photos. A darkroom facility is equipped for both black and white and color photography.

Video facilities include camera, recording and playback equipment as well as a library of pre-recorded films.

Model Shop: Equipped with a variety of heavy and light machinery and a complete selection of hand tools, this facility can accommodate full-scale mock-up and model-scale requirements.

SCHOLARSHIPS/AID

There are two continuing scholarships available for students who have proven ability in the program. Scholarships for both new and continuing students are also currently available for application towards the direct costs of education in the program. Local architects have raised a substantial initial endowment to provide scholarship help on a continuing basis. Development efforts to increase the size of the endowment are on-going. These scholarships will be distributed on both a merit and a need basis and the University's stated philosophy of equal opportunity will ensure that minorities and disadvantaged students are considered.

GRADUATE PROGRAM
Philosophy Statement

The architecture program is dedicated to providing the very best available learning experiences and resources to highly-motivated graduate students *who may have no prior architectural educational experience.*

Its faculty are developing a curriculum that will provide graduates with the intellectual resources and abilities they will need for the practice of architecture in the 21st century. At the same time students will be well grounded in the accumulated history of architecture so that their design work will reflect the *culture* of the architectural profession.

The curriculum is theory-intensive but also practical. Its courses are taught at the graduate level, and capitalize on the undergraduate education of its students. The program exploits both its rapidly-growing urban setting and its connection to the Florida Center for Urban Design and Research. Systematic, faculty-led travel/study is also being developed as a creditable component of the architecture program.

Research and supervised practice opportunities provided in conjunction with the Florida Center for Urban Design and Research and through cooperative work experience in local offices will provide students with practical experiences *before* they graduate. In this way students will have developed marketable skills by the time they graduate.

Program Description

The FAMU/USF Cooperative Master of Architecture Program offered its first courses to students in the Fall 1986 semester. The program is eight semesters long and operates on a three-terms-per-year system. It is possible to complete the required 120 credit-hours of study in two years and two semesters. The program is intended for students without prior course work in architecture, but those with 4-year non-professional baccalaureate degrees in architecture may be admitted with advanced standing that varies with each case. At least seventy-six credit-hours must be earned in residence to qualify for a Master of Architecture degree from this program. The course of study includes:

Design, including thesis	45
History & Theory	15
Graphics	9
Technology:	
Structures	9
Materials & Methods	9
Environmental Technology	9
Related courses	12
Architectural Electives	12
Total credits	120

FACULTY
Administration
Alexander Ratensky, AIA, Dean
David Glasser, AIA, Chairman
Ilene Frank, Architecture Librarian

Professors
David Evan Glasser, AIA, B Arch
Alexander Ratensky, AIA, BA, M Arch

Associate Professors
Deirdre J Hardy, AIA, BA, M Arch
Paul Weir, BS, MS, M Arch

Assistant Professors
James A Moore, BS, MS, M Arch, PhD
Daniel S Powers, B Arch, M Arch

Part-Time Faculty
David A Crane, FAIA, B Arch, MCP
Michael English, BS, MA
Rajan Sen, B Tech, MA Sc, PhD Civil Eng
Sape A Zylstra, BA, BD, PhD

Adjunct Faculty
Michael L Archer, B Des, M Arch
Steven A Cooke, B Des, M Arch
Donna D Gillis, AIA, B Des, M Arch
Stan Meradith, BS, M Arch
Daniel Myers, BS, M Arch
Alberto Picallo, BS, B Arch
Herbert Schmoll, BFA
Frank Setzer, B Arch, MUD
Ed Spivey, BSME, MSME

Southern California Institute of Architecture

SCI-ARC
1800 Berkeley Street
Santa Monica, CA 90404
(213) 829-3482

Application Deadline(s): B Arch M Arch:
March 1
Tuition & Fees: Undgrd: $3400/trimester
Grad: $3400
Endowment: Private

DEGREE PROGRAMS

Degree	Minimum Years for Degree	Accred.	Requirements for Admission	Full-Time Stdnts.	Part-Time Stdnts.	% of Applics. Accptd.	Stdnts. in 1st Year of Program	# of Degrees Conferred
B Arch	5	NAAB	HS diploma, letters of recommendation	267	14	66%	41	46
M Arch 1	3½	NAAB	BA, Interview/portfolio	126	4	60%	42	47
M Arch 2	2		BA in Architecture, Interview/portfolio	20	0	65%	10	4
M Arch 3	1		B Arch, Interview/portfolio	6	0	—	3	2

SCHOOL DEMOGRAPHICS (all degree programs)

Full-Time Faculty	Part-Time Faculty	Full-Time Students	Part-Time Students	Foreign Students	Out-of-State U.S. Stdnts.	Women Students	Minority Students
39	37	419	18	30%	15%	30%	10%

LIBRARY (Tel. No. 213-829-3482)

Type	No. of Volumes	No. of Slides
Arch	10,000	50,000

STUDENT OPPORTUNITIES AND RESOURCES

LIBRARY. The SCI-ARC library is a resource center containing a growing collection of books with special emphasis on current publications, technical and planning publications and a large collection of American and European architectural journals augmented by related journals in such areas as environment, landscape, interiors, and graphics.

MEDIA CENTER. The Media Center is operated as a support facility to enrich and expand existing programs and document major activities such as the SCI-ARC Design Forum. Facilities include audio and video tape production, 35mm slide projection and photographic reproduction equipment. A darkroom is available for general student use.

A collection of audio cassettes and video tapes on local, national and international architects, planners and designers who have participated in SCI-ARC programs is available for student use in the Media Center.

COMPUTER LAB. The Computer Lab provides access to a wide range of application software, from word processing to computer-aided design systems. Currently available hardware includes the IBM-AT, Apple Macintosh, and a variety of output devices including laser printers and pen plotters. The curriculum includes general business and architectural computer applications

and supports the creative use of computers in the design process.

TOPANGA/TUNA CANYON SITE. In 1977, SCI-ARC acquired 120 acres of land in the Topanga and Tuna Canyon area. The immediate purpose is to generate structures, test concepts and develop self-sufficient community processes. The eventual goal is to establish an in-residence research center for scholars and graduate students in search of new concepts.

SPECIAL ACTIVITIES AND PROGRAMS

SCI-ARC conducts a Design Forum which offers students and the general community programs and lectures on architectural issues. Recent Design Forum programs featuring outstanding designers from Europe, Asia and the U.S. have focussed on Japanese Architecture, Architecture as Landscape, Changing Concepts in Space and Architecture, and a special series celebrating Le Corbusier's centenary year.

The SCI-ARC Architectural Gallery opened in May, 1981 with an exhibit entitled Modern Architecture: Mexico. Exhibits are open to the public and have included the work of Alvar Aalto, Peter Cook, Ron Herron, Daniel Liebskind, and Lawrence Halprin.

The Institute for Future Studies is a special program offering graduate studies in issues concerned with human factors, third world development, ocean and space habitation, world resources, and computers. Current Institute research is being conducted under grants from the National Endowment for the Arts and NASA.

SCI-ARC conducts a European Study program at its villa overlooking Lake Lugano in Vico

Morcote, Switzerland. Each session consists of studio and seminar work complemented by travel with members of the architecture faculty. The program is open to third-year students from other schools in the U.S. and abroad.

FACILITIES

SCI-ARC's unique facilities are located in a recycled 20,000-sq.-ft. industrial building whose interiors were designed and built by students and faculty. An "off-the-shelf" flexible scaffolding system provides student study spaces. The large central multi-use space has functioned as a workshop for large construction, seminars, and as an auditorium for up to 300 people, seminar and studio rooms, community design studio, media center, offices, computer room, and library. An adjacent 9,000-sq.-ft. building includes additional studio and seminar space and houses the 1,500-sq.-ft. architectural gallery.

SCHOLARSHIPS/AID

SCI-ARC participates in state and federal financial aid programs as well as offering institute scholarships. Financial assistance is received by approximately 80% of the student body. Federal financial aid available to all qualifying students includes: Guaranteed Student Loans, Pell Grant, SEOG Grant, College Work Study, SLS/PLUS Loans.

Undergraduate California residents may be eligible for Cal Grants under specific qualifying criteria. Graduate California residents may also be eligible for State Graduate Fellowships upon qualification.

Limited funds for scholarships and teaching assistant positions are available to students of exceptional ability who demonstrate financial need. These awards are usually given to continuing students.

UNDERGRADUATE PROGRAM
Philosophy Statement

In general, SCI-ARC best serves those students whose interests and personal characteristics mesh productively with its distinctive educational program. Drive and determination, a capacity for hard work, and a sense of purpose are more important than one's previous record of attainment. Normally any high school graduate may be considered. A student without a high school diploma is welcome to an interview and may enter the program if considered qualified.

Program Description

A basic objective of the undergraduate program is to encourage students to assume increasing responsibility and independence as they progress through the five years. To facilitate this objective, the studio program is divided into two segments. The beginning student spends the first two and one half years in a structured studio sequence. This core program is designed to develop design through skills and experience considered fundamental to architectural education. Upper-division students are given the opportunity of selecting a topical studio each semester from a choice of ten to twelve offered. The topical studios serve to support diversity within the studio program and encourage interaction between upper-division undergraduate and upper-division graduate students. They also permit the school to maintain a balanced student-faculty ratio of 15:1 in the studio program by mixing third-, fourth-, and fifth-year students with second- and third-year graduate students. The studio topics offer a range of urban and architectural issues and viewpoints representative of the diversity within the design faculty.

GRADUATE PROGRAM
Philosophy Statement

SCI-ARC is a genuine alternative, an optimistic one to replace the more institutionalized, professional schools that tend to standardize architectural education. The objective is to explore the nature of architectural education and the broader implications of the discipline (as opposed to the profession) in a social, cultural, political and technological context. The intent is to maintain an ongoing provisional forum for debate about architecture and cities and a confrontation to the most conventional values that exist in the profession.

SCI-ARC does not attach much importance to accepted design methodologies considering that they may preclude the search for ideas and concepts that may lead to new means of expression. It grants individuals in the discipline the opportunity to develop ideas they believe to be important.

Program Description

The school has always been a collective endeavor that reflects everyone's accomplishments. It exists as a body of individuals that are varied and unique in their approach to architecture but are bound together by their commitment to the discipline and their mutual respect, which presupposes the

expectation of a consistently high standard for all work being undertaken. This standard is applied to both faculty and students. The ratio between faculty and students is kept low which encourages a closeness through continual instruction and criticism and results in a continuity of purpose. Currently the studio faculty are among the most active practitioners in the discipline today. The relationship between working and teaching is a very important one that strikes a crucial balance between theory and practice. This is necessary if architecture is to transcend mere utility and become a cultural expression, a critical medium and a forum of knowledge related to the other arts and humanities.

SCI-ARC is a non-profit independent institute that is tuition-financed. By steadfastly maintaining our independence we are able to insulate ourselves from the external pressures that might adversely influence our development, allowing us to always decide our own priorities.

FACULTY
Administration

Michael Rotondi, Director
William M Simonian, Counselor/Admissions
Rose Marie Rabin, Chief Administrative Officer
Arlene Ainbinder, Chief Financial Officer
Robert Mangurian, Chairman, Graduate Division
Coy Howard, Chairman, Undergraduate Program
Kevin McMahon, Library Manager

Professors

Alberto Bertoli, B Arch
Roland Coate, RA, B Arch
Chris Dawson, RIBA, M Arch
Terry Glassman, M Arch
Tony Gwilliam, B Arch, MS
Craig Hodgetts, M Arch
Coy Howard, B Arch, MA Urb Pl
Raymond Kappe, B Arch
Ahde Lahti, MFA
Robert Mangurian, B Arch
Thom Mayne, M Arch
Eric Moss, RA, AIA, M Arch
Michael Rotondi, RA, AIA, Dipl
Glen Small, RA, AIA, B Arch, M Arch
Jim Stafford, B Arch

Associate Professors

Diane Caughey, RA, M Arch
Margaret Crawford, Grad Dipl, PhD
Milica Dedijer, B Arch
Nader Khalili, RA, AIA, M Arch
Heather Kurze, RA, M Arch
David Nixon, RA, AIA, B Arch
Dean Nota, RA, AIA, B Arch
Gary Paige, RA, B Arch
Martin Paull, BS Eng, B Arch
Albert Pope, B Arch, M Arch
John Souza, RA, M Arch
Arnold Stalk, B Arch, M Arch

Assistant Professors

Pamela Burton, ASLA, M Arch
Ben Caffey, B Arch, M Arch

John Clagett, RA, B Arch
Paul Lubowicki, RA, B Arch
Ron McCoy, RA, AIA, M Arch
Martin Mervel, M Arch
Georgia Scott, M Arch
Katherine Spitz, RA, AIA, M Arch
Jay Vanos, M Arch
Randall Wilson, MFA
Andrew Zago, BFA, M Arch

Part-Time Faculty

Steven Albert, RA, AIA
Kiyokazu Arai, M Arch
Bob Barnett, RA, AIA, B Arch, M Arch
Aaron Betsky, BA, M Arch
Kenneth Breisch, MA, PhD
Saul Goldin, BS Eng
Richard Grossman, MA
Alan Hess, BA, M Arch
Dave Hickey, ABD
Yoshio Ikezaki, MFA
Joseph Molloy, BFA
Susan Nardulli, M Arch
Ched Reeder, B Arch, M Arch
Michael Ross, RA, AIA, B Arch, M Arch
Bahram Shirdel, M Arch
David Taubman
Nabih Youssef, MS

Adjunct Faculty

Judith Crook, MFA
Mike Davis
Henry Hirsch, BA, MA Eng
Anna Krajewska-Wieczorex, PhD
Marshall Long, MS, PhD, Eng
Wolf Prix
Kathryn Smith, BA, MA
Michael Sorkin, MA, M Arch
Rachel Strickland, M Arch
Billie Tsien, M Arch
Gerald Wilhelm, B Arch
Tod Williams, BA, MFA

Visiting Faculty

Ann L T Bergren, MA, PhD
Marianne Burkhalter
John Kaliski
Fritz Neumeyer, PhD
Christian Sumi, Dipl
Anthony Vidler

Faculty/SCI-ARC Lugano, Switzerland

Martin Wagner, Director
Mario Botta
Giovanni Brino
Mario Campi
Mario d'Azzo
Aurelio Galfetti
Rafael Gianola
Daniel Herren
Edy Heuber
Luigi Snozzi
Martin Steinmann
Simon Ungers

University of Southern California

School of Architecture
University of Southern California
University Park, Watt Hall 203
Los Angeles, California 90089-0291
(213) 743-2723

Application Deadline(s): February 1 undgrd
                        March 15 grad
Tuition & Fees: Undgrd: $11,498/yr
                Grad: $11,498/yr
Endowment: Private

DEGREE PROGRAMS

Degree	Minimum Years for Degree	Accred.	Requirements for Admission	Full-Time Stdnts.	Part-Time Stdnts.	% of Applics. Accptd.	Stdnts. in 1st Year of Program	# of Degrees Conferred
B Arch	5	NAAB	SAT, hs diploma, statement,	348	0	60%	102	75
M Arch	1½		Prof arch degree, GRE, portfolio	9	0	10%	4	2
MBS	2		1st degree arch/engr,	5	0	60%	2	3
MLA	2		1st degree arch/1 arch, GRE, intro biology and geology, portfolio	2	0	50%	4	2

SCHOOL DEMOGRAPHICS (all degree programs)

Full-Time Faculty	Part-Time Faculty	Full-Time Students	Part-Time Students	Foreign Students	Out-of-State U.S. Stdnts.	Women Students	Minority Students
20	20	364	0	30%	40%	40%	35%

LIBRARY (Tel. No. 213-743-2798)

Type	No. of Volumes	No. of Slides
Art & Arch	55,000	184,000

STUDENT OPPORTUNITIES AND RESOURCES

The University of Southern California is a private university located at the heart of Los Angeles only minutes away from the central business district. The campus is on a beautiful landscaped site next to Exposition Park: the gardens, museums, and sports complex where the 1932 and 1984 Olympics were held. The University enrolls 30,000 students, yet the School of Architecture enjoys the intimacy of a student body of only 400 students. It is the only university-related private School of Architecture in the western United States. The school offers students the supportive environment provided by other such schools on the east coast and in the south.

The School of Architecture offers undergraduate education in architecture, and graduate education in architecture, landscape architecture, and in building science.

The diversity of the student body, from the variety of backgrounds present in California as well as from other parts of the United States and abroad, greatly enriches the educational experience for all students. Approximately one-third of the students are from minority groups and one-third are foreign students. Although nearly 60% of the students are from California, the number of students from other areas in the United States is increasing.

Five of the twenty regular faculty are Fellows of the American Institute of Architects. The faculty has won fourteen national awards for design and more than twenty-five state and regional design awards. Faculty work has been prominent in twenty-seven major exhibitions and in over one hundred and fifty publications. Thirteen major books have been authored by current School of Architecture faculty. Faculty have been recognized for such honors as the National A.I.A. Research Award, the Design Recognition Award from the National Endowment for the Arts, participation in the Venice Biennale and Milan Triennale, and as ACSA Distinguished Professor.

SPECIAL ACTIVITIES AND PROGRAMS

SUMMER PROGRAM: London (1983), Rome (1984, 1985, 1986), Rome/Florence/Venice/Milan/Vienna/Amsterdam and London (1987)

Internship Program for seniors

Field trips to significant places and buildings: Arizona (1985), New York (1986)

Architectural Guild Travelling Fellowships ($3000 for two graduating students)

Extensive schedule of visiting lecturers and critics

Gamble House Student-in-Residence Fellowships

EXPLORATION ARCHITECTURE: Program for high school students, mid-June

Student Thesis Exhibit: Graduating Class

Special Orientation Program for architecture majors

FACILITIES

The on-campus education program is conducted in Harris Hall, designed in 1938, and in Watt Hall, dedicated in 1976.

The new Helen Lindhurst Galleries of Architecture and Fine Arts contains one of the few exhibition spaces in Los Angeles devoted primarily to architecture.

A sun-simulation lab with a large electrically-operated heliodon and a wind-simulation lab with a 30-foot-long wind tunnel are also available.

The school's computer lab allows students the use of lab equipment either to connect to the university mainframe computer or to input and display architecture or site analysis data locally.

The school operates a photography facility and a woodwork and metal shop.

SCHOLARSHIPS/AID

The University provides a need-based financial aid package to all undergraduates admitted to the School of Architecture. Additionally the school awards nearly $200,000 each year in need and merit scholarships and internships. Over 60% of USC undergraduates receive some form of financial aid.

The school attempts to provide required financial assistance to every graduate student qualified for admission.

UNDERGRADUATE PROGRAM
Philosophy Statement

The fundamental premises of the school include: recognition of the interdependence of theory and practice, understanding the basis of architecture as profound response to the human condition and to human experience, respect for the disciplines of visual form and of technology as the means for realization of the objectives of architecture.

The central mission of the School of Architecture at the University of Southern California has been the education of eventual leaders within the profession. A large number of the school's alumni hold positions of leadership in firms and corporations throughout the world. The impact of the school's graduates on the environment of southern California has been particularly great. As this historic mission of the school is extended, vigorous efforts are under

way to continue to meet the complex issues and challenges of contemporary society and to develop images of a future environment that are increasingly humane and supportive.

Program Description

The curriculum has two cycles of study, the first providing a foundation of understanding on which to build a second cycle of advanced studies. Common to both cycles and continuous through the entire ten semesters of the program is the design studio in which projects are engaged as a means for developing the skills, the knowledge and understanding, and the judgment to create appropriate and exemplary architectural designs.

Foundation Program: Years One and Two
Introduction to the discipline of architecture; its subjects, its ideas, its methods, and the skills required for its practice.
Special Integrative Semester
Transition to a more knowing and mature commitment to becoming an architect.
Advanced Program: Years Three and Four
Opportunity to explore specific topics and to develop individual interests and strengths.
Bachelor of Architecture Thesis
Confirmation of the acquisition of skills and knowledge along with clarification of theoretical and professional directions.

The Special Integrative Semester and the Bachelor of Architecture Thesis

Completion of each of the two cycles of the curriculum is marked by a studio program of special significance. The foundation program culminates in the first semester of the third year with a studio project that assists students in summarizing what they have learned and in making the transition toward the more independent studies of the advanced program. The special integrative semester is also a transition to a more knowing and mature commitment to becoming an architect.

The advanced program is designed to encourage students to not only complete their basic education in architecture but also to develop their own interests and their own professional directions. This program culminates with the Bachelor of Architecture thesis. The final semester is devoted to intensive project design studies under the guidance of faculty advisors.

GRADUATE PROGRAM
Philosophy Statement

The School offers three highly individualized thesis-oriented graduate programs with emphasis on the design of urban places and projects.

The Master of Architecture Program emphasizes the study of architecture that contributes to the spatial development and cultural continuity of urban places. Such an architecture creates the continuity of rooms, indoors and out, that can make the city a welcome and supportive context for our lives.

The Master of Building Science program recognizes that exemplary buildings and places come into existence through response to the human condition, requiring good judgment and substantial knowledge about the appropriate and creative use of architectural technology.

The Master of Landscape Architecture program emphasizes the design of humane and supportive urban rooms, responsive to the natural systems and cultural potential of urban places.

Program Description
Master of Architecture

This is an advanced study program. Since each student already possesses a first professional degree (and often other professional experience), the opportunity exists not only to develop more extensive individual knowledge and capabilities, but also to challenge the most significant and important issues facing architecture and urbanism. The typical length of the program is three semesters. Faculty are drawn from all the school's programs as well as from the university at large, including distinguished lecturers and visiting critics.

The M. Arch. program is closely aligned with the other programs of the School of Architecture and with the Master of Planning program of the School of Urban and Regional Planning.

Master of Landscape Architecture

The graduate program in landscape architecture at USC is designed to significantly augment the professional capabilities of students who already possess a first degree in architecture or landscape architecture. The typical length of the program is two years, including 32 units of professional studies, 12 units of electives, and a two-semester thesis.

The program is intended for those with backgrounds in landscape architecture who wish to focus on the issues and projects that are forming our cities, and for those with backgrounds in architecture who wish to develop more extensive knowledge and capability in urban development and design.

The Master of Landscape Architecture program is closely aligned with the other programs of the School of Architecture and with the Master of Planning program of the School of Urban and Regional Planning. Qualified students may be admitted to a dual degree program in landscape architecture and in planning which will normally require an additional semester and summer for completion.

Master of Building Science

The Master in Building Science is intended for students who already possess a first degree in architecture or engineering. The typical length of this program is two years, centering on each student's thesis and supported by research seminars and electives from architecture, engineering, and other related fields.

Study areas include: form options in response to natural forces (sun, wind, seismic); computer-aided design, computer applications in structural design, form finding, analysis and simulation; specialized structures (highrise, longspan, unique forms); static and dynamic simulation models for structure investigation; industrialized construction and automation; solar energy systems; lighting, daylight and color

studies; environmental control system and acoustics, integration of structural, mechanical and electrical systems, their fit and synergy with architectural objectives.

FACULTY
Administration
Robert S Harris, FAIA, Dean, School of Architecture
Goetz G Schierle, AIA, Director, Master of Building Science Program
Amy Ciccone, Head Librarian

Professors
James E Ambrose, M Arch
Robert S Harris, FAIA, MFA
Sam T Hurst, FAIA, M Arch
Ralph Knowles, M Arch
Panos Koulermos, AIA, Dipl Arch
Roger Sherwood, AIA, MS, MRP
Achva Stein, MLA
Emmet Wemple, ASLA, BFA

Associate Professors
Mark Cigolle, AIA, M Arch
Frank Dimster, AIA, MA (UD)
Diane Ghirardo, PhD
Pierre Koenig, FAIA, B Arch
Graeme Morland, Dipl Arch
John Mutlow, AIA, M Arch
Stefanos Polyzoides, M Arch, MUP
Victor Regnier, AIA, M Arch
Goetz G Schierle, AIA, M Arch, Assoc, PhD
Marc Schiler, MS (Arch Sc)

Assistant Professors
Marc Angelil, M Arch
Michael Folonis
Paul Sorum

Adjunct Faculty
Peter de Bretteville, AIA, M Arch
Arthur Golding, AIA, M Arch
Charles A Lagreco, AIA, MFA, Arch
Michael B Lehrer, AIA, M Arch
Norman Millar, M Arch
Jay Nickels, AIA, B Arch
Ron Rose, AIA, M Arch
Dimitry Vergun, MS

Part-Time Faculty
Michael V Carapetian, AIA, Dipl, RIBA II
Edmund Chang, M Arch
Jeffrey Chusid, M Arch
Dana Cuff, PhD (Arch)
Christopher Genik, M Arch
Sarah Graham, M Arch
Randell Makinson, B Arch
Deborah Robbins, AB
John Sorcinelli, B Arch

Southern University

School of Architecture
Southern University and A&M College
P.O. Box 117722
Baton Rouge, Louisiana 70813
(504) 771-3015 or 771-4709

Admissions Office
(504) 771-2430

Application Deadline(s): —
Tuition & Fees: Undgrd: LA res: $562/yr;
    Non-res: $761/yr
    Grad: LA res: $572/yr;
    Non-res: $578/yr
Endowment: State

DEGREE PROGRAMS

Degree	Minimum Years for Degree	Accred.	Requirements for Admission	Full-Time Stdnts.	Part-Time Stdnts.	% of Applics. Accptd.	Stdnts. in 1st Year of Program	# of Degrees Conferred
B Arch	5	NAAB	Completion of all S.U. Junior Division requirements for admission to Senior Division status.	158		100%	49	230

SCHOOL DEMOGRAPHICS (all degree programs)

Full-Time Faculty	Part-Time Faculty	Full-Time Students	Part-Time Students	Foreign Students	Out-of-State U.S. Stdnts.	Women Students	Minority Students
10	3	158		30%	19%	17%	70%

LIBRARY (Tel. No. 504-771-3290)

Type	No. of Volumes	No. of Slides
	6,061	12,822

STUDENT OPPORTUNITIES AND RESOURCES

There are a variety of opportunities, in addition to the curriculum, that are available to students to foster personal development. These include opportunities for student representatives who are elected at each class level to participate in and contribute to most faculty and school committee meetings. The American Institute of Architecture Students (AIAS) is a vital student group that helps to facilitate communications and public relations within the School as well as with other schools and professional organizations. Some of their activities include participation in national and regional conferences, field trips, organized guest lectures, and sponsorship of the annual awards banquet.

SPECIAL ACTIVITIES AND PROGRAMS

A number of courses are offered during the Summer session. Field trips to other cities are held each semester. A limited number of co-operative education positions are available each semester for qualifying students. Individual and group student design competitions are entered throughout the year. An ongoing lecture series includes local architects and engineers. The School has an active chapter of the American Institute of Architecture Students.

FACILITIES

Current facilities of 6100 square feet occupy space in two buildings. A new architecture building has been designed and is scheduled for construction in late 1987. Total square footage will be 61,000.

SCHOLARSHIPS/AID

A limited number of academic scholarships are available. Student work-study positions and several other sources of financial aid are available upon application to the School of Architecture and the Financial Aid Office.

UNDERGRADUATE PROGRAM
Philosophy Statement

The Southern University School of Architecture seeks to prepare students for careers in the environmental design field. While this represents our mission it must be noted that as a mission it is rooted in the realities of the total of our past and present existence. The current general educational objective of the program is that of developing and refining the individual's innate perceptive, descriptive, analytical, conceptual, evaluative and predictive skills and abilities in managing the problem-defining and problem-solving processes required for the ordering of physical space for human use and interaction.

Program Description

The program in architecture is ordered as a two-phase educational process consisting of an orientational and introductory first year and a four-year sequence of intermediate and advanced level educational experiences. The curriculum utilizes a "building block" concept which envisions the first year of introductory studies as the foundation. The process culminates with the awarding of the first professional degree of Bachelor of Architecture.

The baccalaureate program primarily prepares students for gainful employment in architectural firms and other building construction-related agencies and institutions.

Further, the program provides the student with a strong undergraduate foundation for advanced study in architecture, urban planning, landscape architecture and related environmental design fields.

A total of 166 semester-hours are required for graduation from the B Arch degree program. The five years of course work include an essential balance of courses in general education, mathematics, physical and social sciences, arts and humanities, together with professional and technical electives and core curriculum courses in architecture.

FACULTY

Administration

Arthur L Symes, Dean
Dorothy E Davis, Librarian

Professors

Arthur L Symes, D Arch

Associate Professors

Joyce Davis, PhD
E Donald Van Purnell, B Arch

Assistant Professors

John L Delgado, Jr, B Arch
John Desmond, M Arch
Franklin L Lassiter, RA, M Arch
Nelson Longnecker, RA, B Arch
John H Schaeffer, RA, M Arch
Douglas Schneider, RA, B Arch
Charles Ashton Smith, RA, B Arch
Lonnie Wilkinson, M Arch

Part-Time Faculty

Andrew Smith
Patrick Staub, RA, M Arch
Henry L Thurman, RA, MS Arch Engr

University of Southwestern Louisiana

Department of Architecture
School of Art and Architecture
University of Southwestern Louisiana
Lafayette, Louisiana 70504-3850
(318) 231-6225

Admissions Office
Lafayette, Louisiana 70504-1210
(318) 231-6457

Application Deadline(s): U.S. Citizens: 30 days
before start of sem
Non-U.S. Citizens: 90 days
before start of sem
Transfers: March 1 for Fall,
November 1 for Spring
Tuition & Fees: Undgrd: LA Res: $616/sem
Non-Res: $1441/sem
Foreign: $1518/sem
Endowment: State

DEGREE PROGRAMS

Degree	Minimum Years for Degree	Accred.	Requirements for Admission	Full-Time Stdnts.	Part-Time Stdnts.	% of Applics. Accptd.	Stdnts. in 1st Year of Program	# of Degrees Conferred
B Arch	5	NAAB	High School Diploma	287	31	50%	77	30
BFA (Interior Design)	4		High School Diploma	72	10	50%	25	8

SCHOOL DEMOGRAPHICS (all degree programs)

Full-Time Faculty	Part-Time Faculty	Full-Time Students	Part-Time Students	Foreign Students	Out-of-State U.S. Stdnts.	Women Students	Minority Students
15	4	359	41	19%	4%	13%	14%

LIBRARY (Tel. No. 318-231-6396)

Type	No. of Volumes	No. of Slides
University	4,000 (Arch)	50,000 (Arch)

STUDENT OPPORTUNITIES AND RESOURCES

The Department of Architecture, with 400 students, is a fast growing department within an expanding university. The University of Southwestern Louisiana enrolls 15,000 students including 2,000 who come from outside the United States. Lafayette is a small, friendly city of 100,000, located 25 minutes west of New Orleans and 35 minutes east of Houston by air. It is in a corridor that because of its petrochemicals and water resources, is destined to become a highly complex and populous industrial area. The area is rich in cultural activities and is noted for its Cajun culture, French heritage, Mardi Gras, and exquisite food.

The School of Art and Architecture has a diversified, international faculty and cultivates strong relationships with other programs (anthropology, French, humanities, computer science). The campus has excellent facilities and has kept a human scale, reflecting a concern about students that makes it a pleasant place to live and work.

Transfer students are accepted, but are required to have a portfolio of work if any design credit is anticipated.

SPECIAL ACTIVITIES AND PROGRAMS

Varied program of visiting lecturers, workshops, exhibition, etc. sponsored by the Students' Association of the School of Art and Architecture

AIA Student Chapter

Beaux Arts Ball

Architecture Spring Festival (one week)

Awards Night

Weekly Lunches in the Courtyard

Annual Trip to Mexico during Mardi Gras holidays

A new Summer Foreign Study Program in France is available to students and faculty

FACILITIES

At the end of 1976, the school moved into a new building where all of the major courses of the curriculum are taught. The building also houses the offices of the Director, the Audio Visual Library, the Art Museum, the Media Center, and the Workshop. There are also shop facilities available in ceramics, photography, painting, sculpture, printmaking, woodworking, plastics, metals and concrete.

SCHOLARSHIPS/AID

The following scholarships are given in the Department of Architecture: $750 from local building material suppliers, $1000-$3000 a year in AIA scholarships, $1000 for Summer Travel Fellowship, $99.99 from the Architecture faculty (per year) and $1000 a year for four years in University Academic Scholarships for entering freshmen.

UNDERGRADUATE PROGRAM
Philosophy Statement

The School of Art & Architecture is concerned with the professional development of architects, artists, designers, craftsmen, and teachers. Thus, the graphic and plastic arts occupy a unique and autonomous position among the academic disciplines. The relationship between the art and architecture programs allows for an integration of faculty, facilities, equipment, lecturers, libraries, and students which is not only economical but desirable in the sense that the architecture faculty and students alike are in close touch with the arts.

Many of the design projects utilized in the program are more real than hypothetical and are directly related to contemporary social and environmental problems of southwestern Louisiana. Students work directly with city administrators, community action groups, business associations, educational institutions, and the like to solve community problems. Such projects as downtown development, recreation, housing, rehabilitation and campus planning become community service projects.

There is a special emphasis on research and communication at all levels of architectural instruction, wherein the most advanced techniques are employed.

FACULTY
Administration

Gilbert Carner, Acting Director
Edward J Cazayoux, AIA, Department Head

Professors

Edward J Cazayoux, AIA, B Arch, M Arch, MCP
Wilbur D Starr, RA, B Arch, MCP
Rolf G Strahle, AIA, M Arch

Associate Professors

Ruston J Bernard, BA, M Arch
Ethel S Goodstein, AIA, B Arch, MA
Hector Lasala, RA, B Arch, M Arch
George S Loli, AIA, Dottore in Arch

Assistant Professors

Robert W Brown, BID, M Arch
David Courville, AIA, B Arch

Alan Hines, AIA, BED, M Arch
William Merryfield, BA, M Arch
Timothy J Woods, M Arch

Instructor

Charlotte Roberts, RA, BID, MHEc

Part-Time Faculty

Edward Barrier, MA
Herman Gesser, AIA, B Arch, M Arch
Lynn Guidry, AIA, B Arch
Robert Hinkley, PE, MS
Randy J Moore, RA, B Arch
Bulent Ovunc, PhD
David Perkins, FAIA, B Arch

Adjunct Faculty

Beth Woods, BS, MS

Spring Garden College

**Dept. of Architecture
& Interior Design
Spring Garden College
7500 Germantown Avenue
Philadelphia, Pennsylvania 19119
(215) 248-7900 College
(215) 248-7912 Department**

**Admissions Office
(215) 248-7900**

Application Deadline(s): Rolling Enrollment -
Students accepted for
Fall and Spring sems
Tuition & Fees: Undgrd: $6200/yr
Endowment: Private

DEGREE PROGRAMS

Degree	Minimum Years for Degree	Accred.	Requirements for Admission	Full-Time Stdnts.	Part-Time Stdnts.	% of Applics. Accptd.	Stdnts. in 1st Year of Program	# of Degrees Conferred
Architecture AS (Science)	2		4 HS units of English, 3 of Math, 2 of Science	16	5		—	2
BS (Arch)	4		as above	26	1		—	4
B Arch	5	Candidacy Status NAAB	as above	88	5		59	4
Interior Design								
AA (Arts)	2		4 HS units of English, 2 of Math, 2 of Science	—	—		—	—
BA (Arts)	4		as above	29	3		11	4
Construction Management Technology								
AS (Science)	2		4 HS units in English, 2 of Math, 2 of Science	—			—	—
BS	4		as above	75	15		25	19
Civil Engineering Technology								
AS (Science)	2		4 HS units of English, 3 of Math, 2 of Science	—	—		—	—
BS	4		as above	29	8		11	4

SCHOOL DEMOGRAPHICS (all degree programs)

Full-Time Faculty	Part-Time Faculty	Full-Time Students	Part-Time Students	Foreign Students	Out-of-State U.S. Stdnts.	Women Students	Minority Students
8	18	263	37	2%	22%	24%	16%

LIBRARY (Tel. No. 215-248-7900 x526)

Type	No. of Volumes	No. of Slides
Main	22,000 400 periodicals	
Dept'l		3500

STUDENT OPPORTUNITIES AND RESOURCES

Relatively small student body where faculty and students begin to know each other well in a short time. High percentage of female students in design, much less in engineering disciplines.

Located in Mount Airy, almost on outskirts of Philadelphia, close to farm land, Morris Arboretum and away from noise and pollution.

Department makes up 45% of full-time student enrollment at Spring Garden College. Currently, Architecture is largest discipline in College.

Unique relationship of Architecture to Interior Design, Civil Engineering and Construction Management Technology under Chairmanship of Architect.

All faculty practices as architects, engineers, artists, sculptors, surveyors, model makers, photographers, or computer specialists.

Transfer students are accepted but are required to submit (in Architecture and Interior Design) a portfolio so that they may be placed in the design sequence.

The program offers a suburban alternative to the other Architectural Programs in the area; University of Pennsylvania (graduate school);

Drexel (evening program); Temple (inner city campus); Philadelphia College of Art (four-year program in an art school environment).

Students take part in A.I.A.S., canoe contest, A.C.S.A., competitions, exchange program, sports activities, lecture series.

SPECIAL ACTIVITIES AND PROGRAMS

There is a student/faculty exchange program with Bezalel Academy of Arts and Design in Jerusalem, Israel. This Fall, we had a visiting Professor from Bezalel for four months. This Summer, students will be taking an Urban/Design Program in Jerusalem.

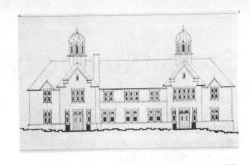

There is an active Career Counseling and Placement Service under Mr. Robert Evans. There are at least three jobs for each student and all our students are employed.

There are Honor Society Awards Programs as well as Dean's and President's lists.

There is an active lecture series in the department which draws on local, national and international personalities. The series is open to the public and is well publicized and well attended.

The Design students are very active in most student activities because of their creative skills.

There are two literary magazines in which our students and faculty participate and contribute.

We have joint degree programs in Architecture, Interior Design, Civil Engineering and Construction Management Technology.

Students participate in fund raising through the various student organizations.

FACILITIES

The Architecture Department has a state-of-the-art Prime C.A.D. System which operates on Medusa Software. There are currently four stations. In addition, there is a Zenith/Auto CAD System and a Textronic Plotter System.

There is a new photographic lab and a model shop. We have a concrete laboratory and are constructing a structural testing laboratory.

We have facilities for duplicating slides and magazines as well as a blueprint machine for student use.

SCHOLARSHIPS/AID

The Financial Aid Office works on the premise that all qualified students should have access to higher education. Spring Garden's comprehensive financial assistance program allows approximately 70% of our students to receive aid.

Included in the aid are federal and state monies, college and other agencies/organizations, in the form of grants, loans, scholarships and employment.

Financial aid filing deadlines are May 1 for Fall and November 1 for Spring.

Scholarships and awards based on merit are available and students are directed to the office of Financial Aid for information.

UNDERGRADUATE PROGRAM
Philosophy Statement

Man has been constantly changing his physical environment since the onset of the urban revolution over nine thousand years ago. Today the rapid alteration of our surroundings is shaping our destiny as never before.

Graduates from the Department's curricula will work in the physical environment, and the environment will be modified by their work. The Department was founded with the conviction that this conscious molding of our surroundings is an awesome responsibility.

The Department's curricula are planned to educate students in the necessary techniques of design and construction. At the same time an understanding of fundamental human values must become a part of everything we do. Each of the Department's programs is complete,

self-sufficient, rigorous and technologically sound. However, structural relations between the programs are strong. They have been designed so that students in one program are exposed to the issues and concerns of students in other department programs.

The structure of the Department seeks to encourage participation in a joyous shared learning process which combines the delights of creation and building with the pleasures of that elusive process called human understanding.

Program Description

Architecture is an ancient art embodying a culture's deepest values and expressing its underlying social concepts.

The tasks of the architect include the research, planning, design and implementation of the shelters and settlements which accommodate human activity. Creative work in architecture is a complex process of analysis and synthesis occurring within the designer's referential framework of art, society, and technology. Accordingly, the study of architecture integrates the poetics of art and truth in design with practical engineering and scientific skills. The built environment, for which architects are responsible, ought to be a fusion of human values and technological achievement, not merely a collection of dispassionate utilitarian objects.

From the freshman year on, students will approach the study of architecture by understanding the products of human skills and endeavor, the inherent qualities of the natural environment, present values, past traditions and aspirations.

Theoretical studies in the physical and natural sciences are taken concurrently and applied to materials and structures, methods of construction, environmental control systems, and ergonomics.

The synthesis of all the essential elements in architecture takes place in the studio. There the students will systematically develop their skills in architectural design. Students are encouraged to express design in a graphic manner as well as through discourse.

Students in the Architecture Program will, during their studies at Spring Garden College, acquire a "way of life" as a person well-versed in the art, craft and humanism of the field. The resulting designs will lead, hopefully, to shelters and settlements rich in humane possibilities.

FACULTY
Administration

Allen I Bernholtz, RA, MRAIC, OAA, MFESAE, ACM, Chairman
Mildred Glushakow, Librarian

Professors

Allen I Bernholtz, MRAIC, B Arch, M Arch
Alexander Messinger, AIA, B Arch, M Arch, MCP, MS
Karl Obermaier, RA, B Arch
Roy Vollmer, RA, B Arch, M Arch

Assistant Professors

Paula Behrens, RA, BA M Arch
Cecelia Denegre, RA, BS, M Arch
David Wang, RA, BA, M Arch

Part-Time Faculty

John Anderson, BS
Warren O Angle, MFA
Linda Brenner, BFA
William Christensen, BS
Raymond Cline, PE, BS, MBA
Leesa Conley-Harding, BSID
Robert Cornelius, BA
Greg Decker, BFA, MFA
John DeFazio, B Arch
Joseph Denegre, M Arch
Lynn Denton, MFA
Daniel Flint, BS
Julie Gabrielli, M Arch
Robin Goodale, MA, MFA
Walter Greene, PE
Gevork Hartoonian, MS, PhD
Gerald Hill, PE, BSME, MEd
Dennis Johnson, RA, BS, B Arch, M Arch/CP
P K Mitra, PE, BE, MS
Sean O'Rourke, M Arch
Susan Pitman, BFA
Ellen Randall, RA, BA, M Arch
Jeri Lynn Robinson, MFA
Andrew Schoerke, RA, B Arch
Dean Sherwin, RIBA, BS, M Arch, MLA
Robert Skaler, RA, B Arch
Jill K Walker, RA, B Arch

Adjunct Faculty

David S Beck, BS, MAT
David H Connolly, MSEE
Mohamed E Elsabbagh, BSEE, MSEE
David X Fitt, MA, PhD
Howard Medoff, PE, BSME, MS
Frank D Quattrone, BA, MA
Anita Y Schwab, BA, MS
Edward Taylor MT(ASCP), BS, MS

State University of New York at Buffalo

School of Architecture
& Environmental Design
State University of New York
Hayes Hall, 3435 Main Street
Buffalo, New York 14214
(716) 831-3483

Admissions Office
(716) 831-3485

Application Deadline(s): February 15
Tuition & Fees: Undgrd: NY res: $1474/yr
Non-res: $3324/yr
Grad: NY res: $2214/yr
Non-res: $3799/yr
Endowment: State

DEGREE PROGRAMS

Degree	Minimum Years for Degree	Accred.*	Requirements for Admission	Full-Time Stdnts.	Part-Time Stdnts.	% of Applics. Accptd.	Stdnts. in 1st Year of Program	# of Degrees Conferred
BPS	4	NYS	64 hrs coll work Portfolio, GPA	101		40%	58	
BAED	4	NYS	2 yrs coll work	80		75%	40	40
M Arch	3½	NAAB	BA/BS non Portfolio	55		50%	17	15
M Arch	2	NAAB	BPS, BA/BS (Arch) Portfolio	57		60%	24	
M Arch	1½	NYS	B Arch Portfolio	7		60%	4	5
M Arch/ Adv Bldg Tech	1½	NYS	B Arch Portfolio	17		60%	9	12
MUP	2	NYS	BA, BS	28		70%	12	12
M Arch/MUP	3	NAAB, NYS	BPS, BA/BS(Arch) Portfolio	5		60%	3	2
M Arch/MBA	3	NAAB, NYS	BPS, BA/BA(Arch) Portfolio, GMAT	5		60%	2	2
BA Design Studies	4	NYS	64 hrs coll work Portfolio	49		50%	25	18

*NYS = New York State Dept. of Education

SCHOOL DEMOGRAPHICS (all degree programs)

Full-Time Faculty	Part-Time Faculty	Full-Time Students	Part-Time Students	Foreign Students	Out-of-State U.S. Stdnts.	Women Students	Minority Students
30	27	404	0	15%	9%	23%	3%

LIBRARY (Tel. No. 716-831-3483)

Type	No. of Volumes	No. of Slides
Special Collection	16,000	

STUDENT OPPORTUNITIES AND RESOURCES

SUNY at Buffalo is one of the four major university centers of the SUNY system. The University provides the full advantages of studies in all major disciplines, a comprehensive library system, computer facilities, student housing, and recreational facilities.

The Buffalo metropolitan area, second-largest in New York State, is rich in architectural heritage and provides a wide range of cultural activities. The School uses Buffalo and the Western New York region as a learning laboratory enriching the "hands-on" component of the professional education programs.

The Department of Architecture is one of three departments in the School of Architecture and Environmental Design. Other departments include the Department of Environmental Design and Planning, which offers an undergraduate degree (Bachelor of Arts in Environmental Design) and a graduate degree (Master of Urban Planning), and the Department of Design Studies, which offers preprofessional courses in design fundamentals and an undergraduate, special-major degree. In addition, several research and educational programs are affiliated with the school: the Center for Integrative Studies, the Center for Comparative Studies in Development Planning, the Center for Regional Studies, and the Architectural Awareness Project for Buffalo.

The Faculty of the Department provide a broad range of expertise offering special areas of electives and graduate study related to urban design, environment-behavior studies, urban ecology, historic preservation/adaptive re-use, computer-aided design, energy studies and advanced building technology.

Undergraduate students transferring from other universities or community colleges are eligible for admission to the Department after completing up to two years of university instruction. Graduate students may transfer up to 12 credits from another university.

SPECIAL ACTIVITIES AND PROGRAMS

AIA Student Chapter
Student Association
Graduate Student Association
Semester lecture series with invited speakers
Topical Conferences
Summer workshops and courses
Student/Practitioner Forums
Field Trips
Professional internship awards
Exhibition and Publication Programs
Visiting Critics

FACILITIES

The school has large studio spaces, a 16,000-volume special library collection, a fully equipped computer-aided design lab, an adaptive-environments lab for research on design Issues related to special populations, a fully equipped photo lab, a wood shop and high bay facility for building component assembly and testing, and an exhibits lounge as well as a student lounge.

SCHOLARSHIPS/AID

The State University has a number of financial aid programs for NYS and out-of-state residents. Separate application should be made to the Office of Financial Aid to Students, 133 Parker Hall, Main Street Campus, SUNY at Buffalo, Buffalo, New York 14214. In addition, the Department of Architecture has a limited number of work-study positions and graduate and teaching assistantships. In any given semester up to 30 graduate students receive some form of assistance.

UNDERGRADUATE PROGRAM
Philosophy Statement

The Department's aim is to develop and educate architects who are visually sensitive, socially aware, environmentally responsible, and technically competent. An architect sensitive to these concerns can respect and respond to cultural roots, identify human wants and needs, translate these into appropriate physical form, and understand how such designs can be implemented and evaluated. The undergraduate program provides the basis for a comprehensive professional education.

Program Description

The Bachelor of Professional Studies is a preprofessional baccalaureate degree designed to provide students with a base of concepts and skills from which further professional studies at a graduate level can be undertaken. It can supplement existing architectural, civil, and construction technology programs of the community colleges of New York.

The program is open to undergraduates who have completed two years of college work and working students with two years of college background. Upon completion of the first two years in the department, undergraduates receive the preprofessional Bachelor of Professional Studies degree. They may then apply for a further two years of graduate study leading to the professional degree of Master of Architecture.

GRADUATE PROGRAM
Philosophy Statement

The Master of Architecture degree may be pursued as either a first or second professional degree. The first professional degree program incorporates the same goals and philosophy as the undergraduate program but also provides students with a comprehensive perspective on the field of architecture and the appropriate skills to make it possible for them to be leaders in the profession. The second professional degree

program allows students to investigate their own areas of special interest, drawing upon the full resources of the Department and the University.

Program Description

The program is open to three groups of students. (1) Graduate students holding a four-year preprofessional degree (BPS, BA, BS or equivalent) from a school of architecture can complete their studies for the M Arch in two years. (2) Graduate students who hold bachelor's degrees in other fields can complete their studies for the M Arch in three-and-one-half years. (3) Graduate students who hold the first professional degree of Bachelor of Architecture or the equivalent can complete their studies for the M Arch as a second professional degree in one to one-and-one-half years.

The Department now offers an M Arch in Advanced Building Technology for holders of a first professional degree in architecture. The program emphasizes the advancement of building technology and building systems, with appropriate application to the needs of both industrially developed and developing societies.

Dual graduate degrees are offered combining the M Arch with either the Master of Urban Planning or the Master of Business Administration. The Department is developing a dual degree agreement with the Civil Engineering Department in Construction Management. In most cases, dual graduate degrees can be earned in two-and-one-half years for students with a Bachelor of Architecture Degree.

FACULTY
Administration

Bruno Freschi, Dean
John S Bis, Associate Dean
Robert G Shibley, AIA, Chairman, Department of Architecture
Jay M Stein, ACIP, Chairman, Department of Planning and Design
Gunter Schmitz, Director, Advanced Building Technology Program
Atilla Bilgutay, Associate Director, Advanced Building Technology Program
Edward Steinfeld, RA, Director, Adaptive Environments Laboratory
Yehuda Kalay, Director, Computer Aided Design/Graphics Laboratory

DEPARTMENT OF ARCHITECTURE FACULTY
Professors

Atilla Bilgutay, MS Civ Eng
William Huff, B Arch, M Arch
Gunter Schmitz, Dipl
Robert G Shibley, B Arch, M Arch UD
Edward Steinfeld, B Arch, M Arch, D Arch

Associate Professors

Dennis Andrejko, B Arch, M Arch
John C Archea, BS, PhD
Elizabeth Cromley, BA, MA, PhD
Gary E Day, B Arch, MUP
Hiroaki Hata, M Arch, M Arch/UD
Yehuda Kalay, B Arch, MSc, PhD
Ulrik Lossing
Lynda Schneekloth, MSLA

Assistant Professors

Lily Chi, M Phil
Anton Harfmann, M Arch
Rashid Mohsini, PhD
Bonnie Ott, BA, M Arch

Part-Time Faculty

Beverly Albert, B Arch, M Arch
Paul Battaglia, BS, M Arch
Donald Blair, BSAS, M Arch
Michael Brill, B Arch
Richard Crandall
Deborah Dennis, M Arch
Joseph Ernst, M Arch
David Giusiana, BA/Arch, M Arch
James Goodson, B Arch
Frederic Houston, M Arch
Christopher Less, B Arch
Theodore Lownie, B Arch
Kenneth MacKay, BA, M Arch
Bruce Majkowski, M Arch
Carl Nuermberger, M Arch
Thomas Payne, MFA
Frances Russo, M Arch
Douglas Scheid, M Arch
Walter Sobieraj, M Arch
Lucien Swerdloff, M Arch
Robert Turley, BSEE

Adjunct Faculty

Walter Bird

DEPARTMENT OF PLANNING AND DESIGN FACULTY
Professors

John S Bis, BA/Des
Harold L Cohen, BA Des
Sam D Cole, D Phil
Donald H Glickman, MS
Magda Cordell McHale
David C Perry, MPA, PhD
Jay M Stein, MA, PhD

Associate Professors

G Scott Danford, PhD
Ibrahim Jammal, M Arch/MCP
Alfred D Price, M Arch/MUP

Assistant Professors

Marilyn L Reeves, PhD
M Beth Tauke, MA/Des, MFA/Des

Adjunct Faculty

William M E Clarkson, MAE
Milton Kaplan, LLB
Andrew Rudnick, MBA, PhD

Syracuse University

School of Architecture
Syracuse University
103 Slocum Hall
Syracuse, New York 13244-1250
(315) 443-2256

Admissions Office
Syracuse University
201 Tolley Administration Building
Syracuse, New York 13244-1120
(315) 443-3611

Application Deadline(s): February 1
Tuition & Fees: Undgrd: $4070 per semester
(1986-87)
Grad: $246 per credit hour
(1986-87)
Endowment: Private

DEGREE PROGRAMS

Degree	Minimum Years for Degree	Accred.	Requirements for Admission	Full-Time Stdnts.	Part-Time Stdnts.	% of Applics. Accptd.	Stdnts. in 1st Year of Program	# of Degrees Conferred
B Arch	5	NAAB	interview, portfolio review	357	13	45%	121	70
M Arch I	3½	NAAB	baccalaureate degree (any field) portfolio	46	1	21%	17	8
M Arch II	1	not applicable	1st prof degree (arch) portfolio	18	0	27%	—	0

SCHOOL DEMOGRAPHICS (all degree programs)

Full-Time Faculty	Part-Time Faculty	Full-Time Students	Part-Time Students	Foreign Students	Out-of-State U.S. Stdnts.	Women Students	Minority Students
28	2	420	14	7%	47%	25%	15.5%

LIBRARY (Tel. No. 315-423-2905)

Type	No. of Volumes	No. of Slides
Art & Arch	53,000	240,000

STUDENT OPPORTUNITIES AND RESOURCES

The School of Architecture's autonomy within the large academic community of Syracuse University offers the best of a small college and the breadth and diversity of choices found in a major university setting.

Syracuse serves over 14,000 undergraduate students and almost 6,000 graduates, coming from every state in the union and 100 foreign countries. There are more than 300 programs of study from which to choose elective course offerings while fulfilling the professional requirements for the B Arch degree. Dual degree programs are possible in many areas; these programs, however, require additional time for completion.

The faculty of the school have studied, taught and practiced architecture in England, France, Switzerland, Italy, Germany and Canada, and in many of the states. Over half are actively engaged in professional practice as licensed architects. The faculty includes professional artists and engineers, and represents unusual strength in architectural history and theory.

SPECIAL ACTIVITIES AND PROGRAMS

Semester or year in Italy

Summer programs abroad

Summer study programs on campus (for make-up or acceleration)

Senior seminar programs

Historic preservation studies available

Visiting professors studio program

School-sponsored lecture series

School-sponsored exhibitions

Student publications

FACILITIES

The School of Architecture is located in Slocum Hall, a building listed in the National Register of Historic Places.

The design studios occupy most of the building's third and fourth floors. Administrative and faculty offices and a display gallery are also located in Slocum Hall, where virtually all the professionally oriented classes in architecture are scheduled. The Architecture Reading Room on the first floor contains pertinent reference and reserve materials as well as current professional publications. The main architecture collection of more than 14,000 volumes is located in nearby Bird Library. Adjacent to the fourth floor studios are a school-operated blueprint facility and a well-equipped model-making workshop for student use.

Syracuse University has an excellent computing network, including four mainframe computers, 100 all-University terminals in public clusters, and hundreds of individual terminals and microcomputers. The School's own computer facility on the third floor of Slocum Hall contains equipment geared to the in-house computer-aided design program.

SCHOLARSHIPS/AID

Syracuse University has $8,230,500 in university scholarships and $3,700,672 in NDSL loans, as well as $19,280,725 in federal/state scholarships and $17,363,210 in Guaranteed Student Loans. Architecture students are eligible for all of these, as well as for approximately $15,000 in aid specifically for architecture students.

UNDERGRADUATE PROGRAM
Philosophy Statement

The School of Architecture at Syracuse emphasizes architecture as a profession. The program, designed to prepare professionals able to respond to different types of involvement and roles in the profession, offers a broad humanistic education as well as the basic skills and understanding required by the practice of architecture.

At Syracuse the architecture program is strongly oriented toward design. It is based on the premise that the architect is the only professional specially educated to give shape and meaning to the environment. The program focuses on synthesizing the innumerable aspects that go into producing a building, with the goal of elevating the facts of mere buildings into the realm of art and ultimately enriching life.

Program Description

The 165-credit-hour B Arch program is organized into three distinct phases: the first three core years, the fourth intermediate year, and the fifth and final year. There are 118 hours of professional architecture course work and 47 hours of non-architecture course work, 29 of which must be in the arts and sciences.

In the core years, the architecture program is sequentially organized and principally skill-oriented, including basic visual and architectural design training and all required basic technology, structural design, and history courses.

The fourth year, after the basic architecture program is completed, is intended as a year of choice, providing opportunities to broaden the student's interests and experiences by participation in the school's off-campus programs abroad. For those remaining on campus, special programs and elective design studios are available.

The fifth and final year includes a course in the legal aspects of professional practice, a summary course in technologies, and a first-semester advanced design studio of the student's choice, usually with a distinguished visiting architect/educator. During the last semester, the entire program culminates in a senior thesis, almost always in the form of a major design project.

GRADUATE PROGRAM
Philosophy Statement

M Arch I Program The three-and-one-half-year Master of Architecture (first professional degree) program encompasses the entire professional component of the undergraduate degree program, but at a more intense pace and with several special courses geared to the broader background and maturity of the graduate student. The program is geared to students with four-year baccalaureate degrees in other disciplines, but can accommodate advanced standing for transfers from four-year architecture programs. Because of the specific design orientation of the program, successful applicants generally tend to have some visual training and are able to offer evidence of this through the submission of a portfolio.

M Arch II Program The M Arch II (second professional degree) program is geared to the highly qualified individuals who have completed a first professional degree and wish to develop advanced design skills. The focus of the program is on architectural design and theory.

Beginning with a three-week session at the University's Syracuse, New York, campus, the program is conducted thereafter entirely in Italy at the Syracuse University Florence Center. There students have the rare opportunity of studying with outstanding architects and critics while surrounded by the rich physical and cultural environment of Italy.

Program Description

M Arch I Program The program totals 115 credits and is divided into two phases. Phase one consists of four semesters that are devoted to acquiring basic architectural skills. Phase two consists of two semesters of advanced design studio, chosen from several studio options, and a seventh and final semester devoted to the thesis.

Four required sequences and a group of professional electives constitute the 115 hours. The first three semesters of the design sequence are structured specifically for graduate students and are coordinated with the two courses in drawing and an introduction to Architecture. After completing these semesters, graduate students join the basic program in the final core year and conclude with design and thesis studios.

M Arch II Program The 30-credit-hour Master of Architecture, second professional degree, program is open to qualified students with a first professional Bachelor or Master of Architecture degree or its equivalent. History and theory are an integral part of the program. The program begins with a three-week intensive preparatory session at Syracuse University, continues to Florence, and culminates in a final project review on the home campus. Classes are taught by Syracuse University faculty and distinguished critics and historians.

The Syracuse University Florence Center provides studios, lecture rooms, a gallery, and its own architecture library. In addition to the M Arch II program, the Center is home to its first professional degree architecture and pre-architecture programs, as well as a number of other undergraduate and graduate programs in studio art, political science and humanities.

FACULTY
Administration

Werner Seligmann, RA, Dean
Arthur W McDonald, RA, Head, Undergraduate
  Architecture

Randall Korman, RA, Head, M Arch I Program
Barbara Opar, Associate Librarian, Fine Arts

Professors

Raymond DiPasquale, AIA, RA, BS Civ Eng, B
  Arch, MSc, Arc Engr
J Francois Gabriel, Dipl
Kermit J Lee, Jr, RA, B Arch
Paul Malo, RA, B Arch
William H Scarbrough, RA, B Arch
Louis Skoler, RA, B Arch
Mary Ann Smith, BFA, MA
Siegfried Snyder, BFA, MFA

Associate Professors

Joel Bostick, RA, B Arch, M Arch
Bruce Coleman, RA, B Arch
Marleen Kay Davis, RA, B Arch, M Arch
Christopher J Gray, RA, Dipl, M Arch
Randall Korman, RA, B Arch, M Arch
Robert A Levy, B Arch, M Arch
Arthur W McDonald, RA, B Arch, M Arch
Mark Shapiro, RA, B Arch, M Arch
Edward J Sichta, BFA, MFA
Patricia Waddy, BA, MA, PhD

Assistant Professors

Theodore Brown, RA, Dipl
Pamela Butz, B Arch, M Arch
Maurice D Cox, B Arch
Thomas K Davis, RA, B Arch, M Arch
Caterina Frisone, RA, B Arch, M Arch
Robert Goodill, B Arch
Susan Henderson, B Arch, M Arch
Chi Wing Lo, B Arch, M Arch
Stuart A Muller, B Arch, M Arch
Cheryl O'Neill, RA, B Arch, M Arch
Richard Role, B Arch
Terry D Steelman, RA, BS, M Arch

Technical University of Nova Scotia

Faculty of Architecture
Technical University of Nova Scotia
P.O. Box 1000
Halifax, Nova Scotia B3J 2X4
(902) 429-8300

Application Deadline(s): July 1
Tuition & Fees: Undgrd: $862 per term
Grad: $829 per term
Endowment: Provincial

DEGREE PROGRAMS

Degree	Minimum Years for Degree	Accred.	Requirements for Admission	Full-Time Stdnts.	Part-Time Stdnts.	% of Applics. Accptd.	Stdnts. in 1st Year of Program	# of Degrees Conferred
BEDS	2 years	—	2 yrs. university, 1 math cr.	104	2	33%	50	52
M Arch	2 years	CAA*	BEDS or equivalent	75	—	—	39	41
M Arch (post prof)	2 years	—	Prof. Degree in Arch	3	—	—	—	0
MURP	2 years	CIP	BEDS or Honours degree	20	—	—	6	5

*Discussing reciprocity between Commonwealth Association of Architects & NAAB (USA) currently. Graduates have special examinations with NAAB.

SCHOOL DEMOGRAPHICS (all degree programs)

Full-Time Faculty	Part-Time Faculty	Full-Time Students	Part-Time Students	Foreign Students	Out-of-State U.S. Stdnts.	Women Students	Minority Students
18	12	202	2	10%	n/a	25%	n/a

LIBRARY (Tel. No. 902-429-8300)

Type	No. of Volumes	No. of Slides
Reference	100,000	15,000

STUDENT OPPORTUNITIES AND RESOURCES

The School of Architecture at the Technical University of Nova Scotia was established in 1961 to serve the Atlantic Region. While it continues to serve its original intention, the School has developed to contribute nationally and internationally to architecture. The primary task of the School is the education of individuals who intend to become professional architects.

Architectual design is the central activity of the BEDS and M Arch programs. It represents the ultimate test of a student's understanding and skill and provides the basis for an integration of the various activities and courses in the School.

Teaching in all subjects is structured so as to enrich the student's view of design. The act of design is taught through projects in the School, practical experience in offices, and studies of the physical environment in Canada and abroad. The majority of the course work is conducted within the School of Architecture by full-time members of the teaching faculty. Specialist knowledge not available within the School is accessible through the Faculty of Engineering at TUNS and faculties at other universities in Halifax.

The BEDS and M Arch together form the full program of professional studies, beginning with a core of the essential and common studies (in the BEDS) and developing into an elective program offering each student individual opportunities. This pattern of moving from the essential to the elective, and from the common to the individual, informs the detailed organization and regulation of the School.

Through its Co-operative Program, the Faculty utilizes the skills and resources of the building professions and industries to provide professional training, proper understanding and use of techniques, a responsible and competent approach to professional practice. Practical experience is an integral part of the Co-operative Program and is achieved through two work periods.

SPECIAL ACTIVITIES AND PROGRAMS

Job placement for co-op work periods

Thesis-related field studies abroad

Research activities both regionally and internationally, through International Development Research Center (IDRC)

FACILITIES

Labs

Computers - main frame PRIME plus personal computers

Audio visual

Photography

Carpentry

Metal working

Resource Center

Slide collection

Library

Easy access to Dalhousie, St. Mary's, and Nova Scotia College of Art and Design

SCHOLARSHIPS/AID

The Governor General's Gold Medal
The Alumni Association Medal
Province of Nova Scotia Bursaries

School of Architecture
Bachelor of Environmental Design Studies Scholarships

The Harry Kitz Fund Scholarship
The Newfoundland Association of Architects Scholarship
The L E Shaw Design Scholarship

Bursaries
The Birks Family Foundation Bursary
The IBM Canada Bursary

M Arch (First Professional Degree) Scholarships
Canada Mortgage and Housing Corporation Graduate Scholarships
The Harry Kitz Fund Scholarship
Mobil Oil Canada Impact and Design Studies Scholarship
O'Brien Foundation Fellowship
The Margaret Dale Phillip Award
Bruce and Dorothy Rosetti Scholarships
Saskatchewan Association of Architects Scholarship Prize
Walter Gardner Stanfield Scholarship
Transportation Development Agency Fellowship
Transport Canada Research and Development Centre Fellowships and Assistantships in Transportation
The Ernest Wilby Memorial Scholarship
Alice E. Wilson Grants

Bursaries
Birks Family Foundation Bursary

Awards
The Henry Adams Medal and Certificate
The Alpha Rho Chi Medal
The Alumni Association Medal
The Alumni Memorial Award
The Governor General's Gold Medal
The Nova Scotia Association of Architects Prize
The NSAA/AUS Book Award
The Royal Architectural Institute of Canada Medal

MURP and M Arch (Post Professional Degree) Scholarships
Atlantic Planners Institute Student Award
Mobil Oil Canada Impact and Design Studies
  Scholarship
Bruce and Dorothy Rosetti Scholarships
Canada Mortgage and Housing Corporation
  Graduate Scholarships
Walter Gardner Stanfield Scholarships
O'Brien Foundation Fellowship
The Margaret Dale Phillip Award
The Roads and Transportation Association of
  Canada Scholarships
Transportation Development Agency Fellowship
Transport Canada Research and Development
  Centre Fellowships and Assistantships in
  Transportation
Alice E Wilson Grants
Technical University of Nova Scotia Part-Time
  Teaching Assistantships
Technical University of Nova Scotia Full-Time
  Teaching Assistantships
Technical University of Nova Scotia Research
  Assistantships
Bell Canada Fellowships
Gulf Oil Canada Graduate Fellowships
Canadian Federation of University Women
  Professional Fellowship
The Canadian Association of University Teachers
  J.H. — The Seward Reid Memorial Fellowship
Bursaries
The Birks Family Foundation Bursary

UNDERGRADUATE PROGRAM
Philosophy Statement

Studios in design aim to develop a student's understanding of the principles that give order to form, and the particular factors that underlie those ordering principles. Students develop their knowledge and understanding through analytical studies of examples drawn from history as well as from current building. The course begins with examples from the immediate environment and proceeds to the study of the important works of individual architects and various historical periods. These analytical studies provide the base which is necessary for the teaching of design, and for the development of a sense of method and skill in design.

Design as a cognitive activity involves the designer's values, knowledge and skills, as well as a variety of functional and other requirements. It is analogous to the activity of a poet, painter, scientist or composer, arising as it does from real concerns and from the desire to address those concerns through the creation of forms, poems, paintings, theories, buildings and places. The teaching of design therefore addresses the questions of an individual's intentions, motivations, knowledge and skills on the one hand, and social preferences, needs and possibilities on the other. The synthesis of these two sets of factors is illustrated throughout the history of architecture. The teaching and learning of design is thus based on the premise that there exists a 'language of design,' whose 'grammar' and 'vocabulary' are essential prerequisites in the study and practice of design.

Program Description
The program consists of studies in several areas:
0. Design
1. Humanities: Theory & Criticism
                    Methodology
                    Architectural History
                    Urban & Regional
                    Planning
                    Landscape Design
2. Technology: Building Environmental
                    Systems
                    Materials &
                    Construction Systems
                    Structural Support
                    Systems
3. Professional Practice
4. Special Studies: Special interest courses
                    Extramural Subjects
                    Personal Projects

The full professional degree program consists of a maximum of four Academic Periods divided into eight terms of fourteen weeks each, and two work periods which total forty-two weeks of practical experience.

The distribution of School terms into Academic Periods (Co-op Periods) is as follows:

BEDS

	Fall	Winter	Summer
Co-op I	Term B1	Term B2	Term B3
	Academic	Academic	Academic
Co-op II	Term B4	Term B5	Term B6
	Work Term	Academic	Academic
	1:14 wks		

M.Arch.

	Fall	Winter
Co-op III	Term M1	Term M2
	Academic	Work Term
		2:28 wks
Co-op IV	Term M3	Term M4
	Academic	Academic

GRADUATE PROGRAM
Program Description

Master of Architecture (M Arch):
1. This is a graduate level program leading to the first professional degree of Master of Architecture. The M Arch degree is awarded after the successful completion of a two year (minimum) program of studies consisting of three terms of residence and one period of work experience. It offers a student the choice of several areas of emphasis. At present, these areas include: Housing, Urban Design; Restoration and Adaptive Re-Use; and Architectural Construction Systems. Other areas of interest might include: Building Science; Landscape Architecture; History and Theory; or Computer Applications to Architecture. Required course work and office experience culminate for each student in an independent graduate-level thesis. Students may take one term of thesis studies at other universities or on individual, independent studies away from TUNS. The thesis may be submitted up to one year after the completion of scheduled classes.
2. The second program leading to the M Arch degree is offered to those candidates already possessing a professional degree in architecture. Ten credits must be gained, usually six for course work and four for a thesis. Applicants are invited to identify a major area of interest and, in consultation with the School, to determine a program of studies and research.

Master of Urban & Rural Planning (MURP):
This is a professional degree, accredited by the Canadian Institute of Planners, awarded after successful completion of a minimum of four academic terms and a prescribed fourteen-week work period.

FACULTY
Administration
Essy Baniassad, ARIBA, MRAIC, Dean of
  Architecture
Kent C Hurley, Assistant Dean and Chairman,
  BEDS Program
Thomas Emodi, RAIA, Chairman, M Arch
  Program

Professors
Essy Baniassad, ARIBA, RAIC, B Arch, MA, PhD
Anthony Jackson, MRAIC, ARIBA, Dipl Arch
Mirko J Macalik, FRAIC, MSc in Arch, P Eng
Peter Manning, FRAIC, AA Dipl, PhD
J Philip McAleer, AB, MFA, PhD
J Grant Wanzel, B Arch, M Arch

Associate Professors
Thomas Emodi, B Arch, MES
Frank J Eppell, MRAIC, Dipl Arch, M Arch
Kent C Hurley, BA, B Arch, MA, Dipl Con Stu
Allen Penney, AA Dipl, MA
Michael C Poulton, BSc, M Phil, MS, PhD
Dimitri Procos, MRAIC, MCIP, B Arch, M Arch
Morton Rubinger, MRAIC, B Arch, M Arch

Assistant Professors
Edwin Cavanagh, BSc, B Arch
Archibald Frost, FICE, FISE, FIHE, P Eng
Frank Palermo, MRAIC, B Arch, M Arch UD
Stephen Parcell, B Arch

Lecturers
David Bessonette, Dipl Elect, B Comm

Part-Time Faculty
Jill Bambury, BEDS, B Arch
Robert Benz, M Arch, UC
Ojars Biskaps, B Arch, M Arch
G E C Brown
John C DeWolf
Joan Doehler, BA, BEDS, B Arch
Michael Grunsky
Peter Henry, BEDS, B Arch
Jennifer Hill, BEDS, B Arch
Brian MacKay-Lyons, BEDS, B Arch, M Arch UD
William MacKinnon
Douglas J Miller
Gordon Ratcliffe
Stephanie White
Ann Wilkie, M Arts, MSc
Allan Willcocks

Adjunct Faculty
Julian Beinart

Temple University

Division of Architecture (084-53)
Temple University
Philadelphia, Pennsylvania 19122
(215) 787-8826

The Office of Undergraduate Admissions (041-09)
Temple University
Philadelphia, Pennsylvania 19122
(215) 787-7200

Application Deadline(s): Fall: June 15
(earlier appl rec)
Spring: November 15
Tuition & Fees: Undgrd: PA Res: Full-Time:
$1650/sem
Non-res: Full-Time:
$2898/sem
Grad: PA Res: Part-Time:
$114/hour
Non-res: Part-Time: $156/hour
Endowment: Public

DEGREE PROGRAMS

Degree	Minimum Years for Degree	Accred.	Requirements for Admission	Full-Time Stdnts.	Part-Time Stdnts.	% of Applics. Accptd.	Stdnts. in 1st Year of Program	# of Degrees Conferred
B Arch	5	NAAB	1050-1100 combined SAT's or portfolio. Upper half of H.S. class. Specific Courses	320	29	40%	95	29
BSc in Arch	4		Same	8	15	50%	NA	5

SCHOOL DEMOGRAPHICS (all degree programs)

Full-Time Faculty	Part-Time Faculty	Full-Time Students	Part-Time Students	Foreign Students	Out-of-State U.S. Stdnts.	Women Students	Minority Students
11	24	328	44	16%	38%	16%	22%

LIBRARY (Tel. No. 215-787-7828)

Type	No. of Volumes	No. of Slides
Branch	7,500	11,000

STUDENT OPPORTUNITIES AND RESOURCES

The Division of Architecture offers the only accredited undergraduate day program in the Philadelphia area. The program is profoundly urban in character, drawing upon the architectural riches of Philadelphia and upon the wealth of resources of one of the nation's leading urban public universities.

The program is an intense one in which students work with senior professionals from their first classes in the program. The student body of 350 has an exceptional sense of identity and commitment to their field. The extremely broad range of students includes those already holding undergraduate or advanced degrees in other fields as well as transfer students from other architectural schools. All minorities and ten foreign countries are represented.

A wide range of housing choices is available on the campus and in the city or its suburbs, often at a somewhat lower cost than in other university communities.

The faculty has a strong professional orientation. Most faculty members are actively engaged in the practice of architecture through their own firms or in association. Faculty work has been recognized through numerous publications, awards and competitions. The diversity represented in the full-time faculty is supplemented by a broad range of adjunct and visiting faculty. Visiting critics and lecturers represent most of the major architectural firms in Philadelphia.

The curriculum itself reflects the impact of the urban setting in the diversity of project sites and problems that the student encounters. The program also benefits from the availability and interest of the many local professionals who participate in juries and in the employment of students.

Temple University has more than 30,000 students at four campus locations. Architecture is taught at the main campus and at the Rome Campus in the Villa Caproni.

SPECIAL ACTIVITIES AND PROGRAMS

Semester in Rome

Architectural study tours to Europe, Central America, and the United States

Regional travel to Boston, New York, Baltimore, and Washington

Student Magazine, *Stanza*

Student lecture and exhibit series

Beaux arts rendering

Advanced standing for students with previous degrees or academic experience

Co-op program under development

Interdisciplinary studios

AIA/S Chapter: Temple Architectural Students Association (TASA)

School participation in the Stewardson Memorial Design competitions

Studio participation in other design competitions

FACILITIES

The Division of Architecture is housed in a modern building on the main campus.

Special facilities include:

Computer graphics laboratory with 3D CAD system and solids modeling system; 12 work stations now available on a local area network

Photographic lab and darkroom

Model shop with wood, clay, and plaster facilities

Branch library including architectural collection

Materials testing and engineering laboratories

Exhibit Hall/Gallery

SCHOLARSHIPS/AID

Loans and scholarships available include national direct student loans, college work-study program, Supplemental Educational Opportunity Grants, Pell Grants, Temple University Grants, including the Presidential Scholars Program and Temple University Outstanding Achievement Grants, PHEAA Grants, the Aaron W. Hardwick Student Aid fund, and the Girard Trust Scholarships. The program conducts an informal referral and placement service for free-lance, part-time, and permanent employment opportunities. A co-op program is under development.

UNDERGRADUATE PROGRAM
Philosophy Statement

The common thread linking all the programs in the Division of Architecture is a commitment to a professionalism founded upon theory. This commitment leads to emphasis upon both what is done and why it is done. The curricula are organized to provide a coordinated sequence of successively more sophisticated opportunities to explore and manipulate the tools of architecture to create meaningful environments.

The five-year Bachelor of Architecture curriculum is designed to prepare students for the professional practice of architecture. The program develops in depth an understanding of human needs and a command of architecture that together enable the student to service the community by shaping its man-made environment in a creative, responsible, and sensitive manner.

The four-year Bachelor of Science in Architecture (Professional Option) allows a student to follow the five-year curriculum for four years. This option is sometimes selected by students whose needs change after entering the program, or those who decide to continue their studies at the graduate level. Through the use of elective options, students in the two four-year options may determine and focus their attention upon a related field within architecture of interest to them.

The four-year Bachelor of Science in Architecture (Technical Option) prepares a student for a role in architecture and related fields through an intensified emphasis upon the technical aspects of architecture. Graduates are qualified for a variety of positions in architecture offices, public service positions in government agencies and for positions in the construction industry and as sales and design architects for manufacturers of building products and equipment.

Program Description

The first two years constitute a common core for all degrees.

In the first year the student takes two drawing and two-dimensional graphics studios and one design studio. In the spring semester the design studio is coordinated with a lecture course which provides the introduction to the study of architecture. Simultaneously the student completes basic requirements in mathematics, composition and the humanities.

In the second year, architectural design studios deal with small- and medium-sized buildings and basic approaches to design. The student begins required courses in building technology and history. In the spring of the second year, students must apply for admittance to the four- and five-year professional programs.

Upon acceptance into the professional program the student continues to develop with an emphasis on both greater rigor and the introduction of new areas of concern and opportunity. Students may take any semester in the third or fourth years in Rome. The fall semester of the third year focuses upon urban design, while the spring studio is an elective studio.

The fall studio of the fourth year focuses upon the integration of design and technology in an intense and thorough manner. Students often produce technical drawings at this point. Extensive use is made of consultants to aid in the integration of both design and technical knowledge previously acquired. Electives continue.

An advanced studio, often taught by a visiting critic, begins the fifth year. Parallel with this studio is an advanced theory seminar and preparation for the undergraduate thesis. In the spring, the thesis studio focuses the combined energies of the faculty and consultants upon the development of the undergraduate thesis projects. The thesis juries culminate the five years of study.

GRADUATE PROGRAM
Philosophy Statement

While Temple University does not have a graduate program as such, many students with bachelor's and even master's degrees are enrolled in the professional program. Every effort is made to recognize the special competencies of graduate-level students. Students with prior degrees may complete the program in four years or less depending upon their individual backgrounds.

Preliminary development of a second professional degree program at the graduate level is now under discussion. Please consult the Division for additional information on this program.

FACULTY
Administration

George L Claflen, Jr, AIA, Chairman
Betsy Tabas, MLS, Librarian

Professor

John Knowles, AIA, B Arch, M Arch, MCP

Associate Professors

George L Claflen, Jr, AIA, B Arch, M Arch, MCP
C William Fox, AIA, M Arch
Emanuel Kelly, RA, B Arch, MCP
Brigitte Knowles, RA, B Arch, M Arch
Norman Krecke, M Arch
John Pron, RA, M Arch

Assistant Professors

Amir Amcri, B Arch, M Arch, PhD
Howard Brunner, MFA
David Cronrath, RA, B Arch, M Arch
J Brooke Harrington, AIA, B Arch

Part-Time Faculty

Peter Batchelor, BSc, M Arch
Alden Blythe, RA, B Arch
Brittain Brewer, RA, B Arch
Roy Decker, RA, B Arch
Mark DeShong, RA, B Arch, M Arch
Curt Dilger, B Arch, M Arch
George Dodds, RA, B Arch, M Arch
Ruth Durack, B Arch, MCP, M Arch
Thomas Han, BA, M Arch
Sally Harrison, RA, M Arch
Caleb Hornbostel, AIA, B Arch, DPLG
Harry Jacobs, AIA, M Arch
David Juppenlatz, PE, B Arch
David Karp, AIA, B Arch
Douglas Kochel, RA, B Arch
Thomas Leidigh, PE, BSCE
Barbara Macauley, RA, B Arch
Romolo Martemucci, RA, B Arch
Muscoe Martin, RA, BA, M Arch
Elizabeth Masters, RA, M Arch
Walter Moleski, RA, B Arch
Chris Nissen, BA, Cert
Peta Raabe, RA, M Arch, MLA
Luis Rivera, RA, BS Arch
Richard Sheward, RA, B Arch
Richard Tyler, BA, MA, PhD
Wesley Wei, RA, B Arch, M Arch
Elizabeth Wilson, Cert

Adjunct Faculty

Thomas Dowd, PE, BSCE, MSCE
Steven Jochum, BSCE
Steven Ridenour, PE, BSME, MSE, DAE
Frederick Schmitt, PhD CE

University of Tennessee - Knoxville

School of Architecture
University of Tennessee
1715 Volunteer Boulevard
Knoxville, Tennessee 37996-2400
(615) 974-5265

Dean of Admissions and Records
The University of Tennessee
320 Student Services Building
Knoxville, Tennessee 37996-0230
(615) 974-2184

Application Deadline(s): August 1st for Fall
Quarter admission;
3 weeks before start
of classes for any
other quarter.
Tuition & Fees: Undgrd: TN Res: $5451/yr.
Non-Res: $7884/yr.
Endowment: Public

DEGREE PROGRAMS

Degree	Minimum Years for Degree	Accred.	Requirements for Admission	Full-Time Stdnts.	Part-Time Stdnts.	% of Applics. Accptd.	Stdnts. in 1st Year of Program	# of Degrees Conferred
B Arch	5	NAAB	ACT, HS Diploma	360	11	63%	111	51
B Arch	3	NAAB	BA or BS w/2.5 GPA	26	1	80%	5	7

SCHOOL DEMOGRAPHICS (all degree programs)

Full-Time Faculty	Part-Time Faculty	Full-Time Students	Part-Time Students	Foreign Students	Out-of-State U.S. Stdnts.	Women Students	Minority Students
24	10	386	12	11%	22%	23%	11%

LIBRARY (Tel. No. 615-974-3275)

Type	No. of Volumes	No. of Slides
Arch	7,700	20,172

STUDENT OPPORTUNITIES AND RESOURCES

The School is centrally located within the southeast region of the country and is near large metropolitan areas such as Cincinnati and Atlanta. Situated in the Tennessee Valley, the School works in cooperation with the Tennessee Valley Authority and Oak Ridge National Laboratory on energy-related issues.

During the academic year advanced students may be given an opportunity to work at locations off-campus by enrolling in Special Design Studies. These programs enable students to gain first-hand experience and work alongside outstanding professional architects while dealing with actual community-based projects. Students may enroll in additional courses at off-campus locations to complete a full term's requirements.

The Lyndhurst Foundation of Chattanooga has contracted with the School to do urban design studies for that city, and each academic term there is one design studio devoted to supporting that program. Also from 1986 through 1989 the School will participate in a major way in Knoxville's "Mainstreet" program funded by the National Trust for Historic Preservation, the U.S. Department of Housing and Urban Development, and the City of Knoxville.

The faculty have a variety of educational backgrounds, including architectural design, architectural civil and mechanical engineering, urban and city planning, architectural history and preservation, and landscape architecture.

Students wishing to transfer into the UT-K School of Architecture are required to have at least a 2.3 grade point average to be considered.

SPECIAL ACTIVITIES AND PROGRAMS

Each year the School offers at least two opportunities for foreign study to its students. In cooperation with the Danish International Student Committee, a program is regularly offered in Copenhagen taught by outstanding Danish architects and educators. Exchange programs are established with Royal Melbourne Institute of Technology, Melbourne, Australia and Chongqing Institute of Architecture and Engineering, Chongqing, Sichuan Province, China. Within the School faculty, a person is assigned responsibility to lead a summer program in Europe. Most recently, for the past two years, the School has offered a program in Yugoslavia in which students and faculty from the Universities of Belgrade and Zagreb join students and faculty from Tennessee in architectural studies.

Students in the School each year publish The University of Tennessee Journal of Architecture. Continuing several years of excellent publications covering work of the School and current thinking in the field, this journal has become a widely recognized part of the School's participation in the profession.

Throughout the academic year, the School organizes an extensive series of special lectures by experts in architecture and related subjects. Annually in the spring a special program called TAAST, "The Annual Architecture Spring Thing," is arranged by students. Within a period of one week the entire School participates in special lectures, seminars, exhibits and informal gatherings.

The School has active student chapters of AIA, CSI, and Tau Sigma Delta. Students from these organizations provide effective student leadership for the program.

A three-month, non-credit internship (service practicum) in an architect's office is required prior to the fifth year. Upon petition, work in an engineer's or contractor's office or related work may be approved.

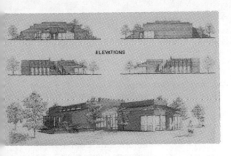
ELEVATIONS

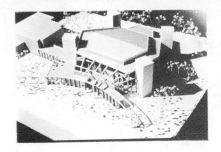

FACILITIES

In the spring of 1981, a new building housing the School of Architecture and shared by the Art Department was completed. The Art and Architecture building contains all the primary activities of the School. It contains as its major feature a large interior mall or street. Opening off this large gathering space, which serves as a campus focal point, are amply designed classrooms, design studios, a reference library which contains extensive slide collections and other reference materials, computer rooms, faculty offices, administrative offices, an elaborate darkroom and studio, a completely equipped workshop, the Ewing Gallery, in which architecture as well as art exhibits are displayed, and a branch of the University Bookstore.

SCHOLARSHIPS/AID

A number of scholarships are made available each year through the Architecture Endowment Fund, the Annual Fund, and the Tennessee Architecture Foundation. Other scholarships have been funded by the Masonry Institute of Tennessee, the General Shale Corporation and other architectural firms, manufacturers of building materials, and other construction-related industries. Also, there are several scholarships awarded based on design competitions within the program of the School. Other scholarships are available through the national headquarters of the American Institute of Architects. Honor students in all the upper four years are eligible for this aid, but it is primarily awarded to students of third- and fourth-year standing. Merit scholarships for outstanding entering freshmen are available through the University's Financial Aid Office.

UNDERGRADUATE PROGRAM
Philosophy Statement

The philosophy of the School of Architecture is a multifaceted one. Its primary reason for existing is its function as a professional education program supporting the architecture profession by seeking to prepare students to meet the needs and requirements of the field in carrying out its work. Serving to prepare leaders in the field of building, understanding and guiding society's best interests in that area, it is incumbent upon the School to address two areas of educational obligation: the provision of a sound general education within a strong undergraduate professional program; and the development of habits of the mind which sharpen the intellectual skills of students through the stimulation of creative imagination, the study of theoretical fundamentals, and rigorous attention to architecture as an intellectual discipline.

Program Description

The program of the School emphasizes the process of learning with the intent of enabling its graduates to adapt to the changing circumstances of our world. How to learn about architecture is as important a matter for the student as learning itself. The curriculum for the Bachelor of Architecture degree includes a combination of required and elective courses which offer the student both a solid professional program of study and a sound general education. While the main focus of the curriculum is on architectural design and the majority of the courses are designed as required, students may use the available architecture electives to expand their knowledge in areas of special interest which include structures, history, preservation, environmental controls and professional practice. Academic non-architecture electives allow students to broaden their education in areas of general interest including the humanities, natural and social sciences or arts. All electives are to be taken only with the approval of the student's advisor.

Students must maintain an overall 2.3 grade point average by the end of their first year in order to maintain "full status" in the program. Delinquent students will be put on "temporary status" and will have one term to raise their GPA's to 2.3, or have a minimum 2.3 on each succeeding term's work until the overall average is raised to 2.3, or be dropped from the program.

Students are required to have all first- and second-year courses satisfactorily completed before entering the third-year design sequence. Also students' progress and design work in second year will be reviewed by a committee of the faculty to determine their readiness for advancement to third year.

The average course load in any term is 16 credit hours. The minimum which may be taken by full-time students is 12 hours; the maximum which may be taken without approval of the Dean is 19 hours.

NOTICE: Beginning in the fall of 1988, the academic program will change from the quarter system to a semester calendar. Transition plans for all curricula are available.

FACULTY
Administration

William J. Lauer, Acting Dean
Jon P Coddington, AIA, Assistant to the Dean

Professors

Gerald I Anderson, RA, M Arch
George F Conley Jr, B Arch
Frederick Grieger, RA, M Arch
Banarsi Kambo, IIA, ASCP, MCP
Richard M Kelso, PE, MS
Joseph A Kersavage, PE, DB Sc
William J Lauer, IES, MS
Anne J Lester, RA, M Arch
Peter Lizon, AIA, PhD Arch
Max A Robinson, AIA, M Arch
William S Shell, RA, M Arch
J Stroud Watson, APA, M Arch
Lawrence M Wodehouse, ARCUK, PhD

Associate Professors

Scott A Kinzy, RA, M Arch
William E Martella, RA, B Arch
Marian S Moffett, PhD
Vojislav Narancic, B Arch
J Stanley Rabun, RA, PE, M Arch

Assistant Professors

Carl H Bovill, RA, M Arch
Jon P Coddington, AIA, B Arch
Michael Kaplan, RA, M Arch
Judith E Reno, M Arch
LaVerne Wells-Bowie, M Arch

Instructor

Shelah M Ware, B Arch

Lecturers

Krzysztof Bojanowski, M Arch
Marek Dunikowski, M Arch
Wojciech Miecznikowski, M Arch

Part-Time Faculty

Joseph W Fortey, PhD
Robert C French, B Arch
Joel M Haden, B Arch
Manuel Herz, AIA, B Arch
Robert D Holsaple, AIA, BS Arch Engr
Morna M Livingston, MFA
Howard A Stucky, RA, B Arch
David L Wooley, AIA, M Arch

Texas A&M University

**Department of Architecture
College of Architecture
& Environmental Design
Texas A&M University
College Station, Texas 77843-3137
(409) 845-1015**

**Office of Admissions
(409) 845-1031**

Application Deadline(s): Undgrd: Fall Sem:
July 15
Spring Sem: Nov 1
Summer Sess: May 1
Grad: Fall Sem: Feb 1
Spring Sem: Sept 1
Summer Sess: May 1
Tuition & Fees: Undgrd: Tx Res: $448/sem
Non-res: $2112/sem
Grad: Tx Res: $350/sem
Non-res: $1600/sem
Endowment: State

DEGREE PROGRAMS

Degree	Minimum Years for Degree	Accred.	Requirements for Admission	Full-Time Stdnts.	Part-Time Stdnts.	% of Applics. Accptd.	Stdnts. in 1st Year of Program	# of Degrees Conferred
BED	4		SAT 1,000, top 25% of HS class	891	50	50%	220	123
M Arch	1		B Arch, Portfolio, GRE of 800, 3.0 GPA	3	0	30%	1	1
M Arch	2	NAAB	BED or equiv., Portfolio, GRE of 800, 3.0 GPA	61	9	54%	23	30
M Arch	3½	NAAB	BA or BS, GRE of 800, 3.0 GPA	14	—	51%	11	0
PhD	3		Master's or equiv., 3.0 GPA, GRE of 1000, portfolio, experience	13	—	10%	5	1

SCHOOL DEMOGRAPHICS (all degree programs)

Full-Time Faculty	Part-Time Faculty	Full-Time Students	Part-Time Students	Foreign Students	Out-of-State U.S. Stdnts.	Women Students	Minority Students
52	7	982	59	15%	15%	29%	3%

LIBRARY (Tel. No. 409-845-5212)

Type	No. of Volumes	No. of Slides
Arch	26,998	63,000

STUDENT OPPORTUNITIES AND RESOURCES

The College of Architecture and Environmental Design is one of ten colleges in a university of some 35,000 students, including 6000 graduate students. The college houses programs in architecture, construction science, environmental design, landscape architecture and urban and regional planning. Formal and informal contacts between programs are an inherent strength of the college.

The University meets the traditional land grant roles of teaching, research and service. Student organizations and programs in athletic, cultural, social and recreational activities provide a rich support for high quality in education. The University has a regular exhibit series, operatic and performing arts society, theatre productions and public radio and television stations.

There is a strong commitment to individual student advising, a mentor program and an honors program in which selected students may participate at the undergraduate level.

The University's location within the state allows excellent contacts with diverse and intensely active architectural firms. Student field trips to Houston, Dallas, Fort Worth, Austin, San Antonio, and Galveston provide frequent opportunities for interaction with the profession and the building industry.

SPECIAL ACTIVITIES AND PROGRAMS

John Miles Rowlett Lecture (annual)

Foreign Studies Program (Florence, Italy)

Visiting Lecturer Programs

Two six-week summer sessions with wide range of required and elective courses

Undergraduate Co-Op Education

Internship programs (for credit) for second-year graduate students

Faculty/student research programs (currently in energy, computer applications, historic preservation, health care planning and design, architectural theory and history)

Professional exam workshops

NCARB design test simulations

Student organizations: AIAS, TAU SIGMA DELTA

FACILITIES

The Technical Reference Center offers architectural reference sources by housing books, research reports, technical documents, and slide collections of art and architecture. A photographic laboratory provides facilities for reproduction of black/white and color prints, and slides and audiovisual endeavors are supported by a video production laboratory. Workshops for metal, plastics, and ceramics are available for creativity and research. The computer facilities include linkage to the University's central Amdahl systems, the college Prime main frame and multiple microcomputer systems. Research facilities include a large artificial sky for daylighting studies.

SCHOLARSHIPS/AID

For the academic year 1986-87, University scholarships totaled $11 million; state and federal grants totaled $6 million. Scholarships in architecture, funded by private donors and the Texas Architectural Foundation, total $30,000+ for undergraduate and graduate students. The Department of Architecture awards approximately

40 scholarships and 30 graduate assistantships each year based on GPR and financial need; fellowships ($8,000) are available for entering graduate students with outstanding academic records.

UNDERGRADUATE PROGRAM
Philosophy Statement

The curriculum in environmental design at Texas A&M University provides opportunities for the study of those disciplines that plan and develop the built environment and that aspire to manage the interface between people and their buildings.

Program Description

The Department of Architecture offers the Bachelor of Environmental Design degree normally requiring four years of undergraduate study. Students study subjects in the arts, humanities, sciences, business, and engineering. They learn skills and acquire knowledge in programming, problem analysis, communications, structures, mechanical equipment, systems, materials, computer technology, history, and design. In the design studio, they learn to assimilate this skill and knowledge. Students choose elective studies in a variety of disciplines, including art, economics, anthropology, mathematics, philosophy, psychology, sociology, geology, geography, physics, business, finance, management, statistics, cost estimating, human factors engineering, landscape architecture, and urban and regional planning. The curriculum is intended to develop students who understand interrelationships between the parts of a building problem, who can analyze and solve complex problems, and who are capable of shifting the focus of their efforts as social needs and technologies change.

Receipt of the baccalaureate degree in environmental design is usually followed by graduate, professional pursuits in architecture or urban and regional planning. Students may also elect or be directed to pursue interests other than professional careers in these fields. Individual interests may be developed within the curriculum through judicious use of the several elective opportunities. For example, programs may be directed toward graduate studies in business, law, or the social sciences or toward paraprofessional careers in the visual and graphic arts or in the design and construction industry.

GRADUATE PROGRAM
Philosophy Statement

The goals of the Department of Architecture are to provide an educational framework for those seeking professional and advanced degrees, to support the profession's need for continuing education, and to pursue opportunities for scholarly inquiry and practical activity in architecture.

Architecture as a profession has been redefined in recent years, and idealism and realism in education have at times seemed alternatives rather than complementary parts of a whole. The department contends that both must be addressed, and therefore the program includes both education and training at the professional level.

Program Description

The department offers the Master of Architecture as a first professional degree, requiring 52 hours of study; the M Arch as a postprofessional degree, requiring 36 credit hours; and the Doctor of Philosophy in Architecture, requiring 96 credit hours beyond the baccalaureate or 64 hours beyond a master's degree. The first-professional-degree program is also available to students from non-design backgrounds after an appropriate period of prerequisite study.

The M Arch first-professional-degree program offers a core curriculum that addresses those issues central to the practice of architecture: design, technology, legal constraints, professional practice, social, physical, and historical contexts, and communication skills. The balance of the program, 27 credit hours, is developed by the student, with the advice and approval of a graduate advisory committee, to further a professional interest area. Current patterns include architectural design, urban design, interior architecture, history and preservation architecture, health facilities design, and management.

The program aims to produce professional attitudes and abilities together with a recognition that architecture is both a highly individual effort and a team endeavor.

The PhD degree is intended to develop academic and research competence of the highest order. Students are expected to enter the program with mature attitude, strong professional experience, and a defined special interest. Current emphases are energy studies, computer applications, health care facilities, and architectural theory.

FACULTY
Administration

Dr. Michael M. McCarthy, ASLA, AILA, Dean
Walter Wendler, RA, Associate Dean
Daniel F MacGilvray, AIA, Associate Dean
Ward V Wells, Interim Head of Department
Paula Bender, Coordinator of Learning Resources

Professors

Lester L Boyer, MS, PhD
Carrol D Claycamp, PE, M Arch
Larry O Degelman, PE, MS
John G Fairey, MFA
John O Greer, AIA, M Arch
W Weston Harper, AIA, M Arch
Rodney C Hill, AIA, M Arch
Karen E Hillier-Woodfin, MFA
W Graham Horsley, MA
Joseph M Hutchinson, MA
Theo S Maffitt, FAIA
George J Mann, AIA, MS Arch
Joseph J McGraw, AICP, CIP, MCP, PhD
Malcolm W F Quantrill, M Arch, PhD
Raymond D Reed, AIA, M Arch

Edward J Romieniec, FAIA, M Arch
Andrew D Seidel, PhD
Alan L Stacell, MFA
Richard E Vrooman, FAIA, M Arch
John W Walker, MFA
David G Woodcock, AIA, RIBA, Dipl TP

Associate Professors

Edwin E Allen, M Arch
Ian D Bishop, PhD
Richard R Davison, Jr, MFA
David C Ekroth, RA, M Arch
Julius M Gribou, AIA, M Arch
Augustus C Hamblett, AIA, M Hist of Arch
Terry R Larsen, MS
Daniel F MacGilvray, AIA
Gerald L Maffei, AIA, M Arch
Joseph L Mashburn, AIA, M Arch
G Joan Moore, M Ed
Vivian L Paul, MA, PhD
Roy C Pledger, RA, M Arch
Larry L Priesmeyer, RA, MUP
Robert J Schiffhauer, MFA
Ward V Wells, M Arch
Walter V Wendler, RA, M Arch
Charles W White, MA, PhD

Assistant Professors

Philip Berke, MS, PhD
Marlene E Heck, M Arch, PhD
Susan M Kirchman, MA
Paul W Mason, MS
M Jana Pereau, MA
John W Rogers, M Arch

Part-Time Faculty

James H Biehn, BS
M Lewis Coody, PE, MS
Roy E Graham, MA
Larry W Grosse, MS
Ronald J Kruhl, PE, MS
Graham B Luhn, B Arch
James H Marsh, PE, M Arch
Albert Pedulla, RA, M Arch
Frederick J Trost, RA, M Arch

Visiting Faculty

James B Asbel, MS
Paolo G Barucchieri, MA
Kelcey Beardsley, M Arch
Paul C Blumenthal, MA
Edward Cunnius, BLA
David G Kenyon, BLA
Kenneth P Larson, RA, MS
Douglas E Oliver, M Arch
Mary C Saslow, MFA
Bijan Youssefzadeh, MA

Texas Tech University

College of Architecture
P.O. Box 4140
Texas Tech University
Lubbock, Texas 79409
(806) 742-3136

Admissions Office
P.O. Box 4350
Texas Tech University
Lubbock, Texas 79409
(806) 742-3661

Application Deadline(s): 30 days prior to start
of semester
Tuition & Fees: Undgrd: $599/sem
Grad: $599/sem
Endowment: State

DEGREE PROGRAMS

Degree	Minimum Years for Degree	Accred.	Requirements for Admission	Full-Time Stdnts.	Part-Time Stdnts.	% of Applics. Accptd.	Stdnts. in 1st Year of Program	# of Degrees Conferred
B Arch	5	NAAB	Conditional: University requirements Unconditional: University requirements to include: 3½ units Math; 4 English; 1 Science	689	91	93%	245	100
M Arch	1		B Arch					
M Arch	2		BA or BS in Architecture					
M Arch	3		Bachelor in unrelated field					

SCHOOL DEMOGRAPHICS (all degree programs)

Full-Time Faculty	Part-Time Faculty	Full-Time Students	Part-Time Students	Foreign Students	Out-of-State U.S. Stdnts.	Women Students	Minority Students
21	10	694	91	7.4%	10.4%	14.4%	16.4%

LIBRARY (Tel. No. 806-742-2599)

Type	No. of Volumes	No. of Slides
Arch	10,000	65,000

STUDENT OPPORTUNITIES AND RESOURCES

Texas Tech University is composed of seven colleges, the Graduate School and the School of Law. Adjacent to the main campus is the Texas Tech University Health Sciences Center. The College of Architecture is the newest college at Texas Tech though architectural studies have been offered on the campus since 1927 and the Bachelor of Architecture program has been continuously accredited since 1957. Exciting growth is anticipated in the years ahead. A College faculty of diverse backgrounds and interests ensures a pluralistic approach to learning while the University provides a broad multi-cultural context for personal explorations.

More than 23,000 students attend classes on the Lubbock campus, which, with 1,839 contiguous acres, is one of the nation's largest. Campus resources include The Museum, the Ranching Heritage Center and the Southwest Collection. The Library, comprised of over 1.3 million volumes, is one of two Regional Depositories for U.S. Government Documents in Texas and the only one situated on a university campus. As a member of OCLC, the Library is instantly linked with over 4,000 other libraries.

The College accepts transfer students based on a portfolio review and maintenance of a 2.25 overall GPA and a 2.50 in architecture courses.

SPECIAL ACTIVITIES AND PROGRAMS

Numerous special activities are available for Architecture majors beginning with pre-registration counseling sessions each summer for entering freshmen and transfer students, culminating in the opportunity for low-interest loans for foreign travel after graduation. Provided each semester are lecture series by outstanding architects and professionals in related fields and field trips to cities around the nation and several foreign countries to observe significant architecture and to assist in urban design/planning projects. Independent summer programs provide students with employment in outstanding architectural firms in the U.S. or study with noted European architects. Gallery exhibits regularly display work of students, faculty, and practicing architects.

Active chapters of AIAS and Tau Sigma Delta enhance a student's opportunities, both professionally and socially. Student publications are issued periodically.

FACILITIES

Computer facilities include computer-aided design and drafting, word processing, and programming as well as terminals connected to mainframe computers. Photographic and graphics production equipment are available for students with assistance from qualified personnel. A complete woodworking shop and metal shop supplement design studios to provide equipment and technical advice to students. Architectural design research laboratories provide special equipment and computing facilities. The College includes its own reference library in addition to the architecture collection of the main University library.

SCHOLARSHIPS/AID

Scholarships are available on a competitive basis at both the undergraduate and graduate levels. Six scholarships are dedicated to students entering from high school. To be eligible for all other scholarships, however, a student must be enrolled in both fall and spring semesters for at least 12 credit hours each semester and must have maintained a minimum of a 3.00 GPA. Some scholarships are specific to a degree program or to a year within the five-year curriculum. Approximately $13,000 in scholarships is awarded annually by the College through support by various professional, business, and alumni organizations.

UNDERGRADUATE PROGRAM
Philosophy Statement

Architecture is a potent force in culture for the projection of human emotion, intellect and spirit. It is the dominant physical presence of civilization—a material synthesis of social, political, artistic, economic and technological concepts. Since buildings are physical manifestations of personal and collective values, the architect must be a student of Mankind. He should promote the dignity of each individual within Society and the integrity of Society within Nature.

The mission of the College is to develop and to foster creativity based upon sound judgment and professionalism. Students are encouraged to explore personally enriching sources of knowledge and to strive for fulfillment of ambitious goals.

Program Description

The professional Bachelor of Architecture degree provides the opportunity for students to specialize in architectural design, urban design or architectural structures. Within the architectural design specialization, students may pursue a concentration in architectural history and historical preservation. Each student develops a thesis in the fifth year through personally focused research and design. Whereas the design specialization may be chosen at any time prior to completing the first three years of the core curriculum, those students interested in the structures specialization should choose it upon their initial enrollment. A dual degree program is offered in cooperation with the Department of Civil Engineering; this results in a degree in Architecture and a degree in Civil Engineering.

Graduates of all the varied specializations offered are prepared to enter the practice of architecture. A core curriculum provides the theoretical knowledge, historical perspective and practical skills essential to architectural design. Further concentrations of study and research provide avenues for students to develop expertise focused upon their individual interests and talents. Ample elective hours encourage exploration of broader humanistic and interdisciplinary issues.

GRADUATE PROGRAM
Philosophy Statement

The professional courses in the Master of Architecture program build solidly upon the strengths of the undergraduate program. Students develop the skills and concepts necessary for success in the practice of architecture and an understanding of the issues confronting architecture now and in the future.

The emphasis of the non-professional degree, research and elective courses vary according to student and faculty interest. The curriculum allows individualized study plans to be formed. Because the program is new and flexible, students are encouraged to extend the traditional boundaries of Architecture.

Program Description

The Master of Architecture degree is available to accredited professional degree recipients and to both pre-professional and non-professional degree holders through three plans.

Plan 1 is for the recipient of a professional (B Arch) degree. The program offers opportunities to complete the requirements for a degree through approximately 30 hours of graduate study. Plan II is for the recipient of a pre-professional degree (a four-year BA or BS in architecture). The program offers opportunities to complete the requirements for a professional degree through approximately 60 hours of graduate study. Plan III is for the recipient of a non-professional degree (a degree in another discipline). The program provides the opportunity to complete the professional degree requirements through approximately 90 hours of graduate study.

For each candidate an individual degree plan will be developed according to appropriate advanced placement and/or leveling requirements. The graduate faculty has identified primary areas of study for the final year of the program. These currently include architecture, historic restoration and preservation, urban design and planning, and computer aided design. Students have the opportunity to become involved with ongoing research projects in these areas.

FACULTY
Administration

R Wayne Drummond, Dean
Bill W Felty, RA, Associate Dean

Professors

R Wayne Drummond, AIA, B Arch, M Arch
Jusuck Koh, RA, RLA, B Arch, MLA, PhD Arch
George T C Peng, AICP, B Arch, M Arch, Dr-Ing
Willard B Robinson, RA, B Arch, M Arch
Elizabeth M Sasser, PhD
A Dudley Thompson, B Arch, MS in Urban Planning
James E White, AIA, B Arch, MS

Associate Professors

Bill W Felty, RA, B Arch
Melvin H Johnson, MFA
Guenter Lehmann, B Arch, M Arch
Joanna W Mross, B Arch, M Arch, Tech, MFA
Robert D Perl, AIA, B Arch, M Arch
Michael G Peters, AIA, B Arch, M Arch
Rinaldo A A Petrini de Monforte, AIA, D Arch, MS (Des), PhD
Virginia M Thompson, B Adv Art & Design
John P White, AIA, B Arch, M Arch

Assistant Professors

Ali Bayegan, B Arch, M Arch
Robert L Coombs, MFA, MA, M Arch
James T Davis, Jr, MA Ed, MFA
David A Driskill, AIA, B Arch, M Arch
Michael Dymond, DBA, M Arch
Glenn E Hill, B Arch, M Arch
W J Danny Nowak, RA, B Arch
Erhard Schuetz, M Arch
Mark Spitzglas, B Arch, BSc, MSc, DrSc
James C Watkins, MFA

Lecturer

Lloyd Lumpkins, B Arch, MBA

Part-Time Faculty

Bill W Cantrell, RA, B Arch
Stephen L Fillipp, AIA, B Arch
Diana J Johnson, BFA, MFA
Michael T Martin, AIA, B Arch
Raymond D Powell, RA, B Arch
Johnny K Worley

University of Texas at Arlington

School of Architecture
and Environmental Design
UTA Box 19108
Arlington, Texas 76019
(817) 273-2801

Graduate - UTA Box 19167
Undergraduate - UTA Box 19088-A
Graduate (817) 273-2688
Undergraduate (817) 273-3565

Application Deadline(s): Grad: U.S. - July 1
International - April 25
Undgrd: July 1
Tuition & Fees: Undgrd: TX Res: $389/12 hours
Non-Res: $1637/12 hours
Grad: TX Res: $389/12 hours
Non-Res: $1637/12 hours
Endowment: State

DEGREE PROGRAMS

Degree	Minimum Years for Degree	Accred.	Requirements for Admission	Full-Time Stdnts.	Part-Time Stdnts.	% of Applics. Accptd.	Stdnts. in 1st Year of Program	# of Degrees Conferred
BS Arch	4		800 SAT (400 min. each part)	600	150	90%	300	115
BS Arch Land Option	4		800 SAT (400 min. each part)	30	15	90%	15	10
BS Arch Urb Des Plan Option	4		800 SAT (400 min. each part)	5	0	100%	3	1
BS Int Des	4		800 SAT (400 min. each part)	65	10	90%	30	15
M Arch Path A	3	NAAB	4 yr degree, GRE, interview	10	3	50%	5	
Path B	2	NAAB	BS Arch, GRE, portfolio	46	16	50%	10	18
Path C	1		B Arch, GRE, portfolio	1	0	100%		
MLA	2		BS/BA, GRE, portfolio	9	9	70%	7	7

SCHOOL DEMOGRAPHICS (all degree programs)

Full-Time Faculty	Part-Time Faculty	Full-Time Students	Part-Time Students	Foreign Students	Out-of-State U.S. Stdnts.	Women Students	Minority Students
23	6	766	203	5.6%	2.8%	33%	10.2%

LIBRARY (Tel. No. 817-273-2387)

Type	No. of Volumes	No. of Slides
Arch/Art	25,000	55,000

STUDENT OPPORTUNITIES AND RESOURCES

Students at the SAED who wish to enter the architecture profession will find over two hundred offices within a radius of 30 miles from the campus, providing excellent opportunities for part-time employment during school years and full-time employment upon graduation. The Master's program is based upon a combined day and night schedule that allows time for study and creative experiences in area offices. The Dallas-Fort Worth area is the heart of a rapidly expanding dynamic economy.

The student body is diverse and talented. Enrollment is sufficiently large to accommodate students with different interests and skills, ranging from the technical to design. The graduate professional program emphasizes advanced design, theory and professional responsibilities and, together with the computer center, provides opportunities for research and studies in theory, design, energy, and building systems.

The SAED offers multidisciplinary studies in landscape architecture and interior design, as well as an option in urban design/planning. Elective course work in these areas is strongly encouraged.

The faculty is diverse and enthusiastic. Their broad range of philosophies is reflected in the studio, which is not dominated by any single design approach. The Architect in Residence Program brings talented critics to further diversify the school's design approach. Specializations are offered in design theory, history of architecture, preservation and energy-related research.

SPECIAL ACTIVITIES AND PROGRAMS

Summer program of study abroad, including tour groups and course work in Rome, England, and other sites.

Weekly Faculty/Guest Lecture Series presents prominent speakers from the USA and abroad.

Beaux-Arts Ball

Alpha Rho Chi fraternity house on campus

AIAS Student Chapter

Student exhibits

Field trips to see current architectural work

Traveling exhibits

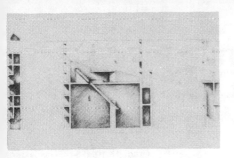 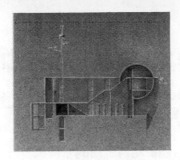 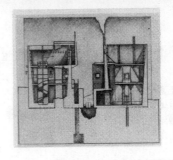

FACILITIES

The SAED moved to a new facility in the Fall of 1986. Resources include a state-of-the-art computer center, an art/architecture library (branch of central library), photographic studios and dark rooms, wood/plastics/metal shop, lecture hall, exhibition gallery, project review spaces, student lounges, open and contained studios, lighting lab, materials lab, and a grand courtyard. The four-story building is adjacent to the arts complex and maintains a central campus location. SAED students may access the building on a 24-hour basis via an I.D. card electronic security system.

SCHOLARSHIPS/AID

Financial assistance is available through work-study programs, graduate teaching and graduate research assistantships, and a number of scholarships awarded to deserving students in the program. Award of assistantships and scholarships entitles out-of-state students to pay tuition at the in-state rate. Twenty-five percent of the students in the professional program received assistantships in the current year. Many others participate in the Practicum Program, working in area architectural offices for credit.

UNDERGRADUATE PROGRAM
Philosophy Statement

The SAED offers a diverse range of educational opportunities leading to professional and related career opportunities. The undergraduate curriculum is structured around a commitment to a broad-based liberal arts education. The model is a 2+2+2. Two years of Basic Studies concomitant for all students interested in the design professions. Two years of Major Studies allowing students to specialize in (and select) a major discipline of Architecture, Interior Design, Landscape Architecture or Urban Design/Planning. A large block of electives allows for further specialization or a diverse range of course offerings. Architecture, Landscape Architecture and Planning students considering a professional career must matriculate to Graduate Studies for the appropriate accredited professional degree. Refer to graduate program and admissions requirements for professional degrees.

Program Description

All undergraduate degree offerings and options require 138 credit hours plus physical education activity courses or equivalents. The undergraduate program in architecture offers options in architecture, landscape architecture and urban design/planning. The undergraduate program in interior design is architecturally based and intended for serious students interested in professional careers which specialize in this area. Specific degree requirements are available on request and are published in both the general University catalog and the SAED course bulletin. Transfer and international students should contact the associate dean's office for specific entrance requirements. Students who hold an undergraduate degree should refer to the graduate options and contact the graduate advisor for degree opportunities and admission requirements. The SAED adheres to equal opportunity admissions standards and encourages minority applicants.

GRADUATE PROGRAM
Philosophy Statement

The program introduces students to professional-level work in research, theory, professional practice, and design. The goal is to enable students to enter the profession with a high level of skills and to provide them with a foundation for sound decision-making throughout their careers. Course work in the thesis program consists of independent study and demonstrates the graduating student's level of overall competence.

Program Description

Students entering the program include those with a four-year pre-professional degree in architecture (Path B), a five-year professional degree in architecture (Path C), and, in increasing numbers, those with a baccalaureate degree in a field other than architecture (Path A). The latter complete an intensive program of study in design, architectural history and technology before undertaking the common core curriculum in Path B.

The core curriculum in Path B consists of 18 hours of design, 15 hours of technology and practice, and 18 hours of electives, of which one course must be taken in each of three specified areas: history and theory, technology and practice, and allied disciplines such as landscape architecture, interior design, or urban design and housing. The Path B curriculum culminates in six or nine hours devoted to one of three options: research thesis, design thesis, or advanced studio.

The Path C curriculum consists of 6 hours of design, 6 hours of history and theory, and 12 hours of electives arranged to provide for an area of specialization or for advanced general studies. The Path C curriculum also culminates in one of three options: research thesis, design thesis, or advanced studio.

Elective opportunities include courses in historic preservation, energy-conscious design, and computer-aided design and graphics. Elective credits may be earned for appropriate experience in professional offices. In addition to the full-time faculty, visiting critics are regularly invited to conduct graduate studio courses.

FACULTY
Administration

Edward M Baum, AIA, RA, Dean
Richard B Ferrier, AIA, RA, Associate Dean
Robert A Gamble, Architectural Librarian

Professors

Anthony C Antoniades, AIA, RA, MS, M Ph
Edward M Baum, RA, M Arch
Richard B Ferrier, AIA, RA, B Arch, MA
Jay C Henry, B Arch, M Arch, PhD
John McDermott, RA, B Arch, MA
Madan Mehta, RA, B Arch, M BS, PhD
Martin Price, AIA, RA, B Arch
Richard Scherr, RA, B Arch, MS
Michael Tatum, BPA
George Wright, FAIA, RA, M Arch

Associate Professors

Bill Boswell, RA, B Arch, M Arch/Urb Des
Chester Duncan, FASCE, PE, MS
George Gintole, B Arch, M Arch
Joe Guy, MFA
Todd Hamilton, RA, B Arch, M Arch
Craig Kuhner, RA, B Arch, M Arch
John Maruszczak, B Arch, M Arch
Richard McBride, RA, B Arch, M Arch
Andrzej Pinno, M Arch
Gary Robinette, RLA, MLA
Dan Spears, RA, B Arch, M Arch
Lee Wright, RA, B Arch, M Arch
Michael Yardley, MA

Assistant Professors

Robert DeJean, RLA, BLA
Truett James, M Arch
Stephen Lawson, M Arch

Instructors

Elfriede Foster, BS

The University of Texas at Austin

School of Architecture
University of Texas
Austin, Texas 78712-1160
(512) 471-1922

Undergraduate Admissions:
Austin, Texas 78712-1159
Graduate Admissions:
P.O. Box 7608
Austin, Texas 78713-7608
(512) 471-1711

Application Deadline(s): February 1 priority;
March 1 non-priority
Tuition & Fees: Undgrd: TX Res:
$475/semester
Non-res: $2250/semester
Grad: TX Res: $435/semester
Non-res: $1995/semester
Endowment: State

DEGREE PROGRAMS

Degree	Minimum Years for Degree	Accred.	Requirements for Admission	Full-Time Stdnts.	Part-Time Stdnts.	% of Applics. Accptd.	Stdnts. in 1st Year of Program	# of Degrees Conferred
BS Arch Studies	4		Class standing, SAT (or ACT),**** (3.00 GPA for transfers, 30 hrs)	7	0	40%	1	11
B Arch*	5	NAAB	Class standing, SAT (or ACT),**** (3.00 GPA for transfers, 30 hrs)	432	56	37%	150	63
1st-Prof'l M Arch	3½**	NAAB	Bacc degree with 3.0 upper-div., GPA, 1000 GRE, portfolio, recs.	91	32	30%	30	47
Postprof' M Arch	1		B Arch with 3.0 upper div. GPA, 1000 GRE, portfolio, recs.	14	0	45%	9	5
MS Arch Studies	1		Bacc degree with 3.0 upper-div GPA, 1000 GRE, portfolio, recs.	6	2	42%	4	1
MS CRP***	2	ACSP	Bacc degree with 3.0 upper-div. GPA, 1000 GRE, recs.	66	23	65%	28	11

*Dual degree programs combine the B Arch with the BS in Architectural Engineering (six-year program), and with the BA Plan II (Liberal Arts Honors Program—5 years with summers).
**The first-professional M Arch program can be foreshortened for students entering with preprofessional degrees in architectural studies.

***The M.S. in Community and Regional Planning is offered as a joint degree with the MA in Latin American Studies, and with the PhD in Geography.

****Texas resident freshmen: Top 10%, or top ¼ with 1000 SAT (24 ACT), or 2nd ¼ with 1100 SAT (27 ACT). Non-resident freshmen: top ¼ with 1100 SAT (27).

SCHOOL DEMOGRAPHICS (all degree programs)

Full-Time Faculty	Part-Time Faculty	Full-Time Students	Part-Time Students	Foreign Students	Out-of-State U.S. Stdnts.	Women Students	Minority Students
35	14	616	113	6%	11.5%*	35%	17%

*10% of undergraduate enrollment; 50% of graduate enrollment

LIBRARY (Tel. No. 512-471-1844)

Type	No. of Volumes	No. of Slides
Arch & Planning	46,150**	154,887

**Plus 95,713 items in the Architectural Drawings Collection

STUDENT OPPORTUNITIES AND RESOURCES

With 700 students, a faculty of about 50, and a supporting staff of 18, the School of Architecture is sizable enough to be a dynamic architectural academy, yet remains small enough to permit intensive interaction among students and faculty. One of the smallest of the 14 schools and colleges of U.T. Austin which enrolls 48,000 students, the School benefits from its small-school atmosphere in the center of the vast resources of a major University. The School's restricted enrollment mandates that 90% of the undergraduate enrollment be Texas residents, although 50% of the graduate students in architecture are from out of state. The School employs up to 35 graduate students per semester as teaching assistants. The faculty is a diverse group of academicians and practitioners from a variety of backgrounds, emphasizing a pluralistic approach to the discipline of architecture. Austin, the state capital, enjoys the Central Texas location along the beautiful Highland Lakes on the Colorado River as it descends from the Texas Hill Country to meet the grassy expanses of the Gulf Plains. Austin's abundant vegetation, its parks and trails along the many waterways, and its temperate subtropical climate support a population of about 500,000 people. Within a 200-mile range are San Antonio, Dallas/Fort Worth, Houston, Galveston, and the Gulf of Mexico.

SPECIAL ACTIVITIES AND PROGRAMS

Summer Academy in Architecture (career discovery program for high school juniors/seniors)
Oxford Summer Study Abroad Program, with tours to other parts of England and continental Europe
European Study Program with VPI each fall, based in London and Switzerland
Winedale Institute in Historic Preservation (five-week in-residence summer program)
Intensive summer entry program for transfer students
Professional Residency Program (optional 7-month internships with architecture firms for advanced students); Planning Internship Program
Career Week (graduating students interview with firms)

Endowed Visiting Lecture/Charrette Series
Visiting Critic studio (optional advanced design studio)
Exhibitions
Architecture and Planning Student Council, which sponsors such events as the annual Beaux Arts Ball and publication of student journal
Dual degree programs combining the B Arch with the architectural engineering degree and with the Liberal Arts Honors degree
Joint Degree Programs combining the master's in planning with the master's in Latin American Studies and with the PhD in geography
School Publications including a biennial *Prospectus*, a semesterly newsletter, and the annual *CENTER: A Journal for Architecture in America*
Symposium each year

FACILITIES

Battle Hall (1911 by Cass Gilbert) housing the Architecture Library, the Architectural Drawings Collection, and the Center for the Study of American Architecture

Sutton Hall (1918 by Cass Gilbert, beautifully renovated in 1982)
Goldsmith Hall (1933 by Paul Cret, expanded and renovated in 1988)
Four computer labs including CAD systems, microcomputers, and terminals interfaced with the University's extensive Computation Center
Student darkroom
Student workshop
Slide Library and Reference Center with audiovisual equipment and slides of architectural works

SCHOLARSHIPS/AID

The University's Office of Student Financial Aid administers a variety of grants, scholarships, loans, work-study and part-time employment programs on the basis of need; apply while applying for admission. The Graduate School awards competitive fellowships and programs for disadvantaged students; applications in admission packet. The U.T. Ex-Students' Association administers the Texas Excellence Awards and other scholarships; applications available in high schools. Various awards are available to students *currently enrolled* in the School of Architecture including scholarships provided by the Texas Architectural Foundation, private endowments, and the AIA. Incoming students should contact local AIA and Ex-Students' chapters and other civic organizations about locally sponsored scholarships.

UNDERGRADUATE PROGRAM
Philosophy Statement

The undergraduate curriculum offers a broad education in professional subjects and in the arts, sciences, and humanities. An emphasis on solving actual and theoretical problems develops the knowledge and skills that link understanding to experience, theory to practice, and art to science in ways that respond to human needs, aspirations, and sensitivities.

Program Description

The School offers a traditional five-year Bachelor of Architecture program requiring ten sequential design studios, other professional courses, and the Basic Education Requirements. Students follow a highly structured curriculum for the first three years and submit a portfolio of their work to the advanced design faculty in order to enter the fourth year. In fourth- and fifth-year design, students select studios focusing on various aspects of architecture or programs such as the Professional Residency Program, study-abroad programs, and/or Visiting Critic studio.

Intensive dual degree programs combine the B Arch with the BS in Architectural Engineering, requiring six years of study, or with the Liberal Arts Honors Program (BA, Plan II), requiring five years of study including summers.

A four-year program leading to the Bachelor of Science in Architectural Studies is offered for students who elect a nonprofessional or pre-professional undergraduate degree focusing on the art and science of architecture without the rigorous curriculum required of the professional degree.

GRADUATE PROGRAM
Philosophy Statement

The School of Architecture strives to attract highly motivated graduate students with strong scholastic achievements in a variety of backgrounds, and to develop in them knowledge, sensitivity, and skill in design and construction so that, as architects, they may effect positive changes to the human environment.

For the graduate student seeking a first professional degree, the School offers a concentration of professional studies for practice in architecture.

For postprofessional graduate students, faculty and resources are available for advanced study and research that allow exploration and preparation for academic careers or the refinement of design philosophies.

Program Description

The *first professional degree program* leading to the Master of Architecture may be completed in 3½ years of concentrated study by students entering with degrees in discipline unrelated to architecture. (For students entering with preprofessional degrees in architectural studies, the required hours of professional coursework are prescribed on the basis of the student's previous work.) Students complete a rigorous four-semester curriculum in design and other professional subjects and, after a satisfactory qualifying review, enter advanced design studios which are taken with advanced undergraduates. The student selects a supervising committee which determines the exact program of study for advanced graduate work including thesis or independent project.

For students holding professional degrees in architecture, the Master of Architecture is a *postprofessional degree* offering several opportunities for advanced study including design, computer simulation, history and theory, historic preservation, and urban design. Based on the student's interests, specific degree requirements are established which are normally completed in thirty semester hours of graduate work (including thesis) under the supervision of a committee of two or more faculty members.

The Master of Science in Architectural Studies degree program offers an advanced academic (nonprofessional) degree for applicants holding degrees in various disciplines with interests in the many facets of architecture that support rather than produce architectural design. Options for study include those described in the previous paragraph.

The Master of Science in Community and Regional Planning degree is normally completed in two years; the degree may be combined with the MA in Latin American Studies in a three-year program or with the PhD in geography in a program requiring three years of study followed by the completion of a doctoral dissertation.

FACULTY
Administration

Hal Box, FAIA, RA, Dean
Richard L Dodge Jr, RA, Associate Dean
Larry A Doll, RA, Assistant Dean
Wayne Attoe, Assistant to the Dean for Graduate Architecture
Lawrence W Speck, AIA, RA, Director, Center for the Study of American Architecture
Terry D Kahn, APA, Director and Graduate Adviser, Graduate Program in Community and Regional Planning
Peter O Coltman, RIBA, Graduate Adviser for Architecture
Eloise McDonald, Architecture Librarian

Professors

Francisco Arumi, PhD
Simon Atkinson, RIBA, RTPI, FRSA, Dipl Arch, Dipl Plan & Des, MA, Urb Reg Stud
Wayne Bell, FAIA, RA, B Arch
Sinclair Black, FAIA, RA, B Arch, M Arch
Hal Box, FAIA, RA, B Arch
James Coote, RA, BA, M Arch
Richard L Dodge, Jr, RA, B Arch, M Arch
Gerlinde Leiding, M Arch
Charles Moore, FAIA, RA, B Arch, MFA, PhD
Sandra Rosenbloom, APA, BA, MPA, PhD
Lawrence W Speck, AIA, RA, BS Arch, M Arch
Richard Swallow, AIA, RA, BS Arch, M Arch
Lance Tatum, AIA, RA, B Arch, M Arch

Associate Professors

Michael Benedikt, B Arch, MED
Kent S Butler, APA, BA, MS, PhD
Owen Cappleman, BA, MFA
Peter O Coltman, RTPI, AIA, RIBA, B Arch, Dipl Town Plan, MS CRP
Larry A Doll, RA, B Arch, M Arch
Buford Duke, AIA, RA, B Arch
Michael Garrison, RA, B Arch, M Arch
Michael Jordan, RA, B Arch, M Arch
Terry D Kahn, APA, BBA, MBA, PhD
Dan Leary, AIA, RA, BS, Arch E, B Arch, M Arch
Roxanne Williamson, BA, MA
Patricia A Wilson, APA, RA, BA, MRP, PhD

Assistant Professors

Anthony Alofsin, M Arch, PhD
Natalye Appel, B Arch, M Arch
Christian Bergum, AIA, B Arch, M Arch, PhD
Amy Glasmeier, BES Plan, MCP, PhD
J L Jinkins, BA, M Arch
Malcolm McCullough, BA, M Arch
Andy Vernooy, AIA, RA, BS, M Arch

Lecturer

Frances Chamberlain, BA, MLA

Part-Time Faculty

D Blake Alexander, RA, B Arch, BS, MA
Wayne Attoe, AIA, BA, B Arch, PhD
Jon A Bowman, AIA, PE, RA, BS Arch E, M Arch
Smilja Milovanovic'-Bertram, AIA, RA, BA, B Arch, M Arch
Terry D Morgan, BS, JD
Robert Renfro, AIA, RA, BBA, BID, M Arch
Keith Shuley, ABA, AIA, BS, B Arch, M Arch, JD

Adjunct Faculty

Natalie deBlois, FAIA, RA, B Arch
Robert Mugerauer, BA, PhD

University of Toronto

**Programme in Architecture
School of Architecture and
 Landscape Architecture**
University of Toronto
230 College Street
Toronto, Ontario M5S 1A1
Canada
(416) 978-5038

University Office of Admissions
315 Bloor Street West
Toronto, Ontario M5S 1A3
Canada
(416) 978-2190

Application Deadline(s): April 1
Tuition & Fees: Undgrd: $1683/yr
Grad: $1686/yr
Endowment: Provincial

DEGREE PROGRAMS

Degree	Minimum Years for Degree	Accred.	Requirements for Admission	Full-Time Stdnts.	Part-Time Stdnts.	% of Applics. Accptd.	Stdnts. in 1st Year of Program	# of Degrees Conferred
B Arch	5	OAA, CAA	Canadian applicants: Acad. report from second. schl, math courses, recommendation. U.S. applicants: HS+CEEB adv. placement or 1 yr. (30 cr) college-level study at accred. inst.	247	14	—	61	56
M Arch	1½-2½	OAA, CAA	Deg. equiv. to UT B Arch with final yr average mid-B or better, portfolio, letter of intent, 3 recs, 1 yr. exp. Other Bacc. degrees may be considered for admission.	6	4	—	4	0

SCHOOL DEMOGRAPHICS (all degree programs)

Full-Time Faculty	Part-Time Faculty	Full-Time Students	Part-Time Students	Foreign Students	Out-of-State U.S. Stdnts.	Women Students	Minority Students
10	39	253	18	3%	—	13%	—

LIBRARY (Tel. No. 416-978-2649)

Type	No. of Volumes	No. of Slides
Arch & Landscape Arch	17,200	10,300

STUDENT OPPORTUNITIES AND RESOURCES

The Faculty of Architecture and Landscape Architecture is on the St. George campus of the University of Toronto, one of the oldest teaching institutions in Canada. The campus is in the center of the city of Toronto, within walking distance of museums, galleries, theaters, and the resources of provincial, city, and metropolitan agencies. The city is, in itself, a source of material for studies in architecture, both in historic and contemporary development. The lively city core is well served by public transportation, and the entire metropolitan area is interlaced by a unique system of open spaces that links a network of ravines with the lake front.

The 34,272-student University provides a wide range of academic and ancillary facilities. Elective courses may be taken in any division of the university, and there are many special lectures and events in disciplines related to architecture: landscape architecture, engineering, fine art, social studies, urban and regional planning, etc.

The University of Toronto has the most extensive university library system in Canada and one of the largest in North America. Students also have access to a number of major libraries and archives in the city.

Faculty members have a diversity of experience and expertise; their academic background is varied. Since the city is home to many outstanding practitioners, the programs draw upon the profession for part-time teaching, tutorship, advanced lecture courses, and reviews of studio work.

SPECIAL ACTIVITIES AND PROGRAMS

The Faculty provides an active program of open symposia, lectures and special projects involving Faculty members and outside participants. Public lectures provide continuing education for both professions. Other institutions in the city, such as the Art Gallery and the Ontario College of Art, offer similar programs. Since Toronto is a major urban center, it frequently is host to major conferences on topics related to studies in architecture.

Short study trips are organized in each year of the undergraduate program, as an extension of the work in the studio.

Study Abroad programs to Italy and France are offered in the fourth year. Students electing to go abroad follow the normal program under the tutorship of a senior faculty member, but draw upon the resources of the city in which they live and work.

There is a close relationship between the program and professional organizations. Since Toronto is a major center for architectural practice, there is opportunity for both formal and informal contact with the profession.

The University Placement Office maintains liaison with potential employers of students and graduates, and the Ontario Association of Architects acts as an informal employment information exchange.

FACILITIES

The Faculty of Architecture and Landscape Architecture is located on the St. George Campus of the University of Toronto with easy access to all University facilities, public transport and the resources of Provincial Government, local and metropolitan agencies.

The administrative office and principal facilities of the Faculty are at 230 College Street. Each student has a work station in the studio, which is always accessible during the school term. Photographic darkrooms, audio-visual equipment, an art studio, woodworking shop and library containing almost 20,000 volumes are located at 230 College Street.

SCHOLARSHIPS/AID

The Government of Ontario provides financial aid to residents of the province who demonstrate need, through the Ontario Student Assistance Program. Application forms and brochures are available in April from the Office of Student Awards.

Loans are available for emergency purposes to students in second and subsequent years from the University of Toronto Alumni Association Loan Fund, Alumni House, 47 Willcocks St., Toronto, Ont. M5S 1A1.

ADMISSION SCHOLARSHIPS

John Yamada Admission Scholarship
Ken Kardiak Memorial Scholarship
4 general scholarships

ARCHITECTURE SCHOLARSHIPS AND AWARDS

The Alpha Rho Chi Medal
Architecture Alumni Awards
The Eric Ross Arthur Scholarship
Frederick Coates Scholarship
The Jack Deutsch Memorial Masonry Scholarship
William S Goulding Memorial Award

George T Goulstone Fellowship
The Harry B Kohl Award
Lieutenant Governor's Medal
Moriyama and Teshima Award
Ontario Association of Architects' Scholarship
Ontario Industrial Roofing Contractors
   Association Scholarship
Para Paints Scholarship
Royal Architectural Institute of Canada Medal
Toronto Architectural Guild Medal
Toronto Society of Architects Prizes
The Jules Wegman Fellowship
The Ernest Wilby Memorial Scholarship

ARCHITECTURE BURSARIES
Frederick Coates Bursaries
Huang and Danczkay Bursary
John Yamada Memorial Bursary

UNDERGRADUATE PROGRAM
Philosophy Statement

Architecture is concerned with environments for life as it is lived around us. Good architecture at once meets and transcends the requirements of our daily lives. In response to the need to accommodate and enhance human activities, architects must assume responsibility for designing the built environment. This implies an understanding of human values and aspirations; a knowledge of the origins and functions of buildings, neighbourhoods and cities; and competence in the means to produce them.

The work of building design is used as an essential vehicle for learning. In the studio, concerns for the cultural origins, social purposes working processes and technical aspects of architecture are brought together. Individuals and groups are charged with the responsibility of researching and advancing experimental solutions to credible and relevant problems. As specific attempts to creatively integrate and apply diverse forms of knowledge and skill, design projects in the studio are continuously subjected to critical examination as part of the learning process.

To support the work in the studio, the basic technical knowledge necessary for professional practice is provided by theoretical and applied courses using various lecture, seminar and workshop formats. Advanced and specialized elective courses in architectural theory, history, building technology, methods, techniques and professional practice allow students to develop special interests within the field, thus enriching, expanding and consolidating the learning experiences of the studio. Cultural and intellectual interests outside the field of architecture are developed through a substantial number of courses elected from the range available in the University at large.

Program Description

Integration of knowledge through project work in the studio represents the fundamental learning experience of an architect irrespective of future role in professional practice. The specifically architectural aspect of the education afforded by the program depends on the consistent provision of appropriate opportunities to effect the process of integration through design. This does not mean that studio courses are the main source of

knowledge or that other program components are less important - it means that studio work, seriously and consistently pursued, is the necessary but not sufficient condition of a good education in architecture. The program clearly distinguishes between studio work, technical and professional knowledge and general knowledge, attempting to strike an effective balance between all components through carefully calculated sequences, conjunctions and cross-relationships. The program structure is based on a 5-year sequence of three distinct curriculum components:
   1) the mandatory studio curriculum;
   2) the mandatory technical and professional curriculum; and
   3) the elective curriculum.

GRADUATE PROGRAM
Philosophy Statement

The post-professional Master of Architecture degree program is directed at mature students who want to: a) acquire specialized expertise in urban design or particular aspects of architectural design, technology or practice; b) pursue advanced study within a scholarly aspect of the field, such as history or theory. Emphasis is placed on individually structured plans of applied study and research culminating in a thesis carried out under the supervision of a specially constituted interdisciplinary committee. With respect to both course work and research, the program is actively supported by the specialized academic resources of graduate departments in related disciplines, by external research and public agencies and by leading specialist practitioners.

Program Description

The degree requirements consist of completion of six one-term courses one of which, the Toronto Workshop, is specified; participation in the non-credit Seminar in Architecture and Urban Design; and completion of a thesis based on research in a specialized technical, professional or scholarly area or in support of an advanced architectural or urban design project.

An advisor selected from the graduate faculty helps the student to choose a University-wide complement of courses in support of the thesis subject and coordinates the student's linkages to other departments and external agencies.

The mandatory non-credit Seminar, which includes presentations by faculty from Architecture and cognate departments and by visitors, is a forum for discussion of philosophical, professional and methodological issues and acts as a social and academic integrator into the University framework and the external world of practice.

The Toronto Workshop takes the form of coordinated case studies devised each year to focus on particular aspects of Toronto architecture and urban design which reflect students' special interests. Besides allowing thesis parameters to be more precisely defined by reference to the well-documented case of Toronto, the Workshop is intended to consolidate graduate level work methods and standards.

Both design and research program options require the submission of a comprehensive study

report in the form of a thesis. The focus of the design option is on an advanced urban or architectural project which must be supported by research into historical, functional, technical and formal parameters resulting in specific programmatic objectives and explicit design criteria. The final thesis document must include the design project, a comprehensive project report and the research material on which it is based.

The focus of the research option is on advanced work in a specialized area of study of the student's choice. Research and scholarship may be in one of several fields including history and theory of architecture and urban design; specialized building types; building technology; conservation; housing; urban development. The broad range of topical areas thus encompassed is feasible because individually structured research programs rely on the resources of other graduate departments, programs, centres and institutes within the University and on the contributions of specialized consultants, practitioners and officials in the city.

The normal period of residence is at least one year, with completion of all requirements in one-and-a-half to two-and-a-half years. A more extended part-time option will be in effect from 1987.

Candidates for admission must hold a professional degree in architecture and should have a minimum of one year of professional experience. Apart from conforming to the academic standards of admission of the School of Graduate Studies, candidates must submit a portfolio and a statement of interest to the Graduate Program in Architecture.

FACULTY
Administration

Anthony Eardley, Dean
Steven T Fong, Programme Chairman
Pamela Manson-Smith, Librarian

Professors

George Baird, FRAIC, OAA, B Arch
Carmen Corneil, B Arch
Anthony Eardley, Dipl, MA
Douglas Lee, RIBA, MRAIC, B Arch
Peter Prangnell, ARIBA, MRAIC, AA Dipl, M Arch
Antonio de Souza Santos, B Arch, M Arch
Blanche van Ginkel, FRAIC, MCIP, ARIBA, RCA,
  B Arch, MCP

Associate Professors

Klaus Dunker, MRAIC, RA, B Arch, M Arch
Steven T Fong, B Arch, M Arch
Jeff Stinson, AASTC, ARAIA, MRAIC, Dipl Arch, MA

Part-Time Faculty

Donovan Pinker, MRTPI, MCIP, B Sc, MCP
Paul Sandori, MRIBA, MRAIC, Dipl Ing Arch
Alan Tregebov, MRAIC, B Arch, M Arch

Adjunct Faculty

Miriam Basset, BS
Trevor Boddy, BA, M Arch
Hans Lucke, D Phil
Joseph Schwaighofer, Dip Ing, MS, PhD, Dr Tech

Tulane University

School of Architecture
Tulane University
6823 St. Charles Avenue
New Orleans, Louisiana 70118
(504) 865-5389

Office of Admissions (for B Arch)
(504) 865-5731

Application Deadline(s): Undgrd: February 1
Grad: April 1
Tuition & Fees: Undgrd: $11,200/yr
Grad: $11,200/yr
Endowment: Private

DEGREE PROGRAMS

Degree	Minimum Years for Degree	Accred.	Requirements for Admission	Full-Time Stdnts.	Part-Time Stdnts.	% of Applics. Accptd.	Stdnts. in 1st Year of Program	# of Degrees Conferred
B Arch	5	NAAB	HS diploma, SAT or ACT scores	326	2	NA	80	41 (1986)
B Arch	3½	NAAB	undergraduate degree other than architecture	22	0	NA	5	4 (1986)
M Arch	1		B Arch	5	0	NA	5	5 (1986)

SCHOOL DEMOGRAPHICS (all degree programs)

Full-Time Faculty	Part-Time Faculty	Full-Time Students	Part-Time Students	Foreign Students	Out-of-State U.S. Stdnts.	Women Students	Minority Students
24	16	353	2	5.4%	77%	32%	15.7%

LIBRARY (Tel. No. 504-865-5391)

Type	No. of Volumes	No. of Slides
Arch Lib	40,000	110,000

+Main Library holdings

STUDENT OPPORTUNITIES AND RESOURCES

In 1981, the School of Architecture received an eight-year, $800,000 grant from the Henry Luce Foundation of New York creating a sponsored professorship dealing with architecture and the humanities. This grant, unique among architecture schools in the country, has allowed an architect/architectural theoretician team to come to the school and work in the interpretation of society through its architectural manifestations. This program encompasses both undergraduate and graduate seminars along with faculty symposia addressing these current and vital issues.

The Junior-Year-Abroad Program offers superior students the opportunity to complete one year of study, usually the fourth, at a cooperating European university, for full credit toward the Bachelor of Architecture degree.

Participation in the program is limited to not more than 5 percent of a given class. In addition, a candidate must have a minimum cumulative average of 3.0 and must have demonstrated during his or her three-year residence at the School of Architecture a superiority in architectural design and general academic excellence including proficiency in the language of instruction of the cooperating school.

The Independent Studies Program is an honors program for fourth- and fifth-year School of Architecture students with at least a 3.0 average. Under this program a student may select a period of independent study as a substitute for all or some portion of the required course work. The time period and a detailed study area definition are to be submitted to the Dean in addition to an explanation of the motive for the particular study, its value to the student's education as an architect, and arrangements necessary to successful engagement.

Special studies directed by a School of Architecture faculty member may be proposed by a student at any time. The subject must be of signal interest to both the student and faculty member and not available to the student through regular curriculum schedules.

Acceptance of the proposal by the Dean must occur before registration of Directed Study. Credit to be allowed and final review of study results are a joint decision by the Dean of the school and the faculty member responsible.

SPECIAL ACTIVITIES AND PROGRAMS

John William Lawrence Memorial Lecture

Junior-Year-Abroad Program (for fourth-year students)

Annual Beaux Arts Ball

Architects Week lectures

Tulane Architecture Review

Work-study opportunities with the Architectural Coalition, the School's research and practice organization

Student Chapter, AIA

Arthur Q. and Mary W. Davis Visiting Critic

Monday Evening Lecture Series

Tau Sigma Delta

Extensive Visiting Critics and Lecturer Program

FACILITIES

The School of Architecture is housed in Richardson Memorial Hall, a turn-of-the-century building, located on the historic Tulane campus in uptown New Orleans. The building features large open drawing studios in two wings on four floors, a computer laboratory, a library, a slide library and space for all School of Architecture activities.

A major renovation completed in 1986 has improved both the public lecture facilities and many of the school's instructional spaces. The facility is open twenty-four hours a day, and each student is provided with work space and equipment.

SCHOLARSHIPS/AID

Tulane University administers a University-wide financial aid program of $18,000,000 which in 1986-87, provided students enrolled in architecture scholarship assistance totaling $920,000, loans totaling $250,000, and work-study employment funds totaling $125,000. One-half of the student body received assistance in meeting the total costs of their education. A limited program of merit scholarship funds is open to entering students.

UNDERGRADUATE PROGRAM
Philosophy Statement

Architecture is the creation of human places. It is at the same time an expression of human values and a context for human activity. Through the design process, architecture addresses interrelated physical, behavioral, and cultural issues that underlie the meaning of our built environment.

Program Description

The School of Architecture maintains a strong relationship with architecture activity in New Orleans. The city's professionals frequently visit the school's studios, and New Orleans' varied architectural heritage provides an invaluable educational laboratory. Students have surveyed important buildings and districts of the city and have successfully participated in campaigns for preservation and sensitive renovation.

The five-year Bachelor of Architecture program emphasizes building design and a broad liberal arts foundation. One-third of the curriculum consists of free electives, allowing students to pursue joint degree programs with the various disciplines in the College of Arts and Sciences and Newcomb College. Joint degrees usually require an additional semester of academic work. A joint degree program with the Graduate School of Business Administration requires two additional semesters.

A special three-year curriculum (including the summer session preceding the first year) leading to the Bachelor of Architecture degree is offered for students who hold degrees in disciplines other than architecture. A minimum residence of two years is required for students who transfer into the School of Architecture.

GRADUATE PROGRAM
Philosophy Statement

The Graduate Program offers a unique opportunity to students with first professional degrees for a one-year individualized course of study combining specialized interests with generalized and collective studies. Mature students are invited to participate in graduate seminars, and colloquia and to define a thesis project oriented in one of three areas: design and theory, historic preservation, or man/environment studies. Graduate students are assigned individual faculty to work with them and are encouraged to take advantage of University resources in the development of their work.

Program Description

In the fall semester graduate students all participate in a design colloquium in which design issues which span the interests and work of each student are explored and discussed in a seminar format with course instructors and visitors. In addition graduate thesis research is undertaken with the goal of developing an extensive and detailed program statement of a proposed thesis project. Graduate students are encouraged to then choose elective courses either within the School of Architecture or at large within the University to augment their particular interests.

In the spring semester an individual thesis project is developed and refined. In the course of this work, a number of faculty members are brought in as critics and advisors and graduate students are given special access to prominent visitors to the school. Elective courses in the spring semester tailored to each student's particular interests are offered to fill out the curriculum.

The graduate program requires mature students with initiative and some professional experience on which to build their educational and theorical search. The program is small in size, a feature which allows individual attention for each graduate student along with the opportunity to interact informally with a large number of faculty.

FACULTY
Administration

Ronald C Filson, RA, FAAR, AIA, Dean
Richard O Powell, R. Eng., Associate Dean

Professors

Geoffrey H Baker, MA, Dipl, PhD
Eugene D Cizek, AIA, RA, SAH, B Arch, MCPUD, D Sci, PhD
Ronald C Filson, AIA, RA, B Arch, Dipl
James R Lamantia, Jr, RA, FAAR, BS (Arch), M Arch
William J Mouton, Jr, PCI, CE, L Surveyor, BS, MSCE
Leo M Oppenheimer, B Arch
Richard O Powell, AIA, R Eng, BME, MSCE, PhD
Ligia Ravé, APS, PhD
David Slovic, AIA, RA, M Arch
William K Turner, FAIA, RA, B Arch, M Arch

Associate Professors

John F Adams, AB, MA
C Errol Barron, AIA, RA, SHA, B Arch, M Arch
Malcolm W Heard, Jr, AIA, BA, B Arch, M Arch
Stephen P Jacobs, RA, B Arch, M Arch
Karen Kingsley, SAH, CAA, NWSA, BA, MA, PhD

Assistant Professors

Michael K Crosby, RA, B Arch, M Arch
Donald F Gatzke, BA, M Arch
Bruce Goodwin, RA, M Arch
John Klingman, RA, BSCE, M Arch
Stephen F Verderber, BS Arch, M Arch, Arch D
Ellen Weiss, BA, MA, PhD

Part-Time Faculty

Bryan Bell, B Arch
Arthur Q Davis, FAIA, RA, B Arch, M Arch
Charles D Deakin, RA
R Allen Eskew, AIA, RA, B Arch, M Arch
David M Leake, RA, B Arch
E Eean McNaughton, RA, B Arch
Nancy B Monroe, RA, M Arch
Grover E Mouton III, FAAR, B Arch, M Arch, Dipl
Martha J Murray, RA, B Arch
Norberto F Nardi, AIA, RA, APA, Dipl Arch, MPUD
R Bradford Rogers, PE, MSCE
John L Schackai, III, RA, B Arch
Milton F Scheuermann, RA, B Arch
Victor E Stillwell, B Arch, M Arch, JD
Luis Vildostegui, B Arch

Adjunct Faculty

Donald Del Cid, M Arch
Michael D Nius, AIA, RA, B Arch

Tuskegee University

Department of Architecture
Tuskegee University
Tuskegee, Alabama 36088
(205) 727-8329

Admissions Office
(205) 727-8580

Application Deadline(s): Open
Tuition & Fees: Undgrd: $2,100/Semester
Grad: $2,100/Semester
Endowment: Private

DEGREE PROGRAMS

Degree	Minimum Years for Degree	Accred.	Requirements for Admission	Full-Time Stdnts.	Part-Time Stdnts.	% of Applics. Accptd.	Stdnts. in 1st Year of Program	# of Degrees Conferred
BA	4	—	HS Diploma	80	0	NA	NA	15
M Arch	2	NAAB	GPA, Portfolio, Interview	13	0	50%	6	6
B Arch	5	—	GPA, Portfolio, Interview	45	0	NA	45	0
BS Const Mgmt	4		HS Diploma	35	0	NA	8	6

SCHOOL DEMOGRAPHICS (all degree programs)

Full-Time Faculty	Part-Time Faculty	Full-Time Students	Part-Time Students	Foreign Students	Out-of-State U.S. Stdnts.	Women Students	Minority Students
9	2	163	—	20%	75%	26%	98%

LIBRARY (Tel. No. 205-727-8351)

Type	No. of Volumes	No. of Slides
Arch	8,200	22,500

STUDENT OPPORTUNITIES AND RESOURCES

One of the key features of the program at Tuskegee University is its relatively small size, which fosters a very personal and informal approach to professional training. The Department has 9 full-time faculty members and an average enrollment of 170 students per year. Students hail from all geographical areas of the country, with the majority coming from the southeast. Alabama residents constitute approximately 25 percent of the total enrollment. Approximately 20 percent of the student body are foreign students and 26 percent are women.

Tuskegee University is located in Tuskegee in east-central Alabama. Interstate 85 provides convenient access. Tuskegee is a two hours' drive from both Atlanta and Birmingham and a 40 minutes' drive from the capital of the state, Montgomery. Architectural and environmental design in the region ranges from complex urban architecture to stately antebellum structures. Tuskegee University's campus is designated as a national historic park site, with three buildings that are historic landmarks.

Tuskegee is a technical, scientific, and professional institution with an average enrollment of 3600 students per year. Instruction is organized under seven major units: College of Arts and Sciences, School of Agriculture and Home Economics, School of Business, School of Education, School of Engineering and Architecture, School of Nursing and Allied Health, and School of Veterinary Medicine.

The Department of Architecture is one of five departments in the School of Engineering and Architecture. The other departments are: Department of Aerospace Science Engineering, Department of Chemical Engineering, Department of Electrical Engineering, and the Department of Mechanical Engineering.

The Department of Architecture offers degrees in two disciplines: Architecture and Construction. The Department's faculty possess expertise in a variety of disciplines, including architectural design, architectural practice, urban design, city and regional planning, civil engineering, construction management, graphic design, and mechanical engineering.

SPECIAL ACTIVITIES AND PROGRAMS

Summer Internship
Energy-Conscious Design Studio
Community Service Projects with Student Involvement
Visiting Lecturer Program
Dual Degree in Architecture and Construction
Learning Resources Center (Modern Audiovisual Facilities)
Photographic Center
Computer Center

A MARINA FOR LAKE WILLCOX

SCHOLARSHIPS/AID

Tuskegee's Extensive Financial Assistance Program includes scholarships, Basic (Pell) and Supplemental Educational Opportunity Grants, National Direct Student Loans, Fellowships, and work-study programs. The program's scope is broad, and the majority of Tuskegee students receive some type of assistance. Additional information and application forms are available from the Financial Aid Office, Tuskegee University, Tuskegee, Alabama 36088.

UNDERGRADUATE PROGRAM
Philosophy Statement

The five-year program offered at Tuskegee provides a broad and conventional architectural training focused on the practice of architecture. The program is a well-rounded liberal education integrated with professional studies. Students are also exposed to other areas of expertise that are related to the environmental design profession. This serves to provide an awareness of the influence that other disciplines have on the physical environment and of career options that may be pursued following receipt of the professional degree.

Program Description

The curriculum is organized as a five-year Bachelor of Architecture Program.

The first year covers a study of visual design elements, color, texture, light, scale, etc., as well as a general examination of architecture and the built environment. Also included are the development of visual and verbal communication skills and the mathematical understanding.

The second year brings an introduction to problem-solving and decision-making techniques, procedures and factors, and a study of physical environmental (qualitative and quantitative) phenomena and their impact upon design. Visual and verbal communication skill development continues. Optional study in general subject areas is provided.

In the third year, development of skills is stressed, together with an increased understanding of the interface between spatial-movement, structural-mechanical, and site-landscape considerations in building design. Strong emphasis is given to a resolution of spiritual, social, and physical user needs. In addition, quantitative structures and mechanical studies are included as are those concerning historical developments. An introduction to programming as well as limited optional studies are provided.

The fourth year provides a more in-depth study of programming and the relating of the user's spiritual - social - physical needs with the other considerations in the physical design process. There is a continuation of theories, quantitative structures studies, and examination of architectural urban development. Optional study in general subjects is provided.

In the final year, the students examine complex architectural problems in a semi-independent design studio. This studio allows the student to apply all knowledge gained from the proceeding four years. In addition, each student completes a terminal project involving the research, programming, and design of an architectural project chosen by the student. The students also take courses in building economics, professional practice, construction, and management.

FACULTY
Administration

Vascar Harris, Dean, School of Engineering and Architecture
Charles Raine, AIA, Associate Dean, Head, Department of Architecture
Vincent McKenzie, Librarian (Architecture)

Professors

Rajesh Sehgal, PA, M Arch, MUD

Associate Professors

Uthman Abdur-Rahman, BSFA, MFA
Timothy H Barrows, AIA, B Arch, MCP
Richard Dozier, AIA, M Arch
Major L Holland, AIA, B Arch
Troy McQueen, BSAE, BSCE, MS
Charles W Raine, AIA, B Arch, MUD

Instructors

Samir Moussalli, MSE

Part-Time Faculty

Harold Bradford, BSCE, MSCE
Jesse Gamble, BS
Robert T Goodwin, Sr, MS
Michael Holmes, MA
Marvin Hughey, B Arch
Tonte Peters, B Arch

University of Utah

Graduate School of Architecture
University of Utah
Salt Lake City, Utah 84112
(801) 581-8254

Application Deadline(s): March 1st
Tuition & Fees: Grad: UT Res: $529*/qtr
Non-res: $1461*/qtr
*Subject to change without
notice.
Endowment: Public

DEGREE PROGRAMS

Degree	Minimum Years for Degree	Accred.	Requirements for Admission	Full-Time Stdnts.	Part-Time Stdnts.	% of Applics. Accptd.	Stdnts. in 1st Year of Program	# of Degrees Conferred
M Arch	3	NAAB	University requirements; BA or BS (in field other than architecture) Minimum 3.0 GPA	137	32	59%	37	14

SCHOOL DEMOGRAPHICS (all degree programs)

Full-Time Faculty	Part-Time Faculty	Full-Time Students	Part-Time Students	Foreign Students	Out-of-State U.S. Stdnts.	Women Students	Minority Students
14	4	137	32	5%	11%	24%	11%

LIBRARY

Type	No. of Volumes	No. of Slides
Main Univ	15,000 (Arch)	40,000 (Arch)

STUDENT OPPORTUNITIES AND RESOURCES

The University of Utah, a state-supported institution, is located on 1,500 acres at the foothills of the majestic Wasatch Mountains which offer superb skiing at world-famous resorts just minutes from the campus. The University is nationally known for its research and liberal education programs and offers over 100 fields of study leading to bachelor's, master's, and doctoral degrees from eleven colleges and five professional schools. Architecture students interact with many departments on the graduate level and in various research areas. A joint degree program has been established with the College of Business in which students receive the M Arch and the MBA.

The faculty is composed of individuals educated at a wide variety of institutions in the United States and other countries. Their fields of interest and specialization, aside from traditional practice, include photography, vernacular architecture, graphics, sculpture, historic preservation, real estate development, computer graphics, acoustics, art history, architectural history, seismics, structures, and engineering.

SPECIAL ACTIVITIES AND PROGRAMS

Community Design Center involvement in Salt Lake City (school and AIA)

Architectural Research Center (ARC), school function operated by faculty

Building Environment and Energy Laboratory

Distinguished speaker lecture series

Field study trips to major cities, national and international

Surveys of historic buildings and engineering structures in Utah

Professional Development Program (workshops for registered professionals and interns)

American Institute of Architects Student Chapter

Utah Architect, an architectural journal

Faculty exchange with other architecture schools

Denmark International Studies program

Joint Master of Architecture/Master of Business Administration program

FACILITIES

The Architecture Building, built in 1970, consists of design studios, lecture rooms, a reference library, a shop, a photographic lab, a model room, an architecture lab, a slide library, a computer lab, a product-sample room, and an exhibition hall, as well as administrative and faculty offices.

SCHOLARSHIPS/AID

Financial assistance is available to graduate students only, in the form of scholarships, assistantships, grants, and loans. Approximately 60% of the graduate students receive some financial assistance.

UNDERGRADUATE PROGRAM
Philosophy Statement

The intent of the Utah program is to expand a student's perception. The student obtains an undergraduate degree in another field while beginning architectural course work. Major study in one of the sciences, technologies, arts, or humanities is encouraged. Undergraduate students wishing to transfer to Utah should do so before their junior year.

GRADUATE PROGRAM
Philosophy Statement

It is the intention of this program that graduates with a variety of backgrounds and interests will achieve professional competence and serve society in the traditional architectural role as well as in other related areas.

Program Description

The Utah program is highly concentrated during the last three years. Studio courses are integrated with laboratory and lecture courses. Professional requirements are supplemented by electives and independent studies. A 3.0 GPA must be maintained. On satisfactory completion of the professional program, including a thesis, the degree Master of Architecture is awarded.

Applicants who hold a BA or BS degree from other institutions, without architecture prerequisites, will require three to four years to complete the M Arch program. Students with a five-year Bachelor of Architecture degree may be admitted to special research studies in computer applications in architecture and design. A minimum of two years in residence will be required.

FACULTY
Administration

Carl Inoway, AIA, RA, Dean
Peter B Atherton, Assistant Dean

Professors

Robert L Bliss, FAIA, RA, B Arch
Stanley W Crawley, PE, RA, M Arch
Robert D Hermanson, AIA, RA, M Arch
Carl Inoway, AIA, RA, M Arch
Thomas B Kass, MFA
Kazuo Matsubayashi, AIA, RA, B Arch
Edward F Smith, AIA, RA, D Arch
John Sugden, AIA, RA, MS Arch

Associate Professors

Peter Goss, PhD
Gordon Hashimoto, AIA, RA, M Arch
Antonio Serrato-Combe, AICP, M Arch
Raymond Snowden, AIA, RA, M Arch

Adjunct Assistant Professors

Peter B Atherton, AB, MA
Gail Della Piana, MFA

Part-Time Faculty

Thomas R Carter, PhD
Leland Irvine, PE, BSEE
Barbara J Richards, MS
Wayne Rossberg, M Arch

Virginia Polytechnic Institute and State University

College of Architecture
and Urban Studies
Virginia Polytechnic Institute
and State University
Blacksburg, Virginia 24061-0205
(703) 961-6415

Office of Admissions
(703) 961-6267

Application Deadline(s): Undgrd: January 1
Grad: March 1
Tuition & Fees: Undgrd: VA res: $2320/yr;
Non-res: $4660/yr
Grad: VA res: $2674/yr;
Non-res: $2944/yr
Endowment: Public

DEGREE PROGRAMS

Degree	Minimum Years for Degree	Accred.	Requirements for Admission	Full-Time Stdnts.	Part-Time Stdnts.	% of Applics. Accptd.	Stdnts. in 1st Year of Program	# of Degrees Conferred
B Arch	5	NAAB	Univ. Req. SAT	747	68	27%	134	109
M Arch	1		Univ. Req. B Arch	11	—	80%	6	32
M Arch	2	NAAB	Univ. Req. preprof. degree in Arch	38	2	70%	21	32
M Arch	3	NAAB	Univ. Req.	77	7	50%	27	32
MS Arch	2		Univ. Req.	9	—	70%	6	0
M of Arts in Urb Aff	1+		Univ. Req. BA or BS	13	4	75%	9	9
M of Urb & Reg Plng	2	AIP	Univ. Req. BA, BS, or prof. degree	29	1	70%	22	8
D of Env Des & Plng	3		Univ. Req. M Arch, ML Arch, or MURP	19	3	40%	6	1
BL Arch	5	LAAB	Univ. Req. SAT	106	9	60%	27	14
ML Arch	1		Univ. Req. BL Arch	1	—	—	1	7
ML Arch	2	LAAB	Univ. Req. preprof. degree in L Arch	11	—	80%	2	7
ML Arch	3	LAAB	Univ. Req.	14	1	60%	6	7
BSBC	4		Univ. Req. SAT	122	3	70%	28	19

SCHOOL DEMOGRAPHICS (all degree programs)

Full-Time Faculty	Part-Time Faculty	Full-Time Students	Part-Time Students	Foreign Students	Out-of-State U.S. Stdnts.	Women Students	Minority Students
68	21	1197	98	NA	NA	NA	NA

LIBRARY (Tel. No. 703-961-6182)

Type	No. of Volumes	No. of Slides
Art & Arch	52,350+	27,000

STUDENT OPPORTUNITIES AND RESOURCES

Virginia Polytechnic Institute and State University, founded in 1872 as a public land-grant institution, carries out a range of responsibilities at the local, state, national and international levels. Its eight academic colleges have a total enrollment of 22,000 students, with students from every state in the union and ninety-eight foreign countries. On the graduate level, both master's and doctoral degrees are offered in almost 70 different areas of concentration. The University is accredited by the Southern Association of Colleges and Schools.

The College of Architecture and Urban Studies has evolved into a comprehensive college of environmental design and planning offering nine interrelated professional degree programs in Architecture, Landscape Architecture, Urban and Regional Planning, and Urban Affairs; an undergraduate program in Building Construction; and a doctor of philosophy in Environmental Design and Planning.

The Architecture programs attract outstanding students at both the undergraduate and graduate levels. The average SAT score of the incoming class for 1987 is 1166, and half of the incoming students ranked among the top 14 percent of their high school class. A limited number of very high quality transfer students is accepted each year. Graduate students come from across the United States and abroad. Each year students participate in exchange programs established between the College and institutions in China, Argentina, etc.

The faculty come to the College from major institutions throughout the world. Their backgrounds and interests range from architectural and art history to industrial design. All members of the faculty hold terminal professional degrees; about one-third are licensed architects or professional engineers.

The Virginia Tech campus is located in Blacksburg, a town of 33,000 situated in the Appalachian Mountains in southwest Virginia. The Roanoke metropolitan area provides convenient airline connections to principal eastern and midwestern cities.

Virginia Tech offers a wide range of cultural and academic programs on campus. Year-round recreational opportunities are provided through the gymnasiums, indoor swimming pool, all-weather tennis courts, and eighteen-hole golf course.

The Blacksburg community is diverse and supports a strong cultural and recreational life. Claytor Lake and the Appalachian Trail are readily accessible for boating, camping, and hiking.

SPECIAL ACTIVITIES AND PROGRAMS

OFF-CAMPUS STUDY PROGRAMS

The Washington-Alexandria Center in Old Town Alexandria just outside Washington, D.C., provides students and faculty an opportunity to live and work in an urban setting. In addition to formal lecture classes and studios, the Center offers research and continuing education opportunities. The Center was recently expanded with the formation of a consortium of faculty and students from architecture schools in the U.S. and Europe. Undergraduate and graduate students may spend one or more semesters in residence.

The European Study Program, based in Basel, Switzerland, offers a summer travel program as well as an opportunity for residential study in the spring and fall terms. The program consists of studios, seminars, and organized travel. Students may select one or more semesters of residence.

The Professional Office Program offers students in the fourth or fifth year the opportunity to spend one or two semesters working in an approved professional architectural office.

LECTURE SERIES

The College supports a dynamic lecture series. Over the last several years, nearly one hundred speakers from throughout the world visited the College, lecturing on topics ranging from contemporary works in architecture to economic development strategies for developing countries.

In addition, each year the Washington-Alexandria Center co-sponsors a lecture series with the Smithsonian Institution.

STUDENT ORGANIZATIONS

The American Institute of Architecture Students has an active chapter within the College which is engaged in a broad range of social and professionally-oriented activities.

COLLEGE PUBLICATIONS

CAUS News, published several times a year, highlights various activities under way in the College and disseminates information on achievements of faculty, student, and alumni, upcoming events, etc.

FACILITIES

The Architecture Program is housed in Cowgill Hall, a modern four-story building designed to suit the specific curriculum needs. The Architecture Library contains over 53,500 volumes and subscribes to over 500 periodicals from around the world. In addition to the slide collection, faculty and students have access to photography, video, animation, graphics, and ceramics facilities and a wood/metal shop. The College Environmental Systems Laboratory contains a boundary layer wind tunnel, a daylight simulation dome, a fiberglass fabrication facility, and machines to work in wood, metal, plaster, etc. In addition to the University's extensive computing facilities, which include the IBM 3090 super computer, the College has access to two CAD systems: the IBM CADAM system and the Computervision CADDS 4X system.

SCHOLARSHIPS/AID

Virginia Tech administers a comprehensive financial aid program, awarding aid to qualified undergraduate and graduate students in the form of scholarships, grants, loans, and employment. Financial assistance available to graduate students also includes fellowships, scholarships awarded by corporations and foundations, and teaching and research assistantships awarded through departments. Fifty-seven percent of Virginia Tech students receive some form of student aid.

Federal programs include the Pell Grant, Supplemental Educational Opportunity Grant, College Work-Study, National Direct Student Loan, and Guaranteed Student Loan programs. State programs include the Virginia College Scholarship Assistance program and the State Council of Higher Education grants and loans.

PHILOSOPHY STATEMENT

The energies of the College are focused on understanding the process and impacts of the many dimensions associated with the translation of human needs and aspirations into three dimensions. Faculty, students, and the resources of the College are intertwined, creating a learning environment that is self-directed, comprehensive, concerned with the development of the whole person, and geared toward individual instruction. The purpose of the program is to engage students in the processes and professional standards of design and management of shaping the human environment. It is concerned with bringing order, vitality, and form to man's surroundings.

It is the intention of the school to expand the role the architect can play in society. This is based upon the belief that the education the architect receives develops problem solving skills which have many applications.

In this light, students are expected to acquire a liberal education, aided by the newly-introduced University core curriculum, as well as master the key elements of professional education, which will enable them to participate in the mainstream of architectural practice.

Undergraduate Program Description

The Architecture curriculum is structured as three successive levels of studies: foundation studies (first year); core professional studies (second and third years); and advanced professional studies (fourth and fifth years). In addition to completion of an acceptable design or research thesis, a total of 147 semester-credit hours is required for the B Arch degree, of which 95 credits are in professional core courses.

The foundation program fosters a dialogue between design action and the designer's attitudes, knowledge, and concerns at all scales of the environment by means of heuristic investigation. The main vehicle for this investigation is the foundation design laboratory, which includes two critical components: a) the media and information systems workshops and b) the general lecture series.

The core professional studies level begins with design theory and process and covers building design as an interactive investigation of human factors, environmental forces, and technology. The first professional laboratory provides experience with practical design problems, and the lecture series exposes the student to background and practical experience in the design and construction of buildings. Special purpose workshops promote proper integration of necessary professional skills.

At the advanced professional studies level, the objective of the fourth year is for the student to summarize and present himself as an architect by completing an external competition, preparing a portfolio, or working on an appropriate field project. The fifth year includes laboratory and studio design exploration and pertinent professional elective courses intended to provide the student the opportunity to develop depth and expertise within a particular area of architecture. The student should be able to demonstrate how he can take a broad view of a situation, explore the relevant factors, develop alternatives, make a judgement, and take action.

Graduate Program Description

M ARCH 1: ADVANCED RESEARCH AND DESIGN CURRICULUM. A three-semester graduate degree program intended for the student with a professional degree (B Arch) in architecture or an equivalent in academic and professional experience. The program provides the opportunity and academic resources necessary to pursue a definitive, experimental design investigation or research in a design-relevant subject area according to the student's special interests. Emphasis is given to preparation of a research thesis or other project document demonstrative of the student's professional accomplishment and potential. A total of 54 semester-credit hours, including credit for 24 hours of advanced standing for fifth-year undergraduate studies, is required for the degree.

M ARCH 2: ADVANCED PROFESSIONAL STUDIES CURRICULUM. A two-year advanced professional degree program intended for the applicant having a non-professional (four-year) baccalaureate degree in architecture or in a pre-architecture curriculum. The first year of the program provides for completion of the student's professional building design and related technical and human factors studies. The second year is reserved for independent research and/or design work, for thesis preparation, and for appropriate elective studies. A total of 54 semester-credit hours is required for the degree.

M ARCH 3: COMPREHENSIVE PROFESSIONAL STUDIES CURRICULUM. A three-year professional degree program is provided for the student with a degree in a field other than architecture. Students complete a sequence of study to provide a foundation of basic environmental design experiences and to promote a preliminary understanding of the discipline. Upon successful completion of the qualifying year, students advance through a sequence of two years of studies providing for development of professional skills, techniques, and opportunities. In addition to the three academic years of this program, students are required to complete one full summer session of study at the Blacksburg Campus, the Washington-Alexandria Center, or the Study Abroad program in Basel, Switzerland. A total of 81 semester-credit hours, consisting of 27 credit-hours earned during the qualifying year and 54 during the professional program, is required for the degree.

MASTER OF SCIENCE IN ARCHITECTURE. The two-year graduate degree program allows students to concentrate on a broad range of architectural and environmental design issues. Students conduct a research-based program which can be expected to contribute to the base of knowledge in the design and planning profession. The program can lead to future study in the PhD program, and advanced standing is awarded for acceptable graduate credits earned at the Master's level. The following options are available in the Master of Science Degree Program: Building Economics and Industry Studies; Building Science; Computer Applications; Construction Management; Environmental and Product Design; International Development Studies; and Urban Design. In addition to the presentation of an acceptable thesis, a total of 54 semester-credit hours is required for the degree.

FACULTY
Administration

Charles W Steger, AIA, RA, AICP, Dean
Dixon B Hanna, AIA, RA, Associate Dean for Finance and Administration
Frederick Krimgold, Associate Dean for Research and Extension
D Eugene Egger, AIA, RA, Assistant Dean for Undergraduate Studies
William W Brown, RA, Chairman, Graduate Architecture Program
Ronald W Daniel, Chairman, Foundation Studies (1st year Architecture)
Robert J Dunay, AIA, RA, Chairman, Advanced Professional Studies (4th-5th year Architecture)
Dennis J Kilper, RA, Chairman, Core Professional Studies (2nd-3rd year Architecture)
Vincent J Cilimberg, Chairman, Building Construction Program
Patrick A Miller, Chairman, Landscape Architecture Program

James R Bohland, Chairman, Urban Affairs and Planning Programs
W David Conn, Chairman, Environmental Design and Planning (PhD) Program
Vickie Kok, Librarian

Professors

Milka Bliznakov, RA, PhD
James R Bohland, PhD
William W Brown, AIA, RA, MCP
Charles H Burchard, FAIA, M Arch
Robert N S Chiang, AIA, M Arch
W David Conn, D Phil-Econ
John W Dickey, PhD
Robert G Dyck, PhD
Patricia A Edwards, PhD
D Eugene Egger, AIA, RA, M Arch
Benjamin H Evans, RA, FAIA, M Arch
Olivio C Ferrari, AIA, Dipl
James E Hackett, PhD
Dennis J Kilper, RA, D Arch
Paul L Knox, PhD
Harry S Ransom, M Arch
Fernando Ruiz, AIA, M Arch
Wolfgang Schueller, M Arch, MSCE
Donald R Sunshine, RA, AIA, M Arch
Francis T Ventre, AIA, PhD
John W Wade, AIA, RA, M Arch
Richard E Zody, PhD

Associate Professors

Larz T Anderson, MCP
Dean R Bork, ML Arch
Walter J Butke, M Arch
Salahuddin Choudhury, M Arch
Vincent J Cilimberg, Bldg Const
Ronald W Daniel, M Arch
A Jack Davis, AIA, RA, M Arch
Donna W Dunay, RA, M Arch
Robert J Dunay, AIA, RA, M Arch
Robert F Graeff, RA, MA
Jaan Holt, M Arch
Jerry Householder, PhD
Jeanne B Howard, PhD
Gregory K Hunt, RA, M Arch
Benjamin C Johnson, ML Arch
Dennis B Jones, RA, MS Arch
John M Levy, PhD
Patrick A Miller, PhD
John Randolph, PhD
Humberto L Rodriguez-Camilloni, PhD
Sara A Rosenberry, PhD
Hans C Rott, M Arch
Robert P Schubert, M Arch
Leonard Singer, MS
Joseph C Wang, AIA, PhD
Richard M Yearwood, PhD

Assistant Professors

John O Browder, PhD
Charlene A Browne, ML Arch
David M Dugas, M Arch
Timothy A Fluck
Maria Karvouni, M Arch
Paul Kelsch, ML Arch
Thomas Koontz, AIA, RA, M Arch
Michael J O'Brien, M Arch
Patsy E Owens, ML Arch
J Scott Poole, M Arch
Holan E Rutland, MS
William E Shepherd, PhD
Jay E Stoeckel, M Arch
Frank H Weiner, B Arch, MS Arch

Lecturers

Ellen Braaten

Part-Time Faculty

Michael Appleby
Lucy Ferrari
Anna M Hardman, PhD
Rengin T Holt, B Arch

Adjunct Faculty

James C Canestaro, M Arch
Peter Disch, Dipl
Rudy Hunziker, Dipl
James Ritter
Fritz Schwarz, Dipl

209

University of Virginia

School of Architecture
Campbell Hall
University of Virginia
Charlottesville, Virginia 22903
(804) 924-3715

Admissions Office
(804) 924-6442

Application Deadline(s): January 15
Undgrd: VA Res:
$2366/yr
Non-res:$5796/yr
Grad: $2366/yr
Non-res: $5796/yr

Tuition & Fees: State

DEGREE PROGRAMS

Degree	Minimum Years for Degree	Accred.	Requirements for Admission	Full-Time Stdnts.	Part-Time Stdnts.	% of Applics. Accptd.	Stdnts. in 1st Year of Program	# of Degrees Conferred
BS Arch	4		HS diploma, SAT, 3 ach tests	305	0	27%[1]	74	79
M Arch	1		B Arch (5-yr), GRE, portfolio, letters	3	0	16%[2]	2	
M Arch	2	NAAB	Bacc degree, GRE, portfolio, letters	19	0	25%[2]	13	27
M Arch	3½	NAAB	Bacc (any field), GRE, portfolio, letters	40	0	18%[2]	14	

[1] 1986–87   [2] 1987–88

SCHOOL DEMOGRAPHICS (all degree programs)

Full-Time Faculty	Part-Time Faculty	Full-Time Students	Part-Time Students	Foreign Students	Out-of-State U.S. Stdnts.	Women Students	Minority Students
23	13	367	0	1%	59%	46%	4%

LIBRARY (Tel. No. 804-924-6601)

Type	No. of Volumes	No. of Slides
Branch	96,689	107,516

STUDENT OPPORTUNITIES AND RESOURCES

The academic programs of the School of Architecture encompass four distinct, yet increasingly interrelated, programs providing a rich setting for professional education. The architecture and landscape architecture programs seek to integrate the intellectual and pragmatic aspects of their disciplines in the belief that design skills must be as responsive to the cultural, historical, and physical context as to functional need. The architectural history program aims to develop an awareness of the value of the past and, in conjunction with the other programs, offers a specialization in historic preservation. The program in urban and environmental planning emphasizes the application of planning theory, processes, and methods in the context of an understanding of political and market forces, resource limitations, and social needs. In addition to the traditional courses offered in each division, the curricula provide ample interdisciplinary opportunities for the exploration of such diverse contemporary issues as energy conservation, social equity, environmental protection, historic preservation, and adaptive reuse.

At the undergraduate level the school offers three degrees, Bachelor of Science (Architecture), Bachelor of Architectural History, and Bachelor of City Planning. In addition, there are four graduate programs leading to the degrees Master of Architecture, Master of Landscape Architecture, Master of Architectural History, and Master of Planning. The programs of the school are accredited by the NAAB, ASLA, and APA; the school holds memberships in the Collegiate Schools of Architecture, the Collegiate Schools of Planning, the Council of Educators in Landscape Architecture, the National Council of Preservation Education, the Society of Architectural Historians, and the National Trust for Historic Preservation.

The full- and part-time faculty numbers about 60, augmented by 20-30 visiting lecturers and critics from this country and abroad who, each year, bring to students their varied perspectives and wide-ranging experience in the fields of architecture, planning, landscape architecture, and architectural history. The student body averages approximately 550 students, of whom about 350 are undergraduates and the remainder graduate students.

The Thomas Jefferson Memorial Foundation Professorship in Architecture has been funded since 1965 by an annual grant from the same foundation, which also has guided the restoration and preservation of Monticello, the home of Thomas Jefferson. The foundation also annually awards a medal and honorarium to a practitioner or teacher of international distinction and has established a number of scholarships for graduate students.

The principal research agencies of the School of Architecture are the Center for Housing and Social Environment (CHASE) and the Institute for Environmental Negotiation (IEN).

SPECIAL ACTIVITIES AND PROGRAMS

Opportunities to study abroad in London, Bath, Vicenza, Venice

Annual lecture series, symposia, and conferences

Modulus, annual school publication

Thomas Jefferson Visiting Professorship

Public service studios

Interdivisional joint programs

Independent study and thesis programs

Extern program

Options in historic preservation and technology and Studies in American Urbanism

Student Design Council

Beaux Arts Ball

FACILITIES

Campbell Hall, the School of Architecture building, provides well-equipped studio work areas, exhibition areas, lecture halls, and seminar rooms. The school also provides a range of support facilities, including a Fine Arts library, computer, mechanical and structural laboratories, a woodworking shop, a photography darkroom, and a student-operated supply store and blueprint shop.

SCHOLARSHIPS/AID

During the 1985–86 session, undergraduate students in the School of Architecture received $125,682 in university scholarship aid, $17,165 in work-study funds, and $255,899 in NDSL funds. Graduate students had $43,500 in fellowships, $15,500 in teaching assistantships, $39,855 in work-study funds, and $347,442 in NDSL funds. In addition, graduate students were funded by special research grants.

UNDERGRADUATE PROGRAM
Philosophy Statement

The undergraduate degree in architecture has as its primary goal the development of a strong cultural and intellectual background in architecture. Emphasis is placed on the role of architecture as a reflection of specific cultural value systems, expressed as idea, as process, and finally as built form. It is in this context that the architecture studio is seen as the distinctive and fundamental basis of an education with a major in architecture. The emphasis in the studio sequence is placed on developing ideas about architecture and their formal resolution and expression in problems of ever-increasing complexity. The undergraduate program couples the development of a strong humanities background with the specific activity of making built form. The program is therefore preprofessional, with the expectation that a majority of students will pursue graduate studies in order to obtain the first professional degree in architecture or related disciplines.

Program Description

The school offers a four-year Bachelor of Science (Architecture) curriculum structured about two primary educational objectives: (1) to develop a liberal arts foundation, including environmental design, and (2) to develop a preprofessional program in architecture with a concentration in design.

The first objective enables students to develop a firm humanistic foundation in liberal arts, which serves as a basis for architecture studies. Elective courses in social sciences, humanities, and natural sciences are required. In addition, students take introductory courses in related architecture subjects.

The second objective enables students to concentrate on architecture as a major in a professional educational discipline. The predominant educational mode is the design studio where work is supported by a series of courses in technology, theory, and history.

The bachelor's program prepares graduates for a variety of professional and/or academic opportunities. Graduates may enter directly into the architecture profession although they may elect to work in related employment areas. Graduates are also prepared to continue graduate study in architecture or related environmental disciplines.

The school places high value on architectural design as a process for improving the physical environment. The program concentrates on developing this method as a synthesizing, creative force in environmental improvement. Each student develops his or her own capabilities and specialization by drawing on a core of professional skills and a broad range of liberal arts experiences.

GRADUATE PROGRAM
Philosophy Statement

The educational intention of the graduate program in architecture is to investigate architecture for its pragmatic realities and the more speculative realm of ideas that comprise the values of the academic community. Architecture is seen as a participant in a system of communication of cultural order, capable of being understood and intelligently manipulated.

Program Description

The Master of Architecture program is open to students with an undergraduate degree in any field of study. There are three distinct paths by which a student can obtain the first professional degree in architecture (M. Arch). Students with a background in an architectural discipline can expect to graduate in one or two years depending on the degree, while students from other disciplines may finish in three or four years depending on their background and abilities. The presence in the school of other graduate curricula in landscape architecture, architecture history, and city planning makes teaching integration with these disciplines possible. There are also offered special options in preservation, architectural technologies and studies in American urbanism.

Design is offered in section laboratories that investigate architectural issues such as design theories, housing, urban design, campus planning, structural studies and general technologies, visual communication, and adaptive use of existing structures. The nature of the various design projects is dependent upon the expertise of the teaching staff involved at the graduate level. These studies investigate all aspects of the architectural problem including design programming and component technology, as well as the traditional concern with form. A diversity of design experiences is encouraged.

FACULTY
Administration

Harry W Porter, Jr, FASLA, Acting Dean
Theo van Groll, Assoc Dean-Student Affairs
Bruce Abbey, RA, Assoc Dean-Academic Affairs
William G Clark, Jr, RA, Chairman of Architecture
Carroll William Westfall, Chairman of Architectural History
Warren T. Byrd, Jr, Chairman of Landscape Architecture
David Phillips, Chairman of Planning
Mario di Valmarana, Director, Preservation Program
Robert D Dripps III, Director, Studies in American Urbanism
Jack Robertson, Fine Arts Librarian

Professors

Bruce Abbey, RA, B Arch, M Arch
William G Clark, Jr., RA, B Arch
Richard C Collins, BA, PhD
James A D Cox, Dipl
Mario di Valmarana, Dott Arch
Robert D Dripps III, AB, M Arch
William M Harris, BS, MUP, PhD
Matthias Kayhoe, RA, BS Arch, M Arch
K Edward Lay, RA, B Arch, M Arch
William H Lucy, BA, MA, PhD
Frederick D Nichols, MA
Harry W Porter Jr, BSLA, MLA
Yale Rabin, BFA, BS, B Arch (Grad)
Jaquelin T Robertson, RA, BA, M Arch
James S Tuley, RA, B Arch
Robert L Vickery Jr, RA, B Jour, M Arch
C William Westfall, BA, MA, PhD
H Kenneth White, RA, Dipl Arch
Richard G Wilson, BA, MA, PhD
William Zuk, BSCE, MSE, PhD

Associate Professors

Michael J Bednar, RA, B Arch, M Arch
Warren Boeschenstein, RA, BA, B Arch, MUD
Warren T Byrd Jr, BS, MLA
Errol Cowan, BS, MBA, PhD
A Bruce Dotson, BA, PhD
Donald E Dougald, RA, BAE, MSAE
Edward R Ford, RA, BS, M Arch
Judith A Kinnard, RA, B Arch
David L Phillips, BS, PhD
John L Ruseau, BS Arch

Assistant Professors

Timothy P Beatley, BCP, MUP, MA, PhD
Gregg D Bleam, BSLA, MLA
Charles E Brownell, BA, MA, M Phil, PhD
Robert W Collin, BA, JD, MSW, MSUB, MLUS
Ellen Dunham-Jones, AB, M Arch
James R Klein, BS, BLA, MLA
W Jude LeBlanc, B Arch, M Arch
John Meder, RA, B Arch, M Arch
Kenneth A Schwartz, RA, B Arch, M Arch
Ellen P Soroka, BFA, M Arch
Daphne G Spain, BA, MA, PhD

Part-Time Faculty

J Norwood Bosserman, RA, BS in Arch, MFA
P Jeff Bushman, RA, BS, M Arch
Nancy N Chambers, BED, M Arch
Bethany J Christenson, BA, M Arch
Charles P Edwards, BSEE
J Murray Howard, B Arch, M Arch, PhD
Joseph G Howe, BSCE, MCE
Yunsheng Huang, Dipl Arch, MS, MA, PhD
Satyendra Huja, BA, MA
John F James, BA, MLA
William M Kelso, BA, MA, PhD
C Timothy Lindstrom, BA, JD
Daniel Montgomery, RA, BS, MRP
Howard H Newlon, BSCE, MSCE
Garland A Okerlund, BA, MLA
Rosser H Payne, BE, ICMA
Lucia B Phinney, BA, M Arch
Constance W Ramirez, BA, MCP, PhD
William D Rieley, BS, MLA
Nancy A Takahashi, BS, MLA, M Arch
Robert W Tucker, BS, MURP
J Marvin Watson, AB, MS

Adjunct Faculty

Clemente di Thiene
Philip Rylands

Thomas Jefferson Professor of Architecture

Demetri Porphyrios, AB, M Arch, PhD

Washington State University

School of Architecture
Carpenter Hall
Washington State University
Pullman, Washington 99164-2220
(509) 335-5539

Application Deadline(s): 3rd Year - February 1
Graduate - Anytime
(Feb 21 Preferred)
Tuition & Fees: (1986-87)
Undgrd: WA res: $803/Sem;
Non-res: $2231/Sem
Grad: $1160/Sem;
Non-res: $2888/Sem
Endowment: State

DEGREE PROGRAMS

Degree	Minimum Years for Degree	Accred.	Requirements for Admission	Full-Time Stdnts.	Part-Time Stdnts.	% of Applics. Accptd.	Stdnts. in 1st Year of Program	# of Degrees Conferred
BS/Arch St*	4		GPA, portfolio (3rd yr)	140 (3-5)	0		150	47
B/Arch*	5	NAAB	GPA, portfolio (3rd yr)	140 (3-5)	0	60%	150	45
MS/Arch**	1		B/Arch, GPA, GRE (TOEFL-Foreign)	4	0	80%		—
BS/Const Mgmt	4		GPA (2nd year)		0	45%	60	25

*B/Arch Grads also receive BS/Arch studies
**MS/Arch commenced Fall Semester, 1987

SCHOOL DEMOGRAPHICS (all degree programs)

Full-Time Faculty	Part-Time Faculty	Full-Time Students	Part-Time Students	Foreign Students	Out-of-State U.S. Stdnts.	Women Students	Minority Students
21	0	520*	0	12%	6%	18%	2%

*Includes first two years of program

LIBRARY (Tel. No. 509-335-4967)

Type	No. of Volumes	No. of Slides
Arch	10,000	45,000

STUDENT OPPORTUNITIES AND RESOURCES

Washington State University is located in the community of Pullman, population 21,500 (17,000 of whom are students). Pullman, located in Palouse wheat country, is 75 miles south of the city of Spokane. To the east is the lake district of northern Idaho with access to rain forests. To the south lies the wilderness area of the Snake River Canyon and to the west, the open plains of the Columbia Basin and the Columbia River, which provides the water for thousands of acres of irrigated farm lands. WSU is thus within two hours' driving time of four unusual natural environments. As a major land-grant institution, WSU is a comprehensive university that offers a wide range of academic choices encompassing over 60 degree-granting programs. There is a continuing university studies program offering correspondence courses, evening classes, and off-campus classes. Interdisciplinary ties can be developed with the Departments of Landscape Architecture, Interior Design, and Regional Planning in other colleges. The College of Engineering offers course work in surveying, advanced structures, traffic, transportation, solar energy, materials science, sanitation, and hydrology.

WSU houses museums of art, natural history, and anthropology. The School of Music and Drama offers varying events of cultural interest. The main library contains 2.5 million volumes and has two branches for science and engineering. The Radio and Television Service is satellite-equipped, broadcasting on PBS. The university supports the Energy Research and Resource Management institutes. The University of Idaho, eight miles away, offers additional academic opportunities, and many courses are cross-listed.

SPECIAL ACTIVITIES AND PROGRAMS

Close relationships with all AIA chapters in the state and Portland, Oregon

Study-abroad program in Copenhagen, Denmark and London, England (alternate years)

Annual field trips (Chicago, San Francisco, Vancouver, etc)

Annual Spring Symposium

Visiting lecturer program

Traveling exhibits

Work-study

Summer internship

FACILITIES

The School of Architecture has been located in Carpenter Hall since the program was initiated in 1913. While it has shared space in that building with many units in the College of Engineering and Architecture, Carpenter Hall will undergo a major renovation beginning in the fall of 1988, and the entire building will house the School of Architecture thereafter.

SCHOLARSHIPS/AID

Tuition scholarships for upper-division students total approximately $3000 and are under the control of the School of Architecture. For further information on scholarships available through the Financial Aid Office, applicants should contact that office. Student loans are available. Scholarships and aid are based on financial need and academic standing.

UNDERGRADUATE PROGRAM
Philosophy Statement

The primary thrust of the school is to provide the best possible undergraduate education for those students who desire to participate in the development of a better built environment through architectural design and practice.

Program Description

The education program is organized in a 2-3 format. There is limited enrollment at the start of the third year. The formal admission procedures take into account student's academic record, potential in design, and stated goals.

At the present time transfer students are accepted into the fourth- or fifth-year programs on a space-available basis only.

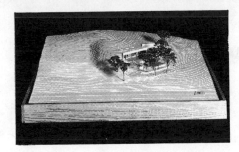

The vehicle for learning lies in the curriculum's organization around the design studio core. The problems vary in complexity on the basis of the faculty's areas of expertise and their perception of the students' ability level.

Emphasis is placed on professional skills and creative analysis. Most students seek professional employment upon leaving the university.

Those students who have the necessary mental capability, motivation, and financial resources are encouraged to attend graduate school at another institution.

The primary role of the faculty is one of managing learning opportunities. The role of the student is to be an active, motivated participant. Learning is a dynamic participatory process that provides enrichment for both the student and the faculty.

BACHELOR OF ARCHITECTURE
Pre-Architecture

Students who enter WSU as freshmen and have an interest in architecture should obtain an adviser in the Department of Architecture through the Curriculum Advisory Program. Specific requirements of the pre-architecture program are:

Complete 60 hours and 2 years of college-level work including the following:

Freshman Year	
First Semester	*Hours*
Math 107 and/or 108	2-5
Com Prof GUR	3
Arch 101 Graphic Communication	3
Hum GUR	3
Env S 101 (Soc S GUR)	3
Second Semester	*Hours*
Math 171 or 206	3-4
Arch 102 Graphic Communication	3
Com Prof GUR	3
Arch 202 Built Environment	3
Elective	3

Sophomore Year	
First Semester	*Hours*
Phys 201 or 101	4
Arch 201 Intro Design	3
Arch 331 Mat and Const	3
Soc S GUR	3
Electives	3
Second Semester	*Hours*
Ph S Elective	3-4
Arch 203 Intro Design II	3
Hum GUR	3
Electives	6

Professional Program

Upon completion of the Pre-Architecture program requirements or their equivalent for transfer students, application must be made for admission to the third year Professional Program (see requirements below). Successful completion of the three-year Professional Program requirements, totaling 90 semester credits minimum, leads to the degree of Bachelor of Architecture. This accredited degree plus three additional years of professional experience and successful completion of the architectural license examination qualifies a person for registration as a licensed architect in the state of Washington.

Professional Program Entry Requirements

1. Satisfactory completion of all Pre-Architecture requirements or their equivalents including 60 semester credits total.

2. Submission of application for entry. Forms and instructions for application are available from the Office of Admissions and must be submitted prior to February 1 preceding fall registration. Transfer students must also submit an Application for Admission to the university. Successful applicants will be notified prior to May 1.

NOTE: Satisfactory progress in the Professional Program requires a grade of C or better be earned in all architectural design and determinants courses in the third, fourth, and fifth years.

Junior Year	
First Semester	*Hours*
Arch 301 Design	4
Arch 307 Determinants	2
Arch 323 History	2
Arch 351 Structures I	3
Arch 353 Struct Sem	1
Elective	3
Second Semester	*Hours*
Arch 303 Design	4
Arch 309 Determinants	2
Arch 324 History	2
Arch 352 Structures II	3
Arch 354 Struct Sem	1
Arch 432 Env Control Bldgs	3

Senior Year	
First Semester	*Hours*
Arch 401 Design	5
Arch 407 Determinants	2
Arch 423 History	2
Arch 433 Env Control II	3
Structures Elective	3
Second Semester	*Hours*
Arch 403 Design	5
Arch 409 Determinants	2
Env Control Elective	1-2
Arch Emphasis Elective	3-4
F A Elective	3

Fifth Year	
First Semester	*Hours*
Arch 411 Design	6
Arch 415 Programming	2
Arch 472 Const Comm	2
Arch Emphasis Elective	3
Elective	2-3
Second Semester	*Hours*
Arch 413 Design	6
Arch 473 Business	2
Arch Emphasis Elective	4
F A Elective	3

GRADUATE PROGRAM
Philosophy Statement

Beginning in the fall of 1987, the School of Architecture initiated a one-year post-professional Master of Science in Architecture degree program. The emphasis of this program is on energy and resource management including cultural resources. The program will require a thesis.

FACULTY
Administration

Reid Miller, Reg Engr, Dean, College of Engineering and Architecture
J William Rudd, AIA, Director, School of Architecture
Ann Warrington, Library Specialist

Professors

Robert B Allen, BS, MS
Tom J Bartuska, RA, B Arch, M Arch
Charles R Burger, RA, B Arch E, B Arch, M Arch
Robert J Patton, RA, B Arch, MFA
J William Rudd, RA, B Arch, MA
David M Scott, RA, BS Arch E, M Arch
S Wayne Williams, RA, B Arch, M Arch

Associate Professors

Kenneth L Carper, RA, B Arch, MS CE
Larry G Fisher, RA, BS Arch E, MS Arch E
Donald R Heil, RA, BS Arch, M Arch
Henry C Matthews, RA, BA, MA Arch, Dipl
Douglas W Menzies, RA, BS Arch E, B Arch, M Arch
Donald N Mirkovich, RA, BA Arch, MA Arch
Sara M Recken, BS, MFA
Kim C Singhrs, BA, MFA

Assistant Professors

J Jeffrey Burnett, BS, BS Arch St, MA Arch
Channell Graham, RA, BS Arch E, M Arch
Gregg Kessler, RA, B Arch, M Arch
Michael S Owen, BA, M Arch
H Rafi Samizay, B Arch, M Arch

Washington University

School of Architecture
Washington University
Campus Box 1079
St. Louis, Missouri 63130
(314) 889-6200

Office of Admissions
(314) 889-6200

Application Deadline(s): Undgrd: Feb. 15
(Early decision
Nov. 1)
Grad: Feb. 15
Tuition & Fees: Undgrd: $11,400/yr
Grad: $11,400/yr
Endowment: Private

DEGREE PROGRAMS

Degree	Minimum Years for Degree	Accred.	Requirements for Admission	Full-Time Stdnts.	Part-Time Stdnts.	% of Applics. Accptd.	Stdnts. in 1st Year of Program	# of Degrees Conferred
BA	4	N Central Assn	HS Diploma	168	—	50%	50	38
M Arch	1-3½	NAAB	BA, BS, or BFA	102	—	60%	—	40
MAUD	1-2		1st Prof. Degree	5	—	60%	5	3

SCHOOL DEMOGRAPHICS (all degree programs)

Full-Time Faculty	Part-Time Faculty	Full-Time Students	Part-Time Students	Foreign Students	Out-of-State U.S. Stdnts.	Women Students	Minority Students
14	37	270	—	17%	67%	31%	12%

LIBRARY (Tel. No. 314-889-5218)

Type	No. of Volumes	No. of Slides
Art & Arch	65,500	90,000

STUDENT OPPORTUNITIES AND RESOURCES

A small but diverse student body (less than 200 undergraduate, 100 plus graduate), and a flexible curriculum which allows for completion of the preprofessional undergraduate and the professional graduate programs in a minimum of 6 or a maximum of 7½ years, provide many educational choices as well as a strong professional focus for entering freshmen, transfer and graduate students. The architecture faculty is composed of a core of full-time members whose fields range widely over the spectrum of professional concerns. Although each has a primary responsibility to the school, all full-time faculty members carry on research or practice. In turn, a number of St. Louis area architects, engineers, planners, and artists serve as part-time members of the faculty. Outstanding visiting professors from abroad and from other parts of the United States serve as full-time faculty members for a semester.

All undergraduate students at the School of Architecture are candidates for the Bachelor of Arts degree offered by the College of Arts and Sciences. This candidacy nurtures the development of a broader education in the liberal arts as students simultaneously pursue their architecture commitments. Architecture students may elect to minor in the arts, literature or languages, philosophy, history, social and behavioral sciences, natural sciences, or mathematics, or in any of a broad range of area studies. Qualified students may combine studies in the School of Engineering toward a bachelor's degree in civil engineering or mechanical engineering with graduate work leading to the Master of Architecture degree. Graduate level studies are enriched with combined programs with the Graduate School of Business Administration leading to M Arch and Master of Business Administration degrees; the School of Engineering leading to M Arch and a Master of Construction Management; and with the George Warren Brown School of Social Work leading to M Arch and Master of Social Work degrees. Graduate studies for the M Arch degree program can also be completed in combination with studies toward the Master of Architecture and Urban Design degree.

Freshman and sophomore year architecture studios have 20 to 30 students. Junior and senior year studios vary from 20 to 22 students. Graduate studios may have as few as 8 or as many as 16 students.

SPECIAL ACTIVITIES AND PROGRAMS

Special activities and programs include, among others, the following:

Summer Architecture Career Discovery program for high school students

Junior Year Abroad program as part of liberal arts studies

Combined programs with other disciplines at both the undergraduate and graduate levels.

Annual student awards and prizes programs.

Summer design studios at the graduate level, abroad and in St. Louis

Professional Studio allows students at the graduate level to gain experience in a St. Louis metropolitan area architectural firm

Visiting Faculty program of long history and distinction

Monday night lecture series

School conducts the Steedman Fellowship Competition for young professional degree holders

School publications include "Approach" and "Architecture News"

FACILITIES

All architecture studios, classes and seminars are conducted in Givens Hall.

Architecture students take all other classes in various buildings composing a University Campus of architectural distinction and quality dating from 1905.

Givens Hall also houses computer labs, photographic labs, and model and construction shops.

Art and Architecture Library, Gallery of Art, and auditorium are located in adjacent Steinberg Hall.

SCHOLARSHIPS/AID

The School of Architecture offers financial aid at both the undergraduate and graduate levels. During the 1986-87 academic year, 60 percent of the need-based undergraduates and 75 percent of the graduate students participated in one or more of the various need-based financial aid programs offered. Three basic types of financial aid are available at the undergraduate level: aid based on financial need, aid based solely on

academic merit, and aid for foreign students. Gifts, loans, and work-study funds make up most undergraduate aid "packages." Financial aid at the graduate level is based on academic excellence and need, and includes tuition remission scholarships, Dean's Scholarships, federally funded loan programs, and university-related loan funds. The Spencer T. Olin Fellowship for Women, as well as the Thurston C. Ely, Edward H. Pelton, Milton L. Zorensky, the Henges Interiors, the George Kassabaum, etc. scholarships are available for graduate students. The Ralph P. Ranft Scholarship is also awarded in conjunction with the St. Louis AIA Chapter. Teaching and research assistantships carrying a stipend of $1,500 per semester are also available. More detailed information may be obtained by contacting the School of Architecture. Washington University encourages and gives full consideration to applicants for admission and financial aid without regard to sex, race, handicap, color, creed, or national origin. University policies and programs are nondiscriminatory.

UNDERGRADUATE PROGRAM
Philosophy Statement

The undergraduate program is designed to provide a wide overview of architecture as both an entity and a process. A general and conceptual focus encourages the development of the means with which to exercise material, aesthetic, and moral choices in the planning and building of a humane environment.

Program Description

The first two years are primarily devoted to studies in the College of Arts and Sciences but also include introductory work in architecture.

The professional curriculum begins at the junior-year level. During the first two years of professional studies, the student is exposed to basic architectural issues through a sequence of studios supported by a number of lecture courses in theory, graphics, history, and structures. Satisfactory completion of this phase qualifies a student for the Bachelor of Arts degree with a major in Architecture awarded by the College of Arts and Sciences. Under this option, only one year of the professional curriculum will be included in the BA degree. Hence, three years instead of two will be spent at the graduate level working toward an M Arch degree.

GRADUATE PROGRAM
Philosophy Statement

The graduate program prepares individuals for architectural practice and concentrates on the development of professional excellence and accountability. Professional skills and attitudes are cultivated as students, in their design studios, courses, and seminars reconcile the multiple determinants that shape the built environment.

Program Description

The Master of Architecture degree is the accredited, professional degree offered by the School of Architecture. Students who hold a BA degree with a major in architecture including two years of studies at the professional curriculum level can complete the requirements for the M Arch degree in a minimum of two years. Work at this advanced level demands an increasingly independent attitude and focuses on a studio sequence, a number of required courses and seminars, and electives that can be taken either at the School of Architecture or at other divisions of the university.

Students who hold an undergraduate degree without a major in architecture (BA, BS, BFA) are admitted to the School of Architecture as candidates for the M Arch degree. Such students may complete the professional studies program in three and one-half years or less (minimum of three). Students who have completed a five-year first professional degree program (B Arch) in an accredited school in the United States or a foreign country are also eligible for admission to the M Arch program and are given advanced placement by the Admissions Committee following evaluation of their applications.

Those holding a first professional degree in architecture or equivalent may qualify for admission to the program leading to the degree of Master of Architecture and Urban Design. This degree is normally awarded upon completion of a calendar-year graduate curriculum devoted to urban design and other aspects of large-scale architecture and planning.

The architectural design studio sequence is the spine of the undergraduate and professional curricula. Aesthetic concerns, technology and social issues come under close examination in such studios where individual achievement as well as peer learning provide vehicles for the development of personal and architectural judgment.

FACULTY
Administration

Constantine E Michaelides, FAIA, Dean
James R Harris, RA, Associate Dean
Davis W van Bakergem, RA, Director URDC
Wayne W Enderling, AIA, Director of Continuing Education
Rodney Henmi, Assistant to the Dean
Linda L Lott, Librarian Art & Architecture

Professors

Irving Engel, RA, MS Arch Sci
Gerald Gutenschwager, AICP, PhD
Sheldon S Helfman, MFA
Udo Kultermann, PhD
Constantine E Michaelides, FAIA, M Arch
Donald C Royse, RA, PhD
Thomas L Thomson, AIA, M Arch

Associate Professors

Iain Fraser, M Arch
Carl B Safe, RA, MED

Assistant Professors

Adrian Luchini, RA, M Arch
James R Harris, RA, M Arch
Rodney Henmi, RA, B Arch
Kevin Hinders, M Arch
Lorens Holm, RA, M Arch
Brian McLaren, MSc
Maya Schali, M Arch
Davis W van Bakergem, RA, B Arch

Part-Time Faculty

Lorenz T Bannes, BSce
William Bricken, M Arch
Janet Brown, PhD
Gerardo Caballero, M Arch
William C Carr, PE, MSSE
Joseph Catalano, M Arch
Mario Luis Corea, RA, M Arch
William J Curtis, PhD
Clark S Davis, AIA, M Arch
Wayne W Enderling, AIA, B Arch
Robert A Fraser, ASLA, MLA
Paul Gawronik, M Arch
Christopher Grubbs, M Arch
Richard Janis, PE, MSME
Gay G Lorberbaum, RA, M Arch
Richard Macias, MLA
Arthur Monsey, PE, DSc
Robert Pettus, BS Arch
Peter Prangnell, RA, M Arch
W Patrick Schuchard, MFA
Ed Schultz, B Tech
James Scott
Ted Smith, MFA
Joseph A Stein, M Arch
William K Tao, MSME
Robert L Vickery, B Arch
Thomas F Walsh
Martha Whitaker, BS
Janet W White, AIA, M Arch
Stephen White, M Arch
Kenneth Worley, MFA
James F Yerges, PhD

Adjunct Faculty

Robert Thorp, PhD
Mark Weil, PhD

University of Washington

Department of Architecture
208 Gould Hall J0-20
University of Washington
Seattle, Washington 98195
(206) 543-4180

Application Deadline(s): Undgrd: January 15th
& May 15th
Grad: February 15th
Tuition & Fees: Undgrd: WA res: $1731/yr
Non-res: $4809/yr
Grad: WA res: $2505/yr
Non-res: $6228/yr
Endowment: Public

DEGREE PROGRAMS

Degree	Minimum Years for Degree	Accred.	Requirements for Admission	Full-Time Stdnts.	Part-Time Stdnts.	% of Applics. Accptd.	Stdnts. in 1st Year of Program	# of Degrees Conferred
BA (prep for arch or other)	4		univ req: 2.5 GPA	185	—	60%	90	80
M Arch	1+		B Arch; GRE; portfolio; letters	5	—	70%	5	3
M Arch	2+	NAAB	BA Arch or equiv; GRE; portfolio; letters	75	—	33%	50	20
M Arch	3+	NAAB	BA or BS; GRE; letters; portfolio recommended	105	—	33%	30	20
M Arch Cert in UD			Concurrent with M Arch					
M Arch Cert in Pres Des			Concurrent with M Arch					

SCHOOL DEMOGRAPHICS (M Arch degree program)

Full-Time Faculty	Part-Time Faculty	Full-Time Students	Part-Time Students	Foreign Students	Out-of-State U.S. Stdnts.	Women Students	Minority Students
23	30	185	—	25%	14%	19%	11%

LIBRARY (Tel. No. 206-543-4067)

Type	No. of Volumes	No. of Slides
College	30,000	70,000

STUDENT OPPORTUNITIES AND RESOURCES

The University of Washington is the oldest state-assisted institution of higher education on the Pacific Coast. Members of the University's teaching and research faculty are known nationally and internationally. The University of Washington is one of the major seats of learning and research in the western United States and ranks among the fine public universities in the country and on the Pacific Rim. For the last 18 years, the University has ranked among the top five institutions and first among public universities in the country in receipt of federal grants and contracts. Located between Lake Washington and Lake Union, the campus and university district form a distinctive enclave within a city that is one of the most picturesque in the nation. Seattle is the major city of the Pacific Northwest, having reached a metropolitan population of over 2 million.

Enrollment at the University is over 30,000, of which about one-fourth are graduate students. There are over 3,000 teaching and research positions and a staff of 12,000 on the 700-acre campus which has 128 buildings. A library collection of over four million volumes is one of the most extensive in the nation.

The Department of Architecture was officially established in 1914 - the nineteenth such department in the nation. At present, the Department, housed in Gould Hall and nearby Architecture Hall, is the largest department in the College of Architecture and Urban Planning, which also includes the Departments of Urban Design and Planning, Landscape Architecture and Building Construction.

SPECIAL ACTIVITIES AND PROGRAMS

Foreign study programs in Italy
Exchange student/visiting graduate student opportunities with Scandanavia, Japan and Germany
Student journal, *Column 5*
Beaux Arts Ball
Visiting lecturers/critics
Regular exhibitions
"Job Book" listing of clients soliciting student help
Summer courses for advanced high school students, university level students and professionals
University Placement Office
Active AIAS
ACSA Summer Institute on Environmental Controls
Annual Awards program
Rome Dinner and Auction
September Intensive
Design Charrette week with distinguished visiting critics

FACILITIES

Newly-renovated Architecture Hall
Review and exhibition space
Architectural library/slide library
Computer facility
Lighting applications laboratory
Environmental Measurements facilities
Design Graphics Laboratory
Photography Laboratory
Wood and metal working shops
Coffee shops in both buildings

SCHOLARSHIPS/AID

The department awards a limited number of scholarships and assistantships each spring quarter for the following academic year. Most awards are based on financial need. Although they are normally available only to students currently enrolled in the graduate program in architecture at the time of the awards, the department has been able to use some scholarships in the recruitment of students applying to the Master of Architecture degree program. A listing and application are available from the department. Other possibilities may be available from the Financial Aid Office, 105 Schmitz Hall, UW, Seattle, Wa. 98195, (206) 543-6101; or The Graduate School, Fellowship Division, 201 Administration Building, UW, Seattle, Wa. 98195, (206) 543-7152.

UNDERGRADUATE PROGRAM
Philosophy Statement

The BA degree program provides the student with a liberal arts education with special preprofessional emphasis in architecture; it does not enable the student to begin a professional career as an architect without further formal study. The program is intended to prepare students for further study in a range of related fields, such as landscape, urban planning, architectural journalism, and interior design and to enable them to compete strongly for graduate study in architecture at this and other schools.

Program Description

The undergraduate BA program requires a 75-credit liberal arts distribution and completion of a nine-credit introductory course before application to the College.

Acceptance as a college major requires junior standing (90 or more credits) and acceptance by the Program Admissions Committee.

The Program includes an interdisciplinary environmental design and planning core. The 45-credit component of the program provides an introduction to environmental design knowledge and beginning skills development and comprises two parts:

a. Core Courses - there are seven required courses for a total of 36 credits.

b. Core Distribution Electives - there are nine credits required which are distributed over two subject areas. The student must take a minimum of one course from each area. The program prepares students to enter the college's professional programs.

Students enrolled in the undergraduate BA program who are interested in preparing for a graduate professional degree program (at the U. of W. or elsewhere) can take up to 45 credits of elective courses offered by the Department of Architecture.

GRADUATE PROGRAM
Philosophy Statement

The Department of Architecture sees its mission as providing education in both the professional and academic aspects of a field that is simultaneously an art and a science. The term "academic" here refers to broader learning and the development of the intellectual capabilities. Professional education equips the student with skills and expertise; academic education exposes the student to values, attitudes and culture.

The Department has consistently held its primary mission to be the preparation of students for a professional role in architecture. "Professional role" has various meanings. Foremost is the traditional role of the architect as the generalist designer, versatile and broadly educated, who is often the leader of a design team which might include planners, engineers, landscape architects and other consultants. Then there are the myriad of other, sometimes more specialized, roles of architects in society - in research, government, development, management, planning, journalism, teaching, etc. While most of these occupations do not require a professional license, they do require an understanding of and exposure to a professional education.

The professional education arm emphasizes the development of skills and expertise required by the practicing architect. Chief among these skills is design, usually taught in studio. Design has been frequently and variously defined, often as the act of synthesizing and integrating many variables into a single solution - an act both rational and intuitive, methodical and inspirational. It is a specific type of problem-solving that relies heavily on spatial and visual modes of thinking and expression. Supporting and informing design studio are a wide range of required and elective courses - graphics, theory, history, structure, building science, person-environment relations, professional practice and others.

As design skill is the backbone of professional education, meaning and values are the life-blood of academic education. It deals in the qualitative realm of ideas and beliefs, as opposed to the quantitative realm of facts and figures. Academic education is the traditional goal of a University, whose ultimate obligation is to preserve, expand

and disseminate knowledge, and to educate citizens who are morally responsible members of society. An essential goal of the M Arch program is to inculcate in the students intellectual honesty and curiosity, and to keep alive in them the humanistic and artistic ideals of our profession and our culture, by teaching them to be clear and critical thinkers. Academic education, like professional education, happens for the student of Architecture most effectively and intensely in studio, where the teacher is not only an instructor but also a role model. In studio, students experience the expression of values by themselves, their fellow students and their teachers in a setting that can be both informal and intense.

Program Description

The Department offers a Master of Architecture degree program based on educating architects who are well-rounded in the liberal arts, possess full command of the practical arts of the profession of architecture, and who assume enlightened, responsible, and imaginative roles in society. The Department of Architecture and related departments offer a range of both survey and specialized courses that cover the many aspects of architecture: design, graphics, structural engineering, building science, history, theory, ecology, sociology, psychology, law and professional practice. The faculty is a large and diverse group of teachers, practitioners, scholars and researchers, who represent a wide spectrum of background, experience, and viewpoints. Permanent faculty members are supplemented by part-time professional practitioners from the region and from around the country, as well as by exchange scholars from foreign institutions.

The graduate program accommodates three groups of undergraduate degree holders: (a) persons holding the five-year Bachelor of Architecture professional degree, who can usually complete an M Arch program in three or four quarters (45 approved credits, including thesis); (b) persons holding a preprofessional four-year degree, such as a Bachelor of Arts in Architecture (or equivalent), who normally will require seven or eight quarters of study; (c) persons with an undergraduate degree in a field other than those mentioned above, who normally will require ten or eleven quarters, over a period of at least three years, to complete the requirements for the degree. This three-year program may vary somewhat in duration and specific course work required, depending on selection of concentration/study areas and prior academic and professional experience. Normally, it requires approximately 40 credits of preparatory work, 36 credits of design studio options, 45 credits of professional electives, and 9 credits of thesis.

Priorities stressed by the faculty reflect changing notions of architecture. The celebration of region - the local blend of climate, topography, vegetation, building materials and practices, culture, history, and mythology - is presently the vertical focus of many design studios within the department. In addition to this vertical studio focus, there is a horizontal theme for each of the 3 years of the M Arch program. Year 1 is "The Dwelling Place", Year 2 "The Public Realm" and Year 3 "The Rich Panoply." These horizontal themes not only help to clarify the student's experience, but also insure that students get a broad and coherent cross-section of design problems and instructors. Both the vertical and horizontal themes are designed to be broad enough to allow for wide latitude of interpretation by the faculty.

To respond to the increasing specialization in the profession, the Department offers two

certificate programs. One is in Preservation Design, the other in Urban Design.

FACULTY

Administration

Gordon Varey, RA, AIA, Dean
Douglas Kelbaugh, RA, AIA, Chairman
Katrina Deines, Associate Dean
Doug Zuberbuhler, RA, AIA, Graduate Program Coordinator
James Donnette, RA, AIA, Associate Dean and College BA Director
Betty Wagner, Librarian

Professors

David Bonsteel, M Arch
Thomas Bosworth, M Arch
Grant Hildebrand, M Arch
Douglas Kelbaugh, M Arch
Folke Nyberg, M Arch
Hermann Pundt, MA, PhD
Claus Seligmann, Dipl Arch
Robert Small, M Arch
Christian Staub, Cert
Philip Thiel, MS Nav Arch
Anne Vernez-Moudon, B Arch, PhD
Astra Zarina, M Arch

Associate Professors

Robert Albrecht, MSCE
Richard Alden, M Arch, PhD
J William Curtis, MA
James Donnette, M Arch
Dean Heerwagen, B Arch, MS
Warren Hill, MA
Ed Lebert, MS
Joel Loveland, B Arch, MAUP
Marietta Millet, M Arch
Arnold Rosner, MSCE
Dennis Ryan, MA, PhD
Robert Sasanoff

Lecturers

Brian Johnson, M Arch
Barry Onouye, MSCE
Andris Vanags, BFA
Doug Zuberbuhler, M Arch

Part-Time Faculty

Barbara Allan
Fred Brown, B Arch
Frank Ching, B Arch
Jennifer Dee, M Arch
Katrina Deines, M Arch
Philip Jacobson, M Arch
Norman Johnston, MCP, PhD
Keith Kolb, M Arch
Elaine Latourelle, M Arch
Wendell Lovett, M Arch
Eric Meng, M Arch
Galen Minah, M Arch
Rich Mohler, M Arch
Daniel Streissguth, M Arch
Roger Williams, M Arch
David Wright, B Arch

Adjunct Faculty

Meredith Clausen, PhD
Ashley Emery, MS, PhD
Leo Fritschen, MS, PhD
Steve Goldblatt, JD
Neil Hawkins, MS, PhD
Charles Kippenhan, MSME, PhD
Asuman Kiyak, MA, PhD
George Rolfe, M Arch
David Streatfield, MLA

University of Waterloo

School of Architecture
University of Waterloo
Waterloo, Ontario, N2L 3G1
Canada
(519) 885-1211 extension 2676

Architecture Admissions
Registrar's Office
University of Waterloo
Waterloo, Ontario, N2L 3G1
Canada
(519) 885-1211 extension 3092

Application Deadline(s): March 15 (Ontario Universities' Application Centre)
Tuition & Fees: Undgrd: First-Year: $830 per term
Upper-Year, Coop: $1093 per term
Endowment: Public

DEGREE PROGRAMS

Degree	Minimum Years for Degree	Accred.	Requirements for Admission	Full-Time Stdnts.	Part-Time Stdnts.	% of Applics. Accptd.	Stdnts. in 1st Year of Program	# of Degrees Conferred
BES	3-2/3		high school diploma, minimum of 75% average (normally), portfolio, interview and English precis writing examination	210	0	7%	60	45
B Arch	2-2/3	*OAA **CAA	completion of BES degree or equivalent	90	0	N/A	45	40

*Recognized by Ontario Association of Architects and Certification Board
**Commonwealth Association of Architectus

SCHOOL DEMOGRAPHICS (all degree programs)

Full-Time Faculty	Part-Time Faculty	Full-Time Students	Part-Time Students	Foreign Students	Out-of-State U.S. Stdnts.	Women Students	Minority Students
19	13	290	0	N/A	N/A	N/A	N/A

LIBRARY (Tel. No. 519-885-1211 X2906)

Type	No. of Volumes	No. of Slides
Map and Design	10,000	+ main univ holdings

STUDENT OPPORTUNITIES AND RESOURCES

With more than 22,000 students, the University of Waterloo is Canada's eighth-largest university. Six innovative faculties, the Integrated Studies Program, and numerous research units have evolved since the university was founded in 1957 and are housed on a 1,000-acre suburban campus in the Kitchener/Waterloo/ Cambridge area. In 1988 the University will open its new, $50-million Davis Computing Research Centre. There are also four church colleges associated with the university: St. Jerome's College (Roman Catholic), Conrad Grebel College (Mennonite), Renison College (Anglican) and St. Paul's United College (United).

The city of Toronto, one of North America's most vital metropolitan areas, with a population of 3 million, is about 100 km from the university and is easily accessible by automobile, bus, and train.

The School of Architecture is one of four units in the Faculty of Environmental Studies (the other three are the School of Urban and Regional Planning, the Department of Geography, and the Department of Environment and Resource Studies) and shares well-equipped facilities with these units including extensive studio space, workshops, exhibition space, and specialized laboratories for work in graphics, cartography, synectics, methods and computer-aided design.

Other facilities and services available to students in the Faculty of Environmental Studies include: the University Map and Design Library, the Ecology Laboratory, darkrooms, the Methods and Design unit, and the Environmental Studies Student Society.

Each year, Waterloo receives more than 800 applications for its 60 first-year positions. At the upper levels, individuals who can meet all of the School's requirements are occasionally admitted as transfer students.

SPECIAL ACTIVITIES AND PROGRAMS

The University of Waterloo was the first university in Canada to introduce the cooperative system of study and continues to have the second-largest coop enrollment in the world. Studying under the coop system, students in the School of Architecture alternate academic terms on campus with work terms off-campus. Beginning in the second year, the program gives students the opportunity to engage in various kinds of work experience within architecture, to travel, to balance an academic view with a real-life view, and to finance part of their education.

Since 1979, the school has operated a fall term, fourth-year Study Abroad Program in Rome. This program, accommodating about 45 students, has gained international recognition for its scholarly work in design, urbanism, history, and theory.

Also, the School offers architectural study tours to Ottawa (first-year), New York (second-year), and Chicago (third-year). And

Waterloo has frequent visiting lecturers and critics from throughout the world.

During 1986-88, the Waterloo School of Architecture is participating in an exchange program with the Department of Architecture at the Nanjing Institute of Technology, The People's Republic of China.

The Architecture Student Society offers ongoing opportunities for participation in the life of the School.

FACILITIES

The School has excellent specialized facilities for undergraduate studies in architecture. These include a newly-established studio/laboratory for courses and research using computers, an innovative graphics centre, faculty and student photographic labs, a large workshop for model building and experimental work with furniture and sculpture, and a Technology Resource Centre.

SCHOLARSHIPS/AID

The School has an active scholarship and awards program. In 1987, more than $10,000 was awarded to assist students with their education. The University's Senate Scholarship Fund is a major source, and this is supplemented with contributions from various corporations, professional organizations, and individuals. An annual scholarship and awards banquet is held each year to honour the recipients. Participants in the scholarship and awards program include the Ontario Association of Architects, Royal Architectural Institute of Canada, Lieutenant Governor of Ontario, Toronto Chapter of Architects, and the Smale Fellowship.

Student aid is available through the Ontario Student Assistance Program and other forms of government aid.

UNDERGRADUATE PROGRAM
Philosophy Statement

Waterloo believes that design and visual concerns must remain at the heart of architectural production. And integral to this are rigorous, critical studies in Cultural History, Technology and the various "landscapes" which we inhabit in the late-twentieth century.

The School of Architecture is committed to producing an architecture of accommodation and confrontation. Architecture should accommodate; it should support day-to-day human activities. Architecture should confront; it should challenge existing patterns. It is this dialogue between the "fitting into" of accommodation and the "cutting through" of confrontation that produces meaning. The strategies used for this production also apply to human and political relationships.

It is these human and political relationships that form the bases of architectural production.

Program Description

The School of Architecture offers two undergraduate programs: a preprofessional, three-year Bachelor of Environmental Studies program and a two-year professional program of study for the Bachelor of Architecture degree. Both programs are on the cooperative system, which consists of alternating periods of academic study and practical work experience.

The preprofessional architecture program comprises six academic terms of study and three four-month cooperative work terms leading to the degree of Bachelor of Environmental Studies (BES). This degree indicates appropriate preparation for four subsequent academic terms of study and two cooperative work terms, one of four months and one of eight months, leading to the degree of Bachelor of Architecture (B Arch).

The purposes of the BES program are to encourage future architects to understand the beliefs and needs of individuals and of society: to be willing to take an active role in the creation and improvement of the environment; to clarify the interaction of seemingly unrelated disciplines; to know the principles and values that surround the creation of any artifact; to comprehend the many forms of creative expression; and to understand the present as part of a historical process. The program aims to increase knowledge and expertise in: (1) theories, methods, and practice of architectural design; (2) technology including computer, physical and material sciences; (3) cultural history; and (4) environmental studies, including both natural and human ecology.

The purpose of the Bachelor of Architecture program is to permit a student who has successfully completed the environmental studies (preprofessional architecture) degree or the equivalent to pursue, in parallel with a prescribed design studio program, courses of study selected by the student and appropriate to his or her capabilities and interests. The final two terms of the program are normally devoted to the undertaking of a thesis project.

The program carefully prepares students for Canadian certification and the professional registration process administered by the Ontario Association of Architects.

GRADUATE PROGRAM
Philosophy Statement

Graduate programs are available in the School of Urban and Regional Planning.

FACULTY
Administration

James H Bater, Dean, Faculty of Environmental Studies
Eric R Haldenby, Director, School of Architecture
Thomas Seebohm, OAA, PE, Associate Director, School of Architecture
Lorenzo Pignatti, Associate Director (Rome), School of Architecture
Reinhold Schuster, P Eng, PhD, Undergraduate Officer, School of Architecture
Jo Beglo, Architecture Librarian

Professors

Anupam Banerji, M Arch
Laurence A Cummings, PhD
Fraser Watts, MRAIC, AA Dipl, MLA

Associate Professors

Michael W Elmitt, Natl Dipl Des
Eric Haldenby, B Arch
Brian Hunt, RIBA, MRAIC, AA Dipl
Donald McIntyre, MRAIC, B Arch
Donald McKay, B Arch
Larry Richards, OAA, MRAIC, M Arch
Reinhold Schuster, P Eng, PhD
Fred S Thompson, MRAIC, M Arch
Robert Wiljer, MA

Assistant Professors

Teresa M Boake, B Arch, M Arch
Om Dutt, P Eng, PhD
Lorenzo Pignatti, B Arch, M Arch
Thomas Seebohm, OAA, P Eng, M Arch, PhD
Ryszard Sliwka, OAA, MAUD
Robert J vanPelt, D Lit

Part-Time Faculty

Richard Andrighetti, B Arch
Brian Boigon, B Arch
James Brown, B Arch
Peter Ferguson, B Arch
Pat Hanson, M Arch
Ronald Keenberg, RCA, BFAED
Wilfrid Lamb, OAA, MRAIC, M Arch
Detlef Mertins, B Arch
Valerio Rynnimeri, B Arch
Jonathan Soules, B Arch
Paul Syme, B Arch
Frederic Urban, BFA, MA

Wentworth Institute of Technology

College of Design and Construction
Wentworth Institute of Technology
550 Huntington Avenue
Boston, Massachusetts 02115
(617) 442-9010

Admissions Office
(617) 442-9010

Application Deadline(s): July 1, for Fall;
November 1, Spring;
March 1, Summer
Tuition & Fees: Undgrd: $3019/sem
Endowment: Private

DEGREE PROGRAMS

Degree	Minimum Years for Degree	Accred.	Requirements for Admission	Full-Time Stdnts.	Part-Time Stdnts.	% of Applics. Accptd.	Stdnts. in 1st Year of Program	# of Degrees Conferred
Assoc in Eng* Arch Eng Tech	2	ABET	High School Diploma, Alg/Geometry, Laboratory Science, 4 yrs. English	320	60	80%	250	80
Bach of Sci** Arch Eng Tech	2 yrs. beyond Assoc	ABET	Min. 64 prerequisite semester credits plus portfolio	120	35	80%	60	40
B Arch	3 yrs. beyond Assoc	seeking NAAB candidacy	min. 64 prerequisite semester credits plus portfolio	110	0	60%	60	First class 1988
Assoc in Applied Sci Int Des	2 yrs.	seeking FIDER candidacy	High School Diploma, Alg/Geometry, Laboratory Science, 4 yrs. English	60	0	80%	30	10
Bach of Sci* Int Des	2 yrs. beyond Assoc	seeking FIDER candidacy	Min. 64 prerequisite semester credits plus portfolio	10	0	60%	10	First class 1989

*Day and Evening Offerings
**Day and Weekend Offerings

SCHOOL DEMOGRAPHICS (all degree programs)

Full-Time Faculty	Part-Time Faculty	Full-Time Students	Part-Time Students	Foreign Students	Out-of-State U.S. Stdnts.	Women Students	Minority Students
21	17	620	95	6%	16%	10%	6%

LIBRARY (Tel. No. 617-442-9010 X344)

Type	No. of Volumes	No. of Slides
Central Library Sys*	64,000	50,000

*Also part of a library consortium of Boston Area.

STUDENT OPPORTUNITIES AND RESOURCES

Wentworth Institute of Technology is an accredited, independent, coeducational school of higher learning comprised of 4 colleges: Arts and Sciences, Design and Construction, Engineering Technology, and Continuing Education. There are approximately 5,000 students in the day, evening and weekend programs.

Wentworth's academic programs are designed on a "2 + 2" structure. Students first matriculate in a two-year Associate degree program and after successful completion of the degree, or successful completion of prerequisite courses, may petition for transfer to a baccalaureate program. All day baccalaureate programs are co-operative education programs requiring at least two semesters of related work experience.

The College of Design and Construction is dedicated to providing educational opportunities to those students interested in careers in the design-build industry. The "hands-on application" approach provides students with an appropriate balance of theory and application. The Department of Architecture provides programs for students interested in Architectural Engineering Technology, Interior Design, Facilities Management and the first professional degree in Architecture. Student may transfer into one of the Department's degree programs for which they have met the necessary admission and prerequisite course requirements. Each Architecture student is assigned a specific advisor who is trained to assist students in meeting their academic objectives.

The diversity of specialties represented within the Department and in the College exposes students to the interdisciplinary approach needed in the architectural profession today. Architecture students can work with students from the College's other disciplines of Building Construction, Civil Engineering and Construction Management through associate clubs and joint course work. The choice of architectural curriculum allows students flexibility and the ability to internally transfer with minimum penalty in making educational selections related to their career aspirations.

As part of the Boston community, our architecture students have many opportunities to view the variety of design and construction projects in the metropolitan area, and to meet the professionals responsible for making this city an architectural leader.

SPECIAL ACTIVITIES AND PROGRAMS

Articulation agreements with a number of community and 2-year private colleges in New England.

Established a program with faculty and professional advisor for assisting students to understand and participate in the new Intern Development Program (IDP) necessary for registration.

Visiting lecturers and critics: leading practitioners are routinely invited to provide lectures and design critiques for the programs.

Career placement office works with students to locate positions for their cooperative semesters and also assists them in locating permanent positions in their selected fields.

College Lecture Series: presentations by local specialists in the areas of construction, development, structural and mechanical engineering, energy conservation, planning, and financing.

College-sponsored student clubs open to all Architecture students including: American Institute of Architects, Associated General Contractors, Associated Builders and Contractors, Solar Club, and Society of Women Engineers.

NCAA Division III and intramural sports.

Department-sponsored design competitions.

Institute clubs (over 50) and student government opportunities.

FACILITIES

Institute facilities available to all students include: dormitories, gymnasium, central library, audio-visual center, dining facilities for commuting students, student center, computer center, learning center.

The College of Design and Construction provides its students with laboratories in light construction, heavy construction, sculpture, concrete testing, Computer-aided design and graphics, soils, structures, and a 141-acre field laboratory for environmental projects, surveying and full-scale construction.

The Department of Architecture provides its Bachelor of Architecture and Bachelor of Science Interior Design students with individual work stations for their design and related projects.

Also available are a variety of classrooms and lecture halls equipped for multi-media and audio-visual equipment, including computer displays.

SCHOLARSHIPS/AID

President's scholarships are available to accepted students of high academic achievement and effective participation in extra-curricular activities. Additional types of financial assistance include Federally Insured Student Loan program, Pell Grants, National Direct Student Loan Awards, College Work Study Program, and Wentworth Scholarships, including: Randall Clark Bean Memorial Scholarship, H. Russell Beatty Memorial Scholarship, The Ralph Christian Bohm Scholarship Fund, Robert Bosch Memorial Scholarship, Bryant Chucking Grinder Company Scholarship, Commonwealth of Massachusetts Matching Scholarship Grants Program, Elizabeth Ann Crowley Scholarship Fund, Albert Dacko Memorial Scholarship Fund, Charles C. Ely Scholarships, Philip A. Eyrick Memorial Scholarship, Raymond P. Foster Memorial Scholarship, William E. Foster Memorial Scholarships, Nelson S. Greely Loan Fund, Charles Hayden Memorial Scholarships (First-Year Students), International Business Machines Corporation Scholarships, Grant Johnson Scholarship, John R. Leighton Scholarship, Salvatore Pesaturo Scholarship, John F. Rich Scholarship, Chester H. Sanford Fund, Joseph C. Simone Memorial Scholarship, Tuition Scholarship Fund, John J. Volpe Scholarship Fund, Wentworth Scholarship Endowment, Wentworth Institute Scholarships (First and Second-Year Students), Miller Reprographics, and Construction Specifications Institute.

All applications and forms pertaining to financial aid administered by Wentworth Institute of Technology must be submitted to the Financial Aid Office prior to May 1st of each year. No financial aid of any sort will be available through Wentworth unless the May 1st deadline is met.

UNDERGRADUATE PROGRAM
Philosophy Statement

Architecture is part of an enormous building industry. It includes construction of not only shelters from rain, sun and wind, but also bridges, subways, moving structures, as well as interior designs and space planning. Architecture is a professional field where input from building sciences, engineering system technologies and design arts are creatively combined in the generation of space and/or building design. Architecture inspires thinking and belief in problem-solving and provides answers to many societal, urban and habitational questions. It utilizes the findings of scientific research and services of relevant engineering fields such as environmental, structural, mechanical, electrical and most recently, the human engineering field.

The instructional methods used at Wentworth Institute of Technology combine hands-on

application with technology. These programs, whether they lead to degrees in architectural engineering technology, interior design or architecture, will foster the development of uniqueness and leadership in the application of building design sciences and system technologies. They will also guide in generating professional confidence and character commensurate with state-of-the-art construction in industry. The unique architectural hands-on approach is employed for effective personal learning and development in areas of material construction technologies, engineered building systems and design production services.

The Department of Architecture, through its offered programs, provides professional training for its students in order to become familiar with programming, schematic design, design development, production of contract documents (working drawings and specifications) and construction and contract administration.

Graduates of these programs may perform a variety of tasks that will include: design; drafting and visual communication; preparation of construction documents and cost estimates; writing of specifications and technical reports; and administration of project construction. Graduates may work directly with architectural and engineering offices, building contractors, or large corporations having their own physical facilities and architectural/engineering teams. Others may pursue the marketing aspects of the profession by joining manufacturers and their product marketing departments.

Program Description

In recent years, environmental planners and designers have broadened their commitment to improving the quality of life through technological advancements. In order to meet current and future challenges, associate and baccalaureate degree programs have been designed with a wide range of pertinent courses in mathematics, computers, sciences, design, and technology. Studio courses stress the development of analytic and logical problem-solving skills, creativity and sensitivity to the aesthetic aspects of design. Technical competency is gained through application courses in materials, construction methods and engineering systems. These also allow the student to transform design solutions into three-dimensional reality. Graphics and business-related courses provide the oral, written and visual communication skills necessary for professional practice.

The Department offers: two-year associate degree programs in Architectural Engineering Technology (Day and Evening) and Interior Design (pre-professional); two-year Bachelor of Science degree programs in Architectural Engineering Technology (day co-op and weekend) and Interior Design (day co-op and evening); and a three-year Bachelor of Architecture (day co-op).

All freshmen enter one of the Department's associate degree programs to prepare for either immediate employment opportunities or for advanced study in the College or Department. Students entering the bachelor degree program must have a minimum of 64 credits of collegiate work in architecture or interior design and prepare a portfolio for review by the faculty.

The professional degree programs in Architecture and Interior Design have been developed to meet the educational and professional needs of the industry for leadership in technology and design. The bachelor degree program in Architectural Engineering Technology has been developed to meet the ever-growing need for architectural technologists in design, engineering, construction and the allied fields. The instruction philosophy of "hands-on" is enhanced by student participation in the day co-op structure of the bachelor degree programs.

FACULTY
Administration

George T Balich, AIA, Dean, College of Design & Construction
Terry M Moor, RA, Department Head, Architecture
Ann Montgomery Smith, Director of Alumni Library

Professors

George T Balich, RA, AIA, B Arch
E Gilman Barker, PE, MS Civ Eng
Stephen Diamond, RA, AIA, M Arch
Walter B Jones, RA, AIA, BS Arch

Associate Professors

Kaffee Kang, RA, M Arch, AIA
Thomas M Lesko, RA, NCARB, B Arch
Thomas Melvin, ME, MS in ME
Terry M Moor, RA, NCARB, B Arch
Robert H Murphy, PE, APA, B Arch

Assistant Professors

Sarah S Dixon, RA, M Arch
John Ellis, M Arch
Valentine Gunasekara, RIBA, RA
Jacalyn Hirsty, LPA, RA, M Arch
Herbert Kronish, RA, AIA, B Arch
Frederick Kuhn, RA, NCARB, M Arch
Richard F Schneider, M Arch
Bernard Webb, RE, B Arch

Part-Time Faculty

Allen J Boemer, RA, NCARB, B Arch
Reaz Haque, M Arch
Deleep Hazra, PE, MSCE
Rodman Henry, AM, PhD
Anthony Kurneta, PhD
David L Liberatore, M Arch
William J Mello, MCARB, RA, B Arch
Donald Oster, RA, NCARB, B Arch
Clarence Passons, RA, AIA, RIBA, RAIA, B Arch, M Arch
R Wendell Phillips, Jr, RA, AIA, B Arch, M Arch
Leonard Saulnier, RA, BAC
John Wood, BSCET

Adjunct Faculty

Richard Heydecker, RA, NCARB, B Arch

University of Wisconsin-Milwaukee

**School of Architecture
& Urban Planning**
University of Wisconsin-Milwaukee
P.O. Box 413
Milwaukee, Wisconsin 53201
(414) 229-4014

Admissions Office
(414) 229-4015

Application Deadline(s): March 1 for Fall
(BSAS, M Arch)
October 1 for Spring
(BSAS, M Arch)
January 1 for Fall
(PhD, Arch)
July 1 for Fall,
November 15 for
Spring (MUP)
Tuition & Fees: Undgrd: WI res: $892/sem;
Non-res: $2617/sem
Grad: WI res: $1265/sem;
Non-res: $3650/sem
Endowment: Public

DEGREE PROGRAMS

Degree	Minimum Years for Degree	Accred.	Requirements for Admission	Full-Time Stdnts.	Part-Time Stdnts.	% of Applics. Accptd.	Stdnts. in 1st Year of Program	# of Degrees Conferred
BSAS	4		Univ. requirements	477	93	68%	113	79
M Arch	2	NAAB	BSAS, GRE, 3.0-GPA, portfolio	67	22	80%	47	31
M Arch	3	NAAB	Bacc degree, GRE, 3.0 GPA, portfolio	29	10	75%	15	16
MUP	2	AICP	Bacc degree, GRE, grad sch adm	20	4	65%	8	7
M Arch/MUP	3	NAAB, AICP	See M Arch above	15	5	80%	5	2
PhD	3		Bacc degree, 3.0 GPA, GRE, resume, research statement, recommendations, examples of work	10	5	17%	3	—

SCHOOL DEMOGRAPHICS (all degree programs)

Full-Time Faculty	Part-Time Faculty	Full-Time Students	Part-Time Students	Foreign Students	Out-of-State U.S. Stdnts.	Women Students	Minority Students
31*	12	618	139	16%	25%	22%	6%

*includes Planning faculty

LIBRARY (Tel. No. 414-229-5239)

Type	No. of Volumes	No. of Slides
Browsing	350	17,000
Reference + main library holdings		

STUDENT OPPORTUNITIES AND RESOURCES

The School of Architecture and Urban Planning offers the only professional program in architecture in Wisconsin that is accredited by the NAAB.

The Milwaukee and Madison campuses compose the doctoral cluster of the University of Wisconsin System. UWM has been designated by the UW System as its campus with an urban mission, and the School of Architecture and Urban Planning as a Center of Excellence.

Milwaukee's city landscape, strong in historical as well as modern architecture, has proved itself to be an excellent learning laboratory for students of architecture and urban planning. Only blocks from Lake Michigan, the campus is surrounded by a residential area with convenient access to downtown. Serving a metropolitan area of rich ethnic diversity and enrolling local, out-of-state and international students from over 35 countries, the School enjoys a heterogeneous student population. Most architecture students are enrolled full-time, and many live in the dormitories or near campus. Transfer students are considered for admission.

SPECIAL ACTIVITIES AND PROGRAMS

Academic credit opportunities for independent study, directed research, and internships
Visiting Critics' studios
Foreign Studies program
Lecture series
Student chapter of AIA
Student employment opportunities on campus through work-study and off campus through local firms and public agencies
Annual Awards Banquet and Ceremony
Small Towns Design-Assistance Project
Faculty Exchange Programs
Publication Series
Invited School in Annual Chicago AIA Student Design Competition
Student Annual Research Awards
Special events, including International Days, Sandcastle competitions, graphics day, etc.
Visiting Scholars

FACILITIES

Graphics laboratory with developing, printing, enlarging, and photographic studio
Computer laboratory with computer graphics, programming and word processing capabilities

Information Center with slide collection, reference materials, and audiovisual equipment
Workshop including facilities for wood, metal, and plastics
Center for Architecture and Urban Planning Research
Student Counseling Office

SCHOLARSHIPS/AID

Various forms of financial assistance are available through both the university and the Department of Architecture. Although most forms of undergraduate financial assistance are based on demonstrated need and administered by the UWM Financial Aids Office, several awards based on academic merit are available to advanced undergraduates and graduate students. These include UWM Alumni Scholarships, University Fellowships, the Advanced Opportunity Program, AIA awards, and Wisconsin Architects Foundation Scholarships. The department also awards teaching and project assistantships to qualified graduate students. Students with work-study eligibility have opportunities to work in the school's various facilities and offices.

UNDERGRADUATE PROGRAM
Philosophy Statement

The city is the ultimate reflection of civilization. The educational philosophy of the school is shaped by the dynamic nature of the city and the need for intelligent and sensitive professionals.

By emphasizing the full scope of what is involved in building and decision-making, the school seeks to develop architects who are better able to deal with the complex and changing needs of society than those whose training includes only short-term technical or vocational skills.

Program Description

The four-year undergraduate program leads to a nonprofessional degree, the Bachelor of Science in Architectural Studies. This degree prepares students for work toward an accredited professional degree in the graduate program, for graduate work in related fields, or for a career in fields associated with the architectural profession.

Admission to the architectural studies major is not considered until the junior year after a student has completed 58 credits of undergraduate liberal arts study including fundamental courses in architectural design and theory and has satisfied University-wide General Education Requirements. Freshmen or sophomores at UWM initially enroll in the department as pre-architecture majors.

The undergraduate degree program includes a core program of three 6-credit studio courses that students take in their junior and senior years. These studios deal with various scales of the physical environment and resolve problems of programming, design, and implementation. The core program also includes four lecture courses treating basic issues related to architectural composition and theory, construction technology, environmental controls, and human behavior.

Each of the core courses is taught by a team of faculty members that represents a broad cross section of expertise in architectural design and construction, planning, landscape architecture, engineering, economics, and environment-behavior studies. In addition, students take a minimum of 18 elective credits selected from other studio, lecture and seminar courses available both inside and outside the department.

GRADUATE PROGRAM
Philosophy Statement

Architecture is the integration of social, technological, and artistic intention in a building in context. In the largest sense, it is an activity intended to enhance the quality of life. It makes places significant contributions to society. To serve the educational objectives of individuals seeking to prepare for the varied roles afforded in the architectural profession as well as the related fields of urban planning and architectural research, consulting, and teaching, the School offers several graduate degree programs.

Program Description

The M Arch (Master of Architecture) degree program is structured to allow students to pursue an educational program that best meets their individual career objectives while establishing a high level of professional competence. Organized around a distribution requirement in the four broad areas of theory, technologies, design, and professional practice, the program integrates these subject areas in the design studios. The School's designation as a Center of Excellence has provided funding for visiting distinguished professionals to teach in design studios. Particular program strengths include building design, adaptive re-use of buildings, environment-behavior studies, and urban design and development.

Students holding a bachelor's degree in architectural studies or an equivalent degree from another accredited school or department of architecture may enroll in the two-year (48-credit) program requiring a minimum of four semesters of full-time work.

Students with undergraduate degrees in disciplines other than architecture may enroll in the three-year (72-credit) program requiring a minimum of six semesters of full-time work.

The MUP (Master of Urban Planning) degree program offers a skills-oriented curriculum preparing students to perform a variety of planning-related jobs in either the public or private sector. Beyond the study of planning theory and methods, this 48-credit program explores substantive areas such as economics, finance, housing, land use, the environment, energy, and transportation.

The School also offers a three-year, 72-credit Joint Master of Architecture/Master of Urban Planning Program. This coordinated program allows students to integrate physical design and planning principles as they apply to areas such as urban design, energy conservation, housing, and environment and behavior.

The PhD Program offers the opportunity for advanced study and research in Architecture. The focus of the Doctoral Program is environment-behavior studies, a multidisciplinary field which utilizes theories and methods from the behavioral and design sciences to explore, understand and enhance the mutual relations between people and the socio-physical environment. Application of environment-behavior research is pursued at various scales including public policy, urban planning and design, and architectural programming, design and evaluation. The PhD Program is appropriate for persons seeking advanced training for research, consulting, professional, or academic careers in environmental planning or design or allied disciplines.

FACULTY
Administration

Carl V Patton, APA, AICP, Dean
Lawrence P Witzling, RA, AIA, APA, Associate Dean
Robert C Greenstreet, RA, RIBA, AFAS, FRSA, ACIArb, Chair
Gary T Moore, Research Director
Mark C Roth, Information Center Director

Professors

Frederick A Jules, RA, AIA, B Arch, M Arch
Amos Rapoport, FRAIA, ARIBA, AIA, B Arch, M Arch, Dipl-Town & Regional Plng

Associate Professors

Uriel Cohen, M Arch, PhD Arch/EBR
Kevin Forseth, MA Arch
David Glasser, RA, AIA, M Arch
Robert C Greenstreet, RA, RIBA, AFAS, FRSA, ACIArb, Dipl Arch, PhD Arch
Miriam Gusevich, B Arch, M Arch
Thomas Hubka, M Arch
Kent M Keegan, RA, AIA, RPE, B Arch, M Sc Arch Eng
Gary T Moore, B Arch, PhD
Jeffrey E Ollswang, RA, AIA, B Arch, M Arch, MS Bldg Sciences
Harvey Z Rabinowitz, RA, B Arch, M Arch
K David Reed, RA, RIBA, Dipl Arch, M City Planning
Douglas C Ryhn, MS Bldg Research
Anthony J Schnarsky, RA, MS Arch
D Michael Utzinger, RA, B Arch, MSc Eng
Harry Van Oudenallen, RA, AIA, M Arch
Gerald D Weisman, B Arch, M Arch, PhD
Lawrence P Witzling, RA, AIA, B Arch, PhD City & Reg Plan

Assistant Professors

Sherry B. Ahrentzen, PhD Social Ecology
Peter Cohan, BA, MFA, M Arch
Don Hanlon, M Arch, MBA
Nancy Hubbard, PhD
Linda Krause, BA, MA, MPhil, PhD
James W Shields, RA, AIA, M Arch
Gil S Snyder, RA, AIA, M Arch
Josef Stagg, B Arch, MED, PhD
Brian Wishne, BA, M Arch

Part-Time Faculty

John Cain, BS Arch, M Arch
M Caren Connolly, MLA
James G Dicker, M Arch
Kevin Kennan, BS, JD, MS Arch, MSUP
Janis LaDouceur, M Arch
James Piwoni, M Arch
Andrew Pressman, M Arch
Hanno Weber, RA, MFA Arch
Dan Wheeler, BFA, B Arch

Adjunct Faculty

Paul E Sprague

Woodbury University

Architecture Program
Woodbury University
7500 Glenoaks Blvd.
Burbank, CA 91510
(818) 767-0888 ext. 330

Application Deadline(s): None
Tuition & Fees: Undgrd: $5970/year
Grad: $5970/year
Endowment: Private

DEGREE PROGRAMS

Degree	Minimum Years for Degree	Accred.	Requirements for Admission	Full-Time Stdnts.	Part-Time Stdnts.	% of Applics. Accptd.	Stdnts. in 1st Year of Program	# of Degrees Conferred
B Arch	5	WASC	High School Graduate	74	0	90%	20	5

SCHOOL DEMOGRAPHICS (all degree programs)

Full-Time Faculty	Part-Time Faculty	Full-Time Students	Part-Time Students	Foreign Students	Out-of-State U.S. Stdnts.	Women Students	Minority Students
2	10	120	10	25%	10%	50%	30%

LIBRARY (Tel. No. 213-482-8491)

Type	No. of Volumes	No. of Slides
Arch & Gen Ed	55,000	5,000

STUDENT OPPORTUNITIES AND RESOURCES

Given its location, just twenty minutes from downtown Los Angeles, Woodbury provides its students with many opportunities to examine some of the most important and exciting architecture of the southwest. In addition, the university is surrounded by many of the largest and most active architectural firms in the country. Finally, our close proximity to some of the major museums such as the Museum of Contemporary Art, the Norton Simon Museum and the Los Angeles County Museum of Art provides the student with ample cultural and architectural experiences.

The Fall of 1987 brings new opportunities to Woodbury and its students as the University moves to a new campus in Los Angeles, near Burbank. The new 22-acre campus, located at the foot of the Verdugo hills, offers students such amenities as a swimming pool, gymnasium, auditorium, athletic field, dormitories and food services, which will enhance the academic environment.

Woodbury University prides itself on being a small, high-quality university which places a great deal of emphasis on student-faculty interaction. Each student is dealt with individually in a caring manner. Architecture design studios and lectures are kept small and intimate to maximize each student's opportunity to extract the most out of each instructor and learning situation.

The architecture program offers a great deal of hands-on computer experience for all of its students. A Vax/11750 super mini computer, very sophisticated architectural software, and a number of terminals are available in the CADD laboratory. Students are encouraged to experiment with this equipment over and above the required courses taken as part of the architecture curriculum.

SPECIAL ACTIVITIES AND PROGRAMS

• American Institute of Architecture Students
The AIAS is an organization of student architects. It fosters a relationship between colleges and universities that offer degrees in architecture. The purpose of the student chapter is to give students exposure to their profession and a voice in the affairs and direction of the American Institute of Architects (AIA). The Woodbury chapter plans seminars and workshops and invites speakers to campus on topics related to the architectural profession.

• The Placement Center offers job placement services to students and alumni. Students are assisted in seeking major-related job placement for practical training while in school. Current job listings are maintained for part-time employment and career opportunities. On-campus and job-site interviews are conducted.

Career counseling is available. Workshops are conducted in the areas of self-assessment, job search techniques, resume writing and interviewing. A wide range of career information is available.

• The Student Activities Office plans and conducts a variety of educational, cultural, social and recreational programs for the University community. This office also advises and assists all student clubs and organizations, plans and coordinates new student orientation for American students, offers housing assistance, coordinates student insurance plans, produces the "Hotline" - a bi-weekly newsletter, and maintains a University activities calendar.

• The International Student Office assists all visa students in their transition into the American culture and Woodbury University. It provides information, forms, and assistance for questions dealing with passports, student visas, and Immigration and Naturalization Service regulations.

FACILITIES

Studio space. The third- and fourth-year Architecture students have assigned work stations in a dedicated studio space. Each student is provided with a studio table and a drafting lamp. Locked storage is available.

As of September 1986, dedicated space will be provided for the third-, fourth-, and fifth-year students.

SCHOLARSHIPS/AID

Assisting students who lack adequate financial resources to attend Woodbury is a primary concern of the University. Various sources of financial aid are available to help meet educational costs: loans, part-time employment, grants, and scholarships. Students generally are awarded a financial aid package consisting of a combination of available funds.

The University packages financial assistance based on the student's financial need. Financial need is considered to be the difference between the cost of attendance at Woodbury and the expected contribution from a student and his/her family. All financial aid is viewed as supplementary to the student's contribution and that of his/her parents and/or spouse.

To determine financial need, the University uses the nationally accepted standards established by the U.S. Department of Education to calculate a fair family contribution. The Student Aid Application for California (SAAC) and Financial Aid Form (FAF) provide the information used to determine the family contribution.

UNDERGRADUATE PROGRAM
Philosophy Statement

Architecture is presented as an applied social science, the fundamental justification of which is the satisfaction of human and social needs. The program derives its position from a humanistic point of view, which promotes a belief in the combined strength of science and human reasoning as the most fruitful approach to problem solving. In the case of architecture, the social, behavioral, and engineering sciences are seen as the providers of information which the architectural student is expected to apply to human-environment problems in the most rational way possible. In this approach, fine art is peripheral to architecture and self-expression, while encouraged, is viewed as subordinate to the larger human issues with which architecture deals.

Program Description

Architecture students at Woodbury University are required to carry a minor degree in Business.

A total of seventeen units of computer-aided design, drafting and microcomputer applications are required.

The courses in the Architecture major consist of five parallel sequences, each of which focuses on an aspect of architecture.

The Design Sequence consists of 21 courses (88 units) which focus on giving the student the ability to analyze, synthesize, evaluate, and communicate architectural design decisions.

The Human Behavior and Environmental Context Sequence consists of four courses (10 units) and deals with the characteristics and behavior of individuals and groups in relation to the physical environment in which they function. This sequence also deals with the process of environmental change and modification relative to human needs and satisfaction.

The Technical Systems and Requirements Sequence consists of 13 courses (57 units) which include all sets of structural elements, operations, and procedures which lend themselves to precise analysis and design. Course content includes structural design in wood, concrete and steel. Students work with building equipment and other devices which are essential to human safety and comfort.

The Practice Sequence consists of nine courses (32 units) and includes the business minor. This sequence encompasses those activities essential to the conduct of the profession of Architecture in society. In particular, the Practice Sequence addresses the organization, management, and documentation of the design, construction and business processes of architecture. Specifically, these include: the design and building processes, laws, codes, and regulations.

Architecture Electives. Students are required to take 27 quarter units of architecture electives or 8% of the total units for graduation.

Business education, through the Business minor, prepares the student for the productive use of his or her creative skills (20 units or 8% of the curriculum).

General Education furnishes the student an opportunity to explore the human experience through the arts and sciences (64 units or 26% of the curriculum).

FACULTY
Administration

Donald J Conway, AIA, Director
Dr William Stanley, Librarian

Professors

Donald Conway, AIA, B Arch
Michael Selditch, B Arch, M Arch
Fay Sueltz, B Arch, M Arch

Part-Time Faculty

Gaila Barnett, AIA, B Arch
Stanley Bertheaud, AIA, B Arch, M Arch
Roderick Butler, M Arch
Geraldine Forbes, AIA, BA, M Arch
Arlene Hopkins, BA, MA, M Arch
Carol Limahelu, B Arch, M Arch
Robert Lowe, AIA
Koje Shoraka, PE, MS Str Eng
Michael Stangl, PE, BS Const Eng
Richard Wheeler, FAIA, B Arts, M Arch

Yale University

School of Architecture
Yale University
180 York Street
New Haven, Connecticut 06520
(203) 432-2288

Admissions Office
(203) 432-2296

Application Deadline(s): January 15
Tuition & Fees: Grad: $11,600/yr
Endowment: Private

DEGREE PROGRAMS

Degree	Minimum Years for Degree	Accred.	Requirements for Admission	Full-Time Stdnts.	Part-Time Stdnts.	% of Applics. Accptd.	Stdnts. in 1st Year of Program	# of Degrees Conferred
M Arch	3	NAAB	Required courses, GRE, Portfolio, Baccalaureate Degree	122	0	17%	40	42
M Arch	2		B Arch Degree, GRE, Portfolio	15	0	15%	7	8
MED	2		Arch or related degree, GRE, Research Proposal	7	0	38%	4	3

SCHOOL DEMOGRAPHICS (all degree programs)

Full-Time Faculty	Part-Time Faculty	Full-Time Students	Part-Time Students	Foreign Students	Out-of-State U.S. Stdnts.	Women Students	Minority Students
12	56	144	0	11%	78%	35%	6%

LIBRARY (Tel. No. 203-432-2640)

Type	No. of Volumes	No. of Slides
Art &	80,000	270,000 Slides
Arch	+75,000	163,000 Photos

STUDENT OPPORTUNITIES AND RESOURCES

The School of Architecture maintains a student enrollment of 140 - 145. Characteristically, the students represent a diversity of undergraduate majors. The architecture curriculum provides opportunity for students to choose electives from among the offerings of the school as well as from the offerings of all other departments at Yale.

SPECIAL ACTIVITIES AND PROGRAMS

Davenport, Saarinen and Bishop Visiting Professorships in Design
Winchester Traveling Fellowship
Gertraud A Wood Traveling Fellowship
Lecture and Exhibition Series
Retrospecta Annual Publication
PERSPECTA (student editors) Architectural Journal
Student participation on the school's committees
Alumni News letter and calendar
First-year building project

FACILITIES

Design Studio individual workstations
Photographic darkroom
Print room
Wood-working shop
Computer Laboratory with 2-D & 3-D graphic workstations
Drawing Archive
Structures Laboratory

SCHOLARSHIPS/AID

In 1986-1987 university scholarships for architecture students totaled $463,331 and university loans totaled $645,900. A comprehensive "Financial Aid Package" is prepared and designed to ensure that no student who is admitted will be denied the opportunity of attending Yale because of financial need.

UNDERGRADUATE PROGRAM
Philosophy Statement

The purpose of the undergraduate major in architecture at Yale is to include the study of architecture within the broader context of liberal arts education.

Program Description

The undergraduate program in architecture is open only to students enrolled in Yale College. A student in the junior year of the Yale architecture major may apply for admission to the intensive major. These students take courses in the first-year professional degree program during their senior year in Yale College.

GRADUATE PROGRAM
Philosophy Statement

The task of architecture is the creation of human environments. It is both an expression of human values and a context for human activity. Through the design process, architecture addresses the interrelated physical, behavioral, and cultural issues that underlie the organization of man's built form. It is architectural design, the comprehensive creative process through which an understanding of these fundamental issues is transformed into a coherent physical environment, that is the focus of the Yale School of Architecture.

The objectives of the School of Architecture reflect the view that architecture is simultaneously an art, an intellectual discipline, and a profession. The program, therefore, is based on the following intentions: (1) to stimulate artistic sensitivity and creative powers; (2) to strengthen intellectual growth and the capacity to respond creatively and responsibly to unique and

changing problems; and (3) to develop skills necessary to the competent practice of architecture.

Students in the Yale School of Architecture have opportunities to become well acquainted with a wide range of major contemporary design approaches. The school does not seek to impose any single design philosophy but rather encourages in each student the development of discernment and an individual approach to design.

Program Description

The School of Architecture offers graduate-level professional education and advanced research opportunities in architecture and allied design fields. An undergraduate major in architecture is offered only to Yale College Students.

In order to further the pursuit of a variety of interests within the study of architecture, the curriculum offers opportunities for work in interrelated fields. Courses in architecture theory, structures, environmental controls, and communication skills serve as a basis for developing a comprehensive approach to architectural design. Courses in architectural theory examine both historical and contemporary attitudes to the design of buildings and cities that may contribute to a design process responsive to its broadest social and cultural context. Structures and environmental controls courses explore, as an integral part of the architectural design process, its physical context: properties of natural forces and materials in their application to building technology. The field of communication media offers an opportunity to develop the tools of visual analysis and expression in architectural design.

The study of a wide variety of important related topics is encouraged by course offerings in the school and the university. Urban design and landscape design are both concerned with the design of the spatial context of an individual building as well as with the impact of this context on individual building design. Urban design studies the relationship of buildings to transportation, land utilization, government policies and economic and social institutions. Landscape design deals with the relationship of buildings to their natural environment: land and water forms, drainage systems, and landscaping. Courses in methodology and research investigate alternative design processes and the generation and management of design information. In the field of development, courses focus on problems of market research, government subsidy programs, financial strategies, and land planning. Courses in community involvement explore the interrelationship of community needs and expectations with governmental, legal, and economic policies as they shape the architectural program and design process.

The growing research capability within the school is fulfilled in the Master of Environmental Design Program, which provides an opportunity for graduate students to research and develop new approaches and solutions to problems involved in the design of our constructed environment. The stress in this area is on the concept of rigorous scholarship and research. The extensive resources of related disciplines within the university are available to MED students. The program aims not only at the development of new insights and information but also at helping to redefine the parameters of the architect's role in terms of modern urban complexities and changing social patterns.

Yale School of Architecture students in the M Arch program who are interested in continued advanced study in an area of specialization in architecture, environmental design, or planning/development are eligible to apply for advanced standing in the Master of Environmental Design (MED) Program. By taking courses that support an area of advanced study during the M Arch, a Yale M Arch graduate can qualify for up to one year's advanced standing toward the MED, which normally requires two years.

FACULTY
Administration

Thomas H Beeby, AIA, Dean
Martin D Gehner, Associate Dean
Nancy S Lambert, Librarian

Professors

Thomas H Beeby, B Arch, M Arch
Kent C Bloomer, BFA, MFA
Martin D Gehner, B Arch, M Arch
Walter D Harris, B Arch, M Arch, PhD
Herman D J Spiegel, BS in Arch, M Eng
King Lui Wu, B Arch, M Arch

Associate Professors

Everett M Barber, Jr, BS
Deborah Berke, B Arch, MUP (Urb Des)
John Jacobson, BA, M Arch
Alan Plattus, BA, M Arch
Alexander Purves, BA, M Arch
George J Ranalli, B Arch, M Arch

Part-Time Faculty

Edward B Allen, BA, M Arch
John Altieri, BS
Donald J Baerman, BA
Diana Balmori, PhD
Jeffrey Berg, BA, M Arch
Larry G Berglund, BME, MSME, PhD

Phillip Bernstein, BA, M Arch
Paul B Brouard, BA, M Arch
Robert S Charney, BA, M Arch
Roger Crowley, BA, B Arch, M Arch
Judy Dimaio, BA, BFA, M Arch
Richard Doerer, BFA, MFA
Turan Duda, BA, M Arch
Timothy H Feresten, BFA, MFA
Stephen Fritzinger, BA, M Arch
Joan A Gilbert, MA, PhD
Jeremy Gilbert-Rolfe, MFA
Paul J Goldberger, BA
Alexander Gorlin, B Arch, M Arch
Philip Grausman, BA, MFA
Steven Harris, BFA, M Arch
John C Herman, B Arch
Michael Horowitz, BA, M Arch
P Kevin Kennon, BA, M Arch
Kenneth Labs, M Arch
Andrea Leers, BA, M Arch
M J Long, BA, M Arch
Paul Lubowicki
Peter B MacKeith, BA, M Arch
Gavin A Macrae-Gibson, BA, MA, M Arch
J Robert Mann, BE
David McMahon, BA, M Arch
Peter Millard, BA, M Arch
Herbert S Newman, M Arch
Cesar Pelli, Dipl in Arch
Patrick L Pinnell, M Arch
Peter G Rolland, BS, MLA
Harold Roth, BA, M Arch
Philip Sherman, AS, BS
Donald R Watson, BA, B Arch, MED
Timothy Wood, B Arch, MFA

Adjunct Faculty

Robert E Apfel, BA, MA, PhD
Esther Da Costa-Meyer, PhD
Francesco Dal Co, Dipl in Arch
Robert Frew, B Arch, MA Sci, PhD
Karsten Harries, BA, PhD
Diane Lewis, B Arch
Jules Prown, PhD
Vincent J Scully, Jr, MA, PhD, LLD

Chaired Visiting Professors

Andreas Brandt, B Arch
Ardvino Cantafora, B Arch, MFA
Michael Dennis, Dipl
Frank O Gehry
Demetri Porphyrios, Dipl

Affiliate Members

Architecture Intermundium

Via Benedetto Marcello 46
Milano 20124   Italy

(392) 278 128

Daniel Libeskind,
Founder and Director

APPROXIMATE NUMBER OF FT STUDENTS, 1986-87 10

NUMBER OF FTE FACULTY 1

ADMISSION REQUIREMENTS An architecture degree or its equivalent or a year-out in an undergraduate or graduate architectural program. Practitioners, professors and researchers in design and theory.

1986-1987 TUITION AND FEES $10,500 (U.S.)

DEGREE OR CERTIFICATE Certificate is issued.

PROGRAM SUMMARY

Architecture Intermundium has been founded as an alternative to conventional schooling and practice. It is located in an intimate and informal private studio. A maximum number of ten persons are admitted each year. The studio provides a working space and a small inter-disciplinary library, bringing together students, post-graduates, professors and practitioners.

Like the early Renaissance workshop where no distinction was yet made between the magical-symbolic and the pragmatic-technical, *Architecture Intermundium* strives to retrieve the poetic, creative dimension of architecture's being and non-being. As such it provides a place where concrete architectural design work and theoretical discussion, scholarship and experiment are integrated into a single whole. *Architecture Intermundium* forms a unique context in which distinguished architects and thinkers can come to share their ideas and works.

The course consists of two independent time periods. The first is from the beginning of October to the end of January (with a winter break). The second is from the beginning of February to the end of May (with a spring break). Preference for admission will be given to those who can attend both periods.

Butler County Community College

Department of Architecture
Oak Hills
Butler, PA 16001

(412) 287-8711

Donald A Drum, PhD,
Chairman of Technology Division
Wayne Shaulis, Professor,
Contact Person

APPROXIMATE NUMBER OF FT STUDENTS, 1986-87 22

NUMBER OF FTE FACULTY 1

ADMISSION REQUIREMENTS High school graduate

1986-1987 TUITION AND FEES $1100

DEGREE OR CERTIFICATE AAS

PROGRAM SUMMARY

The architectural drafting and design curriculum is designed to prepare students for either semiprofessional employment or transfer into architectural programs at other schools. In addition to drawing and graphic skills, mathematics, science, structures, and other support courses are taught. Sixty-six credits are required for the degree. Specific courses include Technical Drawing, Materials and Construction, Architectural Art, Architectural Design, Mechanics, Strength of Materials, Surveying, and Architectural Environment.

Delgado Community College

(City Park Campus)

Engineering Division
(Architecture Department)
615 City Park Avenue
New Orleans, LA 70119

(504) 483-4444

P Victor Mirzai, Head

APPROXIMATE NUMBER OF FT STUDENTS, 1986-87 95

NUMBER OF FTE FACULTY 2

ADMISSION REQUIREMENTS High school diploma

1986-1987 TUITION AND FEES LA Res: $375 Full-time
Non-Res: $975 Full-time

DEGREE OR CERTIFICATE Associate of Science Degree

PROGRAM SUMMARY
Architectural engineering technology deals with the design and construction of homes, factories, schools, stores, and public buildings and projects. Architectural engineering technology is also concerned with the upkeep, repair, modification, and modernization of existing buildings.

The primary objective of the program is to prepare each student for full-time employment as an architectural engineering technician in two years. There are numerous career opportunities in the building construction industry for architectural technicians. The architectural engineering technician may be employed as an architect's or contractor's assistant to aid in the supervision of construction and in making progress inspections; as a building inspector to inspect buildings under construction to ensure compliance with codes, plans, and specifications; as a construction equipment and materials salesman to sell building supplies and equipment; as an estimator to compute quantities and cost of materials and labor; as a materials man to buy and distribute materials on construction jobs; or as a structural draftsman to draft specifications on steel and concrete requirements.

Affiliate
Members

Istanbul Technical University

Faculty of Architecture
Istanbul Technical University
80191 Taksim, Istanbul, Turkey

Istanbul / 145 27 53

Professor Gündüz Atalik,
PhD, Dean

APPROXIMATE NUMBER OF FT STUDENTS, 1986-87 1200

NUMBER OF FTE FACULTY 137

ADMISSION REQUIREMENTS Admission to the University may be granted to all graduates of all high schools of approved standing provided the applicant obtained the necessary ÜSYM (General Inter-University Entrance Examination) scores and majored in science. The student admission quotas for each Department are determined by the University Senate every year. Students are admitted according to the scores received in the "ÜSYM."

Foreign Students
  High School graduates of foreign countries are also admitted according to the announced quotas for foreign students in each Faculty each year. Their high school diplomas must be accepted by the Ministry of Education as equivalent to Turkish diplomas.
  Foreign students must have an adequate knowledge of Turkish. If the number of applicants exceeds the new foreign students quota, a general knowledge test will be given in Turkish, Mathematics, Physics and Chemistry. Acceptance is decided according to the total scores obtained in this test and also admissions allotment set for each Department.

1986-1987 TUITION AND FEES Annually TL. 70,000 for Turkish Students,
TL. 210,000 in foreign currencies for foreigners

DEGREE OR CERTIFICATE Department of Architecture/BS, MS, PhD;
Department of Urban and Regional Planning/BS, MS, PhD

PROGRAM SUMMARY
Undergraduate study leading to Engineering and Architecture diplomas or Degrees consists of compulsory and elective courses, projects, problem sessions, laboratory and workshop training, field applications, seminars and graduate assignments.
  Studies are done according to the Faculty curriculum, which must not exceed 22 hours a week. An additional two hours a week can be taken in courses of general culture. The course load limit does not include the Foreign Language courses.
  The students are also required to complete a minimum of twelve weeks of practical work during their training and vacations in accordance with the rules set by the Faculty Council. Those courses for which studio or practical work is to

be pursued outside the university are in effect after the termination of the summer term within the time periods as specified by the concerned departments.

Graduate Assignment:
  A student of the Dept of Architecture or Dept of Urban and Regional Planning is required to complete an architectural design or Urban and Regional Planning project that will be considered his Graduation Assignment during his/her 8th semester. The study is aimed at evaluating whether the student has reached the desired capacity in terms of approach, development and the final decision within the process of solution of a specific problem and, especially, understanding whether he has attained the ability to exercise his rights and responsibilities granted to him by his Diploma.

Lansing Community College

The Architectural Studies Center
P.O. Box 40010
Lansing, MI 48901

(517) 483-1356

James C Perkins, Director,
Architectural Studies Center

**APPROXIMATE NUMBER OF FT
STUDENTS, 1986-87** 75

NUMBER OF FTE FACULTY 3

ADMISSION REQUIREMENTS College Admission
18 years of age, high school graduate

1986-1987 TUITION AND FEES District Res: $17
per credit
Non-res: $24 per credit
Out-of-state: $34.50 per credit

DEGREE OR CERTIFICATE Associate of Applied
Science Degree in Architecture
Associate of Applied Science Degree in
Landscape Architecture
Associate of Applied Science Degree in
Architecture (Solar Option)

PROGRAM SUMMARY
The Architectural Studies Center at Lansing
Community College offers its students the most
comprehensive program of its type in the nation
with the largest Computer Graphics facility of any
community college in the nation. The concept of
Architectural Studies was instituted to combine
and coordinate existing programs relating to the
study of architecture at Lansing Community
College. The Center offers a series of two-year
Associate of Science Degrees and degree
options designed to prepare students as
technicians in the fields of Architecture,
Landscape Architecture, and Solar Technology.
Additional degree options are also offered for
students who are interested in gaining
preparatory skills needed to work toward an
advanced degree.

A wide variety of courses are available at the
Architectural Studies Center, either for the
various degree programs, or for individual
specialized study. These classes are
supplemented by additional college courses in
Civil Technology, Art, Interior Design, Math,
Science, English and Computer-Aided Design
Technology. All courses are structured and
taught by field-trained professionals using the
latest equipment and teaching techniques.

Students enrolling in classes offered by the
Architectural Studies Center often have different
yet specific career goals. Some students seek
training to work in a support capacity for an
Architectural Engineering or design firm as a
paraprofessional. An equal number of students
use their first two years of college to achieve an
Associate Degree and accumulate skills and
credits to transfer to one of many Bachelor
Degree programs at colleges throughout
Michigan or across the country. Still other
students find their needs fulfilled by taking one or
more of the many specialty classes offered
without prerequisite on a wide range of
architecture-related subjects.

Lehigh University

Department of Art & Architecture
Chandler-Ullmann Hall, #17
Bethlehem, PA 18015

(215) 758-3610

Lucy Gans,
Chairman/Associate Professor
Ivan Zaknic,
Program Chairman/Associate
Professor

**APPROXIMATE NUMBER OF FT
STUDENTS, 1986-87** 50

NUMBER OF FTE FACULTY 7

ADMISSION REQUIREMENTS Admission to
Lehigh University, College of Arts and Sciences

1986-1987 TUITION AND FEES $11,400 per year

DEGREE OR CERTIFICATE BA (Architecture)

PROGRAM SUMMARY
The Department of Art and Architecture is part of
the College of Arts and Sciences. The degree
granted by the university is a liberal arts BA with
a major in architecture.

A major in architecture is designed to give the
student a strong liberal education related to the
problems of the built environment. The major
requirements are in architectural design (22
credits), studio (6 credits), and history and theory
of architecture (15 credits). Courses in calculus (8
credits) and physics (5 credits) are also required.
In addition, courses related to architecture are
recommended in the Division of Urban Studies
and the Departments of Social Relations and
History. It is the interaction of these areas that
defines the character of architectural education
at Lehigh. In all, 62 credits are needed for an
architecture major.

This program is intended primarily for students
who plan to attend graduate schools of
architecture and stresses design as the
architect's essential skill.

The major is also open to students admitted to
the College of Engineering who may take a
double degree of five years, earning a BA
(Architecture) and a BS (Civil Engineering).
Individually structured programs for engineers
are also available which lead to a BS (CE) with a
minor in architecture.

Leicester Polytechnic

School of Architecture
P.O. Box 143
Leicester LE1 9BH, England

(UK) 0533 551551 ext 2334/5

Professor Theo Matoff, Head
Contact Person

**APPROXIMATE NUMBER OF FT
STUDENTS, 1986-87** 200

NUMBER OF FTE FACULTY 20

ADMISSION REQUIREMENTS 6 points from 2/3
'A' (A=5 point, B=4, C=3, D=2, E=1)

1986-1987 TUITION AND FEES UK = £556
Overseas £3,720*
*Waived if School Exchange Programme
Agreement has been ratified

DEGREE OR CERTIFICATE BA (Hons) Degree,
Full-time
BA Degree, Part-time
Diploma, Architecture and Conservation Diploma
(Post-Graduate)

PROGRAM SUMMARY

The Undergraduate Course:
A three-year full-time degree course leading to
a BA Degree with Honours in Architecture, and
giving exemption from Part One of the RIBA
Examination in Architecture, is designed in a way
which responds to the needs of a challenging
profession in a rapidly changing world. The aim
is to develop an integrative approach to
architectural design based on creative ability and
technical competence. Emphasis is given to
self-directed studies and students are
encouraged to participate in student exchange
programmes abroad. The impact of information
technology on design is a major theme of the
work undertaken.

A central concern is the consideration of
contemporary society's needs and to respond to
these requirements with an imaginative and
innovative environment.

The Graduate Course:
The three-year course leads to the award of
the Polytechnic Graduate Diploma in Architecture
- Dip(Leics) - which gives exemption from Part
Two of the RIBA Examination in Architecture.
The course comprises:

1 One year of office-based experience in
  collaboration with the School of Architecture.
2 Two years of full-time study, of which part may

be spent at another institution abroad or in the
UK.

The two academic years of the course
consist of combinations of structured teaching
and self-directed study, including Design
Studies, Technology Studies, Urban Studies,
Professional Studies and a Dissertation Study.
Students are encouraged to determine their
own study programmes by choosing from a
variety of optional study areas including
Computer-Aided Design, Rehabilitation, Design
Technology and topics related to Continuing
Professional Development. A wide selection of
optional Elective Courses reflecting staff
research and interests are also offered.

Research:
Computing facilities are excellent and are used
extensively in research and all courses in the
School. Computer-Aided Architectural Design and
Information Technology are increasingly involved
in research programmes and course work.

The School has established research and
consultancy facilities and many of its activities
are collaborative ventures, both international and
national, with the SERC. These contracts involve
collaborative research links with American
Institutions, e.g. SERI (Colorado), the Building
Research Establishment, the Rutherford-Appleton
Laboratory, and several British Universities.

Miami-Dade Community College/South Campus

Department of Architecture
11011 S.W. 104 Street
Miami, FL 33176

(305) 347-2226

Oscar A Larrauri, AIA,
Chairman & Professor
Rudy A Williams,
Associate Dean of Occupational
Education

APPROXIMATE NUMBER OF FT STUDENTS, 1986-87 450

NUMBER OF FTE FACULTY 9

ADMISSION REQUIREMENTS The following persons are eligible for admission to the credit programs of Miami-Dade Community College:

1. High school graduates—all programs;
2. Transfer students from colleges, universities, and other post-secondary institutions—all programs;
3. Foreign students with education equivalent to U.S. secondary school education and meeting language standards established through College policy and/or procedure—all programs;
4. Persons eighteen years and over who would have graduated prior to 1983 and who do not hold a high school diploma or a high school equivalent (GED) diploma—occupational programs only.

1986-1987 TUITION AND FEES FL Res: $24.50 per credit
Non-Res: $51.00 per credit

DEGREE OR CERTIFICATE Associate in Arts in Pre-Architecture

PROGRAM SUMMARY
Miami-Dade Community College, South Campus, offers the first two years of the five-year Bachelor of Architecture, or the four-year Bachelor of Design degree programs. The student body is a mixture of local, international and minority students with varying abilities. In recognition of this diversity, the architecture program has an education philosophy that starts at a beginning level and quickly accelerates enthusiastic students to a level in which they are soon exercising much creativity, imagination and independence.

The Architecture program is structured to achieve two different levels and philosophies of architectural education:

1. For those students wishing to pursue professional careers, South Campus offers the first two years (Associate in Arts Program) of the four- or five-year baccalaureate degrees. The majority of our students fall into this category. This program stresses traditional coursework, such as design, theory, presentation and drawing, as well as computer applications, materials, structures, math and physics. Students are successfully prepared to enter upper-division architecture programs in universities throughout Florida and the country.
2. For individuals interested in entering architecture as technically-oriented paraprofessionals, the two-year Associate in Science technical program in Architectural Technology emphasizes such coursework as working drawings, computer technology, construction estimating and technical math.

In addition, South Campus also offers the first two years of Interior Design, Building Construction and Landscape Architecture. These programs are also designed for continuation into baccalaureate programs in universities throughout the country.

233

Affiliate Members

Norwalk State Technical College

Architecture Department
181 Richards Avenue
Norwalk, CT 06854

(203) 855-6600

Olga Vallay Szokolay, Chairperson
Architectural Engineering
Technology Department

**APPROXIMATE NUMBER OF FT
STUDENTS, 1986-87** 85

NUMBER OF FTE FACULTY 2

ADMISSION REQUIREMENTS High school
diploma

1986-1987 TUITION AND FEES CT Res: $861
Non-res: $2,826

DEGREE OR CERTIFICATE Associate of Science
in Architectural Engineering Technology

PROGRAM SUMMARY
The Architectural Engineering Technology
program is designed for high school graduates
who wish to pursue careers in the architectural
or construction fields. Graduates of the program
shall have basic skills for employment in
architectural or engineering offices as well as at
construction. They are also prepared to enter at
advanced levels into professional degree
programs elsewhere, in the pursuit of becoming
registered architects.

Parsons School of Design

(A Division of the New School for
   Social Research)
Department of Environmental
   Design
66 Fifth Avenue
New York, NY 10011

(212) 741-8955

James Wines, Chair
Patricia Phillips, Associate Chair
Contact Person

**APPROXIMATE NUMBER OF FT
STUDENTS, 1986-87** 150 BFA

NUMBER OF FTE FACULTY 2

ADMISSION REQUIREMENTS College/high
school transcripts
Written essay
Portfolio

1986-1987 TUITION AND FEES $8,000

DEGREE OR CERTIFICATE BFA
M Arch (beginning Sept. 1988)

PROGRAM SUMMARY
The Department of Environmental Design
provides an interdisciplinary education in design
and architecture studies. The objective of this
department is to encourage the development of
designers who are able to work in a variety of
scales and creative situations including
architecture, interior architecture, furniture
design, and urban design. The emphasis of this
program is the development of individual,
creative strategies through a curricular focus on
invention and conceptual thinking.

   This program in general architecture studies is
designed to encourage inquiry about design
issues and process through intensive studio work
and interdisciplinary study. The nature of this
program prepares students for a range of

creative roles in a variety of professional
capacities. This orientation reflects significant
changes in the design professions; the divisions
between professional disciplines (i.e., architecture
and interior design) have become more fluid
resulting in many more small firms that have
diversified practices.

   The core of the Environmental Design
curriculum is the studio. Studio is complemented
and supported by prescribed and elective
courses in art and architecture history,
technology studies, and fine and applied arts.
This balance not only prepares students for
productive careers but provides a strong
academic foundation for those who choose to do
graduate level studies at Parsons/New School or
other institutions.

The School of the Art Institute of Chicago
Department of Interior Architecture

Columbus Drive and Jackson Blvd.
Chicago, IL 60603

(312) 443-3700

Linda Lee Nelson,
AIA, Chairman

APPROXIMATE NUMBER OF FT STUDENTS, 1986-87 50 (SAIC 1585)

NUMBER OF FTE FACULTY 10 (SAIC 199)

ADMISSION REQUIREMENTS BFA - Application & $25 nonrefundable fee, Portfolio of work (10-15 examples) w/description list, Personal Statement, Transcripts from HS or GED, SAT or ACT scores, letter of recommendation. MFA - Application & $25 fee, Portfolio of work (15-20 examples) w/list, Statement of purpose, Transcripts, 3 letters of recommendation

1986-1987 TUITION AND FEES $3900 per semester (full-time 12-18 credits hours) + student health insurance $150
MFA - $260 per credit hour

DEGREE OR CERTIFICATE Bachelor of Interior Architecture (162 credit hours)
Bachelor of Fine Arts (132 credit hours)
Master of Fine Arts (60 credit hours)

PROGRAM SUMMARY
The Interior Architecture Area at the School of the Art Institute of Chicago, offers a unique approach to studying the art of creating, completing, and/or adapting the environment. The curriculum emphasizes awareness, understanding, and explorative application of the conceptual aspects of the design processs, as well as the development of the necessary technical, theoretical, and psychological skills required of an interior architect.

Two-dimensional, three-dimensional, and four-dimensional conceptualizing are explored in the drawing classes, design classes, professional classes, and general electives which are taught by architects, interior architects, film makers, archaeologists, historians, graphic artists, performance artists, painters, sculptors, etc. The Bachelor of Fine Arts (132 credit hours: 72-Studio; 30-Liberal Arts; 18-Art History; 12-Electives) and the Bachelor of Interior Architecture Fifth-Year Option (requires an additional 30 hours of credit of studio work; the design studio credits are affiliated with professional offices in the Chicago area and include the following classes: Historic Restoration and Preservation, Classical Literacy, Professional Practice, and Studio of Uncertainty) provide a viable and valuable pre-architectural course of study broadened with liberal arts and fine arts. The MFA (60 credit hours: 39-Studio/Graduate Projects; 12-Art History; 9-Electives) emphasizes theoretical explorations of Interior Architecture in the realm of the fine arts.

The Interior Architecture Area emphasizes the use of the real world as the studio. Graduates of the program are creative, holistic thinkers whose experience of fine art combined with the art of interior architecture prepare them to better enter and contribute to the profession of architecture which strives to make the world in which we live a better one.

The city of Chicago is one of the greatest architectural centers in the world. The Merchandise Mart, a few blocks away from the School, has the largest collection of materials, furniture, and fabrics under one roof in the world. The Museum has one of the most comprehensive collections of architectural drawings, prints, and photographs in the country. The students are exposed to the work and critique of visiting artists - practicing professionals from the city and visiting lecturers from all over the world! The Interior Architecture Area serves the city of Chicago, as well as setting an unprecedented example for interior architecture and architecture programs across the country.

Faculty Roster

The following is an alphabetical listing of all faculty members mentioned in association with the programs described in this book. For more information about any individual, refer to the two-page entry of the institution indicated.

Abbate, Cinzia, Rensselaer Polytechnic Institute
Abbey, Bruce, University of Virginia
Abbott, Martha, Kansas State University
Abdur-Rahman, Uthman, Tuskegee University
Abernethy, James, Lawrence Technological University
Abraham, Kent, Catholic University of America
Abraham, Raimund J, The Cooper Union, Pratt Institute
Abreau, Maria, University of Miami
Ackerman, Mitchell, Rhode Island School of Design
Acorn, John T, Clemson University
Adams, Don, Boston Architectural Center
Adams, F Douglas, Rhode Island School of Design
Adams, Graham, University of North Carolina at Charlotte
Adams, J Michael, Drexel University
Adams, John F, Tulane University
Adams, Kathy, Boston Architectural Center
Adams, Stanley, University of Arizona
Adams, William, California State Polytechnic University, Pomona
Adaskin, Gordon, University of Manitoba
Addis, Kory, Boston Architectural Center
Addison, Clarence L, Clemson University
Adegbite, Victor A, Howard University
Adelson, Marvin, University of California, Los Angeles
Aderholdt, Robert W, Auburn University
Affleck, Gavin, McGill University
Affleck, Raymond, McGill University
Agarwal, Nancy, Lawrence Technological University
Agrest, Diana, The Cooper Union
Aho, Arnold J, Mississippi State University
Ahrentzen, Sherry B, University of Wisconsin-Milwaukee
Ainbender, Arlene, Southern California Institute of Architecture
Akin, Omer, Carnegie Mellon University
Akridge, James M, Georgia Institute of Technology
Al-Hamdouni, Khalid, Roger Williams College
Alakiotou, Roula, University of Illinois at Chicago
Albaisa, Adolfo, Boston Architectural Center
Albanese, Charles A, University of Arizona
Albanese, Ralph, New York Institute of Technology
Albert, Beverly, State University of New York at Buffalo
Albert, Steven, Southern California Institute of Architecture
Albrecht, Johann G, University of Illinois at Urbana-Champaign
Albrecht, Robert, University of Washington
Alden, Richard, Pennsylvania State University
Alden, Richard, University of Washington
Alexander, Bertram C, Miami University
Alexander, D Blake, University of Texas at Austin
Alexander, Christopher, University of California, Berkeley
Alexander, Gary, Ohio State University
Alfano Jr, Michael, Florida A&M University
Ali, Mir M, University of Illinois at Urbana-Champaign
Aliber, Jennifer, Boston Architectural Center

Allen, Barbara, University of Hawaii at Manoa
Allen, Barbara, University of Washington
Allen, Douglas, Georgia Institute of Technology
Allen, Edward B, Yale University
Allen, Edwin E, Texas A&M University
Allen, Gerald, Carnegie Mellon University
Allen, Gerald, University of North Carolina at Charlotte
Allen, Phoebe, Louisiana Tech University
Allen, R Gary, New School of Architecture
Allen, Robert B, Washington State University
Allen, William, Lawrence Technological University
Alofsin, Anthony, University of Texas at Austin
Alpern, Robert, Pratt Institute
Alscher, Marcia, Drury College
Altieri, John, Yale University
Altschuler, Alan, Harvard University
Alvarez, Hector, Howard University
Amanzio, Joseph C, California Polytechnic State University, San Luis Obispo
Amatuzzo, Paul, New York, Institute of Technology
Ambrose, James E, University of Southern California
Amcri, Amir, Temple University
Ames, Anthony, Georgia Institute of Technology
Amico, Robert L, University of Notre Dame
Amon, Rene, University of Illinois at Chicago
Amourgis, Spyros, California State Polytechnic University, Pomona
Anderson, Amy, Columbia University
Anderson, Anita, Illinois Institute of Technology
Anderson, Arthur K, Pennsylvania State University
Anderson, Barbara, North Dakota State University
Anderson, Bruce, McGill University
Anderson, Gerald I, University of Tennessee-Knoxville
Anderson, James R, University of Illinois at Urbana-Champaign
Anderson, John, Spring Garden College
Anderson, Larz T, Virginia Polytechnic Institute & State University
Anderson, Lee B, University Minnesota
Anderson, Myron, University of Houston
Anderson, Paul, Florida A&M University
Anderson, Richard, University of New Mexico
Anderson, Richard, Pratt Institute
Anderson, Stanford, Massachusetts Institute of Technology
Anderson, Zane, Roger Williams College
Andino, Aureo, University of Puerto Rico
Ando, Tadao, Ohio State University
Andoh, C K, Prairie View A&M University
Andonian, K S, Carleton University
Andrejasich, Michael J, University of Illinois at Urbana-Champaign
Andrejko, Dennis, State University of New York at Buffalo
Andrews, David, University of Houston
Andrighetti, Richard, University of Waterloo
Angelil, Marc, University of Southern California
Angevine, Eric, Oklahoma State University
Angle, Warren O, Spring Garden College

Anselevicius, George, University of New Mexico
Anthony, Ethan, Roger Williams College
Anthony, Kathryn H, University of Illinois at Urbana-Champaign
Antoniades, Anthony C, University of Texas at Arlington
Antonopoulos, Apostolos M, Boston Architectural Center
Aoki, Paula, Boston Architectural Center
Apfel, Robert E, Yale University
Aponte-Pares, Louis, Pratt Institute
Appel, Natalye, University of Texas at Austin
Appleby, Michael D, Virginia Polytechnic Institute & State University
Arai, Kiyokazu, Southern California Institute of Architecture
Aran, Berge, University of California, Los Angeles
Arce, Hector, University of Puerto Rico
Archea, John C, State University of New York at Buffalo
Archer, Michael L, University of South Florida
Arens, Edward, University of California, Berkeley
Arens, Robert, University of Detroit
Arfaa, Peter F, Drexel University
Armpriest, Diane, University of Cincinnati
Armstrong, Foster, Kent State University
Armstrong, Judith, Drury College
Armstrong, Paul J, University of Illinois at Urbana-Champaign
Aroni, Samuel, University of California, Los Angeles
Aronson, Sherman, Drexel University
Arran, Frank, New Jersey Institute of Technology
Arumi, Francisco, University of Texas at Austin
Asbel, James B, Texas A&M University
Aseltine, Mark, University of Pennsylvania
Ast, Bruno, University of Illinois at Chicago
Atallah, Elie, Boston Architectural Center
Atherton, Peter B, University of Utah
Atkinson, Simon, University of Texas at Austin
Atre, Sharad P, California Polytechnic State University, San Luis Obispo
Attoe, Wayne, University of Texas at Austin
Auerbach, Seymour, Catholic University of America
Auger, Jules, Université de Montréal
Augustine, Robert, Boston Architectural Center
Austin, David, University of Illinois at Chicago
Austin, Richard, University of Nebraska-Lincoln
Axley, James, Massachusetts Institute of Technology
Aynsley, Richard, Georgia Institute of Technology
Bachman, Leonard, University of Houston
Baerman, Donald J, Yale University
Bagnall, James R, California Polytechnic State University, San Luis Obispo
Bahls, Harold, Oregon School of Design
Bailey, Stanley C, Georgia Institute of Technology
Bailey, Virginia S, Rensselaer Polytechnic Institute
Bailkey, Martin, Drury College

Bailyn, Paul, The Cooper Union
Baird, George, McGill University, University of Toronto
Baird, James, Illinois Institute of Technology
Baker, Barry J, University of Hawaii at Manoa
Baker, Eugene R, Lawrence Technological University
Baker, Geoffrey H, Tulane University
Baker, Jack S, University of Illinois at Urbana-Champaign
Baker, Joseph, Laval University
Baker, Josiah, Rice University
Bales, Erv, New Jersey Institute of Technology
Balfour, Alan, Georgia Institute of Technology
Balich, George T, Wentworth Institute of Technology
Ballinger, Barbara, Ball State University
Balmora, Diana, Yale University
Balogh, Tivadar, University of Michigan
Balourdas, Arthur, New School of Architecture
Bambury, Jill, Louisiana State University
Bambury, Jill, Technical University of Nova Scotia
Bancroft, Jerry A, Montana State University
Bancroft, Pamela J, Montana State University
Bandini, Pier, Pennsylvania State University
Banerjee, Solil, Hampton University
Banerji, Anupam, University of Waterloo
Baniassad, Essy, Technical University of Nova Scotia
Bank, Andrew, Boston Architectural Center
Banks, Aubrey, Frank Lloyd Wright School of Architecture
Banner, Ian G, Mississippi State University
Bannes, Lorenz T, Washington University
Baracs, Janos, Université de Montréal
Barber Jr, Everett M, Yale University
Barber, Thomas, Kent State University
Barbier, Edward, Louisiana State University
Barcinski, Derek, Boston Architectural Center
Barcus, C H, Miami University
Bardt, Christopher N, Iowa State University
Barker, E Gilman, Wentworth Institute of Technology
Barker, James F, Clemson University
Barlow Jr, Charles C, Mississippi State University
Barnes, James, Rhode Island School of Design
Barnes, Rebecca, Boston Architectural Center
Barnett, Bob, Southern California Institute of Architecture
Barnett, Gaila, Woodbury University
Barnett, Jonathan, City College of the CUNY, University of Maryland
Barnett, Norman E, University of Michigan
Baron, Robert, University of Idaho
Barr-Kumar, Raj, Howard University
Barreto, Mauricio, Roger Williams College
Barrier, Edward, University of Southwestern Louisiana
Barrios-Cader, Cristina, North Carolina State University
Barron, C Errol, Tulane University
Barrows, Timothy H, Tuskegee University
Barry, William, Boston Architectural Center
Bartels, Thomas, Rensselaer Polytechnic Institute
Barton, Craig, Columbia University
Bartuska, Tom J, Washington State University

Barucchieri, Paolo G, Texas A&M University
Bass, Louis O, Oklahoma State University
Basset, Miriam, University of Toronto
Bassett, George, McGill University
Bassin, Joan, New York Institute of Technology
Bassler, Bruce L, Iowa State University
Batchelor, Peter, North Carolina State University, Temple University
Bater, James H, University of Waterloo
Bates, Robert, Ohio State University
Bator, Dennis, Pratt Institute
Battaglia, Paul, State University of New York at Buffalo
Batterson, Ronald E, California Polytechnic State University, San Luis Obispo
Battipaglia, Robert, New York Institute of Technology
Baum, Edward M, University of Texas at Arlington
Baum, Faith, Drexel University
Bauman, Hansel, Boston Architectural Center
Bauman, William C, University of Oklahoma
Baurer, Clark T, University of Illinois at Urbana-Champaign
Bavinger, Bill A, Rice University
Bayegan, Ali, Texas Tech University
Beardsley, Kelcey, Texas A&M University
Beathea, Robert, Howard University
Beatley, Timothy P, University of Virginia
Beattie, Robert, New York Institute of Technology
Becherer, Richard, Carnegie Mellon University
Bechhoefer, William, University of Maryland
Beck, David S, Spring Garden College
Beck, Ursula, Boston Architectural Center
Beckley, Robert M, University of Michigan
Beckley, Tom, Drury College
Beckman, Richard M, University of Nevada, Las Vegas
Beckum, A Frank, Georgia Institute of Technology
Bedard, Jean-Francois, McGill University
Bedford, Bill, Pratt Institute
Bednar, Michael J, University of Virginia
Bee, Carmi, City College of the CUNY
Beeby, Thomas, University of Illinois at Chicago, Yale University
Beglo, Jo, University of Waterloo
Behar, Roberto, University of Miami
Behrens, Paula, Spring Garden College
Behringer, John, Rhode Island School of Design
Beinart, Julian, Massachusetts Institute of Technology, Technical University of Nova Scotia
Beitz, William J, Lawrence Technological University
Belcher, Clay, University of Kansas
Bell, B, Carleton University
Bell, Bryan, Tulane University
Bell, David, University of Illinois at Chicago
Bell, David H, Rensselaer Polytechnic Institute
Bell, Harold K, Columbia University
Bell, Larry, University of Houston
Bell, Matthew, Cornell University
Bell, Ross, University of Oklahoma
Bell, Stanley M, Andrews University
Bell, Walter, University of Hawaii at Manoa
Bell, Wayne, University of Texas at Austin
Bellalta, Esmee C, University of Notre Dame

Bellalta, Jaime J, University of Notre Dame
Bellantoni, Frank, New York Institute of Technology
Belton, Ralph J, Howard University
Belzile, Claude, Laval University
Beman, Scott D, University of Nebraska-Lincoln
Bemiss, Madge, University of Pennsylvania
Bemiss, Margaret, Drexel University
Bencks, Doug, Boston Architectural Center
Bender, Larry, University of Kentucky
Bender, Paula, Texas A&M University
Bender, Richard, University of California, Berkeley
Benedikt, Michael, University of Texas at Austin
Benes, Miroslav M, Harvard University
Benevengo, Edward, Pratt Institute
Benjamin, Bezaleel, University of Kansas
Benjamin, Gail, Pratt Institute
Bennett, Daniel D, Auburn University
Bennett, Francis, Lawrence Technological University
Bennett, Ralph, University of Maryland
Bennett, Ronald R, University of Nevada, Las Vegas
Bennett, Stephen P, University of Kentucky
Benson, Robert, Miami University
Bentel, Frederick, New York Institute of Technology
Bentel, Maria, New York Institute of Technology
Benton, Charles, University of California, Berkeley
Benz, Robert, Technical University of Nova Scotia
Benzing, Nelson S, University of North Carolina at Charlotte
Berbiglia, John L, Lawrence Technological University
Berg, Jeffrey T, Rhode Island School of Design, Roger Williams College, Yale University
Berg, Robert, Catholic University of America
Bergeson, Donald E, University of Illinois at Urbana-Champaign
Berglund, Larry G, Yale University
Bergren, Ann L T, Southern California Institute of Architecture
Bergum, Christian, University of Texas at Austin
Berke, Deborah, Yale University
Berke, Philip, Texas A&M University
Berman, Joyce, Boston Architectural Center
Berman, Lester, Lawrence Technological University
Berman, Seth, Boston Architectural Center
Bermudez, Eduardo, University of Puerto Rico
Bernard, Michael, Boston Architectural Center
Bernard, Ruston J, University of Southwestern Louisiana
Berndtson, Indira, Frank Lloyd Wright School of Architecture
Bernhard, Robert M, Lawrence Technological University
Bernholtz, Allen I, Spring Garden College
Bernier, Benoit, Laval University
Bernstein, Phillip, Yale University
Bertelsen, Wendle R, Arizona State University
Bertheaud, Stanley, Woodbury University
Berthold, Michael, New York Institute of Technology

Faculty
Roster

Bertoli, Alberto, Southern California Institute of Architecture
Bertomen, Michele, New York Institute of Technology
Bertone, Richard, Boston Architectural Center
Bertoniere Jr, John A, University of Notre Dame
Bessonette, David, Technical University at Nova Scotia
Betancourt, Humberto, University of Puerto Rico
Betsky, Aaron, Southern California Institute of Architecture
Betts, Mary Beth, The Cooper Union
Betts, Richard J, University of Illinois at Urbana-Champaign
Bevans, Ronald D, University of Idaho
Bevington, Christine, Pratt Institute
Bezman, Michel, University of Houston
Bhatt, Vikram, McGill University
Bidigare, Frederick, University of Detroit
Bieber, Baron, Oklahoma State University
Biehn, James H, Texas A&M University
Bihler, Leonard, Illinois Institute of Technology
Bilgutay, Atilla, State University of New York at Buffalo
Billington, Kym, Arizona State University
Binder, Harold, Lawrence Technological University
Binford, Michael W, Harvard University
Bing, Judith, Drexel University
Binkley, James, Catholic University of America
Birch, Lawrence E, Florida A&M University
Bird, Walter, State University of New York at Buffalo
Birkby, Phyllis, New York Institute of Technology
Birkerts, Gunnar G, University of Michigan
Bis, John S, State University of New York at Buffalo
Bishop, Ian D, Texas A&M University
Biskaps, Ojars, Technical University of Nova Scotia
Bissky, Wayne, University of Manitoba
Bisson, P. Richard, Université de Montréal
Bizios, Georgia, North Carolina State University
Bjerregaard, Elmer, Kent State University
Black, Alan, University of Kansas
Black, Sinclair, University of Texas at Austin
Blackburn Jr, James B, Rice University
Blackwell, Gaines T, Auburn University
Blair, Donald, State University of New York at Buffalo
Blake, Christopher, Boston Architectural Center
Blake, Peter, Catholic University of America
Blanchard, Jeffrey N, University of Notre Dame
Blanco, Marino, University of Miami
Bland, John, McGill University
Blanda, Andrew A, Drexel University
Blanton, Paul L, University of Idaho
Blatteau, John, University of Pennsylvania
Blazina, Vesna, Université de Montréal
Bleam, Gregg D, University of Virginia
Blew III, J Miller, Harvard University
Bley, Llewellyn, Boston Architectural Center
Bliss, Rhoda, University of Colorado at Denver
Bliss, Robert L, University of Utah

Bliznakov, Milka, Virginia Polytechnic Institute & State University
Block, David A, Iowa State University
Block, Jane, University of Illinois at Urbana-Champaign
Bloomer, Jennifer, University of Florida, Georgia Institute of Technology
Bloomer, Kent C, Yale University
Blue-Blanton, Cynthia, University of Idaho
Bluestone, Daniel M, Columbia University
Bluestone, H Lawrence, Boston Architectural Center
Blumenthal, Paul C, Texas A&M University
Blythe, Alden, Temple University
Boake, Teresa M, University of Waterloo
Bobenhausen, William, Pratt Institute
Boddy, Trevor, Carleton University, University of Toronto
Bodick, Kirk, University of North Carolina at Charlotte
Boemer, Allen J, Wentworth Institute of Technology
Boeschenstein, Warren, University of Virginia
Bognar, Botond, University of Illinois at Urbana-Champaign
Bohland, James R, Virginia Polytechnic Institute & State University
Boigon, Brian, University of Waterloo
Boisvert, Jean-Claude, Université de Montréal
Bojanowski, Krzysztof, University of Tennessee-Knoxville
Bollack, Francoise, Pratt Institute
Bollinger, Elizabeth, University of Houston
Boltz, Russ E, Lawrence Technological University
Bon, Ranko, Massachusetts Institute of Technology
Bonacker, Joyce, Drury College
Bond Jr, J Max, City College of the CUNY
Bone, Kevin, Columbia University, The Cooper Union
Bonitatibus, Stephen M, Drexel University
Bonner, Robert D, Hampton University
Bonsteel, David, University of Washington
Book, Norman L, Clemson University
Boonyatikarn, Soontorn, University of Colorado at Denver
Booth, Laurence, University of Illinois at Chicago
Borbas, Steve, University of New Mexico
Borchers, Perry E, Ohio State University
Borden, Alfred, Drexel University
Bork, Dean R, Virginia Polytechnic Institute & State University
Borkin, Harold J, University of Michigan
Borner, William, University of Nebraska-Lincoln
Borowski, Michael, Arizona State University
Bosley, Peggy J, California State Polytechnic University, Pomona
Bosserman, J Norwood, University of Virginia
Bostick, Joel, Syracuse University
Boswell, Bill, University of Texas at Arlington
Bosworth, Thomas, University of Washington
Boterf, Chester A, Rice University
Botros, R, Carleton University
Botsai, Elmer E, University of Hawaii at Manoa
Botta, Mario, Southern California Institute of Architecture

Bourdier, Jean-Paul, University of California, Berkeley
Bourque, Paul N, Laval University
Bovill, Carl H, University of Tennessee-Knoxville
Bower, John, University of Pennsylvania
Bower, Zane, Boston Architectural Center
Bowler, William, University of Idaho
Bowman, Jon A, University of Texas at Austin
Bowser, Wayland W, University of Oklahoma
Box, Hal, University of Texas at Austin
Boyer, Christine, The Cooper Union, New Jersey Institute of Technology
Boyer, Lester L, Texas A&M University
Boyer, Yvon, Université de Montréal
Boykowycz, Walter, Carnegie Mellon University
Boylan, Bernard R, University of Notre Dame
Boyle, B Michael, Arizona State University
Bozdogan, Sibel, Rensselaer Polytechnic Institute
Braaten, Ellen, Virginia Polytechnic Institute & State University
Brackney, Kathryn, Georgia Institute of Technology
Bradford, Derek, Rhode Island School of Design
Bradford, Harold, Tuskegee University
Bradford, Sara, Rhode Island School of Design
Bradie, Stefanie, University of Nevada, Las Vegas
Brady, Thomas M, Lawrence Technological University
Braham, Bill, University of Pennsylvania
Brajtberg, Alina, Drexel University
Braly, David, Auburn University
Brand, R G, Carleton University
Brandle, Kurt, University of Michigan
Brandt, Andreas, Yale University
Braun, Robert, New York Institute of Technology
Breisch, Kenneth, Southern California Institute of Architecture
Breisch, Kenneth A, Lawrence Technological University, Southern California Institute of Architecture
Brenner, Linda, Spring Garden College
Brentrup, Dale A, Montana State University
Breslin, Lynne, Pratt Institute
Bressani, M, Carleton University
Brew, Nina, Boston Architectural Center
Brewer, Brittain, Temple University
Bricken, William, Washington University
Bridges, Leon, Morgan State University
Brierly, Cornelia, Frank Lloyd Wright School of Architecture
Briggs, Laura M, Boston Architectural Center
Briggs, William S, Auburn University
Brill, Michael, State University of New York at Buffalo
Briner, Thomas, Miami University
Brink, Lois, University of Colorado at Denver
Brino, Giovanni, Southern California Institute of Architecture
Brinson, David, Louisiana State University
Briscoe, John, University of Oregon
Bristol, Robert F, Rensselaer Polytechnic Institute
Brittain, Richard, University of Arizona
Brock, Linda, Montana State University

Brockway, William, Louisiana State University

Brodeur, Mario, Université de Montréal

Brodie, David A, California Polytechnic State University, San Luis Obispo

Broker, Karen, Rice University

Bronet, Frances, Rensselaer Polytechnic Institute

Brooks II, H Gordon, University of Arkansas

Brooks, Kerry R, Clemson University

Brouard, Paul B, Yale University

Browder, John O, Virginia Polytechnic Institute & State University

Brown, Andrea Clark, University of Illinois at Chicago

Brown, David, Kansas State University

Brown, Don, Boston Architectural Center

Brown, Fred, University of Washington

Brown, G Z, University of Oregon

Brown, G E C, Technical University of Nova Scotia

Brown, Gary, University of California, Berkeley

Brown, James, University of Waterloo

Brown, James P, New School of Architecture

Brown, Janet, Washington University

Brown, Jay Lance, City College of the CUNY

Brown, Keith A, University of Michigan

Brown, Lamar H, Clemson University

Brown, M Gordon, University of Colorado at Denver

Brown, Marshall V, Prairie View A&M University

Brown, Richard E, Drexel University

Brown, Robert W, University of Southwestern Louisiana

Brown, Terry, Miami University

Brown, Theodore, Syracuse University

Brown, William H, California Polytechnic State University, San Luis Obispo

Brown, William W, Virginia Polytechnic Institute & State University

Brown-Manrique, Gerardo, Miami University

Browne, Charlene A, Virginia Polytechnic Institute & State University

Brownell, Charles E, University of Virginia

Brownlow, Douglas, Roger Williams College

Brune, Geoffrey John, University of Houston

Brunken, Alan W, Oklahoma State University

Brunner, Howard, Temple University

Bruno, Gary, New York Institute of Technology

Bruun, Judith, University of Manitoba

Bryan, Harvey, Harvard University

Bryan, Stanley, University of Oregon

Bryant, Dale, Kansas State University

Bryant, John H, Oklahoma State University

Buchloh, Benjamin, Massachusetts Institute of Technology

Bucholtz, Jeffrey, Columbia University

Bucsescu, Dan, Pratt Institute

Buday, Richard, University of Houston

Buege, David, New Jersey Institute of Technology

Bugbee, Gordon, Lawrence Technological University

Buisson, Paul, University of Miami

Bulanda, Andrzej, Pennsylvania State University

Bullock, Robert, Kansas State University

Bumbaru, Dinu, Université de Montréal

Buono, Michael J, University of Arkansas

Burchard, Charles H, Virginia Polytechnic Institute & State University

Burger, Charles R, Washington State University

Burgess, J Hugh, University of Nevada, Las Vegas

Burggraf, Frank B, University of Arkansas

Burke-Vigeland, Madeline, Pratt Institute

Burkhalter, Marianne, Southern California Institute of Architecture

Burks, William, Louisiana State University

Burleson, J Douglas, Auburn University

Burleson, Rebecca, Auburn University

Burnett, J Jeffrey, Washington State University

Burnham, Robert, Kansas State University

Burns, Carol J, Harvard University

Burns, Howard, Harvard University

Burns, Robert P, North Carolina State University

Burton, Alton, Pratt Institute

Burton, Joseph, University of Minnesota

Burton, Pamela, Southern California Institute of Architecture

Buscemi, Louis, New York Institute of Technology

Busch, Robert E, University of Oklahoma

Bushman, P Jeff, University of Virginia

Butke, Walter J, Virginia Polytechnic Institute & State University

Butler, Kent S, University of Texas at Austin

Butler, Roderick, Woodbury University

Buttenweiser, Ann, Columbia University

Butz, Pamela, Syracuse University

Bye, Arthur E, The Cooper Union

Byerly, Peter, Boston Architectural Center

Byrd Jr, Warren T, University of Virginia

Byrne, Elizabeth, University of California, Berkeley

Caballero, Gerardo, Washington University

Caban, Jose R, Clemson University

Cadloff, Joseph, McGill University

Caffey, Ben, Southern California Institute of Architecture

Cahn, Elizabeth, University of Oregon

Cain, John, University of Wisconsin-Milwaukee

Cakiades, George, Pratt Institute

Caldwell, Alfred, Illinois Institute of Technology

Caldwell, P Mack, University of Oklahoma

Callahan, Charles, Boston Architectural Center

Calvert, Floyd O, University of Oklahoma

Calvo, Charles M, California State Polytechnic University, Pomona

Campagna, Robert, New York Institute of Technology

Campbell, Cathryn S, Auburn University

Campbell, Robert, University of North Carolina at Charlotte

Campi, Mario, Southern California Institute of Architecture

Candido, Anthony, The Cooper Union

Canestaro, James C, Virginia Polytechnic Institute & State University

Caney, Steven, Rhode Island School of Design

Canier, Caren, Rensselaer Polytechnic Institute

Cann, Teresa, University of Illinois at Chicago

Cannady, William T, Rice University

Cannon, Susan Cole, North Carolina State University

Cantafora, Ardvino, Yale University

Canter, Steven B, Boston Architectural Center

Cantrell, Bill W, Texas Tech University

Cappellari, Francesco, University of Florida

Cappleman, Owen, University of Texas at Austin

Caradonna, Salvator, New York Institute of Technology

Carapetian, Michael V, University of Southern California

Cardinal-Pett, Clare, Iowa State University

Cardle, James A, University of Nevada, Las Vegas

Carell, Gregory, Boston Architectural Center

Carlton, Caroline, North Carolina State University

Carlyle, Christine, Boston Architectural Center

Carner, Gilbert, University of Southwestern Louisiana

Carney, Richard E, Frank Lloyd Wright School of Architecture

Carpenter, Clyde R, University of Kentucky

Carpenter, Kenneth, Louisiana State University

Carper, Kenneth L, University of Idaho, Washington State University

Carr, Barbara, Pratt Institute

Carr, Robert, Lawrence Technological University

Carr, Steven P, University of Nevada, Las Vegas

Carr, William C, Washington University

Carswell, William, University of Kansas

Carter, Donald, Lawrence Technological University

Carter, Frank C, Carleton University

Carter, Steve, Miami University

Carter, Thomas R, University of Utah

Carter, Virgil R, Oklahoma State University

Cartwright, Virginia, University of Oregon

Caruncho, Juan, University of Miami

Carvalho, Mario, University of Manitoba

Casasco, Victoria, California State Polytechnic University, Pomona

Casbarian, John J, Rice University

Cascieri, Arcangelo, Boston Architectural Center

Casewit, Niccolo, Boston Architectural Center

Casey, Effi, Frank Lloyd Wright School of Archecture

Casey, E Thomas, Frank Lloyd Wright School of Architecture

Cass, Gilbert, University of Pennsylvania

Castro, Eduard, Pratt Institute

Castro, Ricardo, McGill University

Casuscelli, Carlos, Ball State University

Catalano, Joseph, Washington University

Catanese, Anthony James, University of Florida

Caughey, Diane, Southern California Institute of Architecture

Causey, Jeffrey B

Cava, John, Oregon School of Design

Cavanagh, Edwin, Technical University of Nova Scotia

Cavenaugh, William, Rhode Island School of Design, Roger Williams College

Cavin III, Brooks, California State Polytechnic University, Pomona

Faculty Roster

Caylor, Jr, Garth W, Boston Architectural Center
Cazabon, Y, Carleton University
Cazayoux, Edward J, University of Southwestern Louisiana
Cederna, Ann, Catholic University of America
Celik, Zeynep, Columbia University
Cenicacelaya, Javier, University of Miami
Ceo, Rocco, University of Miami
Cerny, Ladislav, University of Minnesota
Chafee, Judith, University of Arizona
Chafee, Richard, Roger Williams College
Chaffers, James A, University of Michigan
Chaikin, George, The Cooper Union
Chamberlain, Frances, University of Texas at Austin
Chambers, Nancy N, University of Virginia
Champlin, Robert, Lawrence Technological University
Chang, Edmund, University of Southern California
Chang, Pao-Chi, Illinois Institute of Technology
Chang, Yih-Ping, Boston Architectural Center
Chang, Yung-Ho, University of Michigan
Chapman, Arthur, California Polytechnic State University, San Luis Obispo
Charlebois, Sophie, Université de Montréal
Charney, Melvin, Université de Montréal
Charney, Robert S, Yale University
Chartier, Scott D, Montana State University
Chasco, David M, Lawrence Technological University
Chase, O Glean, Howard University
Chatas, Nicholas, University of Detroit
Chatterjee, Jay, University of Cincinnati
Chauncey, Joseph W, Iowa State University
Chelz, Anthony, Kansas State University
Chen, Frances M, Princeton University
Chen, John, Howard University
Cherry, Edith, University of New Mexico
Chiang, Robert NLS, Virginia Polytechnic Institute & State University
Chiasson, Pual D C, Catholic University of America
Childress, Cabell, University of Colorado at Denver
Childs, Diane K, Iowa State University
Chimera, Chris, New York Institute of Technology
Ching, Frank, University of Washington
Chiodo, Christopher, Boston Architectural Center
Chiogna, Corinne, Boston Architectural Center
Chirigos, Michael, Carnegie Mellon University
Chomowicz, Fred, The Cooper Union
Chou, Joel, Hampton University
Chou, Winston, Boston Architectural Center
Choudhury, Salahuddin, Virginia Polytechnic Institute & State University
Chowdhury, Ali, Louisiana State University
Chrisney, Margy, Arizona State University
Christensen, George, Arizona State University
Christensen, Keith, Kansas State University
Christensen, William, Spring Garden College
Christenson, Bethany J, University of Virginia
Chuddy, Mark, Roger Williams College
Chusid, Jeffrey, University of Southern California
Chylinski, Richard, California State Polytechnic University, Pomona

Ciconne, Amy, University of Southern California
Cigolle, Mark, University of Southern California
Cilimberg, Vincent J, Virginia Polytechnic Institute & State University
Cimino, Charles, Boston Architectural Center
Cinciripini, Christine, University of California, Los Angeles
Cizek, Eugene D, Tulane University
Claflen Jr, George L, Temple University
Clagett, John, Southern California Institute of Architecture
Clarens, Angel, Howard University
Clark, Alson, University of Southern California
Clark, Camille S, University of Nevada, Las Vegas
Clark, Carol, Pratt Institute
Clark, James, Boston Architectural Center
Clark, Kenneth, University of Arizona
Clark, Lois E, University of Kansas
Clark, Roger H, North Carolina Stata University
Clark, Scott, Boston Architectural Center
Clark, Sylvia, Drexel University
Clark, Thomas A, University of Colorado at Denver
Clark Jr, William G, University of Virginia
Clarke, Keith, Pratt Institute
Clarke, Paul, Miami University
Clarke, Robin P A, University of British Columbia
Clarkson, William M E, State University of New York at Buffalo
Clary, Mark, University of Kentucky
Clause, Thomas R, Iowa State University
Clausen, Meredith, University of Washington
Clay, Ernest H, University of Illinois at Urbana-Champaign
Claycamp, Carrol D, Texas A&M University
Cleary, Richard, Carnegie Mellon University
Cleaveland, John P, Georgia Institute of Technology
Clemence, Roger D, University of Minnesota
Clement, Lorn, Kansas State University
Cline, Ann, Miami University
Cline, Raymond, Spring Garden College
Clink, Maryanne, Lawrence Technological University
Clipson, Colin W, University of Michigan
Close, Richard, Arizona State University
Clouten, Neville H, Andrews University
Coate, Roland, Southern California Institute of Architecture
Coates, Gary, Kansas State University
Coburn, Donald, Boston Architectural Center
Cocozzoli, Gary, Lawrence Technological University
Coddington, Gilbert H, Ohio State University
Coddington, Jon P, University of Tennessee-Knoxville
Cohan, Peter, University of Wisconsin-Milwaukee
Cohen, Andrew, Roger Williams College
Cohen, Harold L, State University of New York at Buffalo
Cohen, Herb, Boston Architectural Center
Cohen, Julie, Carnegie Mellon University
Cohen, Michael, Cornell University
Cohen, Murray, New York Institute of Technology

Cohen, Stuart E, University of Illinois at Chicago, University of Notre Dame
Cohen, Uriel, University of Wisconsin-Milwaukee
Cohlmeyer, Steve, University of Manitoba
Cohn, Clare, New York Institute of Technology
Cohn, Sidney, Pennsylvania State University
Colaco, Joseph, University of Houston, Rice University
Colasuonno, Luis A, California State Polytechnic University, Pomona
Colbert, Charles, Louisiana State University
Colbert, Thomas M, University of Houston
Colby, Barbara, Arizona State University
Cole, Raymond J, University of British Columbia
Cole, Robert, Carnegie Mellon University
Cole, Sam D, State University of New York at Buffalo
Coleman, Bruce, Syracuse University
Collier, Ned, University of Colorado at Denver
Collin, Jacques, University of Manitoba
Collin, Robert W, University of Virginia
Collins, Donald L, Clemson University
Collins, Richard C, University of Virginia
Colliton, Dennis C, North Dakota State University
Colomina, Beatriz, Princeton University
Colquhoun, Alan, Princeton University
Coltman, Peter O, University of Texas at Austin
Comerio, Mary, University of California, Berkeley
Compton, Christopher, Pratt Institute
Conard, Gianne, Drexel University
Condia, Robert B, Oklahoma State University
Condon, Patrick, University of Minnesota
Conley Jr, George F, University of Tennessee-Knoxville
Conley-Harding, Leesa, Spring Garden College
Conn, W David, Virginia Polytechnic Institute & State University
Connah, Neal W, Georgia Institute of Technology
Connell, Arnall T, Georgia Institute of Technology
Connell, Bettye Rose, Georgia Institute of Technology
Connolly, David H, Spring Garden College
Connolly, M Caren, University of Wisconsin-Milwaukee
Connor, Harold W, Oklahoma State University
Connors, Joseph, Columbia University
Conrad, Terry, University of New Mexico
Constant, Caroline Brown, Harvard University
Constantine, Greg, Andrews University
Conway, Donald J, Woodbury University
Conway, Kevin, Boston Architectural Center
Coody, M Lewis, Texas A&M University
Cook, Alan R, Auburn University
Cook, J, Carleton University
Cook, Jeffrey R, Arizona State University
Cook, Patricia, Auburn University
Cooke, Gilbert, Morgan State University
Cooke, Steven A, University of South Florida
Cooledge Jr, Harold N, Clemson University
Coombs, Robert L, Texas Tech University
Cooper, Allan R, California Polytechnic State University, San Luis Obispo
Cooper, Douglas, Carnegie Mellon University

Cooper, James, Boston Architectural Center

Cooper, Mary P, California Polytechnic State University, San Luis Obispo

Cooper, Thomas E, Auburn University

Cooper-Marcus, Clare, University of California, Berkeley

Coote, James, University of Texas at Austin

Copeland, Lee G, University of Pennsylvania

Copito, Benjamin, New York Institute of Technology

Copur, Ulker, Roger Williams College

Corbelletti, Raniero, Pennsylvania State University

Corchado, Samuel, University of Puerto Rico

Cordingley, R Alan, City College of the CUNY

Cordts, Richard, Carnegie Mellon University

Corea, Mario Luis, Washington University

Corkill, Phill, University of Nebraska-Lincoln

Corley, Gregg R, Clemson University

Cormier, Leslie Humm, Boston Architectural Center

Corneil, Carmen, University of Toronto

Cornelius, Robert, Spring Garden College

Corner, Donald B, University of Oregon

Cornoldi, Adriano, University of Pennsylvania

Corsini, Richard, California State Polytechnic University, Pomona

Costanza, Christopher, Boston Architectural Center

Costello, Anthony J, Ball State University

Cottle, Mark, Boston Architectural Center

Courville, David, University of Southwestern Louisiana

Cousin, Jean, Université de Montréal

Cousins, Garnet R, Lawrence Technological University

Covo, David, McGill University

Cowan, Errol, University of Virginia

Cowen, Fred, Boston Architectural Center

Cox, James A D, University of Virginia

Cox, Maurice D, Syracuse University

Cox, Norman, Pratt Institute

Cox, Robert, University of Colorado at Denver

Coxe, Weld, University of Pennsylvania

Craig, Lynn G, Clemson University

Craig, Robert, Georgia Institute of Technology

Crain, Edward T, University of Florida

Crandall, J Sterling, University of Michigan

Crandall, Richard, State University of New York at Buffalo

Crane, David A, University of South Florida

Crane, Gerald E, University of Michigan

Cranz, Galen, University of California, Berkeley

Crawford, Greg, Boston Architectural Center

Crawford, Margaret, Southern California Institute of Architecture

Crawley, Stanley W, University of Utah

Craycroft, Robert C, Mississippi State University

Creager, Fred, University of Hawaii at Manoa

Crenshaw, Richard, Florida A&M University

Crespo, Rafael, University of Puerto Rico

Cresswell, Catherine, Miami University

Crew, Ann, Boston Architectural Center

Cripin, Kent, University of Kansas

Criss, Shannon, Boston Architectural Center

Crista, Heloise, Frank Lloyd Wright School of Architecture

Cromley, Donald, Pratt Institute

Cromley, Elizabeth, State University of New York at Buffalo

Crommett, Eugene, University of Puerto Rico

Crone, John V, University of Arkansas

Cronk, Frank, University of Idaho

Cronrath, David, Temple University

Crook, Judith, Southern California Institute of Architecture

Crosby, Michael K, Tulane University

Cross, Sydney A, Clemson University

Crotser, Charles E, California Polytechnic State University, San Luis Obispo

Crouch, Dora P, Rensselaer Polytechnic Institute

Crout, Durham, Clemson University

Crowe, Norman A, University of Notre Dame

Crowell, Gary J, University of Colorado at Denver

Crowley, Roger, Yale University

Crumlish, Brian J, University of Notre Dame

Crump, Bobbie, Louisiana State University

Crump, Ralph, Cornell University

Cruthers, Evan, University of Hawaii at Manoa

Cuff, Dana, University of Southern California

Culbertson, Margaret, University of Houston

Culley, Bruce, University of Kansas

Culot, Maurice, University of Miami

Culp, Jeffrey D, Ball State University

Culvahouse, Tim, Rhode Island School of Design

Cummings, John, University of Minnesota

Cummings, Laurence A, University of Waterloo

Cunningham, Catherine, California State Polytechnic University, Pomona

Cunningham, R George, Rice University

Cunnius, Edward, Texas A&M University

Cuoco, Daniel, Pratt Institute

Curry, Rex, Pratt Institute

Curry, Terrance, University of Detroit

Curtis, J William, University of Washington

Cutri, Anthony, New School of Architecture

Czarnecki, John, Oregon School of Design

Czarnecki, Mary, Oregon School of Design

Da Costa-Meyer, Esther, Yale University

Da Roza, Gustavo, University of Manitoba

Dadras, Aly, New York Institute of Technology

Dagenhart, Richard, Georgia Institute of Technology

Dagit, Charles E, Drexel University

Dal Co, Francesco, Yale University

Dalibard, J, Carleton University

Dallerba-Ricci, Maria G, University of Kentucky

Dalton, Deborah W, North Carolina State University

Dalton, James E, Kent State University

Daly, Dennis, Boston Architectural Center

Dalzell, John, Boston Architectural Center

Danford, G Scott, State University of New York at Buffalo

Daniel, Ronald W, Virginia Polytechnic Institute & State University

Daniel, Sheri, Mississippi State University

Daniels, Donna, University of Arkansas

Dannecker, John, Boston Architectural Center

Danzinger, Dorothy, California State Polytechnic University, Pomona

Daoust, Renee, Université de Montréal

Darbyshire, Caroline, Boston Architectural Center

Darden, Douglas, New Jersey Institute of Technology

Dart, James, Drexel University

Darvas, Robert M, University of Michigan

Dasta, Anthony J, University of Florida

Dave, Bharat, Carnegie Mellon University

David, Theoharis, Pratt Institute

Davidson, Colin H, Université de Montréal

Davidson, William W, Andrews University

Davies, Howard, McGill University

Davila, Norberto, University of Puerto Rico

Davis, A Jack, Virginia Polytechnic Institute & State University

Davis, Arthur Q, Tulane University

Davis, Clark S, Washington University

Davis, Dorothy E, Southern University

Davis, Howard, University of Oregon

Davis, Ilse, University of Oklahoma

Davis Jr, James T, Texas Tech University

Davis, Joyce, Southern University

Davis, Marleen Kay, Syracuse University

Davis, Martin A, Clemson University

Davis, Michael R, Boston Architectural Center

Davis, Mike, Southern California Institute of Architecture

Davis, Nicholas D, Auburn University

Davis, Robert, Boston Architectural Center

Davis, Sam, University of California, Berkeley

Davis, Thomas K, Syracuse University

Davison Jr, Richard R, Texas A&M University

Dawsari, Elizabeth, Frank Lloyd Wright School of Architecture

Dawson, Chris, Southern California Institute of Architecture

Dawson, Julian, University of Illinois at Chicago

Dawson, William, Carleton University

Day, Gary E, State University of New York at Buffalo

d'Azzo, Mario, Southern California Institute of Architecture

De Forest, Claude, University of Manitoba

de Monchaux, John, Massachusetts Institute of Technology

Deakin, Charles D, Tulane University

Deam, Edward, University of Illinois at Chicago

Deamer, Peggy, Columbia University

Dean, Thomas, University of Kansas

DeAngelo, Tom, University of Minnesota

Deans, John, City College of the CUNY

Debanne, J, Carleton University

Debelius, C A, University of Arkansas

deBlois, Natalie, University of Texas at Austin

Debo, Thomas N, Georgia Institute of Technology

de Bretteville, Peter, University of Southern California

DeCampoli, Giuseppe, City College of the CUNY

DeCesare, Raymond A, Roger Williams College

Decker, Greg, Spring Garden College

Decker, Roy, Temple University

DeConink, Christian, Université de Montréal

Dedijer, Milica, Southern California Institute of Architecture

Dee, Jennifer, University of Washington

DeFazio, John, Spring Garden College

DeFelice, Nicholas, New York Institute of Technology

Degelman, Larry O, Texas A&M University

Faculty Roster

Deger, Stephen C, University of Kentucky
DeGiovanni, Frank, Pratt Institute
Deguchi, Wesley, University of Hawaii at Manoa
Deines, Katrina, University of Washington
DeJean, Robert, University of Texas at Arlington
Deknatel, Charles, Boston Architectural Center
Del Cid, Donald, Tulane University
DeLacaze, Norbert, Boston Architectural Center
Delgado Jr, John L, Southern University
Delgado, Manuel, Boston Architectural Center
Della Piana, Gail, University of Utah
Delle Sante, Ricardo, California State Polytechnic University, Pomona
Dellinger, Martha, University of Arkansas
DeLong, David G, University of Pennsylvania
DelVecchio, Christine, Roger Williams College
DelVecchio, Joseph, Roger Williams College
Demele, Gary, Boston Architectural Center
Demsky, Kathy, Andrews University
Dendrinos, Dimitrios, University of Kansas
Denegre, Cecelia, Spring Garden College
Denegre, Joseph, Spring Garden College
Denel, Mustafa, California Polytechnic State University, San Luis Obispo
Denel, Serim, California Polytechnic State University, San Luis Obispo
Denham, Elam L, University of Arkansas
Denison, Dirk, Illinois Institute of Technology
Dennis, Deborah, State University of New York at Buffalo
Dennis, Michael, Cornell University, Yale University
Dent, Stephen, University of New Mexico
Denton, Lynn, Spring Garden College
deOlmos, Sylvia Muniz, University of Puerto Rico
DePopolo, Margaret, Massachusetts Institute of Technology
der Boghosian, Harry, University of Arizona
Derome, Jacques, Université de Montréal
Derrington, Patrice, Carnegie Mellon University
Desai, Ramesh, Morgan State University
DeSanto, Sam, Pratt Institute
Desch, John, New School of Architecture
DeShong, Mark, Temple University
Deslauriers, Francois, Université de Montréal
Desmond, John, Southern University
Dettloff, John, University of Arizona
Dettmer, Randy C, California Polytechnic State University, San Luis Obispo
DeVilbiss, Edward, Kansas State University
DeWolf, John C, Technical University of Nova Scotia
Dexter, Michael, Pratt Institute
Dhaemers, Margaret, University of California, Berkeley
di Thiene, Clemente, University of Virginia
di Valmarana, Mario, University of Virginia
Diamond, David, New Jersey Institute of Technology, New York Institute of Technology
Diamond, Stephen, Wentworth Institute of Technology
Diaz, Lope Max, University of Puerto Rico
Diaz, Rene F, University of Kansas
Dick, Douglas, Boston Architectural Center

Dicker, James G, University of Wisconsin-Milwaukee
Dickey, John W, Virginia Polytechnic Institute & State University
Dickson, Ellen, University of Illinois at Urbana-Champaign
Dickson, Kip A, California State Polytechnic University, Pomona
diDomenico, John, New York Institute of Technology
DiDonno, Ronald, Pratt Institute
Diehl, Christopher D, Boston Architectural Center
Diehl, Tom, University of Houston
Dietrich, Joel K, University of Oklahoma
Dilger, Curt, Temple University
Diller, Elizabeth, The Cooper Union
Dillon, Mark C, California State Polytechnic University, Pomona
Dimaio, Judy, Yale University
Dimitriu, Livio, Columbia University, New York Institute of Technology, Pratt Institute
Dimitropoulos, Harris, Georgia Institute of Technology
Dimond, Thomas W, Clemson University
Dimster, Frank, University of Southern California
Ding, G Day, California Polytechnic State University, San Luis Obispo
Dinham, Sarah, University of Arizona
DiPasquale, Raymond, Syracuse University
Dipner, Wayne, Ohio State University
DiProperzio, Anthony, New York Institute of Technology
DiSanto, Anthony, New York Institute of Technology
Disch, Peter, Virginia Polytechnic Institute & State University
Dittmar, Gunter, University of Minnesota
Dixon, Russell W, Lawrence Technological University
Dixon, Sarah S, Wentworth Institute of Technology
Dluhosch, Eric, Massachusetts Institute of Technology
Doble-Smith, Ellen, University of Kentucky
Dodds, George, Temple University
Dodge, Anneliese, Frank Lloyd Wright School of Architecture
Dodge, David Elgin, Frank Lloyd Wright School of Architecture
Dodge Jr, Richard L, University of Texas at Austin
Doebele, William A, Harvard University
Doehler, Joan, Technical University of Nova Scotia
Doerer, Richard, Yale University
Doerstling, Steffen R, Auburn University
Doktor, Christopher T, Boston Architectural Center
Dole, Philip, University of Oregon
Dolkart, Andrew, Columbia University
Doll, Larry A, University of Texas at Austin
Dombek, George, Florida A&M University
Domer, Dennis E, University of Kansas
Domeyko, Fernando, Massachusetts Institute of Technology
Dominquez, Karen, Pennsylvania State University
Donnelly, Paul, Roger Williams College
Donnette, James, University of Washington

Dorian-Becnel, Veronica, University of Houston
Dorman, Kendall, Arizona State University
Dorsey-Jones, Margaret, Howard University
Doruk, Birsen, Clemson University
Doruk, Teoman K, Clemson University
Dotson, A Bruce, University of Virginia
Dougald, Donald E, University of Virginia
Doughty, Frank L, University of Arkansas
Douglas, William, University of Kansas
Dowd, Thomas, Temple University
Dowling Elizabeth, Georgia Institute of Technology
Downey, Juan, Pratt Institute
Downing, Frances, University of Colorado at Denver
Doxtater, Dennis, University of Arizona
Doyle, Deborah, University of Illinois at Chicago
Doz, Daniel, Ball State University
Dozier, Richard, Tuskegee University
Dragos, Steve, Arizona State University
Dreyer, Glen, Kent State University
Dripps III, Robert D, Princeton University, University of Virginia
Driskill, David A, Texas Tech University
Drummond, Derek, McGill University
Drummond, R Wayne, Texas Tech University
Dry, Carolyn, University of Illinois at Urbana-Champaign
Du Puy, Karl P, University of Maryland
Dube, Claude, Laval University
Dubicanac, Tom, Carleton University
Dubovsky, Anthony, University of California, Berkeley
Duchesneau, Guy, Laval University
Duda, Turan, Yale University
Dudnik, Elliott, University of Illinois at Chicago
Dueber, Allen, New School of Architecture
Duerk, Donna, California Polytechnic State University, San Luis Obispo
Dugal, Donald, University of Hawaii at Manoa
Dugan, Paula Vaune, Boston Architectural Center
Dugas, David M, Virginia Polytechnic Institute & State University
Dugger, John, Boston Architectural Center
Duke, Buford, University of Texas at Austin
Dunay, Donna W, Virginia Polytechnic Institute & State University
Dunay, Robert, Virginia Polytechnic Institute & State University
Duncan, Chester, University of Texas at Arlington
Duncan, Lane M, Georgia Institute of Technology
Duncan, Robert, University of Nebraska-Lincoln
Dundon, John, Drexel University
Dunham-Jones, Ellen, University of Virginia
Dunikowski, Marek, University of Tennessee-Knoxville
Dunnigan, John, Rhode Island School of Design
Dunwiddie, Foster, University of Minnesota
Durack, Ruth, Temple University
Durfee, Dale, Georgia Institute of Technology
Dutt, Om, University of Waterloo
Dutton, Thomas A, Miami University
Dvorak, Robert, University of Arizona

Dyck, Robert G, Virginia Polytechnic Institute & State University
Dymond, Michael, Texas Tech University
Dynerman, Alan, University of Maryland
Dzidzienyo, Victor, Howard University
Eardley, Anthony, University of Toronto
Easter Jr, James G, University of Houston
Easterling, Keller, Pratt Institute
Eastman, Charles, University of California, Los Angeles
Eaton, Ann, Lawrence Technological University
Ebeltoft, Richard, University of Arizona
Eckstut, Stan, Columbia University
Edwards, Arthur, Pratt Institute
Edwards, Charles P, University of Virginia
Edwards, Gordon, McGill University
Edwards, Patricia A, Virginia Polytechnic Institute & State University
Eflin, Robert D, Clemson University
Egan, M David, Clemson University, University of North Carolina at Charlotte
Egbuchulam, Lambert, Pratt Institute
Egger, D Eugene, Virginia Polytechnic Institute & State University
Eggink, Harry A, Ball State University
Ehresmann, Donald, University of Illinois at Chicago
Eidson, Patricia L, Oklahoma State University
Eijadi, David, Arizona State University
Eisenman, Peter D, The Cooper Union, University of Illinois at Chicago, Ohio State University
Ekroth, David C, Texas A&M University
El-Zoghby, Gamal, Pratt Institute
ElAraby, Kadri, New York Institute of Technology
Elam, Merrill, Georgia Institute of Technology
Elder, Rosalyn, Boston Architectural Center
Eliason, Edward, Pratt Institute
Elkhoury, Rodolphe, Louisiana State University
Elkins, Leslie, University of Houston
Eller, Kenneth, Arizona State University
Ellias, Juanita, New Jersey Institute of Technology
Elliott, Cecil D, North Dakota State University
Elliott, Michael, Georgia Institute of Technology
Ellis, Don, University of Manitoba
Ellis, John, Wentworth Institute of Technology
Ellis Jr, Russell, University of California, Berkeley
Ellis, William, City College of the CUNY
Ellner, Anthony, Arizona State University
Ellwood, Craig, California State Polytechnic University, Pomona
Elmitt, Michael W, University of Waterloo
Elmore, James, Arizona State University
Elnaggar, Ahmed, Howard University
Elnimieri, Majoub, Illinois Institute of Technology
Elsabbagh, Mohamed E, Spring Garden College
Elwell, David, New Jersey Institute of Technology
Emery, Ashley, University of Washington
Emery, E Gene, University of Oklahoma
Emodi, Thomas, Technical University of Nova Scotia
Enderling, Wayne W, Washington University

Eng, William, University of Illinois at Urbana-Champaign
Engel, Irving, Washington University
England, Robert D, Clemson University
Englebrecht, Mark C, Iowa State University
Englehardt, Helen, Pratt Institute
English, Mark, Carnegie Mellon University
English, Michael, University of South Florida
Ennis, Robert B, Drexel University
Eppell, Frank J, Technical University of Nova Scotia
Erdener, Eren, University of Oklahoma
Erdman, Fred, University of Oklahoma
Erginsav, Ozdemir, University of Manitoba
Erhardt, Peter, Andrews University
Eribes, Richard, Arizona State University
Erlitz, Benjamin, Georgia Institute of Technology
Ernest, Michael, University of British Columbia
Ernst, F Gene, Kansas State University
Ernst, Joseph, State University of New York at Buffalo
Ertl, Ted, University of Nebraska-Lincoln
Erwin, William H, University of Illinois at Urbana-Champaign
Eskew, R Allen, Tulane University
Eslami, Manouchehr, New Jersey Institute of Technology
Esterson, Jack, Pratt Institute
Etherington, Bruce, University of Hawaii at Manoa
Etlin, Richard, University of Maryland
Eubanks, Ed, University of Houston
Eubanks, Francis M, Clemson University
Evans, Benjamin H, Virginia Polytechnic Institute & State University
Evans, Deane, Columbia University
Evans, Roseann B, Roger Williams College
Evenson, Norma, University of California, Berkeley
Everett, J Michael, Rhode Island School of Design
Ewald, Ted, Lawrence Technological University
Fabris, Joseph, Frank Lloyd Wright School of Architecture
Fader, Lester, University of Michigan
Fairey, John G, Texas A&M University
Fakelmann, Robert, Louisiana Tech University
Falck, Lindsay, University of Pennsylvania
Falk, Edward L, Clemson University
Falkner, Donald C, North Dakota State University
Falta, P Ladia, Université de Montréal
Fanella, David, University of Illinois at Chicago
Fang, Pen, Roger Williams College
Fantauzzi, Frank, University of Cincinnati, University of Detroit
Faoro, Daniel, Kansas State University
Fardjadi, Homa, University of Pennsylvania
Farley, Richard, University of Pennsylvania
Fash, William L, Georgia Institute of Technology
Faust, Robert L, Auburn University
Favro, Diane, University of California, Los Angeles
Fazio, Michael W, Mississippi State University
Fearon, Robert, Lawrence Technological University
Featherstone, Kenneth A, University of Notre Dame

Federman, Peter, Pratt Institute
Fehlig, Teresa A, Oklahoma State University
Feldman, Roberta, University of Illinois at Chicago
Feldt, Allan G, University of Michigan
Fellows, Jay F, The Cooper Union
Felty, Bill W, Texas Tech University
Fendley, Betty J, Auburn University
Fera, Cesare, Clemson University
Ferber, Miklos, Lawrence Technological University
Feresten, Timothy H, Yale University
Ferguson, Peter, University of Waterloo
Fernau, Richard, University of California, Berkeley
Ferrari, Lucy, Virginia Polytechnic Institute & State University
Ferrari, Olivio C, Virginia Polytechnic Institute & State University
Ferre, Carlos, Boston Architectural Center
Ferrero, Harvey, Lawrence Technological University
Ferrier, Richard B, University of Texas at Arlington
Field, Katherine A, Roger Williams College
Fifield, Michael E, Arizona State University
Fillipp, Stephen L, Texas Tech University
Filson, Ronald C, Tulane University
Findlay, Richard, University of Kansas
Findlay, Robert A, Iowa State University
Findley, Lisa, Arizona State University
Fink, Charles, Rhode Island School of Design
Finn, Scott J, Auburn University
Finnie, John, New York Institute of Technology
Finrow, Gunilla, University of Oregon
Finrow, Jerry, University of Oregon
Fiorenzoli, Giuliano, Pratt Institute
Fischer, M Marie, University of Nebraska-Lincoln
Fischer, Scott E, Auburn University
Fish, Frank, Pratt Institute
Fisher, Larry, University of Idaho, Washington State University
Fisher, Robert A, Ball State University
Fitt, David X, Spring Garden College
Fitzgerald, Ed, University of New Mexico
Fitzpatrick, Thomas R, University of Michigan
Flanders, John, Carleton University
Fleischer, Roland, Pennsylvania State University
Fleites, Maria, University of Miami
Flemming, Ulrich, Carnegie Mellon University
Fleshman, Fredric, University of Houston
Flint, Daniel, Spring Garden College
Flint, Franklin S, University of Arizona
Florian, Paul, University of Illinois at Chicago
Fluck, Timothy A, Virginia Polytechnic Institute & State University
Flynn, Michael, Pratt Institute
Foerster, Bernd, Kansas State University
Fogle, David, University of Maryland
Folkerts, Heiko, New York Institute of Technology
Folonis, Michael W, California State Polytechnic University, Pomona, University of Southern California
Fong, Steven T, University of Toronto
Fonseca, Rory, University of Manitoba
Fontein, Lucie, McGill University
Foote, Jonathan, Montana State University

Faculty Roster

Forbes, Geraldine, Woodbury University
Forbes, Malcolm, Roger Williams College
Ford, Edward R, University of Virginia
Ford, Robert M, Mississippi State University
Ford, Wally B, Rice University
Forjaz, Jose, University of Pennsylvania
Forman, Richard T, Harvard University
Forrester, R Alan, University of Illinois at Urbana-Champaign
Forseth, Kevin, University of Wisconsin-Milwaukee
Forster, Peter, University of Manitoba
Fortey, Joseph W, University of Tennessee-Knoxville
Foster, Elfriede, University of Texas at Arlington
Foster, Maelee T, University of Florida
Fotiadi, Eric, New School of Architecture
Foulkes, Timothy J, Roger Williams College
Fowler, Herbert K, University of Arkansas
Fox, C William, Temple University
Fraker, Harrison, University of Minnesota
Frampton, Kenneth, Columbia University
Franceschi, Carl, Boston Architectural Center
Franck, Karen, New Jersey Institute of Technology
Frank, Ilene, University of South Florida
Frank, Samuel B, Rhode Island School of Design
Frascari, Marco, Georgia Institute of Technology
Frascari, Marco, University of Pennsylvania
Fraser, Iain A, Washington University
Fraser, Robert A, Washington University
Freelon, Phil, North Carolina State University
French, Patricia, University of British Columbia
French, Robert C, University of Tennessee-Knoxville
Frenchman, Dennis, Massachusetts Institute of Technology
Freschi, Bruno, State University of New York at Buffalo
Frew, Robert, Yale University
Frey, Douglas A, Iowa State University
Friedberg, M Paul, City College of the CUNY
Friedman, Abraham, McGill University
Friedman, David, Massachusetts Institute of Technology
Friedman, Jonathan, New York Institute of Technology
Friedman, Laurie, Boston Architectural Center
Friedman, Stephen, Pratt Institute
Frisone, Caterina, Syracuse University
Fritschen, Leo, University of Washington
Fritzinger, Stephen, Yale University
Froehlich, Kurt P, University of Illinois at Urbana-Champaign
Frost, Archibald, Technical University of Nova Scotia
Frost, Wil, University of Hawaii at Manoa
Fuermann, Bryan, University of Illinois at Chicago
Fugitt, W Kim, University of Arkansas
Fuksa, Gerard M, Boston Architectural Center
Fung, Hsin-Ming, California State Polytechnic University, Pomona
Furman, Stuart, New York Institute of Technology
Gaboury, Etienne, University of Manitoba
Gabriel, J Francois, Syracuse University
Gabrielli, Julie, Spring Garden College

Gadau, Lloyd, University of Illinois at Chicago
Gaines, Merrill C, California Polytechnic State University, San Luis Obispo
Gainfort, James R, Pratt Institute
Gainforth, James, Columbia University
Gaitanakis, John A, University of British Columbia
Galati, Craig S, University of Nevada, Las Vegas
Galfetti, Aurelio, Southern California Institute of Architecture
Gallagher, Dennis, Pratt Institute
Gallegos, Phillip, University of Colorado at Denver
Gallis, Michael A, University of North Carolina at Charlotte
Galloway, Thomas D, Iowa State University
Gamble, Jesse, Tuskegee University
Gamble, Robert A, University of Texas at Arlington
Gami, Bharat, New Jersey Institute of Technology
Gandelsonas, Mario, University of Illinois at Chicago
Gang, Jeanne K, Boston Architectural Center
Gans, Deborah, Pratt Institute
Gans-Piazza, Karen, University of Illinois at Urbana-Champaign
Garcia, Pilar, Boston Architectural Center
Gardner, Mark, University of Kansas
Gargus, Jacqueline, Ohio State University
Garland, Catherine A, California State Polytechnic University, Pomona
Garlicki, Marek A, Boston Architectural Center
Garlock, George, University of Nevada, Las Vegas
Garner, Allen, University of Kansas
Garner, Anthony, Rensselaer Polytechnic Institute
Garner, John S, University of Illinois at Urbana-Champaign
Garnham, Harry L, University of Colorado at Denver
Garofalo, Douglas, University of Illinois at Chicago
Garriques, Suzanne, Morgan State University
Garrison, James, Columbia University
Garrison, Michael, University of Texas at Austin
Garrison, William, City College of the Columbia UnivNY
Garrott, Jay G, Drury College
Gartner, Howard S, University of Houston
Gati, William, New York Institute of Technology
Gatschet, Steven C, Drexel University
Gattuso, John, Howard University
Gatzke, Donald F, Tulane University
Gauthier, Maurice, Laval University
Gawronik, Paul, Washington University
Gebert, Gordon, City College of the CUNY
Geddes, Robert, Princeton University
Gehner, Martin D, Yale University
Gehry, Frank O, Yale University
Geiger, Walter, Catholic University of America
Gelabert-Navia, Ana, University of Miami
Gelabert-Navia, Jose A, University of Miami
Gelick, Michael, University of Illinois at Chicago
Genasci, Donald, University of Oregon
Genik, Christopher, California State

Polytechnic University, Pomona, University of Southern California
Gerard, Russ, Boston Architectural Center
Gereke, Kent, University of Manitoba
Gersovitz, Julia, McGill University, Université de Montréal
Gerstner, Robert, University of Illinois at Chicago
Gesser, Herman, University of Southwestern Louisiana
Gesund, Hans, University of Kentucky
Getz, Pamela, Boston Architectural Center
Ghirardo, Diane, University of Southern California
Giaccardo, Marc, Catholic University of America
Giachino, James J, Lawrence Technological University
Gianni, J Benjamin, Ohio State University
Gianola, Rafael, Southern California Institute of Architecture
Gianopulos, Nicholas, University of Pennsylvania
Giardina, Michael, Boston Architectural Center
Gibbons, Dennis, New Jersey Institute of Technology
Gibbs, Dale, University of Nebraska-Lincoln
Giebner, Robert C, University of Arizona
Giese, David F, University of Idaho
Gilbert, Joan A, Yale University
Gilbert-Rolfe, Jeremy, Yale University
Gilfillen, Statler, Boston Architectural Center
Gilje, John, University of Hawaii at Manoa
Gill, Grattan, Roger Williams College
Gilland, Wilmot G, University of Oregon
Gillham, Jonathan, University of Detroit
Gillig, Robert, University of Kentucky
Gillis, Donna D, University of South Florida
Gilmour, James, Boston Architectural Center
Gilson, Channing, California State Polytechnic University, Pomona
Gintole, George, University of Texas at Arlington
Giorgini, Vittorio, Pratt Institute
Giral, Angela, Columbia University
Gisolfi, Peter, City College of the CUNY
Gittings, Kirk, University of New Mexico
Giurgola, Romaldo, Columbia University
Giusiana, David, State University of New York at Buffalo
Givoni, Baruch, University of California, Los Angeles
Glanville, John, University of Manitoba
Glasmeier, Amy, University of Texas at Austin
Glasser, David, University of South Florida
Glasser, David, University of Wisconsin-Milwaukee
Glassman, Terry, Southern California Institute of Architecture
Glaze, Sue, Auburn University
Glennie, William L, Rensselaer Polytechnic Institute
Glenny, Edmund J, Louisiana State University
Gleye, Paul, Montana State University
Glickman, Donald H, State University of New York at Buffalo
Glicksman, Leon, Massachusetts Institute of Technology
Glushakow, Mildred, Spring Garden College
Goddard, Roger R, University of Arkansas
Goehner, Werner, Cornell University

Goetzman, Bruce, University of Cincinnati
Goins, Robert, University of Oklahoma
Golany, Gideon, Pennsylvania State University
Goldberg, Georgia, New Jersey Institute of
Technology
Goldberger, Paul J, Yale University
Goldblatt, Steve, University of Washington
Goldfarb, Lloyd, New York Institute of
Technology
Goldfine, Alex, Pratt Institute
Goldin, Saul, Southern California Institute of
Architecture
Goldman, Glenn, New Jersey Institute of
Technology
Goldsmith, Myron, Illinois Institute of
Technology
Goldsmith, Paul H, Lawrence Technological
University
Goldstein, Peter, Boston Architectural Center
Gomes, Ronald J, University of Nevada, Las
Vegas
Gomez-Ibanez, Jose, Harvard University
Gonzalez, Dario, University of Puerto Rico
Gonzalez, Don J, Lawrence Technological
University
Gonzalez, Jose, University of Puerto Rico
Goodale, Robin, Spring Garden College
Goode, Terrance, University of Oregon
Goodill, Robert, Syracuse University
Goodman, Michael Louis, Pratt Institute
Goodman, Roland, Pratt Institute
Goodson, James, State University of New
York at Buffalo
Goodstein, Ethel S, University of
Southwestern Louisiana
Goodwin, Bruce, Tulane University
Goodwin Sr, Robert T, Tuskegee University
Gordan, Judy O'Buck, New York Institute of
Technology
Gordon, Charles, Carleton University
Gordon, Ezra, University of Illinois at Chicago
Gordon, Raymond, Pratt Institute
Gore, Nils, Boston Architectural Center
Gorlin, Alexander, Yale University
Gorski, Gilbert, Illinois Institute of Technology
Goss, Dean, New York Institute of Technology
Goss, Peter, University of Utah
Goth, David, Ohio State University
Gottfried, Herbert W, Iowa State University
Gourd, Yolaine, Université de Montréal
Gourley, Ronald, University of Arizona
Goyert Jr, Philip R, University of Houston
Grabow, Stephen, University of Kansas
Graeff, Robert F, Virginia Polytechnic Institute
& State University
Graf, Douglas, Ohio State University
Graham, Channell, Washington State
University
Graham, David, University of Minnesota
Graham, Priscilla, Kent State University
Graham, Roy E, Texas A&M University
Graham, Sarah, University of Southern
California
Gralla, Stan W, University of Oklahoma
Gran, Warren, Pratt Institute
Grant, Bradford, University of Cincinnati
Grant, Donald P, California Polytechnic State
University, San Luis Obispo
Grausman, Philip, Yale University
Gravelle, Sarah, University of Detroit
Graves Jr, Charles, Kent State University

Graves, Charles P, University of Kentucky
Graves, Dean, University of Kansas
Graves, Ginny, University of Kansas
Graves, Michael, Princeton University
Graves, Rufus L, California Polytechnic State
University, San Luis Obispo
Gray, Christopher J, Syracuse University
Gray, Jonathan, Carnegie Mellon University
Graybrook, Michael, Carnegie Mellon
University
Grebner, Dennis, University of Minnesota
Green, Ellery C, University of Arizona
Green, O Michael, University of Arkansas
Greenan, Gary, University of Miami
Greenberg, Allan, University of Illinois at
Chicago
Greenberg, Donald, Cornell University
Greenberg, Jon, Lawrence Technological
University
Greenberg, Michael, Pratt Institute
Greenberg, Roberta, Pratt Institute
Greenberger, Alan J, Drexel University
Greene, Walter, Spring Garden College
Greenfield, Sanford R, New Jersey Institute of
Technology
Greenspan, David, University of Illinois at
Chicago
Greenstreet, Robert C, University of
Wisconsin-Milwaukee
Greer, John O, Texas A&M University
Greimel, Karl H, Lawrence Technological
University
Gresla, Eric, Boston Architectural Center
Grey, Keith H, Florida A&M University
Gribou, Julius M, Texas A&M University
Grieger, Frederick, University of
Tennessee-Knoxville
Griffin, David, University of Kansas
Griffin, James B, Drury College
Griffin, Percy, New York Institute of
Technology
Griffin, Robert E, University of Houston
Griffiths, N, Carleton University
Griggs, Charles, University of California, Los
Angeles
Griggs, James K, Carnegie Mellon University
Grimshaw, Rosemary, Massachusetts Institute
of Technology
Groat, Linda N, University of Michigan
Grobson, Gary, Lawrence Technological
University
Groenendaal, Denson, Pennsylvania State
University
Groisser, Leon, Massachusetts Institute of
Technology
Grosse, Larry W, Texas A&M University
Grossman, Richard, Southern California
Institute of Architecture
Groth, Paul, University of California, Berkeley
Groves, J Russell, University of Kentucky
Grubbs, Christopher, Washington University
Gruft, Andrew, University of British Columbia
Grulke, Bruce, Mississippi State University
Grunsky, Michael, Technical University of
Nova Scotia
Grylls, John K, Lawrence Technological
University
Guarino, Margaret, Pratt Institute
Guda, Neil, Kent State University
Guenter, Robert, University of
Nebraska-Lincoln

Guerra, Christopher, Pratt Institute
Guertin, Pierre, Laval University
Guggenheimer, Tobias, Pratt Institute
Guice, Les, Louisiana Tech University
Guida, Harold S, California State Polytechnic
University, Pomona
Guidry, Lynn, University of Southwestern
Louisiana
Guimond, Peter, Rhode Island School of
Design
Guise, David, City College of the CUNY
Gulick, Bob, Oregon School of Design
Gumz, Gary, University of North Carolina at
Charlotte
Gunasekara, Valentine, Wentworth Institute of
Technology
Gunderson, Martin G, University of Florida
Gureckas, Vytenis, Catholic University of
America
Gusevich, Miriam, University of
Wisconsin-Milwaukee
Gussow, Sue F, The Cooper Union
Gutenschwager, Gerald, Washington
University
Gutman, Marta, Columbia University
Gutman, Robert, University of Pennsylvania,
Princeton University
Guy, Joe, University of Texas at Arlington
Gwathmey, Charles, University of North
Carolina at Charlotte
Gwilliam, Tony, Southern California Institute
of Architecture
Gwin, William R, Auburn University
Haase, Ronald W, University of Florida
Habiger, Bob, University of New Mexico
Habraken, N John, Massachusetts Institute of
Technology
Hacker, Arthur E, California State Polytechnic
University, Pomona
Hacker, Thom, Oregon School of Design
Hackett, James E, Virginia Polytechnic
Institute & State University
Hackler, John B, University of Illinois at
Urbana-Champaign
Haden, Joel M, University of
Tennessee-Knoxville
Hadley, Barbara, Catholic University of
America
Haglund, Bruce, University of Idaho
Hahn, Wilhelm, University of Houston
Haider, Jawaid, Pennsylvania State
University
Haider, S G, Carleton University
Haines, Frank, University of Hawaii at Manoa
Haire, William H, Oklahoma State University
Halamar, Paul, Drexel University
Halasz, Imre, Massachusetts Institute of
Technology
Haldenby, Eric, University of Waterloo
Hall, Dennis, University of North Carolina at
Charlotte
Hall III, James, Hampton University
Hall, Jeffrey L, Ball State University
Hall, Richard, Lawrence Technological
University
Hall, Roy, Cornell University
Hall, William, Boston Architectural Center
Hallet, Stanley I, Catholic University of
America
Halpern, Ken, Pratt Institute
Hamblett, Augustus C, Texas A&M University

Faculty Roster

Hamdi, Nabeel, Massachusetts Institute of Technology
Hamilton, Todd, University of Texas at Arlington
Hamme, David C, Drexel University
Hammer, Henry, California Polytechnic State University, San Luis Obispo
Hammond, Bret, Florida A&M University
Hammond, Gerald S, Miami University
Hampton, Warren, University of Arizona
Han, Thomas, Temple University
Hancock, John E, University of Cincinnati
Handlin, David, University of Illinois at Chicago
Hanganu, Dan, McGill University
Hanlon, Don, University of Wisconsin-Milwaukee
Hanna, Dixon B, Virginia Polytechnic Institute & State University
Hannigan, Jeffrey, McGill University
Hanser, David A, Oklahoma State University
Hanson, Pat, University of Waterloo
Haque, Reaz, Wentworth Institute of Technology
Hara, John, University of Hawaii at Manoa
Harden, Cindy, Pratt Institute
Hardin, Mary, Arizona State University
Hardman, Anna M. Virginia Polytechnic Institute & State University
Hardwick, Phillip D, Mississippi State University
Hardy, Deirdre J, University of South Florida
Harfmann, Anton, State University of New York at Buffalo
Hargarve, Terry C, California Polytechnic State University, San Luis Obispo
Hariri, Gisue, Columbia University
Harker, Charles, Kent State University
Harkins, Ellen, Harvard University
Harland, Phyllis, Ball State University
Harmon, Frank, North Carolina State University
Harnish, Benjamin, University of Manitoba
Harp, Cleveland, New Jersey Institute of Technology
Harper, Jason, Rensselaer Polytechnic Institute
Harper, Robert, Rhode Island School of Design
Harper, W Weston, Texas A&M University
Harries, Karsten, Yale University
Harrigan, John E, California Polytechnic State University, San Luis Obispo
Harrington, J Brooke, Drexel University, Temple University
Harrington, Charles, Louisiana Tech University
Harris, Bill, University of New Mexico
Harris, Cyril, Columbia University
Harris, Cyril, University of California, Los Angeles
Harris Jr, Edwin F, North Carolina State University
Harris, Floyd T, University of Nevada, Las Vegas
Harris, Harwell H, North Carolina State University
Harris, James R, Washington University
Harris, Kevin, Louisiana State University
Harris, Robert S, University of Southern California
Harris, Steven, Yale University

Harris, Vascar G, Tuskegee University
Harris, Walter D, Yale University
Harris, William M, University of Virginia
Harrison, Marc, Rhode Island School of Design
Harrison, Robert V M, Mississippi State University
Harrison, Sally, Temple University
Harritos, Harry C, Clemson University
Hart, Janice, Carnegie Mellon University
Hartkopf, Volker, Carnegie Mellon University
Hartmere, Anne, University of California, Los Angeles
Hartnett, Jeffrey, University of Arkansas
Hartoonian, Gevork, Spring Garden College
Hartray Jr, John, Illinois Institute of Technology, University of Illinois at Chicago
Harvey, Christine, Boston Architectural Center
Harvey, Timothy A, Ohio State University
Hascup, George, Cornell University
Hashimoto, Gordon, University of Utah
Hasslein, George J, California Polytechnic State University, San Luis Obispo
Hata, Hiroaki, State University of New York at Buffalo
Hatami, Marvin, University of Colorado at Denver
Hatch, C Richard, New Jersey Institute of Technology
Hatem, David, Boston Architectural Center
Hatlen, Vincen W, North Dakota State University
Haugsoen, Knut, University of Manitoba
Haviland, David S, Rensselaer Polytechnic Institute
Hawk, David L, New Jersey Institute of Technology
Hawkins, Neil, University of Washington
Haycock, Gary, Kansas State University
Hayes, Tim, Louisiana Tech University
Haynes, Timothy, Boston Architectural Center
Hays, K Michael, Harvard University
Haywood, Emmet L, University of Colorado at Denver
Hazra, Deleep, Boston Architectural Center, Wentworth Institute of Technology
Hazzard, Bruce, University of Colorado at Denver
Heard Jr, Malcolm W, Tulane University
Heath, Kingston, University of North Carolina at Charlotte
Heatly, Bob, Oklahoma State University
Heck, Marlene E, Texas A&M University
Hector, Denis, Columbia University, University of Pennsylvania
Heemstra, Howard C, Iowa State University
Heerwagen, Dean, University of Washington
Heggans, Thomas, Howard University
Heil, Donald R, Washington State University
Heinrich, John, Illinois Institute of Technology
Hejduk, John Q, The Cooper Union
Helfman, Sheldon S, Washington University
Helmle, Paul N, California State Polytechnic University, Pomona
Helms, Ronald N, University of Kansas
Helwig, Bruce C D, University of Nebraska-Lincoln
Hemphill, Ryland, Mississippi State University
Henckle, David, University of New Mexico
Henderson, Anne Hoover, University of Oklahoma

Henderson, Arn, University of Oklahoma
Henderson, Richard, The Cooper Union
Henderson, Susan, New Jersey Institute of Technology, Syracuse University
Henderson, Thomas W, Mississippi State University
Henmi, Rodney, Washington University
Hennecke, Jurgen, University of Arizona
Hennessey, Leslie G, University of Kentucky
Henry, Jay C, University of Texas at Arlington
Henry, Peter, Technical University of Nova Scotia
Henry, Robert, New Jersey Institute of Technology
Henry, Rodman, Wentworth Institute of Technology
Hensel, S, Carleton University
Herbert, Daniel, University of Oregon
Herdeg, Klaus, Columbia University
Herman, John C, Yale University
Herman, Maurice, California State Polytechnic University, Pomona
Hermansen, David R, Ball State University
Hermanson, Robert D, University of Utah
Hermanuz, Ghislaine, City College of the CUNY
Hernandez, Jorge, University of Miami
Herren, Daniel, Southern California Institute of Architecture
Hershberger, Robert G, University of Arizona
Herz, Manuel, University of Tennessee-Knoxville
Hess, Alan, Southern California Institute of Architecture
Hess, Gary, New York Institute of Technology
Hess, Ronald, Montana State University
Heuber, Edy, Southern California Institute of Architecture
Heydecker, Richard, Wentworth Institute of Technology
Heyer, Paul, Pratt Institute
Hibbs, Jay, Columbia University
Hickey, Dave, Southern California Institute of Architecture
Hicks, William S, Howard University
Hickson, Ernest, Lawrence Technological University
Higgins, John O, Drexel University
Highlands, Delbert, Carnegie Mellon University
Hight, Charles C, University of North Carolina at Charlotte
Hildebrand, Grant, University of Washington
Hilker, Christine, University of Arkansas
Hill, Charles C, Drury College
Hill, David R, University of Colorado at Denver
Hill, Gerald, Spring Garden College
Hill, Glenn E, Texas Tech University
Hill, Jennifer, Technical University of Nova Scotia
Hill, John deKoven, Frank Lloyd Wright School of Architecture
Hill, John W, University of Maryland
Hill, Orry W, University of Florida
Hill, Patrick P, California Polytechnic State University, San Luis Obispo
Hill, Richard, University of North Carolina at Charlotte
Hill, Rodney C, Texas A&M University
Hill, Steven, University of Oklahoma
Hill, Warren, University of Washington

Hilliard, Edmund N, University of Oklahoma
Hillier-Woodfin, Karen E, Texas A&M University
Himber, Adam, Boston Architectural Center
Hinders, Kevin, Washington University
Hines, Alan, University of Southwestern Louisiana
Hines, Thomas, University of California, Los Angeles
Hing, Allan M, Auburn University
Hinkley, Robert, University of Southwestern Louisiana
Hinrichs, Craig, Miami University
Hinson, Mary Alice Dixon, University of Minnesota
Hirsch, Henry, Southern California Institute of Architecture
Hirsch, Jeff, Boston Architectural Center
Hirschman, Ira, Pratt Institute
Hirshen, Sanford, University of California, Berkeley
Hirshorn, Paul M, Drexel University
Hirsty, Jacalyn, Wentworth Institute of Technology
Hittle, Connie, Ball State University
Hoag, John D, University of Colorado at Denver
Hoag, Richard, Kansas State University
Hoagland, Kenneth L, University of Colorado at Denver
Hochstim, Jan, University of Miami
Hodgden, Lee, Cornell University
Hodgdon, Rosaria, University of Oregon
Hodge, Daniel, University of Kentucky
Hodge, George M, University of Oregon
Hodgell, Murlin R, University of Oklahoma
Hodgetts, Craig, University of Pennsylvania, Southern California Institute of Architecture
Hodgson, James S, Harvard University
Hodne, Thomas H, University of Manitoba
Hodnett Jr, Lewis D, University of Houston
Hoffman, D, Carleton University
Hoffman Jr, Edward, University of Illinois at Chicago
Hofstein, Pascal, New York Institute of Technology
Hogan, James, Boston Architectural Center
Hogan, Robert, Clemson University
Hoistad, Mark, University of Houston
Holden, Jane, Boston Architectural Center
Holder, Thomas J, University of Nevada, Las Vegas
Holl, Steven, Columbia University
Holland, Major L, Tuskegee University
Hollander, Michael, Pratt Institute
Hollein, Hans, Ohio State University
Holleman, Robert, University of Arizona
Holliday, Judith, Cornell University
Holm, Lorens, Washington University
Holmes, John, Roger Williams College
Holmes, Michael, Tuskegee University
Holsaple, Robert D, University of Tennessee-Knoxville
Holt, Jaan, Virginia Polytechnic Institute & State University
Holt, Rengin T, Virginia Polytechnic Institute & State University
Holz, David, Louisiana Tech University
Homolac, Andrea, Boston Architectural Center
Honegger, H, Carleton University
Honikman, Basil, University of Miami
Hoover, Tony, Boston Architectural Center

Hopkins, Arlene, Woodbury University
Hopkins, John K, Andrews University
Horii, Howard, Pratt Institute
Horn, Gerald, Illinois Institute of Technology
Hornbostel, Caleb, Temple University
Horowitz, Michael, Yale University
Horsley, W Graham, Texas A&M University
Horvath, Patricia, Boston Architectural Center
Horwitz, Jamie L, Iowa State University
Householder, Jerry, Virginia Polytechnic Institute & State University
Houston, Frederick, State University of New York at Buffalo
Hovey, David C, Illinois Institute of Technology
Howard, Coy, Southern California Institute of Architecture
Howard, Jeanne B, Virginia Polytechnic Institute & State University
Howard, J Murray, University of Virginia
Howard, Thomas C, North Carolina State University
Howe, Joseph G, University of Virginia
Howell, Sandra, Massachusetts Institute of Technology
Howie, James, Pratt Institute
Hsich, May Beth, Arizona State University
Huang, Yunsheng, University of Virginia
Hubbard, Nancy, University of Wisconsin-Milwaukee
Hubbard, William, Massachusetts Institute of Technology
Hubbell, Kent L, University of Michigan
Hubbs, Michael, Auburn University
Hubka, Thomas, University of Wisconsin-Milwaukee
Hudson, Mark R, Clemson University
Hueber, Eduard, Rensselaer Polytechnic Institute
Huff, Deborah, New York Institute of Technology
Huff, Raymond, Clemson University
Huff, William, State University of New York at Buffalo
Huffman, Craig D, Florida A&M University
Hughes, David, Kent State University
Hughes, Norman, Lawrence Technological University
Hughes II, Rufus R, Georgia Institute of Technology
Hughey, Marvin, Tuskegee University
Hughs, Hank, Boston Architectural Center
Huja, Satyendra, University of Virginia
Hull, Michael, Carnegie Mellon University
Hulvershorn, John K, University of Nebraska-Lincoln
Hummel, Roland L, Rensselaer Polytechnic Institute
Hunnibell, Kenneth, Rhode Island School of Design
Hunsicker, Donald, Boston Architectural Center
Hunt, Brian, University of Waterloo
Hunt, Gregory K, Virginia Polytechnic Institute & State University
Hunt, Robert, Arizona State University
Hunter, Bobby R, University of Oklahoma
Hunter, Robert H, Clemson University
Hunziker, Rudy, Virginia Polytechnic Institute & State University

Hurley, Kent C, Technical University of Nova Scotia
Hurst, Elsie, Boston Architectural Center
Hurst, Sam T, University of Southern California
Hurt, N Jane, Clemson University
Hurtt, Steven W, University of Notre Dame
Husseini, Fayez, Kansas State University
Hussey, Outram, Howard University
Huston, William F, Auburn University
Hutchings, Bruce L, University of Illinois at Urbana-Champaign
Hutchinson, Joseph M, Texas A&M University
Hutton, Dale J, Clemson University
Hutton, Ernest, Pratt Institute
Iacucci, Paola, Columbia University
Iber, Howard, Drury College
Igal, Pratt Institute
Ikenoyama, George K, California Polytechnic State University, San Luis Obispo
Ikezaki, Yoshio, Southern California Institute of Architecture
Illingworth, Curtis D, California Polytechnic State University, San Luis Obispo
Imas, Rodolfo, Columbia University, New York Institute of Technology
Incze, Thomas A, Roger Williams College
Ingersoll, Richard, Rice University
Ingleson, Lewis, University of Hawaii at Manoa
Ingraham, Catherine, University of Illinois at Chicago
Inkpen, David, Oregon School of Design
Inoway, Carl, University of Utah
Inserra, Louis, Pennsylvania State University
Irvine, Leland, University of Utah
Isaacs, Kenneth, University of Illinois at Chicago
Ishikawa, Sara, University of California, Berkeley
Israel, Frank, University of California, Los Angeles
Iyengar, Kuppaswamy, University of California, Los Angeles
Izenour, Stephen, University of Pennsylvania
Jacks, Ernest E, University of Arkansas
Jackson, Anthony, Technical University of Nova Scotia
Jackson, Barry, New Jersey Institute of Technology
Jackson, Hobart, University of Kansas
Jackson, Neil M T, California State Polytechnic University, Pomona
Jacobs, Harry, Temple University
Jacobs, Peter, McGill University
Jacobs, Stephen P, Tulane University
Jacobson, John, Yale University
Jacobson, Philip, University of Washington
Jacquemart, George, Pratt Institute
Jacques, John D, Clemson University
Jadin, Patrick K, Howard University
Jaeger, R Thomas, University of Illinois at Chicago
Jahn, Helmut, University of Illinois at Chicago
Jahnke, William, Kansas State University
Jain, Alka, McGill University
Jakobowski, Joe, Boston Architectural Center
James, John F, University of Virginia
James, Robert, The Cooper Union
James, Truett, University of Texas at Arlington

Faculty
Roster

Jameson, Craig, University of North Carolina at Charlotte
Jameson, Gregory, University of Colorado at Denver
Jammal, Ibrahim, State University of New York at Buffalo
Jammal, Walid E, Boston Architectural Center
Jampen, Pierre, Laval University
Janis, Richard, Washington University
Jara, Cynthia, University of Minnesota
Jarnuskiewicz, Z, Laval University
Jaroszewicz, Mark T, University of Florida
Jarrard-Dimond, Terry, Clemson University —
Jarratt, William R, University of Michigan
Jarrett, James R, City College of the CUNY
Jarzombek, Mark, Cornell University
Jefferson, Euerardo, New Jersey Institute of Technology
Jelin, Gary, Lawrence Technological University
Jencks, Charles, University of California, Los Angeles
Jenkins, William R, University of Houston
Jenkinson, Harold L, North Dakota State University
Jensen, Robert, New York Institute of Technology
Jerger, Edward W, University of Notre Dame
Jersey, Todd, Boston Architectural Center
Jesson, Denis, University of Manitoba
Jeter, Reginald, Louisiana Tech University
Jetter, Cheryl J, Andrews University
Jewell, Linda, Harvard University
Jewett, Wayne, University of Oregon
Jimenez, Ricardo, University of Puerto Rico
Jing, Tian-Fang, Pratt Institute
Jinkins, J L, University of Texas at Austin
Jochum, Steven, Temple University
Jog, Bharati, University of Cincinnati
Johansen, John, Pratt Institute
Johns Jr, Anthony N, Morgan State University
Johns, G Robert, University of New Mexico
Johnson, A Kristine, University of Minnesota
Johnson, Benjamin C, Virginia Polytechnic Institute & State University
Johnson, Brian, University of Washington
Johnson, Craig, University of Minnesota
Johnson, Dane, Lawrence Technological University
Johnson, Dennis, Spring Garden College
Johnson, Diana J, Texas Tech University
Johnson, Jory, University of North Carolina at Charlotte
Johnson, Lauri M, University of Colorado at Denver
Johnson, Louis, Illinois Institute of Technology
Johnson, Lyman, University of Oregon
Johnson, Mark, University of Colorado at Denver
Johnson, Melvin H, Texas Tech University
Johnson, Ralph, Montana State University
Johnson, Ralph B, University of Florida
Johnson, Robert E, University of Michigan
Johnson, Todd, University of Colorado at Denver
Johnston, George B, Georgia Institute of Technology
Johnston, Norman, University of Washington
Johnston, Scott, Miami University
Johnstone, Sandra, Lawrence Technological University

Jojola, Ted, University of New Mexico
Jolly, Charles P, University of Kentucky
Jones, Bernie, University of Colorado at Denver
Jones, Dennis B, Virginia Polytechnic Institute & State University
Jones, Don, Drexel University
Jones, Edward, Princeton University
Jones, E Fay, University of Arkansas
Jones, James, Kansas State University
Jones, Kay Bea, Ohio State University
Jones, Michael, Georgia Institute of Technology
Jones, Nigel, Oklahoma State University
Jones, Robert L, University of Oklahoma
Jones, Walter B, Wentworth Institute of Technology
Jordan, J Peter, University of Hawaii at Manoa
Jordan, Michael, University of Texas at Austin
Jules, Frederick A, University of Wisconsin-Milwaukee
Jullian, Guillaume, Cornell University
Juppenlatz, David, Temple University
Kabriel, R Jay, Catholic University of America
Kaha, Arthur L, University of Illinois at Urbana-Champaign
Kahera, Akel Ismail, Boston Architectural Center
Kahn, Andrea, Carnegie Mellon University
Kahn, Charles, University of Kansas
Kahn, Sabir, Boston Architectural Center
Kahn, Terry D, University of Texas at Austin
Kahn-Leavitt, Johnathan, Boston Architectural Center
Kainlauri, Eino O, Iowa State University
Kajkowski, Charles, University of Nevada, Las Vegas
Kalas, Jan, Pratt Institute
Kalay, Yehuda, State University of New York at Buffalo
Kaliski, John, Southern California Institute of Architecture
Kalisperis, Loukas, Pennsylvania State University
Kalsbeek, James, University of Cincinnati
Kambo, Banarsi, University of Tennessee-Knoxville
Kamphoefner, Henry L, North Carolina State University
Kanda, Shun, Massachusetts Institute of Technology
Kanevsky, Sergei, Pratt Institute
Kang, Kaffee, Wentworth Institute of Technology
Kanouse, Marian, Frank Lloyd Wright School of Architecture
Kantrowitz, Min, University of New Mexico
Kaplan, Kenneth, Columbia University
Kaplan, Michael, University of Tennessee-Knoxville
Kaplan, Milton, State University of New York at Buffalo
Kappe, Raymond, Southern California Institute of Architecture
Karahan, Beyhan, New York Institute of Technology
Karalis, Constantine, Pratt Institute
Karas, Carl, New York Institute of Technology
Karn, Gail W, University of Colorado at Denver

Karp, David, Temple University
Karvouni, Maria, Virginia Polytechnic Institute & State University
Kass, Thomas B, University of Utah
Katavolos, William, Pratt Institute
Kaufman, Edward, Columbia University
Kaufman, Peter, Florida A&M University
Kaul, Mikal, University of Florida
Kawaharada, Michael, University of Hawaii at Manoa
Kayari, E, Carleton University
Kayhoe, Matthias, University of Virginia
Kealy, Hinman, University of Illinois at Chicago
Keating, E Larry, Georgia Institute of Technology
Kecskes, Gary A, Lawrence Technological University
Keegan, Kent M, University of Wisconsin-Milwaukee
Keeland, Burdette, University of Houston
Keenberg, Ronald, University of Waterloo
Keenen, John, New York Institute of Technology
Keiger, Alex, Harvard University
Kelbaugh, Douglas, University of Washington
Kellett, Ronald, University of Oregon
Kelley, Daniel O, Drexel University
Kelley, Eric, University of Colorado at Denver
Kellogg, Richard E, University of Arkansas
Kelly, Brian, University of Maryland
Kelly, Cathie C, University of Nevada, Las Vegas
Kelly, Emanuel, Temple University
Kelly, John A, Georgia Institute of Technology
Kelly, Robert, University of Kentucky
Kelsch, Paul, Virginia Polytechnic Institute & State University
Kelso, Richard M, University of Tennessee-Knoxville
Kelso, William M, University of Virginia
Kemp, Edward V, Louisiana Tech University
Kemp, Harold W, University of Florida
Kendall, Steven, Catholic University of America
Kennan, Kevin, University of Wisconsin-Milwaukee
Kennedy, Michael D, University of Kentucky
Kennedy, Sheila, Harvard University
Kennon, P Kevin, Yale University
Kenyon, David G, Texas A&M University
Keown, Alton C, Auburn University
Kercheval, Anita, Boston Architectural Center
Kerl, D B, Prairie View A&M University
Kerr, Oliver, University of Miami
Kersavage, Joseph A, University of Tennessee-Knoxville
Kesner, Brian B, California Polytechnic State University, San Luis Obispo
Kessler, Gregg, Washington State University
Ketterer, Ann, Carnegie Mellon University
Khalili, Nader, Southern California Institute of Architecture
Kieran, Kevin, Harvard University
Kieran, Stephen, Princeton University
Killian, Dortha L, University of Oklahoma
Killingsworth, Roger, Auburn University
Kilper, Dennis J, Virginia Polytechnic Institute & State University
Kim, C W, New School of Architecture
Kim, Jong-Jim, Arizona State University

Kim, Michael, University of Illinois at Urbana-Champaign
Kimball, Bruce, Arizona State University
Kimberk, Fred Boston Architectural Center
Kindig, Robert W, University of Colorado at Denver
King, Robert, New York Institute of Technology
Kingman, Robert, Andrews University
Kingsley, Karen, Tulane University
Kinnard, Judith A, University of Virginia
Kinney, Leila, Massachusetts Institute of Technology
Kinoshita, Masao, Ohio State University
Kinslow, Thomas, Rensselaer Polytechnic Institute
Kinzey, Bertram Y, University of Florida
Kinzy, Scott A, University of Tennessee-Knoxville
Kipnis, Jeffrey, University of Illinois at Chicago, Ohio State University
Kippenhan, Charles, University of Washington
Kira, Alexander, Cornell University
Kirchman, Susan M, Texas A&M University
Kirkland, Lannis, University of Houston
Kirsis, Valdis, Boston Architectural Center
Kirton, Eric, Boston Architectural Center
Kishimoto, Yuji, Clemson University
Kitamura, Robert E, California Polytechnic State University, San Luis Obispo
Kitchen, Judith L, Ohio State University
Kitzman, Marion J, Iowa State University
Kiyak, Asuman, University of Washington
Klausmeyer, Thomas, Lawrence Technological University
Kleihues, Josef Paul, The Cooper Union
Klein, James R, University of Virginia
Kleinman, Martin R, University of Notre Dame
Kleinsasser, William, University of Oregon
Klenk, Patrick, University of Nevada, Las Vegas
Klingman, John, Tulane University
Klos, Sheila M, University of Oregon
Knight, Alan John, Université de Montréal
Knight, Alyce, New York Institute of Technology
Knight, Charles D, University of Illinois at Urbana-Champaign
Knight, James F, Oklahoma State University
Knight, Roy F, Florida A&M University
Knight, Terry, University of California, Los Angeles
Knowland, Ralph E, Clemson University
Knowles, Bridgett, New Jersey Institute of Technology
Knowles, Brigitte, Temple University
Knowles, John, Temple University
Knowles, Johnathan R, Boston Architectural Center
Knowles, Ralph, University of Southern California
Knox, Paul L, Virginia Polytechnic Institute & State University
Knox, Roderick L, The Cooper Union
Ko, Lawrence, Boston Architectural Center
Ko, Shun-Min, McGill University
Koberg, Donald J, California Polytechnic State University, San Luis Obispo
Koch, Paul, New York Institute of Technology
Kochel, Douglas, Temple University
Kocimski, Karol J, Iowa State University

Kodet, Edward, University of Minnesota
Koehler, Uwe F, Ball State University
Koenig, Pierre, University of Southern California
Koeper, Frederick, California State Polytechnic University, Pomona
Koester, Robert J, Ball State University
Koetter, Alfred H, Harvard University
Koh, Jusuck, Texas Tech University
Kohlen, Kenneth M, California Polytechnic State University, San Luis Obispo
Kok, Vickie, Virginia Polytechnic Institute & State University
Kolb, Keith, University of Washington
Koll, Ann, Pratt Institute
Kolotan, Shulan, Columbia University
Kommers, Peter C, Montana State University
Koontz, Thomas, Virginia Polytechnic Institute & State University
Korllos, Thomas, Kent State University
Korman, Randall, Syracuse University
Kostof, Spiro, University of California, Berkeley
Koulermos, Panos, University of Southern California
Koutsomitis, Nicholas, Pratt Institute
Koverman, John, University of Cincinnati
Kowalewski, Henry S, University of Michigan
Kracauer, Benjamin, Pratt Institute
Krajewska-Wieczorex, Anna, Southern California Institute of Architecture
Krause, Linda, University of Wisconsin-Milwaukee
Krawcyk, Robert, Illinois Institute of Technology
Krecke, Norman, Temple University
Krehbiel, Janet, Illinois Institute of Technology
Kremer, Eugene, Kansas State University
Kremers, Jack, Kent State University
Kriebel, Marjorie, Drexel University
Krieger, Jeffrey, Drexel University
Krimgold, Frederick, Virginia Polytechnic Institute & State University
Krizek, Katherine, New York Institute of Technology
Kroelinger, Michael, Arizona State University
Kroloff, Reed A, Arizona State University
Kroner, Walter M, Rensselaer Polytechnic Institute
Kronish, Herbert, Wentworth Institute of Technology
Kronstadt, Arnold, Catholic University of America
Krstic, Vladimir, Kansas State University
Krueck, Ronald, University of Illinois at Chicago
Krug, Nate, North Dakota State University
Kruhl, Ronald J, Texas A&M University
Kruhly, James, University of Pennsylvania
Kruty, Paul, University of Illinois at Urbana-Champaign
Kubelik, Martin, Cornell University
Kudo, Kunio, Columbia University, New Jersey Institute of Technology
Kudrna, James L, University of Oklahoma
Kugler, Jerry, Princeton University
Kuhn, Dennis, New York Institute of Technology
Kuhn, Frederick, Wentworth Institute of Technology

Kuhner, Craig, University of Texas at Arlington
Kultermann, Udo, Washington University
Kunihiro, George, Columbia University
Kunst, Andrea, Boston Architectural Center
Kunz, Arthur, New York Institute of Technology
Kunze, Donald, Pennsylvania State University
Kupper, Eugene, University of California, Los Angeles
Kupritz, Phillip, University of Illinois at Chicago
Kurneta, Anthony, Wentworth Institute of Technology
Kurze, Heather, Southern California Institute of Architecture
Kuska, James, University of Idaho
Kuska, Sharon, University of Nebraska-Lincoln
Kusnerz, Peg, University of Michigan
Kuth, Byron D, Boston Architectural Center
Kuwabara, B, Carleton University
Labarthe, Suzanne, University of Houston
Labs, Kenneth, Yale University
Lachapelle, Jacques, Université de Montréal
Ladensack, Paul, Arizona State University
LaDouceur, Janis, University of Wisconsin-Milwaukee
Laffely, Ron, Boston Architectural Center
LaFon, Alan B, Auburn University
Laging, Tom, University of Nebraska-Lincoln
Lagorio, Henry, University of California, Berkeley
LaGrassa, Stephen, University of Detroit
Lagreco, Charles A, University of Southern California
LaHaie, Brian J, Auburn University
Lahiji, Nadir, Drexel University, Georgia Institute of Technology, New Jersey Institute of Technology
Lahti, Ahde, Southern California Institute of Architecture
Lahti, Aleksis A, Lawrence Technological University
Laing, Michele, University of Manitoba
Lakeman, Sandra P, California Polytechnic State University, San Luis Obispo
Lalvani, Haresh, Pratt Institute
Lamantia Jr, James R, Tulane University
LaMarche, Jean, Lawrence Technological University
Lamb, Stephen, Pratt Institute
Lamb, Wilfrid, University of Waterloo
Lambert, Nancy S, Yale University
Lambert, P, Carleton University
Lambert, Phyllis, McGill University
Lambla, Kenneth, University of North Carolina at Charlotte
Lambson, R Michelle, University of Kentucky
Lammers, James, University of Minnesota
Lane, Jonathan S, Harvard University
Lanford, Samuel T, University of Illinois at Urbana-Champaign
Lang, Jon T, Drexel University
Lang, Jurg, University of California, Los Angeles
Langdon, Tannys, University of Illinois at Chicago
Lange, Cathleen, Boston Architectural Center
Lange, John H, California Polytechnic State University, San Luis Obispo

Faculty
Roster

Langenbach, Randolph, University of
California, Berkeley
Langendorf, Richard, University of Miami
Lanier, Claire, University of Colorado at
Denver
Lanter, Lewis, Georgia Institute of Technology
Lapanne, Nancy K, University of Maryland
Lapp, Floyd, Pratt Institute
Lapping, Mark, Kansas State University
Laramie, Gregory, Roger Williams College
LaRocca, Joseph, University of Miami
Larocca, Joseph, Pratt Institute
Larochelle, Pierre, Laval University
Larsen, Terry R, Texas A&M University
Larson, Gerald R, University of Cincinnati
Larson, Kenneth P, Texas A&M University
Lasala, Hector, University of Southwestern
Louisiana
Laseau, Paul A, Ball State University
Lassiter, Franklin L, Southern University
Latek, Irena, Université de Montréal
Latour, Alessandra, Columbia University
Latourelle, Elaine, University of Washington
Lauer, Kenneth R, University of Notre Dame
Lauer, William J, University of
Tennessee-Knoxville
Lavandero, Carlos, University of Puerto Rico
LaVine, Lance, University of Minnesota
Lawler, John, Boston Architectural Center
Lawrence, Attila E, University of Nevada, Las
Vegas
Lawrence, Denise L, California State
Polytechnic University, Pomona
Lawrence, Howard Ray, Pennsylvania State
University
Lawson, Elizabeth W, Drexel University
Lawson, Stephen, University of Texas at
Arlington
Lawton, Mary, Boston Architectural Center
Lay, K Edward, University of Virginia
Leaf, Richard, Boston Architectural Center
Leake, David M, Tulane University
Leaney, David B, University of British
Columbia
Leaning, John, Carleton University
Leary, Dan, University of Texas at Austin
Leary, David, University of Kentucky
Leatherbarrow, David, University of
Pennsylvania
Leathers, Winston, University of Manitoba
Leaver, John F, Louisiana State University
Lebduska, John, New Jersey Institute of
Technology
Lebert, Ed, University of Washington
LeBlanc, Christian, Clemson University
Leblanc, Janet B, Clemson University
LeBlanc, W Jude, University of Virginia
Lechner, Norbert, Auburn University
LeClerc, Jean-Claude, Laval University
Ledewitz, Stefanie, Carnegie Mellon
University
Leduc, Maryse, Université de Montréal
Lee, Douglas, University of Toronto
Lee, Jeffrey, North Carolina State University
Lee, John, University of Kansas
Lee, Kenneth S, Ohio State University
Lee Jr, Kermit J, Syracuse University
Lee, Peter R, Clemson University
Lee, Ralph J, California Polytechnic State
University, San Luis Obispo
Lee, Steven, Carnegie Mellon University

Lee, Y S, Pratt Institute
Lee, Yuk, University of Colorado at Denver
Leers, Andrea, Yale University
Leeser, Thomas, Pratt Institute
Leet, Stephen, New York Institute of
Technology
Leffers, Lloyd A, University of Illinois at
Urbana-Champaign
Lehmann, Guenter, Texas Tech University
Lehr, Robert, University of Oklahoma
Lehrer, Michael B, University of Southern
California
Lehrman, Jonas, University of Manitoba
Leidigh, Thomas, Temple University
Leiding, Gerlinde, University of Texas at
Austin
Leighton, Donald, Rhode Island School of
Design
Leira, Angeles, New School of Architecture
Leither, Alan, University of Hawaii at Manoa
LeJeune, Jean-Francois, University of Miami
LeMessurier, William J, Harvard University
Lemieux, Claude, Université de Montréal
LeMoyne, Roy, McGill University
Lemr, John, University of Houston
Lenchner, Yevsey, Pratt Institute
Leon, Bruno, University of Detroit
Leon, Don, Pennsylvania State University
Lepere, Yves, University of Pennsylvania
Lerner, Ralph, Princeton University
LeRoy, Glen, University of Kansas
Lerup, Lars, University of California, Berkeley
Leski, Kyna J, Iowa State University
Lesko, Thomas M, Wentworth Institute of
Technology
Leskosky, Vincent, Kent State University
Lesniewski, Anatoliusz, Georgia Institute of
Technology
Lesnikowski, Wojciech, University of Kansas
Less, Christopher, State University of New
York at Buffalo
Lester, Anne J, University of
Tennessee-Knoxville
Levesque, Raymond, Laval University
Levine, Julius, Catholic University of America
Levine, Richard S, University of Kentucky
Levine, Seymour, McGill University
Levit, Robert, Boston Architectural Center
Levy, Alan, University of Pennsylvania
Levy, John M, Virginia Polytechnic Institute &
State University
Levy, M Emanuel, Pratt Institute
Levy, Robert A, Syracuse University
Lewcock, Ronald, Massachusetts Institute of
Technology
Lewis, Calvin F, Iowa State University
Lewis, David, Carnegie Mellon University
Lewis, David, Mississippi State University
Lewis, Diane H, The Cooper Union, Yale
University
Lewis, Roger, University of Maryland
Lewis, Russell C, Lawrence Technological
University
Lewis, Susan, Boston Architectural Center
Lewis, Susan, Rensselaer Polytechnic
Institute
Lewis, Walter H, University of Illinois at
Urbana-Champaign
L'Hote, Willard, University of Idaho
Liberatore, David L, Wentworth Institute of
Technology

Libeskind, Daniel, Ohio State University
Lifchez, Raymond, University of California,
Berkeley
Liggett, Robin, University of California, Los
Angeles
Ligougne, Alexis, Laval University
Liljequist, Jon, University of Illinois at Chicago
Limahelu, Carol, Woodbury University
Linder, Mark, Georgia Institute of Technology
Lindquist, Mark A, Florida A&M University
Lindsey, Bruce, Carnegie Mellon University
Lindsey, Robert, University of Houston
Lindsey, Shelagh, University of British
Columbia
Lindstrom, C Timothy, University of Virginia
Ling, Moses, Pennsylvania State University
Lingley, John, McGill University
Linton, Harold, Lawrence Technological
University
Liou, Fwu-Shiun, University of Kansas
Lipp, Jean-Jacques, Université de Montréal
Lischewski, Christian, Pratt Institute
Liska, Roger W, Clemson University
Lisle Jr, Forrest F, University of Florida
Little, King K, University of Nebraska-Lincoln
Liu, Leighton, University of Hawaii at Manoa
Livesey, Robert S, Ohio State University
Livingston, Morna M, University of
Tennessee-Knoxville
Lizak, Leonard, Pratt Institute
Lizon, Peter, University of
Tennessee-Knoxville
Llanes, Rolando, University of Miami
Llewellyn, Clark E, Montana State University
Lo, Chi Wang, Syracuse University
Lobell, John, Pratt Institute
Lobell, Mimi, Pratt Institute
Lockard, Kirby, University of Arizona
Lockhart, Kay, University of Minnesota
Lockhart, Kenneth, Frank Lloyd Wright School
of Architecture
Lockhart, Susan, Frank Lloyd Wright School
of Architecture
Lockley, Edward, New York Institute of
Technology
Lockrin, Mark, University of Arkansas
Lodholz, Paul, University of Houston
Loerke, William, University of Maryland
Loftness, Vivian, Carnegie Mellon University
Loftus, James E, Boston Architectural
Center
Logan-Peters, Kay, University of
Nebraska-Lincoln
Logue, Sarah, Frank Lloyd Wright School of
Architecture
Loh, Larry H, California Polytechnic State
University, San Luis Obispo
Loli, George S, University of Southwestern
Louisiana
Lombard, Joanna, University of Miami
London, James B, Clemson University
Long, M J, Yale University
Long, Marshall, Southern California Institute
of Architecture
Long, Randy, Illinois Institute of Technology
Longnecker, Nelson, Southern University
Longoria, Rafael, University of Houston
Lonnman, Bruce E, Ohio State University
Loomis, John, City College of the Columbia
UnivNY
Looney, William B, University of Michigan

Loosle, Richard, Catholic University of America
Lopez, Lillian D, University of Puerto Rico
Lopez-Gottardi, Tomas, University of Miami
Lorberbaum, Gay G, Washington University
Lord, David, California Polytechnic State University, San Luis Obispo
Lorenz, Albert, Pratt Institute
Loss, John, University of Maryland
Lossing, Ulrik, State University of New York at Buffalo
Loten, H S, Carleton University
Lotery, Rex, University of California, Los Angeles
Lott, Linda L, Washington University
Lotti, John, University of Oklahoma
Loveland, Joel, University of Washington
Lovett, Wendell, University of Washington
Lowe, Robert, Woodbury University
Lownie, Theodore, State University of New York at Buffalo
Lu, Paul, University of Maryland
Lubowicki, Paul, Southern California Institute of Architecture, Yale University
Lucas, John, Pennsylvania State University
Lucas, W Max, University of Kansas
Lucchesi, Raymond J, University of Nevada, Las Vegas
Lucke, Hans, University of Toronto
Luckey, Donna, University of Kansas
Lucy, William H, University of Virginia
Lueb, Richard, University of Oklahoma
Luhn, Graham B, Texas A&M University
Lumpkin, Ronald, Florida A&M University
Lumpkins, Lloyd, Texas Tech University
Lumsden, Anthony, University of California, Los Angeles
Lundell, Clark E, Auburn University
Lundman, Douglass, Kansas State University
Lusk, Paul, University of New Mexico
Lustig, Michael, University of Illinois at Chicago
Luther, Charles W, Rhode Island School of Design
Luther, Joseph, University of Nebraska-Lincoln
Luzzaro, Susan, New School of Architecture
Lynch, Robert, Lawrence Technological University
Lytle, Raymond H, University of Illinois at Urbana-Champaign
Macalik, Mirko J, Technical University of Nova Scotia
Macaskill, Ian K, Louisiana Tech University
Macauley, Barbara, Temple University
MacDonald, G, Carleton University
MacDonald, Ian, University of Manitoba
MacDonald, William, Catholic University of America
MacDonald, William, Columbia University
MacDougall, Bonnie, Cornell University
MacGilvray, Daniel F, Texas A&M University
Machado, Rodolfo, Harvard University
Macias, Richard, Washington University
Mack, Mark, University of California, Berkeley
MacKay, Kenneth, State University of New York at Buffalo
MacKay-Lyons, Brian, Technical University of Nova Scotia
MacKeith, Peter B, Yale University
Mackenzie, Archie, Cornell University

Mackey, David L, Ball State University
MacKinnon, William, Technical University of Nova Scotia
MacLean, Robert J, University of North Carolina at Charlotte
MacNeil, J Douglas, University of Arizona
MacNelly, Bruce, Harvard University
Macrae-Gibson, Gavin A, Yale University
Macsai, John, University of Illinois at Chicago
Madden, Kathleen, Pratt Institute
Mader, Laurence M, Andrews University
Madey, Robert, New York Institute of Technology
Madill, Robert, University of Manitoba
Madison, Bernard, Morgan State University
Madru, Daniel E, Boston Architectural Center
Maeda, Jim, Pratt Institute
Maffei, Gerald L, Texas A&M University
Maffitt, Theo S, Texas A&M University
Magyar, Peter, Auburn University
Mahaffey, Sally A, University of Oklahoma
Mahoney, Maureen, Boston Architectural Center
Mahony, Walter, Pratt Institute
Majkowski, Bruce, State University of New York at Buffalo
Major, Judith, University of Kansas
Makela, Taisto, University of Colorado at Denver
Maki, Fumihiko, Ohio State University
Makinson, Randell, University of Southern California
Malamuceanu, Roland, Boston Architectural Center
Malecha, Marvin, California State Polytechnic University, Pomona
Maller, Alexander, University of Nebraska-Lincoln
Mallozzi, Americo, Roger Williams College
Malmgren, Richard, University of Hawaii at Manoa
Malo, Alvaro, Columbia University
Malo, Paul, Syracuse University
Mangurian, Robert, Southern California Institute of Architecture
Mankiewicz, Paul, Pratt Institute
Mann, Dennis A, University of Cincinnati
Mann, George J, Texas A&M University
Mann, J Robert, Yale University
Mann, Thorbjoern, Florida A&M University
Mannello, Peter, Pratt Institute
Manning, Peter, Technical University of Nova Scotia
Manson-Smith, Pamela, University of Toronto
Manzo, Frank, Pratt Institute
Mapily, Jose, Howard University
Marans, Robert W, University of Michigan
Marble, Scott, Columbia University
March, Lionel, University of California, Los Angeles
Marchand, Denys, Université de Montréal
Marcou, George, Catholic University of America
Maricak, Gretchen, Lawrence Technological University
Marino, Robert, Columbia University
Mark, Robert, Princeton University
Markovich, Nicholas, University of New Mexico
Marlow, Michael, Boston Architectural Center
Marpilero, Sandro, Columbia University

Marques, Juan, University of Puerto Rico
Marsan, Jean-Claude, Université de Montréal
Marsh, James H, Texas A&M University
Marshment, Richard S, University of New Mexico
Martella, William E, University of Tennessee-Knoxville
Martemucci, Romolo, North Dakota State University, Temple University
Martens, Steve, North Dakota State University
Martin, F Lester, Louisiana Tech University
Martin, Louis, Université de Montréal
Martin, Mary Catherine, Auburn University
Martin, Michael T, Texas Tech University
Martin, Muscoe, Temple University
Martin, Rochelle, Lawrence Technological University
Martin, Roger, University of Minnesota
Martin, Stephen, Boston Architectural Center
Martin, W Mike, California Polytechnic State University, San Luis Obispo
Martineau, Thomas R, Florida A&M University
Martinez, Emilio, University of Puerto Rico
Martinez, Frank, University of Miami
Martinico, Anthony, University of Detroit
Martinico, Patricia A, University of Detroit
Martorano, Felix, Pratt Institute
Marty, Oscar, University of Puerto Rico
Martyniuk, Osyp, Kent State University
Maruel, Thomas, University of Puerto Rico
Maruszczak, John, University of Texas at Arlington
Maruyama, Kinya, University of Pennsylvania
Marx, Paul, Boston Architectural Center
Marzeki, Yousef, Ohio State University
Marzolf, Kingsbury, University of Michigan
Mashburn, Joseph L, Texas A&M University
Mason, Paul W, Texas A&M University
Masters, Elizabeth, Temple University
Masterson, Charles, Iowa State University
Matero, Frank, Columbia University
Matheu, Chris, University of Pennsylvania
Mathews, Katherine, Pratt Institute
Mathieu-Zatrec, Christian, Pratt Institute
Matsubayashi, Kazuo, University of Utah
Matsuzaki, Eva, University of British Columbia
Matter, Fred S, University of Arizona
Mattern, Gerald, Carnegie Mellon University
Matthews, Henry C, Washington State University
Mattock, Chris, University of British Columbia
Matzkin, Arlene, Drexel University
Matzkin, Donald, Drexel University
Maul, James, California Polytechnic State University, San Luis Obispo
Maves, John H, Iowa State University
Maxwell, Robert M, Princeton University
May, Hayden B, Miami University
May, Paul G, Boston Architectural Center
Mayerovitch, Harry, McGill University
Mayers, Robert, Pratt Institute
Mayne, Rebecca J, Kent State University
Mayne, Thom, Southern California Institute of Architecture
Mayo, James, University of Kansas
McAleer, J Philip, Technical University of Nova Scotia
McAlpine, Robert F, Auburn University
McAuliffe, Mary, University of Cincinnati
McAvin, Margaret, Rhode Island School of Design

Faculty Roster

McBride, Richard, University of Texas at Arlington
McCann, Rachel, Mississippi State University
McCarter, Robert, Columbia University
McCarthy, Michael M, Texas A&M University
McCleary, Peter, New Jersey Institute of Technology, University of Pennsylvania
McClure, George S, Montana State University
McClure, Harlan E, Clemson University
McClure, John, Hampton University
McClure, Kirk, University of Kansas
McClure, Wendy, University of Idaho
McConnell, Robert E, University of Arizona
McCormick, J Michael, Columbia University
McCoubrey, Daniel K, Drexel University
McCoy, John J, Catholic University of America
McCoy, Ron, Southern California Institute of Architecture
McCoy, Thomas, University of Kansas
McCreery, John, Ball State University
McCue, Gerald M, Harvard University
McCullough, Malcolm, Harvard University, University of Texas at Austin
McDermott, John, University of Texas at Arlington
McDonald, Arthur W, Syracuse University
McDonald, Eloise, University of Texas at Austin
McDonald, Richard, Kansas State University
McEwen, Lawrence D, Drexel University
McGinn, Paul, University of Notre Dame
McGinty, Tim, Arizona State University
McGlumphy, James, New Jersey Institute of Technology
McGonagill, Willard L, California Polytechnic State University, San Luis Obispo
McGrath, Brian, New Jersey Institute of Technology
McGraw, James, University of Nebraska-Lincoln
McGraw, Joseph J, Texas A&M University
McGuire, John, Drury College
McHale, Magda Cordell, State University of New York at Buffalo
McHenry, Paul, University of New Mexico
McIntosh, Alistair, Harvard University
McIntosh, Bill, Boston Architectural Center
McIntosh, John, Arizona State University
McIntosh, Patricia, Arizona State University
McInturff, Mark, University of Maryland
McIntyre, Donald, University of Waterloo
McKay, Donald, University of Waterloo
McKay, Sherry, University of British Columbia
McKenna, S, Carleton University
McKenzie, Vincent, Tuskegee University
McKeown, Donald I, Iowa State University
McLachlan, Ken, University of Manitoba
McLane, Patrick, University of Illinois at Urbana-Champaign
McLaren, Brian, Washington University
McLaughlin, Donald J, Montana State University
McLeod, Mary, Columbia University
McLeod, Robert, University of Florida
McMahon, David, Yale University
McMahon, Kevin, Southern California Institute of Architecture
McManus, Joseph, University of Houston
McManus Jr, William W, University of Oklahoma

McMaster, Jane, Ohio State University
McMillan, Bruce, Kansas State University
McMillian, B S, Prairie View A&M University
McMinn, William G, Cornell University
McNamara, Michael, Kansas State University
McNanie, John, Pratt Institute
McNaughton, E Eean, Tulane University
McNeil, Wm Garrison, City College of the CUNY
McNeish, Gilbert, University of Colorado at Denver
McNerney, Michael, New York Institute of Technology
McNeur, L, Carleton University
McPheeters, E Keith, Auburn University
McQueen, Troy, Tuskegee University
McQueen, William L, Roger Williams College
McQuillan, Sheila, New School of Architecture
McRae, John M, Mississippi State University
McSheffrey, Gerald, Arizona State University
McWilliams, Conrad, Kent State University
Mead, Christopher, University of New Mexico
Means Jr, George C, Clemson University
Means, Janice, Lawrence Technological University
Mears, Harriett, Drury College
Meder, John, University of Virginia
Medina, John, University of Miami
Medlin, Larry R, University of Arizona
Medoff, Howard, Spring Garden College
Meehan, Patricia, Boston Architectural Center
Meeker, Robert T, Roger Williams College
Meeks, Lyndon L, University of Nevada, Las Vegas
Mehta, Jaimini, Rensselaer Polytechnic Institute
Mehta, Madan, University of Texas at Arlington
Meier, Richard, University of California, Berkeley
Melanson, Serge, McGill University, Université de Montréal
Melaragno, Michele, University of North Carolina at Charlotte
Mello, William J, Wentworth Institute of Technology
Meltzer, George, New York Institute of Technology
Melvin, Thomas, Wentworth Institute of Technology
Mendelsohn, Stanley B, Ball State University
Meng, Eric, University of Washington
Menzies, Douglas W, Washington State University
Meogrossi, Piero, University of Notre Dame
Meradith, Stan, University of South Florida
Merola, Carmela, Rensselaer Polytechnic Institute
Merritt Jr, Harry C, University of Florida
Merryfield, William, University of Southwestern Louisiana
Mersel, Larry, Pratt Institute
Mertins, Detlef, University of Waterloo
Mervel, Martin, Southern California Institute of Architecture
Messersmith, Linda L, University of Notre Dame
Messinger, Alexander, Spring Garden College
Messmer, Robert, University of Kansas
Metcalf, Robert C C, University of Michigan
Meunier, John C, Arizona State University
Meyer, Bruce F, Ball State University
Meyer, Darrell C, Auburn University

Meyer, Elizabeth K, Harvard University
Meyer, Jacob, Montana State University
Meyer, John, Clemson University
Meyer, Thomas, University of Minnesota
Miao, Nancy, Pratt Institute
Michaelides, Constantine E, Washington University
Michaud, Jean, Laval University
Michel, Louis F, University of Kansas
Michel, Michael, New York Institute of Technology
Mickelson, Keith G, Lawrence Technological University
Midani, Akram, Carnegie Mellon University
Middlebrooks, Joseph, University of Miami
Miecznikowski, Wojciech, University of Tennessee-Knoxville
Mielke, Stephen, Boston Architectural Center
Migneron, Jean-Gabriel, Laval University
Milford, Christopher, Boston Architectural Center
Milford, Gary E, Louisiana Tech University
Millar, Norman, University of Southern California
Millard, Peter, Yale University
Millas, Aristides, University of Miami
Miller, Arthur, Drexel University
Miller, Courtney, Boston Architectural Center
Miller, Douglas J, Technical University of Nova Scotia
Miller, Frank, Massachusetts Institute of Technology
Miller, Iris, Catholic University of America
Miller, H James, University of Illinois at Urbana-Champaign
Miller, James R, Miami University
Miller, John, Cornell University
Miller, Joseph, Catholic University of America
Miller, Patrick A, Virginia Polytechnic Institute & State University
Miller, Reid, Washington State University
Miller, Richard A, Ohio State University
Miller, Rob, Georgia Institute of Technology
Miller, Sandra, California Polytechnic State University, San Luis Obispo
Miller, Steven B, University of Arkansas
Miller, William, Kansas State University
Miller, William, Montana State University
Millet, Marietta, University of Washington
Millman, Richard G, Auburn University
Millon, Henry, Massachusetts Institute of Technology
Milne, G, Carleton University
Milne, Murray, University of California, Los Angeles
Milojevic, Michael, University of British Columbia
Milovanovic-Bertram, Smilja, University of Texas at Austin
Minah, Galen, University of Washington
Minai, Ashgar, Howard University
Mintz, Norman, Pratt Institute
Mirin, Leonard, Cornell University
Mirkovich, Donald N, Washington State University
Miro, Antonio, University of Puerto Rico
Missair, Alfredo R, Ball State University
Mistur, Mark, Rensselaer Polytechnic Institute
Mitchell, Charlie, University of North Carolina at Charlotte
Mitchell, O Jack, Rice University

Mitchell, James, Drexel University
Mitchell, Marvin, New York Institute of Technology
Mitchell, Ron, Roger Williams College
Mitchell, William J, Harvard University
Mitias, Michael, Mississippi State University
Mitra, P K, Spring Garden College
Mixon, John, Rice University
Mizerny, Kenneth J, Drexel University
Mockbee, David W, Mississippi State University
Mockbee, Samuel, Mississippi State University
Moe, Diane R, California State Polytechnic University, Pomona
Moentmann, Elise, Louisiana Tech University
Moffett, Marian S, University of Tennessee-Knoxville
Mohler, Rich, University of Washington
Mohsini, Rashid, State University of New York at Buffalo
Moizer, D, Carleton University
Mol, Hendrick, Auburn University
Moleski, Walter H, Drexel University, University of Pennsylvania, Temple University
Moller, Clifford, Boston Architectural Center
Molloy, Joseph, Southern California Institute of Architecture
Monastero, Philip, New York Institute of Technology
Moneo, Jose Rafael, Harvard University
Monroe, Nancy B, Tulane University
Monsey, Arthur, Washington University
Montalto, James, Kent State University
Montgomery, Daniel, University of Virginia
Montgomery, Roger, University of California, Berkeley
Montgomery, Tim, Miami University
Montooth, Charles, Frank Lloyd Wright School of Architecture
Montooth, Minerva, Frank Lloyd Wright School of Architecture
Moody, Susan K E, University of Arizona
Mooney, Kempton, Georgia Institute of Technology
Mooney, Robert T, University of Illinois at Urbana-Champaign
Mooney, Sandra, Louisiana State University
Moor, Terry M, Wentworth Institute of Technology
Moore, Barry M, University of Houston
Moore, Bruce E, Drury College
Moore, Charles, University of California, Los Angeles, University of Texas at Austin
Moore, Ernest, University of Nebraska-Lincoln
Moore, Fuller, Miami University
Moore, Gary T, University of Wisconsin-Milwaukee
Moore, G Joan, Texas A&M University
Moore, James A, University of South Florida
Moore, Randy J, University of Southwestern Louisiana
Moore, Sandra V, New Jersey Institute of Technology
Moorish, William, University of Minnesota
Moradian, Khosrow, Howard University
Morales, Efrer, University of Puerto Rico
Moran, Robert, Louisiana Tech University
Moreira, Sixto E, California Polytechnic State University, San Luis Obispo

Morgan, Charles F, University of Florida
Morgan, Christopher C, University of North Carolina at Charlotte
Morgan, Kathy I, California State Polytechnic University, Pomona
Morgan, Terry D, University of Texas at Austin
Morganstern, James, Ohio State University
Mori, Toshiko, The Cooper Union
Morisset, Pierre, Université de Montréal
Morland, Graeme, University of Southern California
Morosov, Vladimir, New York Institute of Technology
Morrill, Richard, University of Minnesota
Morris, Deborah, University of Houston
Morrison, Alan, University of Pennsylvania
Morrison, Jon, Drexel University
Morrow, Baker, University of New Mexico
Morse, Mary K, Louisiana Tech University
Morse, Richard H, University of Florida
Morse-Fortier, Leonard, University of Notre Dame
Moss, Eric, Southern California Institute of Architecture
Moss, Eric, O, Rice University
Mossessian, Michel, University of Illinois at Chicago
Mostafavi, Mohsen, University of Pennsylvania
Mostoller, G Michael, New Jersey Institute of Technology
Motley, Susan, Pratt Institute
Mounayar, Michel A, Ball State University
Mount, James, Georgia Institute of Technology
Moursund, Earl, University of Oregon
Moussalli, Samir, Tuskegee University
Mouton III, Grover E, Tulane University
Mouton Jr, William J, Tulane University
Moye, Gary, University of Oregon
Mross, Joanna W, Texas Tech University
Muchow, William, University of Colorado at Denver
Mueller, John, University of Detroit
Mugerauer, Robert, University of Texas at Austin
Muir, Eden, Columbia University
Mukerjea, Rabindra, Iowa State University
Mulcahy, Vincent, Cornell University
Mulfinger, Dale, University of Minnesota
Muller, Stuart A, Syracuse University
Mumford, John M, Clemson University
Munier, Quentin, New York Institute of Technology
Muniz, Pedro, University of Puerto Rico
Murai, Luisa, University of Miami
Muramoto, Katsuhiko, Pennsylvania State University
Murphy, Amy L, Boston Architectural Center
Murphy, Dudley, Drury College
Murphy, John, Boston Architectural Center
Murphy, Robert H, Wentworth Institute of Technology
Murphy, William, University of Illinois at Chicago
Murray, Allan C, Boston Architectural Center
Murray, Irena, McGill University
Murray, Marth J, Tulane University
Murray, Ted A, University of Kansas
Murtagh, William, University of Maryland

Musumano, Kristopher, Boston Architectural Center
Mutlow, John, University of Southern California
Mutunayagam, N Brito, University of Nebraska-Lincoln
Myer, John, Georgia Institute of Technology
Myer, John R, Massachusetts Institute of Technology
Myers, Barton, Arizona State University, University of California, Los Angeles
Myers, Daniel, University of South Florida
Myers, David, Boston Architectural Center
Myers, John, University of Minnesota
Naecker, Paul, Columbia University
Nagle, James, University of Illinois at Chicago
Nakajima, Takashi, Laval University
Nakhjaven, Behzad, Auburn University
Nalbantian, Serge, Drexel University
Nalls, Robert, Drexel University
Nambu, John, Pratt Institute
Naos, Theodore, Catholic University of America
Narancic, Vojislav, University of Tennessee-Knoxville
Nardi, Norberto F, Tulane University
Nardulli, Susan, Southern California Institute of Architecture
Nash, Melvin, Boston Architectural Center
Nashlen, Thomas, Lawrence Technological University
Nassauer, Joan, University of Minnesota
Natapoff, Alan, Boston Architectural Center
Naughton, John, University of Illinois at Chicago
Navin, Thomas, New Jersey Institute of Technology
Navvab, Mojtaba, University of Michigan
Neal, Berna, Arizona State University
Neal, Todd, Boston Architectural Center
Neckar, Lance, University of Minnesota
Neel, Paul R, California Polytechnic State University, San Luis Obispo
Neely, Gretchen, Boston Architectural Center
Neff, Diane, New York Institute of Technology
Neiman, Bennett R, University of Colorado at Denver
Nelson, Carl, University of Manitoba
Nelson, Christian A, Georgia Institute of Technology
Nelson, John A, University of North Carolina at Charlotte
Nelson, R G, University of Idaho
Nemtin, Frances, Frank Lloyd Wright School of Architecture
Nemtin, Stephen, Frank Lloyd Wright School of Architecture
Nepomechie, Marilys, University of Miami
Nereim, Anders, University of Illinois at Chicago
Neski, Barbara, Pratt Institute
Nettleton, Laura, Carnegie Mellon University
Neuenswander Dean, Ohio State University
Neumeyer, Fritz, Southern California Institute of Architecture
Neurmberger, Carl, State University of New York at Buffalo
Neve, Deborah, University of Miami
Nevins, Robert, University of Arizona
Newcomb, Leonard, Rhode Island School of Design

Faculty
Roster

Newlon, Howard H, University of Virginia
Newman, Herbert S, Yale University
Newsome, Carol, California State Polytechnic University, Pomona
Newton, Barry, University of Kansas
Ng, Daniel, Boston Architectural Center
Ng, Oliver, University of Minnesota
Nicholas, Philip, Lawrence Technological University
Nichols, Frederick D, University of Virginia
Nicholson, Benjamin, University of Illinois at Chicago
Nicholson, Joe C, New School of Architecture
Nicita, John, New School of Architecture
Nickels, Jay, University of Southern California
Nielsen, Signe, Pratt Institute
Niland, David L, University of Cincinnati
Nishi, Geoffrey K, Ohio State University
Nishimoto, Taeg, New Jersey Institute of Technology, Pratt Institute
Nissen, Chris, Temple University
Nius, Michael D, Tulane University
Nixon, David, Southern California Institute of Architecture
Nocks, Barry C, Clemson University
Noe, Joyce, University of Hawaii at Manoa
Noffsinger, J P, University of Kentucky
Nolan, Linda P, Florida A&M University
Nordenson, Guy, Columbia University
Nordhaus, Richard, University of New Mexico
Nordquist, Raymond E, California Polytechnic State University, San Luis Obispo
Norford, Leslie, Massachusetts Institute of Technology
Noriega, Claudio, University of Miami
Norman Jr, Herbert P, Clemson University
Norman, Richard B, Clemson University
Norris, Ed, University of New Mexico
Norris-Baker, Carolyn, Kansas State University
North, Virginia, Lawrence Technological University
Northen, Oscar, Hampton University
Northup, Dale, Lawrence Technological University
Nota, Dean, Southern California Institute of Architecture
Notaras, Alec, University of Illinois at Urbana-Champaign
Noteis, Viki, University of Kansas
Novitski, Barbara-Jo, University of Oregon
Nowak, W J Danny, Texas Tech University
Numbers, M Joseph, University of Idaho
Nyberg, Folke, University of Washington
O'Brien, Michael J, Virginia Polytechnic Institute & State University
O'Bryan, Mark, Ohio State University
O'Connell, John, Boston Architectural Center
O'Connell, William J, University of Illinois at Urbana-Champaign
O'Connor, Patrick, New School of Architecture
O'Connor, Thomas, University of Detroit
O'Connor, Timothy, Lawrence Technological University
O'Donnell, Elizabeth, The Cooper Union, New Jersey Institute of Technology
O'Hara, Steve, Oklahoma State University
O'Hear III, James, Catholic University of America
O'Leary, Patricia, University of Arkansas

O'Leary, Theresa, New York Institute of Technology
O'Neal, Robert, Rhode Island School of Design
O'Neil, C Shayne, Rhode Island School of Design
O'Neill, Cheryl, Syracuse University
O'Rourke, Michael J, Rensselaer Polytechnic Institute
O'Rourke, Sean, Spring Garden College
O'Sullivan, Michael J, California State Polytechnic University, Pomona
Obermaier, Karl, Spring Garden College
Ochshorn, Jonathan, Cornell University
Ochsner, Ralph H, University of Kansas
Oden, Fran, University of Oklahoma
Odoerfer, Joseph, University of Detroit
Oh, Grace U, Boston Architectural Center
Oh, Randall, Columbia University
Ojeda, Pablo, University of Puerto Rico
Okerlund, Garland A, University of Virginia
Oliver, Douglas E, Texas A&M University
Oliver, Patricia Belton, California State Polytechnic University, Pomona
Olivieri, Joseph, Lawrence Technological University
Ollswang, Jeffrey E, University of Wisconsin-Milwaukee
Olsen, Donald, University of California, Berkeley
Olson, Donald, University of Houston
Olson, Joann, Miami University
Olson, Robert K, Iowa State University
Olving, Gerhard, University of Michigan
Onishi, Patrick, University of Hawaii at Manoa
Onouye, Barry, University of Washington
Opar, Barbara, Syracuse University
Oppenheim, Irving, Carnegie Mellon University
Oppenheimer, Leo M, Tulane University
Oppermann, A Peter, Louisiana State University
Orens, Stan, New York Institute of Technology
Orgen, Tarik A, Auburn University
Orleans, Peter, Iowa State University
Orlowski, Mark B, Iowa State University
Ormbreck, Harlan K, North Dakota State Universtiy
Orr, Arlyn A, Oklahoma State University
Osler, R E, Carleton University
Osmon, Fred, Arizona State University
Oster, Donald, Wentworth Institute of Technology
Osterberg, Arvid E, Iowa State University
Ostlund, John, Cornell University
Ots, Enn E, Florida A&M University
Ott, Bonnie, State University of New York at Buffalo
Otto, Christian, Cornell University
Oubrerie, Jose, University of Kentucky
Ouellet, Jean, Université de Montréal
Ouintard-Hofstein, Pascal, Pratt Institute
Ousterhout, Robert G, University of Illinois at Urbana-Champaign
Ovaska, Arthur, Cornell University
Overton, Charles T, Iowa State University
Ovunc, Bulent, University of Southwestern Louisiana
Owen, Michael S, Washington State University
Owens, Patsy E, Virginia Polytechnic Institute & State University

Owens-Wilson, Gwen, Kansas State University
Owsley, William G, Miami University
Ozel, Felize, New Jersey Institute of Technology
Pabon, Arleen, University of Puerto Rico
Pace, Rocco, University of Pennsylvania
Padget, Steve, University of Kansas
Padolsky, B, Carleton University
Pagani, Freda, University of British Columbia
Paglione, Vince, University of Illinois at Chicago
Paige, Gary, Southern California Institute of Architecture
Paillet, Michel, University of Illinois at Chicago
Palermo, Frank, Technical University of Nova Scotia
Palmer, A E, Ball State University
Panetta, Daniel L, California Polytechnic State University, San Luis Obispo
Panetta, Mike, Boston Architectural Center
Papademetriou, Peter C, New Jersey Institute of Technology, Rice University
Papanek, Victor, University of Kansas
Paplow, Michael, Ohio State University
Parcell, Stephen, Technical University of Nova Scotia
Pardee Diana, Catholic University of America
Parekh, Mahendra, Morgan State University
Parent, Richard, Ohio State University
Parfitt, M Kevin, Pennsylvania State University
Parisel, Claude, Université de Montréal
Parker, Francis H, Ball State University
Parker, Leonard, University of Minnesota
Parker, Phillip, University of Cincinnati
Parker, Ray K, Auburn University
Parker, Scott, Rensselaer Polytechnic Institute
Parker, Tom, Drury College
Parnass, Harry, Université de Montréal
Parsons, George W, Mississippi State University
Parsons, Peter W, Rensselaer Polytechnic Institute
Parsons, Spencer, Rice University
Passanti, Francesco, Massachusetts Institute of Technology
Passe, Michael, Ohio State University
Passini, Romedi, Université de Montréal
Passons, Clarence, Boston Architectural Center, Wentworth Institute of Technology
Pastalan, Leon, University of Michigan
Pastier, John, McGill University
Pastore, Dominic J, Lawrence Technological University
Patkau, Patricia, University of California, Los Angeles
Patricios, Nicholas, University of Miami
Patten, Lawton M, Iowa State University
Patterson, Gordon W, Clemson University
Patterson, James R, Iowa State University
Patterson, Terry L, University of Oklahoma
Patton, Carl V, University of Wisconsin-Milwaukee
Patton, Robert J, Washington State University
Paul, Vivian L, Texas A&M University
Paull, Martin, Southern California Institute of Architecture
Pavlides, Eleftherios, Roger Williams College
Pavlos, Elliott, Georgia Institute of Technology
Pawlowski, Paul, Rhode Island School of Design

Payne, Ifan, Kansas State University
Payne, Richard, University of Houston
Payne, Rosser H, University of Virginia
Payne, Thomas, State University of New York at Buffalo
Payton, Neil J, Catholic University of America
Pearman, Charles, Cornell University
Pearson, Jeffrey T, University of Kentucky
Pearson, Paul David, City College of the CUNY
Peck-Learned, Elizabeth, Roger Williams College
Pecka, Brian E, North Dakota State University
Pedulla, Albert, Texas A&M University
Peek, William J, Auburn University
Pellecchia, Anthony, University of Colorado at Denver
Pellerin, Earl W, Lawrence Technological University
Pelli, Cesar, Yale University
Pelosi, Robert, Pratt Institute
Pempus, Eric, Kent State University
Pendleton, Ann, Cornell University
Peng, George T C, Texas Tech University
Penn, Alan, Boston Architectural Center
Penney, Allen, Technical University of Nova Scotia
Pentecost III, A Ray, University of Houston
Penuel, James, North Dakota State University
Pepper, Thomas, New York Institute of Technology
Pereau, M Jana, Texas A&M University
Perez-Chanis, Efrain, University of Puerto Rico
Perez-Gomez, Alberto, McGill University
Perkins, Ann Raleigh, Pratt Institute
Perkins, David, University of Southwestern Louisiana
Perkins, John, University of Cincinnati
Perkins, Lawrence, University of Arizona
Perkins, Lawrence, University of Illinois at Chicago
Perkowski, Mary Anne, Boston Architectural Center
Perl, Ann, Columbia University
Perl, Robert D, Texas Tech University
Perrell, Richard, Arizona State University
Perron, Richard, University of Manitoba
Perry, David C, State University of New York at Buffalo
Perry, Edward P, University of Illinois at Urbana-Champaign
Perry, John, University of Houston
Pertuiset, Nicole F, Rensselaer Polytechnic Institute
Pertz, Stuart, Pratt Institute
Peter, John, Hampton University
Peters, Mark, University of Kansas
Peters, Michael G, Texas Tech University
Peters, Patrick A, University of Houston
Peters, Richard F, University of California, Berkeley
Peters, Tom, Cornell University
Peters, Tonte, Tuskegee University
Peters, William Wesley, Frank Lloyd Wright School of Architecture
Peterson, Cynthia, City College of the CUNY
Peterson, Don, University of New Mexico
Peterson, John M, University of Cincinnati
Peterson, John R, Arizona State University
Peterson, Larry L, Florida A&M University
Peting, Donald, University of Oregon

Petrini de Monforte, Rinaldo A A, Texas Tech University
Pettinari, James, University of Oregon
Pettorino, Arthur, New York Institute of Technology
Pettus, Robert, Washington University
Pfeiffer, Bruce Brooks, Frank Lloyd Wright School of Architecture
Pfister, Bruno D, Harvard University
Phelps, Barton, University of California, Los Angeles
Phillips, David L, University of Virginia
Phillips Jr, R Wendell, Wentworth Institute of Technology
Phinney, Lucia B, University of Virginia
Picallo, Alberto, University of South Florida
Piccioni, Pasquale, University of Oregon
Piccolo, Richard A, University of Notre Dame
Piche, Denise, Laval University
Pickard, Edward E, California State Polytechnic University, Pomona
Piene, Otto, Massachusetts Institute of Technology
Pierce, Gifford, University of Idaho
Pignatti, Lorenzo, University of Waterloo
Pillet, Michel, University of New Mexico
Pimlott, Mark, McGill University
Pinkard, Edward, Howard University
Pinker, Donovan, University of Toronto
Pinnell, Patrick L, Yale University
Pinney, Paul M, University of Kentucky
Pinno, Andrzej, University of Texas at Arlington
Piomelli, Rosaria, City College of the CUNY
Pisciotia, Henry, Carnegie Mellon University
Pistorius, Nancy, University of New Mexico
Pitman, Karin, Arizona State University
Pitman, Susan, Spring Garden College
Pitt, David, University of Minnesota
Pittman, Peter, Georgia Institute of Technology
Pitts, J Michael, Louisiana State University
Piwoni, James, University of Wisconsin-Milwaukee
Place, Rodney, Rensselaer Polytechnic Institute
Place, Wayne, North Carolina State University
Plater, Terry, Drexel University
Plater-Zyberk, Elizabeth, University of Miami
Plattus, Alan, Yale University
Playdon, Dennis, Pennsylvania State University
Pledger, Roy C, Texas A&M University
Plesums, Guntis, University of Oregon
Plummer, Henry S, University of Illinois at Urbana-Champaign
Plunz, Richard, Columbia University
Plymale, Keith, University of Kentucky
Po, Ling, Frank Lloyd Wright School of Architecture
Poddubiok, Mark, McGill University
Pohl, Jens G, California Polytechnic State University, San Luis Obispo
Pohlman, Richard W, University of Florida
Pokorny, Jan, Columbia University
Politis, Daphne, Boston Architectural Center
Polk, David, University of Pennsylvania
Polk, George M, Clemson University
Pollack, Richard, Pratt Institute
Pollak, Martha, University of Illinois at Chicago

Pollalis, Spiro N, Harvard University
Pollin, Sigrid, California State Polytechnic University, Pomona
Polshek, James S, Columbia University
Polyzoides, Stefanos, University of Southern California
Poniz, Dusan, Texas A&M University
Ponte, Robert, Princeton University
Poole, J Scott, Virginia Polytechnic Institute & State University
Pope, Albert, Rice University
Pope, Albert, Southern California Institute of Architecture
Popovich, Alan, Pennsylvania State University
Porcaro, Louis, Boston Architectural Center
Porphyrios, Demetri, University of Virginia, Yale University
Porter, Brent, Pratt Institute
Porter Jr, Harry W, University of Virginia
Porter, Marley, Arizona State University
Porter, William L, Massachusetts Institute of Technology
Poster, Charles, University of Arizona
Postiglione, Corey, Illinois Institute of Technology
Poticha, Otto, University of Oregon
Potter, James, University of Nebraska-Lincoln
Poulin, Jean-Luc, Université de Montréal
Poulton, Michael C, Technical University of Nova Scotia
Powell, Raymond D, Texas Tech University
Powell, Richard, Andrews University
Powell, Richard O, Tulane University
Powell, Robert B, Lawrence Technological University
Powers, Daniel S, University of South Florida
Powers, Whitney, Clemson University
Poynter, Dale B, University of Illinois at Urbana-Champaign
Pran, Peter, New York Institute of Technology
Prangnell, Peter, University of Toronto, Washington University
Prantis, Nina, New Jersey Institute of Technology
Prasad, Shivnath, University of Illinois at Urbana-Champaign
Predock, Antoine, Arizona State University
Preiser, Wolfgang, University of New Mexico
Prendeville, Jet, Rice University
Pressman, Andrew, University of Wisconsin-Milwaukee
Prestamo, Felipe J, University of Miami
Pretty, Louis C, Université de Montréal
Price, Alfred D, State University of New York at Buffalo
Price, Daniel, Lawrence Technological University
Price, Linda Rice, University of Oklahoma
Price, Martin, University of Texas at Arlington
Price, V B, University of New Mexico
Priesmeyer, Larry L, Texas A&M University
Pritchard, Honora H, University of Nebraska-Lincoln
Pritchard, Joanna S, Mississippi State University
Prix, Wolf, Southern California Institute of Architecture
Prochazka, Alena, Université de Montréal
Prochazka, Jiri, Laval University
Procos, Dimitri, Technical University of Nova Scotia

Faculty
Roster

Proctor, Le, Boston Architectural Center
Pron, John, Temple University
Prosser, John M, University of Colorado at Denver
Prost, Uwe, University of Maryland
Protzen, Jean-Pierre, University of California, Berkeley
Prowler, Donald, University of Pennsylvania, Princeton University
Prown, Jules, Yale University
Prudon, Theodore, Pratt Institute
Prugh, Peter E, University of Florida
Prussin, Labelle, City College of the CUNY
Puderbaugh, Homer, University of Nebraska-Lincoln
Pugh, Thomas D, Florida A&M University
Pugh, Toby, University of New Mexico
Pulliam, John, University of Idaho
Pundt, Hermann, University of Washington
Purcell, Patrick, Massachusetts Institute of Technology
Purves, Alexander, Yale University
Puttnam, Anthony, Frank Lloyd Wright School of Architecture
Qualls, George, University of Pennsylvania
Quantrill, Malcolm W F, Texas A&M University
Quatman II, G William, University of Kansas
Quattrone, Frank D, Spring Garden College
Quayle, Moura, University of British Columbia
Quennell, Nicholas, Columbia University
Quick, Stephen, Carnegie Mellon University
Quigley, Robert, University of Pennsylvania
Quiles, Edwin, University of Puerto Rico
Quinlan, Charles W, California Polytechnic State University, San Luis Obispo
Quinn, Patrick J, Rensselaer Polytechnic Institute
Quinnan, James, Carnegie Mellon University
Quoidbach, Tracy, Boston Architectural Center
Raabe, Peta, Temple University
Rabin, Rose Marie, Southern California Institute of Architecture
Rabin, Yale, University of Virginia
Rabinowitz, Harvey Z, University of Wisconsin-Milwaukee
Rabins, Michael, University of Illinois at Urbana-Champaign
Rabun, J Stanley, University of Tennessee-Knoxville
Rahman, Sheikh, Roger Williams College
Raine, Charles W, Tuskegee University
Rajkovich, Thomas, University of Illinois at Chicago
Ramberg, Walter D, Catholic University of America
Ramirez, Constance W, University of Virginia
Ramos, Sylvia, University of Puerto Rico
Ramsay, Ronald, North Dakota State University
Ranalli, George J, Yale University
Rand, George, University of California, Los Angeles
Rand, Patrick J, North Carolina State University
Randall, Ellen, Spring Garden College
Randle, Jay W, University of Oklahoma
Randolph, John, Virginia Polytechnic Institute & State University
Ranieri, Elizabeth, Boston Architectural Center
Rankin, A, Carleton University

Ransom, Harry S, Virginia Polytechnic Institute & State University
Rapanos, Dino P, University of British Columbia
Rapkin, Chester, Princeton University
Rapoport, Amos, University of Wisconsin-Milwaukee
Rapp, James R, Arizona State University
Rappaport, Elliot, Lawrence Technological University
Rappe, Wallace, University of Illinois at Chicago
Rashid, Hani, Pratt Institute
Ratcliffe, Gordon, Technical University of Nova Scotia
Ratensky, Alexander, University of South Florida
Rattenbury, John, Frank Lloyd Wright School of Architecture
Rattenbury, Kay, Frank Lloyd Wright School of Architecture
Rattray, Alex, University of Manitoba
Rauma, John, University of Minnesota
Rave, Ligia, Tulane University
Rea, Mark S, Rensselaer Polytechnic Institute
Read, Alice G, Boston Architectural Center
Read, Gray, Drexel University
Reagan, John J, Ohio State University
Recken, Sara M, Washington State University
Reed, K David, University of Wisconsin-Milwaukee
Reed, Raymond D, Texas A&M University
Reeder, Ched, Southern California Institute of Architecture
Reehil, Paul, University of Detroit
Rees, Peter, New Jersey Institute of Technology
Reese, D Nels, University of Idaho
Reeves, F Blair, University of Florida
Reeves, Marilyn L, State University of New York at Buffalo
Refuerzo, Ben, University of California, Los Angeles
Regan, J Thomas, University of Miami
Regelous, Douglas, University of Manitoba
Regenbogen, Thomas, Lawrence Technological University
Regnier, Ireland G, Clemson University
Regnier, Victor, University of Southern California
Reifsteck, Charles R, University of Illinois at Urbana-Champaign
Reiner, M A, Rice University
Reinhard, Robert J, Lawrence Technological University
Reinhardt, James, University of Hawaii at Manoa
Reinholtz, Laun, Andrews University
Reissner, Hugo, University of Kansas
Renfro, Robert, University of Texas at Austin
Reno, Judith E, University of Tennessee-Knoxville
Reshower, Joseph, Georgia Institute of Technology
Reuer, John P, North Carolina State University
Rexing, Ted, University of Nevada, Las Vegas
Reynolds, Douglas D, University of Nevada, Las Vegas
Reynolds, Jerlene A, University of Oklahoma

Reynolds, Frank E, University of Nevada, Las Vegas
Reynolds, John, University of Oregon
Reynolds, Susan, Pratt Institute
Ricci, Leonardo, University of Kentucky
Rice, John S, Iowa State University
Rice, Matthew H, Clemson University
Rich, Steve, Boston Architectural Center
Richard, Roger, McGill University, Université de Montréal
Richards, Barbara J, University of Utah
Richards, Larry, University of Waterloo
Richardson, Bonnie, Arizona State University
Richardson, Gaylord, University of Kansas
Richardson, Henry, Cornell University
Richardson, James, University of Mew Mexico
Richardson, Marc, University of Kansas
Richardson-Smith, Juliet, Princeton University
Richter, Dagmar E, Harvard University
Rickel, Mary, University of Kansas
Ridenour, Steven, Temple University
Ridgdill, Gary D, University of Florida
Rieley, William D, University of Virginia
Rifaat, Shafik I, University of Houston
Rifki, Fatih, North Carolina State University
Riley, John, Roger Williams College
Riley, Robert B, University of Illinois at Urbana-Champaign
Risher Jr, Chris, Mississippi State University
Rittel, Horst, University of California, Berkeley
Ritter, James, Virginia Polytechnic Institute & State University
Ritter, Miles, University of Pennsylvania
Rivelis, Lester, Pratt Institute
Rivera, Jose, University of New Mexico
Rivera, Luis, Temple University
Rivielle, Robert, New York Institute of Technology
Rixey, Victoria, University of Maryland
Roach, Michael S, University of Nebraska-Lincoln
Roark, Randal, Georgia Institute of Technology, University of Florida
Robbins, Deborah, University of Southern California
Roberts, Charlotte, University of Southwestern Louisiana
Roberts, Donald H, Howard University
Roberts, George, University of Idaho
Roberts, Paul, Boston Architectural Center
Roberts, Tom, University of Kansas
Robertson, Jack, University of Virginia
Robertson, Jaquelin T, University of Virginia
Robinette, Gary, University of Texas at Arlington
Robinson, Charles T, Lawrence Technological University
Robinson III, Harry G, Howard University
Robinson, Jeri Lynn, Spring Garden College
Robinson, Julia W, University of Minnesota
Robinson, Laura, Boston Architectural Center
Robinson, Max A, University of Tennessee-Knoxville
Robinson, Paul, University of New Mexico
Robinson, Sidney, University of Illinois at Chicago
Robinson, Willard B, Texas Tech University
Robison, Elwin, Kent State University
Robitaille, Andre, Laval University
Robles, Eduardo, Rice University
Rocafort, Jorge, University of Puerto Rico

Rocah, Louis, University of Illinois at Chicago
Roccanova, Anthony, University of Kentucky
Rochon, Richard, Lawrence Technological University
Rockcastle, Garth, University of Minnesota
Rockhill, Dan, University of Kansas
Rockind, Larry M, Lawrence Technological University
Rockwood, David, Oregon School of Design
Rode, Richard, New York Institute of Technology
Rodgers, J Lee, University of Oklahoma
Rodriguez, David L, Pratt Institute
Rodriguez, Manuel, New School of Architecture
Rodriguez-Camilloni, Humberto L, Virginia Polytechnic Institute & State University
Roehl, Wm H, City College of the CUNY
Roesch, Peter, Illinois Institute of Technology
Roesling, Ralph, New School of Architecture
Roger, Dieter, University of Manitoba
Roger, Gerard, Laval University
Rogers, C R, Boston Architectural Center
Rogers, John W, Texas A&M University
Rogers, R Bradford, Tulane University
Role, Richard, Syracuse University
Rolfe, George, University of Washington
Rolfsen, Gerald, University of British Columbia
Rolin, Rene A, University of Nevada, Las Vegas
Rolland, Peter G, Yale University
Rollet, Karen, University of Arkansas
Rollinger, Alan E, University of Colorado at Denver
Romieniec, Edward J, Texas A&M University
Romm, Stuart, Georgia Institute of Technology
Ronaszegi, Arpad D, Andrews University
Rondinelli, Joseph, Boston Architectural Center
Rorke, Joseph, Frank Lloyd Wright School of Architecture
Rorke, Shawn, Frank Lloyd Wright School of Architecture
Rose, Crystal, University of Hawaii at Manoa
Rose, Ron, University of Southern California
Roseland, Richard J, Iowa State University
Rosenberg, Carl, Massachusetts Institute of Technology, Princeton University
Rosenberry, Sara A, Virginia Polytechnic Institute & State University
Rosenblatt, Paul, Carnegie Mellon University
Rosenbloom, Sandra, University of Texas at Austin
Rosenman, Marvin E, Ball State University
Rosenstein, Norberto, University of Illinois at Chicago
Rosenthal, Gilbert A, Drexel University
Rosner, Arnold, University of Washington
Ross, Catherine, Georgia Institute of Technology
Ross, Don, Oregon School of Design
Ross, Michael, Southern California Institute of Architecture
Ross, William, Kent State University
Rossberg, Wayne, University of Utah
Rost, Steven, Lawrence Technological University
Rotenberg, Jeff, Pratt Institute
Roth, Frederick G, Clemson University
Roth, Harold, Yale University

Roth, Mark C, University of Wisconsin-Milwaukee
Rothblat, Rob, University of Kentucky
Rotondi, Michael, Southern California Institute of Architecture
Rott, Hans C, Virginia Polytechnic Institute & State University
Roumanous, Antoine, University of Kansas
Rowe, Colin, Cornell University
Rowe, Peter G, Harvard University
Rowe, William, Boston Architectural Center
Roy, Arnold, Frank Lloyd Wright School of Architecture
Roy, Doris, Frank Lloyd Wright School of Architecture
Royse, Donald C, Washington University
Rozenberg, Jerzy, University of Kentucky
Rubenstein, Michael, Pratt Institute
Rubinger, Morton, Technical University of Nova Scotia
Rudd, J William, Washington State University
Rudnick, Andrew, State University of New York at Buffalo
Rudolph, Christopher, Illinois Institute of Technology
Ruegger, Werner K, California State Polytechnic University, Pomona
Ruiz, Fernando, Virginia Polytechnic Institute & State University
Rumpel, Peter L, University of Florida
Rundquist, James, Lawrence Technological University
Rusch, Charles, University of Oregon
Ruseau, John L, University of Virginia
Rush, W Mack, Florida A&M University
Rusli, Agus, University of Cincinnati
Russell, William, Georgia Institute of Technology
Russo, Frances, State University of New York at Buffalo
Russo, Kenneth J, Clemson University
Rutland, Holan E, Virginia Polytechnic Institute & State University
Ryan, Deborah, University of North Carolina at Charlotte
Ryan, Dennis, University of Washington
Rybczynski, Witold, McGill University
Rycus, Mitchell J, University of Michigan
Ryder, Donald, City College of the CUNY
Ryhn, Douglas C, University of Wisconsin-Milwaukee
Rylands, Philip, University of Virginia
Rynnimeri, Valerio, University of Waterloo
Saalman, Howard, Carnegie Mellon University
Saccopoulos, Christos, Mississippi State University
Saccopoulos, Kathleen, Mississippi State University
Sachs, Stephen, University of Maryland
Sachs, Stephen F, University of Maryland
Safdle, Moshe, Harvard University
Safe, Carl B, Washington University
Sager, I Dale, Arizona State University
Sager, Stanley, University of New Mexico
Saggio, Nino, Carnegie Mellon University
Saile, David G, Arizona State University
Saitowitz, Stanley, University of California, Berkeley
Saksena, Raj, Roger Williams College
Salmon, David, Cornell University
Salmon, Nick, University of Cincinnati

Salona, Inigo, University of Miami
Salvadori, Mario, Columbia University
Salvaggio, Anthony, University of Houston
Salzman, Stanley, Pratt Institute
Sama, Gloria L, University of Notre Dame
Samizay, M Rafi, Washington State University
Sammons, Thomas C, University of Florida
Samuel, Edward B, Andrews University
Samuels, Burton, Illinois Institute of Technology
Samuels, Danny, Rice University
Samuelson, Robert E, Ohio State University
San Jose, Julio M, New York Institute of Technology
Sanabria, Sergio, Miami University
Sander, Dennis, University of Kansas
Sanders, Joel, Princeton University
Sanders, Linda W, North Carolina State University
Sandori, Paul, University of Toronto
Sands, Ellen, University of Maryland
Sanoff, Henry, North Carolina State University
Santaomasso, Eugene, Columbia University
Santos, Antonio de Souza, University of Toronto
Sapers, Carl M, Harvard University
Saporito, Paul, University of Colorado at Denver
Sappenfield, Charles M, Ball State University
Sasanoff, Robert, University of Washington
Saslow, Mary C, Texas A&M University
Sasser, Elizabeth M, Texas Tech University
Satkowski, Leon, University of Minnesota
Sauda, Eric J, University of North Carolina at Charlotte
Saulnier, Leonard, Wentworth Institute of Technology
Savin, Joseph, Lawrence Technological University
Sawyers, Keith, University of Nebraska-Lincoln
Sayles, Alan, New York Institute of Technology
Scanlon, Joseph, Drexel University
Scarbrough, William H, Syracuse University
Scarpulla, Joseph, New York Institute of Technology
Schaar, Kenneth W, Louisiana Tech University
Schack, Mario, Cornell University
Schackai III, John L, Tulane University
Schade, Rachel, Drexel University
Schaeffer, John H, Southern University
Schaeffer, K H, Boston Architectural Center
Schaeffer, Peter, University of Colorado at Denver
Schafer, Dan, Boston Architectural Center
Schali, Maya, Washington University
Schaller, Arthur W, Ball State University
Scheatzle, David G, Arizona State University
Scheer, Dennis, University of Nebraska-Lincoln
Scheffer, George, University of Florida
Scheid, Douglas, State University of New York at Buffalo
Scheidenhelm, Carl, Boston Architectural Center
Scherer, Jeffrey, University of Minnesota
Scherr, Gerald D, Lawrence Technological University
Scherr, Richard, University of Texas at Arlington

Faculty Roster

Scheuermann, Milton F, Tulane University
Schidlowski, Joseph, Kent State University
Schierle, Goetz G, University of Southern California
Schiffhauer, Robert J, Texas A&M University
Schiler, Marc, University of Southern California
Schiller, Arthur, New York Institute of Technology
Schiller, Gail, University of California, Berkeley
Schiller, Loes, Columbia University
Schipporeit, George, Illinois Institute of Technology
Schlegel, Don, University of New Mexico
Schlesinger, B Frank, University of Maryland
Schluntz, Roger L, Arizona State University
Schmitt, Frederick, Temple University
Schmitt, Gerhard, Carnegie Mellon University
Schmitt, Ronald E, University of Illinois at Urbana-Champaign
Schmitz, Gunter, State University of New York at Buffalo
Schmoll, Herbert, University of South Florida
Schnarsky, Anthony J, University of Wisconsin-Milwaukee
Schnee, Ruth A, Lawrence Technological University
Schneekloth, Lynda, State University of New York at Buffalo
Schneider, Douglas, Southern University
Schneider, Peter, Louisiana Tech University
Schneider, Richard E, University of Florida
Schneider, Richard F, Wentworth Institute of Technology
Schneider-Wessling, Erich, Massachusetts Institute of Technology
Schnell, Thomas, Ohio State University
Schock, Hans-Joachim, University of Oregon
Schoenleber, Robert A, University of Nebraska-Lincoln
Schoerke, Andrew, Spring Garden College
Schnoor, Bryan D, Andrews University
Schodek, Daniel L, Harvard University
Schoeman, Thomas J, University of Nevada, Las Vegas
Schoen, Richard, University of California, Los Angeles
Schoenauer, Norbert, McGill University
Scholfield, David, Lawrence Technological University
Scholz, Gordon, University of Nebraska-Lincoln
Schousboe, Ingvar, University of Illinois at Urbana-Champaign
Schreiber, Stephen, University of Miami
Schriever, Lee, University of Nebraska-Lincoln
Schroeder, Kenneth, University of Illinois at Chicago
Schubert, Robert P, Virginia Polytechnic Institute & State University
Schuchard, W Patrick, Washington University
Schueller, Wolfgang, Virginia Polytechnic Institute & State University
Schuette, Stephen, Clemson University
Schuetz, Erhard, Texas Tech University
Schultz, Ed, Washington University
Schultz, Harvey, Pratt Institute
Schumacher, Sheri L, Auburn University
Schumacher, Thomas, University of Maryland

Schuman, Anthony, New Jersey Institute of Technology
Schuster, Reinhold, University of Waterloo
Schuyler, John, Pratt Institute
Schwab, Anita Y, Spring Garden College
Schwaighofer, Joseph, University of Toronto
Schwarting, J Michael, New York Institute of Technology
Schwartz, Kenneth A, University of Virginia
Schwartz, Martin, Mississippi State University
Schwartz, Ralph C, Lawrence Technological University
Schwartz, Robert, Pratt Institute
Schwarz, Fritz, Virginia Polytechnic Institute & State University
Scicchitano, Frank, New York Institute of Technology
Scofidio, Ricardo M, The Cooper Union
Scogin, Mack, Georgia Institute of Technology
Scott, David M, Washington State University
Scott, Georgia, Southern California Institute of Architecture
Scott, James, Washington University
Scott, Jim, University of Kansas
Scott, Pamela, Cornell University
Scott Jr, William J, University of Michigan
Sculley, Sean W, The Cooper Union
Scully Jr, Vincent J, Yale University
Seager, Andrew R, Ball State University
Seamon, David, Kansas State University
Searle, Colgate, Rhode Island School of Design
Seaton, Richard W, University of British Columbia
Sedletzky, Marcel E, California Polytechnic State University, San Luis Obispo
Seebohm, Thomas, University of Waterloo
Segar, Laurie, Andrews University
Segrest, Robertt, University of Florida, Georgia Institute of Technology
Sehgal, Rajesh, Tuskegee University
Seibold, Llewellyn, Kansas State University
Seidel, Andrew D, Texas A&M University
Seiler, Douglas, Drexel University
Seiler, John A, Harvard University
Seinuk, Ysrael A, The Cooper Union
Seiple, Frank M, California Polytechnic State University, San Luis Obispo
Sekler, Eduard F, Harvard University
Selassie, Molla, University of Illinois at Chicago
Selby, Robert I, University of Illinois at Urbana-Champaign
Selditch, Michael, Woodbury University
Seligmann, Claus, University of Washington
Seligmann, Werner, Syracuse University
Selland, Thomas H, University of Oklahoma
Seltz, Julia, Boston Architectural Center
Sen, Rajan, University of South Florida
Senkevitch Jr, Anatole, University of Michigan
Sennyey, Esteban, University of Puerto Rico
Serrato-Combe, Antonio, University of Utah
Setzer, Frank, University of South Florida
Seydler-Sweatt, Betty-Lee, Lawrence Technological University
Shack, Joel, University of British Columbia
Shadbolt, Douglas, University of British Columbia
Shaeffer, Ronald, Florida A&M University
Shafer, Gary A, Mississippi State University
Shank, Wesley I, Iowa State University

Shannon, Graham F, University of Arkansas
Shao, Paul, Iowa State University
Shapiro, David J, The Cooper Union
Shapiro, John, Pratt Institute
Shapiro, Lindsay, New York Institute of Technology
Shapiro, Mark, Syracuse University
Sharon, H, Carleton University
Sharp, P, Carleton University
Sharpe, David, Illinois Institute of Technology
Shatarah, Rudolph, New York Institute of Technology
Shaul, Mark, North Dakota State University
Shaver, Paul, Illinois Institute of Technology
Shaw, Don, University of Hawaii at Manoa
Shaw, John, Cornell University
Sheesley, Deborah F, Drexel Univrsity
Sheikholeslami, Jahan, Drexel University
Sheine, Judith, New York Institute of Technology
Shekner, Michael, University of Minnesota
Sheldon, Susan, Boston Architectural Center
Shell, William S, University of Tennessee-Knoxville
Shellabarger, Fred, University of Oklahoma
Shellenbarger, Michael, University of Oregon
Shelov, Sidney, Pratt Institute
Sheoris, John V, Lawrence Technological University
Shepard, Herschel E, University of Florida
Shepherd, Michael, Montana State University
Shepherd, William E, Virginia Polytechnic Institute & State University
Sheppard, Adrian, McGill University
Sherman, Bert, Pratt Institute
Sherman, Philip, Yale University
Sherman, Richard, Boston Architectural Center
Sherman, Ted, Pratt Institute
Sherman, William, Rice University
Sherwin, Dean, Spring Garden College
Sherwood, Roger, University of Southern California
Shetty, Rajmohan, Rensselaer Polytechnic Institute
Sheward, Richard, Temple University
Sheydayi, E Yury, Arizona State University
Shibley, Robert G, State University of New York at Buffalo
Shields, James W, University of Wisconsin-Milwaukee
Shiffman, Ronald, Pratt Institute
Shih, Jason C, Louisiana State University
Shinberg, Milton, Catholic University of America
Shirdel, Bahram, Southern California Institute of Architecture
Shirvani, Diane Wilk, University of Colorado at Denver
Shirvani, Hamid, University of Colorado at Denver
Shively, Robert, Kent State University
Shoemaker, Gregory, New York Institute of Technology
Shoemaker, Mark, Pratt Institute
Shogren, Vernon, North Carolina State University
Shopsin, William, Pratt Institute
Shoraka, Koje, Woodbury University
Shorn, Jeffrey, New School of Architecture

Showghi, Dariouche, California State Polytechnic University, Pomona

Shows, Owen, Boston Architectural Center

Shrem, Victor, Lawrence Technological University

Shuley, Keith, University of Texas at Austin

Shuster, Lawrence, University of New Mexico

Shutter, Leigh, Boston Architectural Center

Shuttleworth, John, New Jersey Institute of Technology, Pratt Institute

Sichta, Edward J, Syracuse University

Sideris, Christopher, New York Institute of Technology

Sideris, Terry, New York Institute of Technology

Siebein, Gary D, University of Florida

Siegel, Robert, Boston Architectural Center

Siembieda, William, University of New Mexico

Siepl-Coates, Susanne, Kansas State University

Sijpkes, Pieter, McGill University

Siladi, Wayne E, Boston Architectural Center

Silance, Robert, Clemson University

Silberstein, Benjamin, New York Institute of Technology

Siler, Harry L, Howard University

Silman, Robert, Columbia University

Silverman, Joel, The Cooper Union

Silvetti, Jorge, Harvard University

Simaika, Sam Z, Howard University

Simitch, Andrea, Cornell University

Simmons, Gordon B, University of Cincinnati

Simmons, Harry, Pratt Institute

Simmons, Kenneth, University of California, Berkeley

Simon, James E, University of Illinois at Urbana-Champaign

Simonian, William M, Southern California Institute of Architecture

Sims, Sally, University of Maryland

Singer, Leonard, Virginia Polytechnic Institute & State University

Singhrs, Kim C, Washington State University

Sionis, Paul, Pratt Institute

Siress, Cary L, Boston Architectural Center

Sivak, Steven, Boston Architectural Center

Skaler, Robert, Spring Garden College

Skoler, Louis, Syracuse University

Skyles, Benjamin, Howard University

Slert, Charles, New School of Architecture

Sliwka, Ryszard, University of Waterloo

Slone, Herbert, Kent State University

Slovic, David, Tulane University

Small, Glen, Southern California Institute of Architecture

Small, Robert, University of Washington

Smalter, Janet, University of Kansas

Smart Jr, C Murray, University of Arkansas

Smith, Albert, Georgia Institute of Technology

Smith, Andrew, Southern University

Smith, Ann Montgomery, Wentworth Institute of Technology

Smith C Virgil, Georgia Institute of Technology

Smith, Charles Ashton, Southern University

Smith, David L, University of Cincinnati

Smith, Edward F, University of Utah

Smith, Elizabeth, Pennsylvania State University

Smith, Gil R, Ball State University

Smith, J, Carleton University

Smith, Jeri, New Jersey Institute of Technology

Smith, Joseph N, Georgia Institute of Technology

Smith, Kathryn, Southern California Institute of Architecture

Smith, Mark, University of California, Burkeley

Smith, Mary Ann, Syracuse University

Smith, Maurice, Massachusetts Institute of Technology

Smith, Robert L, University of Illinois at Urbana-Champaign

Smith, Scott, Carnegie Mellon University

Smith, Ted, Washington University

Smith, Terence, Princeton University

Smith, Thomas G, University of Illinois at Chicago

Smith, Young, Arizona State University

Smothers, Fount T, Louisiana State University

Smyth-Pinney, Julia M, University of Kentucky

Snow, Edward, Boston Architectural Center

Snow, James E, University of Arkansas

Snowden, Raymond, University of Utah

Snozzi, Luigi, Southern California Institute of Architecture

Snyder, Clifford H, Lawrence Technological University

Snyder, Gil S, University of Wisconsin-Milwaukee

Snyder, Siegfried, Syracuse University

Snyder, Susan, University of Pennsylvania

Sobel, Walter, Illinois Institute of Technology

Sobieraj, Walter, State University of New York at Buffalo

Sobin, Harris, University of Arizona

Sobrino, Eduardo, University of Puerto Rico

Solarz, Cynthia L, Boston Architectural Center

Soleri, Paolo, Arizona State University

Solis, Manuel M, University of Florida

Solomon, Daniel, University of California, Berkeley

Solomon, Richard, University of Illinois at Chicago

Somerson, Roseanne, Rhode Island School of Design

Soo, Lydia M, University of Illinois at Urbana-Champaign

Sorcinelli, John, University of Southern California

Sordyl, Douglas J, Lawrence Technological University

Sorenson Jr, Henry E, Montana State University

Sorey, Thomas L, University of Oklahoma

Sorkin, Michael, The Cooper Union, University of Illinois at Chicago

Sorkin, Michael, Southern California Institute of Architecture

Soroka, Ellen P, University of Virginia

Sorum, Paul, University of Southern California

Soules, Jonathan, University of Waterloo

Souza, John, Southern California Institute of Architecture

Spaeth, David A, University of Illinois at Chicago, University of Kentucky

Spain, Daphne G, University of Virginia

Spain, Thomas A, University of Miami

Spang, Laurence, Boston Architectural Center

Spangler, Ronald L, Ball State University

Spann, Don, University of Arkansas

Spears, Dan, University of Texas at Arlington

Spears, John, Boston Architectural Center

Specht, Stanley, University of Colorado at Denver

Speck, Lawrence, University of Texas at Austin

Spellman, Catherine, University of Houston

Spencer, John H, Hampton University

Sperr, Otto, Drexel University

Spiegel, Herman D, Yale University

Spiker, David, New Jersey Institute of Technology

Spitz, Katherine, Southern California Institute of Architecture

Spitzglas, Mark, Texas Tech University

Spivey, Ed, University of South Florida

Sporleder, Donald E, University of Notre Dame

Sprague, Paul E, University of Wisconsin-Milwaukee

Spratley, Jocelyn, Hampton University

Spreckelmeyer, Kent, University of Kansas

Spring, Bernard P, Boston Architectural Center

St Florian, Friedrich, Rhode Island School of Design

St Marie, Michael, North Dakota State University

Staats, Jeffrey, Roger Williams College

Stacell, Alan L, A&M University

Stafford, Jim, Southern California Institute of Architecture

Stageberg, James, University of Minnesota

Stagg, Josef, University of Wisconsin-Milwaukee

Stalk, Arnold, Southern California Institute of Architecture

Stamm, William P, University of Arizona

Stammiello, Donafo, University of Colorado at Denver

Stammler, Ursula, University of Kansas

Stamper, Eugene, New Jersey Institute of Technology

Stamper, John W, University of Notre Dame

Stangl, Michael, Woodbury University

Stanley, William, Woodbury University

Stanton, Doug, University of Arkansas

Stanton, Michael, University of Miami

Starr, Wilbur D, University of Southwestern Louisiana

Staub, Christian, University of Washington

Staub, Patrick, Southern University

Stauffer, Thomas, Kent State University

Stedman, Barry N, University of Cincinnati

Steel, Edwin J, Boston Architectural Center

Steelman, Terry D, Syracuse University

Steffian, John Ames, University of Maryland

Steger, Charles W, Virginia Polytechnic Institute & State University

Stein, Achva, University of Southern California

Stein, Jay M, State University of New York at Buffalo

Stein, Joseph A, Washington University

Stein, Richard G, The Cooper Union

Steiner, Frederick R, University of Colorado at Denver

Steinfeld, Edward, State University of New York at Buffalo

Steinitz, Carl F, Harvard University

Steinmann, Martin, Southern California Institute of Architecture

Stephen, George, Boston Architectural Center

Faculty Roster

Stern, Robert A M, Columbia University
Stern, Seth, Rhode Island School of Design
Stern, William, University of Houston
Stevens, Richard A, University of Cincinnati
Stevenson, Andrew, Morgan State University
Stevenson, Ralph, Lawrence Technological University
Steward, W Cecil, University of Nebraska-Lincoln
Stewart, Earl E, North Dakota State University
Stewart, George, California Polytechnic State University, San Luis Obispo
Stilgoe, John, Harvard University
Stillman, David, Princeton University
Stillwell, Victor E, Tulane University
Stinson, Jeff, University of Toronto
Stiny, George, University of California, Los Angeles
Stockham, James A, Clemson University
Stoeckel, Jay E, Virginia Polytechnic Institute & State University
Stoller, Claude, University of California, Berkeley
Stone, Harris, University of Kansas
Stone, Peter F, Florida A&M University
Stone, Vernon F, Iowa State University
Stoneking, Michael, Drexel University
Stoner, Jill, University of California, Berkeley
Story, James, University of North Carolina at Charlotte
Stotesbury, Sidney, Kansas State University
Stousland, Charles E, Miami University
Stout, Henry V, Louisiana Tech University
Strahle, Rolf G, University of Southwestern Louisiana
Strassburg, Steven, Iowa State University
Strauss, Eric, University of Kansas
Streatfield, David, University of Washington
Streeter, Raymond, Kansas State University
Streiby, Sandra, University of Nevada, Las Vegas
Streissguth, Daniel, University of Washington
Strickfaden, Roy J, Lawrence Technological University
Strickland, Rachel, Southern California Institute of Architecture
Strickland, Roy, Columbia University
Strother, Joseph W, Louisiana Tech University
Strumillo, Wladyslaw, Pennsylvania State University
Strutt, J, Carleton University
Stuart, John, California Polytechnic State University, San Luis Obispo
Stucky, Howard A, University of Tennessee-Knoxville
Stuebling, Susan, Roger Williams College
Sturgis, Robert, Boston Architectural Center
Sueltz, Fay, Woodbury University
Sugden, John, University of Utah
Sullivan, Patrick M, California State Polytechnic University, Pomona
Sumi, Christian, Southern California Institute of Architecture
Summers, Luis, Pennsylvania State University
Sumption, Brian, University of Idaho
Sunshine, Donald R, Virginia Polytechnic Institute & State University
Surber, Jim, University of Kansas
Sutherland, Cyrus, University of Arkansas
Sutherland, Martha S, University of Arkansas
Sutton, Gilbert F, Carleton University

Sutton, Richard K, University of Nebraska-Lincoln
Sutton, Sharon E, University of Michigan
Suzuki, Theodore, University of Hawaii at Manoa
Swain, Duncan, McGill University
Swallow, Richard, University of Texas at Austin
Swann, Michael, University of Kansas
Swansen, Vern, California Polytechnic State University, San Luis Obispo
Swanson, Randy, North Dakota State University
Swearingen, Don E, California Polytechnic State University, San Luis Obispo
Swenson, Alfred, Illinois Institute of Technology
Swerdloff, Lucien, State University of New York at Buffalo
Swing, Jack H, University of Illinois at Urbana-Champaign
Swisher, Michael, University of North Carolina at Charlotte
Sykes, Robert D, University of Minnesota
Syme, Paul, University of Waterloo
Symes, Arthur L, Southern University
Szabo, Albert, Harvard University
Szerbaty, Michael, New York Institute of Technology
Szoosz, Merlin, Rhode Island School of Design
Tabas, Betsy, Temple University
Tabb, Phillip, Arizona State University
Taberner, Ian, Lawrence Technological University
Tagiuri, Peter, Rhode Island School of Design
Tai, Lolly, Clemson University
Takahashi, Nancy A, University of Virginia
Takano, Gerald, University of Hawaii at Manoa
Takas, Marianne, Boston Architectural Center
Takeuchi, Arthur, Illinois Institute of Technology
Tang, Stephen, University of Oregon
Tanick, Marshall, University of Minnesota
Tanzer, Kim, University of Florida
Tao, William K, Washington University
Tarrant, Athene, Kent State University
Tate, Ann, University of Miami
Tatum, Lance, University of Texas at Austin
Tatum, Michael, University of Texas at Arlington
Taubman, David, Southern California Institute of Architecture
Tauke, M Beth, State University of New York at Buffalo
Tavis, Richard L, University of Illinois at Urbana-Champaign
Taylor, Anne, University of New Mexico
Taylor, Bradbury W, Boston Architectural Center
Taylor, Edward, Spring Garden College
Taylor, J Robert, Ball State University
Taylor, Joseph, Howard University
Taylor, Robert, Carnegie Mellon University
Taylor, Stephen I, University of British Columbia
Taylor, Thomas A, Oklahoma State University
Taylor, William M, California State Politechnic University, Pomona
Taytslin, Vladimir, Boston Architectural Center

Teague, Edward H, University of Florida
Teasdale, Pierre, Université de Montréal
Tector, John O, North Carolina State University
Templer, Joan, Georgia Institute of Technology
Templer, John, Georgia Institute of Technology
Terian, Sara, Andrews University
Tesar, Paul, North Carolina State University
Tesoro, Andrew, Columbia University
Thaddeus, David, University of Houston
Thaler, Peter, New York Institute of Technology
Thallon, Robert, University of Oregon
Thanhauser, Charles, New Jersey Institute of Technology
Theis, Christopher C, Louisiana State University
Thiel, Philip, University of Washington
Thiratrakoolchai, Sombat, University of Maryland
Thomas, J Bruce, University of Oklahoma
Thompsen, Harold A, North Dakota State University
Thompson, A Dudley, Texas Tech University
Thompson, Donna, Oklahoma State University
Thompson, Fred S, University of Waterloo
Thompson, Harlyn, University of Manitoba
Thompson, Milo, University of Minnesota
Thompson, Virginia M, Texas Tech University
Thompson, William P, University of Manitoba
Thomsen, Charles, University of Manitoba
Thomson, Thomas L, Washington University
Thorbeck, Duane, University of Minnesota
Thorne, Karl S, University of Florida
Thornton, Charles, Pratt Institute
Thorp, Robert, Washington University
Thrower, Jack, University of Pennsylvania
Thurman, Henry L, Southern University
Tice, James, Columbia University
Tichich, Ann, New York Institute of Technology
Tickell, Simon, Drexel University
Tiers, Charles A, University of British Columbia
Tigerman, Stanley, University of Illinois at Chicago
Tillman, Wiley L, University of Florida
Tilson, William L, University of Florida
Timberlake, James, Princeton University
Timme, Robert H, University of Houston
Timmer, Wayne F, Mississippi State University
Tinney, Daniel, University of Miami
Tiseo, Benedetto, Lawrence Technological University
Tittman, John, University of Illinois at Chicago
Tivoli, Octavio, University of Manitoba
Tobias, David, Boston Architectural Center
Tobin, John M, Rensselaer Polytechnic Institute
Tobriner, Stephen, University of California, Berkeley
Todd, Anderson, Rice University
Todd, Kim, University of Nebraska-Lincoln
Tollefson, Lee, University of Minnesota
Tompkins, C Larry, University of Arkansas
Tondino, Gentile, McGill University
Toporek, Walter J, Iowa State University
Torre, Susana, Columbia University
Toruner, Aygen, Laval University

Tountas, Christos, Columbia University
Tracy, Robert H, University of Nevada, Las Vegas
Trafidlo, Ed, Boston Architectural Center
Travis, Diane, University of Illinois at Chicago
Travisano, Fred, New Jersey Institute of Technology
Tredway, Richard L, Oklahoma State University
Treece, T Gerald, University of Houston
Tregebov, Alan, University of Toronto
Treib, Marc, University of California, Berkeley
Trelles, Jorge, University of Miami
Trelles, Luis, University of Miami
Tremaglio, Richard, Massachusetts Institute of Technology
Tremblay, Gilles, Laval University
Trencher, Michael, Pratt Institute
Tringale, Joseph, Boston Architectural Center
Tripp, William, Oregon School of Design
Tropf, Karl, Lawrence Technological University
Trost, Frederick J, Texas A&M University
Trott, Richard W, Ohio State University
Trotti, Guillermo, University of Houston
Troy, Martin, McGill University
Tschumi, Bernard, Columbia University
Tsien, Billie, Southern California Institute of Architecture
Tsolakis, Alkis, Drury College
Tucker, Diane, Oklahoma State University
Tucker, Robert, University of Detroit
Tucker, Robert W, University of Virginia
Tuley, James S, University of Virginia
Turan, Mete, Carnegie Mellon University
Turkel, Norbert, Pratt Institute
Turley, Robert, State University of New York at Buffalo
Turner, James A, University of Michigan
Turner, William K, Tulane University
Tuttle, Arthur N, University of Oklahoma
Tyau, Gordon, University of Hawaii at Manoa
Tyler, Richard, Temple University
Tyng, Ann, University of Pennsylvania
Ubbelohde, Susan, University of Minnesota
Ueland, Mark, Drexel University
Underhill, Michael, Iowa State University
Underwood, James R, Ball State University
Underwood, Max, Arizona State University
Ungers, Simon, Rensselaer Polytechnic Institute
Ungers, Simon, Southern California Institute of Architecture
Upton, Dell, University of California, Berkeley
Urban, Frederic, University of Waterloo
Urbas, Andrea, Ball State University
Ushick, Russell E, Oklahoma State University
Utsey, Glenda, University of Oregon
Utsey, Michael, University of Oregon
Utsunomiya, San, Illinois Institute of Technology
Utzinger, D Michael, University of Wisconsin-Milwaukee
Utzinger, Robert C, Montana State University
Uzman, Zeyn, Lawrence Technological University
Vachon, Emilien, Laval University
Vagle, Royle, Drury College
Vajda, Elizabeth, The Cooper Union
Vajna, Agi, Louisiana State University

Vakalo, Emmanuel-George, University of Michigan
Valella, Orestes, Pratt Institute
Valgora, Gerald L, Boston Architectural Center
Valletto, William, Pratt Institute
Vallhonrat, Carles, Princeton University
Vamosi, Stephen J, University of Cincinnati
van Bakergem, Davis W, Washington University
Van Buren, Clemet T, Roger Williams College
Van der Ryn, Sim, University of California, Berkeley
Van Elslander, Terence, Rensselaer Polytechnic Institute
van Ginkel, Blanche L, University of Toronto
van Groll, Theo, University of Virginia
Van Lengen, Karen, Columbia University
Van Neil, George, Ohio State University
Van Oudenallen, Harry, University of Wisconsin-Milwaukee
Van Purnell, E Donald, Southern University
Van Putten, Lilly, Andrews University
Van Sickle, David, University of Kansas
van Valkenburgh, Michael, Harvard University
Van Wyk, Cornelius, Ohio State University
Vanags, Andris, University of Washington
Vanderklok, Roger, Lawrence Technological University
Vann, R Lindley, University of Maryland
Vanos, Jay, Southern California Institute of Architecture
vanPelt, Robert J, University of Waterloo
Varela, Maria, University of New Mexico
Varenhorst, Glenn E, Clemson University
Varey, Gordon, University of Washington
Varga, Joseph, Lawrence Technological University
Varkonda, Linda, Clemson University
Vatalaro, Michael V, Clemson University
Vaughan, Joseph, Carnegie Mellon University
Vaughan, Terry, University of Pennsylvania
Venn, Robert G, University of North Carolina at Charlotte
Ventre, Francis T, Virginia Polytechnic Institute & State University
Verderber, Stephen F, Tulane University
Verges, Ricardo, Université de Montréal
Vergun, Dimitry, University of Southern California
Vernez-Moudon, Anne, University of Washington
Vernooy, Andy, University of Texas at Austin
Ververka, Mary J, Iowa State University
Vickery Jr, Robert L, University of Virginia
Vickery, Robert L, Washington University
Victoria, Teofilo, University of Miami
Vidler, Anthony, Princeton University, Southern California Institute of Architecture
Vieyra, Daniel, Kent State University
Vigier, Francois, Harvard University
Vildostegui, Luis, Tulane University
Vincent, Sammy, Louisiana State University
Vinci, John, Illinois Institute of Technology, University of Illinois at Chicago
Vinciarelli, Lauretta, Columbia University
Vinokur, Herman, University of Pennsylvania
Vinoly, Rafael, Columbia University
Vitali, Davide, University of Arkansas
Vivoni, Enrique, University of Puerto Rico
Voelker, Cecilia E, Clemson University

Voelker III, William J, University of Illinois at Urbana-Champaign
Vogan, David, Hampton University
Voichysonk, Bernard F, University of Florida
Vollendorf, Dean B, University of North Carolina at Charlotte
Vollmer, Roy, Spring Garden College
von Hoffmann, Alexander, Harvard University
von Rabenau, Burkhard, Ohio State University
Vora, S B, Lawrence Technological University
Voss, Jerrold R, Ohio State University
Vreeland, Thomas, University of California, Los Angeles
Vrooman, Richard E, Texas A&M University
Vuyosevich, Robert D, Ohio State University
Vytlacil, Anne, California Polytechnic State University, San Luis Obispo
Waddy, Patricia, Syracuse University
Wade, John W, Virginia Polytechnic Institute & State University
Wagner, Betty, University of Washington
Wagner, George, Rhode Island School of Design
Wagner, George S, Harvard University
Wagner, Harvey Allen, Roger Williams College
Wagner, Martin, Southern California Institute of Architecture
Wagner, Paul, Frank Lloyd Wright School of Architecture
Wagner, William G, University of Florida
Wahl, M Iver, University of Oklahoma
Waldman, Peter D, Rice University
Walker, Bradford, Boston Architectural Center
Walker, Bradford, Roger Williams College
Walker, Gerald L, Clemson University
Walker, Jill K, Spring Garden College
Walker, John W, Texas A&M University
Walker, Peter E, Harvard University
Walkey, Ronald B, University of British Columbia
Wall, Donald, New Jersey Institute of Technology
Wall, Gerard, Pratt Institute
Wall, Jerry D, University of Arkansas
Wall, Scott, Rice University
Wallace, George, Hampton University
Wallet, Stephen S, New School of Architecture
Wallick, Joan, Pratt Institute
Wallister, David, University of Nevada, Las Vegas
Walsh, Thomas F, Washington University
Walters, David R, University of Oklahoma
Walters, Elizabeth, Pennsylvania State University
Walters, Robert, University of New Mexico
Walters, Sandra, Lawrence Technological University
Walther, William, New York Institute of Technology
Walton, Thomas, Catholic University of America
Wampler, Jan, Massachusetts Institute of Technology
Wandel, Robert N, Ohio State University
Wang, David, Spring Garden College
Wang, Joseph C, Virginia Polytechnic Institute & State University
Wang, Samuel, Clemson University
Wang, Wilfried, Harvard University
Wanzel, J Grant, Technical University of Nova Scotia

Faculty Roster

Warburton, Ralph, University of Miami
Ward, Wesley, California Polytechnic State University, San Luis Obispo
Ware, Shelah M, University of Tennessee-Knoxville
Warfield, James P, University of Illinois at Urbana-Champaign
Warke, Val K, Cornell University
Warner, Ed, Boston Architectural Center
Warner, George, Boston Architectural Center
Warren, Jacqueline, Drury College
Warriner, Kenneth L, Rensselaer Polytechnic Institute
Warrington, Ann, Washington State University
Warshaw, Leonard, Université de Montréal
Washburn, Harold, Rhode Island School of Design
Washington, Clarence, Boston Architectural Center
Wasserman, Barry L, California State Polytechnic University, Pomona
Wasylyshen, Ben, University of Manitoba
Watkins, James C, Texas Tech University
Watson, Donald R, Yale University
Watson, J Marvin, University of Virginia
Watson, Philippe, Laval University
Watson, J Stroud, University of Tennessee-Knoxville
Watts, Carol, Kansas State University
Watts, Donald, Kansas State University
Watts, Fraser, University of Waterloo
Waugh, Scott, University of Houston
Wayne, Kathryn, University of Arizona
Weaver, Mark, Auburn University
Webb, Bernard, Wentworth Institute of Technology
Webb, Bruce C, University of Houston
Webb, Michael, Columbia University, The Cooper Union, Pratt Institute
Weber, Hanno, University of Wisconsin-Milwaukee
Webster, Philip, McGill University
Wee, Susan J, North Dakota State University
Weeks, James, University of Detroit
Weeks, J Stephen, University of Minnesota
Weese, Ben, University of Illinois at Chicago
Weese, Cynthia, University of Illinois at Chicago
Wei, Wesley, Pennsylvania State University, Temple University
Weidemann, Gregory, University of Maryland
Weil, Mark, Washington University
Weile, Regi, The Cooper Union
Weiner, Frank H, Virginia Polytechnic Institute & State University
Weinstein, Joel, Pratt Institute
Weinstein, Richard S, University of California, Los Angeles
Weinz, Susan, Boston Architectural Center
Weir, Paul, University of South Florida
Weisberg, Sarelle, Pratt Institute
Weisenburger, Patricia, Kansas State University
Weisenthal, Howard, California Polytechnic State University, San Luis Obispo
Weisman, Gerald D, University of Wisconsin-Milwaukee
Weisman, Leslie, New Jersey Institute of Technology
Weiss, Ellen, Tulane University

Weiss, Gregory, University of North Carolina at Charlotte
Weiss, Julian, New Jersey Institute of Technology
Weiss, Marion, University of Maryland
Weiss, Peter M, Auburn University
Welch, John, University of Manitoba
Wells, Douglas A, Iowa State University
Wells, Herbert C, University of Nevada, Las Vegas
Wells, Jerry, University of Miami
Wells, Jerry A, Cornell University
Wells, Ward V, Texas A&M University
Wells-Bowie, LaVerne, University of Tennessee-Knoxville
Wemple, Emmet, University of Southern California
Wendler, Walter V, Texas A&M University
Wendt, Eugene, Kansas State University
Werner, William A, University of Michigan
Weslar, Jerry, Boston Architectural Center
Wesley, Richard, University of Pennsylvania
West, Judy, Boston Architectural Center
West, M, Carleton University
West, Troy, New Jersey Institute of Technology
Westberg, John, Arizona State University
Westfall, C William, University of Virginia
Westlake, Paul, Kent State University
Westwood, D, Carleton University
Wheeler, Dan, University of Wisconsin-Milwaukee
Wheeler, Richard, Woodbury University
Whetter, David, University of Manitoba
Whiffen, Marcus, Arizona State University
Whitaker, Martha, Washington University
Whitaker Jr, Richard R, University of Illinois at Chicago
Whitbeck, Elizabeth, Boston Architectural Center
White, Charles W, Texas A&M University
White, Edward T, Florida A&M University
White, Frank S, Rice University
White, H Kenneth, University of Virginia
White, Hubert, University of Illinois at Urbana-Champaign
White, James E, Texas Tech University
White, Janet W, Washington University
White, John P, Texas Tech University
White, Julian T, Louisiana State University
White, Norval, City College of the CUNY
White, Stephanie, Technical University of Nova Scotia
White, Stephen, Washington University
White, Tony R, University of Florida
Whiteman, John, Harvard University
Whitmer, Roger, University of Illinois at Chicago
Whittemore, Leila, Oregon School of Design
Wick, Robert, University of Colorado at Denver
Wickersham, Jay, Boston Architectural Center
Wickersheimer, David J, University of Illinois at Urbana-Champaign
Widdowson, William C, University of Cincinnati
Widrig, Walter, Rice University
Wiencke, William R, Florida A&M University
Wiesenfeld, James, New York Institute of Technology
Wigley, Mark, Princeton University

Wilcox, Peter, University of Oregon
Wilhelm, Gerald, Southern California Institute of Architecture
Wilhelm, Gregory J, California Polytechnic State University, San Luis Obispo
Wiljer, Robert, University of Waterloo
Wilke, Douglas, New York Institute of Technology
Wilkes, Joseph, University of Maryland
Wilkes, Kevin, New Jersey Institute of Technology
Wilkie, Ann, Technical University of Nova Scotia
Wilkinson, Lonnie, Southern University
Willcocks, Allan, Technical University of Nova Scotia
Williams, A Richard, University of Arizona
Williams, A Richard, University of Illinois at Urbana-Champaign
Williams, Barry L, California Polytechnic State University, San Luis Obispo
Williams, Graham, Rensselaer Polytechnic Institute
Williams, Jeffrey K, Oklahoma State University
Williams, Jeneice K, Florida A&M University
Williams, Robert A L, Lawrence Technological University
Williams, Robert L, University of Cincinnati
Williams, Roger, University of Washington
Williams, Steve, Auburn University
Williams, Tod, Southern California Institute of Architecture
Williams, Tod C, The Cooper Union
Williams, S Wayne, Washington State University
Williamson, James, Drexel University
Williamson, James, Georgia Institute of Technology
Williamson, John, Boston Architectural Center
Williamson, Roxanne, University of Texas at Austin
Willig, Max, Illinois Institute of Technology
Willis, Daniel, Pennsylvania State University
Willoughby, Edward, Lawrence Technological University
Wilson, Chris, University of New Mexico
Wilson, Forrest H, Catholic University of America, University of Maryland
Wilson, Randall, Southern California Institute of Architecture
Wilson, T Kelly, Rhode Island School of Design
Wilson, Patricia A, University of Texas at Austin
Wilson, Richard G, University of Virginia
Wilson, Stuart, McGill University
Wilson, Thomas T, Boston Architectural Center
Wiltz, S R, Prairie View A&M University
Winarsky, Ira H, University of Florida
Windley, Paul, Kansas State University
Wineman, Jean, Georgia Institute of Technology
Winkelhake, Claude A, University of Illinois at Urbana-Champaign
Winn, Coulter, New School of Architecture
Winne, Robert F, Rensselaer Polytechnic Institute
Wishne, Brian, University of Wisconsin-Milwaukee
Wisnewska, Miriam, University of Detroit
Wisniewski, Chester, The Cooper Union

Witherspoon, Gayland B, Clemson University
Wittenberg, Gordon, Rice University
Witzling, Lawrence P, University of Wisconsin-Milwaukee
Wodehouse, Lawrence M, University of Tennessee-Knoxville
Wofford, Larry, Oklahoma State University
Wolf, Alan, The Cooper Union
Wolf, Carol, University of Miami
Wolfe, Lawrence, Pennsylvania State University
Wolff, Paul M, California Polytechnic State University, San Luis Obispo
Wolin, Judith, Rhode Island School of Design, Rice University
Wollesen-Wisch, Barbara, Pennsylvania State University
Wolner, Edward, Ball State University
Wolstenholme, T, Carleton University
Wong, Peter, University of North Carolina at Charlotte
Wood, John, Wentworth Institute of Technology
Wood, Peter J, University of Houston
Wood, Thomas R, University of Florida
Wood, Timothy, New Jersey Institute of Technology, Yale University
Wood, Woodruff W, University of British Columbia
Woodard, F Scott, University of Colorado at Denver
Woodard, Kramer, University of New Mexico
Woodbury, Robert, Carnegie Mellon University
Woodcock, David G, Texas A&M University
Woodfin, C Daniel, Ball State University
Woodland, Dennis, Andrews University
Woodridge, Wilson, New Jersey Institute of Technology
Woods, Beth, University of Southwestern Louisiana
Woods, Lebbeus, The Cooper Union
Woods, Mary, Cornell University
Woods, Timothy J, University of Southwestern Louisiana
Woolard, Donald S, California Polytechnic State University, San Luis Obispo
Wooley, David L, University of Tennessee-Knoxville
Woolsey, D Kristine, Arizona State University
Worley, Johnny K, Texas Tech University
Worley, Kenneth, Washington University
Worsdale, Marc, Rensselaer Polytechnic Institute
Wren, Douglas, Laval University
Wright, David, University of Washington

Wright, George, University of Texas at Arlington
Wright, Gwendolyn, Columbia University
Wright, Lee, University of Texas at Arlington
Wright, Michael, Boston Architectural Center
Wright, Robert, Oklahoma State University
Wright, Rodner B, Mississippi State University
Wright, Sylvia, City College of the CUNY
Wright, Ted, University of Nebraska-Lincoln
Wu, Hofu, Arizona State University
Wu, King Lui, Yale University
Wyman, John E, Ball State University
Wyman, Richard V, University of Nevada, Las Vegas
Wyre, Stanley, Lawrence Technological University
Wzacny, Christopher, University of Michigan
Yamashita, Jim, University of Manitoba
Yancey, Keith, Boston Architectural Center
Yang, H S, Prairie View A&M University
Yang, Hanford, Pratt Institute
Yanik, John V, Catholic University of America
Yardley, Michael, University of Texas at Arlington
Yates-Burns, Elysabeth, University of Cincinnati
Yearwood, Richard M, Virginia Polytechnic Institute & State University
Yeh, W H Raymond, University of Oklahoma
Yergens, Milton, North Dakota State University
Yerges, James F, University of Notre Dame, Washington University
Yessios, Christos I, Ohio State University
Yip, Christopher, California Polytechnic State University, San Luis Obispo
Yoder, Wilbur, Rhode Island School of Design
Yonamine, Calvin, University of Hawaii at Manoa
Yonder, Ayse, Pratt Institute
Youkilis, Sanford, University of Miami
Younes, Samir, Catholic University of America
Young, Edmund R, Iowa State University
Young, Jenny, University of Oregon
Young, Joseph L, Clemson University
Young Jr, Paul E, Ohio State University
Young, Richard A, California Polytechnic State University, San Luis Obispo
Youssef, Nabih, Southern California Institute of Architecture
Youssefzadeh, Bijan, Texas A&M University
Ytterberg, Michael, Drexel University
Yudell, Robert, University of California, Los Angeles
Zabarkes, Arthur, Pratt Institute
Zabel, Craig, Pennsylvania State University

Zaffanella, Anna B, Rensselaer Polytechnic Institute
Zago, Andrew, Southern California Institute of Architecture
Zalewski, Waclaw, Massachusetts Institute of Technology
Zambonini, Giuseppe, Georgia Institute of Technology
Zanette, Paul, Boston Architectural Center
Zapata, Carlos, New York Institute of Technology
Zarina, Astra, University of Washington
Zdepski, M Steven, New Jersey Institute of Technology
Zeichmeister, Daniel, Lawrence Technological University
Zeller, Martin, University of Colorado at Denver
Zemanek, John, University of Houston
Zeno, Jaime, University of Puerto Rico
Zeppetelli, Lea, University of Manitoba, McGill University, Université de Montréal
Zilm, Frank, University of Kansas
Zimmer, Norman C, Oregon School of Design
Zimmerman, Bernard, California State Polytechnic University, Pomona
Zimring, Craig, Georgia Institute of Technology
Zissovici, John, Cornell University
Zody, Richard E, Virginia Polytechnic Institute & State University
Zoelly, Pierre, Carnegie Mellon University
Zoldos, John, New Jersey Institute of Technology
Zonars, George B, Lawrence Technological University
Zorko, Jozef, McGill University
Zorr, Paul A, Auburn University
Zrein, Imad A, Boston Architectural Center
Zrudlo, Leo R, Laval University
Zuberbuhler, Doug, University of Washington
Zubizarreta, Ignazio, North Carolina State University
Zuk, Radoslav, McGill University
Zuk, William, University of Virginia
Zuliani, Guido, The Cooper Union
Zunino, Jack W, University of Nevada, Las Vegas
Zurinaga, Raul, University of Puerto Rico
Zweig, Peter J, University of Houston
Zweijski, Jan B, Laval University
Zwirn, Robert, Miami University
Zygas, K Paul, Arizona State University
Zylberg, Leonardo, Columbia University
Zylstra, Sape A, University of South Florida

Schools of Architecture Worldwide

Excluding U.S. and Canada

ALGERIA
Université of Constantine, Ecole Polytechique d'Architecture et d'Urbanisme, B.P. n°2, El-Harrach, *Alger* Ecole d'Architecture de Constantine, *Constantine*

ARGENTINA
Universidad de Belgrano, Facultad de Arquitectura, Cramer 1991, *Buenos Aires*
Facultad de Arquitectura y Urbanismo de Buenos Aires, Peru 294, *Buenos Aires*
Universidad Catolica de Cordoba, Facultad de Arquitectura, Deàn Funes 52-2 do P.E. 228, *Cordoba*
Facultad de Arquitectura y Urbanismo de Cordoba, Avenida Vélez Sarsfield 264, *Cordoba*
Universidad Nacional de la Plata, Calle 7, Esquina 47 y 48, *La Plata*
Universidad de la Provincia de Mar del Plata, Facultad de Arquitectura, Juan B Alberdi 2695, *Mar Del Plata*
Universidad de Mendoza, Facultad de Arquitectura y Urbanismo, Diagonal Hammarskjold 750, DAG, *Mendoza*
Facultad de Ingenieria, Vivienda y Planeamiente de Resistencia, Avenida Las Heras 727, *Resistencia* (Chaco)
Escuela de Arquitectura y Planeamiente de Rosario, Avenida Pellegrini 250, *Rosario* (Provincia de Santa Fe)
Universidad Nacional de Rosario, Facultad de Arquitectura, Berutti 2121, *Rosario* (Provincia de Santa Fe)
Escuela de Arquitectura de San Juan, Jufré, Parque de Mayo, *San Juan*
Universidad Nacional de Tucumán, Facultad de Arquitectura, Ayacucho 482, *San Miguel De Tucumán*
Universidad Católica de Santa Fe, Facultad de Arquitectura, San Martín 1966, *Santa Fe*

AUSTRALIA
South Australian Institute of Technology, School of Architecture and Building, North Terrace, *Adelaide* (South Australia 5000)
University of Adelaide, Faculty of Architecture and Planning, GPO Box 498, *Adelaide* (South Australia 5001)
Deakin University, Division of Architecture, P.O. Box 125, *Belmont* (Victoria 3217)
Western Australia Institute of Technology, Department of Architecture, Kent Street, *South Bentley,* (Western Australia 6102)
Queensland Institute of Technology, Department of Architecture and Industrial Design, GPO Box 2434, George Street, *Brisbane* (Queensland 4001)
University of Queensland, Faculty of Architecture, St. Lucia, *Brisbane* (Queensland 4067)
South Wales Institute of Technology, School of Architecture and Building, P.O. Box 123, *Broadway* (New South Wales 2007)
Canberra College of Advanced Education, School of Environmental Design, P.O. Box 381, *Canberra* (A.C.T. 2601)
Gordon Institute of Technology, Department of Architecture, P.O. Box 122, *Geelong* (Victoria 3220)
University of New South Wales, School of Architecture, P.O. Box 1, *Kensington* (New South Wales 2033)
Papua New Guinea Institute of Technology, P.O. Box 793, *Lae* (Papua New Guinea)
Tasmanian College of Advanced Education, School of Environmental Design and Engineering, P.O. Box 1214, *Launceston* (Tasmania 7250)
Royal Melbourne Institute of Technology, Department of Architecture, 200 La Trobe Street, *Melbourne* (Victoria 3001)
University of Western Australia, Department of Architecture, *Nedlands* (Western Australia 6009)
University of Melbourne, School of Architecture and Building, *Parkville* (Victoria 3052)
University of Newcastle, Faculty of Architecture, *Shortland* (New South Wales 2308)
University of Sydney, School of Architecture, *Sydney* (New South Wales 2006)

AUSTRIA
Technische Hochschule Graz, Fakultät für Bauingenieurwesen und Architektur, Stiermark/Rechbauerstrasse 12, *Graz* A-8010
Universität Innsbrück, Fakultät für Architektur, A-6020, *Innsbrück - Kranebilden*
Akademie für Bildenden Künste, Architekturabteilung, Schillerplatz 3, *Wien* 1010
Technische Hochschule Wien, Fakultät für Bauingenieurwesen und Architektur, Karlsplatz 3, *Wien* 1040
Academie für Angewandte Kunst, Oskar-Kokoschka-Platz 2, A-1010 *Wien*

BANGLADESH
University of Engineering and Technology, Department of Architecture, *Dacca* 2

BELGIUM
Koninklijke Academie voor schone Kunster van Antwerpen, Mutsaerstraat 31,2000 *Antwerpen*
Hoger St. Lukasinstituut Schaarbeek, Paleizenstraat 70, 1080 *Brussels*
Académie Royale des Beaux Arts de Bruxelles, Rue du Midi 144, 1000 *Bruxelles*
Ecole Nationale Supérieure d'Architecture et des Arts Visuels, La Cambre, Abbaye de La Cambre 21, 1050 *Bruxelles*
Institute Supérieur d'Architecture Saint Luc, rue d'Irlande, 57, 1060 *Bruxelles*
Académie Royale des Beaux Arts de Gand, Koninklijke Academie voor schone Kunsten van Gent, Academiestraat 2, 9000 *Gent*
Hoger St. Lukasinstituut Gent, Zwarte Zustersstraat 30, 9000 *Gent*
Hoger Provinciaal Instituut van Hasselt, Elfde Liniestraat 25, 3500 *Hasselt*
Académie Royale des Beaux Arts de Liège, Rue des Anglais 21, 4000 *Liège*
Ecole Supérieure d'Architecture, Académie Royale des Beaux Arts de Liège, Rue Fabri 19, 4000 *Liège*
Université de Liège, Chaire d'Architecture, 7, place du Vingt Août, 4000 *Liège*
Institut Saint Luc de Liège, Rue Sainte Marie 26, 4000 *Liège*
Académie Royale des Beaux Arts de Mons, Rue de Nimy 106, 7000 *Mons*
Université Catholique de Louvain, Place du Levant, 1, B 1348 *Louvain la Neuve*
Departement d'Architecture Faculté Polytechnique, rue de Joncquois, 53, 7000 *Mons*
Institut Saint Luc de Tournai, Chaussée de Tournai 50, 7721 *Ramegnies-Chin*

BOLIVIA
Universidad Mayor de San Simon, Escuela de Arquitectura, Calama Final Este, Casilla n° 558, *Cocha Bamba*
Universidad Mayor de San Andrés, Escuela de Arquitectura, Av. Villazon 1995, Cajon Postal 3072, *La Paz*

BRAZIL
Faculdade de Arquitetura de Barra do Pirai, KM 11 Rodovia Benjamin Ielpo, Cx. Postal 228, 27100 *Barra Do Pirai,* Estado do Rio
Universidade Federal do Parà, Departamento de Arquitetura, Centro de Tecnologia, Travessa Campos Sales 295, *Belem,* PA
Universidade Federal de Minas Gerais, Escola de Arquitetura, Rua Paraiba 697, *Belo Horizonte,* MG
Universidade de Brasilia, Faculdade de Arquitetura e Urbanismo, Campus Universitàrio, Asa Norte, *Brasilia,* D.F.
Universidade Federal do Paranà, Departamento de Arquitetura, Faculdade de Engenharia, Centro Politécnico, Cx. Postal 1.611, 80 000 *Curitiba,* PR
Universidade Federal do Ceará, Curso de Arquitetura e Urbanismo, Centro de Tecnologia, Avenida da Universidade 2890, 60 000 *Fortaleza,* Ceará
Universidade Catolica de Goiàs, Escola da Arquitetura, Praça Universitaria, Goiània 74000, Cx. Postal 86, *Goiania,* GO
Universidade Catolica de Goiàs, Faculdade de Artes e Arquitetura, Rua 94, A. 10, Setor Sul, *Goiania,* Goiàs
Faculdade de Arquitetura e Urbanismo Farias Brito, Praca Teresa Cristina 1, Centro, 07 000 *Guarulhos,*SP
Universidade Estadual de Londrina, Faculdade de Arquitetura e Urbanismo, Rua Alagoas n° 2.001, Cx. Postal 1.530, *Londrina,* PR
Federacào das Faculdades Braz Cubas, Avenida Francisco Rodrigues Filho 1233, 08 700 *Mogi Das Cruzes,* SP

Universidade Federal Fluminense, Curso de Arquitetura, Rua Miguel de Frias S/N° *Niteroi*, Estado do Rio

Universidade Federal do Rio Grande do Sul, Faculdade de Arquitetura, Rua Sarmento Leite, Esquina Oswaldo Aranha, *Porto Alegre*, Rio Grande do Sul

Universidade Federal de Pernambuco, Faculdade de Arquitetura, Edificio dos Institutos Bàsicos, 10° Andar, Cidade Universitària, *Recife*, Pernambuco

Instituto "Bennet de Ensino", Faculdade de Arquitetura, Rua Marques de Abrantes 55, Botafogo *Rio De Janeiro*, GB

Sociedade Universitaria "Silva e Souza", Faculdade de Arquitetura e Urbanismo, Rua Uranos 733, Bonsucesso, Guanabara, 20 000 *Rio De Janeiro*,, GB

Universidade Federal do Rio de Janeiro, Faculdade de Arquitetura e Urbanismo, Cidade Universitària, Ilha do Fundào, Edificio da Arquitetura, *Rio De Janeiro*, GB

Universidade Gama Filho, Faculdade de Arquitetura e Urbanismo, Rua Manoel Vitorino 583, Piedade, *Rio De Janeiro*, GB

Faculdade de Arquitetura e Urbanismo "Santa Ursula", Rua Farani N° 75, Botafogo, *Rio De Janeiro*, GB ZC 01

Universidade da Bahia, Faculdade de Arquitetura, Rua Caetano Moura, 121, Federaçào, 40 000 *Salvador*, Bahia

Faculdade de Arquitetura e Urbanismo de Santos, Rua 7 de Setembro 34, 11 100 *Santos*, SP

Faculdade de Arquitetura e Urbanismo "Elmano Ferreira Veloso", Avenida Sao Joao 1 500, Praça Candido dias Castejon, 12 200 *Sao Jose Dos Campos*, SP

Universidade do Vale do Rio Dos Sinos, Faculdade de Arquitetura, Praca Tiradentes 35, *Sao Leopoldo*, Rio Grande do Sul

Universidade Mackenzie, Faculdade de Arquitetura, Fua Itambé 45, *Sao Paulo*, SP

Universidade de Sao Paulo, Faculdade de Arquitetura e Urbanismo, Cidade Universitária Armando Sales de Oliveiro, Cx. Postal 3225, *Sao Paulo*, SP

BULGARIA
Institut du Génie Civil, Faculté d'Architecture, 1, Rue Hr. Smirnenski, *Sofia*

BURMA
Arts & Science University, University P.O., *Mandalay*

Rangoon Institute of Technology, Department of Architecture, Gyoyone, Insein P.O., *Rangoon*

CHILE
Universidad de Chile, Facultad de Arquitectura, Casilla 10-D, *Santiago*

Universidad Católica de Chile, Facultad de Arquitectura y Bellas Artes, Avenida Bernardo O'Higgins 340, Casilla 114-D, *Santiago*

Universidad Catolica de Valparaiso, Facultad de Arquitectura, Casilla 4059, *Valparaiso*

CHINA, NATIONALIST REPUBLIC OF (TAIWAN)
National Cheng Kung University, Department of Architecture, *Tainan*

CHINA, PEOPLE'S REPUBLIC OF
Hua Nan Polytechnic Institute, Department of Civil Engineering and Architecture, *Canton*

Harbin Institute of Building Construction, *Harbin*

Nanking Polytechnic Institute, Department N°1, *Nanking*

Tsing Hua University, Department of Civil Engineering and Architecture, *Peking*

Tung Chi University, Departgment of Civil Engineering and Architecture, Kiangsu, *Shanghai*

Tientsin University, Department of Civil Engineering and Architecture, *Tientsin*

COLOMBIA
Corporación Universitaria de la Costa, Facultad de Arquitectura, Calle 58 entre cras. 54 y 59 *Barranquilla*

Universidad del Atlántico, Facultad de Arquitectura, Carrera 43 N° 50-53 *Barranquilla*

Universidad Autónoma del Caribe, Facultad de Arquitectura, Carrera 46 N° 88-26 *Barranquilla*

Universidad Simón Bolivar, Facultad de Arquitectura, Calle 68 N° 54-82 *Barranquilla*

Universidad de América, Facultad de Arquitectura, Carrera 5a. N° 10-35 *Bogotá*

Universidad Católica, Facultad de Arquitectura, Avenida 39 N° 16-12 *Bogotá*

Universidad de la Gran Colombia, Facultad de Arquitectura, Carrera 5a. N° 13-39 *Bogotá*

Universidad Javeriana, Facultad de Arquitectura, Carrera 7a. N° 40-62 *Bogotá*

Universidad de Los Andes, Facultad de Arquitectura, Calle 1a. E N° 18-A-10 *Bogotá*

Universidad Nacional, Facultad de Arquitectura, Ciudad Universitaria *Bogotá*

Universidad Piloto, Facultad de Arquitectura, Calle 78 N° 10-54 *Bogotá*

Universidad del Valle, Facultad de Arquitectura, Calle 4a. B N° 36-00 *Cali*

Universidad Nacional, Facultad de Arquitectura, Apartado Aéreo N° 127 *Manizales*

Universidad Nacional, Facultad de Arquitectura, Apartado Aéreo N° 1779 *Medellin*

Universidad Pontificia Bolivariana, Facultad de Arquitectura y Urbanismo, *Medellin*

COSTA RICA
Universidad de Costa Rica, Escuela de Arquitectura, Ciudad Universitaria, *San José*

CUBA
Universidad de La Habana, Escuela de Arquitectura, Ciudad Universitaria "José Antonio Echevarría," Central "Martínez Prieto," Marianao, *La Habana*

Universidad Central de Las Villas, Escuela de Arquitectura, *Santa Clara*, Provincia de Las Villas

Universidad "José Antonio Maceo" de Oriente, Escuela de Arquitectura, *Santiago De Cuba*, Oriente Cuba

CZECHOSLOVAKIA
Ecole Polytechnique Slovaque, Faculté d'Architecture, Place Gottwaldo 2, *Bratislava*

Ecole Supérieure Slovaque des Beaux Arts, Faculté d'Architecture, Place Hiezdeslavovo 18, *Bratislava*

Ecole Polytechnique, Faculté d'Architecture, Barvicova 85, *Brno*

Faculté du Bâtiment, Zikova 4, *Prague* 6, Dejvice

Académie des Beaux Arts, Faculté d'Architecture, U Akademie 4, *Prague* 7

Ecole Supérieure des Arts Décoratifs, Faculté d'Architecture, Place Krasnoarmjeu 80, *Prague* 1

DENMARK
Arkitektskolen i Aarhus, Nörreport 20, 8000 *Aarhus* C

Det Kongelige Danske Kunstakademi, Kunstakademiets Arkitekskole, Kongens Nytorv 3, 1050 *Copenhagen* K

DOMINICAN REPUBLIC
Universidad Autónoma de Santo Domingo, Facultad de Arquitectura, *Santo Domingo*

ECUADOR
Universidad de Cuenca, Escuela de Arquitectura, Apt. 168, *Cuenca*

Universidad de Guayaquil, Escuela de Arquitectura, Calle Chile 900, *Guayaquil*

Universidad Central del Ecuador, Garcia Moreno 887 y Espejo 945, Casilla 166, *Quito*

EL SALVADOR
Universidad de El Salvador, Escuela de Arquitectura, *San Salvador*, América Central

ETHIOPIA
Haile Selassie I University, Department of Architecture and Town Planning, *Addis Ababa*

EGYPT
Université d'Alexandrie, Département d'Architecture, *Alexandrie*

Faculté des Beaux Arts, Section Architecture, *Alexandrie*

Université d'Assyout, Département d'Architecture, *Assyout*

Université d'Alazhar, Ecole d'Urbanisme, *Cairo*

Schools of
Architecture
Worldwide

Faculté des Beaux Arts, Zamalek, Section
d'Architecture, 8 Ismail Mohammed, *Cairo*
Université du Caire, Section d'Architecture,
Guiza, *Cairo*
Université Ein Shams, Section d'Architecture,
Cairo

FINLAND
Arkkitchtiosasto, Oulun Yliopisto,
Aleksanterinkatu 6, 90100 *Oulu* 10
Tampere University of Technology,
Department of Architecture,
Tuomiokirkonatu 19, 33100 *Tampere* 10
Helsinki University of Technology, Department
of Architecture, Otankaari 1X, 02150 *Espoo*
15
Lahti Institute of Technology, Stahlberginkatu
10, 15110 *Lahti* 11

FRANCE
Institut d'Aménagement Régional de
l'Université d'Aix-Marseille, 3, avenue
Robert Schuman, 13100 *Aix En Provence*
Ecole Nationale d'Art Décoratif, Place
Villeneuve, 23200 *Aubusson*
Ecole Nationale des Beaux Arts et Arts
Appliqués à l'Industrie, 1, rue des Beaux
Arts, 18000 *Bourges*
Antenne Pédagogique Expérimentale de
Cergy-Pontoise, Ville Nouvelle, Parking P 2,
95300 *Cergy*
Unité Pédagogique d'Architecture, 2, rue
d'Enfer, 63000 *Clermont-Ferrand*
Institut d'Urbanisme de Paris, Avenue du
Général de Gaulle, 94000 *Créteil*
Ecole Nationale des Beaux Arts, 3, rue
Michelet, 21000 *Dijon*
Faculté des Sciences Sociales, U.E.R.
d'Urbanisme "Urbanisation et
Aménagement", 21, rue Lesdiguières, 38000
Grenoble
Unité Pédagogique d'Architecture, 21, rue
Lesdiguières, 38000 *Grenoble*
Unité Pédagogique d'Architecture, 97,
boulevard Carnot, 59000 *Lille*
Ecole Nationale d'Art Décoratif, 8, place
Winston Churchill, 87000 *Limoges*
Unité Pédagogique d'Architecture, 14, Montée
du Télégraphe, 69246 *Lyon*
Ecole d'Art et d'Architecture, Domaine de
Luminy, 13288 *Marseille* Cedex 02
Unité Pédagogique d'Architecture, Rue N° 1
Lotissement de Lambert, Plandes Quatre
Seigneurs, 34000 *Montpellier*
Ecole Nationale des Beaux Arts et Arts
Appliqués, 1, avenue Boffrand, 54000
Nancy
Unité Pédagogique d'Architecture n° 5, 267,
rue de Courbevoie, 92400 *Nanterre*
Unité Pédagogique d'Architecture "La
Mulotière", Rue Massenet, 44000 *Nantes*
Ecole Nationale d'Art Décoratif, 20, avenue
Stéphen Liégeard, 06000 *Nice*
Centre de Recherche d'Urbanisme (C.R.U.), 4,
avenue du Recteur Poincaré, 75016 *Paris*
Institut d'Etudes Politiques de Paris, Cycle

Supérieur d'Aménagement et d'Urbanisme,
4, rue de l'Abbaye, 75006 *Paris*
Université de Paris VII, Département de
l'Environnement, 2, place Jussieu, Tour
24-34, 3ème Etage, P. 06, 75005 *Paris*
Ecole Nationale Supérieure des Arts
Décoratifs, 31, rue d'Ulm, 75005 *Paris*
Ecole Nationale Supérieure des Beaux Arts,
17, quai Malaquais, 75272 *Paris* Cedex 06
Ecole Spéciale d'Architecture, 254, boulevard
Raspail, 75014 *Paris*
Institut de l'Environnement, 14-20, rue
d'Erasme, 75005 *Paris*
Institut d'Urbanisme de l'Académie de Paris
VIII-Vincennes, Route de la Tourelle, 75012
Paris
Secrétariat des Missions d'Urbanisme et
d'Habitat (S.M.U.H.), 11, rue Chardin, 75016
Paris
Ecole Nationale des Ponts et Chaussées,
Séminaire d'Aménagement Urbain et
Régional, 28, rue des Saints Pères, 75007
Paris
Unité Pédagogique d'Architecture n° 1, 11,
quai Malaquais, 75272 *Paris* Cedex 06
Unité Pédagogique d'Architecture n° 2, 1, rue
Jacques Callot, 75006 *Paris*
Unité Pédagogique d'Architecture n° 4, 13-15,
quai Malaquais, 75006 *Paris*
Unité Pédagogique d'Architecture n° 6, 14,
rue Bonaparte, 75006 *Paris*
Unité Pédagogique d'Architecture n° 7, Grand
Palais des Champs Elysées, Porte C, Cours
de la Reine, 75008 *Paris*
Unité Pédagogique d'Architecture n° 8, 69-71,
rue de Chevaleret, 75013 *Paris*
Unité Pédagogique d'Architecture n°9, 14, rue
Bonaparte, 75006 *Paris*
Unité Pédagogique d'Architecture, 34, rue
Hoche, 35000 *Rennes*
Unité Pédagogique d'Architecture,
Aître-Saint-Maclou, 186, rue de Martainville,
76000 *Rouen*
Unité Pédagogique d'Architecture, 1, rue
Buisson, 42000 *Saint Etienne*
Ecole Nationale Supérieure des Arts et
Industries de Strasbourg, Département de
l'Architecture, 24, boulevard de la Victoire,
67084 *Strasbourg*
Institut d'Architecture et d'Urbanisme, Palais
du Rhin, 3, place de la République, 67000
Strasbourg
Unité Pédagogique d'Architecture, Domaine
de Raba, Cours de la Libération, 33405
Talence
Ecole Nationale des Beaux Arts, 5, quai
Daurade, 31000 *Toulouse*
Unité Pédagogique d'Architecture, Chemin du
Mirail, 31300 *Toulouse Le Mirail*
Université de Tours, Centre d'Etudes
Supérieures de l'Aménagement du
Territoire (C.E.S.A.), Avenue Monge, Parc
Grandmont, 37000 *Tours*
Unité Pédagogique d'Architecture n° 3,
Petites Ecuries du Roy, 2, avenue de Paris,
78000 *Versailles*

GERMAN DEMOCRATIC REPUBLIC
Kunsthochschule Berlin, 112 *Berlin,*
Weissensee Strasse 203 Nr. 20
Technische Universität Dresden, Sektion
Architektur, *Dresden,* 8027,
Mommenstrasse 13
Hochschule für Architektur und Bauwesen,
Sektion Architektur, 53 *Weimar,*
Geschwister Schollstrasse 8

GERMANY, FEDERAL REPUBLIC OF
Technische Hochschule Aachen,
Architekturabteilung, Templergraben 55, 51
Aachen
Werkkunstschule der Stadt Aachen,
Architekturabteilung, Südstrasse 40, 51
Aachen
Fachhochschule Aachen, Goethestrasse 1, 51
Aachen
Staatliche Ingenieurschule für Bauwesen,
Bayernallee 9, Ecke Raererenerstrasse, 51
Aachen
Fachhochschule Augsburg, Baumgartner
Strasse 16, 89 *Augsburg*
Werkkunstschule der Stadt Augsburg,
Maximilianstrasse 52, 89 *Augsburg*
Staatliche Werkkunstschule Berlin,
Architekturabteilung, Strasse der 17 Juni
118, 1 *Berlin* 12
Staatliche Hochschule für Bildende Künste,
Hardenbergstrasse 33, 1 *Berlin* 12
Staatliche Ingenieurschulen, Fachrichtung
Hochbau, Leinestrasse 38/44, 1 *Berlin* 44
Technische Fachhochschule Berlin,
Limburger-strasse 20, 1 *Berlin* 65
Technische Universität Berlin, Fachbereich 8,
Strasse der 17 Juni 135, *Berlin*
Fachhochschule Biberach, Waldseestrasse
34, 795 *Biberach* (Riss)
Staatliche Ingenieurschulen für Bauwesen
Arbeitsamt, 795 *Biberach* (Riss)
Werkkunstschule der Stadt Bielefeld,
Architekturabteilung, Am Sparrenberg 2, 48
Bielefeld
Fachhochschule Bochum, Kohlenstrasse 70,
463 *Bochum*
Technische Universität Braunschweig,
Architekturabteilung, Pockelstrasse 4, 33
Braunschweig
Werkkunstschule der Stadt Braunschweig
(Hochschule), Architekturabteilung,
Breizemer Strasse 230, 33 *Braunschweig*
Hochschule für Gestaltung, Am Wandrahm, 28
Bremen
Hochschule für Technik, Langemarckstrasse
116, 28 *Bremen*
Fachhochschule Nordostniedersachsen,
Fachbereiche Architektur und
Bauingenieurwesen, Harburger Strasse 6,
215 *Buxtehude*
Fachhochschule Coburg,
Friedrich-Streib-Strasse 2, 863 *Coburg*
Werkkunstschule Darmstadt,
Architekturabteilung, Olbrichweg 10, 61
Darmstadt

Fachhochschule Darmstadt, Schöfferstrasse 3, 61 *Darmstadt*

Technische Hochschule Darmstadt, Fakultät für Architektur, Hochschulstrasse 1, 61 *Darmstadt*

Staatsbauschule Darmstadt, Havelstrasse, 61 *Darmstadt*

Fachhochschule Lippe, Abt. Detmold, Schubertplatz 12, 493 *Detmold*

Werkkunstschule Dortmund, Architekturabteilung, Ottostrasse 9, 46 *Dortmund*

Fachhochschule Dortmund, Sonnenstrasse 96, 46 *Dortmund*

Hochschule für Bildende Künste, Staatliche Kunstakademie *Düsseldorf*

Werkkunstschule Düsseldorf, Architekturabteilung, Fürstenwall 100, 4 *Düsseldorf*

Fachhochschule Düsseldorf, Josef-Gockelm Strasse 9, 4 *Düsseldorf*

Fachhochschule Kiel, Fachbereich Bauwesen in Eckernförde, Lorenz-v.-Stein-Ring, 233 *Eckernförde*

Fachhochschule Essen, Schützenbahn 70, 43 *Essen*

Staatliche Ingenieurschule, Fachrichtung Hochbau, Robert Schmidt Strasse 1, 43 *Essen*

Werkkunstschule der Stadt Essen, Folkwangschule für Gestaltung, 43 *Essen-Werden*, Abtei

Fachhochschule Frankfurt, Nibelungenplatz 1, 6 *Frankfurt-am-Main*

Staatliche Hochschule für Bildende Künste, Städelschule, Dürerstrasse 10, 6 *Frankfurt-am-Main*

Fachhochschule Hagen, Haldenerstrasse 182, 58 *Hagen*

Staatliche Ingenieurschule, Fachrichtung Hochbau, Grashofstrasse, 58 *Hagen*

Hochschule für Bildende Künste, Lerchenfeld 2, D 2000 *Hamburg 76*

Freie Akademie der Künste in Hamburg, Hochschulen der Bildenden Künste, Heilwigstrasse 39, 2 *Hamburg 20*

Staatliche Fachhochschule, Fachrichtung Hochbau, Hebebrandstrasse 1, 2 *Hamburg 39*

Staatliche Ingenieurschule, Fachrichtung Hochbau, Steinterplatz 2, 2 *Hamburg 1*

Technische Universität Hannover, Architekturabteilung, Schlosswender Strasse 1, 3 *Hannover*

Werkkunstschule Hannover, Architekturabteilung, Köbelingstrasse 21, 3 *Hannover*

Technische Universität, Fakultät für Bauwesen, Welfengarten 1, 3 *Hannover*

Werkschule Hildesheim, Architekturabteilung, Dammstrasse 45, 32 *Hildesheim*

Fachhochschule Hildesheim, Fachbereiche Architektur und Bauingenieurwesen, Hohnen 2, 32 *Hildesheim*

Gesamthochschule Paderborn, Abt. Höxter, An der Wilhelmshöne, 347 *Höxter*

Staatliche Ingenieurschule für Bauwesen, Möllingerstrasse 3, 347 *Höxter*

Fachhochschule Hildesheim, Fachbereiche Architektur und Bauingenieurwesen, Haarmannplatz 2, 346 *Holzminden*

Gesamthochschule Siegen-Gummersbach, Paul-Bonatz Strasse 9, 593 *Huttental-Weidenau*

Fachhochschule Wiesbaden, Limburger Strasse 2, 627 *Idstein*

Fachhochschule des Landes Rheinland-Pfalz, Morlauterer Strasse 31, 675 *Kaiserslautern*

Staatliche Ingenieurschule, Fachrichtung Hochbau, Villenstrasse 5, 675 *Kaiserslautern*

Fachhochschule Karlsruhe, Moltkestrasse 4, 75 *Karlsruhe*

Universität Karlsruhe, Fakultät für Architektur, 7, 75 *Karlsruhe*

Staatliche Akademie der Bildende Künste, Reinheld-Frank Strasse 81/83, 75 *Karlsruhe*

Technische Hochschule, Kaiserstrasse 12, Postfach 6380, 75 *Karlsruhe*

Staatliche Werkkunstschule Kassel, Architekturabteilung, Eugen Richter Strasse 7, 35 *Kassel*

Architektur Gesamthochscule Kassel, Wilhelmshöher Allee 71, 35 *Kassel*

Gesamthochschule Kassel, Friedrich Ebert Strasse 35, 35 *Kassel*

Fachhochschule Kiel, Fachbereich Gestaltung, Lorenzendamm 6, 23 *Kiel*

Muthesius Werkschule Kiel, Architekturabteilung, Herthastrasse 9, 23 *Kiel-Wik*

Fachhochschule des Landes Rheinland-Pfalz, Abt. Koblenz, Am Finkenherd 4, 54 *Koblenz-Karthause*

Staatliche Ingenieurschule, Fachrichtung Hochbau, 54 *Koblenz-Karthause*

Fachhochschule Köln, Claudiusstrasse 1, 5 *Köln*

Kölner Werkschulen, Ubierring 40, 5 *Köln*

Staatliche Ingenieurschule, Fachrichtung Hochbau, Turmstrasse 7, *Köln-Nippes*

Fachhochschule Konstanz, Brauneggerstrasse 55, 775 *Konstanz*

Werkkunstschule Krefeld, Architekturabteilung, 123, 415 *Krefeld*

Fachhochschule Lippe, Abt. Lage, Langestrasse 124, 491 *Lage*

Staatliche Fachhochschule Lübeck, Fachbereich Bauwesen, Stephensonstrasse 1, 24 *Lübeck*

Staatsbauschule Lübeck, Langer Lehberg 24, 24 *Lübeck*

Fachhochschule des Landes Rheinland-Pfalz, Abt. Mainz 1, Holzstrasse 36, 65 *Mainz*

Fachhochschule Bielefeld, Abt. Minden, Artillerie, 495 *Minden*

Akademie für Angewandte Technik, Oskar-von-Miller-Polytechnikum, Lothstrasse 34, 8 *München 2*

Akademie der Bildenden Künste, Akademiestrasse 2, 8 *München 13*

Technische Hochschule München, Architekturabteilung, Arciss Strasse 21, 8 *München 2*

Fachhochschule Dipl. Ing. C. Weber, Rosental 5, 8 *München 2*

Fachhochschule München, Karlstrasse 6, 8 *München 2*

Werkschule Münster, Architekurabteilung, Sentmaringe, Weg 53, 44 *Münster*

Fachhochschule Münster, Lotharingerstrasse 8-26, 44 *Münster*

Fachhochschule Hannover, Fachbereiche Architektur und Bauingenieurwesen, Abt. Nienburg, Bürgermeister-Stahn-Wall 9, 307 *Nienburg / Weser*

Staatliche Ingenieurschule für Bauwesen, 307 *Nienburg / Weser*

Akademie der Bildenden Künste, Bingstrasse 60, 85 *Nürnberg*

Fachhochschule Nürnberg, Kesslerstrasse 40, 85 *Nürnberg*

Hochschule für Gestaltung, Schlossstrasse, 605 *Offenbach*

Fachhochschule Oldenburg, Fachbereiche Architektur, Bauingenieurwesen und Vermessungswesen, Ofener Strasse 16, 29 *Oldenburg*

Fachhochschule Regensburg, Prüfeningerstrasse 58, 84 *Regensburg*

Fachhochschule Rosenheim, Marienberger Strasse 26, 82 *Rosenheim*

Meisterschule für das Gestaltende Handwerk, Architekturabteilung, Keplerstrasse 3/5, 66 *Saarbrucken*

Fachhochschule des Saarlandes, Abt. Ingenieurwesen, Saaruferstrasse 66, 66 *Saarbrucken*

Staatliche Ingenieurschule, Fachrichrung Hochbau, Dr. Ernst Strasse 19, 59 *Siegen*

Universität Stuttgart, Architekturabteilung, Keplerstrasse 1, 7 *Stuttgart 1*

Fachhochschule für Technik, Kanzleistrasse 29, 7 *Stuttgart*

Technische Hochschule, Fakultät für Bauwesen, Huberstrasse 16, Postfach 560, 7 *Stuttgart 1*

Universität Stuttgart, Institut für Schulbau, Ossietzkystrasse 4, 7 *Stuttgart 1*

Staatliche Akademie der Bildenden Künste, Am Weissenhof 1, 7 *Stuttgart N*

Trierer Werkschule, Architekturabteilung, Paulusplatz 4, 55 *Trier*

Fachhochschule des Landes Rheinland-Pfalz, Abt. Trier, Irminenfreihof 8, 55 *Trier*

Universität Trier-Kaiserslautern, Schneidershof, 55 *Trier*

Hochschule für Gestaltung, Am Hochstäb, 79 *Ulm/Donau*

Werkkunstschule Wiesbaden, Schulberg 10, 62 *Wiesbaden*

Staatliche Ingenieurschule, Fachrichtung Hochbau, Pauluskirchstrasse 7, 56 *Wuppertal-Barmen*

Gesamthochschule Wuppertal, Hofkamp 86, 56 *Wuppertal-Elberfeld*

Werkkunstschule Wuppertal, Architekturabteilung, Corneliusstrasse 26, 56 *Wuppertal-Vohwinkel*

Fachhochschule Würzburg-Schweinfurt, Sanderring 8, 87 *Würzburg*

Schools of Architecture Worldwide

GHANA
University of Science and Technology, Faculty of Architecture, *Kumasi*

GREAT BRITAIN *see* **UNITED KINGDOM**

GREECE
Université Technique Nationale d'Athènes, Faculté d'Architecture, 42, rue Patission *Athens* 147
Université de Thessalonique, Faculté d'Architecture, *Thesaloniki*

GUATEMALA
Universidad de San Carlos de Guatemala, Facultad de Ingenieria, Ciudad Universitaria *Guatemala* 12

HAITI
Université de Haïti, Ecole Polytechnique d'Haïti, *Port Au Prince*

HONG KONG
University of Hong Kong, Department of Architecture, Knowles Building, Pokfulam Road, *Hong Kong*

HUNGARY
Magyar Iparmiivészeti Folskola, Ecole Supézrieure des Arts Décoratifs, Zugligeti ut 11-25, 1121 *Budapest*
Ybl Miklos Epitoipari Foiskola, Ecole Supérieure du Bâtiment "Ybl Miklos", 1183 *Budapest* Thököly ut 74
Université Technique de Budapest, Faculté d'Architecture, Budapesti Miszaki Egyetem, Müegyetem rkp. 3, 1111 *Budapest* XI

INDIA
School of Architecture, University Road, Navarangpura, *Ahmedabad* 9, Gujerat
The M.S. University of Baroda, Department of Architecture, *Baroda* 2, Gujerat
Academy of Architecture, Next to Tyresoles Co. Pvt. Ltd., Behind Ravindra Natya Mandir, Off Sayani Road, Cross Lane, Prahbadevi, *Bombay* 25, Maharashtra
Bandra School of Art, Architecture Section, Saint Martin's Road, *Bombay* 50 AS, Maharashtra
Sir J.J. College of Architecture, Dr. Dadabhai Naoroji Road, *Bombay* 1, Maharashtra
The Chandigarh College of Architecture, *Chandigarh*
The Bengal Engineering College, Architecture Section, P.O. Botanic Garden, *Howrah* 3, West Bengal
The Governmental College of Fine Arts and Architecture, Architecture Section, *Hyderabad* 500028 (A.P.)
The Indian Institute of Technology, Architecture Section, *Kharagpur*, S.E. Rly.
The Madras University, Architecture Section, University Building, Chepauk, *Madras* 5

V.R. College of Engineering, Architecture Section, *Nagpur*
School of Planning and Architecture, Indraprasta, *New Delhi*
The Abhinava Kala Vidyalaya, Architecture Section, Tilak Road, *Poona* 9
The University of Roorkee, Department of Architecture, *Roorkee*

INDONESIA
Catholic University, Department of Architecture, Parahiangan, Djalan Merkeda 32, *Bandung*, Java
Institut Teknologi Bandung, Department of Architecture, Fakultas Teknik Sipil et Perencanaan, Djalan Caneca 10, *Bandung*, Java
University Tarumanagara, Department of Architecture, *Djakarta*
State University of Gadjah Mada, Department of Architecture, Borek, *Jogiakarta*
University Diponegoro, Department of Architecture, *Semarang*
Institut Teknologi Surabaya, Department of Architecture, Djalan Kaliasin 84, *Surabaya*

IRAN
National University of Iran, Faculty of Agriculture, *Teheran*

IRAQ
University of Baghdad, Department of Architecture, College of Engineering, Jadiriya, *Baghdad*
University of Technology, Department of Architecture and Planning, Tel Mohammed, P.O. Box 745, *Baghdad*

IRELAND
College of Technology, Department of Architecture, Bolton Street, *Dublin* 1
University College Dublin, School of Architecture, Earlsfort Terrace, *Dublin* 2

ISRAEL
Technion Israel Institute of Technology, Technion City, *Haifa* 3200

ITALY
Università degli Studi, Facoltà di Architettura, piazza S. Marco 4, *Firenze*
Università degli Studi, Facoltà di Architettura, via all'Opera Pia 11, *Genova*
Politecnico di Milano, Facoltà di Architettura, piazza Leonardo da Vinci 32, *Milano*
Università degli Studi, Facoltà di Architettura, corso Umberto 1, *Napoli*
Università degli Studi, Facoltà di Architettura, via Maqueda, *Palermo*
Facoltà di Architettura, *Pescara*
Istituto Universitario di Architettura, *Reggio Calabria*
Università degli Studi, Facoltà di Architettura, viale Belle Arti, *Roma*
Politecnico di Torino, Facoltà di Architettura, corso Duca degli Abruzzi 24, *Torino*

Istituto Universitario di Architettura, Campazzo dei Tolentini 191, calle Amai 197, *Venezia*

JAMAICA
University of the West Indies, Faculty of Engineering, Mona, *Kingston* 7

JAPAN
Meijo University, Architectural Department, School of Science and Engineering (Daytime Division), 69 Yagotourayama, Tenpakucho; Showa-ku, Nagoya-shi, *Aichi*
Meijo University, Architectural Department, School of Science and Engineering (Nighttime Division), 2-5 Shintomi-cho 1-chome; Nakamura-ku, Nagoya-shi, *Aichi*
Aichi Institute of Technology, Department of Architecture, Yachigusa, Yagusa-cho, Toyota-shi, *Aichi*
Chubu Institute of Technology, Department of Architecture, 1200, Matsumoto-cho, Kasugai-shi, *Aichi*
Chiba Institute of Technology, Department of Architecture, 7-1916 Yatsumachi, Narashino-shi, *Chiba*
Nihon University, Department of Architecture, College of Industrial Technology, 2-1 Izumi-cho 1-chome, Harashino-shi, *Chiba*
Chiba University, Department of Architecture, Faculty of Engineering, 33, Yayoicho 1-chome, Chiba-shi, *Chiba*
Science University of Tokyo, Faculty of Science and Technology, Higashi Kameyama 2641; Yamazaki, Noda-shi, *Chiba*
Fukui Institute of Technology, The Constructive Engineering Course, Department of Technology, 20 Gakuanmachi, Fukui-shi, *Fukui*
Fukui University, Department of Architecture, Faculty of Engineering, 9-1 Bunkyo 3-chome, Fukui-shi, *Fukui*
Fukui University, Department of General Constructive Engineering, Faculty of Engineering, 9-1 Bunkyo 3-chome, Fukui-shi, *Fukui*
Kyushu Kyoritsu University, Department of Architecture, Faculty of Engineering, Jiyugaoka, Oribi-cho, Yahata-ku; Kitakyushu-shi, *Fukuoka*
Kyushu Sangyo University, Department of Architecture, Faculty of Engineering, 327, Matsuka-dai 2-chome, Higashi-ku, Fukuoka-shi, *Fukuoka*
Nishi-Nippon Institute of Technology, Department of Architecture, 1633, Ooaza Aratsu Kanda-cho, Miyako-gun, *Fukuoka*
Kinki University, Department of Architecture, Technical College (Kyushu), Kashiwanomori, Iizuka-shi, *Fukuoka*
Kyushu Institute of Design, Environmental Design Department, Faculty of Design, 226, Ooaza Shiobara, Mirami-ku, Fukuoka-shi, *Fukuoka*
Nihon University, Department of Architecture,

College of Engineering, 1-banchi, Aza Nakagawara, Tokusada; Tamura-cho, Kohriyama-shi, *Fukushima*

Hiroshima University, Department of Architecture, Faculty of Engineering, 8-2, Senda-machi, 3-chome, Hiroshima-shi, *Hiroshima*

Hiroshima Institute of Technology, Department of Architecture, Miyake, Itsukaichi-machi; Saiki-gun, *Hiroshima*

Kinki University, Technical College, 1000, Hiro-cho; Kureshi, *Hiroshima*

Hokkai Educational Institute, Department of Architecture, Faculty of Engineering, Nishi 11-chome, Minami 26-jo, Chuo-ko; Sapporo-shi, *Hokkaido*

Kobe University, Department of Architecture, Faculty of Engineering, Rokkodaimachi, Nada-ku, Kobe-shi, *Hyogo*

Kagoshima University, Architectural Course, Department of Engineering, 52 Kamoike-cho, Kagoshima-shi, *Kagoshima*

Kanagawa University, Department of Architecture, Faculty of Engineering, 27 Rokkakubashi 3-chome, Kanagawa-ku, Yokohama-shi, *Kanagawa*

Kanto Gakuin University, Department of Architecture, Faculty of Technology, *Kanagawa*

Kanto Gakuin University, Department of Environmental Engineering of Architecture, Faculty of Technology, 4834 Mutsuuracho, Kanagawa-ku, Yokohama-shi, *Kanagawa*

Kumamoto University, Department of Architecture, Faculty of Engineering, 39-1 Kurokami-cho 2-chome, Kumamoto-shi, *Kumamoto*

Kumamoto Technical College, Department of Architecture, 2332 Ikeda-cho, Kumamoto-shi, *Kumamoto*

Kyoto University, Department of Architecture, Faculty of Engineering, Yoshida Hon-machi, Sakyo-ku, Kyoto-shi, *Kyoto*

Tohoku Institute, Department of Architecture, 19 Koshiji, Nagamachi, Sendai-shi, *Miyagi*

The College of Naval Architecture of Nagasaki, Department of Architecture, 536 Amiba-cho, Nagasaki-chi, *Nagasaki*

Nara Women's University, Department of Dwelling, Faculty of Home Economics, Nishi-machi, Kitauoya, Nara-shi, *Nara*

Oita Technical College, Ooaza Ichigi, Oita-shi, *Oita*

Osaka University, Department of Architectural Engineering, Faculty of Engineering, Ooaza Yamada-ue, Suita-shi, *Osaka*

Kansai University, Department of Architecture, Faculty of Engineering, Senriyama, Suita-shi, *Osaka*

Kinki University, Department of Architecture, Faculty of Science and Engineering, 321 Kowakae, Higashiosaka-shi, *Osaka*

Osaka City University, Department of Architecture and Architectural Engineering, Faculty of Engineering, 459 Sugimoto-cho, Sumiyoshi-ku, Osaka-shi, *Osaka*

Osaka City University, Department of Housing and Design, Faculty of the Science of Living, 459 Sugimoto-cho, Sumiyoshiku, Osaka-shi, *Osaka*

Tokyo University, Department of Architecture, Faculty of Engineering, 2100, Nakanodai, Kujlral, Kawagoe-shi, *Saitama*

Nihon Institute of Technology, Department of Architecture, 900 Suga, Miyashiro-cho, Minamisaitama-gun, *Saitama*

Ashikaga Institute of Technology, Department of Architecture, Faculty of Engineering, 268-banchi, Daizen-cho, Ashikaga-shi, *Tochigi*

Tokai University, Architectural Department, Faculty of Technology, 28, Tomigaya 2-chome, Shibuya-ku, *Tokyo*

Hosei University, Department of Architecture, College of Engineering, 7-2 Kajinocho 3-chome, Koganei-shi, *Tokyo*

Nihon University, Department of Architecture, College of Science and Engineering, 8 Surugadai 1-chome, Kanda, Chiyoda-ku, *Tokyo*

Musashino Art University, The Department of Architecture, Faculty of Arts, 736 Ogawa-cho 1-chome, Kodaira-shi, *Tokyo*

Kokushikan University, Department of Architecture, Faculty of Engineering, 28-1, Setagaya 4-chome, Setagaya-ku, *Tokyo*

Musashi Institute of Technology, Department of Architecture, Faculty of Engineering, 28-1 Tamazutsumi 1-chome, Setagaya-ku, *Tokyo*

Tokyo University of Science, Department of Architecture, Faculty of Engineering, 1-3 Kagurazaka, Shinjuku-ku, *Tokyo*

University of Tokyo, Department of Architecture, Faculty of Engineering, 3-1, Hongo, 7-chome, Bunkyo-ku, *Tokyo*

Tokyo Metropolitan University, Department of Architecture, Faculty of Technology, 1-1 Fukazawa 2-chome, Setagaya-ku, *Tokyo*

Kogakuin University, Department of Architecture, 24-2 Nishishinjuku, 1-chome, Shinjuku-ku, *Tokyo*

Waseda University, Department of Architecture, School of Science and Engineering, 4-170 Nishiohkubo, Shinjukuku, *Tokyo*

Shibaura Institute of Technology, Department of Architecture, 9-14 Shibaura, 3-chome, Minato-ku, *Tokyo* (J 162)

Tokyo Institute of Technology, Department of Social Engineering, 12-1 Ookayama 2-chome, Meguro-ku, *Tokyo*

Kogakuin University, Hatae Design Laboratory, c/o Department of Architecture, 24-2, Nishishinjuku 1-chome, Shinjuku-ku, *Tokyo*

Japan's Women's University, House Planning and Designs (Department of Home Economics), 8-1 Mejirodai 2-chome, Bunkyo-ku, *Tokyo*

Tokushima University, Department of Construction and Engineering, Faculty of Engineering, Tokushima University, 1, Minamijosanjima 2-chome, Tokushima-shi, *Tokushima*

KENYA
University of Nairobi, Faculty of Architecture, Design & Development, P.O. Box 30197, *Nairobi*

KHMER REPUBLIC
Université Royale des Beaux Arts, Faculté d'Architecture, Boulevard de l'URSS, *Phnom-Penh*
Vithei Samdech Ouk, Faculté d'Architecture et d'Urbanisme, *Phnom-Penh*

KOREA, DEMOCRATIC PEOPLE'S REPUBLIC OF
Chungjin Civil Engineering School, Ranam district, *Chungjin*
Hamhung Civil Engineering School, Bonryong district, *Hamhung*
Wonsan Civil Engineering School, Wonsan, *Kangwon*
Sariwon Civil Engineering School, Sariwon, *Narth Hwanghai*
Botonggang Civil Engineering School, Botonggang district, *Pyong Yang*
Donggaewon Senior Civil Engineering School, Bonggaewon district, *Pyong Yang*
Pyongyang Civil Engineering College, Junggu district, *Pyong Yang*

KOREA, REPUBLIC OF
Kang Won University, Department of Architectural Engineering, College of Engineering, *Choon Chun*
Choong Buk University, Department of Architectural Engineering, College of Engineering, *Choong Ju*
Choong Nam University, Department of Architectural Engineering, College of Engineering, *Choong Nam*
Chung Ju College, Department of Architecture, College of Engineering, *Chung Ju*
Chun-Buk University, Department of Architecture, College of Engineering, *Chun Ju*
Han Sa University, Department of Architectural Engineering, College of Engineering, *Daegu*
Kei Myung University, Department of Architectural Engineering, College of Engineering, *Daegu*
Yong Nam College, Department of Architectural Engineering, College of Engineering, *Daegu*
Mok Won College, Department of Architectural Design, *Dae Jeon*
Choong Nam University, Department of Architectural Engineering, College of Engineering, *Dae Jeon*
Wan Kwang University, Department of Architectural Engineering, College of Engineering, *I Lee*
In Ha University, Department of Architectural Engineering, College of Engineering, *Inchon*

Schools of Architecture Worldwide

Kyeong Sang National University, Department of Architectural Engineering, College of Engineering, *Jin Ju*

Inchon Engineering College, Department of Architectural Engineering, *Inchon*

Kwan Dong College, Department of Architectural Engineering, *Kang Reung*

Chosun University, Department of Architectural Engineering, College of Engineering, *Kwang Ju*

Chun Nam University, Department of Architectural Engineering, College of Engineering, *Kwang Ju*

Gyeong Nam College, Department of Architectural Engineering, *Ma San*

Dong Ah University, Department of Architectural Engineering, College of Engineering, *Pusan*

Pusan University, Department of Architectural Engineering, College of Engineering, *Pusan*

Dong Ee College, Department of Architectural Engineering, *Pusan*

City University of Seoul, Department of Architectural Engineering, *Seoul*

Dong Kuk University, Department of Architectural Engineering, College of Engineering, *Seoul*

Kun Kuk University, Department of Architectural Engineering, College of Engineering, *Seoul*

Kyong Gi University, Department of Architectural Engineering, College of Engineering, *Seoul*

Kyung Hee University, Department of Architectural Engineering, College of Engineering, *Seoul*

Myung Gee University, Department of Architectural Engineering, College of Engineering, *Seoul*

Seoul National University, Department of Architecture, College of Engineering, *Seoul*

Tan Kuk University, Department of Architectural Engineering, College of Engineering, *Seoul*

Younsei University, Department of Architectural Engineering, College of Science and Engineering, *Seoul*

Sung Kyun Kwan University, Department of Architectural Engineering, *Seoul*

Kook Min University, Department of Architecture, College of Architecture and Applied Arts, *Seoul*

Chung Ang University, Department of Architecture, College of Engineering, *Seoul*

Hong Ik University, Department of Architecture, College of Engineering, *Seoul*

Kook Min University, Department of Architecture, College of Engineering, *Seoul*

Korea University, Department of Architecture, College of Engineering, *Seoul*

Seoul National University, Department of Architecture, College of Engineering, Gong Reung-Dong, Dobong-Ku, *Seoul*

Han Yang University, Department of Architecture and Architectural Engineering, College of Engineering, *Seoul*

A Ju Engineering College, Department of Architectural Engineering, *Su Won*

Ulsan Engineering College, Department of Architectural Engineering, *Ulsan*

LEBANON

Académie Libanaise des Beaux Arts, Immeuble Farah, rue Monsseïtbéh, *Beirut*

Université Arabe de Beyrouth, Faculté d'Architecture, P.O. Box 5020, *Beirut*

Institut National des Beaux Arts, Ancien Palais de Justice Bab Idriss, *Beirut*

Ecole Supérieure D'Ingénieurs, B.P. 1514 *Beirut*

Université Américaine, Section d'Architecture Rue Bliss, *Beirut*

MADAGASCAR

Université de Madagascar, Département d'Architecture, B.P. 566, *Madagascar*

MALAYSIA

National Institute of Technology, Faculty of Built Environment, *Kuala Lumpur* 15-01

University Sains Malaysia, School of Housing, Building and Planning, *Pulau Pinang*

MARA Institute of Technology, Department of Architecture, *Shah Alam, Selangor*

MALTA

University of Malta, Department of Architecture and Civil Engineering, TAL-QROQQ, *Msida*

MEXICO

Universidad Autónoma de Aguascalientes, Centro Technológico, Jardín del Estudiante N°1, *Aguascalientes*, Ags.

Universidad Autónoma de Chihuahua, Escuela de Arquitectura, Avenida Colegio Militar S/N, Apartado 1727, *Chihuahua*, Chih.

Universidad Autónoma de Ciudad Juárez, Carrera de Arquitectura, Instituto de Ingenieria y Arquitectura, Avenida Lienzo Charro N°610 NTE, *Ciudad Juárez*, Chih.

Universidad Autónoma del Estado de Morelos, Escuela de Arquitectura, Avenida Universidad 1001, Chamilpa, *Cuernavaca, Mor.*

Instituto Tecnológico y de Estudios Superiores de Occidente A.C., Escuela de Arquitectura, Costa Rica N° 161, *Guadalajara*, Jal.

Universidad de Guadalajara, Instituto Tecnológico, Escuela de Arquitectura, Calzada a Tlaquepaque, *Guadalajara*, Jal.

Universidad de Guadalajara, Escuela de Arquitectura, Apartado Postal 1-3457 Central, Extremo de la Calzada Independencia Norte, *Guadalajara*, Jal.

Universidad Autónoma de Guadalajara, Facultad de Arquitectura, Paseo de Las Aquilas 7000, *Guadalajara*, Jal.

Universidad Autónoma de Guadalajara, Avenida Patria 1201, Apartado Postal 1-440, *Guadalajara*, Jal.

Universidad de Guanajuato, Facultad de Arquitectura, Mendizabel N° 19B, *Guanajuato*, Gto.

Universidad del Bajío, Centro de Arte y Diseño, A.C., Prolongación Avenida de los Insurgentes S/N, *León*, Gto.

Universidad de Yucatán, Escuela de Arquitectura, Ex-Convento de Mejorada, Calle 50 entre 57 y 59, *Mérida*, Yucatán

Universidad Autónoma de Baja California, Escuela de Arquitectura, B.B. Jaurez S/N, Ciudad Universitaria, *Mexicali*, B.C.

Auditorio Nacional, Conescal, Paseo de la Reforma, *México*, D.F.

Universidad Autónoma Metropolitana, División de Ciencias y Artes para el Diseño, Unidad Azcapotzalco, Apartado Postal 16-307, *Mexico* 16, D.F.

Universidad del Tepeyac, Escuela Arquitectura, A.C., Callao N° 842, Col. Lindavista, *México* 14, D.F.

Universidad Anáhuac, Escuela de Arquitectura, Lomas Anáhuac, *Mexico* 10, D.F.

Universidad Iberoamericana, Escuela de Arquitectura, División de Arte, Departamento de Arquitectura y Urbanismo, Avenida Cerro de Las Torres N° 395, *México* 21, D.F.

Universidad la Salle, Escuela Mexicana de Arquitectura, Benjamin Franklin N° 47, *México* 18, D.F.

Universidad Nacional Autónoma de México, Escuela Nacional de Arquitectura, Ciudad Universitaria, *México* 20, D.F.

Instituto Politécnico Nacional, Escuela Superior de Ingenieria y Arquitectura, Unidad Profesional de Zacatenco, Edificio N° 5, *México* 14, D.F.

Universidad Intercontinental, Facultad de Arquitectura, Avenida Insurgentes Sur 4135, *México* 21, D.F.

Instituto Superior de Arquitectura, Avenida Insurgentes Sur 1027 *México*, D.F.

Universidad Autónoma Metropolitana, Programa de Arquitectura, División de Ciencias y Artes para el Diseño, Unidad Xochimilco, Canal Nacional y Calzada del Hueso, *México* 20, D.F.

Universidad Nacional Autónoma de México, Programa de Arquitectura Aragon, Calle Norte 80-A 6727, Col. San Pedro el Chico, *México* 14, D.F.

Universidad Nacional Autónoma de México, Unidad Académica de Autogobierno, Ciudad Universitaria, *México* 20, D.F.

Universidad Nacional Autónoma de México, Escuela Nacional de Arquitectura, Ciudad Universitaria, *México*, D.F.

Instituto Tecnológico y de Estudios Superiores de Monterrey, Departamento de Arquitectura, Sucursal Correos "J," *Monterrey*, N.L.

Universidad Regiomontana, Escuela de Arquitectura, Unidad Aldama, Aldama Sur 744, *Monterrey*, N.L.

Universidad de Nuevo León, Facultad de Arquitectura, Ciudad Universitaria de Nueva León, *Monterrey,* N.L.

Universidad de Monterrey, Avenida Gonzalitos N&SO 300, Sur Monterrey, *Monterrey,* N.L.

Programa de Arquitectura, Avenida Alcanfores S/N, Santa Cruz Acatlán, *Naucalpan, Estado de México*

Universidad Autónoma de Oaxaca, Escuela de Arquitectura, Plaza de la Danza, Independencia y 5 de Mayo, *Oaxaca,* Oax.

Universidad "Benito Juárez," Escuela de Arquitectura, Avenida Independencia y M. Alcalá, *Oaxaca,* Oax.

Universidad Autónoma de Puebla, Escuela de Arquitectura, Ciudad Universitaria, Montes 4, Sur N° 104, *Puebla,* Pue.

Universidad Popular Autónoma del Estado de Puebla, Escuela de Arquitectura, 9 Poniente 1517, *Puebla,* Pue.

Universidad Autónoma de Coahuila, Escuela Arquitectura, Unidad Campo Redondo Edificio "D," Apartado 308, *Saltillo,* Coah.

Universidad Autónoma de San Luis Potosí, Nino Artirllero y Diagonal Sur, *San Luis Potosí,* S.L.P.

Universidad Autónoma de Nuevo León, Facultad de Arquitectura, Aparado Postal 533, *San Nicolás de los Garza,* N.L.

Arenal 906 Ote, Col. Tamaulipas, *Tampico,* Tamaulipas

Escuela de Arquitectura del Instituto Politécnico Nacional, Fuente de Leones N° 28, *Tecamachalco,* Estado de México

Universidad Autónoma del Estado de México, Escuela de Arquitectura, Avenida Constituyentes, *Toluca,* Estado de México

Universidad Autónoma del Estado de México, Facultad de Arquitectura y Arte, Ciudad Universitaria, Cerro de Coatepec, *Toluca,* Estado de México

Universidad Autónoma de Chiapas, Escuela de Arquitectura, Boulevard Belisario Dominguez Km. 154, Arpartado Postal 61, *Tuxtla Gutierrez,* Chiapas

Escuela Arquitectura del Instituto Colón, Carretera Veracruz-Boticaria, Kilómetro 1½, *Veracruz,* Ver.

Universidad Veracruzana, Facultad de Arquitectura, Lomas del Estadio, Zona Universitaria, *Xalapa,* Ver.

NEPAL
Tribhubana University, Department of Architecture, *Kirtipur - Kathmandu*

NETHERLANDS
Academie van Bouwkunst, Waterlooplein 67, 1011 PB *Amsterdam*

Academie van Bouwkunst, Sonsbeekweg 22, 6814 BC *Arnhem*

Technische Hogeschool, Afdeling Bouwkunde, Berlageweg 1, 2628 CR *Delft*

Technische Hogeschool te Eindhoven, Afdeling Bouwkunde, Den Dolech 2, 5600 MB *Eindhoven*

Academie van Bouwkunst, Hoge der A 12, 9712 AC *Groningen*

Academie van Bouwkunst, Capucijnenstraat 98, 6211 RT *Maastricht*

Academie van Bouwkunst, Bospolderplein 16, 3025 EM *Rotterdam*

Academie van Bouwkunst, Volstraat 60, 5021 SE *Tilburg*

NEW ZEALAND
University of Auckland, The School of Architecture, P.O. Box 2175, Private Bag, *Auckland*

Victoria University of Wellington, School of Architecture, Private Bag, *Wellington* 1

NICARAGUA
Universidad Nacional de Nicarague, Facultad de Arquitectura, *Managua*

NIGERIA
University of Nigeria, Department of Architecture, Enugu Campus, East Central State, *Enugu*

University of Lagos, Department of Architecture, Faculty of Environmental Design, Akoka, Yaba, *Lagos*

Amahdu Bello University, Department of Architecture, Faculty of Environmental Design, *Zaria*

NORWAY
Arkitekthogskolen i Oslo, St. Olavs gate 4, *Oslo* 1

Norges Tekniske Hogskole, Universitetet i Trondheim, Arkitektavdelingen, N 7034 *Trondheim*

PAKISTAN
National College of Engineering and Technology, Department of Architecture, M.A. Jinnah Road, *Karachi* 5

National College of Arts, Department of Architecture, Shahran-e-Quaid Azam, *Lahore*

Pakistan University of Engineering and Technology, Department of Architecture, Grand Trunk Road, *Lahore*

PANAMA
Universidad de Panama, Faculdad de Arquitectura, Apartado Postal 3277, *Panama* 3

PARAGUAY
Universidad Nacional de Asunción, Colon 73, *Asuncion*

PERU
Universidad Nacional "San Augustin", Escuela Profesional de Arquitectura, Siglo XX n° 225, *Arequipa*

Facultad de Ingeniera de la Universidad Nacional de "San Antonio Abad" del Cuzco, Sección de Arquitectura, Avenida Cultura, *Cuzco*

Universidad Nacional del Centro del Peru, Facultad de Arquitectura y Planeamiento, Calle Real 160, *Huancayo*

Universidad Nacional "Federico Villarreal", Facultad de Arquitectura, Nicolas Pierola 262, *Lima*

Universidad Nacional de Ingeniera, Facultad de Arquitectura, Casilla 1301, *Lima*

PHILIPPINES
University of San Carlos, Department of Architecture, P. del Rosario Street, *Cebu City*

University of Santo Tomás, The Catholic University of Philippines, College of Architecture and Fine Arts, *Manila*

Adamson University, Department of Architecture, 959 San Maralino, Ermita, *Manila*

Feati University, Department of Architecture, *Manila*

Mapua Institute of Technology, School of Planning and Architecture, Intramuros, *Manila*

University of the Philippines, College of Architecture, Diliman, *Quezon City*

Araneta University, College of Architecture, Vietoneta Park, *Rizal*

University of the Philippines, Department of Architecture, Diliman, *Rizal*

POLAND
Politechnika Gdanska, Instytut Architektury i Urbanistyki, ul. Majakowskiego 11/12, 80-321 *Gdansk*

Wydzial Projektowania Plastycznego, Panstwowa Wyzsza Szkola Sztuk Plastycznych, Targ Weglowy, 80-838 *Gdansk*

Politechnika Slaska, Wydzial Budownictwa i Architektury, ul. Katowicka 5, 44-100 *Gliwice*

Adademia Sztuk Pieknych, ul. Humberia 3, 31-121 *Krakow*

Politechnika Krakowska, Wydzial Architektury, ul. Warszawska 24, 31-155 *Krakow*

Wydzial Budownictwa Ladowego, Oddzial Architektury, ul. Piotrowo 5, 61-138 *Poznan*

Wydzial Projektowania Plastycznego, Panstowowa Wyzsza Szkola Sztuk Pieknych, ul. Marcinkowskiego 29, 61-745 *Poznan*

Politechnika Szczecinska, Wydzial Budownictwa i Architektury, Aleja Piastow 17, 70-310 *Szczecin*

Instytut Urbanistyki i Architektury, 01 Krolewska 27, Nr kod 00-060 skr. poczt. 245, *Warszawa*

Politechnika Warszawska, Wydzial Architektury, ul. Koszykowa 55, 00-659 *Warszawa*

Akademia Sztuk Pieknych, Wydzial Projektowania Plastycznego, Krakowskie Przedmiescie 5, 00-068 *Warszawa*

Wydzial Projektowania Plastycznego, Panstwowa Wyzsza Szkola Sztuk

Schools of Architecture Worldwide

Plastycznych, Plac Polski 3/4, 50-156 *Wroclaw*
Politechnika Wroclawska, Wydzial Architektury, Boteslawa Prussa 53-55, 50-137 *Wroclaw*

PORTUGAL
Escola Superior de Belas Artes de Lisboa, Largo da Biblioteca, *Lisboa* 1
Escola Superior de Belas Artes do Porto, Ave. Rodrigues de Freitas 265, *Porto*

ROMANIA
Scoala Tehnica de Arhitectura si constructii, Strada Progresului N° 56, *Baia Mare,* Reguinea Maramures
Institutul de Arhitectura "Ion Mincu", Strada Academiei nr 18-20, Sectorul 1, *Bucarest*
Scoala medie de Arhitectura, Strada Occidentului N° 10, *Bucarest,* Raion 30 Decembrie
Centrul scolar de constructii, Strada Armata Rosio N° 74, *Cluj,* Reguinea Cluj
Institutul Politehnic, Sectia Arhitectura, Strada Emil Isac nr 15, *Cluj,* Jud. Cluj
Institutul Politehnic, Sectia Arhitectura, *Iasi,* Jud. Iasi
Centrul scolar de constructii, Strada Dr. Victor Babes nr 11 Tg. *Mures,* Reguinea Mures Autonoma Maghiara
Centrul scolar de constructii, Strada Paltinisului nr 1, *Oradea,* Reguinea Crisana
Institutul Politehnic "Traian Vuia", *Timisoara,* Jud. Timisoara

SENEGAL
Ecole d'Architecture et d'Urbanisme, P.B. 3111, *Dakar*

SINGAPORE
National University of Singapore, Faculty of Architecture and Buildings, Lady Hill Campus, Lady Hill Road, *Singapore* 10

SOUTH AFRICA
University of the Orange Free State, School of Architecture, P.O. Box 339, *Bloemfontein*
University of Cape Town, School of Architecture, Private Bag, Rondebosch, *Cape Town*
University of Natal, School of Architecture, King George V Avenue, *Durban,* Natal
University of the Witwatersrand, Faculty of Architecture, Milner Park, John Moffat Building, *Johannesburg*
University of Port Elizabeth, School of Architecture, P.O. Box 1600, *Port Elizabeth*
University of Pretoria, Department of Architecture, Hillcrest, *Pretoria*

SPAIN
Escuela Técnica Superior de Arquitectura, Avenida Generalísimo Franco, 1001, *Barcelona* 14
Universitat Politécnica de Barcelona, Diagonal 649, *Barcelona* 28

Escuela Técnica Superior de Arquitectura, Plaza de Tomàs Morales, s/n, *Las Palmas de Gran Canaria*
Escuela Técnica Superior de Arquitectura, Ciudad Universitaria, Avenida Martín Fierro, s/n, *Madrid* 3
Escuela Técnica Superior de Arquitectura, Ciudad Universitaria de Navarra, Santo Domingo, *Pamplona*
Escuela Técnica Superior de Arquitectura, Avenida Reina Mercedes, 31, *Sevilla*
Universidad Politécnica de Valencia, Escuela Tecnica Superior de Arquitectura, Plaza Galicia 4, *Valencia* 10
Facultad de Ciencias Exactas de la Facultad de Valladolid, Escuela Técnica Superior de Arquitectura, *Valladolid*

SRI LANKA
Institute of Practical Technology, Department of Architecture, *Katubedde*

SUDAN
University of Khartoum, Faculty of Engineering and Architecture, P.O. Box 321, *Khartoum*
R.S.B.C.A., P.O. Box 720, *Khartoum*

SWEDEN
Chalmers University of Technology, School of Architecture, Fack, 40220 *Goteborg* 5
The Institute of Technology, Institute of Architecture, Box 725, S 22007 *Lund*
Kungliga Tekniska Högskolan, Fack, 10044 *Stockholm* 70
The National Swedish Institute for Building Research, Box 27163, 10252 *Stockholm* 27

SWITZERLAND
Ecole d'Architecture de l'Université de Genève, 9 Boulevard Hèlvétique, 1205 *Genève*
Ecole Polytechnique Fédérale de Lausanne, 33 Avenue de Cour, 1007 *Lausanne*
E.T.H. Zürich, Abteilung für Architektur, Leonhard Strasse 33, 8006 *Zürich*

SYRIA
Université d'Alep, Faculté de Génie et d'Architecture, *Alep*
Université de Damas, Faculté des Beaux Arts, Place el Tahrir, *Damas*

THAILAND
Chulalongkorn University, Faculty of Architecture, Phya Thai Road, *Bangkok* 5
King Mongkut's Institute of Technology, Faculty of Architecture, Ladkrabang District, *Bangkok*
Northern Technical Institute, Division of Architecture, Department of Design, *Cheingmai*
Dhonburi Technical Institute, Architecture Engineering Division, Department of Civil Technology, *Dhonburi*

College of Design and Construction, Faculty of Architecture and Urbanisme, Bangplud, *Dhonburi*
Northeastern Technical Institute, Division of Architecture, Department of Design, Nakorn, *Rajsima*
Southern Technical Institute, Architectural Division, Department of Civil Technology, *Sonpkha*

TOGO
Ecole Africaine et Mauricienne d'Architecture, Division of Architecture, BP 2067, *Lome*

TUNISIA
Institut Technologique d'Art, d'Architecture et d'Urbanisme de Tunisie, (I.T.A.A.U.T.), Section Architecture et Urbanisme, Route de l'Armée Nationale, *Tunis*

TURKEY
Orta Dogu Teknik Universitesi, Mimarlik Bölümü Baskanligi, *Ankara*
Devlet Güzel Sanatlar Akademisi, Mimarlik Yüksek Okulu Müdürlügü, *Besiktas - Istanbul*
Ege Universitesi, Mühendislik Bilimleri Fakültesi Mühendislik ve Mimarlik, Yüksek Okulu Müdürlügü, *Buca - Izmir*
Devlet Güzel Sanatlar Akademisi, Mimarlik Bölümü Baskanligi, *Findikli - Istanbul*
Ege Universitesi, Mühendislik Bilimleri Fakültesi Mühendislik ve Mimarlik Adademisi, Mimarlik Bölümü Baskanligi, *Izmir*
Devlet Mühendislik ve Mimarlik Akademisi, Mimarlik Bölümü Baskanligi, *Konya*
Itü Mühendislik-Mimarlik Fakültesi, Mimarlik Bölümü Baskanligi, *Macka - Istanbul*
Ankara Devlet Mühendislik ve Mimarlik Akademisi, Mühendislik ve Mimarlik, Yüksek Okulu, Mimarlik Bölümü Baskanligi, *Maltepe - Ankara*
Istanbul Teknik Universitesi, Mimarlik Fakültesi Dekanligi, *Taskisla - Istanbul*
Karadeniz Teknik Universitesi, Insaat ve Mimarlik Fakültesi Mimarlik Bölümü Baskanligi, *Trabzon*
Istanbul Devlet Mühendislik ve Mimarlik Akademisi, Mimarlik Bölümü Baskanligi, *Yildiz - Istanbul*

UNITED KINGDOM
Robert Gordon's Institute of Technology, Scott Sutherland School of Architecture, Garthdee, *Aberdeen* AB9 2QB
University of Bath, School of Architecture and Building Technology, Claverton Down, *Bath* BA2 7AY
The Queen's University of Belfast, Department of Architecture and Planning, *Belfast* BT7 1NN (Northern Ireland)
Birmingham School of Architecture, Art and Design Centre, Corporation Street, *Birmingham* B4 7BX

Brighton Polytechnic, School of Architecture, Grand Parade, *Brighton* BN2 2JY

University of Cambridge School of Architecture, 1 Scroope Terrace, *Cambridge* CB2 1 PX

City of Canterbury College of Art, School of Architecture, New Dover Road, *Canterbury,* Kent

University of Wales Institute of Science and Technology, The Welsh School of Architecture, Cathays Park, *Cardiff* CF1 3NU

The Gloucestershire College of Art, The School of Architecture, Landscape and Planning, Pittville, *Cheltenham*

Thames Polytechnic, School of Architecture, Oakfield Lane, *Dartford,* Kent

Duncan of Jordanstone College of Art, School of Architecture and Town Planning, Perth Road, *Dundee* DD1 4HT

Heriot-Watt University, Department of Architecture, Edinburgh College of Art, Lauriston Place, *Edinburgh* EH3 9DF

University of Edinburgh, Department of Architecture, 20 Chambers, *Edinburgh* EH1 1JZ

Glasgow School of Art and Glasgow University, Mackintosh School, 177 Renfrew Street, *Glasgow* G3 6RQ

University of Strathclyde, Department of Architecture and Building Science, 131 Rottenrow, *Glasgow* G4 0NG

Huddersfield Polytechnic, The Department of Architecture, School of Architecture, Queensgate, *Huddersfield* HD1 3DH

Regional College of Art, School of Architecture, Anlaby Road, *Kingston Upon Hull*

Kingston Polytechnic, School of Architecture and Civic Design, Knights Park, *Kingston Upon Thames* Surrey KT1 2QJ

Leeds Polytechnic, Department of Architectural Studies, *Leeds* LS2 8BN

Leicester Polytechnic, School of Architecture, P.O. Box 143, Clephan Building, *Leicester* LE1 9BH

Liverpool Polytechnic, The Department of Architecture and Surveying, 53-55 Victoria Street, *Liverpool* L1 6EY

University of Liverpool, Liverpool School of Architecture, P.O. Box 147, *Liverpool* L69 3BX

Architectural Association School of Architecture, 34-36 Bedford Square, *London* WC1

North East London Polytechnic, Department of Architecture, Faculty of Environmental Studies, *London* E15 3EA

The Polytechnic of Central London, The Department of Architecture, Surveying and Town Planning, 35 Marylebone Road, *London* NW1 5LS

The Polytechnic of North London School of Architecture, Department of Architecture, Surveying, Building & Interior Design, Holloway, *London* N7 8DB

University of London, Bartlett School of Architecture, University College, Wates House, 22 Gordon Street, *London* WC1

Polytechnic of the South Bank, Wandsworth Road, *London* SW8 2JZ

Manchester Polytechnic, School of Architecture, Department of Environmental Design, Faculty of Art and Design, Cavendish Street, All Saints, *Manchester* M15 6BR

University of Manchester, School of Architecture, *Manchester* M13 9PL

The University, School of Architecture, *Newcastle Upon Tyne* NE1 7RU

University of Nottingham, Department of Architecture, University Park, *Nottingham* NG7 2RD

Oxford Polytechnic, School of Architecture, Headington Road, *Oxford* OX3 OBP

Plymouth Polytechnic, The School of Architecture, Notte Street, *Plymouth* PL1 2AR

Portsmouth Polytechnic, School of Architecture, King Henry 1 Street, *Portsmouth,* Hants

University of Sheffield, Department of Architecture, The Arts Tower, *Sheffield* S10 2TN

USSR

Ecole Polytechnique de Kazakhie, 22 rue Ouniversitetskaïa, *Alma - Ata*

Ecole Polytechnique d'Azerbaïdjan, 25 prospekt Narimanova, *Bakou*

Ecole Polytechnique de Tadjikistan, 5a prospekt Kouïbychev, *Duchanbe*

Ecole Polytechnique d'Erevan, 105 rue Terian, *Erevan*

Ecole Polytechnique de Kaunas, 35 rue Donellaïtchie, *Kaunas*

Ecole d'Ingénieurs de Kharkov, 40 rue Soumskaïa, *Kharkov*

Ecole des Beaux Arts de Kiev, 20 rue Smirnova Lastotchkina, *Kiev*

Ecole d'Ingénieurs de Kiev, 78 Boulevard Chevtchenko, *Kiev*

Ecole d'Ingénieurs de Leningrad, 4 rue 2e Krasnoarmoiskaïa, *Léningrad*

Ecole de Peinture, Sculpture et Architecture Répine, 17 quai Ouniversitetskaïa, *Leningrad* B-34

Ecole Polytechnique de Lvov, 12 rue Mira, *Lvov*

Ecole Polytechnique de Biélorussie, 65 Léninski prospekt, *Minsk*

Institut d'Architecture de Moscou, 11 rue Zdanov, *Moscou*

Ecole d'Ingénieurs de Novossibirsk Kouïbyegev, 113 rue Léningradskaïa, *Novossibirsk*

Ecole Polytechnique de Riga, 70 rue Lénine, *Riga*

Ecole d'Ingénieurs de Rostov, 162 rue Sotsialistitchoskaïa, *Rostov/Don*

Ecole Polytechnique de l'Oural Kirov 2, Vtouzgorodok, *Sverdlovsk*

Ecole Polytechnique de Tachkent, 16 rue Assakinskaïa, *Tachkent*

Ecole des Beaux Arts de la R.S.S. d'Estonie, 11 Tartousskoé chossé, *Tallin*

Ecole des Beaux Arts de Tbilissi, 22 rue Griboédov, *Tbilissi*

Ecole Polytechnique de Georgie, 98 rue Lénine, *Tbilissi*

Ecole des Beaux Arts de la R.S.S. de Lituanie, 6 rue Tiesos, *Vilnus*

URUGUAY

Universidad de la Republica, Facultad de Arquitectura, Avenida 18 de Julio 1824, *Montevideo*

VENEZUELA

Universidad Simón Bolívar, Departamento de Diseño y Estudios Urbanos, *Caracas* D.F.

Universidad Central de Venezuela, Facultad de Arquitectura y Urbanismo, Ciudad Universitaria, *Caracas* D.F.

Universidad del Zulia, Facultad de Arquitectura, carretera de Ziruma, Via el Mojan, *Maracaibo*

Universidad de Los Andes, Facultad de Arquitectura, *Merida*

VIETNAM, SOCIALIST REPUBLIC OF

Ecole Nationale Supérieure des Beaux Arts, *Gia Dinh*

Ecole Secondaire d'Architecture et de Construction, *Hanoi*

Ecole Supérieure d'Architecture, Ministère d'Architecture, *Hanoi*

Ecole Polytechnique de Hanoi, Faculté d'Ingénieurs Constructeurs, *Hanoi*

Université of Ho Chi Minh City, Département d'Architecture, 3 Cong-Truong Chien-Si, *Ho Chi Minh City*

Truong Daihoc Kiên true, *Xuan-Hoa*

YUGOSLAVIA

Arhitektonski Fakultet, Bulevar revolucije 73, 11000 *Belgrade*

Fakulteta za Arhitekturo, Cojzeva 5, 61000 *Ljubljana*

Arhitektonsko-Urbanisticki Fakultet, Hosana Brkica 2, 71000 *Sarajevo*

Université des Républiques Socialistes de Macédoine, Arhitektonsko-gradezen Fakultet, Faculté d'Architecture, Rade Koncar 16, 91000 *Skopje*

Arhitektonski Fakultet, Kaciceva, 26, 41000 *Zagreb*

ZAIRE

Université Nouvelle du Zaïre, I.B.T.P., B.P. 8249, *Kinshasa*

ACSA Members and Affiliates